Financing Health Care

Financing Health Care

Volume I

edited by

Ullrich K. Hoffmeyer

National Economic Research Associates, London

and

Thomas R. McCarthy

National Economic Research Associates, Los Angeles

KLUWER ACADEMIC PUBLISHERS

DORDRECHT / BOSTON / LONDON

Library of Congress Cataloging-in-Publication Data

Financing health care / edited by Ullrich K. Hoffmeyer and Thomas R.
McCarthy.
      p.   cm.
   ISBN 0-7923-3067-6 (set)
      1. Medical care--Finance--Case studies. 2. Insurance, Health-
   -Government policy--Case studies. 3. Health care reform--Economic
   aspects. 4. Medical care, Cost of--Forecasting.   I. Hoffmeyer,
   Ullrich K. II. McCarthy, Thomas R., 1950-   .
   RA411.F57 1994
   338.4'33621--dc20   94-30382
ISBN 0-7923-3065-X (Volume I)
ISBN 0-7923-3067-6 (Set of 2 volumes)

Published by Kluwer Academic Publishers,
P.O. Box 17, 3300 AA Dordrecht, The Netherlands.

Kluwer Academic Publishers incorporates
the publishing programmes of
D. Reidel, Martinus Nijhoff, Dr W. Junk and MTP Press.

Sold and distributed in the U.S.A. and Canada
by Kluwer Academic Publishers,
101 Philip Drive, Norwell, MA 02061, U.S.A.

In all other countries, sold and distributed
by Kluwer Academic Publishers Group,
P.O. Box 322, 3300 AH Dordrecht, The Netherlands.

2-0995-150 ts

Printed on acid-free paper

Printed in the Netherlands

TABLE OF CONTENTS

Chapters 4 to 15 are tabulated on the following page.

CHAPTER 16
THE ROLE OF THE EUROPEAN COMMUNITY   1,295

CHAPTER 17
GLOSSARY   1,393

LIST OF CHARTS AND TABLES

Chapter 12: The Health Care System in Sweden

Chapter 13: The Health Care System in Switzerland

LIST OF COUNTRY SPECIFIC ANNEXES

PREFACE

Background

No country has it quite right. While none of the health care systems we report on in these two volumes are on the verge of collapse, all face the same set of urgent problems. These problems threaten either to reduce the quality of care now being delivered or drain the public coffers. In short, the demand for health care is outpacing the ability to supply it in every industrialised nation.

What propels the growth in demand? The main factors appear to be an ageing population, improving medical technology and real income growth. All of these are in many ways positive developments. Ageing is what happens when a health care system is working well so that lifespans increase. Medical technology, while often expensive, saves lives and pain. Rising income is the fruit of gains in economic productivity, and what better way to spend it than on health?

Where then is the problem? It lies mainly in the way that health care is financed and delivered. Health care markets are dominated by insurance, whether publicly or privately provided. This, too, is hardly a defect. Insurance is necessary when losses are unpredictable and the consequences of those losses may be financially catastrophic. But it is also well-established that patients and providers are likely to behave differently when an insurer is paying the bill. In most countries, the major insurer is the government, mainly to ensure the equitable distribution of care. So the insurance problem becomes a budgetary problem, which makes the problem much more troublesome. The more the government moves to assure the equitable financing and delivery of health care, the greater the potential for regulatory solutions and economic distortions.

The health care systems of the world offer different approaches to providing health care and there are lessons to be learned from these differences. But, more important than the differences, the world is united by a universal need for solutions to the health care financing problem. So far, no single country has it quite right. The key to reorganising health care systems requires finding an acceptable balance between the efficiency with which care is financed and delivered and the equity or social solidarity of the system.

In 1992, National Economic Research Associates (NERA), an international economic research consultancy, was commissioned to analyse the health care systems of twelve industrialised countries. The primary goal of that assignment was to increase understanding of the economic issues underlying health care reform, and why this process is so difficult to do well. NERA was given three major tasks to reach this goal. First we were asked to observe the strengths and weaknesses of different health care systems and to evaluate reforms now being undertaken or considered. Second, NERA was asked to forecast health care expenditure in these countries on the assumption that the *status quo* in each system prevailed; that is, no major restructuring and no acceleration of reform. Finally, and most importantly, NERA was challenged to devise a 'model health care system'. This blueprint could then be used to help to evaluate the long-term reform proposals being offered around the world.

These two volumes present the results of our research. They provide an analysis of the twelve health care systems in their current form, and a programme for structural reform of eight of these systems.

Structure of the Study

Chapter 1 presents a summary of the entire study, including an overview of the health systems studied, a description of our model health care system that we call the 'NERA Prototype', and a brief synopsis of short-term reform proposals for the health care systems of a number of countries.

Rising costs are a feature of each of the health care systems we studied. In Chapter 2 we examine what causes costs to rise and we make *status quo* forecasts of future need for health care and of future health expenditure. The results of these forecasts help to set the context for considering future reforms.

In Chapter 3 we present an analysis of economic issues involved in evaluating health care systems. This chapter was written after we had examined each county's health care system, giving us a sound understanding of what worked and what did not in a wide range of countries, from which we could then design a blueprint for the model system. The 'NERA Prototype' cannot be simplistically applied to all countries; the history and cultural diversity of each country will make reforms to each system unique. However, we believe that the NERA Prototype serves as a useful benchmark against which to compare an existing system, and for evaluating proposed reforms.

Chapters 4 through 15 provide individual country studies. These countries appear in alphabetical order, and fall into one of two categories:

- *Major countries* are Canada, France, Germany, Japan, the Netherlands, Switzerland, the United Kingdom, and the United States. These countries were the focus of our research and we have made reform recommendations for each.

- *Reference countries* are Italy, New Zealand, Spain and Sweden. These countries expanded our understanding of health care systems and reforms, but we did not develop specific reform recommendations for these countries.

Each country chapter has a similar structure. Following an introduction, Section 2, *Structure of the Health Care System*, is an overview of the finance and delivery sides of each system. Section 3, *Analysis of Individual Sectors*, describes the roles, objectives and incentives of the main sectors in the system: the physician, hospital and pharmaceutical sectors, as well as patients, payers, and governments. Section 4, *Intersectoral Analysis*, considers the consistency of these objectives and incentives, and identifies pressure points arising from inconsistencies. Section 5, *Analysis of Health Care Policy*, deals with recent health care policy developments.

For *major countries*, there follow three sections outlining our recommended reforms. These recommendations flow from a comparison of the existing system with the NERA Prototype. Section 6, *Constraints on Reform*, gives a short prognosis of the likelihood of change, and what factors might constrain appropriate reform. Then Sections 7 and 8 spell out our reform recommendations, first as short-term steps, and then as long-term objectives.

Chapter 16 discusses the history, and possible future direction, of the European Community (now European Union) in the health care systems of member countries. Given the increasing integration of countries within the European Union, an analysis of France, Germany, Italy, the Netherlands, Spain and the United Kingdom would be incomplete without such a chapter.

Finally, a glossary provides definitions of terms used throughout this study.

Technical Details

The study is current to December 1992, except in five instances. Chapter 4, Canada, includes discussion of bill C-91, passed in 1993. Chapter 6, Germany, has been updated to include the passage of the 1993 Health Care Act. Both Chapter 11, Spain, and Chapter 15, the United States, include discussion of events up to April 1993. Chapter 13, Switzerland, is current to the middle of 1993.

Throughout this report, monetary values are given in local currency and in 1990 US$. Conversions are made at 1990 Purchasing Power Parities. Figures in 1990 US$ are effectively equivalent to 1990 ECUs, for while the $/ECU exchange rate was 1ECU = $1.382 at 6 August 1992, Purchasing Power Parity in 1990 suggests a rate of 1 ECU = $1.021.

About NERA

National Economic Research Associates (NERA) is a major economic consultancy with offices across the United States, in the United Kingdom and in Spain. In addition to our work in health care, NERA specialises in the energy, telecommunications, water, and transport sectors; and, in regulatory and competition policy economics in all sectors.

This study was produced by approximately twenty economists from our offices in London, New York, Washington, Los Angeles and Madrid. We were assisted by our sister company, William M. Mercer Ltd. of Japan, and by Remit Consultants Ltd. in London.

Thanks

We wish to acknowledge our gratitude to many people who have made this study possible.

We are grateful to the *Pharmaceutical Partners for Better Health Care* for their sponsorship of this study. The *Partners* are a recently established group of research-based pharmaceutical companies from Europe, the United States and Japan. The companies which sponsored the Financing Health Care study are listed below. In particular, we are grateful to the Steering Committee, chaired by Thomas Cueni, for their support and constructive comments. The responsibility for the research and the conclusions drawn rests however with NERA.

We are also greatly indebted to the many health professionals, academics, and policy advisors from each country surveyed who gave of their time in interviews, provided source material, reviewed drafts and assisted us with many helpful insights. The opinions expressed in this study are, of course, our own.

The OECD has given permission for us to use their health care data, for which we are grateful. This cross-country data source enabled us to make more robust comparisons between countries than would have been possible using individual countries' data, and formed the basis of our forecasts.

We also thank Marie Stratta and Maja de Keijzer from Kluwer Academic Publishers who have worked closely with us to convert the study into this publication.

And finally we say thank you to David Tripp, Adam Lloyd and Vicky Naldrett from NERA for the many months they spent preparing this manuscript for publication.

Ullrich Hoffmeyer
Thomas McCarthy

National Economic Research Associates
May 1994

SPONSORS OF THE STUDY

AB Astra
Akzo/Organon Int. bv
American Home Products
Bayer AG
Boehringer Ingelheim
Boehringer Mannheim
Chugai Pharmaceutical Co., Ltd.
Ciba-Geigy Ltd.
Daiichi
Eisai Co., Ltd.
Fujisawa
Glaxo Holdings plc.
Hoechst AG
F. Hoffmann-La Roche Ltd.
Johnson & Johnson
Knoll AG
Eli Lilly & Co.
Menarini SA

Merck and Co., Inc.
Pfizer Inc.
Rhône Poulenc
Roussel Uclaf
Sandoz
Sankyo
Sanofi
Schering AG
Schering-Plough Corporation
Sigma Tau
SmithKline Beecham
Syntex Corporation
Takeda Chemical Industries, Ltd.
Tanabe Seiyaku
The Upjohn Company
Warner-Lambert Company
Yamanouchi

CHAPTER 1
SUMMARY AND OVERVIEW

Ullrich Hoffmeyer

National Economic Research Associates
London

Thomas McCarthy

National Economic Research Associates
Los Angeles

1.1   INTRODUCTION

For the remainder of this century and the beginning of the next, health care systems in the developed world will rely increasingly on market-based incentives as the means to contain costs and allocate resources. Governments will retain control over the redistribution of funds from rich to poor but will relinquish to the market the insurance and provision of health care services. This is our prediction and also our advice.

Many state-run public utilities were inefficient and costly to governments and to consumers twenty years ago. It was then believed that their services were so essential or that the threat of monopoly was so great that only government could oversee them. Even in these cumbersome industries, history has proven that structural reform could improve efficiency and reduce the fiscal burden they created.

Similar reform is possible in health care. We can look to the marketplace for models to reform health care.

The need for reform of health care finance is acute in most countries. The demand for health care continues to outstrip the funds available - partly because of aging populations, and partly because of improvements in medical technology, causing patients to clamour for the latest and best equipment regardless of cost.

Our research over the past year in twelve countries has given us a clear sense that the limits to government financing and provision of health care are at hand. Our forecasts of the demand and supply in these countries reveal excess demand, indicating that, when health care competes with other claims on national budgets, governments will spend less on health care than its citizens individually would spend if they had the choice. We believe that the best solutions to these problems are increased information and choice for patients while placing insurers and providers in competition to provide optimal levels of care at competitive prices.

Each nation we have studied is different from all others in its unique history, institutions and in the social contract between citizens and government. (These studies are summarised in Section 1.2) For this reason, 'competition' is no answer in and of itself. Our suggestions about reform are carefully tailored to each country's particular social and political setting.

The United States is a problematic exception to every generalization about health care. It *has* largely relied on market forces and the results have turned out badly. This unhappy example has probably delayed the reform of health care financing elsewhere. American citizens live without the protection that citizens of other developed nations enjoy, and the expense and insecurity of the American system seem also to counsel against competition.

That would be a mistaken conclusion. We hope that the new administration's policymakers reason rightly that excess capacity and perverse incentives, not reliance on the market, are what lie behind the high costs of the US system. We believe that if a new system that balances competition and regulation is allowed to work unencumbered by administered prices and artificial entry barriers, it will succeed in bringing down the cost of health care in America while increasing access to those presently uninsured.

Our conclusion about competition does not have ideological origins. Appreciating that many modern societies place a high value on an equitable sharing of the health care burden, we were prepared to find a large role for government in even an ideal system. We have found instead that a model health care system (which we call the 'Prototype') calls for government to set the institutional priority for subsidising the poor and the sick. Every citizen's right to a guaranteed health care package is an essential feature of the system. With the proper institutions in place, the system promises an efficient allocation of resources even when the solidarity 'setting' is high. This model, summarised in Section 1.3 and discussed in full in Chapter 3, forms the basis for many of the suggestions for interim reform in individual countries, summarised in Section 1.4.

Health care in industrialised countries has not heretofore been organised in free markets, like so many other essential services, because 'market failures' appear to disqualify private enterprise as the means to allocate resources in this sector. For example:

- Patients do not choose to become sick; social solidarity in most modern societies implies a degree of buffering against adversity. We do not wish to let the full cost of care fall heavily on low-income households. Left to themselves, markets do not automatically subsidise the poor or the infirm.

- Patients regularly rely on physicians to make decisions about treatments so the normal conditions of demand are interrupted. Under some payment methods, doctors and hospitals have a financial incentive to over-provide care. Insurance and third-party payment further reduces sensitivity to cost and price. The outcome is a tendency to excessive care and cost inflation.

Why then is government not the answer, especially in view of the loyalty to single-payer systems we observe in the United Kingdom, Canada and Japan? Government-run systems, for one thing, are not immune to cost pressures. Our studies reveal that the need for cost-containing reforms has been common to all countries as the increasing demands for better care conflict with fiscal constraints. Moreover, when centralised systems try to contain costs by artificial pricing or setting caps on global expenditure, distortions arise which seriously compromise the delivery of the appropriate level of service. For example:

- In Japan a typical doctor's visit lasts less than five minutes as physicians cram dozens of patients per day into their calendars in order to hold up their incomes in the face of artificial prices. Patients wait hours for outpatient hospital care.

- In the UK and Canada, shortages of funds cause hospitals to close their doors to some patients before year end and impede the acquisition of potential lifesaving devices.

- In Germany, physicians and hospitals which are reimbursed for each medical service they perform have little incentive to use resources efficiently. Some competition between insurers exists, but this takes the form of a generous interpretation of benefits, not reduced premiums.

The chief reason for advocating reforms that redirect health care systems toward market-based resource allocation is to correct distortions of this nature by allowing patients and physicians to exercise informed choice. In reformed systems the incentives of insurers and providers can be set to reward efficiency and the market power of insurers can be offset by that of providers. Although market failures do not evaporate, they can be counteracted by instituting pro-competitive incentives. This is the essence of our reform suggestions. For example, under these proposals for health care reform:

- government-run health care funding authorities in tax-financed health care systems (such as Canada, New Zealand, Spain, the UK and Sweden) would be given more autonomy in order to become independent financing authorities in a health care market; whereas,

- insurance funds in social insurance-based health care systems (such as France, Germany, Japan and the Netherlands) would be put on an equal footing in order to allow them to assume a more commercial role as insurers, eventually leading to competition.

Generally, we advocate allowing private companies to provide health insurance and to contract with providers. Health insurance must be mandatory however. A means for subsidizing health insurance premiums of low-income households must be provided. All citizens must have access to basic health care services irrespective of their ability to pay. In our Prototype the government collects income-graduated premiums and an independent central fund divides the pool among private insurers in relation to the risks they bear. Individuals must also pay premiums directly to their insurers who may risk rate. When consumers can shop for insurance, insurers compete to provide the best coverage at the lowest cost. This is the essential source of efficiency in competitive health care systems. Our interim reform recommendations move in this direction, slowly in the case of countries where the satisfaction in centrally managed systems is high, rapidly in nations that are ripe for change.

At the end of our proposed 'reform paths', governments will have set up the institutional framework needed for health care markets to work well, defined a guaranteed health care package to which all citizens are entitled, and assumed responsibility for collecting the income-related portion of each citizen's health care payments that makes the system equitable. The government has a continuing role in assuring safety, quality and fairness.

1.2 HEALTH CARE SYSTEMS IN TWELVE COUNTRIES: AN OVERVIEW

1.2.1 Comparison of Health Care Systems

1.2.1.1 Introduction

Industrialised countries all face pressures to reform the finance and delivery side of their health care systems. The one universal driver for reform is cost. Even those countries that rate high in public satisfaction (Canada, the Netherlands, Germany and France) are in the process of considering reforms.

The growing demand for health care is imposing unacceptable costs on those who must fund the expenditures. Resistance to these costs manifests itself in different ways in each country. In the United States where concern abounds over the rising cost of the government programmes *Medicare* and *Medicaid*, the burden of health care falls on employers and wage-earners who are the main payers of insurance premiums.

Similarly, in France, Germany or Italy, where much of the funding comes from payments to compulsory sickness funds or national insurance contributions, there is equal concern about escalating costs. In other countries, like the United Kingdom and Canada, health costs are financed mainly from general taxation. In these, the immediate concern shows in patients' dissatisfaction about services; for instance, about waiting lists or cut-backs in government-funded services.

All of these issues translate into pressures on national or local budgets. They displace other desirable expenditures and create deficits or cause unacceptable tax increases. In Europe, obligations under the Maastricht treaty are intensifying the pressure to reduce national budget deficits.

The objective of this section is to seek out what we can learn from observing health care systems in twelve countries. Any reform of the health care systems must take account of the way in which people and organisations in these systems respond to regulations, stimuli and incentives. Short of experimentation, which is difficult, the only way to understand this is by observing how people respond in various circumstances in the real world of health care. The emphasis in this section is, therefore, on evidence rather than hypothesis.

This section is not intended to be a comprehensive guide to the health care systems of the twelve countries examined in this study. Readers are advised to read the summaries at the beginning of each Country Study (Chapters 4-15).

1.2.1.2 Classes of Health Care Systems

The countries under study are Canada, France, Germany, Italy, Japan, the Netherlands, New Zealand, Spain, Sweden, Switzerland, the United Kingdom and the United States. In all countries individuals (patients) predominantly rely on third parties (insurers) for the financing of health care services delivered by providers (physicians, hospitals).

All countries have their own institutional and organisational arrangements, as well as their own history, which have all contributed to the development of the countries' health care systems. Nevertheless, in a simplified classification scheme, three generic financing models of health care can be identified as follows:[1]

1. *Predominantly Tax-Funded Health Care Systems*

These are systems which raise health care funds through general or dedicated payroll taxes. Funds are collected by a central authority, usually the national government which transfers these in a variety of ways to regional authorities. Regional authorities act as third party payers by financing health care providers, e.g. general practitioners and hospitals. Examples of countries belonging to this generic class are Canada, Italy, New Zealand, Spain, Sweden and the UK. Of these, Canada and Sweden have regional authorities that collect tax revenues directly. A special funding mechanism exists in the UK, where some general practitioners are providers *as well as* funders of care.

2. *Predominantly Social Insurance-Based Health Care Systems*

In France, Germany, Japan and the Netherlands, participants pay insurance premiums to sickness funds. These funds are not for profit and are compulsory. (People may also supplement them voluntarily.) Where the fund is open to all, competition between funds exists; where membership is restricted, little or no competition exists. Funds reimburse physicians and

---

[1]   Hurst identifies seven sub-systems of health care systems. See Hurst, J. (1992): "The Reform of Health Care - A Comparative Analysis of Seven OECD Countries", *Health Policy Studies*, No. 2, OECD, Paris.

hospitals via negotiated contracts, which specify how payment is made as well as the amount.

Sickness fund premiums typically differ (sometimes substantially) between funds. This reflects the differences in the risk structure of the funds' members. France and, most prominently, the Netherlands rely on a central risk adjustment mechanism to balance premiums across funds. Germany currently adjusts premiums only for some members of its population (but is planning further changes), while Japan relies on government subsidies to partially equalise these. A further complexity relates to France, where payments for some services are made directly from sickness funds to patients, who then pay providers.

3.   *Predominantly Voluntary Insurance-Based Health Care System*

The United States and Switzerland belong to this group. In these countries health insurance is, at present, not universally mandatory. Health care finance is raised by (sometimes competing private) insurance companies which then reimburse providers for services delivered to their members. Reimbursement methods vary considerably in the US, and may include ownership of providers by the insurer.

Competing health insurers set their premiums according to the risk characteristics of the individuals, or groups of individuals through employment. Consequently, poor people with high expected health care costs are often unable to afford insurance.

1.2.1.3 Reimbursement of Providers

Providers of health care services are general practitioners (usually the first point of call for patients), specialists, and hospitals. The health care systems of all countries studied, regardless of their financing structure, rely on a mix of private and public provision. In many countries, general practitioners are usually self-employed professionals, while clinicians are salaried employees. In other countries even physicians are salaried. In all countries public, private and voluntary not-for-profit hospitals co-exist.

Reimbursement methods for primary services fall into three broad categories:

*   *Fee-for-service:* Physicians receive retrospective payment for each act of medical service they provide. The payment for different services is usually stated in a tariff list.

9

- *Capitation Payments:* Physicians receive a fixed fee for every patient they are registered to treat. The capitation fee can be varied for different demographic groups and can also include a risk-sharing component (US).

- *Salary:* Physicians are employed by health authorities and receive a fixed salary for services provided to patients.

Hospitals are typically reimbursed by one or a combination of the following methods:

- *Cost-per-case:* This involves estimating the likely bundle of services that will be required in treating any particular class of cases, combining this with their costs (fee-for-service schedule), and arriving at a price for treating a case that will, on average, cover the cost.

- *Per diem rate:* Hospitals receive a uniform sum per day for the entire duration of the hospital inpatient stay.

- *Global budget:* A fixed sum is paid to a hospital during the course of a year with the obligation to meet demand for services within this budget during the year. A global budget can be set unilaterally by a funder, or negotiated between provider and funder at local or regional levels.

- *Fee-for-service:* Hospitals receive retrospective payment for each treatment they provide.

Charts 1.1, 1.2 and 1.3 show in graphical form the main relationships between patients, funders and providers in the three generic models. They are simplified versions of the countries health care systems. For example, a number of countries outside the US also have substantial private insurance markets for health care in addition to their public systems.

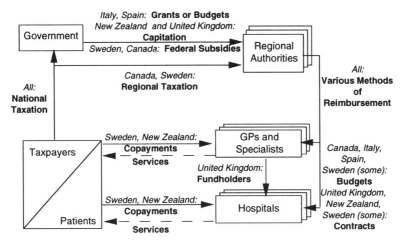

CHART 1.1
Generic Model 1: Tax-Funded Health Care Systems
Canada, Italy, New Zealand, Spain, Sweden, UK

In Chart 1.1 the Taxpayer - Government relationship for each country is as follows:

- Canada: Provincial payroll taxes and federal grants (10 provinces, 2 territories);

- Italy: National social security contributions and grants from national taxation (21 regions, 600 health care units);

- New Zealand: National taxation (4 regional health authorities);

- Spain: National taxation and social security contributions (6 independent regions, 1 organisation for 11 regions);

- Sweden: Regional taxation and national insurance contributions (26 country councils);

- UK: National taxation and national insurance contributions (16 regional and 190 district health authorities).

11

CHART 1.2
Generic Model 2: Social Insurance-Based Health Care Systems
France, Germany, Japan, Netherlands

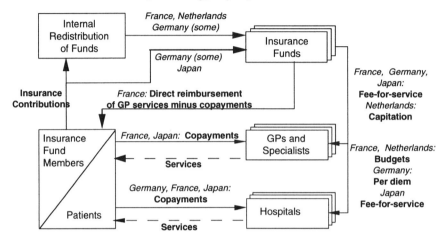

In Chart 1.2 the Insurance Fund Member - Insurance Fund relationship for each country is as follows:

- France: Compulsory income-related insurance contributions to non-competing sickness funds (internal redistribution of funds) and voluntary contributions to competing *mutuelles*, which offer insurance against copayments;

- Germany: Compulsory income-related insurance contributions to non-competing sickness funds, *or* compulsory and voluntary contributions to competing substitute funds (limited internal redistribution of funds);

- Netherlands: Compulsory income-related insurance contributions to the central fund *and* flat-fee payments to competing insurance funds. Capitation payments from central fund to insurance funds;

- Japan: Compulsory income-related insurance contributions and/or government subsidies to non-competing insurance funds (no internal redistribution of funds but tax-subsidies).

12

CHART 1.3
Generic Model 3: Voluntary Insurance-Based Health Care Systems
USA, Switzerland

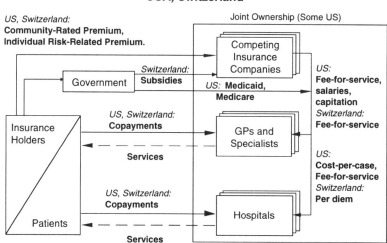

1.2.2 Performance and Output of Health Care Systems

No reliable and widely accepted measure exists which would evaluate the performance of a country's health care system, and would allow one to arrive at comparisons of health care systems. Table 1.1 lists a range of measures that can serve as **proxies** for the performance of health care systems. These are related to the **objectives** of health care systems.

- *'Health care expenditure (HCE) as a percentage of gross domestic product (GDP)'*, and *'HCE per capita'* are measures for **macroeconomic efficiency** of health care systems. Table 1.1 shows that between 1980 and 1990, HCE as a percentage of GDP has risen substantially in France, Canada and the United States only. In many countries the increase was marginal. HCE per capita figures are relatively consistent across countries, apart from the US, where it is substantially higher. In Mediterranean countries and New Zealand they are notably below the average.

- **Microeconomic efficiency** can be evaluated by comparing, for example, *'physician visits per head'*. Table 1.1 shows that on this measure Germany, Italy and Japan are almost twice the average. A possible

13

Table 1.1
Performance of Health Care Systems

	MACRO-PERFORMANCE			MICRO-PERFORMANCE	SOCIAL SOLIDARITY	HEALTH STATUS		SATISFACTION
	HCE as a Percentage of GDP (1980)	HCE as a Percentage of GDP (1990)	HCE per capita, PPP¹ $US (1990)	Physician Visits per head per year (Various Years)	Percentage covered by Public Schemes (Various Years)	PLYL² (Various Years)	Perinatal Mortality³ (Various Years)	Percentage of population Generally Satisfied⁴
Canada	7.4	9.0	1795	6.6	100	3977	7.6	56
France	7.6	8.9	1379	7.2	99	4434	8.9	41
Germany	8.4	8.1	1287	11.5	92	4039	6.4	41
Italy	6.8	7.6	1113	11.0	100	4034	11.0	12
Japan	6.4	6.5	1113	12.9	100	2890	5.7	29
Netherlands	8.0	8.1	1182	5.5	69	3499	9.7	47
New Zealand	7.2	7.2	853	na	100	5198	8.5	na
Spain	5.6	6.6	730	4.0	99	4368	10.0	21
Sweden	9.4	8.7	1421	2.8	100	3375	6.8	32
Switzerland	7.3	7.8	1640	6.0	100	3718	7.1	na
United Kingdom	5.6	6.1	909	5.7	100	4060	9.0	27
United States	9.3	12.4	2566	5.3	44	5479	9.7	10
Average	7.4	8.1	1304	7.3	96	4123	8.5	32

1 PPP (Purchasing Power Parity): notional exchange rates derived from the price of a representative bundle of goods and services in different countries.
2 PLYL (Potential Life Years Lost): the number of deaths under the age of 65 which are "avoidable" given current medical knowledge multiplied by (65 - the age of the deceased), as a rate per 100,000 person years of life, as estimated by the World Health Organisation. This is therefore a weighted measure of premature mortality. The figure quoted is the unweighted average of the male and female PLYL, for the latest year when data was available.
3 Number of stillbirths from the 28th week of pregnancy and of infants dead in the first week of life per 1,000 live and stillbirths.
4 See Blendon et al. (1990,1991).
na Not available.
Source: OECD (1991).

explanation is that in two of these countries, Germany and Japan, doctors are paid on a fee-for-service basis, while in Germany and Italy visits to general practitioners attract no copayments.

- *'The percentage of the population covered by public schemes'* is a proxy for the performance on **social solidarity** of a health care system. All countries, bar the United States, score high on this measure. The lower figures for Germany and the Netherlands indicate the availability of voluntary private opt-out schemes.

- The aggregate **health status** of the population can be measured in a variety of ways, of which two are presented in Table 1.1. For *'potential life years lost'* Japan and the United States are low and high outliers, respectively. Northern European countries and Japan generally score high on *'perinatal mortality'*.

- Finally, *'satisfaction with the health care system'* is a measure sometimes quoted as a proxy for the **outcome** of a health care system. The last column of Table 1.1 indicates the results of a widely quoted survey.[2] There are reservations about both the survey methods and the interpretation of the results. For example, it is likely that people being asked about their satisfaction in different countries have widely differing awareness of the cost to them of the services they are getting.

1.2.3   Observations of Countries

1.2.3.1   *Private and Public Role in Funding*

In no country in our study is health care funded either wholly from public sources or wholly privately. At one extreme, in the United States a little over 40 percent of funding comes from public sources, principally to finance the *Medicare* and *Medicaid* programmes. The highest incidence of public funding is Sweden's 89 percent. It is interesting to note that in the country with the lowest commitment to public funding, the United States, such funding nevertheless amounts to 5.3 percent of GDP, much the same proportion as in the United Kingdom, and that the health status of the population of the two countries seems broadly similar.

---

[2]   Blendon, R., Leitman, R., Morrison, I. and Donelan, K. (1990), "Satisfaction with Health Systems in Ten Nations", *Health Affairs*, Summer, pp. 185-192; Blendon, R., Donelan, K., Jovell, A., Pellise, L. and Costas Lobardia, E. (1991), "Spain's Citizens Assess Their Health Care System", *Health Affairs*, Fall, pp. 216-228.

It should also be noted that the real economic issue about funding is not whether it is 'public' or 'private' but whether it is compulsory or voluntary. For example, copayments (one-half of all 'private' spending in France) are clearly not voluntary. Consequently, voluntary health spending in France is probably a lower proportion of GDP than in the United Kingdom. The same point is relevant in an organisational sense. Hence, German sickness funds are self-governing organisations to which contributions are compulsory. It appears that non-state funding organisations can serve the needs of the population by providing adequate health care services to all. Transferring a funding system from the public sector to the private sector need not change the 'voluntary/compulsory' nature of the system so long as individuals' contributions remain mandatory.

There is some evidence from our studies that countries with high satisfaction ratings are those that combine substantial public financing of health care with quite high private expenditures and/or private provision. Canada, the Netherlands, and Germany all have private health expenditure in excess of 2 percent of GDP - higher than any other country in the survey except the United States where there is no universal public provision. What is not clear is whether this satisfaction arises from the effect of private expenditure increasing total health care spending (which it seems to) or from the extra choice available to individuals through their private outlays (or, as is the case in Italy, their ability to choose private provision at public expense).

1.2.3.2 *Private and Public Role in Provision*

Public funding of health care is not synonymous with public provision. For example, in Canada 74 percent of health care funding comes from central and provincial governments, yet over half of all hospitals are not owned by public authorities. The majority of these are voluntary, non-profit and have religious affiliations. In addition, they have to comply with strict rules, such as accepting all patients regardless of ability to pay. Indeed they are so closely contracted into the public health care system that they are actually classified as 'public'. The fact remains that they are privately-owned hospitals that deliver a publicly-funded service.

This happens in other countries. In much of southern Italy, the state health system relies heavily on private hospitals: indeed, 11 percent of all Italy's state-funded patients are treated in private for-profit hospitals, and 87 percent of private hospitals' income is from public funds. In France, virtually all private hospitals have contracts to treat patients under the public health system. In Japan, most hospitals and clinics are privately owned.

Private hospitals, through contracts, can have a role in providing publicly-funded health services. The reverse is also true. Private payers can buy services from public hospitals, as happens in the United Kingdom and in Spain. There is no evidence that militates against either of these arrangements.

Note too, that in most countries, except Sweden, publicly-funded primary care is provided by doctors who are, at least legally, private and independent contractors.

1.2.3.3   Defining a Guaranteed Health Care Package

All countries in our study define a Guaranteed Health Care Package (GHCP),[3] explicitly or implicitly, and often generously. For example, the Canada Health Act sets out the services that must be covered in provincial plans if they are to receive federal funding. Similarly the United States defines the services available through the *Medicare* and *Medicaid* plans, although that application of a GHCP does not extend into the privately insured sector or to the millions without insurance. In Germany and Switzerland the GHCP is defined in the respective Health Care Act, while Japan has a National Uniform Reimbursement Fee Schedule which defines services.

Definitions of the services included in GHCPs tend to be wide and vague. Often new services get included merely by clinicians deciding that a treatment has become appropriate and the financing system should be expanded to accommodate it, or that is should displace another treatment within a 'fixed' overall budget. Moreover, attempts to tighten definitions in explicit ways have been fraught with difficulty. Nevertheless, existing GHCPs are seldom fully comprehensive, and they do differ between countries. For example, the Canadian package does not include the purchase of medicines, whereas the United Kingdom does, with a minority of copayments. Also in some countries GHCPs include free primary care (e.g. the United Kingdom) while in others, such as France and New Zealand, they do not.

The evidence is that GHCPs can be defined, even if rather loosely at present. There are also signs in some countries (e.g. Germany) of their definitions being

---

[3]   A GHCP is defined as a list of medical conditions, treatment of which are made available to all citizens regardless of their ability to pay.

tightened in response to cost pressures. In others (e.g. Switzerland) the definition is being broadened.

1.2.3.4 Competitive Insurance and the GHCP

Our studies do not reveal whether competing insurers can deliver a universally available health care package. That approach has scarcely been tried anywhere yet, although the Netherlands and New Zealand are moving towards such systems.

A minor exception exists in Germany where some white collar workers are eligible to join more than one statutory sickness fund. They have a choice they exercise without detriment to their right to the GHCP. Universality is ensured by the requirement that everyone must belong to one of the sickness funds.

A recurring issue is that individuals have widely differing degrees of health risk. Different systems treat this issue differently. Private insurance schemes normally risk rate by dividing their individual members into different risk categories, for example by age bands, and by taking account of their health histories. However, this approach cannot be a basis for providing universal uniform coverage based on ability to pay. Hence, such schemes cannot be used to provide a GHCP, and nowhere in our study do they do so (perhaps with the notable exception of Switzerland).

The extreme opposite way of handling the diversity of health risks is to put them all together into the largest possible pool so that they average out. That is essentially what happens in single-payer national health schemes, such as those in the United Kingdom, New Zealand (at present) and Canada.

Between these two extremes are multiple-payer schemes providing a GHCP, such as those in France, Germany, the Netherlands, and Japan. Such sickness funds are obliged to take all eligible applicants, regardless of individual health status. Hence, any particular fund may face an overall membership risk which differs from those of other funds.

That problem can be addressed in two ways. In Germany, everyone in the same fund pays the same percentage of income, regardless of their individual risk. However, premiums across funds vary, so that some charge higher percentages of income than others. A similar approach is followed in Japan. A different approach, which is essentially that followed in the Netherlands and

France, is to compensate individual funds for the risk profile they actually face, so that the members of all funds can be charged the same premiums.

In the German and Dutch systems, multiple non-profit payers provide a GHCP to all comers without assessing individual risk. In principle, competing for-profit payers could provide a GHCP on the same basis, if suitable rules were introduced. However, this approach has not yet been tried in any of the countries in our study, although some (such as Switzerland) are taking steps in this direction.

1.2.3.5 *Remuneration of Primary Physicians*

In most of the countries studied, primary physicians are normally independent professionals, usually partly or wholly contracted to provide publicly-funded care. An exception is Sweden where a large proportion of primary doctors are salaried public employees.

The commonest way of remunerating primary doctors (a definition which includes most non-hospital specialists in countries like the United States and Italy) is on a fee-for-service basis. This is standard or widespread in Canada, France, Germany, Japan, Switzerland, the United States and, effectively, New Zealand. The other main method is capitation payments, which are used, often with specific allowances, in Italy, the Netherlands and the United Kingdom. Spain uses a combination of capitation and salary.

A priori expectation is that fee-for-service will encourage the over-provision of service to patients; and that capitation payments encourage the opposite. Throughout our study there is indeed strong anecdotal evidence that fee-for-service does in practice encourage over-provision. This seems particularly so when doctors' incomes come under pressure, either because of attempts to cut public expenditure or because of competitive pressures in over-supplied markets. Canada is experimenting with increasing use of capitation as an attempt to control costs.

It is far less clear from our studies that capitation payment systems actually lead to under-provision of necessary medical care. This may be partly because of the countervailing effect of medical ethics. But capitation creates incentives which may, at the margin, interfere with best-practice medicine. There is anecdotal evidence (e.g. from Italy) that doctors paid by capitation tend to pander to patients' wishes for medication, and to refer patients to hospital for treatment which might better have been given in the doctor's surgery. For example, doctors paid by capitation tend to have less equipment for minor surgery. Putting primary physicians at "risk" for the services they provide and refer out of their office, as is the case with many HMO contracts in the US, can provide incentives to under-provide.

1.2.3.6 Remuneration of Hospitals and Clinicians

The method whereby hospitals are remunerated is still, in general, less important than the incentives faced by their clinicians, who take most of the decisions about how to allocate available resources. This is too sweeping a statement even for a general overview, because the position is being changed by the introduction of prospective payment systems. These have been implemented by organisations such as *Medicare* and managed care insurers in the United States and private insurers in many other countries. They significantly change the incentives facing those who take spending decisions in hospitals, including the clinicians who work in them or use them for treating their patients. However, prospective payment systems are still the exception rather than the rule internationally.

Most publicly-funded hospitals are given global budgets out of which to meet the demands put upon them. In Germany and Switzerland, however, they are paid on a *per diem* basis whilst in Japan fee-for-service is standard. Private hospitals are usually paid on some mixture of fee-for-service and *per diem*.

It is argued that global budgets provide an incentive for hospitals to be efficient so as to deliver as much care as possible out of their budget. Unfortunately, that incentive often does not reach down to the individual doctors who actually make treatment decisions. In some countries like Italy and Spain, budgets are regularly overspent and topped up retrospectively; hence their incentives are weakened. In some countries where budgets appear to work better, like the United Kingdom, clinicians perceive their effect as 'underfunding'. Global budget shortfalls in Canada and the UK sometimes cause hospitals to close their doors to some patients before year end.

One way in which hospital managers can restrain the spending of their clinicians is by tolerating 'bed blockers'. These are patients well on their way to recovery who are permitted to stay in acute care hospitals, incurring relatively low treatment costs, for longer than is strictly necessary. This represents a waste of resources, as they could recuperate elsewhere at lower cost. This is identified as a problem in Canada, the United Kingdom and

Japan. A variant occurs in Germany where *per diem* payments also encourage public hospitals to lengthen patient stays.

Private hospitals are usually paid through a mixture of fee-for-service and *per diem* rates. These are often monitored quite closely when paid by private insurance funders, who equip themselves with the expertise to judge hospital costings. This is evidence that the introduction of expert purchasers into the system may be one important way to improve efficiency.

Hospital clinicians are most generally paid salaries supplemented, in some cases, by fee-for-service payments. They do not generally face personal financial risks. Yet their decisions are central to the expenditure and efficiency of their hospital. This problem is being addressed in the United Kingdom by the government's Resource Management Initiative, which seeks to involve hospital doctors more directly in the business management of the services they provide. In the United States, as mentioned above, funders such as *Medicare* and health maintenance organisations, are seeking to have more influence over the decisions of hospital doctors.

1.2.3.7 Copayments

Copayments[4] on purchases for services and of medicines and appliances are widespread but not universal in publicly-funded health care systems.

One extreme is Canada where there are no copayments on services covered by the GHCP; they would be regarded as violating conditions stipulated by the Canada Health Act, and would result in the termination of federal contributions to the provinces. There are, however, copayments on some supplementary services covered by the provincial plans, and this tendency is increasing. In the United Kingdom, copayments are confined to optical and dental services, together with a minority of prescriptions for medicines.

The other extreme is a country like France where copayments and user charges are widespread and substantial. They are even levied on primary care and hospital treatment. In consequence, it is normal practice to insure against such charges in France, whereas in a country like the United Kingdom that does not happen. In Japan, copayments are widespread and range from 10 to 30 percent, depending on the compulsory insurance scheme.

---

[4] The terms *copayments* and *cost-sharing* are used synonymously throughout this report.

Our observations suggest that the use of copayments to restrain demand faces practical limits. In some countries, social considerations require that they be kept too low to have much effect. When copayment rates rise they lose their impact because people take out insurance against them. There is evidence that copayments can help to moderate excessive demand if used within an appropriate range. The practical question is whether, in particular countries, a level can be found which is high enough to have a beneficial impact without being so high as to convert the system, unintentionally, onto an insurance basis.

1.2.3.8 Diffusion of Medical Technology

Although the use of advanced medical technology is associated with high-income countries, new medical facilities and equipment usually diffuse fastest in countries with substantial private funding and providing institutions.

Canada has in total considerably fewer high technology medical facilities per head than the neighbouring United States. This is ascribed to the control over new investments exercised in a single-payer funding system. Bureaucracies are inherently less responsive to demands for new treatments than are market-oriented system of competing funders.

We find supporting evidence in the experience of the United Kingdom and Italy. In the United Kingdom, a significant proportion of advanced technology equipment, such as Magnetic Resonance Imaging scanners, has been funded by charitable donations rather than by public investment funds. In Italy, most new technology is introduced first in the substantial private hospital sector, with public hospitals being forced to follow in order to remain competitive.

These observations do not imply that the private approach leads to optimal installation of advanced medical facilities. In both the United States and parts of Italy, such facilities are too many and under-utilised, leading to inefficient investment in new technologies in some areas. The most acute problem arises when the 'gatekeeper' physicians, who decide on the use of the facilities, also have a financial interest in their use. This can be either because the equipment is installed in their own clinics or because they are rewarded, with fees or inducements, for referring patients to them.

The evidence is, therefore, that the private sector tends to introduce the latest technology faster. The rate of introduction of new medicines is another story.

At present, that depends mainly on the regulatory regime rather than on the structure of the health care market.

1.2.4   Conclusions

1.2.4.1   Cost Drivers

The fundamental causes of upward pressure on health care costs appear to be:[5]

- rapid medical technological progress, which widens the range of potentially beneficial treatments, combined with increasing demands for better care; and,

- aging populations who require more care (in countries where they are still aging fast).

These factors are not adequately offset by incentives for patients or providers to restrain excessive utilisation.

Rapid changes in technology, in terms of both equipment and treatment methods (e.g. new drugs), are widening the scope of available medical treatment, and hence the potential demand for health care. The best use of these opportunities depends on having a system that responds to consumer demands and leads to efficient investment in new technologies.

In some countries, the high cost of health care is ascribed partly to the rising relative cost of inputs such as doctors. There could be three reasons for this:

- increasing skills and specialisation in medical personnel; or,

- shortages of supply, or artificially raised prices, caused by restrictive practices; or,

- excess utilisation of existing physician resources.

In general, we do not think that restrictive entry is being used to raise the price of doctors' services artificially. But, it does appear, for instance in Canada, that where there is monopoly power in the supply of medical services, this results in higher costs for these services. In the past,

---

[5]   The largest elements of health care spending are, in descending order: hospitals including facilities; medical equipment and the payment of hospital specialists; primary care; and the purchase of medicines. Hospital care is typically between 40 and 50 percent of the total, primary care 15 to 25 percent and pharmaceuticals 8 to 25 per cent.

governments have sought to offset such monopoly power by introducing monopsony power on the purchasing side. An alternative which is now being explored in, for example, the United Kingdom and New Zealand, is to force doctors, and other providers, into a more competitive environment in which they have to negotiate individual contracts.

In all the countries in our study it is doctors, more than any other group, who take the day-to-day decisions which in the end determine the total level of health care spending in a country. This applies whether funding is by government, by multiple sickness funds or by competing insurers. Even in an extreme case, such as the United Kingdom, it is the cumulative effects of the prescribing and referring recommendations of general practitioners (GPs), together with the individual decisions about treatment taken by hospital clinicians, that mainly determine the demand for care. If these requirements exceed the centrally allocated funding, waiting lists build up. At some point these become politically unacceptable and additional public or private funds get allocated.

Since doctors ultimately determine the level and pattern of health care spending, it is vital that they are given financial and other incentives that encourage them to allocate resources optimally. The most appropriate incentive structures may depend on circumstances; but the evidence favours some element of capitation payment with provisions for risk for primary physicians, or, better perhaps, a fee-for-service structure with a patient copayment element. For hospital care the evidence favours a move towards prospective cost-per-case payments so far as the information systems are in place to calculate average costs.

1.2.4.2 Convergence of Health Care Systems

Public and private approaches to the funding and provision of health care are not mutually exclusive. All countries combine the two approaches and they appear to be able to complement one another.

The allocation of resources to health care in general and, within that, to particular elements of the provider system, is a function of the health care funding organisations. Public, single-payer systems do not seem able to generate sufficient incentives for efficiency nor, in some countries, can they always control total spending. Private insurance funding systems have more incentives to be efficient but often fail to provide universal coverage. This suggests that some combination of these approaches is needed.

All the countries studied are in the throes of some kind of reform of their health care systems. Moreover, there appear to be signs of convergence in the changes they are making. The United States has, for some time, been moving away from a pure and unregulated system of competing private insurers and providers. Countries such as Sweden, Canada, New Zealand and the United Kingdom, which were the archetypical public providers of care, are seeking to introduce more competition and efficiency into their systems. Somewhere in the middle there may be common ground towards which everyone may be heading in the long-run.

1.3 THE ECONOMICS OF HEALTH REFORM: SUMMARY OF A PROTOTYPE

1.3.1 Markets and Governments

1.3.1.1 Introduction

This section provides a brief guide to the economics of health care reform. The main features of an 'ideal' health care system, the **Prototype**, are introduced. It aspires to achieve the best possible balance between two objectives of health care systems, namely efficiency and social solidarity. Some lessons are drawn in applying the Prototype to real world health care systems.

Readers are recommended to read Chapter 3 for a full and detailed presentation of the arguments underlying the recommendations of the Prototype.

1.3.1.2 Competitive Markets and Health Care Systems

The economic characteristics of health care in most industrialised countries can be described as follows:

1. **Large numbers of people** participate in health care systems. Health care services are demanded by a multiplicity of actual and potential consumers (that is, patients); and are supplied by a significant number of providers (that is, primary care physicians, hospitals, nursing homes, pharmacists).

2. In few cases do health care services form a natural **monopoly**. The total costs of providing a health care service are not necessarily lower when a single institution provides the service, rather than two or more.[6]

3. Health care is overwhelmingly consumed **individually**. In most cases each individual pays for and consumes health care without affecting the consumption levels, or the health status, of other individuals.[7]

---

[6]   There are very few exceptions to this rule. *Haemoglobinopathy* (the prenatal analysis of blood disorders) is an example: in most countries the service is centralised with a single institute.

[7]   The main exception to this rule relates to public health issues, and communicable diseases, such as AIDS.

These three traits also characterise **competitive markets**, suggesting that competition could be the most efficient way to allocate resources for health care. In such a market, suppliers of health care would compete for consumers, and consumers would choose which health care services to pay for. Suppliers would quote prices related to the cost of the service they offered, and consumers would express their preference for different health care services, according to their needs and their budget. As a result, prices determined in the market would influence the type, quality and level of health care services provided to individual consumers.

1.3.1.3 Government Intervention

The major reason for intervention by governments in health care systems is the desire to achieve a degree of **social solidarity**[8] among citizens in the provision of health care. The argument is as follows:

1. For any single individual, the need for health care services is typically **unpredictable**, but, in the event of actual need, the expense can be significant, or potentially bankrupting.

2. Unpredictability of health care costs leads individuals to seek health care **insurance**. In a competitive health care market, competing health care insurance companies will charge health care insurance premiums for each person (or groups of persons), which are equal to the expected level of health care costs for that individual (or group).

3. In such a market, premiums will vary from person to person, depending on their **risk characteristics**, and regardless of their income levels. As a result, some individuals may be unable to afford to buy health care insurance.

Most societies regard it as unacceptable that those who cannot afford health care should go without. Since a completely competitive market is unable to offer satisfactory methods to redistribute incomes from the those who can afford to pay for health care to those who cannot, **governments or social insurance plans** have assumed a major role in many health care systems.

---

[8]   Social solidarity in this context means that, as far as health care is concerned, all citizens are treated in a fair and equitable manner.

1.3.1.4   Efficiency or Social Solidarity?

For the reasons set out above, many health care systems have turned to governments or regulated insurance funds as the preferred funders, and sometimes, providers, of health care services. This approach trades some of the advantages of consumer-responsive private provision for those of greater security for the individual and social solidarity.

It also creates new problems. In a **regulated** market for health care insurance, premiums are based on *average* expected costs of a group of individuals. Insurance companies have an incentive to pick the good risks within that group, i.e. those individuals who are intrinsically 'healthy', and therefore likely to incur lower than average health care costs.[9]   At the same time, healthy individuals may prefer to pay for their health care needs as and when they arise and may opt out of social insurance schemes altogether. This would leave the 'sick' only in social insurance schemes, and tends to further disadvantage them, since they are often also the poor.

These adverse effects of regulated markets are why in most countries regulation is even further extended by:

- obliging insurance companies to accept all individuals, regardless of risk, at a common premium (which may be income-related); and,

- by obliging all individuals to take out insurance, even if the premium they contribute is larger than their expected costs of health care.[10]

Mandatory insurance pools, however, curtail the scope for competition for the funding and provision of health care. In such government-sponsored systems, consumers have limited scope to express their preferences.   Choice is an important element in achieving economic efficiency, since the expression of choice provides signals of satisfaction or dissatisfaction to funders and providers of health care, as well as suppliers of medical technology and medicines. Markets, or other decentralised systems, are usually better suited to responding to consumer demands.

---

[9]   This process is called 'risk-selection'.

[10]   Some countries go so far by creating a single mandatory insurance pool, i.e. a national health service, in which the government takes over the role of funding health care.

The central problem of organising health care systems can therefore be described as finding a reasonable and acceptable balance between efficiency and social solidarity.

1.3.2 Objectives of Health Care Reform

The purpose of health care reform is to reorganise health care systems in a way which will lead them to achieve the following goals:

On Efficiency

1. Health care systems should be designed to encourage efficient funding and provision of health care services. The amount and the mix of health care services should reflect the informed preferences of consumers. Providers and consumers should not be encouraged by inappropriate incentives to deliver or consume more or less health care than is economically efficient.

2. Health care systems should be responsive to new opportunities and needs, as expressed by patients and providers. Services should be provided with high professional standards, using cost -effective medical technology and medicines. The health care system should encourage innovation of improved treatments.

In the next section we introduce the outline of a model health care system that is designed to achieve these objectives.

1.3.3 Outline of a Health Care Prototype

1.3.3.1 Definition

The health care model introduced here is called the Prototype. Its purpose is to describe an 'ideal' health care system in an abstract world. Although in principle designed as a health care model for industrialised countries, the description of the model is strictly conceptual, i.e. unconstrained by political, social, cultural or other institutional arrangements of any existing nation.

On Social Solidarity

3. Health care systems should be financed in a way that allows all members of society access to essential services regardless of their ability to pay. This means that within health care systems a redistribution of funds must take place, from those who can afford to pay for these services to those who cannot afford to pay.

4. Access to services, regardless of ability to pay, need not extend to all aspects of health care, but should cover at least a guaranteed package of health care services. Society must, therefore, reach an agreement on how such a guaranteed health care package is to be defined.

1.3.3.2 *General Features*

The Prototype consists of fifteen Recommendations, which are described in detail in Chapter 3 of this study. Its general features are described in the following box.

The main participants of the health care system are (1) the funders, (2) the providers, (3) the government, (4) the patients, and (5) the suppliers of medical technology and medicines. The following sections describe their roles and relationships in more detail.

Coverage

1. Universal comprehensive coverage for a Guaranteed Health Care Package is mandatory.

Structure

2. Individuals enrol with an insurance fund of their choice for the GHCP. The insurer must accept all comers.

Funding

3. Funding for the GHCP comes from three sources:

    First, a premium related to income, but not to risk, is paid to a central fund. From the central fund, each insurance fund receives a fixed, risk-adjusted capitation payment per patient enrolled.

    Second, individuals pay a risk-related premium to the insurance fund of their choice. That premium varies between funds.

    Third, copayments for all services within the GHCP are mandatory.

Incentives

4. Insurance funds reimburse providers for services delivered to their members. Reimbursement levels will be determined through negotiated contracts, or market-determined list prices.

1.3.3.3 *Coverage*

The function of financing health care rests largely with insurance funds, not with the government. The statutory role of insurance funds is to purchase, on behalf of their members, services which are included in a Guaranteed Health Care Package (GHCP). The GHCP defines the rights of the insured and reflects society's view of social solidarity.

A GHCP is defined as a list of medical conditions, treatment of which are made available to all citizens regardless of their ability to pay. One possible method of defining a *truly basic* GHCP is to include only those conditions which satisfy the following three criteria:

1. withholding any form of treatment for the condition presents a threat to the health status of the patient;

2. treatment of the condition is expensive, relative to normal income levels; and

3. it is unreasonable to expect every patient to fund the treatment by accruing savings over previous years.

Other definitions are possible. All health care plans offered by insurance funds to prospective members must include, as a minimum, the GHCP. Individuals are not permitted to seek coverage with a health care plan that excludes any services in return for a lower premium.

Insurance for the GHCP with one of the insurance funds is mandatory for every citizen. Insurance funds have to accept every individual who applies for coverage for the GHCP.

1.3.3.4 Funding

Insurance funds will charge their members a contribution in return for offering coverage of health care expenses for services within the GHCP. The contribution will come from two sources. In addition, insurance fund members copay for services which they use:

1. One part of the insurance fund contribution will be a fee that is related only to income. The fee will be collected by the government as a dedicated payroll tax and passed on to a central fund. The central fund then pays out to each insurance fund a risk-adjusted capitation fee for each individual enrolled with the fund.

2. A second part of the contribution will be a premium which individuals will pay directly to their insurance fund. This premium will vary between funds. Variation will depend on two conditions:

    •   *Any remaining risk characteristics that have not been taken account for by the central fund.* These must not relate to factors outside the individual's control (in particular chronic or acquired medical conditions, or demographic factors such as age), which must be taken into account by the risk adjustment mechanism used by the central fund. Instead, remaining risk characteristics should only relate to life-style factors (e.g. smoking) which have deliberately been excluded from the capitation formula.

- *The efficiency of competing insurance funds to purchase health care services on behalf of their members.* This is intentional. In a competitive health care market, direct payments by patients to insurance funds will provide funds with an incentive to respond to patients' preferences. They are therefore expected to purchase high quality, cost-effective treatments.

3. The third part of the contribution to the GHCP consists of mandatory patient copayments. Copayments will, in principle, apply to all patients and all treatments. Beyond an income-related limit per annum they are equal to that upper limit.

Each country will decide on which proportions of the projected total health care expenditure should (on average) be financed from the three sources of finance. This decision can be updated if necessary.[11]

Insurance funds are free to offer to their members services that are either not covered by the GHCP, or, if they are covered by the GHCP, provide more choice or higher quality (e.g. single rooms in hospitals). Premiums for any additional services will be set by insurers in a competitive market.

1.3.3.5 Reimbursement of Providers

The delivery of services rests with providers. This includes primary care physicians, hospitals, nursing and community homes, and producers and distributors of medicines. All potential providers are given unregulated entry to the health care market, subject to medical qualification requirements.

Providers and suppliers of medicines are reimbursed by purchasers, i.e. insurance funds. They will supply their services through two different routes:

1. open market sales made at list prices. List prices are likely to be quoted on the basis of cost-per-case payments for hospitals; fee-for-service payments for physicians; and prices per units for suppliers of medical aids, technology and medicines; or,

2. contracts negotiated between individual providers (e.g. hospitals) or groups of providers (e.g. physicians) with individual purchasers.

---

[11]   In the Netherlands, which is currently introducing a system similar to that of the Prototype, a decision was taken as follows: 85 percent of health care expenditure is to be financed through an income-related fee, while 15 percent is to be financed through direct payments by individuals to insurance funds. There are no copayments.

Purchasers are free to discontinue a contractual relationship with a provider at the end of contractual period, and are not obliged to commence a contractual relationship with a new provider.

1.3.3.6 The Role of the Government

The government's role is limited in the health care system. Its main role is to ensure that all existing insurance funds and providers, as well as all new insurance funds and providers, meet certain requirements. The government will also set up an agency to oversee, and if necessary regulate, competition amongst insurance funds and providers. The tasks of the agency include investigating collusion and approving of mergers. The government will be responsible for medical teaching facilities. It will also set up a medicines approval agency.

In addition, the government will set up a purchasing agency on behalf of those consumers who cannot be expected to express informed preferences in the health care market (e.g. the mentally disabled). In accordance with the social solidarity concept, this purchasing agency will be financed from the central fund.

The government will oversee and confirm the definition of the GHCP and the specification of the risk adjustment formula used by the central fund. The central fund itself is administered by the insurance funds, who may wish to update the risk adjustment formula from time to time.

Chart 1.4 provides an outline of the NERA prototypical health care system.

1.3.4 Adopting the Prototype

1.3.4.1 The Prototype as a Guide to Reform

The Prototype may serve as a guide to health care reform for countries that are conceptually similar to that underlying the Prototype's assumptions, i.e. industrialised countries with market institutions (laws of contract and intellectual property rights, for example). Comparison of existing systems with the Prototype helps to highlight any differences and to identify areas where reform is required.

Although the Prototype constitutes an 'end-point' for reform policies, this end-point may not be reached in the real world for a long time. In particular, the funding mechanism of the Prototype consists of an intricate mechanism, which

Chart 1.4
The Prototype - Outline

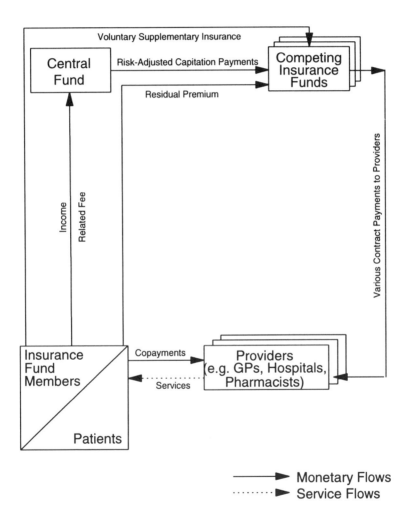

is unlikely to be easily applied to various countries without a major overhaul of the entire existing system. Other Prototype recommendations may not be acceptable on purely political grounds, even though they could be implemented relatively easily.

In Section 1.4, we try to identify short-term reform policies that would convert existing health care systems into transitional systems located somewhere between the *status quo* and the Prototype. In this section we briefly point out implications for long-term reform of existing health care systems, in particular with regard to the competitive funding structure envisaged by the Prototype.

1.3.4.2 Long-Term Reform of Health Care Systems

In **Predominantly Tax-Funded Health Care Systems** (e.g. Canada, Italy, New Zealand, Spain, Sweden and the United Kingdom) the role of financing health care services normally rests with regional authorities. These regional authorities could in the long-run become the predecessors of competing insurance funds. Tax-based systems *always* have a risk-compensating mechanism between authorities (with the government usually performing the role of a central fund). In contrast to the Prototype, tax-based systems typically lack autonomous funding authorities; although, as the example of GP Fundholders in the United Kingdom demonstrates, an element of independent funding can be introduced in such systems, which in the long-run may lead to some form of competition.

In **tax-funded systems the main reform step is, therefore, to transform existing regional health authorities,** *first - in the short-run*, **into independent decentralised purchasing authorities, and,** *second - in the long-run*, **into competing insurers.**

In **Predominantly Social Insurance-Based Systems** (e.g. France, Germany, Japan and the Netherlands) the role of financing health care services rests overwhelmingly with semi-autonomous, not-for-profit insurance funds. In some countries, these insurance funds already compete to some extent; in others they do not. In contrast to the Prototype, social insurance-based systems usually do not have in place a comprehensive risk-compensating mechanism between funds (although all countries either have established quasi-compensation principles, or are planning to establish these).

The main reform step in social insurance-based systems is therefore, *first - in the short-run*, **to establish some form of compensation of premiums**

between funds (e.g. through balance payments between funds);[12] and, *second - in the long run*, to encourage the development of independent, decentralised and commercially oriented funds with opportunities for increased competition.

In **Predominantly Voluntary Insurance-Based Systems** (eg. the United States and Switzerland) the role of financing health care rests overwhelmingly with competing private for-profit insurance companies. No compensating mechanism between funds exists. In the absence of government intervention (for example through tax credits) such systems typically lead to some people being unable to afford insurance. In contrast to the Prototype, such systems do not offer mandatory insurance for a Guaranteed Health Care Package to all citizens regardless of their ability to pay.

The main reform step in voluntary insurance-based system is therefore to introduce a universal, mandatory health insurance scheme.

In all systems, whether tax-funded or based on social or voluntary insurance, health care services are usually delivered by a mix of public, voluntary and private providers. In many countries, including the Netherlands, Germany, the UK, Sweden and the US, providers operate increasingly as independent, and to some extent competing, businesses. This is entirely consistent with the Prototype.

These developments suggest that any reform programme intended to strengthen the autonomy and independence of the funding side of health care systems is likely to be more complex and difficult to implement than any similar type of reform which targets the delivery side of health care systems.

If the funding side of health care systems is not reformed, governments are more likely to intervene whenever a real or perceived funding crisis emerges. Any such government intervention is likely to take the form of global budgets as a measure for containing costs in the health care system. This prospect underlines the importance of implementing health care reform that will lead to health care markets built around independent purchasers, autonomous providers, and sovereign patients. Section 1.4 suggests possible short-term reform steps for a number of countries.

---

[12]   In some countries, direct tax credits to insurance fund members or other forms of subsidies are also a possibility.

1.4   REFORM OF HEALTH CARE SYSTEMS: A SYNOPSIS

1.4.1   Pressures for Reform

There are pressures for health care reform in all the countries included in the study, but they vary greatly in intensity. A crude classification of countries looks as follows:

TABLE 1.2 PRESSURE FOR REFORM OF HEALTH CARE SYSTEMS		
Strong	**Intermediate**	**Weak**
United States United Kingdom New Zealand Switzerland	Netherlands Sweden Germany Canada Italy Spain	Japan France

The major factor behind the pressure for reform is concern about present or future health care costs and the ability of expenditure to meet the rising demand in health care services.

In the **United States**, health care reform is one of the biggest issues on the political agenda of President Clinton. The new administration is faced with the problem of providing universal access to health care services (some 31 million Americans are currently uninsured, and millions of others are under-insured), while at the same time reducing the federal budget deficit. Costs for medical services continue to rise relentlessly, due in part to the substantial over-provision of low-benefit, high-cost care. Tax subsidies to employer health care benefits lead to excessive insurance coverage for some, which, in turn, leads to consumption levels of health care beyond what is necessary on medical grounds. The emphasis on cost containment and expanded access now dominates the reform debate in the US.

In **Canada**, there is also increasing pressure to meet the financing needs of the health care system, albeit to a much lesser extent than in the US. In response to such pressures, some provinces have reduced the number of supplementary services covered. Rationing for some services is commonplace. For example, in the early 1990s, the government of Ontario allowed patients to seek treatment for cardiac surgery in the US to cut down on waiting lists, effectively using the US system as a 'safety valve'. Policymakers recognise the need for reform in the near future to avert a possible funding crisis due to the federal government's inability to increase contributions to the provinces.

European health care systems also face challenges, albeit to different degrees. In the **United Kingdom**, for example, the main problem is underfunding, not lack of access. Public expenditure controls work; but for the country's National Health Service (NHS) they sometimes work in an arbitrary manner creating biased allocation of resources. Recent reforms attempt to address this problem by introducing a quasi-market into the NHS, but the system is cash-limited. Waiting lists for some ailments encourage patients to seek private treatment instead of treatment under the NHS.

By contrast, in **Germany**, the problem is rather one of over-supply of services. Doctors and hospitals have few incentives to use resources efficiently. The fee-for-services reimbursement for primary physicians within capped budgets leads to a rapidly expanding volume of services. This usually translates into increases in overall budgets for physicians in the next financial year. Until recently, hospitals had a statutory right to have their costs reimbursed by insurance funds, which eliminated any incentive for cost-efficient provision of service. Some competition between funds exists. However, this often leads to generous interpretations of an already bountiful list of health care entitlements, rather than to a reduction in premiums. In the past, the government intervened on a number of occasions by passing a succession of cost containment acts; only recently has this given way to a more rational approach to structural reform of the health care system.

In **France**, discussions on the need for reforming the health care system are also urgent. The country has an extremely fragmented health care system, with little focus in policy decision making, which has led to increasing financial pressure on the French sickness funds. Although the French government in the past appears to have successfully emphasised a firm central control, there is now increasing and widespread anxiety about the costs of the French health care system.

The need for reform is fully recognised in the **Netherlands**. A health care reform programme is currently being implemented, albeit slowly. The main problem of the old system is that care is financed from different sources: acute care is financed by sickness funds or private health insurers; home care is financed through a national programme; family assistance and nursing care is predominantly paid out of the national budget; and social work is paid for by municipal budgets. This uncoordinated finance structure makes it difficult to achieve an efficient health care system. As a result, the Dutch government in the past tried to contain costs through a number of regulations, which have largely proved to be unworkable.

Switzerland is currently debating a complete overhaul of its health care system; if accepted by referendum it would constitute only the second main reform programme since the establishment of the country's health insurance scheme in 1911. In the European context Switzerland is unique. Its health care system is a distant relative of the US system, and, not surprisingly, it suffers from similar problems. In particular, health care premiums are not linked to income of the insured. Instead, insurance funds have been allowed to set premiums according to (selected) risk factors. As a result there are considerable premium differentials between and within health insurance funds. In recent years, the federal government has been forced to step in and to pass a series of emergency resolutions which are intended not only to control the increases in health care expenditure, but also to reduce the growing inequalities of premium contributions. At the same time, the government has submitted to Parliament detailed proposals for structural health care reform.

By contrast, in **Sweden**, the current crisis of the health care system has to be seen from a wider political point of view. The country is currently re-examining its role as an advanced welfare state. This re-examination was prompted by a variety of factors, in particular the sluggish growth of GDP in recent years. To overcome its current economic difficulties, and to prepare the country for eventual entry into the European Community, Sweden has to regain its competitiveness. To do so it has to lower taxes, including those raised by the regional authorities for health care purposes. This has led the national government to pass legislation in 1991 and 1992, effectively prohibiting regional authorities from increasing their tax rates.

Given its rapidly aging population and the worsening economic conditions, even **Japan** finds it difficult to maintain its policy of containing growth of health care spending to a level determined by the growth in national income. The aging of the Japanese population leads to an increasing need for long-term care institutions. Mispricing within the uniform fee schedule has resulted in long waiting times at some hospitals and an oversupply of medicines, tests and some procedural services, while at the same time there is under-provision of consultative services and physical deterioration of medical facilities.

1.4.2   Constraints on Reform

There are several impediments to rapid reform of health care systems. In countries such as Germany, Canada, and France, there is general satisfaction with the existing system; a wide range of treatments is available to a high standard. Thus, generating public support for the difficult task of health reform is likely to be difficult. Japan, with its preference for incremental change, may well be the best example of this constraint. Even modest reforms may be difficult to justify, given the country's impressive health outcomes and modest costs.

Further, in the countries mentioned above and also in the Netherlands and the United Kingdom, there is broad political support for the underlying aims and values of the existing health care system, especially in respect to social solidarity. Reforms which could be construed as limiting access to health services, or creating a two-tier system, could prove politically unattractive, unless the financial difficulties of the NHS become much more pressing than they are present. By contrast, in Switzerland a relatively strong emphasis on individual responsibility favours per head health insurance premiums over income-linked contributions even though the risk-rated individual premiums are contributing to the current disintegration of the Swiss health care system.

There are interest groups within each health system that are likely to resist moves in the direction of the Prototype. In Canada, France, Japan, and the UK, government intervention in all areas of health care is pronounced. One reason for this has been to maintain tight control over the cost of the system. As the health care sector has not faced an efficient set of financial incentives, cost containment policies have been the only means to prevent cost escalation. It is unlikely that these powerful bureaucracies would easily relinquish their role. Indeed, this has been the experience with the UK Treasury during the recent reforms of the NHS.

Some groups of medical professionals are also likely to resist change. Many such professional associations have rules that inhibit competition between providers by, for example, banning advertising. A health care market introduces transparency over both cost and quality in a way that could undermine the influence (and incomes) of some professionals relative to others. It is perhaps not unfair to say that many medical professionals believe that they know what the public ought to want.

A move towards more competitive market arrangements would require a substantial change of culture for providers and insurance funds. Presently, especially in continental Europe, decisions over allocation of resources are typically settled by powerful interest groups in centralised negotiations. This has led to inappropriate price signals and collusion to maintain monopolies. Moving to a competitive environment will entail substantial changes in decision making and management processes at all levels within these organisations.

The definition of a Guaranteed Health Care Package (GHCP) may also prove problematic. While most countries have an existing GHCP, albeit sometimes vaguely defined, three problems arise. First, in some countries, notably Germany and Canada, the GHCP is very generous. It may be necessary to reduce the coverage of the package in order to constrain costs, or to ensure that the guaranteed package only covers services that are demonstrably effective. Second, in those countries, such as the UK, where the GHCP is currently only implicitly defined, there would be substantial pressure during the definition process from a variety of interest groups for coverage to be widened. Finally, a number of countries, such as France and Canada, place importance on the freedom to choose the doctor or hospital at which to receive treatment. Constraining this choice, either in the definition of the GHCP or through an insurer providing access to some providers and not others, will be difficult to implement in some countries.

A final and widespread constraint is risk aversion. Health care is politically sensitive and the consequences of reforms going wrong could be severe for their initiators. The risks are exacerbated by severe shortages of management skills in a sector which has been dominated by medical experts who were not expected to address economic and commercial issues. Hence, it is always tempting for policymakers to use a sticking plaster even when more radical treatment is indicated.

1.4.3   Reform Steps

1.4.3.1   Short-Term Steps Towards the Prototype

We have identified several reform proposals designed to enhance the efficiency and social solidarity of existing health care systems. Of these reform proposals, some apply to all countries while others apply to a single country only. Chart 1.5 lists these reform proposals, and indicates whether or not they apply to each of the twelve countries included in the study.

The reform proposals are designed to address the main deficiencies of existing health care systems. Implementing the reforms listed for each country can be expected to lead to improved performance of that country's health care system. The guiding principles for the reform steps proposed in Chart 1.5 have been derived from the Prototype. Thus, implementation of the reform steps listed is meant to move a country's existing health care system towards the system outlined by the Prototype, but without necessarily reaching it. The emphasis has been on the introduction of practical steps, rather than wholesale conversions of systems. Nevertheless, some steps proposed for some countries would amount to radical health care reform that would require dramatic policy initiatives. The establishment of a mandatory universal insurance scheme for the United States is an example of a radical reform which is nonetheless realistic under current conditions.

Before presenting a short-term reform programme for seven major countries, we analyse the exact nature of the individual reform steps.

1.4.3.2   Reform Proposals

1.4.3.2.1   Introduction

The reform steps, which apply to individual countries in different ways, can be classified as belonging to one of the following groups:

- *Coverage* is a social solidarity measure. It spells out the reform steps that are necessary to ensure that each member of the population of a country has access to health care facilities for a defined set of services regardless of ability to pay.

- *Structure* comprises reform proposals that are intended to alter the institutions of a country's health care system. Given the diversity of health care systems, structural reforms have to take into account the existing organisational arrangements within a country in order to arrive at specific proposals for each country.

- *Funding* introduces reform proposals intended to alter the macro-performance of a country's health care system. Such reforms can serve as a precursor of more substantial structural reforms.

- Finally, *incentive*-related reforms introduce a set of financial changes intended to alter the economic behaviour of providers and consumers of health care.

Chart 1.5
Reform Steps

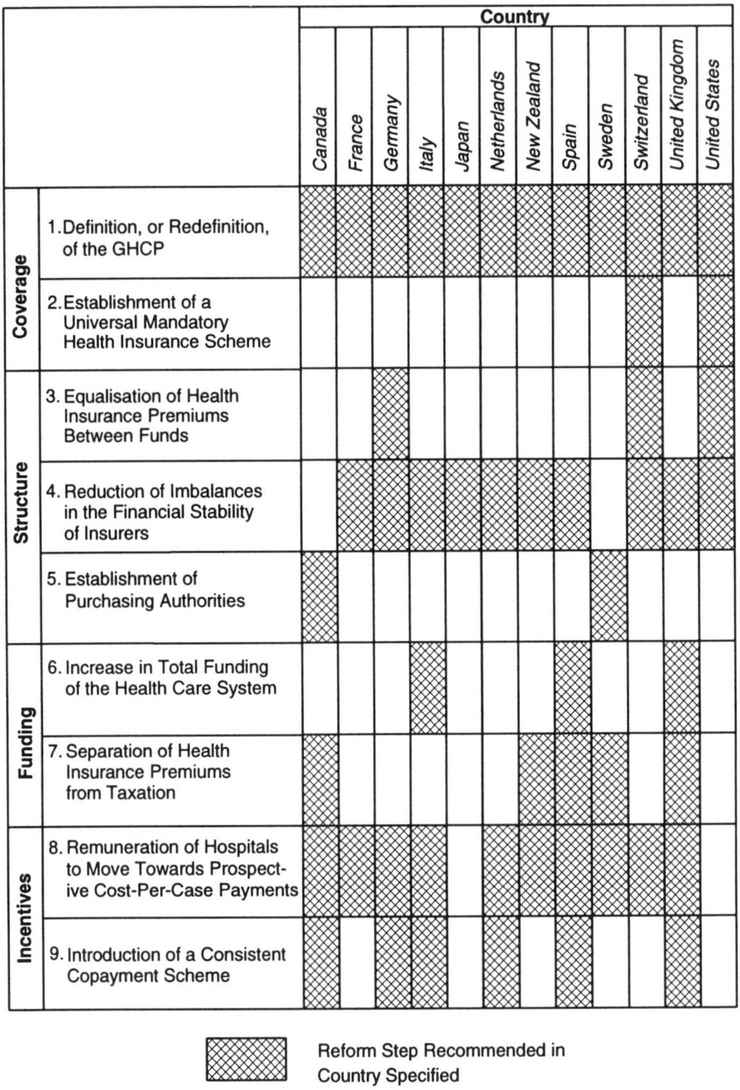

		Country											
		Canada	France	Germany	Italy	Japan	Netherlands	New Zealand	Spain	Sweden	Switzerland	United Kingdom	United States
Coverage	1. Definition, or Redefinition, of the GHCP	X	X	X			X	X		X	X		X
	2. Establishment of a Universal Mandatory Health Insurance Scheme										X		X
Structure	3. Equalisation of Health Insurance Premiums Between Funds			X									
	4. Reduction of Imbalances in the Financial Stability of Insurers		X	X	X	X	X	X	X				X
	5. Establishment of Purchasing Authorities	X									X		
Funding	6. Increase in Total Funding of the Health Care System					X				X		X	
	7. Separation of Health Insurance Premiums from Taxation	X					X	X		X	X		
Incentives	8. Remuneration of Hospitals to Move Towards Prospective Cost-Per-Case Payments	X	X	X	X		X	X	X	X	X		X
	9. Introduction of a Consistent Copayment Scheme	X		X	X		X	X	X		X		X

 Reform Step Recommended in Country Specified

The performance of a health care system during a transitional period from the *status quo* to a reform model may be worse than under the *status quo*. The danger is that under such circumstances, the reform progress will be disrupted, and may never resume again, leaving behind a health care system in which everybody is worse off. The experience of the reforms in the UK, for example, show that the expectation was that the health care reforms would lead to increases in the efficiency of the system, and thus help avoid funding crises. In the event, funding had to be increased substantially during the early stages of the reforms. Similarly, the reforms in the Netherlands, designed to decentralise funding and provision of health care, required some form of centralisation of funding during the transitional stages.

1.4.3.2.2   Definition, or Redefinition, of the GHCP

The purpose of a GHCP is to provide all citizens with essential health care coverage. This reform proposal applies to every country included in the study. Currently, few countries spell out explicitly:

- medical conditions that will be treated regardless of an individual's ability to pay (this is our preferred option); or,

- health care treatments that will be provided to individuals; or,

- nature and type of health care services that are available to individuals.

Those countries that have produced lists of entitlements (usually in terms of services, rather than conditions) tend to formulate these in a vague manner. This often leads to generous interpretations. Consequently, the GHCP is either not guaranteed to all (manifesting itself in unrealistically long waiting lists) or else can only be provided at escalating costs.

1.4.3.2.3   Establishment of a Universal Mandatory Health Insurance
               Scheme

Mandatory insurance is required to ensure that all members of society contribute to the provision of their own health care, as well as to the care of those who are poor and ill. This reform proposal applies to Switzerland and the United States. In all other countries included in our study, forms of health insurance exist which cover the majority of people.

1.4.3.2.4 Equalisation of Health Insurance Premiums Between Funds

The equalisation of premium revenues between insurance funds is necessary to prevent insurance funds from risk-selecting their members. Risk-rating may result in growing divergences of premiums between funds, to the point where health care is not affordable for some.

This reform proposal applies, by definition, only to social and voluntary insurance-based health care systems, not to tax-funded systems. In tax-funded systems, the government has already taken over the role of a central fund. Of the four social insurance-based systems included in the study, the Netherlands is in the process of establishing a central fund. France has a precursor to the central fund (the *Régime Générale*), while Japan relies on subsidies to some funds (primarily the *NHI*). Until recently, Germany had no compensation mechanism between sickness funds (except for pensioners), but under the recently introduced health care reforms this will change. In the United States some form of compensation of premiums between funding institutions will become necessary if mandatory insurance is introduced. Switzerland has recently introduced the concept of risk-adjustment between insurance funds and, as far as subsidies are concerned, between cantons.

1.4.3.2.5 Reduction of Imbalances in the Financial Stability of Insurers

Once a central fund has been established (whether it be the national government in tax-funded systems or a compensation mechanism between funds in social insurance-based systems), purchasers (whether they are regional authorities or individual insurance funds) will receive a capitated budget. This budget relates their income to their expected health care expenditure. As a result, they will be able to purchase health care effectively, and on equal terms, on behalf of their members. This reform proposal is intended to lead to a more active role for regional authorities charged with purchasing. Similarly, it is intended to lead to a 'commercialisation' of sickness funds. In both cases, the reform proposal is the prerequisite for the subsequent introduction of competition between purchasing authorities.

In all countries, bar Canada and Sweden, work on risk-adjusted capitation formulas is progressing. In the Netherlands, the United Kingdom, New Zealand, Germany and Switzerland, it is already well under way. If the United States moves toward the managed competition model now favoured, a risk-adjusted formula for reallocating premiums will be required.

Canada and Sweden are special cases. Both rely predominantly on regional health services. Regional authorities (provinces in Canada, county councils in Sweden) collect tax revenues dedicated to health care. The next reform proposal applies exclusively to these countries.[13]

1.4.3.2.6   Establishment of Purchasing Authorities

The average population of a Canadian province is approximately 2.7 million; that of a Swedish county council is 330,000. In both countries the distribution of the population across regions is uneven. Such geographical entities look too small to sustain independent tax-raising health care systems with desirable competitive and incentive structures. Therefore, in order to bring reform proposals for the two countries into line with those of other countries, the suggestion is to establish purchasing authorities much along the same lines as the present regional funding authorities. These would then receive a capitated budget from their national government. As a result of these changes, equality of health care contributions across regional authorities would be increased, while at the same time income of regional authorities would better match the expected health care expenditure.

1.4.3.2.7   Increase in Total Funding of the Health Care System

In some countries, most notably Italy, Spain and the United Kingdom, there are indications of underfunding of the health care system. In Italy and the United Kingdom this leads patients to jump existing waiting lists by seeking private treatment. In Spain, health care expenditure per capita is the lowest of all countries included in the study. It is conceivable that increased funding by the central government matched by the introduction of copayments will lead to significant improvements in social solidarity and efficiency of the health care system. Currently, none of the three countries have copayments for primary or hospital services.

---

[13]   For the United States the issue is different. If a mandatory insurance scheme were introduced, the need for a capitation formula depends on the nature of the compensation mechanism. If a central fund were introduced, then funds will flow from that fund to competing insurers, and capitation calculations would be needed. If, on the other hand, compensation payments take the form of tax credits to individuals, no compensation mechanism between insurance companies needs to take place, and hence, no capitation payments are required.

1.4.3.2.8   Separation of Health Insurance Premiums from Taxation

The reason for this reform proposal is that a separation of health insurance contributions from general taxation will increase the transparency of existing health care costs.   Rises in health care spending will predominantly be financed through increased insurance contributions, rather than out of general taxation.   The proposal is also a prerequisite before insurance funds can be introduced in countries which do not have these.   Once insurance funds have been established, it will become necessary to identify the contribution rate that is necessary to finance the provision of a GHCP.

Of the countries included in the study, Canada, New Zealand, Spain, Sweden and the United Kingdom would have to introduce full insurance contributions. Spain switched from a principally national insurance-based system to a tax system in the 1980s; under our proposed reforms this change would have to be reversed.

1.4.3.2.9   Remuneration of Hospitals to Move Towards Prospective
             Cost-Per-Case Payments

On balance, a health care system which in structure is close to the Prototype, would appear to work best if remuneration of hospitals were based on cost-per-case payments that are calculated prospectively. In all countries, bar Japan and the United States, this would lead to some changes. In some countries, e.g. Germany, cost-per-case payments have been introduced recently for a number of specialities.   The United States has progressed furthest with Diagnosis Related Groups (DRGs) now being an established element of the US health care system. The DRG system is not perfect, but its adoption would represent an improvement for most countries.

Because of the tendency to under-provide in capitation arrangements, the development of more complex pricing arrangements should accompany these reforms.[14]

---

[14]   It is generally difficult to recommend a universal reimbursement method for primary physicians that is applicable to all countries. However, on balance, they might include a capitation element for those services which physicians *themselves* provide.

1.4.3.2.10   Introduction of a Consistent Copayment Scheme

Copayments help to reduce the inefficient use of health care services by consumers. They strengthen the individual responsibility of patients in deciding about the levels of health care consumption. The Prototype recommends the introduction of a copayment structure that pertains to all services, but applies only to a maximum, income-determined, level. The proposal would require the introduction of copayments in a number of countries that currently do not impose these on primary and hospital services: Canada, Italy, the Netherlands, Spain and the United Kingdom. In Germany, they should be extended to cover GP services. With the adoption of a well-specified GHCP, a more consistent copayment policy could be adopted in those countries which now apply them.

1.4.3.3 Country-Specific Reform Programmes

In the following Tables 1.3 to 1.11 we present an analysis of short- or medium-term reform steps indicated in eight major countries in order to move the existing health care system in the direction of the Prototype. The eight countries are Canada, France, Germany, Japan, the Netherlands, Switzerland, the United Kingdom and the United States. Steps taken by the European Community to facilitate the reform process in Europe are also listed.

Table 1.3: Interim Reform Steps in Canada

The Canadian health care system currently operates in a satisfactory manner. It has the popular support of the majority of Canadian citizens and has been suggested by some as a model for the United States. However, Canadian provinces face increasing cost pressures as federal contributions are likely to decrease. In the absence of reforms Canada will not be able to afford its current level of benefits without increases in funding.

Reform Proposals

1.   Redefinition of the GHCP

In practice, Canada has a GHCP that is prescribed in the Canada Health Act. This, however, is defined in terms of services, rather than conditions, and covers too broad a range of entitlements. In particular, conditions which are inexpensive to treat (relative to normal income levels) and where non-treatment does not lead to a deterioration of the health status need not be included in the GHCP.

2. Establishment of Purchasing Authorities

The single-payer insurance system of Canada has weaknesses due to the administered nature of decisions on fees, budgets, caps and capital expenditures. There are no market mechanisms for signalling potential problems with resource allocation. Relying on the political process and on monopsony power is inefficient. We propose replacing the single-payer system with purchasing authorities which may eventually be transformed into competing insurance funds. Currently, health care is the responsibility of the provinces. In the long run, however, the federal government, as a precursor to a central fund, might assume increasing responsibility for health care funding. This might be a first step towards establishing provincial and territorial purchasing authorities.

3. Separation of Health Insurance Premiums from Taxation

The single public payer model leads to a lack of information about the costs of health care services and a lack of incentives for consumers to seek out the information. Introducing health insurance premiums would enable Canadian citizens to better evaluate the costs of the benefits they receive.

4. Remuneration of Hospitals to Move Towards Prospective Cost-Per-Case Payments

The current method of funding hospitals through global budgets leads to quality reductions, the wrong mix of services being produced, bed-blockers, and waiting lists for services. Some of these distortions would be reduced by switching to prospective cost-per-case payments. Additionally, there may be scope for reforming the current reimbursement method for physicians, for example, by introducing an element of capitation for services provided by the doctor.

5. Introduction of a Consistent Copayment Schedule

At present, patients pay nothing out of pocket for their medical care. This creates incentives to consume too many medical services. Copayments would help by reducing this incentive. They should cover all services, in particular primary and hospital services. Currently, the introduction of copayments on GHCP services violates provisions of the Canada Health Act.

50

Table 1.4: Interim Reform Steps in France

France has arguably one of the most complex health care systems of all the countries included in this study, which already contains some of the more intricate elements of the Prototype. Under the present sickness fund system, the Régime Générale makes transfer payments to funds with a less favourable income and expenditure balance. The Régime Générale, therefore, could become a predecessor of an institution which assumes the role of the central fund in the NERA Prototype. The firm central control by the government over many aspects of health care finance would have to be relaxed to bring the health care system into line with the Prototype.

Reform Proposals

1.   *Redefinition of the GHCP*

The current French health care system specifies a very comprehensive range of services. The list of reimbursable items (*la nomenclature*) includes a broad range of treatments, including fringe therapies. The list of services which are reimbursable under the French system is rather generous and some restrictions would have to be introduced. Several services, such as homeopathic treatments, may be straightforward candidates for exclusion (although they are very popular in France). For others, the criteria suggested in the Prototype to determine exclusion from the GHCP (e.g. no deterioration of the health status in case of non-treatment, no catastrophic expenses associated with treatment) will be difficult to apply. The eventual list of services included in the GHCP would need to satisfy the strong belief in social solidarity held by the French population.

2.   *Reduction of Imbalances in the Financial Stability of Insurers*

At present, individuals do not have the freedom to select their sickness fund. Open enrolment (either for individuals, or, possibly *in the short-run*, for employers) for existing funds should be introduced, and the setting up of new funds should be encouraged. At the same time the *Régime Générale* should assume the role of the central fund and would distribute insurance premiums to individual funds according to a capitation formula. This would be a first step for French insurers away from government direction and a step towards eventual competition. Choice of sickness funds may be acceptable to the French public, but not necessarily to the French government.

3.   *Remuneration of Hospitals to Move Towards Prospective Cost-Per-Case Payments*

At present, the Ministry of Health lays down the total to be spent on public hospitals after which a budget for each hospital is negotiated by the board of each hospital and the government; sickness funds are informed about the outcome. Under our proposals, the negotiations would take place between the hospitals and the sickness funds. The government would play a minor role only, or none at all. A prerequisite for this to happen is to strengthen the French sickness funds (Proposal 3 above) and to grant them more independence and autonomy.

Table 1.5: Interim Reform Steps in Germany

Although superficially like the Prototype, major changes would be needed to the German health care system to bring it in line with the Prototype. There appears to be growing recognition that a structural reform programme, rather than a continuation of cost containment acts, is necessary. Such a reform programme should overhaul the financing structure of the system. Only recently have measures been introduced to reform the hospital sector, by creating incentives for more efficiency. At the same time, doctors' incomes have declined steeply despite the significant rise in the volume of services. The country's generous list of reimbursable services induces patients to inefficient use and weakens individual responsibility. The rising costs of integrating the former East Germany into the Federal Republic are likely to lead to an increase in tensions.

Reform Proposals

1. Redefinition of the GHCP

Of all countries included in the study, Germany has perhaps the most generously defined GHCP. Defined largely in terms of acute services, it nevertheless fails at the same time to include long-term care. As a result, some of those who require long-term care facilities can not afford it (or become dependent on social welfare). Others simply abuse the generosity of the system. A comprehensive redefinition of the GHCP therefore appears to be necessary, and failure to reach agreement on its new format may jeopardise the success of any other reform step.

A cursory glance at the Health Care Reform Act, which lists entitlements, reveals services that might reasonably be excluded from the new GHCP; these include parts of preventative care, spa visits, early diagnosis tests, death benefits, domestic help and nursing care. Monetary sickness benefits, which have little do to with either definition or intention of a GHCP should also be excluded. In its place a list of specific conditions (including long-term care for the infirm) should be introduced.

2. Equalisation of Health Insurance Premiums Between Funds

The latest Health Care Reform Act, which came into effect in January 1993, appears to recognise the importance of establishing a compensation mechanism between sickness funds. Given the complex arrangements in

Germany - some funds compete while others do not - a situation has been created whereby funds are not under pressure to reduce insurance premiums; rather they tend to offer generous interpretations of GHCP services. Equalisation of premiums is a prerequisite for a more active involvement of funds in purchasing of health care services; it is also a first step to a competitive health care market without the scope for risk selection by funds.

3.   *Reduction of Imbalances in the Financial Stability of Insurers*

The introduction of a compensation mechanism between funds is likely to lead to the development of a capitation formula which will become the basis for compensation payments. The ultimate aim should be to reform the funding side of the German health care system in a way which leads to the establishment of nationwide operating insurance funds receiving an income which matches the health care expenditure of their clients. Under such arrangements, competition between funds can be expected to lead to greater efficiency of the German health care system.

4.   *Remuneration of Hospitals to Move Towards Prospective Cost-Per-Case Payments*

First steps have already been taken. The latest Health Care Reform Act progressively abolishes *per diem* rates, replacing them with cost-per-case payments, initially for a range of 200 specialities.

5.   *Introduction of a Consistent Copayment Schedule*

Per capita visits to primary physicians in Germany are among the highest in the world. The government should seriously consider the extension of copayments to cover primary care services.

Table 1.6: Interim Reform Steps in Japan

Japan is arguably the country which least requires any major reform programme for its health care system. On most available indicators measuring performance and output of health care systems, Japan fares exceptionally well. The country operates a well managed social insurance-based health care system, in which the government has taken over the compensation function between funds. It also determines the prices for health care services through a national Reimbursement Fee Schedule. Nevertheless, the rapid aging of the Japanese population may require some structural changes to the Japanese health care system in the future.

Reform Proposals

1.   *Redefinition of the GHCP*

The Japanese GHCP currently consists of almost all medical goods and services, apart from normal childbirth, inoculations and physicals. However, some expensive, highly advanced or rarely used treatments are not covered under the Japanese system. It is only when the price of these treatments comes down that they are covered. For that reason, and in view of the uniform copayment scheme that reduces unnecessary use of health care facilities, few if any changes to the Japanese GHCP appear to be necessary. However, at present some funds provide supplementary benefits (outside the GHCP) and some adjustments may be required to eliminate differences in benefits funds offer.

2.   *Reduction of Imbalances in the Financial Stability of Insurers*

In the Japanese context, this reform proposal amounts to a gradual elimination of the imbalances of financial stability among insurers. Typically, Employee Health Insurance (EHI) plans are financially strong due to the relatively high incomes and youth of the insured, whereas the National Health Insurance (NHI) plans are financially weak since they insure large proportions of the unemployed and retired elderly. Although the government has introduced reforms intended to share the burden more equally among the two classes of funds, there remains a certain lack of equity in the system which is likely to get worse in the long run, given the demographic forecasts for Japan. The reform path for Japan spells out the details of a more equitable distribution of funds between funds which would match their income with the expected health care expenditure.

3.   *Introduction of 'Balance Billing' as a Supplementary Remuneration Method for Physicians and Specialists*

At present no medical institution may charge more than a uniform fee listed on a centrally negotiated schedule. This rigid reimbursement schedule should be converted into a 'balance billing' schedule, by lifting the ceiling on the reimbursement fee schedule. This would mean that patients could be charged more than the reimbursement rate, with the residual amount to be paid out of pocket or by supplementary insurance. The effect would be to enhance patients' choice and provide them with the opportunity to consume better care within the constraints of their willingness to pay.

4.   *'Privatisation' of Long-Term Care*

Long-term care should be split off from the medical sector entirely and be provided predominantly by private sector nursing care institutions. The current distortions created by the reimbursement fee schedule leads to excessive referrals and bed-blocking in acute hospitals by the elderly. Funds earmarked for long-term care inside the health care system should be diverted to subsidise patients' payments to private nursing care facilities as a transitional measure.

Table 1.7: Interim Reform Steps in the Netherlands

In many aspects the current Dutch health care reform programme is similar to NERA's Prototype. It should therefore be studied carefully and lessons should be drawn as individual reform steps are implemented. The reform process is slow and complex. The control and allocation of health care funds first needs to be centralised, before it can be decentralised. Only then will a truly competitive mandatory universal health care system emerge. During the transition period several problems require attention. Among them is the resistance of some private insurers to becoming indistinguishable from public funds. The reform process started in 1989 and is not expected to be completed until 1995.

Reform Proposals

1. Redefinition of the GHCP

The problems of defining a GHCP are fully recognised in the Netherlands. A Committee on *Choices in Health Care* has submitted a first report to the government in 1992 on the redefinition of the country's GHCP. There is some evidence that this will indeed cover only basic care, and will be described in functional, rather than institutional terms.

2. Reduction of Imbalances in the Financial Stability of Insurers

Work on the capitation formula, which will become the basis for the allocation of funds from the central fund to the insurance funds, is also under way at present. One concern is how the formula can be designed to prevent 'cream-skimming', that is, risk-selection by competing insurance funds, in particular since the residual direct payments are based on a community-rated flat fee rather than an individual risk-rated premium.

3. Remuneration of Hospitals to Move Towards Prospective Cost-Per-Case Payments

Currently, Dutch hospitals receive a global budget although hospital-based specialists are paid on a fee-for-service basis. In due course, the method of reimbursement will be left to the participants in the health care market, e.g. hospitals and insurance funds. Reimbursement methods include a range of options. It is possible that prospective cost-per-case payments become a widely used reimbursement method.

4.   Introduction of a Consistent Copayment Scheme

Perhaps surprisingly, patient copayments in the Netherlands are currently limited to some classes of medicines, and do not apply to primary or hospital care services. It is not clear whether, in the competitive health care market, insurance companies will be able to determine whether or not patients copay for services. The discussion of copayments in the Prototype suggests that, for the GHCP, copayments should be made mandatory.

Table 1.8: Interim Reform Steps in Switzerland

Within Europe Switzerland's health care system is unique. Health insurance is not universally mandatory (although effectively the system covers the entire population), and health care premiums are not directly linked to income levels of the insured.   The freedom of insurers to risk select has led to the disintegration of the Swiss health care system. At present it is regulated by a series of emergency resolutions passed by the federal Government. Detailed proposals for health care reform are also currently debated by Parliament. Since all major changes to legislation in Switzerland have to be approved by popular vote it is unclear whether reforms will eventually be implemented.

Reform Proposals

1.   Redefinition of the GHCP

Switzerland is the only country for which NERA proposes an expansion, rather than contraction, of the list of explicitly defined reimbursable benefits. The current catalogue of benefits dates back to 1911 when health insurance was introduced and makes little or no reference to nursing home care and care for the chronically ill. There is general agreement in Switzerland that such care should be covered by the insurance system. Similarly, hospital care benefits should be made unlimited in duration which it is currently not.   NERA recommends, however, that the newly defined catalogue of benefits should not only be legally binding, but should also be sealed at this level.

2.   Establishment of Mandatory Insurance Scheme Covering the Population

Health insurance is currently not mandatory in all parts of Switzerland; yet some 99 percent of the population are members of insurance funds. However, if health care costs continue to rise, then at some point in the future people on very high income levels and, if the option exists, people on very low income levels may decide not to take out health insurance. This would undermine the social solidarity objective of the health care system.   Therefore, health insurance should be made mandatory throughout Switzerland.

3.   Degree of Equalisation of Premiums Between Funds to Be Introduced

A global risk-adjustment mechanism across funds has been introduced in 1992. It intends to balance premiums between funds by transferring money from funds with a high proportion of 'low risk' members to funds with a high proportion of 'high risk' members. Such a procedure is also envisaged to play an integral part in the new health insurance act which is currently debated by Parliament. NERA endorses the establishment of a risk-adjustment mechanism.

4.   Reduction of Imbalances in the Financial Stability of Insurers

Under the current reform proposals, subsidies from federal and cantonal sources remain a source of income for funds. It is envisaged that in the future these subsidies will be targeted more directly to people on low incomes in order to link premium contributions to ability to pay. This means that while the risk-adjustment mechanism is intended to balance premiums *between* insurance funds, subsidies will be allocated in a way to balance premiums *within* funds. NERA endorses this proposal but prefers an administration scheme for subsidies which provides better opportunities for competition among funds.

5.   Remuneration of Hospitals to Move Towards Prospective Cost-Per-Case Payments

Currently hospitals are reimbursed through *per diem* rates. These should be progressively abolished and replaced by US or German style cost-per-case payments.

Table 1.9: Interim Reform Steps in the United Kingdom

Major health care reforms were introduced in 1991. They were designed to increase efficiency by stimulating competition between providers; and, through the establishment of GP Fundholders, to a limited extent between purchasers. The UK model constitutes the basis for the health care reforms in New Zealand introduced in 1992. Other countries are likely to follow. The reforms can be described as steps in the direction of the NERA Prototype. However, the UK government maintains strong central control over the financing and delivery side of the health care system. Under the NERA Prototype, it would have to relinquish some of its powers.

Reform Proposals

1.   Redefinition of the GHCP

There exists a GHCP, but it is not codified in any precise sense, and it is not identical in all parts of the country. Health care facilities are poorly distributed, which results in excessive waiting lists for some (even essential) services in some regions. The government attempts to improve the situation by targeting conditions and setting standards for health status improvements, but so far no comprehensive and universally available list of treatments has been forthcoming. We recommend that work on a GHCP commences; this is desirable as it would facilitate the working of the NHS internal market.

2. Reduction of Imbalances in the Financial Stability of Insurers

Under the reforms, it is planned that purchasers (e.g. District Health Authorities and GP Fundholders) receive a capitated budget from central government. So far the introduction of such capitated budgets has been slow. The transition to capitation should be implemented as quickly as possible, as it is the prerequisite for purchasers to play a more active role in the market and to influence providers' behaviour. In the long run, capitated payments (financed through health insurance premiums) could lead to increased competition between Districts and GP Fundholders for insurance members.

3. Increase of Total Funding of the Health Care System

There is evidence that the health care system in the UK is underfunded. Health care expenditure per capita is lower than in any other European country in the study bar Spain; and health care expenditure as a percentage of GDP is the lowest of all the countries included in the study. It is conceivable that increased funding (perhaps complemented by the introduction of copayments) would increase both efficiency and equity of the health care system.

4. Separation of Health Insurance Premiums from Taxation

A fully separate structure of health care insurance premiums sufficient to cover the costs of the NHS should be introduced. This change would be accompanied by a compensating reduction in taxation. This would increase the transparency of NHS funding and facilitate later reforms.

5. Remuneration of Hospitals to Move Towards Prospective Cost-per-Case Payments

The present predominant form of block contracts between purchasers and providers should give way to contracts based on prospective cost-per-case payments. This would improve the incentive structure and the financial situation of many hospitals but might require increased funding.

6. Introduction of a Consistent Copayment Scheme

More extensive use should be made cf copayments to cover primary and hospital services, not just medicines, dental and eye treatments. However, the introduction of copayments should be matched with an increase in central funding by the government.

Table 1.10: Interim Reform Steps in the United States

An outlier in any classification, the health care system of the United States comprises the best and the worst aspects of any system. Our proposals for the United States collapse to a single proposal, which is to introduce mandatory universal insurance coverage for the 34 to 37 million Americans who are currently not insured. On the positive side, the US health care system is exemplary in the development and diffusion of medical technology; it has an established track record in the use of prospective cost-per-case payments for hospital services; and it employs a variety of reimbursement methods for other providers. The prospects for significant reforms are excellent, although there are huge pressures for short-run cost containment measures due to the anticipated impact of health care reform for the budget deficit.

Reform Proposals

1.   Definition of a GHCP

The necessity of defining a GHCP, which would become the standard bundle of services offered by insurers, follows directly from the introduction of a mandatory minimum insurance scheme for all Americans. Unlike European countries, where the definition of the GHCP is often vague and subject to different interpretations (but, to varying degrees, guaranteed by the government), the United States may well become the first country to explicitly define a minimum scope of entitlements.

2.   Introduction of a Mandatory Insurance Scheme Covering the Population

Indications are that the new administration of President Clinton will make the introduction of a mandatory health care scheme covering the entire population a priority of his policy agenda. To minimise budgetary impacts, universal coverage will most likely be phased in over several years.

3.   Degree of Equalisation of Premiums Between Funds to Be Introduced; and,
4.   Reduction of Imbalances in the Financial Stability of Insurers

One of the major issues in introducing a mandatory insurance scheme relates to risk adjustments among funds. There are various possibilities for doing this. The Prototype recommends the establishment of a central fund which distributes risk adjusted capitated payments to insurance funds. Tax credits to individuals are an alternative but carry the risk that high-risk individuals may still not be able to afford to pay for their health care.

It is expected that the US reforms will begin by adopting a 'managed competition' model with a single insurance pool in each state or metropolitan area for those having difficulty obtaining insurance. This pool, called the

59

'Health Insurance Purchasing Cooperative' (HIPC) must implement a risk adjustment program to remove the incentives of insurers to risk select. This program would be developed by a centralised regulator under most managed competition plans.

Table 1.11: Interim Reform Steps in the European Community

There is no such thing as a European-wide health care system. However, the European Community could facilitate the adoption of similar reforms throughout Europe.

Reform Proposals

1.   Assisting in the Definition of an EC-wide GHCP

The European Community could issue Recommendations and eventually Directives to achieve a harmonisation of the basic packages of treatments available in European countries, and the harmonisation of the control of the quality of treatments offered.

2.   Enforcing Mandatory Health Insurance Schemes

The European Community could issue a Directive that would make it compulsory for Member States to have mandatory health insurance schemes. This would ensure that existing EC Members keep a mandatory health insurance scheme and that new EC Members create one as a precondition to becoming a member of the Community.

3.   European-wide Operating Insurance Funds

The European Community will make sure that insurance funds are allowed to operate across borders and could contribute to the monitoring and the regulation of these funds.

CHAPTER 2

PROJECTIONS OF HEALTH CARE NEED AND FUNDING

Penelope Rowlatt
Adam Lloyd

National Economic Research Associates
London

2.1   INTRODUCTION

Part of this study of health care funding across developed countries has consisted of constructing projections of the future paths of 'need'[1] and expenditure on health care in each of the countries surveyed. The object of this exercise was to identify any countries that were likely to experience serious funding pressures during the next decade.   The projections are predicated upon the *status quo* structure and therefore involve projecting a continuation of past trends in the factors that influence health care 'need' and expenditure.

Unsurprisingly, the data suggest that if past trends were to continue, health care expenditure would take an increasing share of GDP in all the countries of the study.   Further, 'need' would increase faster than the politically acceptable level of expenditure in many of the countries. On the basis of these past trends (and, of course, the *status quo* has already been disrupted by reform in some of the countries) the United Kingdom, the Netherlands and Spain are identified as the most vulnerable to funding crises. France and Italy are next in line. In Canada, Germany, Japan and Sweden it seems likely that if the *status quo* structure of health care funding is politically acceptable, sufficient funds will be available to meet 'need'. In Switzerland, the structure of the system has been such that funding for health care has been determined by what people want to spend, rather than by political expediency. If this market structure continues to be acceptable, it seems unlikely that there will be a funding crisis. In the United States our modelling suggests that if the market continued to work in the way it has in the past, then 'need' would be met in broadly the way it has been met in the past. But it seems that this market structure is no longer politically acceptable.

In this chapter the methodology used to construct the projections is described and the results summarised. There are four annexes. Annex 2.1 gives an overview of the factors causing changes in health care 'need'. Further details of the model estimation are noted in Annex 2.2. Annex 2.3 contains a country by country description of the results of the model and in Annex 2.4 there is a bibliography for this chapter.

---

[1]   This term is defined in Section 2.2.2.

2.2 WHAT DETERMINES HEALTH CARE EXPENDITURE?

2.2.1 Supply and Need

In order to make forecasts, a model is required. The model needs to address such questions as: what determines the quantity of money spent on health care? who takes the decisions that determine how much money is spent? what are the factors that influence these decisions?

There are two distinct classes of model that could explain the path of health care expenditure. One looks at the demand-side:

- what is the likely future 'need' for health care?

- on what does this 'need' depend?

- how much would it cost to fulfil this 'need'? and,

- is the 'need' fulfilled? Or is some form of rationing taking place, perhaps by price, perhaps by some other, non-price, method?

Care must be taken to define the concept 'need' in an appropriate manner (see Section 2.2.2).

The other class of model looks at the supply-side:

- how are the funds provided?

- are there political or other constraints on the quantity of funds available?

Clearly there can be a tension between the output of these two approaches, which look at the two sides of the market and will not necessarily produce the same answer. It is this tension upon which we want to focus.

The question to be addressed in the forecasting exercise is therefore the following:

If in the future the supply of funds is constrained by political expediency in broadly the same way as in the past, and if the extent of the 'need' for health care continues to grow in broadly the same way as in the past, then will an unsustainable tension develop?

Put another way, the question is this:

Is some more formalised type of rationing going to be needed in the future? Or are the ad hoc rationing processes that have been operating in the past adequate to cope with, say, the next ten years?

Before moving on it will be helpful to spell out more precisely what is meant by the term 'need', for its meaning is slightly different from that in normal usage.

2.2.2   The Concept of Need

The concept of 'need' in the context of health care has attracted a great deal of controversy. The definition proposed by Williams (1978) is a useful starting point. He said:

" . . . a need exists so long as the marginal productivity of treatment is positive"

The term 'productivity' in this definition relates to the physiological impact of treatment. An important aspect of this definition of 'need' is the implication that the 'need' for treatment must be capable of being met, given existing technology.

This definition is useful here because it has a number of implications which throw light on the variables that are relevant in modelling the demand for funds. For example, it means that:

- the level of 'need' depends on the state of medical technology (each new procedure or advance in medical technology creates a higher level of 'need');

- the realisation of 'need' depends on its identification; first, the individuals concerned must present themselves for treatment, then there must be confirmation of the 'need' by a medical examination.

This leads to a related concept, that of 'wants'. 'Wants' are defined as 'perceived need'. 'Wants' may be greater or less than 'need': people may 'want' more treatment than they in fact 'need'; on the other hand they may 'need' more treatment than they 'want'. The relation between 'wants' and 'need' will change over time as a result of education and changes in expectations. It is also affected by physician practices and fashions because of the role doctors play in determining 'need'.

However, economists generally look at 'demand' rather than something called 'need' or 'wants'. 'Demand' is different from both 'wants' and 'need'. It refers to the quantity of a good or service that a consumer will purchase at a given price. Payment for health care services (at the point of delivery) is often made, in part or in full, by a third party (the insurer, public or private) rather than by the consumer. Thus the price of health care to the consumer at the point of delivery is often zero. If the price is zero, then 'demand' is the same as 'wants'. Of course, this demand may not be met because the provision of health care may be supply constrained: that is, supply might be rationed by some factor other than price.

The relationship between 'need', 'wants' and 'demand', can be summarised thus:

NEED	=	capacity to benefit from appropriate treatment;
WANTS	=	perceived need;
DEMAND	=	wants, modified by the effect of price.

'Demand' may be greater or less than 'need', but it will not exceed 'wants'.

Annex 2.1 describes some of the factors determined largely or wholly outside the health care system which drive health care 'need'.

2.3   OTHER PEOPLES' WORK

Before describing our own work, the main results of some other peoples' modelling are briefly reviewed. In summary, however, there is just one, very clear, well-established statistical fact relating to health care expenditure: its correlation with GDP. No other robust and stable correlations have yet been found.

Newhouse (1977) found that GDP per head accounted for around 90 percent of the variation in health care spending per head across the OECD countries. He also found that the income elasticity of health care expenditure is generally slightly greater than unity: if GDP per head in one country is 1 percent higher than in another country then health care expenditure per head is likely to be slightly more than 1 percent higher. This suggests that health care is what is called a luxury good: the richer a society is, the greater is the share of health care expenditure in total expenditure.

Nobody has yet made a convincing case for the significance of any other variable besides GDP per head. And that is not for lack of trying. In the mid 1980s **Leu** set about trying to discover:

> "whether factors other than income are important quantitatively
> in explaining the variance of medical care expenditure across
> countries" (Leu, 1986, p.41)

He experimented with a great number of both demand-related variables and supply-related variables. He found that GDP per head was overwhelmingly the most important determinant of health care expenditure per head across the OECD countries in 1974. There were one or two other variables that were statistically significant in explaining the variation across countries, given this one year's data.

Gerdtham et al. (1988) re-examined this work using the same 1974 data and also using data for 1983. Their work broadly confirmed the Leu finding regarding the importance of GDP per head but did not, in general, support his findings regarding the other variables.

Getzen and Poullier (1991) published the result of using panel data (cross-section and time series combined) to estimate the trend relationship between income (GDP) and spending on health care. They used data across 17 countries over the period 1960 to 1987. The estimate of the income elasticity from such an approach combines the estimate across countries with any change in the estimate over time. They obtained an estimate of 1.5 for the income elasticity, implying that a 1 percent increase in GDP has generally been associated with a rise of around 1.5 percent in health care expenditure.

2.4 THE MODELS IN THEORY

Generally, our approach has been to construct two models of the path of health care expenditure, one looking at the supply of funds and the other looking at health care 'need' or 'demand'. The equations are estimated over the period during which there is circumstantial evidence suggesting that 'need' was met by expenditure. We are aware that it is unusual (although not unprecedented) to use one set of data to estimate two equations. This can be justified by the assumption that whereas for most countries expenditure expanded to cover growth in 'need' in the early years of the sample, in many countries it has ceased to do so in recent years.

2.4.1 A Model of the Supply of Funds

First, a very simple model of the amount of expenditure on health care that is politically acceptable in a country has been constructed. This answers the question:

> *what has been the relationship between health care expenditure and GDP?*

or, more precisely:

> *by how much has health care expenditure increased when GDP has risen?*

To answer this question the following equation has been estimated:

$$\ln HCE_t = a_0 + a_1 \ln GDP_t + u_t \tag{1}$$

where: HCE_t is real health care expenditure in year t;
GDP_t is real gross domestic product; and
u_t is the random residual.

2.4.2 A Model of 'Need'

The model used for the other side of the market is, generally, a model of 'need', not 'demand'. In most countries the person who decides on the health care to be provided has not been constrained by a budget constraint and a price. (This is not the case in the US or in Switzerland, so in these countries a price variable has been included in some of the equations estimated. The results are shown in Annex 2.2.)

The equation for 'need' takes account of only three factors, the age distribution of the population (because the elderly usually have more expensive needs than younger people, see Annex 2.1), and technology changes and quality improvements (these two are jointly proxied by a time trend).

The question the modelling has addressed is therefore:

> *what has been the trend in health care expenditure **after** correction for the age structure of the population?*

The question is answered by estimating the equation:

$$\ln(HCE_t/DEM_t) = b_o + b_1 T + w_t \qquad (2)$$

where
$$DEM_t = POP1_t + 2(POP2_t) + 4(POP3_t) + 8(POP4_t) \qquad (3)$$

and $POP1_t$ is the number of people aged less than 65 in year t;
   $POP2_t$ is the number aged 65 or over but less than 75;
   $POP3_t$ is the number aged 75 or over but less than 80;
   $POP4_t$ is the number aged 80 or over;
   T is the time trend; and
   w_t is the random residual.

The time trend in this equation picks up the trend increase in the real cost of health care, and projections made using this equation implicitly assume that this will rise in the future at the same rate as it has in the past.

The weights in the definition of the DEM variable are based on evidence about the relationship between health care costs and age in a number of countries. For example, there is evidence that in some of the countries examined about 6 to 10 times as much is spent on people aged 80 or over as is spent on people aged less than 65.[2]

Chart 2.1 shows the proportion of people over 65 in the countries studied for years from 1960 to 1990, along with projections for 2000.

---

[2]   Robinson, Spiby and Beardshaw (1990) estimate that in the UK those aged over 65 account for nearly four times as much spending per capita as those under 65. The estimates of the relative cost of the aged for Japan given in Fujino (1987) are consistent with this. Estimates of the relative weights of those over 65 can be derived from data in Anderson and Knickman (1984), who offer some age-specific figures for expenditure per head, derived from Medicare data. Data for health care expenditure by age from Sweden are broadly consistent in the years 1976 and 1985, see Culyer, Evans, von der Schulenburg, van de Wen and Weisbrod (1991). None of these sources gives a complete breakdown by age, so judgement has been exercised in the choice of these weights.

Chart 2.1
Percentage of Population over 65

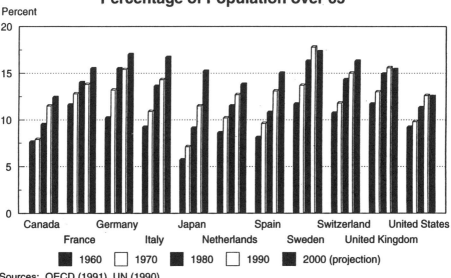

Sources: OECD (1991), UN (1990)

The interpretation of equation 2 is not simple. There are at least five factors that are bound together in the time trend and may cause any forecast based on the equation estimated over the past to be wrong:

- if health care expenditure has been increasingly constrained in the later years of the estimation period, then the equation will underestimate the trend (this is why some of the equations are estimated over truncated periods);

- if there were gaps in health care coverage in the early years, then these equations will overestimate the trend;

- if the quality of care was lower in the early years but has been adjusting towards a long-run acceptable level, and so were not to increase in the same way in the future, then the trend will be over-estimated;

- if the real cost of health care moves in a different way in the future to the trend in the past, the projection will be wrong; and,

- finally, if technological developments were to speed up or slow down in the future, then obviously the forecasts will be wrong.

2.4.3   Combining the Models

Where these models give similar figures for 'need' and for expenditure, it is presumed that the market in health care services was approximately in equilibrium. It is assumed that this is the case over the estimation period common to both equations. However, this is not necessarily the case, either in the later part of the data period or in the future. The equations have therefore been estimated only over the period for which it seems likely that such an equilibrium existed.

The juxtaposition of the forecasts given by the two models in any future year indicates the extent of the likely funding 'crunch'. This being so, the probability of a funding crisis, according to the model, depends on five factors:

- the likely future growth of GDP (the faster GDP grows the more room there is to increase expenditure on health care);

- the estimate of the relation between GDP and the politically acceptable level of funding (the higher the estimated elasticity the more funding will be available for health care);

- the forecast of the future age distribution of the population;

- the assumed dependence of 'need' on the age distribution (in general, the more health care the elderly need the more likely a 'crunch' is to occur, since the number of old people is increasing in most countries); and,

- the assumption about the future trend increase in 'need' (the faster the trend growth assumed, the sooner it will seem likely that the 'crunch' will occur).

If the expected increase in 'need' requires significantly more funds than appear to be politically acceptable then some form of rationing is likely to be required.

2.5 THE MODELS IN PRACTICE

2.5.1 Data

The countries covered are: Canada, France, Germany, Italy, Japan, the Netherlands, Spain, Sweden, Switzerland, the United Kingdom, and the United States.
The data for New Zealand were not sufficient to allow projections to be made.

The dependent variable used in estimating the equations is:

lnHCE   the logarithm of real expenditure on health care. Real
            expenditure on health care has been derived by deflating
            nominal expenditure on health care using the GDP price
            deflator. Figures for nominal expenditure on health care and
            for the GDP deflator come from OECD (1991, 1993). The
            coverage of the health care expenditure series is therefore that
            of the OECD rather than that of the national source.

For the supply-side equation the following explanatory variable is used:

lnGDP   the logarithm of real gross domestic product (GDP). Real GDP
            is derived from nominal GDP by deflating using the GDP price
            deflator. Data for 1960 to 1990 come from OECD (1991). Data
            for 1991 come from OECD (1992a). Forecasts of the growth rate
            of real GDP, needed in order to make the projections, are taken
            from Consensus Economics (August 1992). This provides
            annual forecasts for the years 1992 to 1997 and a forecast of the
            average growth rate for the following five years for each of the
            G7 nations (Canada, France, Germany, Italy, Japan, the United
            Kingdom and the United States). For smaller nations,
            Consensus Economics has short range forecasts (two years).
            NERA has projected GDP growth subsequent to this as the
            average rate of growth in GDP over the previous decade.

The demand-side model uses the following data series:

T   a time trend. This acts as a proxy for the effects of technical
            change and quality improvements.

lnDEM   the logarithm of a constructed demographic variable (DEM).
            The series for DEM is calculated by assigning a weighting to

individuals according to their age band. The data for DEM thus indicate the total number of health care 'need' points allocated to the whole population of the country. The point values used are shown below:

Age group	Weight
aged less than 65:	1
aged 65 or over but less than 75:	2
aged 75 or over but less than 80:	4
aged 80 or over:	8

Data for the numbers of people in each age band come from OECD (1991). Five-yearly forecasts of changes in the numbers in each age band, needed for the health care need projections, are derived from forecasts in United Nations (1988 and 1990). The figures have been linearly interpolated between the five year forecasts.

Experiments were performed with two further variables.

DEF   the government deficit as a share of GDP. Data for nominal GDP come from OECD (1991). Data for the nominal deficit come from IMF (1981, 1991, and 1992). In most of the countries studied the estimated coefficient on DEF was positive, not negative as is required by the theory. The variable was omitted, see Annex 2.2.

lnPRICE   the logarithm of an index of the real unit cost of health care. The data for health care unit costs are taken from OECD (1991, 1993). This series is deflated by the GDP deflator, to give an index of movements in the price of health care relative to the general price level, see OECD (1991). This variable is used in modelling the demand for health care in the US and Switzerland (see Annex 2.2).

2.5.2   Estimation Periods

The equations for health care 'need' (or 'demand') and expenditure in the eleven countries have been estimated over a variety of sample periods. Most start in 1960, but the finishing dates range from 1983 to 1991 (the latest data available for most countries is for 1990).

Through the 1960s and 1970s, expenditure on health care grew rapidly in most of the countries studied. However, since the early 1980s, and increasingly in more recent years, most countries have made efforts to contain the growth of expenditure on health care. Clearly, including periods in which expenditure cuts are politically motivated and where the data reflect the increasing use of rationing will bias downwards the estimate of the trend increase in 'need'. Periods in which it is thought that politically motivated pressure has prevented expenditure from increasing in response to an increase in 'need' have been excluded from estimation.

If the periods of rationing were included in the estimation period, then institutional attempts to hold down expenditure might erroneously be interpreted as the effect of demand-side factors. The coefficient estimates in the 'need' equation would thus be biased downwards, and the trend effect of technology changes might be underestimated.

The end points chosen for the estimation periods are based on information regarding the individual health care systems. The reasons for those chosen for each country are spelt out in Annex 2.3. The end points are:

End date for estimation of 'need' (or 'demand') equations:

Canada, France, Germany, Sweden, UK:	1986
Netherlands, Spain:	1983
Italy, US, Japan:	1990
Switzerland:	1991

For the majority of the study countries, the increase in government pressure has been gradual. The choice of a cutoff date is not, therefore, obvious or unambiguous. Fortunately, the results of the regressions are sufficiently stable that altering the cutoff date by one or two years causes only marginal differences in the estimated parameters.

2.5.3   Results

Table 2.1 summarises the results of estimating the equations.

Table 2.1: Estimated Coefficients

	GDP Elasticity	Time Trend (percent)
Canada	1.4	4.4
France	1.7	5.3
Germany	1.9	4.9
Italy	1.9	5.3
Japan	1.5	6.9
Netherlands	2.0	6.2
Spain	2.3	9.5
Sweden	2.1	4.6
Switzerland	1.4	1.6
United Kingdom	1.8	3.4
United States	2.0	4.4

The estimated GDP elasticity is the value taken by a_1 in the equation for the supply of funds (equation 1). It indicates the percentage increase in health care funding which would be expected if GDP increased by one percent. Table 2.1 shows that the value of this elasticity varies quite considerably across the study countries, from 1.4 in Canada and Switzerland to 2.3 in Spain. The estimated GDP elasticities for the majority of the countries, however, are in the region of 1.7 to 2.0.

The estimated trend rise in health care 'need' is given by the estimate of b_1 in equation 2. It indicates the annual rate at which the 'need' for health care expenditure has been increasing over time, after adjustment for changes in the age profile of the population. The variation across the countries in the estimates of this trend is also quite large, from 1.6 percent in Switzerland to 9.5 percent in Spain. The majority of estimates, however, fall between 4 and 6 percent.

Annex 2.2 provides additional details regarding the estimation of the equations, including alternative formulations of these models that were tested.

2.6   THE PROJECTIONS

2.6.1   Projections of 'Need' and the Availability of Funds

Charts 2.2 and 2.3 show past expenditure on health care as a share of GDP over time for all the countries of the study, along with the projections of the supply of funds in the year 2000. Expenditure for the US and the UK have been included in both charts to facilitate comparison. Expenditure on health care as a percentage of GDP is expected to increase in all the countries studied. Estimates of the funds available for expenditure on health care in 2000 vary from 7.3 percent of GDP (in the UK) to 15.1 percent of GDP (in the US).

Table 2.2 shows the supply of funds and 'need' (or 'demand') in 1990 alongside the projections for the year 2000.[3] Chart 2.4 presents the same results in chart form for the year 2000. The difference between the projections of supply and 'need' provides an estimate of the funding shortfall. The size of the projected funding shortfall varies from 0.1 percent of GDP (in Switzerland) to around 9 percent of GDP (in the UK).

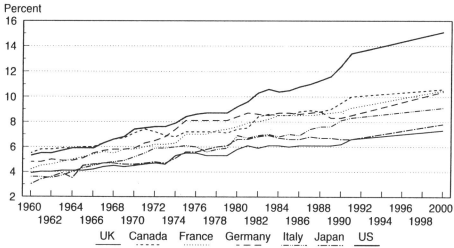

Chart 2.2
Expenditure on Health Care as a Share of GDP

Source: OECD (1993) and projections by NERA

---

[3]   The projection of 'Need' in **Japan** in 2000 is the average of 'need' in eight other countries from the study; in the **UK** in 2000 it is the average for the EC countries covered; the projections for **Switzerland** are of 'demand' and the relationship between expenditure and GDP (see Annex 2.3).

Chart 2.3
Expenditure on Health Care as a Share of GDP

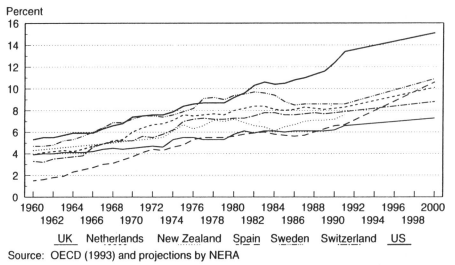

UK Netherlands New Zealand Spain Sweden Switzerland US

Source: OECD (1993) and projections by NERA

Table 2.2: Summary of Projections, Percentage of GDP

	1990			2000		
	Actual Expenditure	'Need' or 'Demand'	Short -fall	Politically Acceptable Expenditure	'Need' or 'Demand'	Short -fall
Canada	9.0	10.2	1.2	10.6	13.5	2.9
France	8.9	11.1	2.2	10.5	15.2	4.7
Germany	8.1	11.0	2.9	10.4	14.2	3.8
Italy	7.6	8.7	1.1	9.1	12.9	3.8
Japan	6.5	11.0	4.5	7.8	13.7	5.9
Netherlands	8.1	12.2	4.1	10.1	18.1	8.0
Spain	6.6	10.3	2.7	10.6	17.2	6.6
Sweden	8.7	12.7	4.0	10.9	16.7	5.8
Switzerland	7.8	7.8	-	8.4	8.5	0.1
UK	6.1	9.0	2.9	7.3	16.5	9.2
USA	12.4	12.5	0.1	15.1	17.1	2.0

Chart 2.4
Supply and Need Extrapolated to 2000
in PPP $US 1990

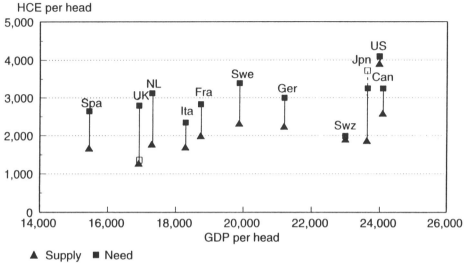

▲ Supply ■ Need

Note: 'Need' in 2000 in the UK and in Japan is forecast by reference to the projections in other countries, rather then by extrapolating past expenditure. Using the extrapolation methodology would give estimated 'need' of $1,400 in the UK and £3,800 in Japan. In Switzerland we have projected 'demand' and the relationship between expenditure and GDP.

Where there is a projection that the funding shortfall will increase, either:

• expenditure on health care relative to GDP will expand to reach a higher level than was previously 'acceptable' within the *status quo* structure; or

• there will be an increase in the efficiency with which care is provided; or,

• there will be a decline in the quality of care provided or a contraction in the scope of care offered.

2.6.2   Conclusions

The conclusions for each country are spelt out in Annex 2.3. In summary, they are the following.

• In **the UK, the Netherlands, Spain, Japan** and **Sweden**, the models suggest that there was already a significant shortfall between 'need' and the supply of funds in 1990. This shortfall is not expected to increase markedly in **Sweden** or **Japan**. Since the present situation seems sustainable in these countries, we conclude that a funding crisis is unlikely. In the **Netherlands, Spain**, and **the UK**, however, if the status quo of the estimation period had continued the shortfall would have been significantly larger in 2000. The projections therefore suggest that if a funding crisis in each of these countries had not already occurred, there would have been one within the next ten years.

- In **France** and in **Italy**, the estimated shortfall was not great in 1990, but the projection for 'need' diverges quite sharply from supply over the next ten years. Both of these countries are therefore likely to experience some funding problems.

- Although the projected shortfall in 2000 for **Canada** and **Germany** is almost as large as that for **France** and **Italy**, it is not that different from the estimated shortfall for 1990. This is because the strong GDP growth expected in both **Canada** and **Germany** results in an estimated supply of funds which almost keeps pace with the expected growth in 'need'. Funding crises therefore appear to be less likely in these countries. The projected increase in shortfall may well be containable within the *status quo* structure.

- In the **United States** 'need' and supply appear not to have diverged significantly over time. Our projections suggest that this would continue to be the case, leading to the conclusion is that no serious funding problem should occur in the US. However, such a conclusion rests on two assumptions: first, that the US allows the relationship between health care expenditure and GDP to be the same in the future as it has been in the past (that is, when GDP rises 1 percent in real terms health care expenditure rises 2 percent) and second, that there is no structural change in the system resulting in an increase in the share of the population with health care needs covered by insurance. Neither of these assumptions seems to be justified.

- In **Switzerland**, although the share of GDP allocated to health care is expected to rise, it seems unlikely that this will cause serious political pressures. The projection, which assumes a continuation of the market-clearing system, therefore suggests there is unlikely to be a funding crisis.

80

ANNEX 2.1 FACTORS DRIVING 'NEED'

2.1.1   Introduction

This annex summarises the factors thought most likely to influence the 'need'[4] for expenditure on health care. It deals first with technological change and second with demographic factors. It then goes on to address expectations, changes in epidemiology, environmental factors and the effect of culture.

2.1.2   Technological Change

Much of the increase in the 'need' for expenditure on health care over the last 20 years can be explained by the development of new medical techniques. Further, it is expected that this trend will continue. Some specific areas of high-tech medicine where rapid developments are expected are identified by Robinson, Spiby and Beardshaw (1990); they are: less invasive techniques in place of open surgery, transplantation surgery, biotechnology, the development of vaccines and pharmaceuticals, and imaging technology.

Technological change in health care is often initiated by discoveries in primary science. It follows that there is considerable unpredictability associated with the rate and timing of the advent of technological change. The same is not necessarily true, however, of the transformation of this into useable form: the investment in innovation required to embody new ideas into new clinical techniques will be motivated partly by economic factors. Any explicit projection of the likely future rate of technical change across different countries would need to take account of the ways in which the individual systems foster such change and of the incentives for innovation that they create.

New technology has two main effects in medicine: it increases the range of diseases which can be treated, and it offers new techniques which may substitute for existing therapy. Many new processes will both provide new treatment for a disease and displace a less effective therapy. Insofar as new techniques enhance treatment, they (paradoxically) increase 'need' and are unambiguously cost-increasing. When they displace an existing therapy the net effect on costs is not clear.

New technology may have an effect on the running costs, capital costs, and level of remuneration of employees.

---

[4]   'Need' is defined in Section 2.2.2.

The effect of new technology on running costs is indeterminate: it may increase or decrease them. Some new techniques will reduce running costs. Examples are the substitution of drug therapies for surgery, earlier detection and thus easier cure of some ailments, and non-invasive surgery which is often less expensive than invasive surgery (once the necessary equipment has been purchased). Other new techniques may increase running costs. The detection of diseases early enough to permit treatment gives a better prognosis, but may increase costs; further, the cure of some diseases leaves the patient to incur further health care 'need' in the future.

New technology almost always increases capital and development costs. The development of new treatments, and research into ways of combatting previously incurable conditions, requires a large investment with no certain return. Further, the use of imaging and scanning techniques requires a large initial capital investment. Generally, the use of more sophisticated techniques means that the health care system has to finance larger capital costs.

Finally, the ever more advanced technology used in health care means that the operators of the technology require increasingly sophisticated skills. The wages of doctors and technicians may be expected to increase in real terms (that is, after adjustment for inflation) as the skills demanded of them grow.

On balance, it is generally the case that the increased use of new technology increases the real cost of medical services.

2.1.3   Demography

2.1.3.1   Population Growth

Based on projections of fertility and mortality trends, the Population Division of the United Nations Secretariat (United Nations, 1987) has forecast that the growth of the total population of the developed world will slow from the rate of 0.5 percent a year today, to around 0.3 percent a year by 2020. Population growth implies a rise in health care 'need'. However, since the resources available for allocation to health care should increase as the population grows, this is not necessarily a cause of concern.

Changes in demographic structure will, however, put pressure on health care expenditure.

2.1.3.2 The Ageing Population

Due to increases in life expectancy and decreasing birth rates, the average age of the population in developed countries is rising, and is expected to continue to do so.[5]

Life expectancy at birth in the developed world has increased steadily over the last forty years: from 66 years in 1950 to 72 in 1985. It is forecast to increase further, to almost 78 years, by 2025. However, this rise in life expectancy is not distributed evenly across the study countries. In recent years it has increased fastest in Japan (which now has the highest life expectancy in the world by a small margin) and more slowly in the UK and the US. In 1987 life expectancy in the countries in this study ranged from 71 to 75 years for males and from 77 to 81 years for females.

The effect of greater life expectancy on the average age of the population is compounded by a falling birth rate. The number of births per 1,000 population in the developed world was almost a third lower in 1985 than in the early 1950s. Fertility rates in Western Europe and North America are now close to the replacement rate.[6] It is expected to fall further. However, increased life expectancy means that the proportion of the old, and especially of the 'very old', will increase substantially over the next ten to twenty years. The number of people aged over 65 in the developed world is expected to reach 17 percent of the population by 2025, with the number over 75 reaching about 7 percent. The corresponding figures in 1985 were 11 percent and 3 percent.

Significant variations in the existing demographic characteristics of the study countries have implications for the extent to which the populations of these countries are expected to age in the future. Of the study countries, Sweden currently has the highest number of people aged over 65 (18 percent of the population), while New Zealand has the lowest (10 percent). Whereas these shares are both expected to rise in the future, the rise in New Zealand will be greater than that in Sweden. The implication is that the effect of ageing on the 'need' for health care expenditure in nations which currently have relatively young populations (New Zealand, Canada and Japan) is likely to be greater

---

[5]   Unless otherwise stated, data in this sub-section comes from United Nations (1987).

[6]   The rate which, if continued indefinitely (and given constant mortality), will lead to no change in the population size.

83

than on those that already have a high proportion of elderly people (Sweden, the UK, and Germany). The latter group has already experienced a more substantial increase in pressure on resources from the ageing of the population.

2.1.3.3   Age and Utilisation

Older people use more health care services than younger people and the very old are especially heavy users of health care. Robinson et al. (1990) estimate that those aged 65 and over in the UK consume around four times as much health care as those under 65. Other data also suggest that health care costs increase rapidly above the age of 65: Anderson and Knickman (1984) analyse Medicare data to show that health care expenditure on the old increases rapidly with age in the US. Fujino (1987) states that in Japan, the rate of disease is 400 per thousand for those aged 65 to 74 and 550 per thousand for those aged above 75. Old people also often need different types of care to the young. In particular, as the proportion of old people increases, so the demand for residential, long term, and community care will rise.

The expected ageing of the population is widely cited as one of the major determinants of the future path of health care spending. However, this is not directly apparent from the data. The wide dispersion of demographic structures in the study countries might be expected to lead to a visible relationship between the proportion of elderly in the population and spending on health care per head. But there is no apparent correlation between this demographic variable and health care expenditure per head in the data for 1987, the latest year for which demographic information is available for all the countries in our study.

2.1.3.4   Age and Culture

The response of societies to the increased pressure on resources that demographic change will bring is strongly influenced by cultural factors. Attitudes to the 'correct' treatment of elderly dependants vary between countries and over time. In the West, the progressive breakdown of the traditional family structure means that the responsibility for caring for the elderly is diffused, and hospitalisation has become more common. In Japan, there is a deeply rooted aversion to the institutionalisation of family members, which brings shame on the relatives: the result is that in Japan the elderly are more often cared for at home.

2.1.4 Expectations

Expectations alter over time. Where health care is concerned, expectations of benefits are increasing and patients are becoming more demanding of the health care system; 'wants' are expanding in relation to 'need'.[7] Patient expectations may also be a factor in explaining different patterns of health care provision in different countries.

2.1.4.1 *Technology*

As medical technology has advanced, there has been a corresponding increase in the standard of health care which is expected. Improved technology means that more ailments can be treated, so patients are less likely to accept that nothing can be done for their complaint. The pressure to treat, even when the value of the therapy is marginal, is increasing.

2.1.4.2 *Education*

The education of a population affects their health care 'wants'. Knowing more about what treatments are available leads patients to expect a better standard of care and to expect to be offered treatment for more conditions.

2.1.4.3 *Income*

Increases in real incomes are likely to have an impact on health care 'demand'. As the budget constraint eases, either for the individual or for the economy as a whole, the opportunity cost of health care falls (other things being equal) and there is an increase in the amount of health care that people expect.

2.1.4.4 *Culture*

In countries such as Canada and the UK, there is an ingrained expectation that health care will be provided free at the point of delivery, and that equity will be an important consideration in the allocation of resources for health care. In the US, however, a different view is taken of the relative importance of equity and individual choice, and Americans appear to be satisfied with a much less equitable distribution of health care.

---

[7]   See Section 2.2.2.

2.1.4.5 Malpractice

Enhanced expectations of what medicine can achieve leads to increased disappointment when medicine or its practitioners fail to deliver. Litigation following a failure of treatment can therefore be expected to increase. The practice of 'defensive medicine' (tests and practices that reduce the likelihood of an unfavourable outcome for the doctor if litigation takes place) appears to be an important cause of the rise in health care expenditure in the US.

2.1.5 Changes in Epidemiology

Increased wealth leads to changes in the incidence of disease. Proper sanitation, housing, and cleanliness come with the increasing wealth of a society, and make it less likely that people will catch infectious diseases. Improved diet make infectious diseases less likely to be fatal. Kawakita (1989) notes a decline of the death rate[8] in Japan from infectious diseases over the last century and ascribes this partly to factors such as 'social environment, food education, food level' which are associated with increased wealth in a country. The counterpart of the decline in deaths from infectious disease among the young is an increase in deaths from causes such as cancer, heart disease, and strokes which tend to affect the old.

While there are unlikely to be further rapid changes in the main causes of death, two points should be noted. First, in developed societies smoking, drinking and accidents are the causes of a significant percentage of deaths before the age of 65. Social pressures to reduce, in particular, smoking, could therefore have an impact on the occurrence of premature death in developed countries.

Secondly, the effects of 'new' diseases are difficult to predict. The effect of AIDS (Acquired Immune Deficiency Syndrome) is one of the biggest unknowns in the projection of expenditure. The course of the epidemic is unpredictable, and the cost of treatment is likely to be substantial. Medicines currently available address containment of the disease, not cure. Equally important, it is impossible to forecast when some other new illness such as AIDS will arise.

---

[8] The number of deaths per 100,000 in the population per year.

2.1.6   Environmental Factors

Environmental factors are unlikely to have a substantial effect on the time profile of health care expenditure within a country, but may explain some part of the difference in expenditure between countries. Thus, the degree of **urbanisation** of a society affects both the real cost of providing care (for example, by reducing travel costs) and the type of illness experienced. Other environmental factors, such as **climate** and **pollution** may have a significant influence on health 'need' in some countries but are not expected to have a significant effect on health care expenditure in the countries of this study.

2.1.7   Culture

Cultural factors can have considerable bearing on health care 'wants' in addition to the effect that they have on the institutions which provide health care. However, cultural differences are unlikely to alter quickly or systematically over the next ten years, so they are more relevant to differences in the level of perceived 'need' between countries than to the rate of growth of health care expenditure in a country.

2.1.7.1   Culture and the Need for Health Care

Culture can affect the 'need' for health care through lifestyle and diet. The Japanese diet has historically been very low in fat, and this has resulted in low rates of morbidity and mortality from heart disease and other cardio-vascular problems. Within Europe, there is a clear distinction between the health of the Mediterranean nations and that of the Northern countries (above the 'olive line'). This is believed to be due to different cultural norms in lifestyle, work and diet. There may also be cultural influences on the perception of what constitutes health.

2.1.7.2   Culture and Health Care Wants

Culture and historical accident also affect the perception of health care 'need', and of what constitutes appropriate treatment. This is closely tied to expectations (discussed above) but includes other idiosyncrasies. Examples would be the German sick funds offering spa cures as part of their coverage, and the fact that some American insurers will now pay for chiropractors, who are regarded as providing 'fringe' medicine in some other countries.

2.1.7.3 *Culture and the Costs of Meeting Health Care Wants*

Cultural attitudes may also affect the cost of meeting health care 'wants'. The status which society affords doctors and other health care professionals influences their pay and conditions, and therefore affects the level of health care spending. Social preferences may also have a role: for example, in many countries (e.g. Britain) public opinion is strongly opposed to the use of price (copayments) as a means of rationing health care.

2.1.8   Conclusion

The most important factors influencing the 'need' for health care expenditure in the future are technological change, changes in demographic structure and increased expectations of benefit from health care. Other factors that are relevant include changes in epidemiology, changes in environmental factors and changes in culture.

ANNEX 2.2 FURTHER ESTIMATION RESULTS

A number of alternative specifications for the equations described in this chapter were explored in addition to the ones described in the main text. This Annex summarises the results of investigating two alternative specifications for the equation modelling the funds available for health care. It also reports on the estimation of equations for 'demand' in the US and Switzerland.

The models used to make the projections and described in the main text are very simple. Thee specifications below offer more complex explanations of health care expenditure. The results of these investigations, and the reasons why it was thought not to be appropriate to use these models to make projections, are described below.

2.2.1 The Role of the Government Deficit

Almost all governments have a role in the financing of health care. This is clearly visible in national health systems, less so in other types of system. However, even in insurance based systems government subsidies, investment funds and other contributions are often significant.

The supply-side model is predicated on the assumption that GDP is relevant to the supply of funds for health care. However, the supply of funds may also be affected by the financial position of government. One way to examine this proposition is to ask:

> Does the extent of the government's financial deficit affect the amount
> of funds allocated for expenditure on health care?

When the government is experiencing financial pressures from other sources and running a substantial deficit it is likely that downward pressure will be exerted on health care expenditure. If this were the case, then in years when the government deficit is large, the funds available for expenditure on health care would be lower than they would otherwise have been, while when the deficit is small or when there is a surplus, there might be more funds available for health care.

Since higher health care expenditure will itself will lead to a larger government deficit, the equation that includes the government deficit will suffer from simultaneity. It is therefore important to use two stage least squares (2SLS) when estimating this equation.

In order to examine whether this significantly affects health care expenditure, we estimated equation A1 below using 2SLS. This is the supply equation (equation 1 of Section 2.4 above), with an extra explanatory variable :

$$\ln HCE_t = a_0 + a_1 \ln GDP_t + a_2 DEF + u_t \qquad (A1)$$

where HCE_t is health care expenditure in year t;
GDP_t is gross domestic product;
DEF_t is the general government deficit (percentage of GDP); and,
u_t is the random residual.

Table 2.3: Instrumental Variables with Lagged Explanatory Variables

	Ordinary Least Squares				2SLS			Period of
	C	GDP	DEF		C	GDP	DEF	Equations
Canada	-7.1	1.35	0.006		-7.2	1.36	0.002	1960-90
	(18.9)	(44.5)	(1.0)		(14.1)	(32.4)	(0.2)	
France	-12.6	1.65	0.025		-12.1	1.61	0.044	1960-90
	(53.3)	(105)	(5.9)		(29.6)	(58.5)	(4.0)	
Germany	-13.4	1.75	0.040		-13.5	1.76	0.043	1960-90
	(25.3)	(46.7)	(4.9)		(19.6)	(35.9)	(3.2)	
Italy	-17.1	1.70	0.012		-21.6	1.92	-0.005	1960-90
	(9.3)	(18.2)	(1.8)		(4.6)	(8.0)	(0.3)	
Japan	-9.6	1.34	0.031		-8.8	1.30	0.043	1961-89
	(18.0)	(47.1)	(5.2)		(11.9)	(32.5)	(4.6)	
Netherlands	-14.0	1.89	0.005		-14.4	1.92	0.001	1960-90
	(25.0)	(42.0)	(0.9)		(20.8)	(34.4)	(0.1)	
Spain	-22.6	2.15	0.008		-22.9	2.17	<0.001	1962-90
	(22.9)	(36.3)	(0.8)		(20.1)	(31.6)	(<0.1)	
Sweden	-13.7	1.82	0.017		-13.7	1.82	0.015	1960-90
	(22.1)	(39.5)	(5.8)		(19.7)	(35.2)	(4.3)	
UK	-11.4	1.67	0.015		-11.5	1.67	0.019	1960-90
	(25.1)	(46.1)	(4.8)		(22.8)	(41.7)	(4.6)	
USA	-14.7	1.81	0.029		-16.3	1.92	0.011	1960-90
	(26.2)	(47.3)	(4.8)		(13.8)	(23.7)	(0.7)	

Estimation of this equation using lagged values of the explanatory variables as instrumental variables resulted in estimates of a_2 which were generally positive and in some cases statistically significant, see Table 2.3. This implies that an increase in the government deficit is accompanied by an increase in expenditure on health care.

This variable (DEF) was excluded from further consideration.

2.2.2   Dynamic Specifications

The estimation results presented in Annex 2.3 describe the correlation between health care expenditure and GDP in the same year. However, the relationship between the variables may be better explained by last year's GDP, for there may be a time lag between a change in GDP and a change in expenditure on health care.

To investigate the hypothesis that there may be lags in the relationship we estimated an equation which contains the contemporaneous values of the variable ln GDP, the values of this variable in each of the two previous years, and each of the two previous years' values of ln HCE:

$$\ln\text{HCE}_t = a_0 + a_1 \ln\text{GDP}_t + a_2 \ln\text{HCE}_{t-1} + a_3 \ln\text{GDP}_{t-1}$$
$$+ a_4 \ln\text{HCE}_{t-2} + a_5 \ln\text{GDP}_{t-2} + u_t \tag{A2}$$

where HCE_t is real health care expenditure in year t;

   GDP_t is real gross domestic product, are defined as above;

   t-1 is the year prior to year t;

   t-2 is the year two years before year t; and

   u_t is the random residual.

The equation was tested to see if various parameter restrictions were rejected by the data.

For most countries the parameter estimates in this equation suggested that the best explanation of health care expenditure this year is health care expenditure last year. However, the relationship between health care expenditure and GDP is more of the nature of a broad correlation; a change in expenditure on health care is unlikely to be directly caused by a change in the level of GDP. A problem that arises when a dynamic equation is estimated in these circumstances is the possibility of a downward bias in the estimated values of the coefficients in the exogenous variable (in this case GDP) due to "errors in variables".

In the course of estimating this equation we also tested a simple **error correction specification (A3)**. This is a special case of equation A2 with constraints imposed on the values of some of the coefficients:

$$\Delta \ln HCE_t = b_0 + b_1 \Delta \ln GDP_t + b_2 \{\ln HCE_{t-1} - b_3 \ln GDP_{t-1}\} + u_t \qquad \text{(A3)}$$

where $\Delta \ln HCE_t = \ln HCE_t - \ln HCE_{t-1}$
$\Delta \ln GDP_t = \ln GDP_t - \ln GDP_{t-1}$
u_t is the random residual

and the parameter b_3 is constrained to take the value of the estimate of a_1 from the equation:

$$\ln HCE_t = a_0 + a_1 \ln GDP_t + u_t \qquad \text{(A4)}$$

described in Section 2.4.1.

Equation A3 can be given the following interpretation. If b_3 is interpreted as the 'trend' or long-run elasticity relating GDP to expenditure on health care, then the term in curly brackets is the difference between the long-run trend value and the actual value in the last period. The interpretation of the equation is therefore that the growth in HCE this year (the left-hand-side variable) will be related to this year's growth in GDP (the term in $\Delta \ln GDP_t$), modified by a 'correction' factor which depends on how different last year's expenditure on health care was from the long-run expected value.

The dynamic specification had mixed success in explaining historical health care expenditure in the countries of the study. The general dynamic equation (A2) performed quite well. An F-test (of the joint significance of parameters) rejects the deletion of the lagged variables in the majority of countries. The error correction model (A3) produced more varied results. This equation was not rejected as a simplification of (A2) in about half of the countries studied. In addition, the estimate of the coefficient b_1 on the exogenous variable in $\Delta \ln GDP$ was in all cases much smaller than the estimate of b_3. It was rejected as a forecasting equation because:

- the use of this specification when the data are subject to measurement error, as in the present case, is likely to lead to an underestimate of the short-run GDP elasticity and an overestimate of the time taken to return to equilibrium; and,

- we are more interested in the long-term relationship between HCE and GDP than we are in the dynamics of adjustment on an annual basis. The key relationship is therefore the long-run one between HCE and GDP. The long term projections of equations A3 and A4 are in any case the same.

We therefore based our projections of HCE on the simple regression without the error correction model.

2.2.3   Inclusion of a Price Effect

2.2.3.1   Introduction

The projections of health care expenditure for each country assume that the unit cost of health care will not have a major impact on the utilisation of health care services. This is because the view taken was that most countries do not have sufficiently widespread cost-sharing for this to be a significant determinant of demand.[9]

There are, however, exceptions to this assumption. Both the United States and Switzerland have health care systems in which cost-sharing is normal for a wide variety of health care services, and copayments at the point of delivery are normal. This means that changes in the copayments paid by patients should influence 'demand', and so affect total expenditure on health care. Below, we describe the investigation of price effects on health care expenditure in these countries.

In these countries people often take an explicit decision regarding the extent of their expenditure on health care and pay a substantial part of the cost of their medical care themselves, either at the point of delivery or in the form of an insurance premium or both. Further, studies that relate health care expenditure to the level of copayment provides evidence supporting an influence of the price of the service on the consumption of care.[10] It therefore seemed worth experimenting with the effects of including a cost indicator in the equation for 'need' in these countries, effectively transforming it into an equation for 'demand'.

---

[9]   There is a further, conceptual, question regarding the role of the 'price' of health care. The type of services provided now are often different from those that were provided 20 years ago. The health care 'price' index is therefore an indicator of health care costs; it is not an indicator of the price of a well-defined service.

[10]   See NERA (1992).

2.2.3.2 The United States

The equation estimated in the US implicitly assumes the copayments faced by patients move in line with the OECD cost index:

$$\ln(HCE_t/DEM_t) = b_o + b_1 T + b_2 \ln PRICE_t + w_t \qquad (A5)$$

where HCE_t is real health care expenditure in year t;

  DEM_t is the weighted demographic variable defined in Section 2.4.2;

  T is the time trend;

  $PRICE_t$ is the OECD index of the real unit cost of health care; and,

  w_t is the random residual.

The price index used is deflated by the GDP deflator. This index, which is defined to be 100 in 1985, increased from 78 in 1960 to 88 in 1980, and then rose more quickly, reaching 114 in 1990.

If the cost of services had no effect on the quantity of health care consumed, then expenditure on health care would reflect any increase in unit cost (other things being equal) and the coefficient on the price index in equation A4 would be plus unity.

Over the period 1960 to 1990, the estimated value of this coefficient is -0.3 (see Table 2.4). It is significantly different from plus unity, and implies that the price elasticity of health care expenditure is -1.3.

In making the projections we have implicitly assumed that real unit costs increase at the same trend rate in the future as they have on average in the past.

```
┌──────────────────────────────────────────────────────────────────────────┐
```

Table 2.4: Regression Results for the United States

Dependent Variable: ln(HCE/DEM)

Explanatory Variables:

Intercept	-3.20	-0.89	0.96	-0.88	0.58	-0.87
T	4.3	4.7	4.9	4.5	4.8	4.4
	(12.4)	(42.4)	(21.7)	(50.0)	(28.2)	(62.2)
lnPRICE	0.53	-	-0.42	-	-0.34	-
	(1.0)		(1.8)		(2.4)	
R^2	0.989	0.988	0.991	0.990	0.994	0.993
SEE	0.0351	0.0350	0.0350	0.0364	0.0328	0.0354
PERIOD	1960-82	1960-82	1960-86	1960-86	1960-90	1960-90

(the numbers in brackets under the coefficients are t-statistics)

2.2.3.3 Switzerland

In Switzerland also, citizens enjoy a considerable degree of choice over the insurance package they purchase and are not restricted to one government determined package only. The equation implicitly assumes that the copayments faced by patients have moved broadly in line with the OECD cost index:

$$\ln(HCE_t/DEM_t) = b_0 + b_1T + b_2\ln PRICE + w_t \qquad (A6)[11]$$

Over the period 1974 to 1990 the estimated value of the coefficient on the price variable is 0.01 (see Table 2.5), and significantly different from plus unity. This implies that the price elasticity of health care expenditure is -1.0. If the results of estimating equation A6 over different periods are examined, the estimate of the elasticity can be seen to have increased over time. One possible explanation of this is that the relationship between real unit costs and copayments faced by patients may have changed.

[11]   See equation A5 above for a description of the terms used. This equation is a restatement of the demand equation in section 2.3.10 in Annex 2.3.

95

Table 2.5: Regression Results for Switzerland

Dependent variable: ln(HCE/DEM)

Explanatory Variables:

Intercept	-8.36	-3.37	-2.28	0.456	1.42
T	0.6	1.0	1.2	1.6	1.7
	(0.7)	(4.5)	(6.6)	(12.6)	(9.2)
lnPRICE	1.97	0.86	0.61	-0.01	-0.22
	(4.1)	(6.1)	(4.4)	(0.1)	(0.9)
R^2	0.799	0.802	0.840	0.941	0.926
SEE	0.112	0.026	0.020	0.012	0.011
PERIOD	1960-90	1970-90	1972-90	1974-90	1980-90

(the numbers in brackets under the coefficients are t-statistics)

The projection of the future value of real unit costs in the health care sector does not affect projections of health care expenditure based on this equation.

The fact that the coefficient on lnPRICE is close to zero and not significant means that this variable can be removed with very little effect on the estimated time trend. Excluding the cost variable from both sides of equation 2 and re-estimating gives:

$$ln(HCE/DEM) \quad = \quad 0.42 + 1.6\ T$$
$$(28.0) \qquad\qquad \text{(A7)}$$

$$R^2 = 0.981 \quad SE = 0.011 \quad \text{Period: 1974 to 1990}$$

We have used this equation in making projections for the demand for health care in Switzerland.

ANNEX 2.3 COUNTRY SPECIFIC RESULTS

2.3.1   Canada

2.3.1.1   Estimation Period

There are a number of factors which suggest that, increasingly, the 'need' for health care in Canada is not being met. For example, since the middle of the 1980s, the health care systems of Canadian provinces have increasingly been reducing the range of the services they offer that are not mandatory under the Canada Health Act. Over the last five years copayments for pharmaceuticals have been introduced or increased.[12] There have been increased efforts to control expenditure on primary physicians.[13] The existence of queues has become increasingly apparent, especially following press coverage of the deaths of patients waiting for cardiovascular surgery in Toronto in 1988.[14] Further, examination of the data shows that the growth of health care expenditure slowed after 1986 (see Chart 2.5).

The equations for the supply and 'need' for funds for health care in Canada have therefore been estimated over the period 1960 to 1986.

2.3.1.2   Estimation Results

The result of estimating the supply equation over the period 1960 to 1986 is:[15]

$$\text{lnHCE} = \begin{array}{cc} -7.18 & + \quad 1.36 \;\; \text{lnGDP} \\ (20.3) & (48.5) \end{array}$$

$$R^2 = 0.99 \qquad SE = 0.05 \quad \text{Period: } 1960 \text{ to } 1986$$

Chow predictions $F_{(4,25)} = 0.23$ Chow stability $F_{(2,27)} = 0.30$

The estimated value of the elasticity of the supply of funds for health care with respect to changes in GDP is thus 1.36. When estimated over the period 1960 to 1990 (and thus not abstracting from the effects of recent attempts to reduce

---

[12]   See Section 4.5.3.

[13]   See Section 4.3.4.

[14]   See Section 4.4.1.

[15]   T-statistics in parentheses.

costs) the data give an estimated GDP elasticity of 1.37. The data up to 1990 support the hypothesis that the relationship between GDP and health care expenditure is stable. Together with Switzerland, Canada has the lowest GDP elasticity of all eleven countries for which we have made projections in our study (see Table 2.1).

The result of estimating the demand-side equation is:

$$\text{lnHCE} = \text{lnDEM} - 0.86 + 4.4\,\text{T}$$
$$(50.2) \quad (40.6)$$

$$R^2 = 0.99 \quad SE = 0.04 \quad \text{Period: } 1960 \text{ to } 1986$$

$$\text{Chow predictions } F(4,25) = 2.83 \quad \text{Chow stability } F(2,27) = 6.09$$

The estimated trend increase in health care expenditure per head of the population, after correction for demographic changes, is 4.4 percent per year. Only the UK and Switzerland among our countries have lower estimated time trends (see Table 2.1). There is a sharp difference between the estimated time trends before and after 1984: during the period 1984 to 1990 health care expenditure, corrected for demographic change, increased at an annual rate of 2.6 percent. Estimating over the whole 30 year period gives a time trend of 4.2 percent.

2.3.1.3   The Projections

It is forecast by Consensus Economics (1992) that GDP in Canada will grow at 3.2 percent a year in real terms on average over the next decade. As the estimate of the elasticity of health care expenditure to GDP is 1.36, this suggests that the 'acceptable' quantity of funds allocated to health care will increase by over 50 percent in real terms during the next ten years. This implies that total expenditure on health care would reach around C\$90 bn (1990 prices) by the year 2000, which is 10.6 percent of the forecast for GDP.

United Nations forecasts imply that the demographic variable DEM will increase by 1.0 percent a year on average over the next ten years. (Between 1960 and 1990 its average increase was 1.7 percent a year.) The ageing of the population is thus expected to cause an increase of about 11 percent in health care 'need' over the next decade. Although this is larger than the increase expected for demographic reasons in most other study countries, it represents only a small share of the 50 percent increase in funds projected as being acceptable.

The projections of health care 'need' and of the supply of funds are illustrated in Chart 2.5.[16] 'Need' is estimated to be 10.2 percent of GDP in 1990. If this increases at the trend rate of 4.4 percent per year, then 'need' will reach 13.5 percent of GDP by 2000. The shortfall between expenditure and 'need' in 2000 is therefore projected at 3.3 percent of GDP. The development of this funding shortfall is sensitive to the rate at which 'need' is assumed to expand in the future. If it were to expand at 2.0 percent instead of 4.4 percent a year, then the funding gap would disappear by the year 2000.

Chart 2.5
Demand for Health Care and Funds Provided
Projections for Canada

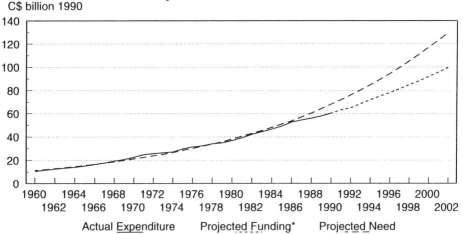

C$ billion 1990

Actual Expenditure   Projected Funding*   Projected Need

* Set to be coincident with actual expenditure in 1990

Because the evidence of unmet 'need' in the Canadian system at present is not compelling, we believe that this pressure may be containable within the *status quo* structure, albeit at a cost. Canada will, however, have a strong incentive to seek opportunities to reduce inefficiencies in its health care system.

---

[16]   We have no data for health care expenditure in 1991 compatible with our historical series, so an estimate is required. If we used the model equation, the fall in GDP in the 1991 recession would imply a sharp fall in the estimated supply of funds, but this did not happen in the previous recession. The projection for health care expenditure in 1991 was therefore based on the estimated trend increase.

2.3.2   France

2.3.2.1   Estimation Period

There is evidence of increasing constraints on the funding of health care in France. For example, the ending of *per diem* payments to hospitals from 1984,[17] the introduction of copayments for inpatient care in 1982, and increases in the scope of pharmaceutical copayments in 1976 (and again in 1986) bear witness to recent downward pressure on health care expenditure in France.[18] Perhaps more important, the government has been making strenuous efforts to restrain the annual increase in the level of the fee-for-service payments made to primary care physicians. Indeed, the data suggest that the relationship between health care expenditure and GDP may have changed in the 1980s, with health care expenditure rising at a somewhat slower rate than might have been expected based on previous historic trends.

The equations for the supply and 'need' for funds for health care in France have therefore been estimated over the period 1960 to 1986.

2.3.2.2   Estimation Results

The result of estimating the supply equation over the period 1960 to 1986 is:[19]

$$\mathbf{lnHCE} = -13.0 + 1.68 \ \mathbf{lnGDP}$$
$$(33.2) \quad (64.6)$$

$$R^2 = 0.99 \quad SE = 0.04 \quad Period: \ 1960 \ to \ 1986$$

$$Chow \ predictions \ F_{(4,25)} = 0.21 \quad Chow \ stability \ F_{(2,27)} = 0.45$$

The estimated value of the elasticity of the supply of funds for health care with respect to changes in GDP is thus 1.68. When estimated over the period 1960 to 1990 (and thus not abstracting from the effects of recent attempts to reduce costs) the data give an estimated GDP elasticity of 1.69. The equation is stable, as demonstrated by the Chow test on the accuracy of the predictions for the years 1987 to 1990 and the Chow test for stability of the coefficient estimates. The data up to 1990 do not, therefore, support the hypothesis that the

---

[17]   See Section 5.3.5.2.

[18]   See Section 5.5.1.4.

[19]   T-statistics in parentheses.

relationship between GDP and health care expenditure has significantly altered.

The result of estimating the demand-side equation is:

$$\ln HCE = \ln DEM + \underset{(13.5)}{0.372} + \underset{(30.9)}{5.3} \ T$$

$$R^2 = 0.97 \qquad SE = 0.07 \qquad \text{Period: 1960 to 1986}$$

$$\text{Chow predictions } F(4,25) = 4.88 \qquad \text{Chow stability } F(2,27) = 10.53$$

The estimated trend increase in health care expenditure per head of the population, after correcting for demographic changes, is 5.3 percent per year. There is a sharp difference between the estimated time trends before and after 1984: during the period 1984 to 1990 health care 'need' has grown at an estimated rate of 2.6 percent. Estimating over the whole 30 year period gives a trend growth rate of 4.9 percent.

2.3.2.3 The Projections

It is forecast by Consensus Economics (1992) that GDP in France will grow at 2.8 percent a year in real terms on average over the next decade. As the estimate of the elasticity of health care expenditure to GDP is 1.68, this suggests that the 'acceptable' quantity of funds allocated to health care will increase by over 50 percent in real terms during the next ten years. This implies that total expenditure on health care would reach around FF 950 bn (1990 prices) by the year 2000, which is 10.5 percent of the forecast for GDP.

Demographic change on its own will not make large inroads into this sum, since France already has a relatively old population. United Nations forecasts imply that the demographic variable DEM will increase by only 0.4 percent a year on average over the next ten years. (Between 1960 and 1990 its average increase was 1.1 percent a year.) The ageing of the population is thus expected to cause an increase of only about 4 percent in health care 'need' over the next decade.

The projections of health care 'need' and the supply of funds are illustrated in Chart 2.6. This suggests that since the early 1980s the system has come under increasing pressure, as expenditure has failed to keep pace with the expansion of 'need'. This is consistent with the evidence that the French government is perpetually making efforts to control costs. The system appears to have coped fairly well with the increased pressure thus far: satisfaction with the system is still relatively high,[20] although there is an escalating debate about the maintenance of quality. However, 'need' is estimated to be 11.1 percent of GDP in 1990, and is projected on the *status quo* assumptions to increase to 15.2 percent in 2000.

Chart 2.6
Demand for Health Care and Funds Provided
Projections for France

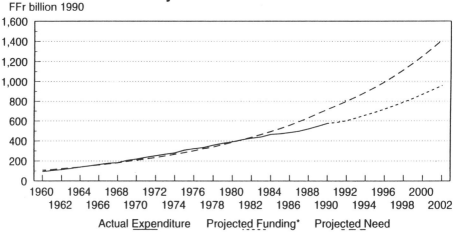

FFr billion 1990

Actual Expenditure   Projected Funding*   Projected Need

* Set to be coincident with actual expenditure in 1990

The development of the funding shortfall is sensitive to the rate at which the 'need' is assumed to expand in the future. If 'need' were to expand at 1.5 percent instead of at 5.3 percent a year, then the funding gap would disappear by the year 2000.

One way in which this tension might be resolved would be through continued expansion in the share of health care which is privately financed: private expenditure on health care increased from around 20 percent of the total in 1981 to 26 percent in 1990.[21] If the implied contraction in the share financed by the public sector were to continue, total expenditure on health care might increase to meet 'need'.

---

[20]   See Blendon *et al.* (1990).

[21]   OECD (1991).

2.3.3 Germany[22]

2.3.3.1 Estimation Period

Over the last decade a series of cost containment acts have been passed in Germany.[23] Each has succeeded in containing expenditure on health care for one or two years, but expenditure has then returned to its upward trend. This has resulted in the share of GDP spent on health care falling from 8.7 percent in 1981 to 8.1 percent in 1990.[24] Further, the Health Care Act of 1989 cited stable sickness fund contribution rates as an objective. In the light of this, the equations for the supply and 'need' for funds have been estimated over the period 1960 to 1986.

2.3.3.2 Estimation Results

The result of estimating the supply equation over the period 1960 to 1986 is:[25]

$$\text{lnHCE} = -15.6 + 1.91 \text{ lnGDP}$$
$$\quad\quad\quad (26.3) \quad (45.6)$$

$$R^2 = 0.99 \quad\quad SE = 0.05 \quad\quad \text{Period: } 1960 \text{ to } 1986$$

$$\text{Chow predictions } F(4,25) = 5.18 \quad\quad \text{Chow stability } F(2,27) = 10.50$$

The estimated value of the elasticity of the supply of funds for health care with respect to changes in GDP is thus 1.91. When estimated over the period 1960 to 1990 (and thus not abstracting from the effects of recent attempts to reduce costs) the data give an estimated GDP elasticity of 1.83. The Chow predictions test rejects the hypothesis that the data for the years 1987 to 1990 would have been generated by this equation and the stability of the coefficient estimates is rejected by the Chow stability test. This indicates that the relationship between GDP and health care expenditure has changed to a significant extent, perhaps due to the successful containment of expenditure by cost controls in the last decade.

---

[22] The projections presented here take no account of the implications of German unification.

[23] Since 1990 expenditure has again grown rapidly. See Section 6.5.1.

[24] OECD (1991).

[25] T-statistics in parentheses.

The fit of the relationship between the equation's predictions and actual expenditure over the estimation period (1960 to 1986) is good (with a standard error of around 5 percent), in spite of fluctuations of expenditure around its trend. Outside the fitted period, from 1987 to 1990, real expenditure is lower than the equation predicts, especially in 1989 and 1990, when the 1989 Health Care Act restricted expenditure.

The result of estimating the demand-side equation is:

$$\text{lnHCE} = \text{lnDEM} - 0.54 + 4.9 \text{ T}$$
$$(17.1) \quad (24.7)$$

$$R^2 = 0.96 \quad SE = 0.08 \quad \text{Period: } 1960 \text{ to } 1986$$

$$\text{Chow predictions } F(4,25) = 7.13 \quad \text{Chow stability } F(2,27) = 15.03$$

The estimated trend increase in health care expenditure per head of the population, after correction for demographic changes, is 4.9 percent per year. There is a sharp difference between the estimated time trends before and after 1986: during the period 1986 to 1990 health care 'need' has an estimated time trend of -0.1 percent. Estimating over the whole 30 year period gives a time trend of 4.3 percent.

2.3.3.3 The Projections

It is forecast by Consensus Economics (1992) that GDP in Germany will grow at 3.1 percent a year in real terms on average during the next decade. As the estimate of the elasticity of health care expenditure to GDP is 1.91, this suggests that the 'acceptable' quantity of funds allocated to health care will increase by over 75 percent in real terms during the next ten years. This implies that total expenditure on health care would reach almost DM 330 bn (1990 prices) by the year 2000, which is 10.4 percent of the forecast for GDP. This represents a very rapid increase in health care expenditure. It is, of course, predicted on the assumption that the high elasticity of health care expenditure to GDP growth observed over the period 1960 to 1986 will continue (the *status quo* assumption).

Demographic change on its own will make negligible inroads into this sum. United Nations forecasts imply that the demographic variable DEM will increase by less than 0.1 percent a year on average over the next ten years. (Between 1960 and 1990 its average increase was 1.0 percent a year.) The ageing of the population is thus expected to cause an increase of less than 1 percent in health care 'needs' over the next decade.[26]

The projections of health care 'need' and the supply of funds are illustrated in Chart 2.7. 'Need' is estimated to be 11.0 percent of GDP in 1990. If this increases at the trend rate of 4.9 percent per year, then 'need' will reach 14.2 percent of GDP by 2000. The shortfall between expenditure and 'need' is therefore estimated to be 2.9 percent of GDP in 1990. This shortfall is projected to be 3.8 percent of forecast GDP in 2000.

Chart 2.7
Demand for Health Care and Funds Provided
Projections for Germany

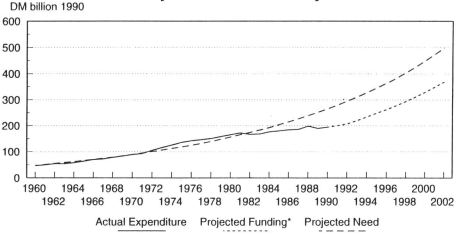

DM billion 1990

Actual Expenditure   Projected Funding*   Projected Need

* Set to be coincident with actual expenditure in 1990

This suggests that the cost control efforts of the last decade have been rather successful in restraining the cost of health care, as the level of expenditure has expanded at a slower rate than the estimated rate of increase in 'need' without queues developing and without a reduction in the scope of benefits provided. However, financial pressure on the medical profession has become more intense over this period with, for example, a fall in the income of doctors relative to average earnings.[27]

---

[26]   The UN made these demographic projections without allowing for the inclusion of Eastern Germany, or of the large influx of East Europeans into the Federal Republic in 1990 and 1991.

[27]   See Section 1.3.4.

105

If the real cost of meeting 'need' were to continue rising at the rate it did on average between 1960 and 1986, then the scenario shown on Chart 2.7 will pertain. In this case the funding shortfall in the German health care system would remain at around the current level for the foreseeable future. In these circumstances we would expect the financial stringency of the last few years to continue. While this might result in a progressive, gradual decline in the quality or scope of the care offered, a crisis appears unlikely. The development of the funding shortfall is, however, sensitive to the rate at which the 'need' is assumed to expand in the future. If 'need' were to expand at 2.0 percent instead of 4.4 percent a year, then the funding gap would disappear by the year 2000.

In addition, if the cost control efforts of recent years signify a change in the relationship between GDP and willingness to spend on health care, then a funding problem would develop during the next decade. The current reform proposals in Germany suggest that such a change in political perception may indeed have occurred.

2.3.4   Italy

2.3.4.1 Estimation Period

Experience in other countries suggests that health care systems which have a single dominant payer tend to have lower expenditure on health care than more decentralised systems. The SSN, which came into existence in 1978, currently finances around three-quarters of health care in Italy and can be viewed as such a dominant payer.[28] So it might be expected that health care expenditure would grow at a slower rate after about 1980.

Indeed, the SSN has made several efforts to contain costs. For example, physician reimbursement was changed from a fee-for-service to a capitation basis in 1978;[29] a ceiling for the SSN drugs bill was introduced in 1984;[30] and copayments for hospitals were introduced in 1989[31] (although both the latter measures were later withdrawn). However, the data suggest that, in spite of

---

[28]   The SSN was effectively formed in December 1978, See Section 7.2.1.

[29]   See Section 7.3.4.2.

[30]   See Section 7.3.5.2.

[31]   See Section 7.3.6.2.

this circumstantial evidence, there was no change in the relationship between health care expenditure and GDP.

The equations for the supply and 'need' for funds for health care in Italy have been estimated over the period 1960 to 1990. In addition the equations have been estimated from 1960 to 1980 and from 1980 to 1990, to allow a test of the effects of the formation of the SSN on the provision of funding. The conclusion is that there is no statistical evidence to support a structural change.

2.3.4.2 Estimation Results

The result of estimating the supply equation over the period 1960 to 1990 is:[32]

$$lnHCE \ = \ - \ 20.0 \ + \ 1.85 \ lnGDP$$
$$(24.4) \quad (45.6)$$

$$R^2 \ = \ 0.99 \qquad SE = 0.069 \qquad Period: \ 1960 \ to \ 1990$$

$$Chow \ predictions \ F(4,25) = 0.29 \qquad Chow \ stability \ F(2,27) = 1.70^{33}$$

The estimated value of the elasticity of the supply of funds for health care with respect to changes in GDP is 1.85. When estimated over the period 1960 to 1980 (and thus abstracting from the effects of the SSN) the data give an estimated GDP elasticity of 1.92. The Chow tests on the accuracy of the predictions of this equation for the years 1981 to 1990 and for stability of the coefficient parameters imply that the hypothesis that the equation is stable from 1960 to 1990 cannot be rejected, suggesting that the establishment of the SSN has not significantly altered the relationship between health care financing and GDP.

The result of estimating the demand-side equation is:

$$lnHCE \ = \ lnDEM \ + \ 5.28 \ + \ 5.3 \ T$$
$$(135.6) \quad (25.2)$$

$$R^2 \ = \ 0.96 \qquad SE \ = \ 0.11 \qquad Period: \ 1960 \ to \ 1990$$

$$Chow \ predictions \ F(4,25) = 2.72 \qquad Chow \ stability \ F(2,27) = 18.3$$

---

[32]   T-statistics in parentheses.

[33]   The Chow tests are based on the results of the regression run over the period 1960-1980.

The estimated trend increase in health care expenditure per head of the population, after correction for demographic changes, is 5.3 percent per year. Estimating this equation over the period 1960 to 1980 gives a larger estimate of the time trend, at 6.6 percent, while using the period 1980 to 1990 puts it at 3.1 percent. The Chow tests reject the hypothesis that this equation is stable over the whole period.

2.3.4.3   The Projections

It is forecast by Consensus Economics (1992) that GDP in Italy will grow at 2.5 percent a year in real terms on average over the next decade. As the estimate of the elasticity of health care expenditure to GDP is 1.85, this suggests that the 'acceptable' quantity of funds allocated to health care will increase by over 60 percent in real terms during the next ten years. This implies that total expenditure on health care would reach around Lira 150 tn (1990 prices) by the year 2000, which is 9.1 percent of the forecast for GDP.

Demographic change on its own will not make large inroads into this sum. United Nations forecasts imply that the demographic variable DEM will increase by 0.8 percent a year on average over the next ten years. (Between 1960 and 1990 its average increase was 0.9 percent a year.) The ageing of the population is thus expected to cause an increase of about 8 percent in health care 'need' over the next decade.

The projections of health care 'need' and the supply of funds are illustrated in Chart 2.8. 'Need' is estimated to be 8.7 percent of GDP in 1990. If this increases at the trend rate of 5.3 percent a year, then 'need' will reach 12.9 percent of GDP by 2000. The shortfall between 'need' and expenditure in 2000 is therefore projected to be 3.8 percent of GDP. Only if 'need' were to grow more slowly, say at 4 percent a year, would the problem of financing health care in 2000 be manageable within the *status quo* structure. If trends continue to operate in the future in the same way as they have in the past, then there will be a serious funding crisis in Italy within the next ten years.

However, Chart 2.8 shows that the time trend underestimates expenditure before the mid 1970s, and overestimates it from the mid 1980s onwards. Prior to 1978 the time trend (estimated to be 6.6 percent in 1960-1980) would be expected to overstate the rate of growth of 'need' as coverage was being progressively expanded. After the establishment of the SSN the time trend (estimated to be 3.1 percent in 1980-1990) probably understates the growth of 'need', as the slow-down in GDP growth put more pressure on the budget.

Chart 2.8
Demand for Health Care and Funds Provided
Projections for Italy

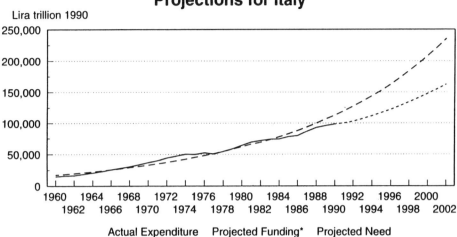

* Set to be coincident with actual expenditure in 1990

This *status quo* projection rests, of course, on the assumption that the relationship between GDP and expenditure on health care continues to be the same as it was in the period 1960 to 1990. However, the Italian government is under pressure to reduce its budget deficit to below what has been politically acceptable in the past. This is already causing considerable political disruption, and public expenditure on health care is likely to come under further pressure. If the private sector does not expand to fill this funding shortfall, then the crisis implied by the projections may arrive more quickly.

2.3.5   Japan

2.3.5.1   Estimation Period

There is evidence that the government has, in recent years, attempted to limit the growth of health care expenditure in Japan. Measures include: increases in copayments in 1977, 1982, 1984 and 1986; amendments to the Medical Services Act to restrict hospital capacity in 1985;[34] and, the reductions in drug prices imposed by the government.[35] Further, examination of the data suggest that the relationship between health care expenditure and GDP may

---

[34]   See Annex 8.2 for chronology of the Japanese health care system.

[35]   See Table 8.5.

have changed in the 1980s, with health care expenditure rising at a somewhat slower rate than might have been expected. Including this period would risk confusing government cost controls for a slowdown in the growth of need, therefore give an under-estimate of the *status quo* trend.

However, at the beginning of the period, the coverage and scope of health care expenditure were expanding. Including the early period would therefore give an over-estimate of the *status quo* trend.

The equations for the supply and 'need' for funds for health care in Japan have been estimated over the period 1960 to 1990. In addition the equations have been estimated from 1960 to 1980 and from 1980 to 1990, to allow tests for structural changes in the funding of health care.

2.3.5.2   Estimation Results

The result of estimating the supply equation over the period 1960 to 1990 is:[36]

$$\textbf{lnHCE} = - \textbf{11.5} + \textbf{1.45 lnGDP}$$
$$(23.3) \qquad (55.9)$$

$$R^2 = 0.99 \qquad SE = 0.08 \qquad \text{Period: 1960 to 1990}$$

$$\text{Chow predictions } F(8,21) = 0.41 \qquad \text{Chow Stability } F(2,27) = 1.90^{[37]}$$

The estimated value of the elasticity of the supply of funds for health care with respect to changes in real GDP is 1.45. When estimated over the period 1960 to 1980 (and thus ignoring the slowdown in the growth of health care expenditure during the 1980's) the data give an estimated GDP elasticity of 1.42. The equation is stable, as demonstrated by the Chow test on the accuracy of the predictions for the years 1981 to 1990 and the Chow test of the stability of the coefficient estimates.

---

[36]   T-statistics in parentheses.

[37]   The Chow tests are based on the results of the regression run over the period 1960-1980.

The result of estimating the demand-side equation is:

$$\text{lnHCE} = \text{lnDEM} + \underset{(53.1)}{3.221} + \underset{(20.8)}{6.9} \ \text{T}$$

$$R^2 = 0.94 \quad SE = 0.165 \quad \text{Period: 1960 to 1990}$$

$$\text{Chow predictions } F(8,21) = 4.32 \quad \text{Chow Stability } F(2,27) = 22.11$$

The estimated trend increase in health care expenditure per head of the population, after correction for demographic change, is 6.9 percent per year. There is a sharp difference between the estimated time trends before and after 1982: the period 1960 to 1982 has an average trend growth rate of 8.5 percent a year; the period 1982 to 1990 has an estimated trend rate of 2.9 percent.

2.3.5.3   The Projections

It is forecast by Consensus Economics (1992) that GDP in Japan will grow at 3.8 percent a year in real terms on average over the next decade. As the estimate of the elasticity of health care expenditure to GDP is 1.45, this suggests that the 'acceptable' quantity of funds allocated to health care will increase by 60 percent in real terms during the next ten years. This implies that total expenditure on health care would reach almost 50 tn Yen (1990 prices) by the year 2000, which is 7.8 percent of the forecast for GDP.

The Japanese population is aging more rapidly than that of any of the other study countries, but the demographic variable suggests that the majority of the effects of this change will not be felt in the forecast period. United Nations forecasts imply that the demographic variable DEM will increase by 1.0 percent a year on average over the next ten years. (Between 1960 and 1990 its average increase was 1.4 percent a year.) The ageing of the population is thus expected to cause an increase of about 11 percent in health care 'need' over the next decade.

The majority of the other countries in the study currently have higher health care spending per head than Japan, and all except the UK have higher spending as a share of GDP; however, the estimated time trend for Japan is 6.9 percent per year, while in most of the other countries in the study it is between 4 and 5.5 percent. As a result, the projection of 'need' in the year 2000 derived from the estimated time trend in Japan is higher than that estimated for other countries, even though the starting point is very low.

An alternative projection of 'need' in Japan has therefore been made. This used the average of the estimated 'need' in eight other countries (Canada, France, Germany, Italy, the Netherlands, Spain, Sweden, the United States). This projection for 'need' in Japan has been constructed by combining estimated 'need' per head in each of these countries (in PPP $US 1990 per head) using relative population figures (adjusted for age structure) as weights.

The projections of health care 'need' and of the supply of funds are illustrated in Chart 2.9. 'Need' is estimated at 11.0 percent of GDP in 1990, and is projected to increase to 13.7 percent of GDP by 2000.

Chart 2.9
Demand for Health Care and Funds Provided
Projections for Japan

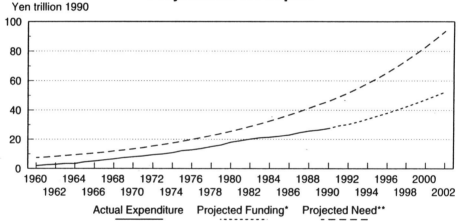

Yen trillion 1990

Actual Expenditure   Projected Funding*   Projected Need**

* Set to be coincident with actual expenditure in 1990
** Based on average of projected 'need' per head in eight other countries

Given this projection of 'need', the Japanese health care system does not face a large increase in its funding shortfall: the increase from the present level, estimated at 4.5 percent of GDP to the 5.9 percent of the projections is modest compared to that in some of the other countries. It seems unlikely that a crisis will be caused by this relatively small increase in the pressure on health care expenditure.

2.3.6   The Netherlands

2.3.6.1   *Estimation Period*

The government in the Netherlands has become increasingly closely involved in health care planning: in 1982 pharmaceutical lists were introduced;[38] in 1983 global budgets were introduced for hospitals (the budget formulae were changed in 1985 and again in 1988);[39] municipalities have used a system of permits to control the number of GPs;[40] and direct involvement has increased through the steady expansion in the number of services offered under AWBZ. The most dramatic effects of cost control measures were seen in 1984, when health care expenditure fell from 8.4 to 8.1 percent of GDP. Further, examination of the data shows that the rate of growth of health care expenditure slowed in the early 1980s (see Chart 2.10).

The equations for the supply and 'need' for funds for health care in the Netherlands have been estimated over the period 1960 to 1983.

2.3.6.2   *Estimation Results*

The result of estimating the supply equation over the period 1960 to 1983 is:[41]

$$\text{lnHCE} = -15.3 + 1.99 \ \text{lnGDP}$$
$$(35.4) \quad (58.1)$$

$$R^2 = 0.99 \quad SE = 0.04 \quad \text{Period: } 1960 \text{ to } 1983$$

$$\text{Chow predictions } F_{(4,25)} = 2.99 \quad \text{Chow stability } F_{(2,27)} = 12.38$$

The estimated value of the elasticity of the supply of funds for health care with respect to changes in GDP is thus 1.99. When estimated over the period 1960 to 1990 (and thus not abstracting from the effects of recent attempts to reduce costs) the data give an estimated GDP elasticity of 1.91. The Chow test on the stability of the coefficient estimates indicates rejection. This supports the hypothesis that there was a change in the relationship between health care

---

[38]   See Section 9.3.6.

[39]   See Section 9.3.5.

[40]   See Section 9.3.4.

[41]   T-statistics in parentheses.

finance and GDP in the early 1980s. Expenditure on health care grew more slowly than predicted by the equation in the years 1984 to 1990.

The result of estimating the demand-side equation is:

$$\text{lnHCE} = \text{lnDEM} - \underset{(15.5)}{0.691} + \underset{(19.7)}{6.2}\ T$$

$$R^2 = 0.95 \quad SE = 0.11 \quad \text{Period: 1960 to 1983}$$

$$\text{Chow predictions } F(4,25) = 6.63 \quad \text{Chow stability } F(2,27) = 28.43$$

The estimated trend increase in health care expenditure per head of the population, after correction for demographic factors, is 6.2 percent per year. There is a sharp difference between the estimated time trends before and after 1983; during the period 1983 to 1990 health care 'need' has an estimated time trend of only 1.2 percent. Estimating over the whole 30 year period gives a time trend of 4.6 percent.

2.3.6.3   *The Projections*

It is forecast that GDP in the Netherlands will grow at 2.4 percent a year in real terms on average over the next decade.[42] As the estimate of the elasticity of health care expenditure to GDP is 1.99, this suggests that the 'acceptable' quantity of funds allocated to health care will increase by almost 60 percent in real terms during the next ten years. This implies that total expenditure on health care would reach almost Guilders 65 bn (1990 prices) by the year 2000, which is 10.1 percent of the forecast for GDP.

Demographic change on its own will not make large inroads into this sum, since the Netherlands already has a relatively old population. United Nations forecasts imply that the demographic variable DEM will increase by only 0.8 percent a year on average over the next ten years. (Between 1960 and 1990 its average increase was 1.3 percent a year.) The ageing of the population is thus expected to cause an increase of only about 9 percent in health care 'need' over the next decade.

---

[42]   Consensus Economics (1992). This forecast does not cover the whole period to 2000. Growth has therefore been projected at the average over the previous ten years.

Chart 2.10
Demand for Health Care and Funds Provided
Projections for the Netherlands

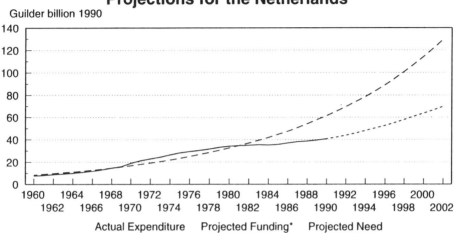

Guilder billion 1990

Actual Expenditure   Projected Funding*   Projected Need

* Set to be coincident with actual expenditure in 1990

The projections of health care 'need' and of the supply of funds are illustrated in Chart 2.10. 'Need' is estimated at 12.2 percent of GDP in 1990. If this increases at the trend rate of 6.2 percent a year, then 'need' will reach 18.1 percent of GDP by 2000. (If need expands at 0.2 percent instead of 6.2 percent a year, the funding gap will disappear by the year 2000.) This suggests that since the early 1980s the system has come under increasing pressure, as expenditure has failed to keep pace with the expansion of 'need'. This is consistent with the evidence that the Dutch government has for some time been making efforts to control costs. The reforms which are currently being implemented are the latest in a series of attempts by government to restrain health care expenditure.

The conclusion is that *if* trends and institutions were to operate in the future in the same way as they did in the period 1960 to 1983, then a funding crisis would be expected in the Netherlands. However, the reforms of the health care system already in train in the Netherlands suggest that the structure which is dubbed the *status quo* for the purpose of this analysis has already been disrupted.

115

2.3.7   Spain

2.3.7.1   Estimation Period

Major political events have shaped the growth of health care expenditure in Spain.   The data show that the expenditure on health care in Spain grew rapidly in the 1960s and early 1970s, possibly due to expansion in coverage, and much less quickly from around 1978.   It seems likely that health care expenditure would grow slowly at a time of economic stringency, such as after the death of General Franco in 1975.   However, health care expenditure continued to grow very slowly until 1987 in spite of the fact that GDP growth resumed in the mid 1980s.   This suggests that political attempts to constrain spending may have met with some success.   There is also some circumstantial evidence of recent government attempts to reduce expenditure.   For example, there have been increases in the level of copayments on pharmaceuticals, from 10 percent in 1978 to 40 percent in 1980;[43] waiting lists have lengthened;[44] and there has been a series of budget crises in 1983, 1989, and 1992.

After consideration of these factors, it was decided that the equations for the supply and 'need' for funds for health care in Spain should be estimated over the period 1960 to 1983.

2.3.7.2   Estimation Results

The result of estimating the supply equation over the period 1960 to 1983 is:[45]

$$\text{lnHCE} = -25.4 + 2.32 \ \text{lnGDP}$$
$$\quad\quad\quad\quad (50.1) \quad (76.5)$$

$$R^2 = 1.00 \quad \text{SE} = 0.05 \quad \text{Period: 1960 to 1983}$$

$$\text{Chow predictions } F_{(4,25)} = 7.11 \quad \text{Chow stability } F_{(2,27)} = 27.15$$

The estimated value of the elasticity of the supply of funds for health care with respect to changes in GDP is 2.32.   This is the highest GDP elasticity estimate in our study (see Table 2.1).   When estimated over the period 1960 to 1990 the data give an estimated GDP elasticity of 2.20.   The Chow tests for accuracy of

---

[43]   See Section 11.3.6.

[44]   See Section 11.3.2.

[45]   T-statistics in parentheses.

predictions and for parameter stability both indicate rejection, suggesting that the relationship between GDP and health care expenditure has indeed changed during the 1980s. Expenditure on health care grew more slowly than predicted by this equation in the years 1985 to 1990.

The result of estimating the demand-side equation is:

$$\textbf{lnHCE} \quad = \quad \textbf{lnDEM} \quad + \quad \underset{(18.2)}{1.594} \quad + \quad \underset{(15.5)}{9.5 \text{ T}}$$

$$R^2 \ = \ 0.92 \qquad SE \ = \ 0.21 \qquad \text{Period: 1960 to 1983}$$

$$\text{Chow predictions } F(4,25) = 3.85 \qquad \text{Chow stability } F(2,27) = 16.18$$

The estimated trend increase in health care expenditure per head of the population, after correction for demographic changes, is 9.5 percent per year. This is the highest trend estimate in our study (see Table 2.1). There is a sharp difference between the estimated trend before and after 1983; health care expenditure in the period 1983 to 1990 has an estimated trend of 4.6 percent. Estimating over the whole 30 year period gives a time trend of 7.2 percent.

2.3.7.3   The Projections

It is forecast that GDP in Spain will grow at 3.9 percent a year in real terms on average over the next decade.[46] As the estimate of the elasticity of health care expenditure to GDP is 2.32, this suggests that the 'acceptable' quantity of funds allocated to health care will increase by over 140 percent in real terms during the next ten years. This implies that total expenditure on health care would reach around Ptas 7.7 tn (1990 prices) by the year 2000, which is 10.6 percent of the forecast for GDP. It is interesting to note that health care expenditure in Spain is comparatively high, given its level of GDP.

Demographic change on its own will not make large inroads into this sum. United Nations forecasts imply that the demographic variable DEM will increase by only 0.7 percent a year on average over the next ten years. (Between 1960 and 1990 its average increase was 1.3 percent a year.) The ageing of the population is thus expected to cause an increase of only about 7 percent in health care 'need' over the next decade.

---

[46]   Consensus Economics (1992). This forecast does not cover the whole period to 2000. Growth has therefore been projected at the average over the previous ten years.

The projections of health care 'need' and of the supply of funds are illustrated in Chart 2.11. 'Need' is estimated at 10.3 percent of GDP in 1990. If need increases at the trend rate of 9.5 percent a year, then 'need' will reach 17.2 percent of GDP by 2000. The shortfall of funding relative to 'need' is projected to increase from 3.7 percent of GDP in 1990 to 6.6 percent in 2000. It seems unlikely that this would have been sustainable without structural changes, such as the Abril reforms. Further, there is continued political pressure to control the government deficit.

Chart 2.11
Demand for Health Care and Funds Provided
Projections for Spain

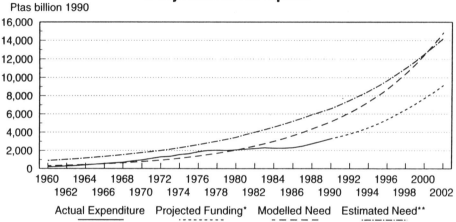

Ptas billion 1990

Actual Expenditure   Projected Funding*   Modelled Need   Estimated Need**

* Set to be coincident with actual expenditure in 1990
** Based on average of projected 'need' per head in 4 EC nations

Expenditure on health care in Spain in 1990 was only 76 percent of the EC average (in 1980 it was 64 percent).[47] To check this projection, we have also plotted the average of the estimates of health care 'need' per head, adjusted for age distribution, in Germany, France, Italy, and the Netherlands on Chart 2.11. It intersects the *status quo* projection of 'need' in Spain around the year 2000. If Spanish health care 'need' tracks the *status quo* projections, it will reach the level of the average of these countries at around that time.

---

[47]   Consensus Economics (1992). This forecast does not cover the whole period to 2000. Growth has therefore been projected at the average over the previous ten years.

118

2.3.8   Sweden

2.3.8.1   Estimation Period

There is evidence that expenditure on health care in the Sweden has increasingly been constrained for political reasons in the 1980s. The Health Care and Medical Services Act of 1982 (amended in 1985) reorganised the system, and in 1988 a law was passed freezing the tax rates levied by the county councils which are largely responsible for financing health care.[48]

The equations for the supply and 'need' for funds for health care in Sweden have been estimated over the period 1960 to 1986.

2.3.8.2   Estimation Results

The result of estimating the supply equation over the period 1960 to 1986 is:[49]

$$\textbf{lnHCE} \;=\; -16.9 \;+\; 2.07 \;\textbf{lnGDP}$$
$$\qquad\qquad (26.2)\quad (42.9)$$

$$R^2 \;=\; 0.99 \qquad SE = 0.05 \qquad \text{Period: } 1960 \text{ to } 1986$$

$$\text{Chow predictions } F(4,25) = 6.47 \qquad \text{Chow stability } F(2,27) = 13.94$$

The estimated value of the elasticity of the supply of funds for health care with respect to changes in GDP is 2.07. When estimated over the period 1960 to 1990 (and thus not abstracting from the effects of recent attempts to reduce costs) the data give an estimated GDP elasticity of 1.94. The Chow statistics test the hypothesis that there has been no change in the relationship between health care finance and GDP. The values indicate that this hypothesis is rejected. Expenditure on health care grew more slowly than predicted by the equation in the years 1985 to 1990.

---

[48]   See Section 12.3.3.3.

[49]   T-statistics in parentheses.

The result of estimating the demand-side equation is:

$$\text{lnHCE} = \text{lnDEM} + \underset{(19.5)}{0.832} + \underset{(17.3)}{4.6 \text{ T}}$$

$$R^2 = 0.92 \quad SE = 0.11 \quad \text{Period: } 1960 \text{ to } 1986$$

$$\text{Chow predictions } F(4,25) = 4.21 \quad \text{Chow stability } F(2,27) = 9.10$$

The estimated trend increase in health care expenditure per head of the population, after correction for demographic changes, is 4.6 percent per year. There is a sharp difference between the estimated time trends before and after 1986: during the period 1986 to 1990 health care 'need' has an estimated time trend of 1.5 percent. Estimating over the whole 30 year period gives a time trend of 4.0 percent. The Chow tests reject the hypothesis that the parameters of the equation are unchanged over the sample period.

2.3.8.3 The Projections

It is forecast that GDP in Sweden will grow at 2.2 percent a year in real terms on average over the next decade.[50] As the estimate of the elasticity of health care expenditure to GDP is 2.07, this suggests that the 'acceptable' quantity of funds allocated to health care will increase by 55 percent in real terms during the next ten years. This implies that total expenditure on health care would reach around Kroner 190 bn (1990 prices) by the year 2000, which is 10.9 percent of the forecast for GDP.

Demographic change on its own will not make large inroads into this sum, since Sweden has the oldest population of any of the countries in our study. United Nations forecasts imply that the demographic variable DEM will increase by only 0.3 percent a year on average over the next ten years. (Between 1960 and 1990 its average increase was 1.0 percent a year.) The ageing of the population is thus expected to cause an increase of only about 3 percent in health care 'need' over the next decade.

The projections of health care 'need' and of the supply of funds are illustrated in Chart 2.12. 'Need' is estimated to be 12.7 percent of GDP in 1990. If this increases at the trend rate of 4.6 percent a year, then 'need' will reach 16.7 percent of GDP by 2000. The shortfall between 'need' and funding is projected

---

[50]   Consensus Economics (1992). This forecast does not cover the whole period to 2000. Growth has therefore been projected at the average over the previous ten years.

to increase from around 4 percent of GDP in 1990 to almost 6 percent of GDP in 2000. This suggests that since the middle of the 1980s expenditure has failed to keep pace with the expansion of 'need'.

Chart 2.12
Demand for Health Care and Funds Provided
Projections for Sweden

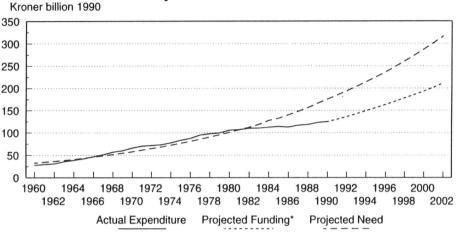

Kroner billion 1990

Actual Expenditure   Projected Funding*   Projected Need

* Set to be coincident with actual expenditure in 1990

In fact, the present shortfall seems to have been absorbed without threatening the stability of the system: waiting lists are not excessive,[51] and there is a general consensus in Sweden that the system is still delivering quality care.[52] There is, however, some evidence that the system is under strain: the Blendon survey revealed that a large percentage of people in Sweden thought that their health care system needed 'fundamental reform', even though there was only a small percentage who felt that complete rebuilding was required.[53] Further, several reform options are currently being considered in Sweden. The main motivation for change does *not*, however, appear to be concern about the overall level of health care costs. It is rather the result of political debate about the provision of social services and the role of the state in Swedish society.

---

[51]   See Section 12.3.5.

[52]   See Section 12.5.2.

[53]   Blendon *et al.* (1990) and Section 12.3.2.

121

Because the evidence suggests that the present 'need' is acceptable, we believe that an increase in the gap between 'need' and the supply of funds of the magnitude shown in the projections should be containable within the *status quo* structure.

2.3.9 Switzerland

2.3.9.1 Estimation Period

In the other countries which we have studied, there is evidence of administrative constraints which succeed in restricting the overall level of health care spending. By contrast, in Switzerland citizens enjoy a considerable degree of choice over the insurance package they purchase and are not restricted to one government determined package only. We have therefore taken the view that, over the data period used (1960 to 1991), it has been the 'demand' for health care that has determined the quantity purchased. In this regard, the market for health care in Switzerland seems to be similar to that for most other economic goods, but differs from most other health care systems.

Over the early part of the period (1960 to 1974) expenditure on health care increased quickly, as the number of people covered by insurance increased. The proportion of the population registered with a licensed sickness insurance fund increased from 74 percent in 1960 to 94 percent in 1974. The equations for the relationship between health care expenditure and GDP, and for the 'demand' for health care in Switzerland have been estimated over the period starting in 1974. The period ends at the last available data point: 1990 for the 'demand' equation, and 1991 for the GDP equation.

2.3.9.2 Estimation Results

The result of estimating the relationship between health care expenditure and GDP over the period 1974 to 1991, is:[54]

$$\text{lnHCE} = -7.1 + 1.36 \text{ lnGDP}$$
$$(12.2)$$

$$R^2 = 0.90 \qquad SE = 0.05 \qquad \text{Period: 1974 to 1991}$$

---

[54]   T-statistics in parentheses.

The estimated value of the elasticity of the supply of funds for health care with respect to changes in GDP is 1.36. This is the lowest GDP elasticity estimate in our study (see Table 2.1). When estimated over the period 1960 to 1991 (and thus not abstracting from the slowdown in the growth in expenditure) the data give an estimated GDP elasticity of 2.34.

The results of estimating the 'demand' equation over the period 1974 to 1990 are:

$$\text{lnHCE} = \text{lnDEM} + 0.46 + 1.6\,\text{T} - 0.01\,\text{lnPRICE}$$
$$\qquad\qquad\qquad\qquad\quad (12.6) \qquad (0.1)$$

$$R^2 = 0.941 \quad \text{SE} = 0.012 \quad \text{Period: 1974 to 1990}$$

The estimated trend increase in the real value of health care expenditure per head of the population (health care expenditure corrected for the OECD estimate of unit cost and for demographic changes) is 1.6 percent per year, once the effects of changes in cost have been taken into account. There is a sharp difference between the estimated value of the time trend before and after 1974: during the period 1960 to 1974 the annual increase in the real value of health care expenditure per head (corrected for demographic change and for changes in unit cost) was 8.0 percent.

The coefficient on lnPRICE is -0.01 (and not significantly different from zero). This suggests that the effect of the unit cost of health care on expenditure is very small. Hence, the elasticity of the volume of care demanded with respect to cost is estimated to be close to minus unity. That is, a 1 percent increase in unit cost would cause volume to fall by 1 percent, and so total expenditure would not change.

2.3.9.3   *The Projections*

It is forecast that GDP in Switzerland will grow at only 1.2 percent a year in real terms on average over the next decade.[55] As the estimate of the elasticity of health care expenditure to GDP is 1.36, this suggests that the 'acceptable' quantity of funds allocated to health care will increase by around 20 percent in real terms during the next ten years. This implies that total expenditure on health care would reach almost Swiss Franc 29 bn (1990 prices) by the year 2000, which is 8.4 percent of the forecast for GDP.

---

[55]   Consensus Economics (1992). This forecast does not cover the whole period to 2000. Growth has therefore been projected at the average over the previous ten years.

Demographic change alone is likely to lead to some growth in health care expenditure in Switzerland over the next ten years. United Nations forecasts imply that the demographic variable DEM will increase by 0.7 percent a year on average over the next ten years. (Between 1960 and 1990 its average increase was 1.3 percent a year.) The ageing of the population is thus expected to cause an increase of about 7 percent in health care expenditure over the next decade.

Health care expenditure per person, adjusted for demographic change, is projected to increase at 1.6 per cent a year. On this basis, expenditure on health care would increase from 7.8 percent of GDP in 1990 to 8.5 percent of GDP by the year 2000. Chart 2.13 shows the track of this equation, together with the projection of the GDP equation.

Chart 2.13
Demand for Health Care and GDP Relationship
Projections for Switzerland

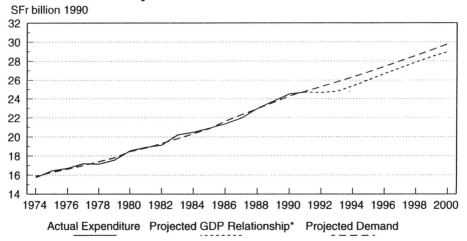

SFr billion 1990

Actual Expenditure   Projected GDP Relationship*   Projected Demand

* Set to be coincident with actual expenditure in 1991

If the relationship between health care expenditure and GDP can be interpreted as indicating the politically acceptable level of health care expenditure, then this outcome suggests that there will be no shortfall between the acceptable level of expenditure and the level of demand in 2000.

2.3.10 United Kingdom

2.3.10.1 Estimation Period

Most expenditure on health care in the United Kingdom is controlled by political expedient. The cabinet decides the sum that it wishes to spend on the NHS, and adjusts its policies to control total expenditure over time. A larger than usual funding shortfall in 1987 led to a review of the health service, and so to reforms which are currently being implemented in the UK.

Examining the data suggests that the relationship between health care expenditure and GDP may have changed in the late 1980s, with health care expenditure rising at a somewhat slower rate than might have been expected, from previous historic trends.

The equations for the supply and 'need' for funds for health care in the UK have been estimated over the period 1960 to 1986.

2.3.10.2 Estimation Results

The result of estimating the supply equation over the period 1960 to 1986 is:[56]

$$\text{lnHCE} = -13.0 + 1.80 \text{ lnGDP}$$
$$(19.7) \quad (34.0)$$

$$R^2 = 0.98 \quad SE = 0.05 \quad \text{Period: } 1960 \text{ to } 1986$$

Chow predictions $F_{(4,25)} = 2.98$ Chow stability $F_{(2,27)} = 6.04$

The estimated value of the elasticity of the supply of funds for health care with respect to changes in GDP is 1.80. When estimated over the period 1960 to 1990 the data give an estimated GDP elasticity slightly lower, at 1.69. Further, the data support the hypothesis that the relationship between GDP and expenditure on health care has changed during this period. This is shown by the Chow test which rejects parameter stability. From 1986 to 1990 expenditure on health care grew more slowly than predicted by the equation.

---

[56]   T-statistics in parentheses.

The result of estimating the demand-side equation is:

$$\text{lnHCE} = \text{lnDEM} - 2.16 + 3.4\,\text{T}$$
$$\phantom{\text{lnHCE} = \text{lnDEM} -\ } (142.2)\quad (35.4)$$

$$R^2 = 0.98 \qquad SE = 0.04 \qquad \text{Period: 1960 to 1986}$$

$$\text{Chow predictions } F_{(4,25)} = 1.54 \qquad \text{Chow stability } F_{(2,27)} = 3.27$$

The estimated annual trend increase in health care expenditure per head of the population, after correction for demographic changes, is 3.4 percent per year. There is no significant difference between the estimated time trends before and after 1986: the period 1986 to 1990 has an estimated time trend of 3.0 percent. Estimating over the whole 30 year period gives a time trend of 3.2 percent. The UK has one of the lowest time trends estimated for the study countries (see Table 2.1).

2.3.10.3 The Projections

It is forecast by Consensus Economics (1992) that GDP in the UK will grow at 2.0 percent a year in real terms on average over the next decade. As the estimate of the elasticity of health care expenditure to GDP is 1.80, this suggests that the 'acceptable' quantity of funds allocated to health care will increase by around 40 percent in real terms during the next ten years. This implies that total expenditure on health care would reach around £45 bn (1990 prices) by the year 2000, which is 7.3 percent of the forecast for GDP.[57]

Demographic change on its own will not make large inroads into this sum, since the UK already has a relatively old population. United Nations forecasts imply that the demographic variable DEM will increase by only 0.3 percent a year on average over the next ten years. (Between 1960 and 1990 its average increase was 0.7 percent a year.) The ageing of the population is thus expected to cause an increase of only about 2.5 percent in health care 'need' over the next decade.

---

[57] We have no data for health care expenditure in 1991 compatible with our historical series, so an estimate is required. If we used the model equation, the fall in GDP in the 1991 recession would imply a sharp fall in the estimated supply of funds, but this did not happen in the previous recession. The projection for health care expenditure in 1991 was therefore based on the estimated trend increase.

The problems that have been observed in the UK health care sector in recent years, most spectacularly the 1987 funding crisis, suggest that expenditure on health care has been heavily constrained in recent years. Further, the majority of the other countries in the study have higher health care spending per head, and the estimated time trend for the UK is only 3.4 percent per year compared to estimates in the range 4 to 5.5 percent for most of the other countries. The projection of 'need' in the year 2000 derived from the estimated equation for the UK is far lower than that estimated for other countries (see Chart 2.14), suggesting that the data have been constrained by political factors for some time and the methodology used in other countries may not be appropriate for these data.

Chart 2.14
Demand for Health Care and Funds Provided
Projections for the United Kingdom

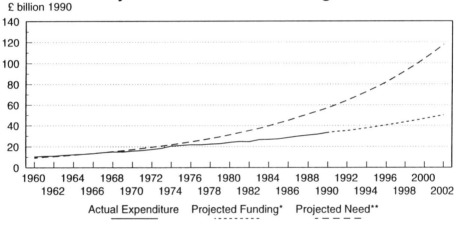

£ billion 1990

Actual Expenditure   Projected Funding*   Projected Need**

* Set to be coincident with actual expenditure in 1990
** Based on average of projected 'need' per head in 4 EC nations

We have therefore made an alternative projection of 'need' in the UK, using the weighted average of the estimated 'need' for health care expenditure per head in five other EC countries (France, Germany, Italy, the Netherlands, and Spain).

The path of this estimate of 'need' is shown in Chart 2.14. This suggests that the 'need' for health care expenditure is currently around 9 percent of GDP, and that it will increase to over 16 percent of GDP by the year 2000. On this estimate, the funding shortfall in 1990 amounted to almost half of actual health care expenditure, and it will increase to over 100 percent of health care expenditure by 2000. This is a larger shortfall than in any of the other countries in our study.

2.3.11   United States

2.3.11.1 Estimation Period

There is circumstantial evidence of increasing downward pressure on health care expenditure in the US. In the 1980s the Federal government began to put pressure on health care expenditure. Initially this was through the introduction of DRGs for the treatment of Medicare recipients (from 1983 onwards). More recently pressure can be seen in the introduction of the RBRVS, in joint purchasing of pharmaceuticals by government agencies, and in the practice of inviting competing bids for provision of services.[58] In spite of this, examining the data shows very little evidence a slowdown in the rate of growth of expenditure on health care.

The equations for the supply of funds and the demand for health care in the USA have been estimated over the period 1960 to 1990.

2.3.11.2 Estimation Results

The result of estimating the supply equation for the US over the period 1960 to 1990 is:[59]

$$lnHCE = -16.7 + 1.95 \ lnGDP$$
$$(32.8) \quad (57.1)$$

$$R^2 = 0.99 \quad SE = 0.05 \quad Period: \ 1960 \ to \ 1990$$

$$Chow \ predictions \ F(4,25) = 0.32 \quad Chow \ stability \ F(2,27) = 0.43[60]$$

The estimated value of the elasticity of the supply of funds for health care with respect to changes in GDP is thus 1.95. When estimated over the period 1960 to 1986 (to test for effects of federal government efforts to restrain health care expenditure) the data give an estimated GDP elasticity of 1.97. The Chow tests on the accuracy of the predictions for the years 1987 to 1990 and on the

---

[58]   See Section 15.3.3.

[59]   T-statistics in parentheses.

[60]   The Chow tests are based on the results of the regression over the period 1960-1986.

128

stability of the coefficient parameters imply that the hypothesis that the equation is stable over this period cannot be rejected.

The result of estimating the demand-side equations are:

$$\ln HCE = \ln DEM - 0.868 + 4.4\,T$$
$$(66.6) \quad (62.2)$$

$$R^2 = 0.99 \quad SE = 0.04 \quad \text{Period: } 1960 \text{ to } 1990$$

$$\text{Chow predictions } F(4,25) = 0.61 \quad \text{Chow stability } F(2,27) = 1.31$$

and:

$$\ln HCE = \ln DEM + 0.58 + 4.8\,T - 0.34\,\ln PRICE$$
$$(12.6) \quad (7.4)$$

$$R^2 = 0.994 \quad SE = 0.033 \quad \text{Period: } 1960 \text{ to } 1990$$

In the equation that omits the price variable the estimated trend increase in health care expenditure per head of the population, after correction for demographic change, is 4.4 percent per year. Over the period 1960 to 1986 the estimated time trend is similar, at 4.5 percent per year. The period 1986 to 1990 has an estimated time trend of 4.8 percent. The Chow tests on the accuracy of the predictions for the years 1987 to 1990 and on the stability of the coefficient parameters imply that the hypothesis that the equation is stable over this period cannot be rejected.

The estimated coefficient on the variable lnPRICE was -0.34 when the period 1960 to 1990 was used for estimation, and was significantly different from plus unity.[61] In making the projections it has implicitly been assumed that real health care costs increase at the same trend rate as on average in the past.

2.3.11.3 The Projections

It is forecast by Consensus Economics (1992) that GDP in the US will grow at 2.5 percent a year in real terms on average over the next decade. As the estimate of the elasticity of health care expenditure to GDP is 1.95, this suggests that the 'acceptable' quantity of funds allocated to health care will increase by around 60 percent in real terms during the next ten years. This

---

[61] If price had no effect on the quantity consumed, then health care expenditure would be proportional to price. In this case the coefficient on lnPRICE would be plus unity. See Annex 2.2, Section 2.2.3 for a further description of the role of PRICE.

implies that total expenditure on health care would reach around $1.1 tn (1990 prices) by the year 2000, which is 15.1 percent of the forecast for GDP.

Demographic change on its own will not make large inroads into this sum. United Nations forecasts imply that the demographic variable DEM will increase by 0.8 percent a year on average over the next ten years. (Between 1960 and 1990 its average increase was 1.4 percent a year.) The ageing of the population is thus expected to cause an increase of about 8 percent in health care 'need' over the next decade.

The projections of health care 'need' and the supply of funds are illustrated in Chart 2.15.[62] 'Demand' is estimated to be 12.5 percent of GDP in 1990. If this increases at 4.4 percent a year,[63] then 'demand' will reach 17.1 percent of GDP by 2000. Chart 2.15 shows that the equations representing 'demand' and the supply of funds are very close throughout the period of the study. This supports the intuition that in the US in the past health care expenditure has been largely determined by 'demand', with people consuming the health care they can afford, rather than being constrained by political factors.

The conclusion is that the extrapolation of the *status quo* structure over the period to 2000 would imply a continuation of the growth in expenditure. However, there is clearly pressure for a change in the structure.

---

[62]   We have no data for health care expenditure in 1991 compatible with our historical series, so an estimate is required. If we used the model equation, the fall in GDP in the 1991 recession would imply a sharp fall in the estimated supply of funds, but this did not happen in the previous recession in 1982. The projection for health care expenditure in 1991 was therefore based on the estimated trend increase.

[63]   This is equal to a trend rate of 4.8 percent a year reduced by copayments that increase at around one percent a year in real terms.

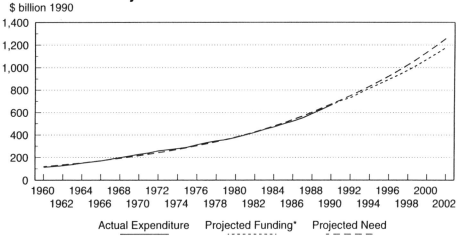

Chart 2.15
Demand for Health Care and Funds Provided
Projections for the United States

Actual Expenditure   Projected Funding*   Projected Need

* Set to be coincident with actual expenditure in 1990

ANNEX 2.4 BIBLIOGRAPHY

Anderson, G., and Knickman, J. (1984), "Adverse Selection Under a Voucher System: Grouping Medicare Recipients by Level of Expenditure", *Inquiry*, Summer, pp. 135-143.

Consensus Economics (1992), "Long Term Forecasts", *Consensus Forecasts: a digest of International Economic Forecasts (October)*, Consensus Economics Inc., London.

Culyer, A. J., Evans, R. G., von der Schulenburg, J. M., van de Wen, W., Weisbrod, B. (1991), "International Review of the Swedish Health Care System", *Den Svenska Sjukvarden, Occasional Paper Nr 34*, Stockholm.

Fujino, S. (1987), "Health economics in Japan: Prospects for the future", in Teeling Smith, G., (ed), *Health Economics: Prospects for the Future*, Crook Helm, London.

Gerdtham, U., Andersson, F., Sogaard, J., Jonsson, B. (1988), *Econometric Analysis of Health Care Expenditures: A Cross-Section Study of the OECD-Countries*, CMT Report, Linkoping University.

Getzen, T. E. and Poullier, J-P. (1991), "An Income-Weighted International Average for Comparative Analysis of Health Expenditures", *International Journal of Health Planning and Management*, 6:1.

IMF (1981), *International Financial Statistics Yearbook 1981*, Washington, DC.

IMF (1991), *International Financial Statistics Yearbook 1991*, Washington, DC.

IMF (1992), *International Financial Statistics*, (August), Washington, DC.

Kawakita, H.(1989), "Healthcare Services in Japan", *International Hospital Federation*, Vol 25 number 2, pp. 11-25.

Leu, R.E., (1986), The Public-Private Mix and International Health Care Costs, *Public and Private Health Care Services: Complementarities and Conflicts*, Eds. Culyer A.J. and Jonsson B., Basil Blackwell, Oxford.

NERA (1992), *The Impact of Cost Sharing for Medical Care and Pharmaceuticals: Evidence from the Literature*.

Newhouse, J. P. (1977), "Medical-Care Expenditure: A Cross-National Survey", *Journal of Human Resources*, Number 12, pp. 115-125.

OECD (1990), *Health Care Systems in Transition*, Paris.

OECD (1991), (1993) *OECD Health Data: comparative analysis of health systems, version 1.01 & version 1.5* (software package), Paris.

OECD (1992a), *Main Economic Indicators*, August, Paris.

OECD (1992b), *Historical Statistics 1960-1990*, Paris.

Robinson, R., Spiby, J. and Beardshaw, V. (1990), "*Expected Developments in Health Needs, Science and Technology*" (a paper prepared for the Council of Europe), Mimeo, King's Fund, London.

United Nations (1987), "World Demographic Trends", *World Health Statistics Quarterly*, 40, pp. 6-21.

United Nations (1988), *Global Estimates of Population by Sex and Age*, New York.

United Nations (1990), *World Population Prospects*, New York.

Williams, A. (1978), "'need' - an economic exegesis", in Culyer, A.J. and Wright, K.G. (eds), *Economic Aspects of Health Services*, Oxford, Martin Robertson.

CHAPTER 3

THE ECONOMICS OF HEALTH CARE REFORM: A PROTOTYPE

Thomas McCarthy

National Economic Research Associates
Los Angeles

Ullrich Hoffmeyer

National Economic Research Associates
London

3.1   INTRODUCTION

> *"Prototype: an original thing or*
> *person in relation to a copy, imitation,*
> *representation,   later   specimen,*
> *improved form, etc.; trial model,*
> *preliminary version".*

The Concise Oxford Dictionary

3.1.1   The Problem

At the broadest level, all nations face the same problem in the financing and delivery of health care: that is the fundamental economic conflict of unlimited wants, but scarce resources. No matter how wealthy a nation is, there are demands and desires that will go unsatisfied.

Scarcity is of course not a problem unique to health care. All goods and services compete for scarce resources. The reality of modern health care systems is that in some countries large and increasing amounts of resources have been flowing into the health care sector, while in others expenditure has been controlled in apparently arbitrary and perhaps unjustified ways. The question for the policy maker is whether the resources committed to health care are too large, too small or about right. Policy makers in many nations feel that their health care systems are inefficient in some significant way, and our own research confirms that impression. With reform, it is felt, "more health care could be purchased for the same resource spending", or "more resources would be made available". So why is reform of the health care sector such a difficult task, and why is a consensus on the best approach to reform so hard to reach?

Beyond scarcity, there are several features of health care which make reform difficult and uncertain in its effects. They include significant information problems for patients, providers and the funders of health care; the complicated effects of third party payment on patient and provider incentives; society's concern for an equitable distribution of health care services; and the complex politics that follow when governments try to alter resource flows: after all, money spent on health care, whether efficiently spent or not, is revenue for some provider and (usually) a benefit for some patient. These complications spawn a wide variety of reform solutions and divisive debates over how best to organise a health care system.

How then should a nation decide how much of its scarce resources to devote to health care and how much to other goods and services? And how should a nation choose the mix of services to be produced and for whom? There appear to be at least as many answers as there are health care systems in the world. The purpose of this paper is not to enumerate the full range of possibilities, but rather to examine those issues that are common to developed economies when confronting the problem of scarce resources available for health care. Then, having examined these issues, we will attempt to outline a prototypical health care system which tackles these issues, taking into account several key considerations. These considerations include not only the need to produce health care services efficiently, but also how to distribute those services fairly.

We conclude that there are <u>not</u> a wide variety of options available for sensible long-run health care reform. Our recommended Prototype requires five essential elements of health care reform. These are:

1. Mandatory health insurance coverage for all citizens under a guaranteed health care package, with premiums based on ability to pay, not health risk.

2. Reliance on competitive provider markets to encourage efficiency and innovation in health care delivery.

3. Reliance on competitive insurance markets to encourage efficiency and innovation in the financing of health care.

4. A risk-adjustment mechanism between health insurers to discourage competition by risk selection.

5. Meaningful financial incentives for consumers to stimulate informed shopping for both insurance coverage and medical care.

In our view, any significant reform must include these elements if a long-run, self-balancing health care system is to be achieved.

3.1.2   Reforming a Health Care System

3.1.2.1   *Preferences and Efficiency*

Though the problem in health care is often expressed as cost containment, simple cost-cutting and budget-balancing should not be the goal of health care reform. We seek a different type of balance, one that weighs the benefits and costs of using resources in the health care system.

Thus the 'best' health care system is one that is organised to satisfy consumers' preferences as completely as possible within the constraints of consumers' willingness to pay for health care, and not one that simply reduces expenditures. There can be no single goal expressed as 'the percentage of gross domestic product' that every country should strive to attain.

Economic efficiency dictates that resources should flow into the production of health care services as long as consumers are willing to pay more for these services than for other products that could be produced with the same resources. This requires that consumer preferences are regularly measured and acknowledged. It also requires that the system be 'transparent'; that is, consumers and providers of health care understand the costs of the services they are using or delivering. Without such signals, one cannot be certain whether the outcome approaches the economically efficient outcome. With the right signals, the mix of goods and services being produced will tend toward the best result for consumers in the economy.

3.1.2.2   *Market Failures and Social Solidarity*

The reasonable performance of an economic system depends on the absence of 'market failures', or on the effects of such failures being mitigated by government regulation and/or the appropriate design of institutions. In health care one of the major potential market failures which policy has to confront is information asymmetry. Patients are usually dependent on physicians for their understanding of the ailment and the likely implications of alternative treatments. Similarly, insurers need to rely on the good faith of potential clients and providers declaring medical histories and risks.

Another reason why markets may fail relates to the 'moral hazard' problem, which arises when services are provided free at the point of delivery as a result of being covered by an insurance policy. Mainly, this stems from the fact that it is very difficult to know when a particular service is justified, i.e.

when the expected benefits of a procedure exceed its costs. This is because information problems may result in a type and mix of services not always being known beforehand and the insurer often having difficulty determining whether care was necessary even after the event.

The possibility of excess use, or what might be labelled the degree of moral hazard, is smaller the more inelastic is the demand for a particular type of health care. This is equivalent to saying that if the lower price really does not change the patient's behaviour much (e.g. demand for appendectomies), the moral hazard problem is small. That is, the patient, in this example, consumes almost the same amount despite the price reduction. Whatever the elasticity, the moral hazard problem reflects an important issue for health care cost containment; the tendency to consume a substantial amount of care whose cost is significantly higher than its expected benefits.

The moral hazard 'excess' can take many forms other than higher quantities - greater comfort and amenities of service; less consumer search to find the lowest price; and higher quality. Since one measure of quality is the amount by which the uncertainty about the illness has been reduced, this means a substantial amount of potentially very expensive care can be demanded at a zero or near zero price. This may involve expensive technology to remove any last doubts that the physician has provided the most appropriate care.

Furthermore, health care markets need to be organised so as to satisfy society's sense of equity or social solidarity. An unregulated competitive market in health care insurance will not satisfy this concern. Social solidarity, or alternatively social concern and responsibility, comprises society's views on equity, justice and fairness. As far as health care is concerned, this does not typically mean absolute equality for all. But for a health care system to be socially acceptable, it usually requires that access to essential health care services be available regardless of ability to pay. This can be expected to lead to an outcome which is different from that which would be produced by a free market. One important point to remember is that, whatever society's definition of social solidarity, health care should be provided in an efficient manner.

3.1.2.3   Funding and Provision

There are two components to any health care system: funding (which combines insurance and purchasing), and provision. Because health care needs are not easily predicted by individuals and sometimes have severe financial consequences, health care in many countries is funded in large part through public or private insurance schemes. Each scheme represents an alternative method for pooling the risk of becoming ill. Without insurance, the unhappy alternative would be large out-of-pocket payments by patients, leading to a need for excessive savings to fund these expected payments, and to the poor being denied care altogether, which would be regarded as morally repugnant in most countries.

Some of the reform proposals we have studied in several countries are directed at health care funding, where the emphasis is on the 'rules of the game' of the insurance contract terms.   Others focus more on provision.   The funding scheme that a country chooses, together with the structure and regulation of the provider system, will ultimately determine how much care will be produced, what kind of care it will be and who will receive it.

Simply stated, the goal of a number of 'structural' health care reforms is to specify the rules of the game on the funding side so as to encourage the efficient and equitable delivery of health care. This is often accomplished by changing the incentives contained in the insurance and reimbursement arrangements. For example, paying doctors and hospitals on a fee-for-service basis gives them extra income for providing extra treatments. The result is an incentive to over-prescribe and over-consume health care services. Changing the payment from fee-for-service to a cost-per-case measure such as a fixed payment for each Diagnosis Related Group (DRG) encourages hospitals to provide fewer services and shorten the average length of stay. But which incentives and payment mechanisms should be preferred?

The rules that are most appropriate in one country may not be the best for another country. In part, this flows from differences in the degree of social solidarity that must be satisfied. For instance, most developed nations believe that, as a society, each citizen must receive an acceptable minimum level of services, which may be at a high level. Such a nation will wish to provide uniform care up to that standard to all whether or not individual citizens would benefit from having greater choice. Another reason for different 'rules' in different countries is that patients and providers may have substantially different responses to the same type of economic incentives, such as

141

copayments or fee-for-service reimbursements. Furthermore, an important factor is the size and internal diversity of the 'nation' being considered. Many proposed reforms are based on ideas supported more by economic theory than by experience and fact. In some cases, this is simply because a particular 'good idea' has never been tried. Thus, the reform debate often varies based on the usual contest of ideas among students of health care systems. Finally, history also helps to explain the specific set of rules being used in a given country and may further affect the choice of reform likely to be most appropriate.

This insight is important in understanding the economics of health care reform. As our studies of the twelve countries demonstrate, there are significant differences between the systems currently operating, or in serious contemplation by reformers. The United States (US) and the Switzerland systems are the only two in which the majority of health care is provided through competing private insurance companies, and, in the US, a large number of people are uninsured or underinsured. In many European systems, and also in Canada and New Zealand, all or virtually all of the citizens are covered by health insurance that is provided by the government or by tightly regulated non-profit insurance funds. By this means citizens are secure in the knowledge that their ability to receive necessary treatment will not be put at risk by a lack of money. All systems depend in varying degrees upon the political process to set the bounds of government expenditures, which are substantial even in the USA. This can lead to shortages and other mismatches between what patients want and what they get.

3.1.3   Outline

The outline of the remainder of this chapter is as follows. In Section 3.2 we spell out the role of markets in health care, and point to the central problem of health care systems that can lead to inefficiencies and inequity, and hence to the need for government interference.

In Section 3.3 we spell out the objectives of a health care system that need to be taken into account when designing a prototypical health care system.

In Section 3.4 we review some of the main current proposals for reforming health care funding, and consider the main advantages and disadvantages.

Section 3.5 presents our recommendations for an efficient and equitable health care system. The analysis proceeds in several steps. First, we introduce proposals for the funding side of a health care system (Section 3.5.1). The proposals include an example of the funding mechanism (Section 3.5.2). This is followed by recommendations for the provider side of a health care system (Section 3.5.3). This is followed by an analysis of the likely nature of transactions in the health care market (Section 3.5.4). Next we spell out the appropriate role and functions of the government in the health care system (Section 3.5.5). Then we assess the responsibilities of patients in the health care system, in particular with respect to copayments (Section 3.5.6). Dynamic aspects are being dealt with in the next section on innovation and technology (Section 3.5.7).

In Section 3.6 we make some cautionary remarks about the likely problems of persuading individual countries to converge towards a health care system similar to that recommended by NERA.

There are five Annexes which analyse some important topics in more detail. They deal with: social solidarity, the definition of a Guaranteed Health Care Package (GHCP), the nature of health care insurance, reimbursement methods for health care services, and competition policy.

3.2 MARKETS AND GOVERNMENTS

"That any sane nation, having observed that you could provide for the supply of bread by giving bakers a pecuniary interest in baking for you, should go on to give a surgeon a pecuniary interest in cutting off your leg, is enough to make one despair of political humanity."

George Bernard Shaw:
The Doctor's Dilemma

3.2.1 Health Care Markets

The economic characteristics of health care services provided and purchased in most industrialised countries can be described as follows:

1. Health care systems are characterised by a **multiplicity of actual and potential consumers** (that is, patients) who demand health care; and a large number of providers (hospitals, primary care physicians, specialists, paramedics, nursing and community homes) which supply health care.

2. In virtually no case does the provision of a health care service constitute a **natural monopoly**. That is to say, the total costs of providing a certain health care service are not necessarily lower when a single institution provides the entire service for a society, rather than two or more institutions. A possible exception relates to some specialised services (e.g. heart transplants), where a concentration of the entire service in a small number of facilities (as opposed to a larger number) may be more cost-effective.

3. Health care is overwhelmingly consumed **individually, rather than collectively**. This means that in most cases each individual pays for, and consumes, health care without affecting the consumption level of any other individual. The main exception to this concerns the consumption of some public health services (e.g. clean water), where the benefits of one individual paying for them accrue to other individuals regardless of whether or not they pay for these services.

4. There are few **external effects** in health care, i.e. the health status of an individual does not in general affect the health status of any other

individual. That is to say that the health status of individuals depends primarily on factors peculiar to themselves, including their own consumption levels of health care, but not on that of any other individual. The main exception to this concerns the prevention or cure of communicable diseases.[1]

This description of the conditions in which health care services are provided and consumed suggests that there is scope for using **competitive markets** as the most efficient way of allocating resources. Suppliers of health care would compete for consumers and consumers would choose which health care services to pay for. Suppliers would quote prices related to the cost of the services they offered and consumers would express their preference for different health care services, according to their budget and needs. As a result, prices determined in the market would influence the type, quality and level of health care services provided to individual consumers.

Observation of real health care systems suggests that few countries are prepared to leave the provision of health care to the market, however. The operation of free markets raises other problems which require attention from governments.

3.2.2   The Equity of Provision

The major reason for government intervention in health care markets is the desire to achieve a degree of equity among citizens in the provision of health care.

1.   For any single individual, the need for health care services is typically **unpredictable** but, in the event of actual need, the expense can be significant, or potentially bankrupting.

2.   The unpredictability of health care costs will lead many individuals to seek health care **insurance**. However, in a free market, competing health care insurance companies will charge health care insurance premiums for each person (or for groups of similar persons) which are equal to the expected level of health care costs for that individual (or group). Premiums will vary from person to person, depending only upon their risk characteristics and regardless of their income levels. As

---

[1]   The same is not necessarily true for the welfare of an individual which may depend on the consumption levels of other individuals.

a result, some individuals may be unable to afford to buy health care insurance.

3.   On the social level, a society may regard it as **unacceptable that those who cannot afford health care should go without**. Hence, most countries do not opt for a free market in health care services, but set up instead a system in which individuals contribute to the costs of health care, or health care insurance, at a rate which is related to their level of income. Since the free market is unable to offer satisfactory methods to redistribute incomes in this way, the government assumes a major role within the system.

One reason why so many countries accept government provision of health care services or insurance is that patients are not often responsible for reductions in their health status. Illness is frequently an accident of environment or genetics and cannot usually be attributed to mistaken behaviour on the part of the patient. Forcing people to pay for all their health care directly, or charging high insurance premiums to people who are bad risks, is viewed as unfair if there is nothing they can do to improve the situation, since the charges merely compound their bad fortune. Governments and social insurance plans therefore take over the costs of treatment as a means for equalising the welfare of its citizens with respect to health status, regardless of their income.[2]

3.2.3   Risk Selection

For the reasons set out above, many national health care systems have turned to governments or regulated insurance funds as the preferred funder of health care and, sometimes, as the provider of services. This approach involves trading off some of the advantages of consumer-responsive private provision for those of greater security for the individual and social solidarity.

Regulation, however, creates new problems. In particular, in a regulated market for health care insurance, premiums are based on the *average* expected costs of a group of individuals. Insurance companies have an incentive to pick the good risks within that group, i.e. those individuals who are intrinsically 'healthy' and therefore likely to incur lower than average health care costs.

---

[2]   This raises the issue of whether a person who practices a lifestyle known to be unhealthy should be included in this safety net or be forced to pay a differential insurance premium. Smoking and drug addiction are examples. Society must make the value judgments necessary to determine who should be covered and what premium should be paid.

Insurance companies may also try to deny cover to bad risks (those identifiable now as likely to incur higher than average costs in the future). This behaviour by the insurance companies is called 'risk selection'.

At the same time, regulation causes problems for individuals. A health care premium set at the average expected cost of a group of individuals will be less than the cost of a bad risk, but more that the cost of a good risk. Bad risks will be encouraged to take out insurance, whilst good risks may prefer to pay for their health care needs when they arise. Insurance companies are therefore only approached by bad risks. This process is called 'adverse selection'.

Risk selection and adverse selection create a major problem for market-based health care reforms. Competition in the health sector will only work if insurance companies can set premiums equal to the expected health care costs of each individual. This is inconsistent with the aims of equity, which require a system of common, or income-related premiums. However, such premiums will lead to risk selection and adverse selection, which also tend to disadvantage high risk groups. The regulation of the insurance market is therefore usually extended to prevent both risk selection and adverse selection by limiting the degree of competition in provision of health care services in two ways:

- by obliging insurance companies to accept all individuals, regardless of risk, at a common premium (which may be income-related); and

- by obliging all individuals to take out insurance, even if the premium they contribute is larger than their expected costs of health care.

Some countries have imposed these obligations by creating a 'single payer' for major parts of the health care system, i.e. a single mandatory insurance pool, such as the provincial systems in Canada or the National Health Service in the United Kingdom. Other countries, such as Germany, France, Sweden, Italy and the Netherlands, have used a sick fund system, which assigns each citizen to one of several 'single payers' on the grounds of geography or occupation. Both these systems levy what is called a 'community rated' premium, by requiring all members to contribute equally (or according to income). Hence, their contribution is related to income, but independent of their health status, an outcome which is generally deemed equitable, and in some cases is considered so important that it is enshrined in the country's constitution.

3.2.4   Efficiency and Equity

In choosing a structure for health care systems, we do not treat government provision and private market provision as polar choices. There are lessons to be learned from both approaches. In general, we argue that there is a long-standing preference to organise economic activity by reliance on the market process. Markets have a demonstrated propensity to achieve widespread benefits by allowing decentralised decision makers to signal their preferences as buyers and sellers. Markets are generally more efficient than national governments at identifying consumer preferences, responding to change, and finding innovative solutions.

In contrast, governments are generally not well suited to provide for choice. They are typically slow to respond to consumer signals. In part, this is because government bureaucracies generally lack the incentive to see that citizens are satisfied on a day-to-day, personal level. Choice is an important element in achieving economic efficiency, since the expression of choice provides signals of satisfaction or dissatisfaction to suppliers. Markets, or other decentralised systems, are usually better suited to responding to consumer demands, especially when consumers have different preferences.

The central problem of health care is thus often described as the trade-off between efficiency and equity (social solidarity). We believe that this characterisation can be exaggerated. It is possible to develop a health care system that is efficient as well as equitable, at least in reasonable measure. Our review of the health care systems in industrialised countries reveals that many nations are moving to accomplish this outcome. The point of convergence centres around sharing the financial risk between funders, patients and providers to make each more aware of the cost of care, but, at the same time guaranteeing each citizen access to a range of health care services at a cost that is considered to be fair.

The central problem of health care can therefore be described as finding a reasonable and acceptable balance between efficiency and equity or social solidarity.

These concepts of efficiency and social solidarity will be defined in section 3.3.

3.3 OBJECTIVES OF HEALTH CARE SYSTEMS

"Society becomes more wholesome, more serene, and spiritually healthier, if it knows that its citizens have at the back of their consciousness the knowledge that not only themselves, but all their fellows, have access when ill, to the best that medical skill can provide".

Aneurin Bevan[3]

"The fulfilment of our national purpose depends on promoting and assuring the highest level of health attainable for every person ... and marshalling of all health resources to assure comprehensive health services of high quality for every person".

United States Congress, 1966

3.3.1 Introduction

Ideally, there would exist a perfect model of health care financing and delivery system that each nation might comfortably adopt as its own (or at least measure its own against). We do not believe that such a single ideal model exists. However, we do conclude that there are many common problems in designing and reforming health care systems and that there are broad lessons that all systems should consider. There is a series of choices that each country must make when structuring its health care system. The chosen structures should be those which best accomplish the goals of the system. These goals are assumed to be efficiency and social solidarity.

The discussion which follows deals mainly with the economics of reform. The economic concepts that we explain in this and the next section provide the basic principles needed to propose, consider and choose among reform

---

[3]   Quoted in Foot (1975)

proposals. Section 3.5 presents a hypothetical, ideal health care system designed by the application of the economic principles. If soundly based, this ideal health care system may serve as a yardstick against which to measure reform proposals in each country.

We begin by defining some key concepts and principles.

3.3.2 Efficiency

3.3.2.1 Three Forms of Efficiency

Economic efficiency consists of three separate, but closely related, concepts: productive efficiency; efficiency in consumption; and dynamic efficiency. In each case, attaining efficiency depends on, among other things, there being appropriate market signals concerning the allocation of resources. A key feature in this is the relative prices of goods and services. For example, if the same level of goods and services could be produced more cheaply using a different, cheaper input, then the process is not efficient in the productive sense. Similarly, if consumers are indifferent between a cheap and an expensive good, they will purchase the cheaper one thus increasing the efficiency of their consumption. The price signals relating to dynamic efficiency are inter-temporal, involving the expected return on capital: more resources should be used in research and development today if future benefits of the new products are expected to outweigh the cost of not consuming more goods today.

3.3.2.2 Productive Efficiency

Productive efficiency is attained when producers use the least-cost combination of inputs. This involves two separate requirements. First, the least cost type of production must be chosen. Second, there must be no wastage of inputs: the quantities of the inputs used should be no more than necessary.

Often, there are alternative methods by which health care can be produced. For instance, cataract surgery can usually be produced with equal quality by admitting the patient to the hospital or by using a day surgery centre. Productive efficiency requires that the least-cost site of care be used: in this case, this is often the day surgery centre. To encourage the appropriate method of production to be chosen, providers need to be mindful of the relative resource costs of the alternatives. Otherwise, the care will be produced at excess costs and production will not be efficient.

One way of encouraging productive efficiency is to ensure that the industry structure gives producers an incentive to minimize costs, while maintaining the quality of care. Pressure to reduce costs can be exercised by ensuring that remuneration is through prospective reimbursements; these set the amount to be paid for an episode of health care before the service is performed. Thus, the introduction of fixed payments to hospitals by DRG in the USA has led to shorter lengths-of-stay and relatively more day surgery. Another way in which health care systems should encourage productive efficiency is to ensure that the system of financing and remuneration does not create distorted incentives, e.g. to use one form of treatment when another would be more cost-effective.

3.3.2.3 Efficiency in Consumption

Efficiency in consumption requires that the 'right' levels of the different types of goods and services are consumed (including products of different qualities). In standard competitive consumer goods markets, this means that consumers are assumed to have considered the costs and benefits of a wide range of the goods and services available to them and have decided which to buy based on which give them the most benefit per amount paid - given their preferences.

The usual way of achieving efficiency in consumption involves allowing the expression of choice across alternatives for well informed individuals in the light of market price signals. Consumers can achieve a greater level of satisfaction for the same level of expenditure if lower priced goods can be substituted for higher priced goods and still produce the same benefits to the consumer. In such an instance, the consumer will be able to divert spending to other products, and will achieve a higher real income as a result.

Applied to health care, this means that, for example, if a medical treatment can effect the same cure in the same time as a surgical treatment that is more expensive in terms of resource costs, efficiency in consumption can be increased by substituting medicine for surgery. If, however, the consumer's health insurance scheme pays for surgery but not for medicine, the relative price signal the consumer receives is distorted. That is, it is at variance with the resource cost and is giving an erroneous signal. A choice which is inefficient from society's point of view is likely to be made.

To the extent that society decides that health care should be provided according to the health needs of its citizens, as distinct from their ability to pay, it cannot use market prices charged to the patient as the sole method for allocating health care resources. That would lead systematically to the wrong outcome, and would therefore be inefficient. Other means of ensuring efficiency have to be found.[4]

3.3.2.4 Dynamic Efficiency

There are two parts to dynamic efficiency. First, dynamic efficiency requires that the right share of current resources be allocated to research and development and to investment for efficient future production. This type of dynamic efficiency is achieved if the net present value of the current and future stream of benefits expected with the existing allocation of funds to research, development and investment exceeds the benefit that would accrue if more funds were spent on providing goods and services for current consumption. If the expected future profits following current expenditure on research and development by pharmaceutical companies are sufficiently great, today's researchers will acquire enough funds to divert current resources into this type of investment.

Second, dynamic efficiency requires that there are incentives to improve and maintain productive efficiency and allocative efficiency of consumption over time. This means that the legal framework, the regulatory framework and the system of intellectual property rights should be such as to encourage the development of these forms of efficiency. For example, the legal framework

---

[4]   Some observations are relevant regarding whether competitive health care markets are workable in the face of information problems and whether consumption efficiency is possible in health care markets:

    (1)   Consumer demands for information create a market for someone to respond by producing the desired information. An example are the publication of so called 'Pill Books' in Japan, to provide consumers with information about the medicines doctors dispense without explanation. Governments in some countries have also joined in providing information by sponsoring studies on appropriate protocols for treating various illnesses.

    (2)   Even with information problems, a relevant policy question is whether government can in some way correct the underlying source of the information problem by, for instance, relying on physicians as agents for their patients.

    (3)   Health care systems should be as 'transparent' as possible, whether the system is based on government provision or private market provision. Consumers cannot make properly informed political choices or informed economic choices if they do not know what the system costs relative to the benefits they draw from the system. Transparency is extremely important if resources are to be channelled in and out of the health sector on a rational basis, whether by government or by market signals.

should not be such as to encourage excessive precautionary expenditure in anticipation of a threat of litigation, which is a problem in the USA.

3.3.2.5   Conclusions on Efficiency

Economic efficiency is achieved when the three conditions listed above are simultaneously and consistently achieved. That is, if suppliers have an incentive to purchase the minimum necessary amounts of relatively low priced inputs, in order to make lower priced (but appropriate quality) products for consumers, then greater economic efficiency results. Similarly, if consumers or their agents are receiving, and acting on, realistic price signals relating to resource costs, they will be enhancing economic efficiency. Finally, if the right amount of resources is being invested to produce sufficiently valuable future products, economic efficiency will be enhanced by those resources being shifted away from consumption today.[5]

---

[5] An example of efficiency in health care is as follows. Suppose that an excess demand for lithotripsy develops as patients diagnosed as having kidney stones, informed about the benefits of this treatment and with funds available to pay for it, begin to line up for treatment. Under a market-based delivery system, suppliers observe these patients who come to their door with money in hand, offering to pay more for timely treatment. If capacity is tight, suppliers may make the judgment that they should buy a new lithotripter to satisfy the higher demand. Depending on financial control systems within the provider market, the proposal will be evaluated, and presumably approved. If necessary, additional funding may be sought from capital markets. Thus, the people with the problem signal that they are willing to pay more for lithotripters and resources flow into the sector.

A centrally regulated delivery system will be likely to respond differently, and sometimes more slowly. If the hospital is given a global budget or similar capital constraint, the process of responding to increased demand is different and less flexible. Doctors and hospital administrators observe that waiting lists grow. They appeal to the regulator for additional capital funds to take care of this growing demand. If the regulator does not have excess funds, he/she must in turn appeal to the central authority for funds. If this department's budget is also currently in balance, more funds must be sought from elsewhere in the political system. Indeed, ultimately voters must register their demand for more health care resources through the political process.

In this system, how can the lithotripsy patients find the support they need to buy the lithotripter they would otherwise be willing to pay for? With a market-based system, consumer signals are likely to be easier to read and it is likely that they will be responded to more rapidly. The lithotripsy patents can express their demand for more lithotripters without waiting for others to join their cause. Thus, the amount and mix of services is likely to be closer to the amounts and mix desired by those able to pay.

3.3.3 Social Solidarity

Social solidarity expresses the relations of mutual dependence that exist between individuals in society, and the consequence which this has for the distribution of wealth among them. In health care, social solidarity encompasses the idea that everybody is entitled to receive proper medical attention and care, regardless of their ability to pay, and means that individual citizens should be treated equally in equal circumstances. The basis for social solidarity is partly political, but rests more fundamentally on values such as fairness and justice. Thus, to deny someone access to health care facilities not only violates political rights and promotes inequity, it is also rejected by society's sense of justice. Annex 3.1 spells out these ideas in further detail.

The most obvious rationale underlying social solidarity is ethical. Simply stated, it means that we care, and ought to care, about the health and welfare of our fellow citizens. There are several reasons for this. One is a simple moral imperative, perhaps based on religious beliefs. Another may be an implicit social contract that we 'take care of our own'. A related reason concerns equal opportunity within the society as part of the social contract. One's health status in part determines one's income. As with education, withholding health services compromises an individual's ability to become a productive member of society, earn a livelihood and prosper. Another reason is more pragmatic: healthy members of society are more productive and less of a burden to the state if medical disability and the consequent income loss can be avoided.

There is no doubt that the guarantee of subsidised health services to the sick or poor by the government is part of the social contract in all the countries we have studied. Even in the United States, where the health care system is based largely on private enterprise, *Medicare* and *Medicaid* partly fulfil this obligation, albeit in a costly and inefficient way. Nations vary greatly in the way government sees to the insurance of individuals against the expenses arising from ill-health, but all modern societies define some standard of health care service to which the poorest citizen is entitled as a right.

3.3.4 Goals of a Health Care System

While trade-offs between efficiency and social solidarity are sometimes unavoidable, economic analysis helps to identify opportunities for, say, greater efficiency with no loss in social solidarity. When such costless gains are not possible, specifying the nature of the solidarity-efficiency trade-off also provides important information to voters and policy makers.

Health care systems should be designed in a way which will lead them to achieve the following goals:

On Efficiency

1. The amount and the mix of health care services delivered by providers should reflect the informed preferences of consumers. Providers and consumers should not be encouraged by inappropriate incentives to deliver or consume more or less health care than is economically efficient.

2. Health care systems should be designed to encourage efficient provision of health care services, and should be set in a context of social policies which also help to improve the health status of the people.

3. The health care system should be responsive to new opportunities and needs, as expressed by consumers and their agents. This includes that services are provided to high professional standards, using the best medical technology available, wherever this is cost-effective. The health care system should encourage research and development of new and improved treatments.

On Social Solidarity

1. Health care systems should be financed in a way which allows all members of society access to essential services regardless of their ability to pay. This means that within health care systems a redistribution of funds must take place, from those who can afford to pay for these services to those who, in the absence of support, cannot afford to pay.

2. Access to services, regardless of the ability to pay, need not extend to all aspects of health care, but should cover at least a guaranteed package of health care services. Society must therefore reach an agreement on how such a guaranteed health care package is to be defined.

An additional objective might be to design a health care system that avoids unnecessary government regulation. This means that the health care system should, as far as possible, be self-regulating and self-adjusting to consumers' preferences and needs. Other than regulatory supervision when necessary, the role of the government should be minimised.[6]

Economists have little guidance to offer on how to rank or prioritise these objectives if and when trade-offs between them exist. It is essentially a political decision for each country to decide what 'weighting' should be apportioned to each of them. This means that in some countries certain objectives may be considered more important than others. These decisions are likely to depend on the history of the country, as well as its socio-political framework and the values of its citizens.

The prototypical health care system that we recommend therefore exhibits sufficient flexibility to allow individual countries to find a reasonable balance between the benefits of competition and the value of social solidarity.[7] This does not mean that there is an optimal 'trade-off point' between efficiency and social solidarity which countries have to locate. Even within a system that is primarily concerned with social solidarity, a range of options for improving efficiency exists. Similarly, in a system that is predominantly focused on efficiency, options for enhancing solidarity are likely to be found. However, rather than assessing every possible option (or permutation of options), our recommendations for a prototypical health care system are designed in a way to ensure a balance between the objectives of the system.

---

[6]   Other objectives might be ease of administration and capability of implementation. However, since we are concerned here with long-term developments and do not focus specifically on any particular country, these are subsidiary objectives.

[7]   Contributions to the debate on efficiency and equity in the UK include: Maynard and Williams (1984) and Culyer (1991).

3.4   OPTIONS FOR FUNDING HEALTH CARE

> *"He that will not apply new remedies,*
> *must expect new evils, for time is the*
> *greatest innovator; and if time of*
> *course alters things to the worse and*
> *wisdom and counsel shall not alter*
> *them to the better, what shall be the*
> *end?"*
>
> **Francis Bacon:** Of Innovation

3.4.1   Introduction

In this section we assess some options for funding health care that have been suggested in the economic literature. To restate, the central problem is that a freely competitive health care market, while theoretically attractive, generally leads to risk selection by insurers. It therefore fails to meet society's desired level of social solidarity. Non-market solutions, on the other hand, generally lead to productive inefficiencies and a poor allocation of resources.

It is perhaps not surprising that most proposals emphasise some objectives of health care systems at the expense of others. For the purpose of our analysis, we introduce two generic classes from the set of reform options, and point to their deficiencies.

3.4.2   The Competitive Approach - Individual Risk Rating

The first approach envisages a **competitive market for health care insurance and health care delivery**. Its characteristics are as follows:[8]

General Features

A.   There is mandatory basic coverage, through individual or family insurance plans.

B.   All insurance plans must provide a Guaranteed Health Care Package, that is a range of services to which everybody is entitled regardless of their ability to pay. Additional services can be offered for a higher premium.

C.   Individuals seek coverage in an essentially private insurance market. Their premium would therefore be based on an assessment of individual risk.

Special Features

D.   Universal tax credits or vouchers would be used to compensate those with low incomes but high health care premiums.

E.   Some proposals, though not all, also recommend that high risk individuals, who have failed to buy, or cannot afford, insurance, would obtain fall-back coverage through a subsidised assigned risk pool.

The main disadvantage of the competitive approach is as follows. By shifting social solidarity considerations onto the government, a health care system that may otherwise operate through internal checks and balances may lose this feature, and may instead invite excessive government regulation. This is because governments may not be able to set tax credits at their appropriate level. Tax credits are at their appropriate level if, first, they allow people

---

[8]   See, for example Pauly, Danzon, Feldstein, and Hoff (1991), Leu (1992), Aaron (1991a) and Pauly (1986).

access to services within the Guaranteed Health Care Package;[9] if, second, they minimise additional government interference; and if, third, they provide incentives for individuals to search for the 'right' insurance policy. These three conditions may not be fulfilled:

1.   If the tax credits which qualifying individuals receive are set at a fixed level, then risk-adjustment may be inadequate. As a consequence, those individuals whose premiums (significantly) exceed their tax credits would not be able to afford health care. This situation is all the more likely to arise if a government is under pressure to control public spending. In that case, it may be tempted to reduce tax credits for needy individuals as one contribution to public spending cuts.[10,11]

2.   If tax credits are based on each qualifying individual's expected health care cost (i.e. on health care need), then an individual's risk would be assessed from two sources, namely their insurance company and the government. In such a situation, the government may decide to assume the health insurance function for such individuals altogether. It may do so for two reasons:

  •   If the government's risk assessment differs from that of an insurance company, the insurance company will want to charge an additional premium (or else is unlikely to insure the individual). This discrimination may appear politically unacceptable. As a consequence, the government may be forced to step in as an insurer.

  •   The transaction and administrative costs of determining the individual's risk from two sources may be high in comparison to the transaction and administrative costs that would arise if the government assumes the insurance function itself.[12]

---

[9]   The Guaranteed Health Care Package is further explained in Section 3.5.1.

[10]   The temptation for governments to reduce tax credits, or not to increase them in line with increases in premiums, may be substantial. This underlines the importance of the objective of designing a health care system which does not rely too heavily on government intervention.

[11]   A similar argument holds if (flat) tax credits are replaced by (proportional) tax allowances.

[12]   If, for example, society were to agree that all women should qualify for tax credits (or tax allowances), since the expected health care costs of females exceeds that of males (for similar risk categories), then the government would have to assess an appropriate tax credit level for at least fifty percent of the population.

159

As a result, the health care system is likely to establish a government financed fall-back fund for uninsurable individuals, or those for which no agreement can be reached between insurance companies and the government. A fall-back fund, however, could be perceived as consisting of a 'dumping ground for social outcasts'. A visible distinction within society between those citizens who are insurable and those who are not may fail to meet society's standard for solidarity.

3.   If high risk, low income individuals receive a tax credit, or equivalent support, that is always equal to their premium, they do not have a strong incentive to search for the cheapest insurance plan covering the Guaranteed Health Care Package. Under such circumstances, insurance funds may charge higher premiums than they would do otherwise, since they know that the premiums they charge are completely covered by tax credits.[13] In this case, the escalation of health care costs is simply transferred into public budgets. This may be a source of inefficiency.

This option may also put the government into a monopsony position, where it may be able to dictate lower premiums than a competitive market structure would bring about. As a result, some insurance funds may be driven out of the market.[14] Alternatively, the government may invite bids from insurance companies, allocate the insuree to the insurance fund that offers the lowest premium, and reimburse the

---

[13]   The incentive for an insurance fund to charge a higher premium than individual risk-rating would prescribe may not be very strong in a competitive market. However, the insurance fund and the applicant might collude by charging the government a premium for the applicant which is higher than it would be if the applicant would pay, and splitting the difference.

[14]   There is one further reason why we do not recommend a system which relies on tax credits. This reason relates to an emerging European wide health care market, as part of the increasing European integration. A further objective of the prototypical health care system could be established, namely that it should allow health care insurance companies to offer insurance policies to individuals in all member states of the European Community. Successive life and non-life insurance Directives of the European Community have indeed led to substantial progress towards a Single European insurance market. Thus, cross-border activities of health care funds may develop in the future.

However, if a health care system were to develop in the future which relies on tax credits for those who cannot afford coverage, then the likelihood for such cross-border activities is reduced. This is because, in general, a system of tax credits would require a much deeper degree of tax harmonisation than is currently envisaged in the short to medium term by the European Community. A system of tax credits may also require large unilateral transfers towards the poorest countries in the European Community. This might be consistent with a broad interpretation of the objective of 'economic and social cohesion' of the Treaty of Rome (*Article 130A*), but would probably not be politically and economically feasible.

insurance company with the full premium. As a result, the insurance companies have an incentive to compete for lower premiums. This solution, however, appears to be impractical since the government is likely to have to perform this role for the majority of people (e.g. women, the elderly, the chronically ill etc.).

These arguments suggest that governments may find it difficult to provide a framework that allows a competitive health insurance market to operate in an acceptable manner. However, if societies can agree how tax credits and other subsidies should be distributed, to provide compensation for low income and high risk, a free market in health insurance may provide access to a Guaranteed Health Care Package for all.

3.4.3   The Solidarity Approach - Community Risk Rating

The social solidarity approach relies less on competitive forces, but rather emphasises **affordability and accessibility of health care services to all members of society**. Variants of the solidarity approach include the following characteristics:[15]

General Features

A.   Health care insurance is mandatory or automatic. Individuals become members of insurance pools, or are covered by a national or regional scheme. Membership may be limited by employment, or location of residence; or may be based on random selection or random assignment; or may cover an entire nation.

B.   Each insurance fund provides access to a Guaranteed Health Care Package. Funds are not allowed to risk-select, but must accept all applicants who are a member of at least one of those groups on which the insurance fund is based.

C.   Insurance funds are allowed to offer benefits over and above the Guaranteed Health Care Package. Premiums for these services may be based on individual risk-rating.

Special Features

D.   Premiums are set by insurance funds on the basis of income only and not the risk characteristics of the individual. They therefore contain an element of cross-subsidy between pool members.

Most health care systems that have insurance funds, and indeed most national health services, are variants of this type. In the case of the latter only one government-owned fund exists (e.g. the National Health Service in the United

---

[15]   See, for example: Enthoven (1988), Enthoven and Kronick (1989), Diamond (1992) and Culyer (1990).

Kingdom). That fund receives its premiums through compulsory national insurance contributions and tax receipts based on income, expenditure and capital gains.

The main disadvantages of the solidarity approach are as follows:

1. In the absence of competitive forces on the funding side, the system may not be very responsive to consumers' preferences. Most members of society (at the same income levels) would pay the same percentage of their income and be entitled to receive similar or the same benefits. Furthermore, if the GHCP is defined in a way that includes virtually all health care services, individuals may have no incentive to search for an appropriate health care insurance plan or accept restrictions that could lower their premiums. In fact, in some health care systems, they may not have any choice over the insurance fund to which they belong.

2. Health care expenses are overwhelmingly, or even exclusively, linked to income, rather than to health care needs. This means that if the economy grows, more resources are available for health care if the ratio of premium to income remains stable. Similarly, if the economy contracts, fewer resources for health care may be available (unless premiums increase, or governments intervene). By contrast, the actual health care need may relate inversely to increases in income levels.[16]

3. In the case of a single insurance fund, which is an extreme variant of this approach, the possibility arises that the fund - which might be the government -allocates a single global budget to health care, or several budgets to different types of health care provision. In this case it is possible that the designated budget is not sufficient to cover the costs of all services which consumers demand. In this case, those who wish to consume and pay for more health care may have little or no scope for choosing an alternative insurance fund, and would normally buy cover in the supplementary private insurance market. The resulting monopsony may cause distortions such as excessive shortages and queues, which are both inefficient and deceptive.[17] Patients waste their valuable time and suffer more discomfort, but these costs are not

---

[16]   There is some evidence that in time of economic depression and higher unemployment, more health care is consumed than in time of economic prosperity.

[17]   Where resources are scarce, and access to health services is on the basis of need rather than ability to pay the full price, some queuing or other prioritisation will be necessary, and may be efficient.

registered as such in any systematic accounting framework. The total costs of such health care systems is therefore usually understated.

This does not mean that the solidarity approach cannot be made to work sufficiently well under any circumstances. Indeed, in several countries the entire population already has access to a Guaranteed Health Care Package, although supplemental privately financed health care is available, and is increasingly used to supplement the Guaranteed Health Care Package. There has, however, been growing discontent with such approaches, particularly over the lack of incentives for efficiency. Recent reform policies addressing these issues include the development of the internal market in the United Kingdom; the shift towards prospective cost-per-case payments for hospital services in Germany; and moves towards contractual agreements for services designed to improve allocative and productive efficiency (e.g. some reform policies in Sweden and New Zealand). These are examples of movements toward a mixed system which introduces incentives to compete into a social solidarity model.

3.4.4 The Mixed Approach - Funding from Two Sources

The mixed approach attempts to combine aspects of the two approaches categorised above. Although there is as yet no working example, several reform proposals fall into this category, thereby introducing an element of convergence among health care systems. One suggestion is particularly attractive; the so-called **Dekker** plan for the Netherlands.[18] The plan proposes the **introduction of regulated competition among health care providers and health care insurers.** Its main characteristics are shown in the box below.[19]

---

[18]   Its implementation by Government is also known as the *Simon* plan, or '*Stelselwijziging*' (system reform).

[19]   See, for example, Ministry of Welfare, Health and Cultural Affairs (1989), Lapre (1988), van de Ven (1990) and Schut, Greenberg and van de Ven (1991).

General Features

A. Comprehensive insurance coverage for a Guaranteed Health Care Package is mandatory.

B. Individuals enrol with an insurance fund of their choice for the Guaranteed Health Care Package. The insurer must accept all comers.

C. Individuals may purchase supplementary insurance for services not included in the Guaranteed Health Care Package. Premiums for these services will be set in the competitive market.

Special Features

D. Funding for the Guaranteed Health Care Package comes from two sources:

- First, a premium related to income but not to risk is paid to a central fund. From the central fund each insurance fund receives a fixed risk-adjusted capitation payment per patient enrolled.

- Second, each individual pays a flat fee directly to the insurance fund of their choice. That fee may vary between funds.

The key purpose of the reform plan for the Netherlands is to strike an acceptable balance between competition and social solidarity. Social solidarity is maintained through the central fund, whose premiums are related only to income, and are hence independent of risk factors; and by the obligation for insurance funds to charge a community-rated flat rate premium. The risk-adjustment process of the central fund is supposed to neutralise the insurers' incentives for preferred risk selection. Finally, competitive elements are introduced into the system through the flat premium that individuals pay directly to their insurer. This is intended to generate an incentive for insurers to become prudent buyers of health care by selecting efficient providers of health care and negotiating terms of contracts with them.[20]

Hence, there are two distinct sources of finance in this model. One part of the premium consists of a direct payment by the individual to the insurance fund of his or her choice. The remainder of the premium is paid indirectly to the insurance fund and includes an element of subsidisation to low income, high risk patients from contributions by other citizens.

One particular problem in this system is then to decide what percentage of expected total health care funding should come from the each source. This is a predominantly political decision, since it will determine the extent of the subsidisation. In the case of the Netherlands, a decision was taken to allocate initially 85 percent of funding to the first source (the contribution to the central fund), and 15 percent to the second source (direct payments to the insurance funds).

---

[20] To some extent the contracting process may lead to limited provider plans such as the American Health Maintenance Organisations (HMOs) or Preferred Provider Organisations (PPOs). This is consistent with the intentions of the reforms.

3.5 RECOMMENDATIONS FOR THE DESIGN OF A HEALTH CARE SYSTEM

3.5.1 The Funding Side of a Health Care System

Building on the analysis in Section 3.4, we now proceed to outline our recommendations for reform of the funding side of health care. In this section we present recommendations on the financing of the funders of health care, noting that in Section 3.5.6 an additional source of funding, namely patient copayments, is introduced.

Recommendation 1:   *A Guaranteed Health Care Package (GHCP) should be defined, detailing the services that society intends that everyone should be entitled to, regardless of their ability to pay.*

A GHCP is a bundle of services which becomes the standard minimum commodity traded in the health care insurance market. It needs to be defined, so that if and when insurance companies compete for customers for essential health care cover, they are required to offer an insurance plan that covers at the minimum the GHCP. The GHCP defines the rights of the insured, and reflects, in part, society's view of social solidarity. It defines a level of health care entitlements that no one should lack for financial reasons.

If a health care service is included in the GHCP it means that everybody in society contributes to the provision of that service, regardless of whether he or she ever actually uses this service. It follows that it is not possible for any individual to seek coverage with a health care plan that excludes any of the GHCP services in return for a lower premium, and that the scope for competing insurance funds is increased if the GHCP is defined at a low level.

On the other hand, individuals will make different contributions to the provision of the GHCP for all members of society. These contributions will depend on their ability to pay for the GHCP, *as well as* their expected utilisation of the GHCP.

The GHCP may include only minimal emergency and catastrophic care; or it may include a range of health care services, including long term care (nursing home care, care for mentally and physically disabled people), and health care related to social welfare (e.g. old people's homes). It is for individual countries to define a level of basic health care services which in their view constitutes an adequate GHCP. This decision becomes therefore part of the social contract between citizens of a nation.

Some general principles on possible alternative definitions of the GHCP can be stated. For example, the Dutch Commission which was set up to look into this issue, recommends that the GHCP should be defined in **functional terms** rather than specific **institutional** terms.[21] Functional terms may specify for example *nature* of care (e.g. primary or secondary care), *content* of care (e.g. components of care included in treatments), and *extent* of care (e.g. limits in its provision). On the other hand, the GHCP does not need to define exhaustively all institutional terms, such as *who* will give the care (e.g. is there a free choice of doctor), *where* it will be given (e.g. is there a free choice of hospital), and under *what conditions* (e.g. immediate access to providers on weekends) it will be given. These specifics may largely be stated in the individual's health insurance policy. Some regulation may be required to ensure minimum standards of the following kind:

- The quality of medical care must be assured.

- Services within the GHCP should be available without undue waiting time (waiting time may be specified in the insurance plan of the individual, but must be linked to the severity of the illness).

- Services should be made available at a convenient location (depending on the severity of the illness).

- Services should be provided with minimal psycho-social barriers to be overcome (i.e. treatment should be dignified and take into account differences in racial and ethnic backgrounds, or languages).

Generally, we recommend that the GHCP should be specified as a **list of conditions**, treatment for each of which is reimbursable through the GHCP. This means that this list is not specified in terms of *health care services which are required to treat the conditions*. Nor is it defined in terms of *institutions where treatment is provided*. By defining the GHCP in terms of conditions, rather than treatments or institutions, it will be left to the participants of the health care market to allocate health care resources; i.e. the participants of the health care system will determine what therapies should be provided at which institutions to provide treatment for the conditions. Specifying the GHCP in this way will ensure that new medical technologies and alternative institutional

---

[21]   Government Committee on Choices in Health Care (1992), p.17.

arrangements in the delivery of care, both of which offer additional benefits or cost-savings, will be speedily introduced.

Clearly the definition of a GHCP in terms of conditions is a difficult and politically sensitive task. Apart from the Netherlands, New Zealand is also in the process of explicitly defining a GHCP. So far, neither country has published a list of conditions which are included in the GHCP. There is, however, agreement that the GHCP should be limited to a basic, rather than a generous, list of services.

The following table presents an example of how a *basic* list of GHCP conditions might be compiled (other methods of defining a GHCP are perfectly well possible). Rather than specifying the conditions themselves, the table suggests that, in order for a **condition** to be included in the GHCP, it must pass the following three tests:

1. withholding any form of **treatment for the condition** must present a threat to the health status of the patient, or of others;

2. any **treatment of the condition** must be expensive, relative to normal income levels; and,

3. it must be unreasonable to expect every patient to fund any form of **treatment for that condition** by accruing savings over previous years.

The last criterion applies to certain types of geriatric treatments, which patients can anticipate and where insurance is not therefore required. Citizens are expected to contribute to the cost of maintaining themselves in old age by amassing a savings fund during their working lifetime. Some people will convert this fund into an annuity, as protection against the risk that they exhaust their savings by living longer than expected. However, this is an aspect of life insurance which is adequately covered by the financial sector.[22] The GHCP would only be liable to provide such treatment to people who could not have anticipated the need, i.e. people who require the treatment whilst below a certain age.

---

[22]   The Government might be involved if there were an issue of income distribution, but such concerns would be addressed under social policy, not health policy.

Table 3.1: A Possible Definition of a GHCP

In deciding whether or not a **condition** should be included in the GHCP, the following three criteria might be used:

A.   Is the inclusion of *any treatment for the condition* within the GHCP likely to prevent irreversible decline in health status for certain individuals, or for the public at large?

B.   Is *any treatment for the condition* catastrophically expensive, compared with normal income levels, such that an individual would find it difficult to finance the service, even with support from others such as relatives?

C.   Is it unreasonable to expect individuals to fund *any treatment for the condition* by saving up over their working lives, either because the need for the treatment may arise before they retire, or because it is a uncommon occurrence, even in old age?

If the answer to *all* of these questions is 'yes', the *condition*, not the treatment, should be included in the GHCP. If the answer to *any* of these questions is 'no', the condition should be excluded.

Insurance funds will then *translate the list of* **conditions**, *specified under the GHCP, into a list of* **services** *for which they reimburse providers.* Application of the three criteria to a common range of health care services suggests the following division [Square brackets indicate the reason for exclusion]. The services listed purely serve as examples; and insurance funds may well specify further services in the GHCP (such as health checks), if only because these may be cost-effective.

Services Likely to be Reimbursed under the GHCP	*Services Likely not to be Reimbursed under the GHCP*
	(1) Health Checks and Immunisations (*They would, however, be mandatory*)
(2) Most services for children, including neo-natal care	
(3) Most benefits in kind for adults - accident and emergency care - ambulatory care - hospital inpatient/outpatient care - maternity care - geriatric care	(3) Some benefits in kind for adults - special amenities **[A]** - free choice of (some) providers **[A]** - cosmetic surgery **[A]** - age limit for some services, e.g. renal failure, coronary heart disease **[C]**

	(4) Most dental care, in particular cosmetic dentures, crowns, bridges **[B]**
(5) Mental care institutions Rehabilitation institutions Chronic disability institutions	(5) Old people's homes **[C]** (*these could be financed out of social welfare*)
(6) Prescription medicines	(6) OTC medicines **[A,B]**
(7) 'Expensive' medical aids	(7) 'Non-expensive' medical aids **[B]**
	(8) Opticians services, glasses, lenses **[B]**
	(9) Psychiatric services and psychoanalysis **[B]**
	(10) Paramedical services, e.g. physiotherapy, occupational therapy, spa visits, except as part of an acute treatment **[B]**
	(11) Homeopathic services **[A,B]**
	(12) *In Vitro Fertilisation* **[A,B]**
	(13) Abortions, except on medical grounds **[A,B]**
(14) Transport costs in case provider choice is not free	(14) All benefits in cash **[A,C]** (*some of these could be financed by employers*)

Some care would have to be taken not to define conditions in too much detail. Thus if the condition *'normal cold'* is excluded from the GHCP (on grounds that it does not pass the second criteria, as people can reasonably be expected to pay for its treatment), but *'pneumonia'* is included in the GHCP, then some doctors may specify the former condition as the latter, in order not to have the patient paying for its treatment.

171

The GHCP does not include any cash benefits for general use by the patient.[23] Nor is the decision to include or exclude specific conditions on the basis of an economic cost-benefit analysis of its treatment. Purely economic criteria are not used as a basis for choice, because, at present, research into the costs and benefits of treatments for conditions is not advanced to such a degree that its results are widely accepted. For the foreseeable future, they should therefore not be used as the basis for decisions on which particular conditions are included in, or excluded from, the GHCP.

Annex 3.2 provides further guidance on how a GHCP might be defined. Approaches which include an assessment of costs and benefits of treatments as the basis for a decision on the inclusion of a service within the GHCP are presented in that Annex.

Recommendation 2: *The function of financing health care rests mainly with insurance funds, even within the GHCP. The statutory role of insurance funds is to purchase or otherwise provide the services included in the GHCP on behalf of their members. Funds may be for-profit or not-for-profit organisations. Market entry is open for new insurers who meet certain requirements specified by the government, as regulator of the system.*

Insurance funds must meet credentialling requirements before they are awarded a license by the government. They operate under supervision of a government department or agency set up for that purpose. Health insurance funds are basically mutual aid societies. Regulation may need to be in place to ensure their financial viability and to govern funds' access (if any) to capital markets.

Recommendation 2 is designed to set up a health care insurance system that is largely self-governing and self-regulating. A self-governing and self-regulating insurance fund system is a system in which the government sets the rules, but does not intervene directly in the funding or providing of health care (as would be the case, for example, if the government were to give tax

---

[23] Regulation may be in place which obliges employers to continue to pay wages to employees during sickness up to a maximum period. The underlying rationale is that paying sickness money is not necessarily a function of a health insurance scheme. Similar considerations have led to the exclusion of old people's homes from the GHCP (not to be confused with geriatric care which is included in the GHCP) on the grounds that such homes should come under the responsibility of social welfare institutions.

credits). It means that premiums for health insurance, and prices for health services, are set in a health care market. To that effect, a system of insurance funds will be set up whose statutory role is to sell health insurance plans (which cover the GHCP and other supplementary plans) to customers, and to buy health care (in accordance with the specifications in the health insurance plans) from providers. Insurance funds may wish to operate region-wide, nation-wide, or, possibly at some stage, e.g. in the European context, across national boundaries.[24]

Based on Recommendation 2, a health care financing system would therefore be established that is largely independent from the government. Governments might be free to set up their own funds if they wish, but only if they compete on equal terms with private or other voluntary non-profit funds. Recommendation 2 is intended to ensure long term stability of the organisational structure of the system.[25]

Recommendation 3: *Insurance for the GHCP with one of the insurance funds is mandatory for every citizen. Insurance funds have to accept every individual who applies for coverage for the GHCP.*

Mandatory health care insurance restricts individuals' choices. The main reasons for mandating compulsory insurance for the GHCP are:

1. it forces every individual of society to contribute to his or her individual health care, which they might not do if health insurance was not mandatory; and,

2. it ensures that health care is provided to the poor and severely ill, who could not afford to pay for it themselves. Otherwise, society would have to meet the health care costs of those who fall ill but have not taken out health care insurance, or else deny such individuals health care. The latter outcome would be unacceptable in most societies.

---

[24] Regulation may be needed to ensure that each insurance company offers one insurance plan which only includes the GHCP by itself. Otherwise, companies may be able effectively to risk-select based on income.

[25] Long term stability may not be guaranteed in mixed private/public systems where governments have an exclusive role, such as becoming the sole funders for some members of society which are otherwise not insurable. In that case, it is possible that governments may attempt to alter the structure of the health care system through a sequence of short term interventions. Furthermore, if governments compete, they may undermine the private sector by providing implicit subsidies.

Insurance funds have to accept all comers.[26] They are not allowed to deny coverage to anybody, subject to an agreement being reached on the premium that the individual pays. This is dealt with in Recommendation 4.

On the other hand, individuals are free to change membership from one to another health care fund. Some regulation may be needed to set an upper limit on how often members are allowed to switch funds, say, per annum. Individuals may wish to change an insurance fund for several reasons. These include dissatisfaction with the premium they are being charged, dissatisfaction with the range and types of health care insurance plans being offered over and above the GHCP by the fund, or dissatisfaction with those providers that a particular fund (and a particular insurance plan) has contracted with as the source of health care delivery.

Annex 3.3 analyses the special nature of insurance in health care.

Recommendation 4:   *Insurance funds will charge their members a premium to cover their health care expenses for services within the GHCP. That premium will come from two sources:*

    A.   *One part of the premium will be a fee that is related only to income.*

    B.   *The remainder of the premium will come from individual contributions based on individual risk.*

  A political decision will be taken by society on the respective share of the two sources of funding. That is to say, society decides which share (x) of the projected total health care expenditure for any given year should be financed through income contributions. The remaining share of (1-x) then constitutes that part of the contribution which is based on individual risk.

---

[26]   To minimise the transaction costs of a large number of individuals searching for an insurance policy, some standardisation could be introduced of the following kind:

    (1)   All insurees provide relevant information about themselves (say, through standardised questionnaires). This information could then be distributed to insurers.

    (2)   The government could intervene and prescribe a class of characteristics which insurance funds are allowed to use in their assessment of the individual's risk.

This system of funding the GHCP from two sources attempts to satisfy any nation's social concerns, while at the same time introducing competition into health care financing.[27] Each individual is granted access to the GHCP in return for (1) a basic fee (in relation to income) levied by, or on behalf of, a central fund, plus (2) a supplementary premium charged by competing insurance funds (to reflect differences in the residual risk of the individual and the efficiency of each fund).[28] Reliance on the income-related basic fee will foster social solidarity; greater emphasis on supplementary premiums increases the influence of competition. The proportion of the total cost met from each source is a political decision: within federal systems, different decisions could be reached in different regions, without compromising the overall system.

> *Comment No. 1: Note that insurance funds are allowed to differentiate that part of the premium which individuals pay directly to the fund. This premium component will therefore vary according to what funds estimate to be the residual predictable risk of the insured. Because of this, insurance funds have no incentive to risk-select. The resulting differences in premiums may however, depending on the level of x, be a fraction of what they would be in a completely competitive insurance market.*

> *Comment No 2: Note that in this system the size of overall health care expenditure is **not** fixed. Only the shares of the two sources of funding are fixed. Cost-containment pressures come mainly from competitive forces, but not from spending caps.*

The first funding source requires individuals who apply for coverage with an insurance fund to disclose their income to the central fund.[29] This may be problematic if individuals do not reveal their true income (say, by producing tax returns, or other evidence of income). The most efficient way to administer the system is to allow the government to collect the funds itself in the form of taxes, national insurance contributions or the equivalent. The government will

---

[27]   Patient co-payments are the third source of funding in this system. They are introduced in Section 3.5.6.

[28]   Pensioners would pay a contribution related to their pensions. Unemployed people would pay a contribution related to their unemployment benefits. Only children up to a certain age would be exempt (see Recommendation 5 which discusses the characteristic of the risk-adjustment formula of the Central Fund).

[29]   Another reason why individuals need to reveal their incomes to the central fund is to allow the government to set the upper limits for co-payments (see Section 3.5.6).

then pass the money to the central fund which is administered by the insurance funds themselves.

The basis for the calculation of the income-related fee will in most countries be the basis used for income tax. Some countries may prefer to base health insurance contributions on earnings (i.e. wages), rather than income. This is consistent with the Prototype. Individual countries may also decide to introduce an upper limit on the income-related fee (i.e. to cap the fee). This would mean that the income related fee for higher income earners, whose income exceeds a limit, consists of a flat fee.

In general, the aim of the Prototype is to individualise the burden of health insurance payments as much as possible. There will, however, be limits in achieving this objective. In most countries it will only be feasible to base health insurance contributions on the *income per household*. (A household is defined as a single person, or a legal relationship between two individuals and their children.) This means that non income-earning partners as well as children (up to a certain age) are entitled to receive all health care benefits within the GHCP through the income-earner's contribution. To allow for a higher percentage rate for the health insurance fee for married couples and/or couples with children may conflict with social policies, and would also be difficult to administer. Additional regulations could, however, be introduced to tackle a number of emerging problems.

- One emerging issue is that, under the system proposed, partners of high income earners are automatically insured, while partners of low income earners contributing to the household income are not. In order to ensure a higher degree of fairness in contributions, regulations may be put in place whereby insurance contributions are not capped, but are lowered to a smaller percentage contribution over and above a certain income level. This would ensure that high income earners would contribute more to the health care expenses of other members of society (including their partners). Similarly, regulations may be in place whereby partners on low (additional) incomes pay less towards their health insurance, or may be exempt from insurance payments altogether.

- Another emerging issue concerns the fact that children (who have high health care costs during their early years) are exempt from payments. Here regulation could be in place which would allow an insurance fund to charge a marginally higher direct residual premium to parents to cover parts of the expected additional health care costs of these households. However, this regulation assumes that legal responsibility for children can be established. In general, if it is accepted that most people will have children at some stage during their lives, then the level of subsidies which individuals receive (during child-rearing years) may be on parity with those which they contribute (before and after the child-rearing years), considered over the life-time of individuals.

- Another issue arises with respect to contributions of special groups. In general, we recommend that all members of society pay *themselves* for their health insurance. This allows them to choose their insurance fund, even if their contributions are to a large extent subsidised by the governments. Thus, we recommend that pensioners should pay a contribution from their pension payments. Similarly, unemployed persons should pay a contribution from their unemployment benefits, and students should pay a contribution from grants which they receive.

- Foreign nationals who are residents in a country must also seek coverage with an insurance fund. Unemployed foreigners, immigrants and others will also become members of an insurance fund. Their premiums are likely to be paid in most cases by the social welfare system of the country of immigration. The government may wish to make available some money to pay for the health care of those who, for whatever reason, have failed to sign up with an insurance fund and have fallen ill before they can be compelled to join an insurance fund.[30]

- Health insurance premiums of income earning individuals may or may not be partly paid by employers. The case for or against employer contributions is largely dependent on the tax systems in place in various countries. Our recommendation is that health insurance premiums should be paid in full by individuals themselves rather than their employers whenever this is possible. If, however, countries opt for employers' contributions to the health insurance fees of their employees, than these fees should be treated as an employment cost, and so be deductible for corporation tax, but taxable as income of the employee. In any case, employers' contributions should only cover the fees for the GHCP, but not of services over and above the GHCP. Employees should not receive income tax relief on their own GHCP contribution, which is itself a quasi-tax. Employers' contributions to that part of the health insurance premium of a health care insurance

---

[30]   In other words, not joining an insurance fund should be made a punishable offence.

plan which covers services over and above the GHCP are benefits in kind offered by the employer. Consequently, these should again be tax deductible as far as the employer is concerned, but should be taxed as income of the recipient. It would be distortionary to offer tax relief to individuals paying voluntary insurance contributions for care outside the GHCP.

Recommendation 5:   *A central fund, or re-insurance scheme, should be set up to provide the insurance funds with a risk-adjustment service. Its operations would fall into two parts:*

      A.   *The central fund would receive all income-related premiums paid by individuals, and would pay out to each insurance fund a risk-adjusted capitation fee for each individual enrolled in the fund.*

      B.   *For 'low' or 'moderate' levels of x, funds would be obliged to seek re-insurance to cover their expenses associated with patients who incur unexpectedly high costs.*

In essence, this means that each insurance fund receives a fixed risk-adjusted amount for each citizen who signs up with the insurance fund.[31] This fixed amount pays only for contributions to the GHCP, and not for any supplementary insurance.

---

[31]   Under these proposals, each citizen hands over an income-related premium to a central fund, and a direct premium to a selected insurance fund. The central fund then **pays the selected insurance fund** a supplementary premium related to the risk characteristics of the person concerned (after allowing for any direct premiums which were risk related). The *Pauly-Danzon* scheme is a variant of this approach, whereby each citizen hands over an income-related sum to the Income Tax Service. The Income Tax Service then **returns this revenue to the citizens**, in the form of a risk-related tax credit, and the citizens pay a single premium to their selected insurance fund, which is related to their own risk characteristics. **The Income Tax Service and the citizen together take over the role of the central fund.** This scheme allows more competition between insurance funds, since they receive all their revenues from potential patients and none from a central source. However, it is also more prone to moral hazard; under most formulations of social solidarity, a citizen who spends the tax credit on items other than health care is still likely to receive treatment at the expense of society. When the central fund makes payments direct to the insurance fund, insurance funds compete for customers on a different basis, but the scope for moral hazard is eliminated. Each government may accord a different emphasis to the desirability of free competition, versus the dangers of moral hazard, and will favour one approach or the other accordingly.

Even if funds are not allowed to risk-select, but are required to accept all comers, the distribution of high- and low-cost individuals (i.e. of 'sick' and 'healthy' individuals) will be uneven across funds. The function of the central fund is therefore to compensate funds with a large proportion of high-cost individuals by transferring money to them from funds with a low proportion of high-cost individuals. The more balanced the risk structure is across funds (for example, because there is a small number of large funds), the more modest the risk-adjustment payments will be.

In order for insurance funds to properly risk-adjust premium payments they receive, a well designed risk-adjustment formula is required. The formula will become the basis for the calculations of risk-related compensation payments which funds receive or pay.

One of the issues to be resolved in order to make the two source funding approach work concerns the question of which factors should be included in the risk-adjustment formula, and, by implication, which factors should be at the discretion of insurance funds to determine the residual premium. The answer to this question is that the risk-adjustment formula used by the central fund to calculate capitated fees for groups of individuals should include those characteristics which are:

- easily identifiable;
- reliable in measurement;
- good predictors of (differences in) health care expenditures; and,
- related to society's perception of social solidarity.

The latter point means that due regard should be given to those risk characteristics which account for differences in health expenditure, but for which an individual cannot be held responsible. Chronic diseases or birth defects are examples of illnesses which lead to higher than average health expenditure, but society may agree that such costs should be shared by all instead of being paid by the individual concerned. Similarly, for children, who do not pay premiums, the funds would receive an adjusted payment per enrolled child from the central fund.

In contrast, insurance funds, when determining the risk related residual premium, should not be constrained in their choice of factors to be taken into account; at least as long as they are assured that the central fund's formula (which they determine themselves) is accurate. Accuracy means that the predictability of an individual's health care expenses cannot be improved by using the same variables again for the determination of the residual premium.[32] This would suggest that any remaining explainable variance of an individual's health care expenses is essentially due to life-style factors (of course the largest of all unexplainable factors is chance).[33]

One problem hereby is that the progress in the search for potential risk-adjusters may generate variables which increase the explanatory part of the variance of an individual's health care expenses, but which society regards as unacceptable grounds for premium differentiation. One such factor might be *'prior utilisation of health care facilities'*. Studies indicate that the inclusion of this variable significantly increases the predictability of health care expenses. It would be difficult, if not impossible, to prohibit insurance funds from using this variable, given that prior utilisation data will be routinely available to them. It is furthermore a problematic variable in that differences in prior utilisation may reflect differences in doctors' practice. In order to exclude such problems it appears necessary to differentiate between chronic diseases which lead to continuous high utilisation of services, or one-off acute conditions which do not. It is therefore in the insurance funds' interest to share the risk for patients with chronic conditions by accounting for that risk characteristic into the central fund's formula.

---

[32] Research shows that the maximum explainable variance in annual health care expenditure per individual is approximately 15 to 20 percent. See van de Van and van Vliet (1992), van Vliet and van de Ven (1992), Becham (1992) and Newhouse, Manning, Keeler and Sloss (1989).

These studies show that in order to develop a risk-adjustment formula that eliminates the use of 'undesirable' factors for the determination of the residual premium by insurance companies, it is important to have a good predictor of individual health care expenditure. Note that in the NERA Prototype model 'cream skimming' is less likely to constitute a problem since insurance companies can always determine the residual premium on an individual, rather than a community, basis.

The studies by van de Ven and van Vliet describe the simultaneous predictive power of various risk- adjusting factors given the maximum explanatory power of 15 to 20 percent:

Age, Gender, Region		2.6 percent
Socio-Economic Factors	*plus*	0.4 percent
Prior Utilisation	*plus*	4.1 percent
Physical Impairment/Health Status Measures	*plus*	3.8 percent
Total		**10.9 percent**

[33] Differentiations of the residual premium will of course mainly relate to differences in efficiency with which insurance companies purchase health care services.

180

In summary, a possible distinction of risk factors which determines an insurance fund's revenues for different customer risk categories might be as follows:

Table 3.2: Possible Risk Characteristics	
Accounted for in the Risk-Adjustment Formula of the Central Fund	**Accounted for in the Individual's Residual Premium**
(1) *Income*, e.g. Wages, Salaries [a,B]	(1) *Life-Style Factors*, e.g. Smoking, Alcohol Consumption [A,B]
(2) *Demographic Factors*, e.g. Age, Gender, Children [A,B]	(2) *Disease Factors, if Not Medically Controlled*, e.g. Blood Pressure, Cholesterol Levels, Cardiac Function [a,b]
(3) *Geographic Factors*, e.g. Region, Urban versus Rural [a,B]	
(4) *Chronic or Acquired Medical Conditions*, e.g. Rheumatism, Heart Condition, Diabetes, Asthma, Cancer, AIDS, Consequences of an Accident [A,b]	(3) *Prior Utilisation other then Chronic Medical Conditions and Disability Status*, e.g. Number of Hospitalisations [A,b]
(5) *Disability Status*, e.g. Birth Defects [A,B]	
(6) *Socio-Economic Factors*, e.g. Income, Education, Employment, Marital Status [a,B]	

Square brackets indicate the following qualifications:

[A] Powerful Predictor
[a] Poor Predictor
[B] Relatively Easily Obtainable Characteristic
[b] Requires Medical Examination to Verify Characteristic: *Some characteristics, such as chronic or acquired medical conditions may be difficult to verify. In that case the benefits of including these in the risk-adjustment formula may be outweighed by the administrative costs in obtaining these characteristics.*

Once the criteria for the risk-adjustment formula have been specified, the specification should be approved by the government. Note that it will be in their interest to arrive at an appropriate mechanism that compensates them adequately for any number of *ex ante* higher cost individuals as balanced against the reduced reimbursements for the low risks which they take on.

Furthermore, funds should be able to review the parameters of the formula on a regular basis.

In addition to a central fund, insurance funds may be obliged to seek re-insurance to cover them against any residual risk. Re-insurance is advisable for countries that opt for a high proportion of health care expenses to be funded through individually risk-rated premiums. Individual risk-rating relates premiums of individuals to their expected health care costs. It thus reduces the necessity of establishing a central fund that compensates funds for individuals whose premiums do not match their expected health care costs. However, funds may wish to seek re-insurance for high-cost patients.

Adjustment payments made by either the central fund or paid out under the re-insurance scheme should be determined **prospectively**, not retrospectively. Under a prospective payment regulation funds have an incentive for a correct assessment of the risk-rated premium and for efficient purchasing of health care services for their members. Under retrospective payment arrangements funds would be able to shift incurred expenses to the central fund or the re-insurer.

> *Comment: Because insurance funds are allowed to risk differentiate part of the premium, they could be made obliged to make explicit which risk factors they use for that differentiation. In that case, the risk-adjustment formula could be reviewed in subsequent years to include some of these factors. As a result of this, the variance in premiums across risk categories will diminish.*

Recommendation 6: *A safety net should be set up to ensure health care is provided to those few remaining individuals who are unable to cope with the proposed system. The safety net would apply in the following cases:*

> *A.* *Special concessions should be available to those individuals, who, despite the safeguards in the system for those on low incomes and with poor health, are unable to afford coverage. They may apply for an affordable rate with an insurance fund. Either the discount would be subsidised by all other members of that particular fund; or, alternatively, the fund would receive*

> *compensation payments from other insurance funds via the central fund.*

    B.   *An agency would be set up to aid mentally disabled people, and other members of society who, for whatever reason, are unable to make the appropriate decisions within the health care system. The main function of this agency would be to purchase health care insurance on behalf of these individuals.*

As far as the first part of the recommendation is concerned, this is intended to act as a safeguard for those who cannot afford health care. Such a situation can basically only arise if society decides to give little or insufficient consideration to income-related funding. In this case, Recommendation 6 would stipulate that in that case individuals may apply for a premium that reflects their ability to pay, and that the expected health costs are shared within the community. In effect, this means that the role of the re-distributive fund as envisaged in these proposals has to be strengthened.[34]

As far as the second part of the recommendation is concerned, an agency would be set up to handle the affairs of some individuals in society which require special attention. The function of the agency would be to play the role of an agent on behalf of those who cannot participate as rational decision makers in the health care system, such as children not covered by parental contributions, the senile and others who are incapacitated. The agency would provide other functions as well for these individuals. It would be obliged to act on behalf of the individuals on those matters which society must decide. The most important of these decisions is the health care to be sought for each individual, and, at a broad political level, the definition of which services are to be included in the GHCP, and the level of x.

---

[34]   Or, in fact, it has to be established. This relates to the extreme case where x equals 0, which means that funds are not raised through an income related fee, and that hence no central fund exists in the original system.

Recommendation 7: *Insurance funds are free to offer to their members services that are either:*

A.   *not covered by the GHCP; or,*

B.   *that are covered by the GHCP, but which provide more choice or higher quality.*

Premiums for any additional services will be set by the insurer in whatever manner they see fit.

The first part of the recommendation helps to ensure that services that are not included in the GHCP, but for which there is demand, will be available to individuals who wish to pay for these. Since such services are not included in the GHCP, by definition there is less concern about those individuals who cannot afford those services. Depending on the definition of the GHCP, it can be reasonably expected that decisions on consumption levels of services excluded from the GHCP can be left to individuals, even if this means that no consumption takes place. Subsidisation between premiums for those services which are included in the GHCP and those which are excluded should be prohibited, so that the premiums for such services are likely to relate to the risk of the individual consumer.[35]

The reason for the second part of the recommendation is as follows. As specified in Recommendation 1, the GHCP is to be defined in functional terms, leaving several aspects of the delivery of care to the individual health care contract. Examples of insurance contract terms for supplementary benefits might include private rooms in hospitals, immediate treatment within 24 hours for non-acute ailments, or a nationwide or even international choice of providers. If individuals wish to purchase health care insurance that includes services over and above those specified in the GHCP, then they should be charged the (actuarial value of the) full incremental costs for these supplementary benefits.

Charts 3.1, 3.2 and 3.3 present the 'build-up structure' of the funding side of NERA's Prototype. In following sections these charts will be updated as the roles of the other participants of the health care system will be explained.

---

[35]   Regulation may have to be introduced to discourage insurance funds from only offering supplementary insurance, but not GHCP coverage (or effectively overprice coverage for the GHCP). In practice, most individuals are likely to purchase an integrated package (with includes the GHCP, but offers some supplementary benefits) from one insurance fund only.

Chart 3.1
Income-Related Insurance Premia

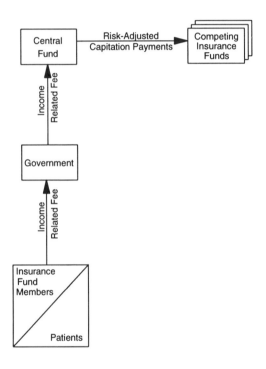

Chart 3.2
Risk-Related Insurance Premia

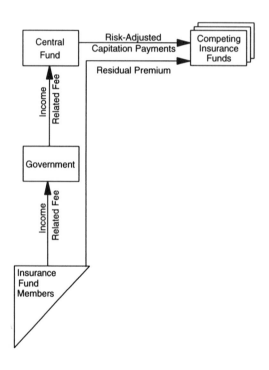

Chart 3.3
Insurance for Services not in GHCP

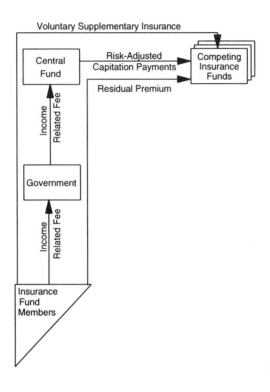

3.5.2   An Example of the Funding Mechanism

3.5.2.1   The Two-Source Funding Mechanism

In practical terms the funding side of the Prototype system, as outlined in Recommendations 1 to 7 so far, would work as follows. Society decides on the proportion of *x*. Say *x* equals *0.9*. The insurance funds project health care expenditure for the coming financial year. Assume that the projected health care expenditure is *100*. Then *0.9 * 100*, or *90*, is expected to be financed through income-related fees. In order to generate a level of funding equal to *90*, a percentage of income needs to be calculated which every member of society has to pay. The government will collect this income-related fee and will transfer the payments to a central fund. The central fund will pay the insurance funds a capitated fee which relates to the risk characteristics, and hence to the expected health care costs, of the individuals enrolled with the insurance funds.

The remaining part of the projected health care expenditure, i.e. *(1-0.9) * 100*, or *10*, will be raised through direct contributions of insurance fund members to individual funds. This part of the health care expenditure varies across individuals. It is dependent on two factors, namely: any difference between the risk-related capitation paid by the central fund to the insurance fund and the insurance fund's own assessment of an individual's expected costs (note that individuals can shop for another insurance plan with a different fund if they disagree with that decision); and the efficiency with which the fund purchases health care on behalf of its customers. The expected total revenue raised this way will be *10*, but individual contributions will diverge from the average contribution.

Setting the value of the cut-off point *x* is a political decision that rests with the citizens of each individual country.[36] Economists can make no recommendations on an 'optimal' level of *x*. However, we recommend that in order to reap the benefits of the system, *x* should not be set at its lower level of *0* since this would lead to an entirely competitive insurance market with little or no safeguards for those who cannot afford to pay their premiums (see

---

[36]   In general the prototype allows for a rich range of actual systems depending on the split between income-related fee and risk-related premium, and the number of risk categories allowed for. One special case of this generic class has already been set forward: if insurers were obliged to only offer a single risk class for the second source of funding (i.e. the individual risk rating would be replaced by a flat fee), and *x* were set at *0.85*, then the prototype leads to a system as suggested by the Dekker proposals for the Netherlands.

Recommendation 6 on this issue). Under those circumstances, it is likely that the government would be asked to intervene on behalf of those who cannot afford health care.[37]

The arguments against setting the upper level for x at 1 are less strong. The possibility for a nation to decide that it wishes to raise all funds from income-related fees should not be excluded altogether. However, if a country decides to exclude direct payments to insurance funds, the potential for competition among insurance funds is significantly diminished, and so are the incentives for efficiency.[38]

3.5.2.2 The Risk-Adjustment Mechanism

The risk-adjustment formula of the central fund is specified in a way to discriminate between different risk category of the population. For each member of each risk category the central fund pays a risk-related capitation payment to the member's insurance fund. This will work as follows:

Assume that there are four individuals in a country; Ms A, Mr B, Ms C and Mr D. Each individual has health insurance with one of four competing funds, called (for convenience) a, b, c and d, so that Ms A is insured with fund a and so on.

The following characteristics are known:

---

[37]   Because insurance funds do not receive their total income from income-related and risk-adjusted premiums, but also from direct payments of their members, there will be no role for 'niche' funds in this system. Niche funds are funds with a small membership of generally bad risks. Such funds can be expected to disappear in the health care system outlined here.

[38]   As a consequence the country may wish to set up a limited number of funds, or in fact a single fund only. In this case, we would recommend that the single payer system be decentralised. That is to say payments should be channelled to different geographical entities which will then purchase health care on behalf of patients taking into account local and regional parameters. This at least allows some variation in managing the system and avoids too much central authority which might exaggerate the need for uniformity.

Name	Risk Characteristics	Income Per Annum [$]	Expected Health Care Costs Per Annum [$]
Ms A	*poor and very sick*	5,000	4,500
Mr B	*rich and sick*	45,000	4,400
Ms C	*poor and healthy, non-smoker*	5,000	300
Mr D	*rich and healthy, smoker*	45,000	800
All		**100,000**	**10,000**

This means that total expected health care costs are 10 percent of gross national product.

Suppose that x has been set at 0.9. This means that $9,000 have to be raised through income-related fees, and $1,000 have to be raised through direct contributions of the insured to their insurance funds, based on risk.

All income-related fees are collected by the government and transferred to the central fund. The central fund then pays a capitation fee for each member of each insurance fund. The capitation payment will depend on risk factors (such as chronic diseases), but not on life-style factors (e.g. smoking).

Suppose the insurance funds agree on the following capitation payments from the central fund:

Accounts of the Central Fund

From	Income-Related Fee Paid to Central Fund, i.e. 9 Percent of Income [$]	To Insurance Fund	Risk-Adjusted Capitation Fee Paid by Central Fund [$]
Ms A	450	a	4,490
Mr B	4,050	b	4,250
Ms C	450	c	250
Mr D	4,050	d	10
All	**9,000**		**9,000**

By subtracting the capitation payments which each insurance fund receives from the expected health care costs, each insurance fund calculates the direct premiums which it will collect from the individuals, as follows:

Accounts of Insurance Funds

From	Risk-Adjusted Capitation Fee [$]	Expected Health Care Costs [$]	Required Residual Payment [$]	Insurance Fund
Ms A	4,490	4,500	10	a
Mr B	4,250	4,400	150	b
Ms C	250	300	50	c
Mr D	10	800	790	d
All	9,000	10,000	1,000	

The total payments of each individual are therefore:

Accounts of Insurance Members

Name	Income-Related Fee [$]	Risk-Related Premium [$]	Total Contribution [$]	Percentage of Income [Percent]
Ms A	450	10	460	9.2
Mr B	4,050	150	4,200	9.3
Ms C	450	50	500	10.0
Mr D	4,050	790	4,840	10.8
All	9,000	1,000	10,000	10.0

This example serves to demonstrate that the risk-adjustment formula must be specified in way to be able to discriminate between risk categories. In this example:

- healthy Ms C and healthy Mr D both pay more than sick Ms A and sick Mr B;

- rich Mr B pays more than poor Ms A (approximately same health status);

- rich Mr D pays more than poor Ms C (approximately same health status, but Mr D smokes).

If some insurance funds (say, *a* and *b*) are more efficient in purchasing health care for their members than others (say, *c* and *d*), then the risk-related premiums will be different, and hence the percentage of income which individuals pay will be different. This is the intention of the two source funding approach.

The calculation example has to be interpreted with care, and no general conclusions can be drawn from its specific results. All that can be deduced from it is that for the four risk categories defined in the example, the central fund uses the following weighting factors in its risk-adjustment formula:

the '*Very Sick*' risk category is being allocated **49.9 percent** of resources;
the '*Sick*' category is being allocated **47.2 percent** of resources;
the '*Healthy, Non-Smoker*' category is being allocated **2.8 percent** of resources;
the '*Healthy, Smoker*' category is being allocated **0.1 percent** of resources.

3.5.2.3 Summary

This completes the example. To summarise, the main reason why we propose a dual source of funding is as follows. The decision on the proportions of the two funding sources is arrived at by a democratic process. This process allows the balance between efficiency and social solidarity to be kept under review, while at the same time minimising government interference. When deciding on the appropriate level of x, each member of society will have to take into account their own potential future health status, and possibly that of their children, as well as their preferences for health care and the way it is being financed. In contrast, if x were fixed at its upper bound, efficiency losses are likely to result, whereas if it were fixed at its lower bound, it would require the government to support those who cannot afford coverage.

3.5.3   The Provider Side of a Health Care System

In this section we present recommendations for the provision of health care, as opposed to the funding.

Recommendation 8:   *The delivery of health care services rests with providers, including primary care physicians, hospitals, nursing and community centres, and producers and distributors of medicines. Providers will sell their services primarily to insurers. The quantities of goods and the level of services, their quality and their prices will be either determined through open market sales made at list prices, or will be specified in legally binding contracts concluded between individual insurance funds and individual providers. Some providers, such as primary physicians, may be allowed to negotiate contracts collectively. Providers therefore have an incentive to compete on the basis of the quality and the price of their services.*

The aim of this recommendation is to establish 'expert purchasers'. Insurance funds will become expert purchasers by accumulating knowledge on the most cost-effective ways of providing health care of acceptable quality, taking into account a variety of factors. Such factors may include the long term cost effects of conducting a preventative care campaign, comparative cost schedules of different providers, or the effects of substituting surgery by drug therapy or vice versa. Insurance funds competing for members will therefore have an incentive to establish cost-effective ways of purchasing health care on behalf of their members. To do this they will attempt to influence the referral patterns of general practitioners, as well as the cost-schedules of hospital specialists, and the service they provide.[39] There will be a need for effective quality assurance, to prevent cost-cutting from going too far in cases in which the patient is relatively ill-informed.

Competition on the delivery side of the emerging health care market will stimulate productive efficiency. Since patients are allowed to make choices, it will also produce market signals between suppliers and demanders that are

---

[39]   Providers and producers may negotiate different prices with different purchasers if price differentiation is legal.

essential to stimulate allocative efficiency, i.e. the appropriate amount and mix of health care services, given patients' preferences.

Some providers, such as primary physicians, may be allowed to negotiate contracts collectively as this minimises transaction costs. If collective negotiations take place, they should not allow the formation of a cartel. Collective arrangements with physicians could be agreed on the local level, or, preferably, with groups of specialists (e.g. gynaecologists, dentists, etc.).

To underline the importance of the contents of health care contracts, and in order to assist purchasers and providers in the process of planning health care, health care contracts should be legally enforceable. This means that penalties for non-compliance with respect to the contents of health care contracts will have to be in place. Legal specifications of health care contracts should be based on the legal system of that country in which they are concluded.

Recommendation 9: *The way in which providers are reimbursed by purchasers is subject to negotiations between the two parties. Purchasers of health care are free to discontinue a contractual relationship with a provider at the end of a contractual period. Similarly, they are not obliged to commence a contractual relationship with a new provider.*

We recommend that within the framework of a regulated market, the appropriate reimbursement methods for providers should be left to the participants. In the absence of monopolistic providers or monopsonistic purchasers, contracts are likely to emerge that will share risk appropriately between the two parties, taking into account factors such as treatment methods, substitution of procedures, waiting lists, new technologies, as well as local and other parameters.[40]

Reimbursement methods include:

- fee-for-service payment;
- cost-per-case payment;
- *per diem* rates;

---

[40] It may be that the government, or some expert agent of the patient, wishes to review all contracts, and their operation, to prevent providers and purchasers colluding to defraud the patients.

- budgets (calculated prospectively or retrospectively);
- capitation fees;
- salaries; or,
- any combination of these.

While some reimbursement methods usually create better incentives than others, no generalisation is possible whereby a single payment method is preferred under all circumstances anywhere at any time.[41] Hence there is no need to regulate against or in favour of any of these.[42] Annex 3.4 details the advantages and disadvantages of several reimbursement methods for health care services.

We recommend that insurance funds should not become owners of provider units, nor accept commission from them, mainly because this may create market distortions and encourage anti-competitive behaviour. It may furthermore create a situation where cost-cutting pressures lead to the

---

[41]   Payment for the services of primary physicians and specialists is typically by fee-for-service payment, salaries, capitation payments, or a hybrid of these. Each engenders different incentives and allocates risk in different ways. For example, fee-for-service payments give a GP a pecuniary interest to provide treatments beyond what is perhaps necessary. However, doctors faces the risk of reduced income if none of their patients become sick (which is a desirable outcome). Salaries reduce the financial incentive of providers to provide high quality care. While capitation payments give GPs an incentive to keep their patient population healthy (so they do not visit the doctor), they also give GPs an incentive to pass patients onto specialists quickly, even though this may be more expensive.

Likewise, different means of paying hospitals also give these a financial incentive to provide treatment in different ways. For example, *per diem* rates pay hospitals more for each extra day a patient is in hospital, while a cost-per-case payment pays nothing more for a long hospital stay, as the rate is set prospectively. Thus shorter, and therefore cheaper, hospital stays are encouraged by the latter method of payment, but in this case the hospital bears the risk of the severity of a patient's illness resulting in a longer stay even though this is beyond the hospital's control.

In a competitive market, an insurer will want to choose a method of payment that allocates risk effectively between the provider and the payer. Different combinations of the payment mechanisms above will be optimal in different situations for paying for different forms of care.

[42]   For example, clinicians may receive a financial incentive to treat an ailment in the manner best suited to minimising costs while maintaining a quality level which is consistent with medical requirements. If incentives are sufficiently powerful, they may reinforce the doctor's natural desire to heal while at the same time ensuring that resources are not wasted. This suggests that the clinician may receive a prospective payment to cover the total costs of treating the patient (assuming that the patient falls into a treatment category for which cost-per-case payments are feasible). He would then be expected to purchase the necessary inputs, and keep the remainder as his or her own remuneration. This reimbursement method might, however, allocate a substantial residual risk to the clinician.

lowering of quality in the provision of services to an inefficient and intolerable level. Such a situation is likely to be prolonged in the absence of a separation between the provider and the insurance fund. On the other hand, insurance funds and provider units may establish a relationship of 'mutual preference'. Under such an agreement, the insurance fund would carry some of the risk in fluctuations in demand for services, in return for lower treatment costs. This is entirely consistent with Recommendation 9, as long as providers and insurance funds are separate legal and managerial entities, and collusion between them is prevented.

Regulation might, however, be in place to guarantee some providers (e.g. individual primary physicians) a minimum length of accreditation with a purchaser, if providers appear to be unable to negotiate the appropriate contracts. This may be necessary if, for example, individual physicians establishing their own practice are to amortise at least some of their initial investment expenditure.[43]

> *Comment: Recommendation 1, the definition of a GHCP, in conjunction with Recommendation 9, freedom of negotiating, means that patients have a choice of provider, unless they decide to opt for a health care insurance plan (consistent with GHCP requirements) that restricts their choice of provider.*

Recommendation 10: *All potential providers are given unregulated entry to the health care market subject to meeting medical qualification requirements, which will be continuously checked. This includes private, for-profit hospitals, as well as new provider forms, such as medical centres. Capital expenditure programs are financed mainly by contractual income and from funds raised by providers on the capital markets, but not by the government.*

---

[43] Whether or not individual GPs are able to negotiate appropriate contracts with insurance funds is likely to depend on several factors, including the structure of the market for GP services. This may give rise to some issues which may require anti-trust regulation, e.g. in situations where insurance funds are in a position to insist on exclusive and/or short-term contracts. Under the prototype, it is generally not possible for a GP not to be accredited with one or several insurance funds, unless he or she relies entirely on private income. Such a situation can only emerge under an insurance contract which gives patients free choice of which GP they wish to consult (this is likely to be specified as a supplementary benefit).

The main purpose of Recommendation 10 is to put public, semi-public, voluntary and private providers on an equal footing. The government can establish providers units if it wishes to do so, provided that they compete on equal terms with private providers.

All providers should expect to cover their costs through contractual income and patient copayments. No provider should have preferential access to capital funds at little or no cost (with the possible exception of donated assets or gifts). Instead, providers should be allowed to raise capital for investment purposes on the capital markets, and include these costs in their contract prices. Some co-ordination among providers concerning large investment plans could be allowed. To that effect, but only for this purpose, co-operation among providers should be encouraged.[44]

Charts 3.4 and 3.5 present the updated version of Chart 3.3; in Chart 3.4 the provider side of the NERA Prototype is introduced, while in Chart 3.5 the funding and delivery sides of the Prototype have been combined.

---

[44] To ensure 'level playing field' between public and private providers may require governments to levy capital charges on public hospitals, as well as tax harmonisations between public and private providers.

Chart 3.4
Delivery of Health Care

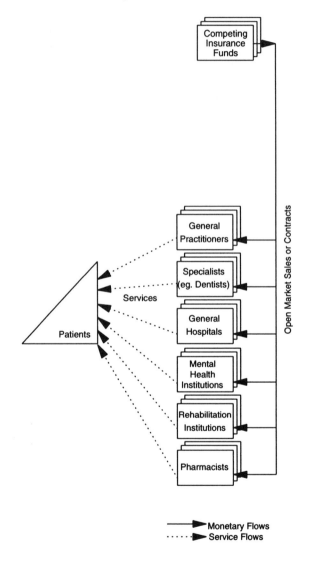

Chart 3.5
Competitive Financing of Health Care

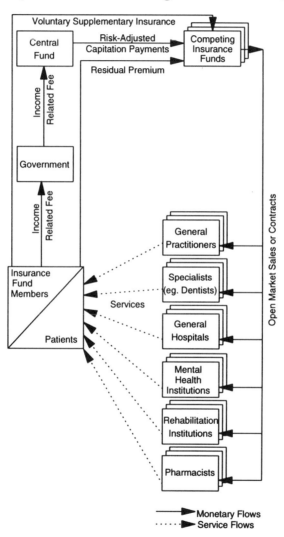

3.5.4 Forms of Transactions in the Health Care Market

3.5.4.1 Introduction

Our recommendations for the structure of the funding and provider components of the health care system lead to the establishment of a market in health care products and services. The market will consist of thousands of transactions between providers and purchasers in the goods and services that make up the necessary treatments. This market will encourage efficiency in the supply of health care, provided that there are enough players on both sides of the market to permit true competition.[45]

If providers (individually or jointly) establish some monopoly power, they will charge too much; if purchasers (individually or jointly) operate a monopsony, they will depress prices. These price distortions will affect the demand and supply of health care and will prevent an efficient use of resources. To resolve such problems, some regulatory intervention by government may be necessary.[46]

In a competitive market, however, the prices and terms for each transaction can be negotiated by the buyer and seller. This section explains how this process might work for different forms of health care products. It therefore provides an illustration of how Recommendations 8 to 10 are likely to work in practice.

3.5.4.2 Economic Purchasing

The simplest form of transaction requires all sellers to state a price for the product and for the buyers to decide where to buy the product so as to minimise the cost. This system would be consistent with the NERA Prototype. Insurance funds pay for services and products, but it is doctors and patients who usually decide what health care is required. Since patients make proportionate copayments on all their health care expenditure (see Section 3.5.6 below), they will have an incentive to choose the cheapest source of treatment, and insurance companies will normally be prepared to leave the selection of treatment to the doctor and patient.[47]

---

[45]   Competition must be compatible with legal requirements; i.e. anti-trust laws have to be enforced.

[46]   See Fuchs (1988) and Appleby, Little, Ranade, Robinson and Salter (1991).

[47]   Patient co-payments are introduced in Recommendation 13.

In this system, the price lists set up by providers can take many forms. To encourage efficiency, insurers might prefer to deal with providers who quote prices on the following basis (although others are perfectly possible):

- for hospital services: *prospective cost-per-case*;

- for primary physician services: *fee-for-service*;[48] and,

- for medical aids, medical technology and medicines: *list prices per unit*.

3.5.4.3 Negotiated Prices

This simple approach is liable to be complicated, however, by the desire of purchasers and providers to negotiate special terms on a one-to-one basis, in recognition of their own special needs and characteristics. Individual contracts might contain any of the following provisions:

- Prices and/or volumes might be fixed in advance, in order to reduce risk over costs and revenues.

- The terms of delivery might require special attention, e.g. minimum or maximum quantities, contract-specific quality provisions, advance notice to be given by the purchaser, required speed of response by the provider, etc.

- Large contracts might reduce transactions costs, and provide scope for bulk discounts and terms designed to foster a long term relationship between supplier and customer.

Negotiating special deals of this type is one way in which insurance funds can gain a competitive edge over their rivals. For example, a prime consideration will be the ability of insurance funds to forecast the health care needs of their policy holders, in order to secure guaranteed prices in advance, and to avoid paying a premium for health care provided at short notice.

---

[48] For primary physicians the advantages of fee-for-service payments are less pronounced than, say, those of prospective cost-per-case payments for hospitals. The fee-for-service payment method should be complemented with a significant co-payment element. Alternatively, an element of capitation payment for those services which physicians provide themselves may be appropriate.

3.5.4.4   Extra Contractual Referrals

Insurers and providers cannot hope to anticipate health care needs so accurately that all requirements are covered by contracts negotiated in advance. From time to time, a patient will need some form of health care for which the insurer has no contract. Such needs are referred to in the UK as 'Extra Contractual Referrals' and the Department of Health was initially surprised how large a feature they were of the new system.[49] Under the NERA Prototype there will also be cases where a doctor wishes a patient to have a treatment for which the insurer has no contract, or has a contract with a different supplier.

Under these circumstances, insurance funds will want to ensure that the doctor and the patient select the treatment economically, as far as the insurer is concerned. This may require some form of guidance to the doctor to use providers with whom a contract is in place. However, this will not always be possible or advisable, and some other basis must be used for setting prices and reimbursement levels. In such cases, obviously, published price lists will prove invaluable, especially where the urgency of the case precludes any negotiation over terms (e.g. accident and emergency cases).

The doctor and the patient will then only need to consider the prices quoted by each health care provider, or supplier of medicines, and the terms of reimbursement offered by the insurer. In the case of purely proportional copayments, as for the GHCP, the patient will have an incentive to choose the most cost-effective form of treatment. (Any contracts between insurance funds and providers will have to be keenly priced to encourage their use by patients). For treatments outside the GHCP, the insurer may use other methods to guide patient choice, such as fixed reimbursement levels. However, the scope for the insurance funds to impose restrictions on access to treatment will be limited by the scope for competitors to offer a better insurance plan with a wider range of suppliers.

---

[49]   Each hospital in the UK is required to negotiate reimbursement levels for services which it provides with its main purchasers. Main purchasers are usually the host district health authority and neighbouring authorities since these send patients in significant numbers to the hospital. In addition, each hospital is required to publish a price list, detailing prices and services which apply to patients who are resident in district health authorities with whom the hospital has not concluded a contract.

3.5.4.5   Implications for Providers

Providers will supply their services through two different routes: contracts negotiated with individual purchasers; and open market sales (extra contractual referrals) made at list prices. The availability of supplies at published list prices means that contract prices are likely to be lower than list prices. However, the key to negotiating a remunerative contract is to provide the purchaser with added value, by tailoring the terms of delivery to the individual requirements of the purchaser. In this respect, therefore, relations between supplier and customer in the market for health care services will resemble those in any other competitive market.

3.5.5   The Responsibilities of the Government

The system recommended here makes as much use as possible of the beneficial effect of competitive markets. The keystones of the proposal are (1) competing providers and (2) competing insurance funds. However, the desire to meet certain social objectives means that governments will be unable to leave all decisions to individual persons and corporations. The government will therefore have to pass legislation to enact some basic rules.

Recommendation 11: In order to provide universal access to the GHCP, the government will intervene in the market for health insurance in the following ways:

    A.   Every individual must be obliged to take out health insurance from an accredited insurance fund, to cover the GHCP.

    B.   Every accredited insurance fund must be obliged to accept all requests for enrolment on reasonable terms.

    C.   Every individual must be obliged to pay over to the central fund a premium related to his or her income, and to nominate an insurance fund as recipient of a risk-adjusted payout; or every insurance fund must be required to collect an income-related premium from every individual enrolled, on behalf of the central fund and in return for a risk-adjusted premium.

> D. *A Guaranteed Health Care Package will be defined which will include mandatory copayments.*

These obligations must be imposed by law, as they will not arise out of a competitive market framework. Together, they ensure that every individual is given access to the GHCP, in return for a basic fee related to income, plus a residual premium charged by the insurance fund. The residual premium may reflect the risk characteristics of the individual, but only to the extent that they are not already reflected in the risk-adjusted payout of the central fund. If the central fund provides complete adjustment for risk, the residual premiums will only reflect differences in the efficiency of the competing insurance funds.

The final definition of the GHCP, as stated in Recommendation 11D, follows a decision by society on its exact specification. This specification will be enacted through democratic institutions.

Beyond imposing these obligations, the role of government can then be limited to supervision and provision of certain services with widespread benefits. These supervisory and service provision arrangements mainly need to be in place in order to guarantee that the market participants act according to the roles that have been prescribed to them. Hence, we recommend that these functions should be allocated to the government. They include:

Recommendation 12: In this health care system the main operational functions of the government will be as follows:

> A. *The government should set up an agency to oversee, and if necessary regulate, competition amongst insurance funds and amongst providers. The task of the agency would be to adapt existing or new anti-trust legislation to the health care system. In particular, this includes a ban on cartels and arrangements that are designed to benefit some participants of the health care system at the expense of others. This includes merger approval. Furthermore, this agency would also be charged with supervising, and approving, the risk-adjustment formula for*

the central fund, and auditing the process to guard against abuse.

B.   The government should set up an audit agency. The audit agency will be charged with the task of ensuring that all insurance plans offered by the insurance funds meet certain credentialling requirements. Furthermore, the audit agency may be charged with the task of inspecting providers to ensure that acceptable quality services are provided.

C.   The government should set up a separate agency that will act as the agent of the mentally disabled, and others who are unable fully to participate in the health care system. This agency will purchase health care on behalf of its members and will represent their interests in those matters that require a decision by society.

D.   To the extent that teaching and research is not financed from private funds, the government will assume some responsibility of financing these. This includes funding medical and nursing schools, as well as some research activities carried out at hospitals or elsewhere.

E.   The government will have responsibility for public health issues, in particular the prevention of communicable diseases.

F.   The government will also maintain a licensing agency, that will grant licenses to all participants in the health care system, e.g. insurance funds and providers. This agency will also act as the medicines approval agency.

G.   The government will assist in collecting the income-related fee which it then transfers to the central fund.

Thus the role of the government is in line with that which it assumes in many other markets, i.e. the role of a legislator, supervisor, and, where necessary, regulator. Legislation may be required to enact the necessary pro-competition and quality regulation policies. Annex 3.5 provides some examples of regulatory authorities in some countries that are charged with the implementation of competition policies. Supervision is required to ensure that the participants of the health care system act according to their roles. Finally, regulation may be required in special circumstances where the health care system may otherwise fail. In the system outlined here, the likelihood of market failures that necessitate government intervention are minimised.

Chart 3.6 presents the latest update of the Prototype in graphical form, which now includes the funding side, the provider side, and the role of the government.

Chart 3.6
The Role of Government

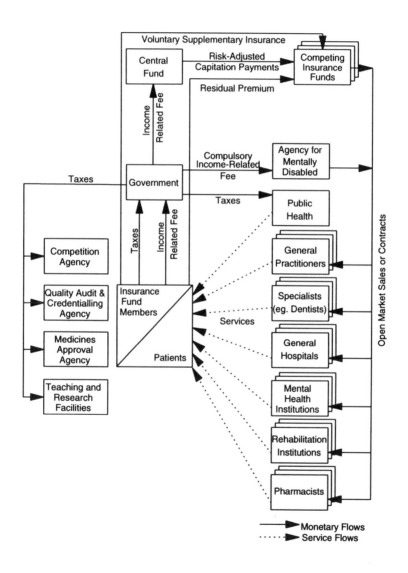

3.5.6   The Responsibilities of Patients

In this section we present our recommendations about the responsibilities of patients. Two responsibilities are presented here which are both intended to enhance the role of the patient as a consumer of health care, e.g. to strengthen consumer sovereignty. While the second of these recommendations deals with the establishment of consumer organisations, we turn first to the recommendation which considers appropriate cost-sharing arrangements between patients and their insurance funds.

Cost-sharing arrangements, or copayments, describe the way in which costs for health care are shared between the purchasers and the patients themselves. An important function of copayments is to strengthen the individual responsibility of patients by making them more aware about the costs of the services which they consume. This function relates to the so-called moral hazard problem. In health care, moral hazard arises when patients consume more health care than is economically efficient, either because they have no incentive to take reasonable care to avoid the necessity of consuming health care, or because the price at the point of service is below cost, or zero which leads to unrestrained demand. In both cases, imposing direct payments on the consumer at the point of delivery of health care can act as restraint to demand, and hence lead to economically more efficient levels of consumption.

A cap on copayments is a provision of insurance that prevents copayments from becoming an unbearable financial burden to the sick or poor. In Japan, for example, copayments are an efficient aspect of health care financing. Patients pay a fixed percentage for all insured medical goods and services. The co-insurance rate for an individual varies between 10 and 30 percent, averaging about 20 percent nationwide, depending on the individual's insurance plan. The maximum any individual pays in copayments per month at present is ¥60,000 ($480).

The effect of copayments may be observed from the failed experiment to eliminate them for the elderly in Japan. In 1973 the Japanese government decided that the elderly should be able to obtain medical services free of copayments. Before that decision, *per capita* visits were no greater for the elderly than for other adults. Once the co-insurance payment was eliminated, the frequency of hospital visits by the elderly increased drastically. Copayments were restored in 1982 with the objective of reestablishing a degree of cost consciousness among older patients. Presently, copayments for those over 65 equal ¥400 ($3.20) per day for inpatient care and ¥800 ($6.40) per month for outpatient care. Officials in the Japanese Ministry of Health and Welfare believe that this low threshold leaves too little responsibility with patients, and contemplate further increases in the rate.

Some other interesting conclusions can be drawn from various experiments on copayments in the USA (see Table 3.3), which tend to confirm that the introduction of copayments reduces the levels of consumption of health services.

Table 3.3: Findings from Studies of the Effects of Copayments in US Health Care[50]

Overall Findings

1. Overall price elasticities appear to be -0.1 to -0.2 for medical services and -0.1 to -0.3 for pharmaceuticals.

Medical Services

2. Introduction of a 25% coinsurance plan cut visits to the doctor by 27% and hospital admissions by 18%. A 95% coinsurance plan achieved cuts of 40% and 22% respectively.

3. Reductions in total costs of medical services tend to be achieved by falls in the number of episodes, not in the cost per episode.

4. Copayments had little or no impact on the choice of provider.

Pharmaceuticals

5. Introduction of a 25% copayment plan cut the number of prescriptions by 18%.

6. Patients responded to a copayment by cutting 'essential' and 'discretionary' usage of particular drugs by the same amount. Patients responded to a copayment by cutting 'appropriate' and 'inappropriate' usage of antibiotics by the same amount.

7. Copayments caused a bigger fall in usage of 'discretionary' types of drug, than of 'essential' types.

8. Differential copayments for generic and brand name drugs caused switching towards generic drugs, but little effect on total drug usage.

---

[50] Based on: Foxman, Valdez, Lohr *et al.* (1987), Harris, Stergachis and Ried (1990), Leibowitz, Manning and Newhouse (1983), Lohr, Brook, Kamberg, Goldberg, Leibowitz, Keesey, Reboussin and Newhouse, (1986), Manning, Newhouse, Duan, Keeler, Leibowitz and Marquis (1987), Marquis (1985), Smith (1992) and Weiner, Lyles, Steinwachs and Hall (1991).

209

The objectives of efficient and socially acceptable arrangements of copayments are therefore as follows:

Objectives of Copayments

1.   Copayments strengthen individual responsibility of patients in deciding about their levels of health care consumption, taking into account their ability to pay; and thus reinforce the balance of efficiency and social solidarity;

2.   they help to reduce an inefficient use of health care facilities by consumers;

3.   if applied consistently across all health care services, they encourage patients and doctors to adopt the most cost-effective treatment; and,

4.   they imply recognition of the need for flexibility in the choice of treatment, which may be lost under strict quantity or price restricting schemes with no copayments.

The constraints which need to be imposed on the copayment structure are:

1.   For services within the GHCP, there should be no premium differentiation that is exclusively due to copayments;

2.   There should be as few exempt categories to copayments as possible, either for patients or for treatments;

3.   No patient should face copayments which are potentially bankrupting.[51]

---

[51]   This does not mean that patients belonging to different risk categories should make the same copayment contributions. The requirement that higher health care expenditure of sick people is subsidised by society has been introduced in the funding structure of the Prototype. Here we are concerned with efficient consumption levels of health care services, which we seek to establish through copayments. This means that sick people will have higher copayment bills than healthy people.

Building on the objectives of copayments, and taking account of the constraints on copayments, the following recommendation for the prototypical health care system spells out the desirable structure of copayments.

Recommendation 13: Copayments for health care services included in the GHCP should be made mandatory for each insurance plan offered by each insurance fund. Furthermore, copayments should:

    A.   in principle, apply to all patients and all treatments;

    B.   use a comparable basis for different health care services as the basis for their calculation;

    C.   be calculated as a percentage point of health care expenditures; and,

    D.   apply only up to an income-related upper limit (beyond which copayments are equal to the upper limit).

The reasoning behind the first part of Recommendation 13, i.e. that copayment should be made mandatory for GHCP services, is as follows. Suppose an insurance fund is allowed to offer consumers a choice of two insurance options for a particular service within the GHCP. One option includes a copayment and commands a lower premium, while the other option excludes a copayment, but commands a higher premium. In those circumstances, patients would assess their individual risk in deciding whether they would purchase the first or the second option. It is likely that low risk individuals would opt for copayments, thereby raising the premiums for high risk individuals, i.e. those who expect to consume the service and hence do not wish, or cannot afford, to opt for copayments. As a result, the service would be primarily funded by those who need it, and not (or only marginally) by those who expect not to consume it. This means that the service has effectively dropped out of the GHCP. Because of the contradiction, copayments for services within the GHCP cannot be made optional.[52] They should therefore be made

---

[52]   The argument is partially based on Rothschild and Stiglitz (1976).

mandatory.[53] This provision therefore takes account of the first constraint, namely that there should be no premium differentiation that is only due to copayments.

The reasoning behind the second part of Recommendation 13 is as follows:

A.   In principle, copayments should apply to all patients and all treatments (there may be specially defined exemptions). Excluding some patients may lead to a gradual increase in the number of people who qualify (or try to qualify) for exempt status, such that ultimately few if any patients are obliged to copay. Excluding treatments from the copayment scheme may lead to the substitution of some treatments or providers by others, namely those which do not command copayments. This may be both undesirable and inefficient.[54] Recommendation 13A therefore takes account of the second constraint.

B.   Copayments should be calculated by taking the expenditures for health care services as the basis. This requires prices for health care services to be of similar magnitude. Otherwise a single 'large' copayment, say a 1 percent copayment on the price of a major surgery treatment, would immediately push the *sum* of copayments above that upper limit, which is required to protect patients from bankruptcy.

In most cases finding a common currency does not constitute a problem. Thus, the basis for the calculation of a copayment for primary care services should be the price per GP consultation; for a prescription, it should be the price of the medicine;[55] while for

---

[53]   Making copayments mandatory for a range of services within the GHCP is one method of effectively banning insurance against copayments. This is because, an insurance fund who offers insurance against copayments (for a higher premium) offers a different type of insurance plan covering the GHCP, namely one that does not include copayments. This is a contradiction to the regulation that makes copayments mandatory for some services in every insurance plan covering the GHCP.

[54]   For example, imposing copayments on visits to general practitioners, but not on visits to hospital outpatient departments, can be expected to lead to an increase in the number of outpatient visits at the expense of GP visits. This may not be cost-effective, if the costs of treatment with the GP are lower than the costs of treatment in a hospital.

[55]   If multiple prescriptions of medicines command different copayments, then additional instructions may be needed. For example, if medicines are covered by proportional copayments up to a maximum level, but additional prescriptions command lower copayments, then additional instructions are required to specify which copayment applies to which medicine (first).

hospital inpatient care, it might be a *per diem* rate, rather than the price of the treatment.

Note that finding a common currency for copayments for different health care services means that no exemption categories for treatments have to be defined.

C.   The total copayments for each patient should be calculated as a percentage point which is applied to the price of each health care service.[56] Alternatively, copayments for different health care services may be calculated by using different percentage points.

D.   Un upper annual limit on the sum of copayments per year should be set to avoid that high risk patients have unlimited, and potentially bankrupting, obligations to pay for health care (e.g. those who are chronically sick). The upper annual limit should be dependent upon the income of insurance fund members, such that high income people pay more copayment than low income people (for the same consumption levels).

Insurance fund members will be categorised according to income bands by the central fund, which collects the income-related fee. The central fund then informs the insurance fund about the upper limit of copayments which apply to each insurance fund member. The reimbursement of providers then occurs in either of two ways:

1.   the provider invoices patients directly. Patient claim back from their insurance funds any copayments which exceeds their upper annual limit.

2.   The insurance fund initially funds the entire costs of the provider, and then invoices the patient for the copayment up to the upper annual limit.

---

[56]   An alternative method would be to set different copayment percentage points, whereby the percentage points would vary with patients' incomes. The reasoning behind this method is that high income people may not reduce their consumption levels of health care services to the same extent as low income patients do, since their welfare is affected to a different degree. Under this method, patients would not have to disclose their income to their insurance fund. Rather, patients would be categorised according to *income bands* by the central fund, which collects the income-related fee. The central fund would then inform the insurance fund of the percentage point which applies for the insurance fund member.

In mathematical terms, the copayment structure suggested is as follows:

---

if $0 \leq \Sigma_i\, p_i \leq M(y)$,   then $c = \alpha\, [\Sigma_i\, p_i]$;

if $M(y) < \Sigma_i\, p_i$,   then $c = \alpha\, [M(y)]$;

where:

α = copayment percentage point, $0 < \alpha \leq 1$;

p_i = price of health care service i;

$\Sigma_i\, p_i$ = sum of health care prices per annum per patient;

y = annual income of patient;

$M(y)$ = upper per annum limit of *sum* of health care prices (dependent on annual income y of patient), at which further copayments cease to apply;

c = total copayments per annum.

For services which do not fall into the GHCP, there are less restrictions on the structure of copayments. This is spelt out in Recommendation 14.

<u>Recommendation 14</u>: *For services not included in the GHCP, or for supplementary benefits of services included in the GHCP, insurance funds are allowed to offer insurance plans that include optional cost-sharing arrangements.*

The argument outlined in the first part of Recommendation 13 does not apply to services that are not included in the GHCP. Hence optional copayments may be introduced on services outside the GHCP.[57] Furthermore, where the cost-per-case of a treatment is well known in advance, the copayment could equal the excess of the medical bill, quoted to the patient, over that price. The differential would tend to cover such things as the cost of supplementary amenities which patients have consumed during their in-patient stay.

---

[57]   The general conclusion of the economics literature on cost-sharing is that consumers are moderately sensitive to cost-sharing provisions and that cost-sharing does offer a useful tool in constraining utilization. As a rough rule of thumb, a ten percent increase in the price of medical care leads to a two percent decrease in utilization. Cost sharing also reduces health care expenses by reducing the number of provider contacts; that is, compared to free care, people cut back on the number of visits to the doctor or the number of admissions to the hospital when faced with a significant copayment (25 percent).

Finally, insurance funds may wish to introduce finely tuned penalties for those patients who have opted for copayments for supplementary services, but who, in the event of actual treatment, default. An efficient solution would entail that insurance funds provide coverage for the services specified in the insurance plan, regardless of whether patients fulfil their cost-sharing obligations or not. Consumers would therefore have a guarantee of receiving the health care benefits they have opted for. However, in the event of a patient defaulting, the insurance fund would have the right to place the insuree into another plan; namely one that commands fewer copayment options (or none), but higher premiums. In addition, regulation would be needed to ensure that defaulters could not switch to a different fund. If it is known to consumers that the insurance fund is entitled to such action, they will chose their individual insurance plan with care. Outcomes such as these are described in the economic literature as 'reputational equilibria'.[58]

The next recommendation deals with the establishment of patients' organisations.

Recommendation 15: Consumers of health care should be encouraged to establish private consumer organisations to monitor the developments in the health care system.

Consumers, that is patients, should be encouraged to set up private organisations which would closely monitor insurance funds. In particular, they would note cases where insurance funds appear to attempt to risk select despite the safeguards included in the health care system, or engage in any other unethical practices. The organisation may wish to scrutinise the risk characteristics which insurance funds use to assess individuals' risks, or which form the basis of the lower and upper copayment limit. The organisation should be private, but might wish to collaborate with the audit agency set up by the government.[59]

Consumer organisations could also issue moral guidelines or ethical codes relating to issues such as quality of services contracted for by insurance funds, procedures for handling complaints, access for people with disabilities etc.

---

[58]   See, for example Barro and Gordon (1983) or Kreps and Wilson (1982).

[59]   Regulation could be in place which would oblige insurance funds to disclose their rates for standardised risk categories. The consumer organisation, together with the audit agency of the government, could then examine these on a regular basis.

Furthermore, they would give ample publicity to any situation that may arise which is a violation of the ethical code. As a result, an insurance fund that operates in such way may acquire a bad reputation, which might result in a loss of individuals willing to become insured with that fund. Similarly, a provider that violates the code may loose contracts and thus income.[60]

Chart 3.7 presents again in graphical form the latest updated version of the Prototype; it now contains a description of the roles of the funding side, the provider side, the government and patients.

3.5.7   The Role of Innovation and Technology

3.5.7.1   The Reward for Innovative Products

Medical technology has made a huge contribution to improving the quality of life for large sections of the modern world.[61] This has been achieved through continuous and painstaking research and development. The NERA Prototype uses competitive markets to promote efficiency, but must also encourage this research effort to continue, in order to support innovation for the future. In this section we are therefore concerned with the dynamic, rather than the static, properties of the Prototype.

Expenditure on Research and Development (R&D) is an investment. Money spent now is expected to produce real benefits in the future, in the form of new products for which consumers are willing to pay the market price (above the cost of production). Today's expenditure on R&D is therefore recouped in the revenues from tomorrow's products.

---

[60]   See van de Ven and van Vliet (1992), p. 30, 40.

[61]   Examples of technologies relevant to health care services which have been developed in the past, and are likely to proliferate further in the future are the following:

- Laser Technology;
- Neurosciences;
- Genetic Screening;
- Vaccines and Antibodies;
- Minimally Invasive Surgery;
- Medical Imaging;
- Transplants; and,
- Pharmaceuticals.

Also of importance are developments in telecommunications and increased use of computers. Source: Hoare (1992), p. 5.

Chart 3.7
The Role of Patients and Cost-Sharing

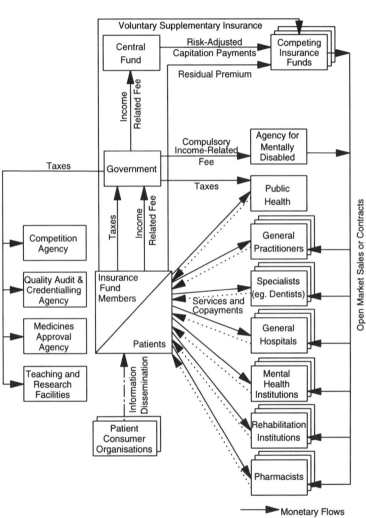

217

The ability of innovators to charge a market price is limited by the customers' valuation of the product, which may depend, for instance, on the cost of alternatives. However, innovators must not be prevented from charging a price equal to the customers' valuation by competition from cheap copies, nor by government regulations which restrict the price that can be charged.

If other manufacturers are allowed to profit from the innovation, the incentive to spend money on R&D will be diminished, and innovation will cease. This is the economic rationale for governments to allow patents for new products and processes, which provide the innovator with some protection against imitative competition (in the form of 'free-riding' on others research success).

The extent of the protection is limited: formally, it is only valid for a fixed number of years, so that others may eventually benefit from cheaper copies of the innovation, once the original innovator has had the opportunity to earn a return on the original R&D expenditure; moreover, the value of a patented product may be undermined by the discovery of close substitutes which can be sold more cheaply.

The competition from substitutes (during the period of patent protection) and copies (after the patent expires) makes it important that the innovator is allowed to charge a price they wish to set when the product is first launched. In the area of medical technology, some governments appear reluctant to accept this, claiming that medical innovations should have low prices, so as to be available to all. This policy of price control would discourage medical R&D, if it were not usually linked with equivalent policies to support the revenues of innovators in the later stages of a medical product's life. For example, governments, in the past, have discouraged competition from 'parallel imports', or resisted requests by competitors to licence the manufacture of copies (i.e. generics). As a result, the prices and revenues of medical products often follow the more stable 'regulated' path shown in Charts 3.8 and 3.9, in which R&D is paid for partly out of the additional revenues earned by old products.

3.5.7.2   Riskiness in R&D

The previous section described how manufacturers of medicines will be able to set prices for innovative products to provide a return on R&D expenditure. It is of course widely acknowledged that not all R&D expenditure results in a valuable product. R&D is risky, sometimes producing only products which have a limited advantage over existing ones, or no new products at all.

Chart 3.8
Rewarding Innovation: Alternative Paths for Price

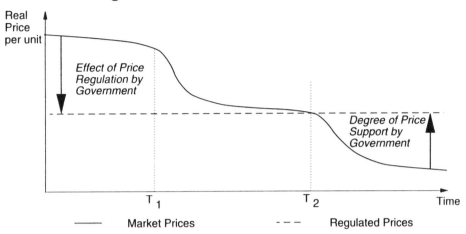

At Time T1 a competing product enters the market
At Time T2 the patent expires and generic products enter the market

Chart 3.9
Rewarding Innovation: Alternative Paths for Revenue

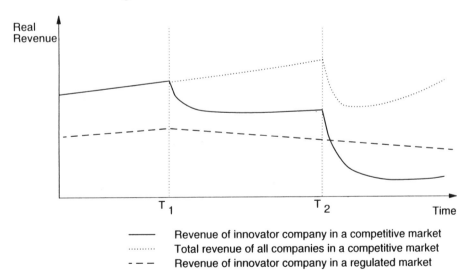

At Time T1 a competing product enters the market
At Time T2 the patent expires and generic products enter the market

The variability of returns applies to all R&D, not just R&D in the health care sector. Experience suggests that successes and failures balance out over time, so that the high profits earned on valuable new products cover the losses on fruitless R&D. A company that conducts a large portfolio of R&D projects can therefore usually expect to recoup the expenditure overall, taking one year with another.

However, some companies will be more successful than others. The successful companies will earn higher returns and may grow; the less successful companies may shrink. This is the expected outcome of competition in R&D (although mere 'luck' plays a role), in that it rewards and encourages effective research.

3.5.7.3 Take-Up of Innovation

The process set out above depends on the willingness of consumers to pay market prices for innovative products. The NERA Prototype allows such innovations to be taken up, even though patients purchase much of their health care through insurance companies where governments may no longer be able to offer price support in the market for pharmaceuticals and other medical technologies.

Innovations in medical technology may provide additional benefits for consumers and/or may reduce the cost of treatment, compared with alternatives. Each of these groups of products will find a market under the NERA Prototype, provided that information about the products is widely available.

Products which provide **additional benefits to patients** will be taken up as long as patients value the benefits more highly than the cost of the product. In such cases, they will either pay for the product directly, or search around for insurance plans which offer the product as part of the treatment plan, in return for a higher premium. The new product may be included within the GHCP, in which case the basic premium will rise, or the product may be offered as a separate service, in return for a supplementary premium. In both cases, it is essential that patients can effectively be made aware of the benefits of the new product.

Other products **reduce the cost of treatment**. In such cases, it will normally be the insurance companies that take the lead in encouraging their adoption, so that they can reduce their premiums. A major exception might arise in the case of products whose effects on costs is only long-term, e.g. the use of medicines to reduce the probability of developing a condition in later life. An insurance fund might avoid spending money on preventive care, in the hope that the patient will have switched to another insurance fund, when costs of curative treatment arise. However, patients could prevent this from happening, by paying more for insurance plans which offered long-term health care, provided only that they were aware of the options, and of the long-term consequences of omitting preventive care. Furthermore, consumer organisations are likely to point out to their members the advantages of long-term care plans.

Realistically, very few patients have sufficient access to medical research to be able to compare insurance plans in this manner. Insurers themselves make great efforts to convince potential customers that they have their long-term interests at heart, but patients may find such claims difficult to assess. To ensure that patients press for the take-up of innovations which offer immediate patient benefits, or long-term cost-savings, it may be necessary to provide, or encourage, alternative sources of information.

One possibility is for patients to apply to a second, independent doctor for advice on the appropriate insurance plan, or form of treatment. Nothing in the Prototype prevents a patient paying for a second opinion in this manner. However, general information on medical technology has some 'public good' characteristics, which means that it may be more efficient to set up a single information source which advises all patients, instead of requiring each individual to seek out information separately.

In order for the health care system to rapidly introduce innovative new technologies and beneficial new treatments, it is essential that the manufacturers of medical technology and therapies, including medicines, have access to all information channels to promote their products and services to insurers, providers and consumers (subject to ethical guidelines); and that these products and services have unrestricted entry to the market, subject to an approval process based only on requirements for safety and efficacy.

This completes our description of the prototypical health care system. Chart 3.10 presents the complete version of the Prototype, which includes funders, providers, the government, patients and the manufacturers of medical technology and medicines.

Chart 3.10
The Flow of Information

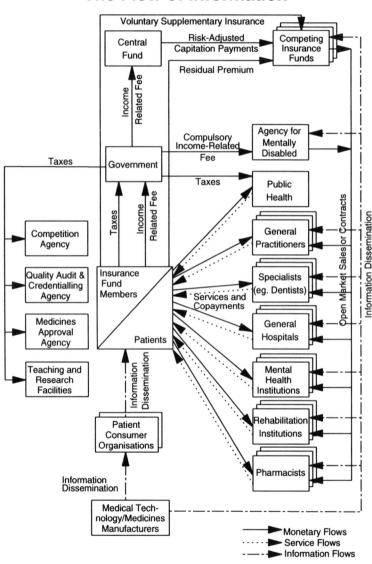

3.6   PATH DEPENDENCY AND CONVERGENCE

"The innovator makes enemies of all those who prospered under the old order, and only lukewarm support is forthcoming from those who would prosper under the new. Their support is lukewarm ... because men are generally incredulous, never trusting new things unless they have tested them by experience."

Machiavelli: The Prince

It would be naive, and wrong, to propose that the same health care system simply be adopted by each country. History cannot be ignored when considering reform paths for specific countries. This goes beyond the obvious difficulties of convincing a political system to override vested interests. Not all the recommendations outlined above will be politically acceptable in some countries in the long run, if ever. Nevertheless, the recommendations with respect to a prototypical health care system are useful because they set a standard against which existing systems and reform proposals can be evaluated.

This suggests that the 'rules' that are most appropriate for the health care sector in one country may not be the best set of rules for another country. In part, this flows from differences in the degree of social solidarity. For instance, some nations may prefer to provide uniform care to all up to a high standard, whether or not individual citizens would benefit from having greater choice.

Another reason for different 'rules' in different countries is that patients and providers may have substantially different responses to the same type of economic incentives, such as copayments or fee-for-service reimbursements. A further important factor is the size and internal diversity of the 'nation' being considered. Finally, history also helps to explain the specific set of rules being used in a given country and may well affect the choice of reform likely to be most appropriate.

Economists recognise the concept of 'path dependency', i.e. that the most efficient course of action for institutions with identical goals will depend on the starting point, and the path by which the present situation has been reached. Thus, for example, a company whose reputation for innovation and financial strength is high, may rationally choose a different business strategy from a competitor seeking the same goals in the same industry but plagued by perceptions that it is vulnerable to takeover or bankruptcy. The underlying economics is the same in the two cases; but the short and medium term priorities may well be quite different.

This insight is extremely important in understanding the economics of health care reform. Many proposed elements of the Prototype are based on ideas supported more by economic theory than by experience and fact. In some cases, this may simply be because a particular 'good idea' has never been tried. But as the studies of the twelve countries on which our research is focused demonstrate, there are great differences between the health care systems currently operating.

For example, the United States and Switzerland are the only health care systems in which the majority of health care is provided through competing private insurance companies. In the US there are also large numbers of people who are uninsured, or under-insured. But even the United States, as reflected in a wide variety of reform proposals, now seeks to increase access to those who cannot afford care. Most of these solutions require more collective activity, particularly on the financing side.[62]

There are notable signs of convergence. This includes the widespread agreement in the US, for example, that to seek to strengthen the solidarity aspect in the US health care system is paramount. The result is that all of the reform plans currently under discussion involve some movement in the direction of European-type systems. All serious reform proposals seek to improve the equity of the system by extending health care coverage to more or all citizens.

Some would seek to improve equity by extending further the role of *Medicare* and *Medicaid*, which are supported by taxation. Other proposals would increase the extent to which private insurance companies and health organisations are regulated, requiring them to accept poor risks at subsidised rates or compensating them for doing so through a central re-financing arrangement.

---

[62]   See, for example Fuchs (1991), Taylor and Reinhardt (1991) and Reinhardt (1991).

Outside the US, several countries studied are considering ways of increasing the extent to which their systems are open to competitive forces. In some, notably the UK, the emphasis is on establishing an 'internal market' in which health care providers compete for work from various purchasers predominantly financed from taxation or national insurance contributions. In others, of which the Netherlands is the prime example, attention is also being given to encouraging competition between privately owned but effectively regulated insurance funds for the assignment of financing part of the GHCP. Germany is considering increasing the scope of competition among sickness funds as a possible reform option. In all countries apart from the US, we note that the role of supplemental insurance and health care (i.e. health care purchased by private decision-takers, to add to or improve on the GHCP provided or regulated by the government) is increasing, and likely to continue to do so.

Political conflict over redistribution can also be expected. It is often pointed out that a dollar of spending is someone else's dollar of revenue. Beyond the institutional adjustment costs, there are groups that will win and groups that will lose out under any reform. Thus, redistribution will create vested interests as those who may be asked to increase their contributions may resist, and those now receiving the subsidies may be asked to accept restrictions.

ANNEX 3.1 ON SOCIAL SOLIDARITY[63]

3.1.1 Utilitarianism and Efficiency

The concept on which much of economic analysis is based is 'utility'. Utility intends to measure, by way of an ordinal comparison, different states of an individual's well being with a view of arriving at a conclusion as to which of several states is the most preferable. By comparing the benefits associated with utility of a given state to the costs of that state, economic theory arrives at conclusions regarding the allocative efficiency of that state.

Definitions of utility range form "happiness" and "pleasure, absence of pain" to "a person's conception of his or her well being". Note that according to the latter definition it does not matter if the conception which the person has is 'wrong' by some other standard (e.g. a preference for an unhealthy diet). Rather, utilitarianism assumes that the satisfaction of desires has its value irrespective of moral relations between persons of a joint undertaking.

Welfarism is a related concept to utilitarianism. Welfarism usually is defined as the "sum of individual utilities" which is meant to be a measure of social welfare. Alternative social states can then be ordered in terms of the value of the sum of individual utilities. One of the problems that welfarism poses is the aggregation of individual utilities as a means to determine the social welfare. This is problematic if it involves the pair-wise comparison of alternatives, which may lead to no overall majority for any of them.

However, in general utilitarianism stands for the maximisation of utility of society by adding the utility levels of individuals. If society can choose from various different states of nature, then it is best off by choosing that state which maximises its utility (as the sum of individual utilities in that state).

3.1.2 Critique of Utilitarianism

Utilitarianism can be criticized on several grounds. The most prominent critical comments made are summarised below:

---

[63] This annex is based on Mill (1863), Rawls (1958), Rawls (1971), Sen (1970), Sen (1973), Sen (1975), Sen (1977), Sen (1979), Sen (1980) and Sen and Williams (1982).

3.1.2.1 Utilitarianism Leads to Inequality

Utilitarianism can advocate extremely radical redistributions. Generally it favours a redistribution of benefits (say of income, wealth or any other good, such as health) to those members of society who have the capacity of benefiting most from the redistribution. This may result in a shifting of benefits to those who may already be in the possession of a larger share of the overall benefits. It therefore can lead to an extremely unequal distribution of benefits. In the case of health care, for example, it may mean that additional health care should be provided to those who have a higher capacity to benefit from the additional resources made available, irrespective of the health status they enjoy (which may already be appreciably higher than that of other citizens).

3.1.2.2 Utilitarianism Violates Fundamental Values

Justice: Utilitarianism permits to argue in favour of slavery, if it can be shown that the advantages of slave-holders outweigh the disadvantage of slaves so that overall utility is maximised in the state of slavery. The example shows that utilitarianism cannot rule out such outcomes.

Integrity: Some argue that in the example given above, the fact that slave-holders' utilities are considered in the first place, and that there is no mechanism to rule out some states on ground of some ethical consideration, violates the value of integrity.

Liberty: It can also be shown that the application of utilitarianism violates the value of liberty. In particular, it can be shown that the value of liberalism ("nobody should be forced to do things they do not want to do", and "everybody should be permitted to do things they want to do") may be incompatible with utilitarianism.

Fairness: Utilitarianism also is not concerned with the value of fairness. Fairness is defined as a practice such that if nobody feels that, by participating in it, they or any of the others are taken advantage of, or forced to give in to claims which they do not regard as legitimate.

3.1.3 Alternative Concepts

Because of the obvious disadvantages of utilitarianism as a basis for choice where ethical considerations play a role, other concepts have been developed. Many of these concepts broadly fall into the category of social solidarity, in that they take account of values other than efficiency (in the form of utility maximisation).

3.1.3.1 *The Social Contract*

The best known alternative to the utilitarian approach is that of a social contract. Under a social contract, rational individuals decide among themselves about the conception of justice at a point when nobody knows his or her position in society, nor his or her place in the distribution of natural talents and abilities. A recent exponent of this approach has been John Rawls. In a Rawlsian system, for example, it can be shown that some positions in society, such as that of slave-holders, would not be considered as an option for choice.

In a Rawlsian world, justice becomes an important concept as a counterweight to utilitarianism. Justice is defined as a state where the following two principles hold:

- Each person participating in it or affected by it has an equal right to the most extensive liberty compatible with a like liberty for all; and,

- Inequalities are arbitrary, unless it is reasonable to expect that they will work out for everyone's advantage and provided the position and offices to which they attach, or from which they may be gained, are open to all.

From there, Rawls goes on to show that a state of affairs is just (in the sense of not violating the two principles of justice) if social and economic inequalities are to be arranged so that they are both (a) to the greatest benefit of the least advantaged and (b) attached to positions and offices open to all under conditions of fair equality of opportunity.

3.1.3.2 *Sympathy and Commitment*

Another form of introducing the notion of social solidarity into utilitarian theory is to point to concepts such as sympathy and commitment which may, so to speak, be included as explanatory variables in the utility function of an individual.

In this context sympathy concerns a direct interest in the utility of others. In other words, sympathetic action (e.g. a mandatory insurance scheme based on income-related fees) improves one's own welfare. In economic theory this is the case of an externality.

Commitment on the other hand can be defined as a concern for others that does not affect one's own welfare. Nevertheless, one is ready to do something to stop it, since otherwise one's sense of justice would be violated. In this approach, the individual chooses a lower level of personal welfare in return for the establishment of some fundamental value.

While it may be difficult to differentiate between sympathy and commitment, in general sympathy makes claims for groups to which the individual is closely connected (e.g. family, friends, communities, peer groups, social classes, or firms), while commitment makes claims for larger (and possibly anonymous) groups. Both therefore reflect varying degrees of social solidarity, and both are in contrast to orthodox utilitarianism, based solely on self-interest.

ANNEX 3.2 ON THE DEFINITION OF THE GHCP[64]

3.2.1 Introduction

There are a number of different approaches that can be taken to arrive at a definition of a Guaranteed Health Care Package (GHCP). The central problem is how to prioritise services so that a decision can be made whether a particular service should be included in the GHCP or not, and the related question who should make the decision. This Annex describes how the approaches work, and assesses their advantages and disadvantages.

3.2.2 Bottom up

3.2.2.1 Description

The 'bottom-up' approach attempts to draw up a list of treatments to be covered by the GHCP, by identifying those treatments which should be excluded from the GHCP. In practice this approach will often end up identifying the circumstances in which a treatment should or should not be included, rather than ruling out broad classes of treatment.

3.2.2.2 Assessment

In countries that have an extensive GHCP it may be more sensible to focus on what should not be included rather than what should. While this should lead to the same outcome as the 'top down' approach (it should not matter whether you begin by including or excluding everything), there are claimed advantages for the 'bottom up' approach.

First, it is possible to do an amount of bottom up rationing on the basis of only a few studies, and then exclude the services which emerge as marginal. It can be argued that the loss of efficiency caused by not analysing all the available treatments is small, as doctors have a fair idea of what is and is not effective even before the formal analysis begins. In a system where rationing is not a major issue, the expense of large-scale exploration of the costs and benefits of treatments may not be justified.

---

[64] This annex is based on Bridgeport Group (1992), Culyer and Wagstaff (1992), Health Service Commission (HSC) (1992), Honigsbaum (1992), Government Committee on Choices in Health Care (1992), Kind, Rosser and Williams (1982), Minister of Health, New Zealand (1991) and Williams (1985).

Bottom up rationing has also differed in the traditional way that it has been applied. Bottom up analysis has traditionally taken a more desegregated view than other approaches (see below), which is possible as there are fewer alternatives to examine. An example would be excluding classes of patients from certain treatments, rather than removing the treatment 'en bloc'.

3.2.3 Use of QALYs

3.2.3.1 Description

The use of *Quality Adjusted Life Years* (QALYs) is an attempt to derive a single measure which considers both changes in the expected length of life and changes in the quality of life, in order to compare the effectiveness of actions which result in different bundles of improvement in life expectancy and quality.

To adjust life years for quality involves valuing years according to the quality of well-being experienced in those years. To assess this we compare the value of a year of life of a particular quality (e.g. expressed as 'bedridden but able to perform basic self-care'), with two bench-marks: a year of life in good health, and death. By allocating death a value of zero and unimpaired health a value of one, comparisons can be used to give a quality of well being value to other states of health, such as partial disablement, discomfort, or the need for regular medication. These values are being used to build up a quality index. Most health states will be expected to be allocated values between zero and one, with poor quality of life scoring low values, and states with only minor impairments being allocated values close to one. It should be noted that studies have shown that large numbers of people allocate certain states (for example permanent coma) a value of less than zero - these states are perceived to be worse than death.

Once a set of values for various qualities of life has been established, different medical procedures can be compared by looking at the change in the patient's expected number of QALYs which results. For example a cancer therapy which increases life expectancy from one year to two, but which cuts the quality of life from 0.7 to 0.4 due to serious side effects would be preferable to no treatment, as:

QALYs with no treatment = 1 year x 0.7 (quality of life) = 0.7
QALYs with treatment = 2 years x 0.4 (quality of life) = 0.8

However, if it were possible to effect symptomatic relief (increasing the quality of life to close to 1), this might be preferable, even if life expectancy were unchanged:

QALYs with symptoms relieved = 1 year x 1 (quality of life) = 1

This assertion is, to some, controversial. In particular, medical personnel often hold strongly to the idea that their job is to preserve life. However, the use of QALYs asserts that the function of medicine is also to reduce suffering. These two objectives are traded-off already by physicians when choosing treatments for terminal care.

QALYs can also be used for decisions on the allocation of funding between treatments for different patients. Given information on the likely changes in the length and quality of life which results from a treatment, the treatment's cost, and a scale which rates the quality of the resulting life, we can calculate the cost per QALY for each proposed treatment. An example of assessed cost per QALY is as follows:

Treatment	*Cost per QALY gained in 1985 £*
Pacemaker implant for atrioventricular heart block	*700*
Hip replacement	*750*
Kidney transplantation	*3,000*
Hospital haemodialysis	*14,000*

3.2.3.2 Assessment

- The use of QALYs in allocating funds may result in people dying, while money is spent on minor complaints (e.g. haemodialysis versus hip replacement, above). However, everyday choices in health care result in such outcomes already.

- To be practicable, the QALY approach is applied to large categories of treatment. This neglects the fact that the benefits of the same treatment differ vastly between cases - in some cases a kidney transplant may be more cost-effective than some hip replacements. Calculating QALYs gained for classes of treatment ignores this diversity.

• The derivation of the value of years of imperfect health is dubious; it is normally based on various types of hypothetical choices. Responses to this type of question may not reflect true preferences, as most people have no relevant experience.

• The use of a single value may not be appropriate. The cost in terms of quality of life of a minor disability will be much higher to an athlete than to someone else.

• The use of QALYs requires that we know the costs and results of a treatment, and the results of not treating. Data, especially on the effects of not treating, can be very hard to find. To use QALYs properly, however, requires that this information is available for all the treatments being considered.

• The application of QALYs is politically explosive. QALY analysis tends to give treatments such as transplant surgery and intensive care for very premature babies low priority (they are expensive and often not effective). This may seem to be publicly unacceptable.

3.2.4   The Oregon Approach

3.2.4.1 Description

In May 1991 the Oregon Health Services Commission (HSC) produced a report 'Prioritisation of Health Services' which has attracted global attention as an attempt to systematically address the issue of rationing health care. The report was the result of an eighteen month process of analysis, public consultation and political debate. It listed over 700 services in order of priority. The state Legislature subsequently announced that their Medicaid programme (state-funded medicine for the poor) would cover services only as far as number 587 on this list. Other services would not be offered, and Medicaid recipients will have to buy them privately, or do without.

The Oregon scheme assesses treatments as follows. Procedures were assigned to one of seventeen categories according to the effectiveness of treatment, whether the condition was acute or chronic, and the consequences of failure to treat. The categories, together with types of preventative care, were then ranked in order of priority: ranging from the treatment of acute fatal conditions, where treatment resulted in complete recovery (Rank 1) through to the treatment of fatal and non-fatal conditions, where treatment resulted in minimal or no improvement in the quality of life (Rank 17).

The criteria used in ranking these categories were derived from a series of open public consultations, but administered by the Commission alone. The treatments within each category were then ranked within their categories, according to a cost-benefit analysis.

Numerous panels of physicians and other providers reviewed the work, and suggested a large number of changes to the overall list. Many items from lower ranked categories were promoted, and some treatments from the highest ranked categories were moved towards the bottom of the list. The Commission also applied a test of 'reasonableness' to the list, resulting in further adjustments, primarily on the basis of ease of prevention and treatment.

The result of this process was a list which the Commission completed in February 1991. It was accepted in principle by the Legislature, which calculated that its available Medicaid funds could cover the first 587 items. The items which Oregon will not fund include life support for very premature babies, medical treatment for end-stage HIV disease and AIDS, some transplants, and in-vitro fertilisation. Some common medical procedures such as medical therapy for bronchitis, and haemorrhoidectomy are also not covered.

3.2.4.2 Assessment

The Oregon proposal is an example of the usefulness and drawbacks of discretion in fund allocation. In the absence of good quality quantifiable information on the costs and benefits of treatments, doctors were able to modify priorities based on their compassion, concern, and experience. However, this discretion also allowed anomalies to creep in. Looking at the costs and benefits of transplant surgery shows that it is less effective at improving quality of life than more mundane treatments: however, transplants are often popular or even glamorous. This area poses questions which are difficult to face. Oregon's rationing procedure is less open and accountable as a result.

The authors of the Oregon proposal intended to canvass public opinion as far as possible in order to provide an open and fair system of rationing. However, a large proportion of those attending the public meetings were themselves health care workers, and statements from the general public and from Medicaid recipients were too poorly informed to do more than reflect 'the general tone of public needs and concern'. The practicability of Oregon-style rationing has also been questioned: two puzzles being how doctors are to interpret the groups into which therapies are divided (when does medical treatment of AIDS become end-stage, and thus no longer funded?), and how will doctors respond to co-morbidities (when a patient is admitted suffering from more than one complaint) if only one ailment is covered? This places some onerous decisions in the hands of doctors.

ANNEX 3.3 ON THE NATURE OF HEALTH CARE INSURANCE

3.3.1 Introduction

Insurance serves an important economic function. Uncertain events, such as fires and heart attacks, often lead to significant financial losses. Without insurance, people would be forced to save large amounts of money in advance of what is, by definition, an unpredictable event. This would lead to inefficient patterns of savings in the sense that total savings would exceed the total amount needed to cover the aggregate cost of the risks which actually emerge. Moreover, people who suffered a serious loss of health would be forced to give up many important goods and services at the time of their health loss in order to shift the money from these purchases to the purchase of health care. Thus, the financial burden of the health loss could not be smoothed out without health insurance.

3.3.2 Asymmetric Information

Another reason for the special nature of health care insurance is related to the fundamental information problems which exist in health care. These include:

3.3.2.1 The Insurer Does Not Know Potentially How Sick A Subscriber Might Be.

The patient knows more about his or her potential for illness and may be able to hide this information from the insurer. Thus, the insuree can choose a low premium insurer knowing that his or her claims with be higher than his or her contributions to the fund. This problem is called adverse selection, which is one type of inefficiency found mostly in private insurance markets where consumers have choice.

3.3.2.2 Insurers Do Not Know How Sick A Patient Is.

Diagnosis is not always easy or precise. A severe headache may have stress and tension as its source or it may derive from a brain tumour. An insurer cannot pay an lump-sum indemnity for a diagnosis called 'headache' until a final diagnosis is made, which may be long after treatment has begun.

*3.3.2.3 Physicians, Insurers And Patients Do Not Know The Production Process
For Restoring Health.*

This means that the insurer cannot pay until someone states how big the loss
is. Traditionally, this has been the physician or the hospital and the final
number is not known until *after the care has been provided*. This is called
retrospective reimbursement, which generally encourages inefficiency.

*3.3.2.4 Patients Have Only A Limited Ability To Evaluate The Benefits Of Any
Given Provider Or Any Given Medical Procedure.*

This means that the patient does not always know what to buy or how much.
The main consequence on the delivery side is that the patient must establish
an agency relationship with a physician and, particularly for specialty care,
cannot efficiently 'shop' for medical care without such an 'agent'. Thus, much
of health care reform must confront the issue of proper incentives to the
physician as agent.

3.3.3 Risk Rating

Despite the informational problems outlined above, insurance funds are
typically able to estimate with reasonable accuracy what percent of people will
require health care in any given year, as long as the group of people is large
and the general demographics (e.g., age and gender) of the group are known.
Thus, most people are willing to pay a relatively small amount each year to
buy health insurance and avoid potentially very large financial losses should
they become seriously ill. Insurance allows individuals to transfer income
from their 'well' state (when the sacrifice in terms of reduced income is
relatively small) to their 'sick' state (when the income is especially needed).

In general, consumers of most types of insurance are charged insurance
premiums which reflect the risk that they present to the insurer. Thus, a home
with a sprinkler system and fire alarms will cost less to insure against fires
than one that does not have these features since the likely damage from a fire
is reduced. Using the risk category of the insuree to set the level of premium
is called risk-rating. In health care, while it would clearly be efficient for
insurers to charge premiums which reflect the risk of the individual, many
countries feel that it would be unfair to charge high risk individuals, such as
chronically ill people, the highest premiums when they are the ones who can
least afford large premiums. As a result, some countries choose to pool all
citizens and, in effect, charge everyone the same price for insurance coverage
to avoid the perceived inequities which can result from risk-rating. This

approach is called community rating since individuals pay the expected average loss based on the characteristics of the community as a whole, not their individual characteristics. Thus, one reason the role of insurance in health care differs from its role in other markets is reflected in the desire of many policy makers to supplant an efficient form of insurance based on risk-rating with a more equitable form, community rating.

3.3.4 Benefits

Health insurance, whether publicly or privately funded, is also different from other forms of insurance in terms of how the benefits are delivered to people who suffer a loss. In the case of fire insurance, a claim is made on the insurer following a loss due to fire. An insurance adjustor inspects the site of the fire, confirms the loss and estimates what the costs of repair will be. The adjustor then usually issues a cheque to the home owner in the form of a lump-sum payment called an indemnity. The home owner can then put that money to the highest use according to his or her preferences. In many cases, the money is used to rebuild the same basic house that was lost in the fire but a smaller home could be chosen if, for instance, the home owner's children have recently left home. If so, the remaining money is then available for the purchase of other goods and services which yield greater value than the benefits that would be derived from rebuilding the same 'large' house. The lump sum is efficient from the consumer's point of view because this insurance reimbursement methodology allows the consumer to buy the mix of goods and services which most closely fits his or her tastes.

In contrast, health insurance benefits, whether provided publicly or privately, are provided to consumers as a lowering of the price at the point of service. That is, rather than a lump-sum indemnity to help cover the costs of restoring someone's health, the insurance usually provides for free care (or relatively small copayments) for the patient when he or she receives the care. The zero or near-zero price may encourage excess consumption of health care. Rather than being given a lump-sum of money to help finance the care in a time of need and facing the full price of the care when deciding where to buy the care and how much care to buy, the insurance benefit signals to the patient that the care is (nearly) free compared to every other good or service.

ANNEX 3.4 ON REIMBURSEMENT METHODS FOR HEALTH CARE SERVICES[65]

3.4.1 Primary Care Physicians

3.4.1.1 Fee-for-Service

With a fee-for-service schedule a price is set against each service that is available from a provider, that is, there is a tariff list. Fee-for-service schedules can be set by providers (as in the US), they can be set by payers (as in the Netherlands) or they can be negotiated between payers and providers at varying levels of centralisation (as in Germany or Japan). Since the treatment provided to any particular patient usually involves a varying bundle of services, the approach leaves open the question of volume and thus the overall level of funding. With this form of remuneration there is an incentive to expand volume, so supplier-induced demand becomes a problem.

Under fee-for-service payment, the provider has a financial incentive to over-provide. And the patient is likely to be content with this if he/she pays nothing at the point of delivery. As a perfect agent for the patient, the physician would provide all care which had any expected positive benefit to the patient. As a profit maximiser, the physician may go further, he/she may provide all care that does not obviously have an expected negative benefit, subject to resource constraints and given that the fee contains a margin for the doctor.

Fee-for-service is popular with the provider because it gives him/her a degree of control over income. But, of course, it creates a financing and resource problem: there will be an excessive utilization of high-cost, low-benefit care.

In most circumstances, this is an inappropriate method of payment: the physician is a self-interested individual, and there is an incentive for him/her to provide too much care; it involves no structural constraints which force either the patient or the provider to balance the costs and the benefits of the care. However, to the extent that society wishes to encourage the consumption of some types of preventive care (eg. an annual physical check for people over 40 or well-baby care), fee-for-service is an appropriate method for stimulating this.

---

[65]   This annex is based on Aaron (1991) and Ham, Robinson and Benzeval (1990).

3.4.1.2 *Simple Capitation*

In its simplest form, capitation gives the primary care physician a budget for performing the gate-keeper role for each patient on his/her books. For performing other services the physician may be remunerated on a cost-per-case basis, or in some other way. The size of the capitation payment may be set by the physician, or it may be laid down by the payer or the government. If the capitation fee depends on factors such as age, and sex, it will approximate more accurately to the likely cost of performing this role for the patient and this will reduce the opportunity for income maximisation by risk selection.

Capitation of this simplest sort is arguably the best way to pay a primary care physician for the gatekeeper role. However, it needs to be combined with freedom of access: freedom to consult another doctor at will. Then, whenever the patient feels the quality of service is in some way inadequate, he/she can try another doctor. Without this freedom of entry and exit, the doctor has an incentive to economise on the time spent with the patient.

3.4.1.3 *Capitated Risk Arrangements*

Under capitated risk arrangements, the physician is paid a fixed annual (or monthly) sum per patient on his/her list and expected to meet the bill for the patient's expenditures on health care out of this sum. This means that he/she will only provide care when it is clear to all that the benefit is equal to or greater than the cost. Thus, the physician becomes a double agent: he/she continues to be the agent for the patient by evaluating the patient's health care needs but is also an agent for the insurer for whom he/she evaluates the costs of care.

Since the physician is the best informed person in the system, it is appropriate that he/she should be the one to weigh the costs and benefits in this way. However, since the physician is concerned to continue in the role of agent to the insurance fund, he/she also has an incentive to provide less care than might be in the patient's best interests. There is an incentive to under-provide care under this capitation arrangement.

This incentive to under-provide is countered by four forces: medical ethics, medical training, the threat of malpractice law suits and the informed patients. However, there is nothing to prevent insurance funds and the doctors contracted to them from educating the patient and involving him/her in the medical care decision with a view to encouraging economy of health care.

240

3.4.1.4 Salary

There is little incentive to perform effectively with payment by salary. The physician has no financial incentive to act as the patient's agent. This means that the economic incentive is for the physician to follow his/her own labour-leisure tradeoff. Thus, most salary arrangements include performance incentives, because work effort and output must be monitored in order to make a salary arrangement work well.

An alternative arrangement is to give the physician a share of the profits earned by the organization for which he/she works. However, such an arrangement functions much like a risk-capitation since the physician shares in any savings made by keeping utilization down.

3.4.2 Hospital Care

3.4.2.1 Global Budgets

A global budget is a fixed sum which is paid to a provider during the course of a year. With it goes the obligation to meet demand within the fixed budget during the year.

A global budget can be set unilaterally by the payer (UK, Sweden), presumably taking account of representations from the provider concerning expected costs and expected volume. It can alternatively be negotiated between representatives of payers and providers at the national level (Netherlands), or regional or local level (Germany) or it could be negotiated by one individual payer (sick fund or voluntary private insurance fund) with each individual provider (HMOs in the US).

Global budgets do not fit easily into mixed competitive delivery systems where one hospital may be used by patients from different sick funds or from voluntary private insurance funds as it is not clear how much each payer should pay. A points system which allows fee-for-service charges to be derived which are consistent with the global budget can be used to solve this problem.

Global budgets give little incentive to achieve efficiency unless the budget level happens to be 'right', which is very difficult to achieve, and the obligation to supply (meet demand) has teeth. Even when the obligation to supply is effective, global budgets allow providers to relax quality standards rather than devote effort to cost control.

Global budgets are very effective tools for controlling expenditure. They create some incentive for productive efficiency, but can lead to quality reductions and a wrong mix of services (e.g. bed-blockers). However, with global budgets the question arises as to what happens if there is an overrun, or if there is a surplus, or if demand is not met and sub-optimal queuing results.

3.4.2.2 Cost-Per-Case

Cost-per-case involves estimating the likely bundle of services that will be required in treating any particular class of case, combining this with their costs (fee-for-service schedule) and arriving at a price for treating a case that will, on average, cover the cost. This payment is then made to the provider, regardless of the bundle of services which the physician finally uses in the treatment of any particular case. The services covered by a cost-per-case may include: hospital services chosen for the patient by the doctor, the doctor's own time, and follow-up care resulting from the same incident.

Thus the cost-per-case method encompasses responsibility for all care delivered during an episode of care (e.g. normal delivery or open heart operation with catheterization), including any readmission tied to the original admission. Whether the hospital or the physician should receive the payment would largely be determined in the market for sharing risk.

The main problem with such an approach is that it is currently difficult to define a 'case' or an 'episode'. Thus, it is difficult to set a fee prospectively. However, the cost could be determined retrospectively.

Cost-per-case payments involve a cross-subsidy. Within a single case group, some patients with a certain condition will require much more treatment than others, with correspondingly higher costs. The cost-per-case that the provider receives is, however, the same. These patients are being cross-subsidised by lower-cost individuals. This cross-subsidy gives providers an incentive to turn away patients who look likely to be more expensive than their fee. This would involve reluctance to treat the more serious and complicated cases within a classification.

With cost-per-case pricing the provider bears the case cost risk. As the fee for a treatment is set before the full cost of the individual treatments needed is known, the provider is bearing the risk that the patient will be more or less than averagely expensive. It is because the provider is the only person that can manage this risk that cost-per-case has desirable efficiency properties. However, there is always a residual unavoidable risk, and this can be considerable for conditions which are serious or complicated. This risk must be pooled. Providers who are being paid on a cost-per-case basis will combine to pool the risk.

Like many prospective pricing systems, this method of charging has good incentives for efficiency. It can be combined with a competitive, mixed funding and delivery structure; it does not lead to excess volume. However, it could lead to a reduction in quality: providers can manipulate the quantity, and more particularly the quality, of the care in ways which are not easy to observe, and very difficult to prove. It is important to strengthen the ways in which quality can be monitored. There is a danger that patients may get low-cost, low-value treatment. This issue is particularly serious when the patient dies (for terminal care, a provider makes more profit when the patient dies more quickly than expected - this is not an incentive we want to see in our hospitals).

3.4.2.3 Contracting

One way that risk can be off loaded is through contracting. In the UK system 'cost and volume' contracts offer a provider a guaranteed payment in return for an undertaking to treat a certain number of patients within specified treatment groups. Some risks are difficult to pool in this manner. Examples are specialised services which are required by purchasers only very rarely. The variance of their demand is therefore very high, and a cost and volume contract is not practicable.

3.4.2.4 Fee-for-Service

As in the case of primary care physicians, paying hospitals their fee-for-service list prices leads to "piecework" and encourages excess utilization.

3.4.2.5 Administered Prices

When there is no competition, perhaps because of geographical considerations, then it may be necessary for the government to set ceilings for prices.

However, administratively-set reimbursements should be avoided wherever competition among providers is workable, and prices should be set in a competitive market. This is because the incentives in a competitive market tend to produce a lower cost, better quality outcome. Administered prices, such as negotiated physician fees or DRG rates for hospitals, are unlikely to reflect resource costs and thus will not give the proper signals to participants in the market.

ANNEX 3.5 ON COMPETITION POLICY[66]

3.5.1 Competition Policy in the United States

3.5.1.1 Introduction

The USA has the longest and most active history of anti-trust activity. The main legal regulations determining US anti-trust policy are listed below:

- The Sherman Act (1890), which illegalised "restraint of trade", banned monopolies, and enabled anyone injured by anti-competitive behaviour to bring an action for damages.

- The Clayton Act (1914), which illegalised price discrimination and mergers which lessened competition.

- The Robinson-Patman Act (1936), which strengthened the provisions of the Clayton Act against price discrimination, in an attempt to protect small firms with less bargaining power than more powerful rivals.

The Federal Trade Commission (FTC), established by the Federal Trade Commission Act, is the main Federal antitrust executive. It shares responsibility for antitrust enforcement with the Department of Justice.

US anti-trust policy was not turned towards health care with any frequency until the mid to late 1970's. Possible reasons for this include the exemption of insurance industries from most anti-trust legislation (McCarran-Ferguson Act, 1945); a reluctance to regard learned professions as liable for anti-trust action; and the fact that the Federal Trade Commission in its founding legislation had no competence to act against non-profit organisations.

However, in the 1980's, health care was an area of intense anti-trust activity, in three main areas:

3.5.1.2 Codes of Practice

The American Medical Association had declared advertising and a number of contracting practices (eg one doctor undercutting others' prices) to be unethical. These regulations were declared illegal by the United States Supreme Court.

---

[66]   This annex is based on Lovell, White and Durrant (1988), Manches & Co (brochure), Office of Fair Trading (1973, 1976, 1980) and Schut, Greenberg and van de Ven (1991).

3.5.1.3 Boycotts

The early history of HMOs has a number of cases of physicians boycotting the participants in HMO schemes, by for example denying physicians participating in HMOs hospital privileges, or refusing them registration with insurers. These arrangements were successfully broken up by the FTC.

3.5.1.4 Hospital Mergers

Hospital mergers may be investigated on the grounds that they reduce competition for hospital services. Significant mergers have been blocked for this reason.

3.5.2 Competition Policy in the European Community

European Community competition law is defined by two articles in the treaty of Rome. The main features of these rules are:

- *Article 85:* Article 85 prohibits agreements between undertakings which have a significant detrimental effect on competition.

- *Article 86:* Article 86 prohibits the abuse of a dominant position.

In addition, a later regulation imposed by the Council of Ministers gives the Commission the power to block certain classes of merger which are judged to be likely to reduce competition (Regulation 4064/89, OJ, 1989, L395). This took effect on 31 September 1990.

The bulk of enforcement is done by the Commission, which also has the power to issue injunctions and impose significant fines (around $15 million in at least one case). The application of EC law is, in general, limited to activities which affect trade between member states, or where the activity involves participants in more than one state. "Activities affecting trade" has, in the past, been interpreted very widely: however, little interest has been shown by the Commission in health care, and this seems likely to continue for as long as member states retail the diversity of health care organisation which we see today.

3.5.3   Competition Policy in the United Kingdom

3.5.3.1 Institutions

The United Kingdom (UK) is the European state which has the most active history of competition policy. UK regulations have evolved over time, with a large number of pieces of legislation. The two main organisations in charge of competition policy are the Monopolies and Mergers Commission (MMC) and the Office of Fair Trading (OFT). The MMC can investigate public bodies as well as the effects of mergers and monopoly situations as in the previous section. In these activities the MMC is required to determine whether an arrangement or merger is 'against the public interest': UK competition policy has therefore evolved in a case-by-case manner. The OFT was set up in 1973, and acts as a 'watchdog'. It must be informed of certain classes of restrictive agreements between firms and of mergers.

There are three principal elements of the framework of competition policy in the UK:

- The Fair Trading Act, 1973 (the 1973 Act);
- the Restrictive Trade Practices Act, 1976 (the 1976 Act); and,
- the Competition Act, 1980 (the 1980 Act).

3.5.3.2 The 1973 Act

The 1973 Act empowers the MMC to investigate and report on matters referred to it by the Secretary of State or the Director General of Fair Trading (DGFT). Sections 6 to 8 of the Act contain powers to investigate monopoly situations, defined as a situation in which:

> *"at least a quarter of all [reference] goods which are supplied in the UK are supplied by one and the same person, or are supplied to one and the same person." [Section 6(1)(a)]";*

or in which:

> *"at least a quarter of all [reference] goods which are supplied in the UK are supplied by [or to] members of one and the same group of interconnected bodies corporate" [Section 6(1)(b)]";*

or in which:

> *"at least one quarter of all [reference] goods which are supplied in the UK are supplied by [or to] members of one and the same group consisting of two or more such persons who whether voluntarily or not, and whether by agreement*

or not, so conduct their respective affairs as in any way to prevent, restrict or distort competition ..." [Sections 6(1)(c) and 6(2)]

The provisions of Sections 6(1)(c) and 6(2) cover what are referred to in Section 11 of the 1973 Act as a "complex" monopoly situation. The trigger for the complex monopoly is the possible existence of a line of conduct common to a group of companies which has allegedly adverse effects on competition.

There is no time limit laid down for monopoly references under Sections 6 to 8 of the 1973 Act; the time scale for the enquiry is specified at the time of the reference. It is unusual for a reference to be completed in less than about 9 months and it may extend over 18 months or two years.

If the MMC finds that a monopoly situation exists and is likely to operate against the public interest, it is required to consider remedies and to make recommendations. An adverse public interest finding acts as a trigger for the application by the Secretary of State of powers under Section 56 of the Act to make orders aimed at remedying the adverse effects identified by the Commission.

3.5.3.3 The 1976 Act

The 1976 Act, which consolidated the provisions of several Acts relating to concerted practices passed between 1956 (the date of the original Restrictive Trade Practices Act) and 1973, provides for the registration and subsequent judicial investigation of agreements affecting the supply of goods and services in the UK between two or more persons, under which certain types of restriction are accepted. The restrictions include prices to be charged and terms and conditions of supply. Any agreement containing relevant restrictions must be registered with the DGFT before the date on which restrictions covered by the agreement become effective.

There is a presumption in the Act that any registerable agreement is against the public interest, so that once an agreement is referred to the Court, the onus is on the parties to prove that it is not. They must do so by reference to specific criteria in the Act, known as gateways, which relate mainly to alleged benefits flowing from the agreement.

3.5.3.4 The 1980 Act

The 1980 Act provides for a two stage investigation of anti-competitive practices, defined in Section 2(1) as a course of conduct "likely to have the effect of restricting, distorting or preventing competition".

The first stage of the process involves an enquiry which is conducted by DGFT. If he concludes that the conduct in question is anti-competitive, then he may accept an undertaking from the organisation concerned which remedies the difficulty. If a satisfactory undertaking is not forthcoming, then the DGFT may refer the matter to the MMC for investigation.

The MMC then reexamines whether or not the course of conduct is anti-competitive, and, if so, whether it adversely affects the public interest. If the Commission finds the practice to be against the public interest, and if the Secretary of State concludes that the adverse effects could be eliminated if some specified action were taken, then the Secretary of Sate may require the DGFT to negotiate an appropriate undertaking with the organisation concerned. If such an undertaking cannot be negotiated, or is not being complied with, then the Secretary of State may then make an order under Section 10 of the Act.

The MMC has undertaken various investigations of the health care market. These include an examination of the effects of a merger between BUPA, the UK's largest private health insurer, and a chain of private hospitals, and an investigation into restrictions on advertising by medical specialists.

249

ANNEX 3.6 BIBLIOGRAPHY

Aaron, H. J. (1991a), "Choosing From the Health Care Reform Menu", *Journal of American Health Policy*, pp. 23-27.

Aaron, H. J. (1991b), *Serious and Unstable Conditions: Financing America's Health Care*, The Brookings Institution, Washington.

Appleby, J., Little, V., Ranade, W., Robinson, R. and Salter J. (1991), "How Do We Measure Competition", *NAHAT Project Paper*, No 2.

Barro, R. and Gordon, D. (1983), "Rules, Discretion and Reputation in a Model of Monetary Policy", *Journal of Monetary Economics*, pp. 101-121.

Becham, L. (1992), "Genetic Testing has Little Effect on US Health Insurance", *British Medical Journal*, p. 1244.

Bridgeport Group (1992), *The Core Debate - Review of Submission*, Wellington.

Chipman, J. (1987), "Compensation Principle", in Eatwell, J., Milgate, M., Newman, P. (eds.), *The New Palgrave Dictionary of Economics*, London, Macmillan.

Choices in Health Care (1992), "A Report by the Government Committee on Choices in Health Care" (The Dunning Report), Rijswijk, The Netherlands.

Culyer, A. J. (1990), "The Internal Market: An Acceptable Means to a Desirable End", *Centre for Health Economics Discussion Paper*, No. 67.

Culyer, A. J. (1991), "The Promise of a Reformed NHS: An Economist's Angle", *British Medical Journal*, 25 May, pp. 1253-1256.

Culyer, A. J. and Wagstaff, A. (1992), "QALYs versus HYSs: A Theoretical Exposition", *Centre For Health Economics Discussion Paper*, No. 99.

Diamond, P. (1992), "Organizing the Health Insurance Market", *Econometrica*, 60, pp. 1233-1254.

Enthoven, A. (1988), *Theory and Practice of Managed Competition in Health Care Finance*, North Holland.

Enthoven, A. and Kronick, R. (1989), "A Consumer-Choice Health Plan for the 1990's" *New England Journal of Medicine*, 5 January, pp. 29-37, and 12 January, pp. 94-101.

Foot, M. (1975), *Aneurin Bevan, 1945-1960*, Paladin, London.

Foxman, B., Valdez, R., Lohr K. et al. (1987), "The Effect of Cost Sharing on the Use of Antibiotics in Ambulatory Care: Results from a Population-based Randomized Controlled Trial," *Journal of Chronic Diseases*, 40, pp. 429-437.

Fuchs, V. (1988), "The 'Competition' Revolution in Health Care", *Health Affairs*, Summer, pp. 5-24.

Fuchs, V. (1991), "National Health Insurance Revisited", *Health Affairs*, Winter, pp. 7-17.

Government Committee on Choices in Health Care (1992), *Choices in Health Care* (The Dunning Report), Rijswijk.

Ham, C., Robinson, R. and Benzeval, M. (1990), *Health Check: Health Care Reforms in an International Context*, King's Fund Institute, London.

Harris, B., Stergachis, A., Ried, L., (1990), "The Effect of Drug Copayments on Utilization and Cost of Pharmaceuticals in a Health Maintenance Organisation," *Medical Care*, 28, pp. 907-917.

Health Service Commission (HSC) (1992), *Prioritisation of Health Services* A Report to the Governor and Legislature, Portland, Oregon.

Hoare, J. (1992), "Tidal Wave: New Technology, Medicine and the NHS", King's Fund Centre.

Honigsbaum, F. (1992), *Who Shall Live? Who Shall Die?*, King's Fund College Papers, London.

Kind, P., Rosser and Williams, A. (1982), "Valuation of Quality of Life: Some Psychometric Evidence", in Jones-Lee, M.W. (ed.), *The Value of Life and Safety*, Amsterdam, North Holland.

Kreps, D. and Wilson, R. (1982), "Reputation and Imperfect Information", *Journal of Economic Theory*, pp. 253-279.

Lapre, R. (1988), "A Change of Direction in the Dutch Health Care System" *Health Policy*, pp. 21-32.

Leibowitz, A., Manning, W. and Newhouse, J. (1983), *The Demand for Prescription Drugs as a Function of Cost Sharing*, Santa Monica, The Rand Corporation.

Leu, R. (1992), "Leistungswettbewerb im Gesundheitswesen", *Neue Züricher Zeitung*, 25/26 April, No. 96, pp. 33.

Lohr, K., Brook, R., Kamberg, C., Goldberg, G., Leibowitz, A., Keesey, J., Reboussin D. and J. Newhouse (1986), "Use of Medical Care in the Rand Health Insurance Experiment: Diagnosis and Service-specific Analyses in a Randomized Controlled Trial," *Medical Care* (Supplement), 24(9), pp. S1-S87.

Lovell, White, Durrant (1988), *An Introduction to EEC Competition Laws*.

Manches & Co, *The Competition Rules of the European Community*, Brochure.

Manning W., Newhouse, J., Duan, M., Keeler, E., Leibowitz, A. and Marquis, S. (1987), "Health Insurance and the Demand for Medical Care: Evidence from a Randomized Experiment", *The American Economic Review*, 77(3), pp. 251-277.

Marquis, S. (1985), "Cost Sharing and Provider Choice," *Journal of Health Economics*, 4, pp. 135-157.

Maynard, A. and Williams, A. (1984), "Privatisation and the National Health Service", in Le Grand, J. and Robinson, R. (eds.), *Privatisation and the Welfare State*, London, George Allen and Unwin.

Mill, J. S. (1863), *Utilitarianism*, London, Parker, Son & Bourn.

Minister of Health, New Zealand (1991), *The Core Debate - Stage One: How We Define the Core*, Wellington.

Ministry of Welfare, Health and Cultural Affairs (1989), *Health Insurance in the Netherlands*, Rijswijk.

Newhouse, J. P., Manning, W. G., Keeler, E. B., Sloss, E. M. (1989), "Adjusting Capitation Rates Using Objective Health Measures and Prior Utilization", *Health Care Financing Review*, p. 41-54.

Office of Fair Trading (1973), *Mergers - A Guide to the Procedures under the Fair Trading Act 1973*.

Office of Fair Trading (1976), *Restrictive Trade Practices - Provisions of the Restrictive Trade Practice Act 1976*.

Office of Fair Trading (1980), *Anti-Competitive Practices - A Guide to the Provisions of the Competition Act 1980*.

Pauly, M. (1986), "Taxation, Health Insurance, and Market Failure in the Medical Economy", *Journal of Economic Literature*, June 1986, pp. 629-675.

Pauly, M., Danzon, P., Feldstein, P. and Hoff, J. (1991), "A Plan for 'Responsible Health Insurance'", *Health Affairs*, Spring 1991, pp. 5-25.

Rawls, J. (1958), "Justice as Fairness", *Philosophical Review*, pp. 164-194.

Rawls, J. (1971), *A Theory of Justice*, Cambridge, Mass., Harvard University Press.

Reinhardt, U. (1991), "Breaking American Health Policy Gridlock", *Health Affairs*, Summer, pp. 96-103.

Rothschild, M. and Stiglitz, J. (1976), "Equilibrium in Competitive Insurance Markets: An Essay on the Economics of Imperfect Information", *Quarterly Journal of Economics*, pp. 629-649.

Schut, F., Greenberg, W. and van de Ven, W. (1991), "Antitrust Policy in the Dutch Health Care System and the Relevance of EEC Competition Policy and U.S. Antitrust Practice" *Health Policy*, pp. 257-284.

Sen, A. K. (1970), "The Impossibility of a Paretian Liberal", *Journal of Political Economy*, pp. 152-157.

Sen, A. K. (1973), *On Economic Inequality*, Oxford, Oxford University Press.

Sen, A. K. (1975), "Rawls versus Bentham", in Daniels, N. (ed.) *Reading Rawls: Critical Studies of 'A Theory of Justice'*, Oxford, Basil Blackwell.

Sen, A. K. (1977), "Rational Fools: A Critique of the Behavioural Foundations of Economic Theory", *Philosophy and Public Affairs*, pp. 317-344.

Sen, A. K. (1979), "Intertemporal Comparisons of Welfare", in Boskin, M. J. (ed.) *Economics and Human Welfare*, New York, Academic Press.

Sen, A. K. (1980), "Equality of What?", in McMurrin, S. (ed.) *The Tanner Lectures on Human Values*, Cambridge, Cambridge University Press.

Sen, A. K. and Williams, B. (eds.) (1982), *Utilitarianism and Beyond*, Cambridge, Cambridge University Press.

Smith, D. (1992), "The Effects of Copayments and Generic Substitution on the Use and Costs of Prescription Drugs" (unpublished manuscript).

Stocking, B. (1992), "The Future Starts Here", *The Health Service Journal*, 1 October., p. 28.

Taylor, H. and Reinhardt, U. (1991), "Does the System Fit?", *Health Management Quarterly*, pp. 2-10.

van de Ven, W. and van Vliet, R. (1992) "How We Can Prevent Cream Skimming in a Competitive Health Insurance Market", in Zweifel, P. and Frech, H. [eds.] *Health Economics Worldwide*, Kluwer Academic Publishers, The Netherlands, p. 23-46.

van de Ven, W. (1990), "From Regulated Cartel to Regulated Competition", *European Economic Review*, pp. 632-645.

van Vliet, R. and van de Ven, W. (1992) "Towards a Capitation Formula for Competing Health Insurers. An Empirical Analysis", *Social Science Medicine*, p. 1035-1048.

Weiner, J., Lyles, A., Steinwachs, D. and Hall, K. (1991), "Impact of Managed Care on Prescription Drug Use," *Health Affairs*, 10(1), pp. 140-154.

Williams, A. (1985), "Economics of Coronary Artery Bypass Grafting", *British Medical Journal*, pp. 326-329.

CHAPTER 4

THE HEALTH CARE SYSTEM IN CANADA

Richard Rozek
Carla Mulhern

National Economic Research Associates
Washington DC

4.1   SUMMARY

Structure

The health care system in Canada is a universal access, single payer, public insurance system for basic benefits.   It is comprised of 12 individual health care plans administered by each of the 10 provinces and 2 territories. Funding comes from a combination of federal government, provincial government and private support. The Federal Government has five criteria for a provincial plan to be eligible for federal contributions: public administration, comprehensiveness, universality, portability and accessibility.   Supplemental private insurance is available for uncovered services, but private insurance is not permitted for services covered by provincial plans.

Aggregate Level of Expenditure

Each province individually determines the extent of coverage it will provide in addition to the federally-mandated basic services (established in the "comprehensiveness" criterion). Therefore, the overall level of expenditure on health care in Canada is primarily determined by the provincial governments. In 1991, per capita spending on health care in Canada was C\$2,473. The cost of the Canadian system in terms of the share of GNP devoted to health care is 10.2 percent.

Incentives

Primary Care Physicians: Most physicians are paid on a fee-for-service basis with fee schedules determined through negotiation between the provincial medical association and the provincial Ministry of Health. In general, fee-for-service payment of physicians encourages provision of services in excess of the efficient level.

Hospitals: Hospitals operate under annual global budgets with additional provincial government review of capital expenditures. Global budgets give hospitals an incentive to control costs. However, they also create an incentive for hospitals to use acute care beds for long-term low-intensity patients (bed-blockers).   The need for government approval to obtain access to certain medical technologies reduces the rate of technological diffusion.

Patients: Patients have a choice of providers. They pay zero price at the point of delivery for all federally-mandated basic services. Copayments exist for some additional services such as medicines provided to the elderly. General lack of knowledge about health care costs and the zero price gives patients an incentive to consume more health care than is efficient.

Medicines: Generally, physicians prescribe medicines and pharmacists dispense. With exceptions for the elderly and needy, Canadians pay for medicines out-of-pocket or through private insurance. The Patented Medicine Prices Review Board (PMPRB) sets maximum allowable price increases for existing products and monitors the price levels of new products.

Issues

In addition to the issues arising directly from the distorted incentives of physicians, hospitals and patients, the following potential problems for the health care system arise:

- The recession in Canada has caused the Federal Government to freeze its contributions to the provincial plans, putting pressure on the provincial governments to contain costs or increase revenues.

- The single-payer structure is inflexible. Due to lack of market-based signals, it is slow to respond to changing environments.

- Queue-based rationing of services leads to waiting lists for some procedures.

- The aging of the Canadian population means that funding health care will continue as a problem into the next century.

- There is a general maldistribution of physicians, with plentiful supply in urban areas, but shortages in rural areas.

Current Reforms

Currently, in Canada, the following reforms are being considered to address the distortions and issues described above:

- creating managed care alternatives;

- shifting emphasis from traditional physicians and hospital services to community-based care;

- increasing cost-sharing by patients;

- shifting resources from primary care services to health promotion;

- exploring alternative methods of compensation for physicians;

- implementing incentive schemes to attract physicians to rural areas; and

- better management of queues for hospital services.

Political Environment

The health care system is the single most supported of all social programs in Canada. Indeed, it is widely believed in Canada that no government that tried to do away with the universal coverage of health care services could be re-elected.

NERA's Reform Proposals

Characteristics of the existing Canadian health care system introduce distortions. These include: the single, public payer; lack of information about the cost of health care services; methods of reimbursement for health care providers; and centralised health care decision-making. Reforms to minimise or eliminate these distortions would enable Canadian citizens to receive more health care benefits for a given level of spending.

In suggesting reforms for the Canadian system, we must bear in mind that two major goals of any health care system are equity and efficiency. We suggest that first the standard for equity be established according to the culture and politics of the individual country. Given the equity standard, we seek well-designed market-oriented incentives to maximise efficiency.

Most likely, neither a strictly private nor a strictly public system can fulfil the equity and efficiency goals of Canada. Although the Canadian health care system operates in a satisfactory manner on the whole, it is a relatively 'public' system and as such, it may benefit from greater reliance on the private sector for financing and increased competition among providers.

In Sections 4.7 and 4.8, we identify several reforms that will enhance the efficiency of the Canadian health care system and bring it into line with the NERA Prototype system. Some of these reforms are either underway currently or could be implemented without changes to existing Canadian legislation (short-run reforms). However, some of these reform recommendations may not be politically feasible in the short run. Some may be impossible to implement without major changes to the Canada Health Act or other existing legislation (long-term reforms). We present long-term reform recommendations to describe a possible future direction for the Canadian

259

health care system. This does not mean that Canadians should delay action on those reforms that are feasible in the short run. Any improvement in efficiency today will ease the financial burden of providing health care.

4.2   STRUCTURE OF THE HEALTH CARE SYSTEM

4.2.1   The Health Care System in Context

Prior to 1947, Canada[1] had a health care system similar to that in the US; namely, private competitive insurance markets on the financing side and fee-for-service providers on the delivery side.[2] This privately-funded system has evolved into a publicly-funded system based on single insurers, the provincial governments.[3]   Each province administers its own public health insurance scheme;[4] the Federal and provincial governments share the costs. Currently, the Federal Government contributes approximately 35 percent of total public funding for health services; thereby giving it considerable leverage over the provincial plans.   The Federal Government funds are conditional on compliance with the national criteria established in the Canada Health Act.

Creating a government run system for buying basic health care has had an impact on the delivery side as well. The provincial governments bargain collectively with physicians over fee schedules, set global operating budgets for hospitals and approve their capital expenditure.

The Canada Health Act forms the basis for the Canadian system as it operates today.[5] The Act describes the five criteria for a provincial plan to be eligible for a federal subsidy:

---

[1] Canada has ten provinces: Alberta, British Columbia, Manitoba, New Brunswick, Newfoundland, Nova Scotia, Ontario, Prince Edward Island, Québec, Saskatchewan, and two territories: Northwest and Yukon. Throughout this report, the term "provincial" will refer to both provinces and territories.

[2] In 1947, Saskatchewan introduced a hospitalization plan for all residents financed by a combination of premiums and general taxes (Shah, 1990). British Columbia introduced a similar plan in 1949. By 1957, two other provinces, Alberta and Newfoundland, had hospital insurance programs in place (Coyte, 1990).   Hospital insurance paved the way for comprehensive medical insurance. For a more detailed discussion of the evolution of Canada's health care system, see Brown (1987).

[3] Under Sections 91 and 92 of the British North American Act, 1867, the provision of hospital and medical care in Canada is a provincial concern (Shah, 1990).

[4] All provinces had public medical insurance by January 1971. The two territories followed within one year (Neuschler, 1990).

[5] The Canada Health Act replaces the Hospital Insurance and Diagnostic Services Act, 1957, and the Medical Care Act, 1966, which provided federal funding for hospital and medical (physician) services, respectively.

- Public Administration - Each provincial plan must be run by a non-profit, public authority accountable to the provincial government.

- Comprehensiveness - Provinces must provide comprehensive insurance coverage for all necessary physician and hospital services, and surgical-dental services rendered in hospitals.

- Universality - Insured services must be universally available to all residents of the province on uniform terms and conditions. For new residents, the waiting period to entitlement cannot exceed three months.

- Portability - Each provincial plan must be portable between provinces, so that the eligible residents are covered while they are temporarily absent from the province.

- Accessibility - Reasonable access to insured health services is not to be precluded or impaired by charges or other mechanisms. Also, reasonable compensation must be made to physicians and dentists for providing insured health services.[6]

These federal criteria insure that, although there are twelve separate health plans in Canada, they are largely similar in that all provinces provide insurance for medically necessary services to all citizens at zero price at the point of delivery. All provincial plans provide coverage for the following hospital services:

- accommodations and meals;
- necessary nursing services;
- laboratory, radiological and other diagnostic procedures;
- biologicals and related preparations;
- use of operating room, case room and anaesthetic facilities;
- routine surgical supplies; and
- use of radiotherapy and physiotherapy services.

In addition, all provincial plans cover all medically-required services provided by medical practitioners and dental services for which hospitalization is necessary.

---

[6]   The accessibility condition was added in 1984. The public administration, comprehensiveness, universality and portability conditions were carried over from the Medical Care Act of 1966.

There are some differences among provincial plans. For example, Alberta and British Columbia charge an insurance premium. However, to comply with the federal conditions described in the Canada Health Act, these provinces cannot deny coverage for nonpayment of the premium. Therefore, these premiums are effectively additional taxes serving only to raise revenues for the provinces. Some employers pay the premiums as part of a private group insurance plan. Other differences exist among provincial plans, such as the fee schedules for physician services and the scope of services covered.

Private health insurance is permitted for health care services not covered by the provincial insurance plans. These uncovered services can include charges for: private and semi-private rooms in public facilities; cosmetic surgery not included in the provincial plans; dental care;[7] prescription medicines;[8] eyeglasses or contact lenses; and all treatment in privately-owned facilities.

4.2.2 General Features of the Finance System

The Canadian health care system is primarily funded by the provincial and Federal governments, largely through tax revenues. In 1991, the public sector accounted for approximately 72 percent of total health care expenditures in Canada. Federal government spending was 24 percent of the total; provincial government spending was 46 percent; local government spending and worker's compensation schemes accounted for the remaining 2 percent (see Chart 4.1). The size of the Federal Government's contribution to each province is determined by an "indexed per capita block grant" approach outlined in the Federal Provincial Fiscal Arrangements and Established Programs Act, 1977. The grants are based on the Federal Government's national average per capita payment in fiscal year 1975-1976 and are increased annually by the average nominal growth in GNP.[9] This indexed amount is multiplied by the population of each province to determine each province's entitlement.

---

[7]   There is no national dental insurance plan in Canada. Federal legislation has established a cost-sharing program with provinces under the Canada Assistance Act to provide dental services to the needy (Federation Dentaire Internationale, 1990).

[8]   Some provinces cover prescription medicines for the elderly or needy.

[9]   The 1977 Act provided for an annual escalation factor equal to the nominal growth in GNP. However, as part of a federal deficit reduction strategy, the annual escalation factor was reduced by two percentage points in 1986 and a third percentage point in 1989. The federal government has frozen its per capita contribution to provincial health care spending at the fiscal 1989-1990 level for the fiscal years 1990-1991 and 1991-1992 (Neuschler, 1990). Also, the 1991 budget extended the freeze through fiscal year 1994-1995.

Chart 4.1
Expenditure on Health Care in Canada, 1991

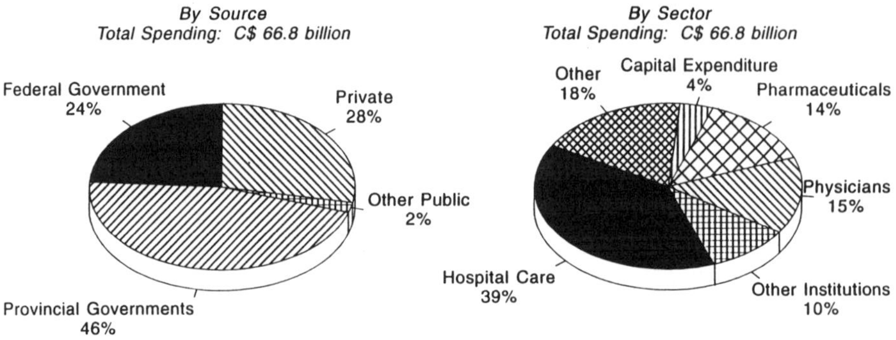

By Source
Total Spending: C$ 66.8 billion

By Sector
Total Spending: C$ 66.8 billion

Federal Government
24%

Private
28%

Other Public
2%

Provincial Governments
46%

Other
18%

Capital Expenditure
4%

Pharmaceuticals
14%

Physicians
15%

Hospital Care
39%

Other Institutions
10%

Source: Health and Welfare Canada (1993)

The Federal Government contribution is independent of the total expenditures on health services in the individual provinces; increases in provincial health care costs are not passed directly through to the Federal Government. This was not always the case. The 1977 Act replaced a "matching grant" system, established in 1966, under which the Federal Government contributed approximately one-half of total government payments for health care costs.[10] The change in 1977 was introduced as a cost-control measure since the open-ended nature of the matching grant approach limited the provinces' incentives to control costs.

After the shift in 1977 to the indexed per capita grant system there was an increase in extra billing and user fees as provinces searched for additional ways to raise revenues. This followed a perceived reduction in the accessibility of health care services. Therefore, the 1984 Canada Health Act contained a provision to allow the Federal Government to deduct from the block grants to each province any funds raised through extra billing and user fees. Currently, extra-billing by physicians is prohibited throughout Canada and copayments are permitted only for services which are additional to the basic services provided by the provincial plans.

The federal contribution as a percentage of total public expenditures on health care has declined from 45 percent in 1979 to 33 percent in 1991. Total public sector (provincial and federal) spending as a percentage of total national health

---

[10]   Shah (1990).

expenditures is approximately 72 percent. Thus, there is increasing pressure on provinces to bear the financial burden of financing health care. Direct provincial government spending as a percentage of total spending has increased from 39 percent in 1979 to 46 percent in 1991.[11] Currently, health care costs account for roughly one-third of provincial government budgets.[12] As the federal share has been falling, provincial Ministries of Health have had to experiment with ways to reduce costs and/or raise revenues.

In 1975, private sources accounted for 24 percent of total health care expenditures in Canada.[13] By 1991, this percentage had risen to 28 percent.[14] Most Canadian employers offer supplemental health insurance as an employee benefit. In 1985, 65 percent of Canadians had some form of private insurance.[15] Employer-provided health insurance in Canada has preferential tax status in that it is not taxed as income to the employee (as is the case in the US).

This insurance typically covers out-patient prescription medicines, dental[16] and vision care, the additional charge for a private or semi-private hospital room, medical devices, ambulances and other transportation, special nursing, medical expenses incurred outside Canada in excess of amounts covered by government plans and certain services beyond the limits of government plans (e.g., podiatry and chiropractic services).[17]

[11] Health and Welfare Canada (1993).

[12] House of Commons Canada (1991).

[13] These sources include spending by private individuals, firms, voluntary organizations and private insurance plans (Health and Welfare Canada, 1990).

[14] Health and Welfare Canada (1993).

[15] House of Commons Canada (1991).

[16] A 1988 survey stated that approximately seven million Canadians have private dental insurance, most of whom are covered through an employee dental plan (Federation Dentaire Internationale, 1990).

[17] Neuschler (1990).

4.2.3   General Features of the Delivery System

Canada is a country of approximately 27 million people in which the major causes of death are heart disease and cancer. In Canada, people have the right to choose their primary care physician and they are encouraged to contact a general practitioner for a reference when specialist treatment is needed.

In 1989, there were approximately 59,400 physicians in Canada, 2.2 per thousand of the population (the average over our study countries is 2.4 per thousand).[18] Of these, 46 percent are general practitioners. Over the last decade, the increase in the number of physicians in Canada has outpaced the growth of the general population. There is some concern about what is seen as the plentiful supply of physicians in Canada, although this phenomenon varies greatly by geographic region.

On average, 50 percent of physicians were in solo practice in 1984, ranging from 43 percent in Québec to 57 percent in Ontario.[19] Generally, physicians in Canada are paid on a fee-for-service basis. Fee schedules are negotiated annually between the provincial medical associations and the provincial governments.

As emphasis on cost containment and preventive health care increases, Canada is experimenting with alternative forms of delivery of physician services. These include:

- Community Health Centres (CHC) - Currently, there are CHCs in all provinces. These centres place a great emphasis on prevention and are designed to integrate health and social services. They provide a wide range of services such as medical, dental, social and nursing. Physicians, as well as all other health professionals, are salaried. CHCs were formed in the 1970s to provide a point of access to the health care system for people who do not have regular contact with a general practitioner.[20] Provincial health authorities now view the CHCs as generally providing low cost alternatives to emergency room visits for some health problems; for example CHCs may be a substitute for some

---

[18]   OECD (1991).

[19]   Hasting and Vayda (1989).

[20]   For example, a generally healthy person may not have a regular physician. Such a person could use the CHC for the occasional health problem.

emergency room visits. Patients that do not require relatively high-intensity care at an acute-care hospital would be treated more cost-effectively in a CHC.[21]

- Health Services Organizations (HSO) - These exist only in Ontario. They are organized by two or more physicians as a form of group practice. Physicians are paid on a capitation basis.

- Comprehensive Health Organization (CHO) - As of 1990 there were no functioning CHOs, but the Ontario government was experimenting with the process of funding new pilot CHOs[22] and a CHO in Fort Frances, Ontario could be operating in 1992.[23] The CHO concept is similar to the Health Maintenance Organizations (HMO) in the US. They provide a wide range of services such as medical, hospital and home care. They would place great emphasis on disease prevention and health promotion. Where possible, institutional care is replaced with ambulatory and community-based care. CHOs could receive their funding from the provincial health insurance plans on a capitation basis, with physicians compensated either by fee-for-service, capitation or salary. CHOs are designed to serve populations of 15,000 and over in large or medium urban communities.[24]

Recently, some physicians have opened private ambulatory-surgery clinics designed to treat patients who otherwise would face a long wait for surgery through the public system, for example, cataract patients. The surgeon's fee is covered by the provincial health plan. Any charges for the use of the facility must be paid by the patients directly.[25]

---

[21] Manitoba Health (1992).

[22] Shah (1990).

[23] Ontario Ministry of Health (1991).

[24] One concern with establishing CHOs is whether a consumer selecting a CHO will be bound to remain with the CHO for a period of time. If the patient is able to seek care outside the CHO, the ability of the managed-care entity to contain costs is diminished.

[25] Neuschler (1990).

Of the 1,227 hospitals in Canada, 1,121 are public.[26] Their primary source of revenues is the annual global budget they negotiate with the provincial health plans. These hospitals also generate revenues from private/semi-private room charges and donations obtained through foundations. These "public" hospitals are owned by: municipal or county corporations (29.5 percent); provincial authorities (13.7 percent); voluntary, non-profit organizations (45.8 percent) and religious orders (11.0 percent).

An additional 44 hospitals are controlled by the Federal Government. These hospitals are operated by: the Department of Veterans Affairs (1); Health and Welfare Canada (9); Industrial - Crown Corporations (1); the Department of National Defence - Military (30); and the Solicitor General of Canada - Correctional Service (3).

The remaining 62 hospitals in Canada are private.[27] Private hospitals are operated for profit and patients pay for services directly. These hospitals are not for general acute-care patients. They tend to be specialized institutions; for example, cosmetic surgery, hernia procedures and alcoholism treatment.

4.2.4 Inputs and Outputs of the System

4.2.4.1 Spending

In 1991, total national health expenditures were approximately C\$67 billion. (\$56 bn 1990).[28] Total health expenditures (unadjusted for any possible measurement problems), as a percentage of GNP, have increased from 5.5 percent to 9.2 percent from 1960 to 1990. During the decade 1980 to 1990, total health expenditures as a percentage of GNP increased from 7.5 to 9.7 percent.

---

[26]   A public hospital is defined as one which "is not operated for profit, accepts all patients regardless of their ability to pay, and is recognized as a public hospital by the province in which it is located." Although hospitals operated by the federal government are federally owned, they are grouped in a separate classification (Canadian Hospital Association, 1991, p. 10).

[27]   A private hospital is defined as one "which ordinarily restricts its admissions to patients paying for the care provided, at rates determined by the management" (Canadian Hospital Association, 1991, p. 10).

[28]   OECD data show that in 1987, total health expenditures in Canada were C\$44.7 billion in 1985 dollars and C\$53.2 billion (\$67 billion) in 1990 dollars.

In 1991, this increased further to 10.2 percent. Growth in health expenditures has consistently outpaced growth in GNP.[29]

The reported share of GNP in Canada devoted to health care may understate the actual share. Krasny and Ferrier adjusted health care expenditure for under-reporting of capital costs, labour costs, R & D expenditure as well as the younger Canadian population relative to the US. They conclude that adjusted health expenditure as a percent of GNP is 10.6 percent for Canada compared to 11.1 percent of GNP in the US.[30]

Of the approximately C$67 billion ($56 bn 1990) spent on health care in 1991, 39 percent was spent on hospital care, 10 percent on other institutions, 15 percent on physicians, 14 percent on medicines, 4 percent on capital expenditure, and 18 percent on other categories[31] (see Chart 4.1).

4.2.4.2 Mortality[32]

Between 1941 and 1990 life expectancy at birth increased from 63 to 74 years for males, and from 66 to 80 years for females.[33] In 1990 life expectancy at age 60 was 19 years for males and 24 for females. These figures are similar to the corresponding averages in the countries under study (74 and 80 years at birth, 19 and 23 years at 60).

Infant mortality in Canada has declined from 61 deaths per 1,000 live births in 1941 to 6.8 deaths per 1,000 live births in 1990.[34] The unweighted average infant mortality for the countries under study is 7.2 deaths per 1000 live births.

---

[29]   Health and Welfare Canada (1993).

[30]   Krasny and Ferrier (1991).

[31]   Health and Welfare Canada (1993).

[32]   Mortality data are widely used as measures of quality of the health care system especially when making inter-country comparisons. However, socio-economic factors (such as income level and distribution), past and present nutrition levels, dietary fashions and genetic differences may influence mortality independent of the health care system. Mortality data are clearly imperfect measures of the quality of a health care system.

[33]   OECD (1991).

[34]   OECD (1991).

4.3   ANALYSIS OF INDIVIDUAL SECTORS

4.3.1   Key Participants in the Health Care System

The key participants in the Canadian health care system are:

- the citizens of Canada (both as patients and taxpayers);
- the governments (payers);
- physicians;
- hospitals; and,
- the pharmaceutical industry.

Of course, there are a number of other participants with stakes in the health care system such as nursing homes, private insurers and manufacturers of medical devices. However, we will focus on the key participants in this section. The main relationships between these participants, and the flows of finance and services between them, are shown in Chart 4.2.

4.3.2   Patients

The principle behind Canada's health care policy is that Canadians "...should not make the sick bear the financial burden of health care..."[35] Health care should be publicly administered, comprehensive, universal, portable and accessible. Canadians expect that those with higher incomes will subsidize those with lower incomes and the healthy will subsidize the sick.[36]

Canadians have an egalitarian notion of equity. Equity in the provision of health care services means that a citizen's access to care is **not affected** by the citizen's ability to pay. This is a different definition of equity than the notion that merely sets a floor beneath which no-one should be allowed to fall. Equity, for Canadians, means no two-tiered health system. Canada is the only major industrialised country that explicitly prohibits a two-tiered system. The Canadian health care system does not allow the purchase of supplemental private insurance for services covered by the provincial plans. Therefore,

---

[35]   Department of National Health and Welfare (1983), p. 7.

[36]   This is the goal for Canadian health policy; however, there does not appear to be any empirical evidence on the distributive effects of the Canadian health care system.

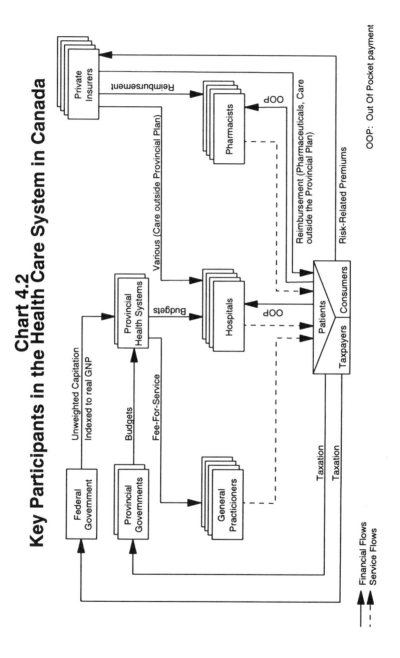

Chart 4.2
Key Participants in the Health Care System in Canada

OOP: Out Of Pocket payment

Canadian citizens have access to the same level of care regardless of income.[37] This equity standard is embodied in the five criteria described in the Canada Health Act.

The health care system in Canada is the most popular government program. It is a source of national pride. According to a ten-nation survey performed by Louis Harris and Associates,[38] only 5 percent of Canadians perceived a need completely to rebuild their health care system. This contrasted with 29 percent of Americans and 40 percent of Italians. Of the ten nations surveyed, Canada had the largest proportion satisfied with their current system.[39] Our interviews confirm a high level of satisfaction with the existing single-payer system in Canada.

Patients receive services but do not observe the costs of service. When funds are inadequate, the Canadian system rations health care through queuing. One way to measure the extent of rationing is to examine the waiting lists for procedures and treatments. In a recent survey of waiting times for specific surgical procedures, Walker et al. (1992) found "that the total estimated number of people waiting for surgery during 1991 was 260,721" (this is 1.0 percent of the population) and commented "that substantial waiting for health services is a reality in Canada". They also said; "Social costs associated with increased time spent waiting for treatment are primarily associated with prolonged pain, anxiety, physical disability, and the inconvenience of being able to schedule treatments when the patients' opportunity cost of time ... is low".[40] We do not have data on the extent of waiting in a broad set of countries for comparison; however, in the U.K. 1.3 percent of the population were waiting for surgery in 1985.[41]

---

[37] Although the Canadian system is based on the egalitarian notion of equity, some Canadians are able to circumvent the system. Some people seek treatment in the US for procedures that are either unavailable in Canada, or for which there are long waiting lists.

[38] The survey was conducted in 1988 for the U.S., Canada and the U.K. The remaining seven nations - the Netherlands, Italy, West Germany, France, Sweden, Australia and Japan - were surveyed in 1990.

[39] Blendon, Leitman, Morrison, and Donelan (1990).

[40] Walker et al. (1992), p. 11.

[41] Walker et al. (1992), p. 23.

The objective of Canadians, in their role of ultimate payer, is to fulfil efficiently the goals of the Canada Health Act. However, as taxpayers, they are generally unaware of the costs of their health care system. The federal and provincial governments collect taxes from Canadians without specifying the amounts to be used for each of the various government programs (although four provinces have taxes paid identified as "health taxes" that are paid by employers, these are in fact merely additional sources of revenue). Thus, there are information gaps and choice gaps in the Canadian system. Canadians lack:

- information about costs, benefits and cost-effectiveness of treatments;

- the ability to choose alternative levels of support for health care services; and

- the ability to choose a form of controlling moral hazard (copayments, length of physician visits, wait for services).

4.3.3 Payers

4.3.3.1 Federal Government

A key restriction in the Canadian health care system is that it does not allow private insurance for services that are covered by the provincial plans. This restriction eliminates the possibility of a "two-tier" health care system and prohibits the use of private insurance for "queue-jumping", as in the UK. However, there are some services not covered by the provincial plans, so that there is a role for private insurance, which accounts for about one quarter of total health care expenditure.

Health and Welfare Canada is the federal agency with responsibility for health care. Health and Welfare Canada's mission is two-fold: (i) to promote, preserve and restore the health of Canadians; and (ii) to provide social security and social welfare to Canadians. The health aspect of Health and Welfare Canada is under the jurisdiction of the Deputy Minister of Health and is divided into four main branches, with an assistant deputy minister heading each branch:

- Health Services and Promotion;
- Medical Services;
- Health Protection;
- Fitness and Amateur Sport.

The major goals of the Health Services and Promotion branch are equity of access to adequate health care and promotion of healthy lifestyles. This branch achieves its goal of equity of access to adequate health care through the leverage provided by its financial contributions to each province. The magnitudes of these federal contributions are determined according to the Federal Provincial Fiscal Arrangements and Established Programs Act, 1977, described in Section 4.2.2. A special unit of the branch exists to address issues of health promotion. This is an expanding area within the agency and in the provinces as well. The idea behind the emphasis on health promotion is that expenditure on encouraging healthy lifestyles today will reduce the need for more costly health interventions later.

The Medical Services Branch is responsible for health care and public health services for Indians, Inuit and all residents of the Yukon and Northwest Territories. It is also responsible for quarantine and immigration medical services, the health of civil servants, a national prosthetics service and civil aviation medicine.

The Health Protection Branch is responsible for "protecting the public against unsafe foods, drugs, cosmetics, medical and radiation-emitting devices, harmful microbes, technological and social environments deleterious to health, environmental pollutants and contaminants of all kinds, and fraudulent drugs and devices".[42] Among other responsibilities, this branch regulates the manufacture and distribution of medicines in Canada.

The Fitness and Amateur Sports Branch seeks to raise the fitness level of Canadians. It endeavours to increase participation in physical recreation and amateur sports.

4.3.3.2 Provincial Governments

Constitutionally, the provincial governments have primary responsibility for the financing and delivery of health care. Provincial health ministries carry out these responsibilities. Methods of organizing, financing and administering health ministries vary from province to province.

The provincial health ministries bear the bulk of the costs of the Canadian health care system. They also have significant control over the quality and quantity of care consumed. Provincial health ministries negotiate physician

---

[42]   Shah (1990), p. 87.

fee schedules with the provincial medical associations as well as the level of capital spending and the annual global operating budgets of hospitals.

The fee-for-service nature of the payment scheme for physicians and the zero price to patients at the point of health care delivery creates incentives to expand the amount of physician services consumed. Provincial governments have tried various methods of exerting control over the quantity of physician services consumed in addition to their existing control over fees. For example, some provinces have placed ceilings on the amount that general practitioners can bill the provincial plan for their services (see Section 4.3.4).[43] These give physicians the incentive to limit the supply of services, which, in turn, reduces the total amount of physician services consumed.

Through the use of global operating budgets and controls on capital expenditures, provincial governments determine the rate of adopting and diffusing medical technology. For example, provincial governments determine access to Magnetic Resonance Imaging (MRI) by controlling which hospitals install the underlying equipment and receive continuing operating funds for the equipment.

4.3.3.3 Private Sector

Private sector expenditure includes spending by individuals, firms and voluntary organizations as well as private insurance plans.[44] It accounts for an increasing percentage of total health care expenditure in Canada.[45]

Private insurers cover supplemental hospital, medical, dental services, expenses incurred while travelling outside of Canada,[46] and prescription medicines not included in the provincial plans. They are prohibited from covering services included in the provincial plans. Private insurance can be

---

[43]   Differences in the manner in which provinces impose ceilings will be discussed later.

[44]   Health and Welfare Canada (1990).

[45]   In 1987, private sources accounted for 24 percent of total health care expenditures. By 1991, this percentage had risen to 28 percent.

[46]   Most provincial plans will reimburse patients for hospital and medical expenses incurred while travelling outside of Canada at the rates at which they would have received comparable treatment in Canada. Many Canadians have private insurance to cover the additional costs of treatment in other countries. It is interesting to note that Canadian banks are cutting back on out-of-country insurance coverage offered to certain credit card holders.

purchased by individuals or their employers; most private insurance is purchased in group plans by employers.[47]

Approximately 98 percent of Canadian employers offer supplemental health insurance.[48] The largest private insurer is Blue Cross. Others include Great West Life, Confederation Life, and Sun Life. Prescription medicines account for 70-80 percent of expenditures covered by private health insurance. Indeed, the bulk of all private spending is for medicines and appliances (41 percent).[49] The remainder consists of spending on institutional and related services (24 percent); dentists (19 percent); physicians and other professionals (3 percent); and other health expenses (13 percent).[50,51]

4.3.4 Primary Health Care Sector

In 1991, spending on physician services accounted for approximately 15 percent of total Canadian health expenditures.[52]

Canadians are free to choose their primary care physicians. In general, patients first contact a general practitioner when they are ill. The general practitioner then makes referrals to specialists when necessary. However, on some occasions, patients contact specialists directly.[53] As gatekeepers for patients requiring hospital services, most general practitioners have privileges at one or more hospitals.

In Canada, almost all physicians are paid on a fee-for-service basis by the provincial medical plans according to schedules negotiated periodically

---

[47] Blue Cross is the only private insurer that sells to individuals.

[48] In Canada, as in the U.S., employer-provided health insurance is tax-deductible and does not appear as income for the employee.

[49] The category includes prescription and non-prescription medicines, eye-glasses, hearing aids and appliances and other prostheses.

[50] Other health expenses include spending on care that is not primarily related to the care of individual pre-payment administration, public health, capital expenditure, health research and miscellaneous health costs.

[51] Health and Welfare Canada (1990).

[52] Health and Welfare Canada (1993).

[53] In order to discourage this practice, specialists are reimbursed only at the rate of a general practitioner for patients with no referral (Consumer Reports, 1992).

between provincial governments and provincial medical associations.[54] There are, however, some alternative arrangements for the delivery of physician services under which physicians are paid by salary or capitation. For example, physicians employed by hospitals (radiologists, pathologists and anaesthesiologists) receive salaries. Ontario and Québec have taken the lead in experimenting with alternative delivery systems such as CHCs, HSOs and CHOs. However, Canadian physicians are paid primarily on a fee-for-service basis by the provincial governments.

Since fee-for-service reimbursement sets fixed prices for medical services, physicians can control the level of their revenues only by adjusting the quantity of services provided. Therefore, fee-for-service reimbursement creates an incentive for physicians to increase the volume of services and to unbundle services. Furthermore, since patients receive medical services at a zero price at the point of delivery, they may be requesting specific treatments. There is some evidence to support the existence of an increased number of billable units of medical services in Canada.[55] Between 1971 and 1985, utilization per physician grew 25 percent in Canada and 7 percent in the US, where the majority of physicians are not paid on a fee-for-service basis.[56] Additional evidence of excess utilization of physician services is the comparison of physician contacts per capita. Physician contacts per capita in Canada are 25 percent higher than in the US and nearly two and one-half times the number for Sweden, but are less than two thirds those in Japan, Germany and Italy.

Although there is no formal system of third-party payer review of physician's recommendations in Canada, there is a mechanism by which excessive physician billings can be detected. The provincial governments periodically review physician billings and compare the billings of physicians with similar practice characteristics. Physicians at the extremes may be required to explain their practice patterns to the provincial government. This process merely detects outliers. It may be that Canada could lower health care costs by instituting more extensive utilization review through such practices as

---

[54] The provincial medical association represents all physicians. The association has a negotiating team that determines the negotiating position, which balances the interests of all physician groups.

[55] "Canadian physicians perform about 20 percent more diagnostic and therapeutic procedures per patient than Americans and have 56 percent more office visits", (*The Washington Post*, March 22, 1992).

[56] Barer, Evans and Labelle (1988).

monitoring providers, requiring pre-authorization for surgery and encouraging patients to obtain second opinions. The cost-savings of such programs seem likely to justify the efforts.

The number of practising physicians in Canada has been increasing. In 1979, the Canadian population per practising physician was 656. In 1989, this figure had fallen to 515.[57] The supply of physicians is increasing at a rate of 1.5 to 2 percent per capita per year contrasted with a rate of increase of physician use of about 0.3 percent per capita per year.[58] These statistics have led to some concern about a plentiful supply of physicians in Canada (it is, in fact, close to the average of the 11 countries in this study). However, this tends to be more of an issue in urban areas, with physicians distributed scarcely in rural areas. A recent study found that professional incentives and personal lifestyle factors "strongly favour concentration [of physicians] in urban practice settings".[59]

Some provinces are taking steps to correct the plentiful supply of physicians and their geographic maldistribution. For example, Québec and Manitoba have placed limits on medical school enrolments in an effort to curb the supply of new physicians. In 1983, British Columbia tried to place restrictions on the number of physicians permitted to bill the provincial medical plan. However, this policy met with significant opposition in the medical community and was subsequently overturned.

In the last ten years, Québec has provided incentives for physicians to locate in areas that are in greater relative need of their services. For example, the provincial government in Québec offers to reimburse a new, recently-trained physician at only 70 percent of the established fee schedule if the physician locates in an urban area such as downtown Montreal; conversely, the government reimburses 120 percent of the negotiated fees if the physician locates in certain rural areas. After the first five years in practice, a physician is free to practice in any location with no restrictions on reimbursement. New Brunswick initiated a similar program in July 1990.[60]

---

[57]   House of Commons Canada (1991).

[58]   Evans (1987).

[59]   Barer and Stoddart (1991), p. 13.

[60]   Canada Health Act Annual Report (1991).

In an attempt to control increases in utilization of physician services, several provinces are experimenting with expenditure caps/targets for physician fees paid by the province. In Québec, the provincial government establishes ceilings on the quarterly gross billings of individual general practitioners. Quarterly as opposed to annual ceilings ensure that physicians are available to treat patients throughout the year. Any billings in excess of these ceilings are reimbursed at only 25 percent. British Columbia, Alberta, Saskatchewan, Manitoba, New Brunswick and Ontario have established limits on total billings by individual physicians. In British Columbia, the recent threat of such caps on revenues prompted physicians to strike.[61]

Canadian physicians earn significantly less income than their US counterparts. In 1987, the average income of a Canadian physician was C$101,800 ($91,600 1990) and the average income of a US physician was $132,300 ($151,500 1990).[62] Canadian physicians earn about the same as physicians in Germany (using 1990, PPP exchange rates) and significantly more than physicians in France, Japan, New Zealand, the UK and Sweden. However, Canadian medical school enrolments are on the rise, and "physicians remain Canada's highest paid professionals".[63]

Differences in the institutional features governing physicians' behaviour between the US and the other countries, including Canada, may explain inter-country differences in income. For example, US physicians face greater risk or uncertainty than other countries' physicians in at least three ways. First, due to the litigious nature of US society, physicians in the US face a much greater risk of a malpractice lawsuit and resulting damage to their reputations and future income, than do other countries' doctors.[64] Second, in addition to their duties as medical care providers, US physicians must act as bill collectors. In this role, they face a risk of non-payment for services. In Canada, physicians are guaranteed payment for their services by the provincial government. An advantage of the current Canadian system over the previous

---

[61]   Michael Walker refers to a province-wide strike by health care workers and a one-day strike by doctors to register their discontent with the provincial government's caps on billings. This strike was ongoing at the time he wrote the article, Summer 1992 (Walker, 1992).

[62]   Poullier (1989).

[63]   Iglehart (1990), p. 567.

[64]   "Canadian physicians are sued for malpractice about one fifth as often as their US counterparts. The average fee paid by Canadian physicians for malpractice insurance is one ninth as high as that paid by US physicians ... " (Coyte, et al., 1991).

US style system that existed in Canada is that the physician is no longer a bill-collector. Finally, most other countries subsidise the education of their physicians to a much greater extent than the US.[65] Therefore, physicians in other countries begin their practices with relatively little debt compared to their US counterparts.[66] US physicians willing to invest in medical education expect a greater income.

4.3.5   Hospital Sector

In 1991, hospitals accounted for 39 percent of total health expenditure in Canada. There are 1,227 hospitals in Canada[67] classified by status or licence as: public, federal or private. Public hospitals are not operated for profit, accept all patients regardless of ability to pay, and are recognized as public by the provincial government. Although hospitals operated by the Federal Government are publicly owned, they are grouped in a separate classification. Private hospitals admit patients who pay for the services provided either through private insurance or out-of-pocket.

Within each status classification, hospitals can be further categorized by controlling body. Public hospitals can be controlled by any of the following: cities, towns, counties, municipalities (municipal); the provincial government (provincial); non-profit, non-religious, non-government, voluntary organizations (lay); or churches or religious orders (religious). Federal hospitals can be controlled by one of the following government departments: the Department of Veterans Affairs (DVA); Health and Welfare Canada (HWC); Industrial (crown corporations); the Department of National Defence (DND); the Solicitor General of Canada (Correctional Service Canada). Private hospitals are categorized under the following types of controlling body: for-profit organizations (proprietary); religious; municipal; or provincial.

---

[65]   "Canadians highest medical tuition is $3,200 a year. Montreal's illustrious McGill University charges $1,600." In contrast, George Washington University (GWU), albeit one of the most costly in the U.S., has a current tuition charge of $27,500. Less expensive than GWU although significantly more expensive than Canadian universities are the Mayo Medical School and Johns Hopkins, with annual tuition charges of $15,600 and $17,500, respectively (*The Washington Post*, July 21, 1992).

[66]   An example of a new Canadian doctor's typical total debt upon graduation is approximately $16,000 compared to the average US medical student's burden of $46,000 (*Los Angeles Times*, July 16, 1992).

[67]   Canadian Hospital Association (1991).

These 1,227 hospitals provide a total of 182,222 beds (7.0 per thousand of the population), of which 96.2 percent are in public hospitals, 1.4 percent are in federal hospitals and 2.4 percent are in private hospitals. As of 1988-1989, the average occupancy rate for all public hospitals in Canada was 81 percent. However, overall occupancy rates vary widely by province from 36 percent in the Northwest Territories to 86 percent in Québec.[68] According to OECD data, in 1987 the average occupancy rate in Canadian hospitals was 83 percent.

In Canada, the provincial governments fund the operating expenses of public hospitals through global budgets negotiated annually by the hospital and the provincial Ministry of Health. Hospitals receive periodic lump-sum payments. In addition to funds provided by the provincial governments, hospitals obtain revenues through charges covered by private insurance and donations.

Global budgeting can provide a powerful incentive to contain costs. In general, this incentive has positive effects on efficiency since it creates an incentive for hospitals to explore the following: outpatient as opposed to inpatient care; bulk purchasing of medicines; contracting out services such as laundry and meal services (rather than providing them internally); and merging departments with similar functions.[69]

However, a hospital's emphasis on cost-containment can have an adverse impact on the nature of service provided. For example, hospitals may seek to keep beds occupied by patients requiring low-intensity care, preventing physicians from using acute-care beds for short-term patients who are often in greater need of care. These "bed-blockers" are of two types: patients who are not discharged expediently after a period of high-intensity care, and patients who require only low-intensity care.[70]

These patients therefore have daily medical requirements that are well below average in cost. These patients are typically over 65 years of age, and their lengths of stay exceed 60 days. In general, bed-blockers pose an economic problem if care could be provided at lower cost elsewhere or if they keep out a patient with a higher value use for the bed.

---

[68] Canadian Hospital Association (1991).

[69] US General Accounting Office (1991).

[70] They are typically over 65 years of age, and their lengths of stay exceed 60 days.

The elderly patients currently blocking beds in acute-care hospitals could be adequately treated, at lower cost, either at home, or in other specialized institutions such as CHCs or long-term care facilities. The recent Standing Committee report acknowledges the need for a reallocation of public funds. Several witnesses proposed to shift funds away from costly hospital care toward community and home-care services.[71]

The Ontario Ministry of Health estimates that bed-blockers occupy approximately 15 percent of acute-care beds.[72] The comparative average length-of-stay data for hospital patients in Canada and the US provide some evidence supporting the existence of a bed-blocker problem. The average length-of-stay for all disease categories was over 75 percent higher in Canada (11.4 days) than in the US (6.4 days).[73] But it should be noted that across the countries in our study length-of-stay is shortest in the US, highest in Japan and broadly the same in Canada as in all the other countries.

Data regarding the length of stay of elderly patients in the US and two Canadian provinces also supports the existence of bed-blockers. In 1985, one percent of elderly patients stayed over 60 days in US hospitals. This is considerably less than the corresponding data for Canada. In Ontario, 2.9 percent of elderly patients stayed over 60 days and in Manitoba, the corresponding figure was five percent.[74,75]

Bed-blockers exacerbate the queuing problem and, thus, have an adverse impact on the overall quality and mix of hospital services provided. More general problems with global budgeting are as follows: it discourages bottom-up responsibility for controlling costs; it encourages a growth mentality; and it fails to address inequities in hospital budgets.[76]

---

[71]   House of Commons Canada (1991).

[72]   US General Accounting Office (1991).

[73]   Poullier (1989).

[74]   Data for the US and Ontario are for all hospitals excluding rehabilitation and long-term hospitals. Data for Manitoba exclude stays in personal care units, geriatrics and extended treatment hospitals.

[75]   Newhouse, Anderson and Roos (1988).

[76]   US General Accounting Office (1991).

Long-term needs such as major renovation or equipment acquisition are not included in these global operating budgets and are subject to provincial approval based on a "needs assessment." Most of the funding for these projects comes from the province, although the hospital is usually required to fund some portion of the cost (10 to 40 percent).[77] If a hospital raises sufficient private funds to purchase a new piece of medical equipment, the provincial government must still provide the necessary additional operating expenses in the global budget.

Through the process of needs assessment, provincial governments control the diffusion of medical technology. Perhaps as a consequence of this government control over access to high technology for hospitals, the availability of some major technologies in Canada is lower than that in the US. For example, Canada has substantially fewer units per capita than the US of open-heart surgery, cardiac catheterization, organ transplantation, radiation therapy, extracorporeal shock-wave lithotripsy and magnetic resonance imaging (MRI).[78] A comparison of availability of MRIs in the Toronto and Washington DC metropolitan areas (areas of similar size and population) shows that Toronto has five MRIs, whereas the metropolitan Washington area has 35. Lack of access to technology can be a problem in Canada. Walter Kucharzyle, Chairman of Radiology at the University of Toronto states, "I can point to about a dozen cases a year at my centre where someone's health was directly jeopardised because they couldn't get an MRI". He claims that Toronto should have at least 14 MRI to deliver a minimum standard of quality care.[79]

4.3.6 Pharmaceutical Sector

4.3.6.1 Structure of the Pharmaceutical Sector

In 1991, expenditure on pharmaceuticals accounted for 13.8 percent of total health care spending in Canada;[80] that is, total sales were C$9.2 billion ($7.7 bn 1990). Canada is a net importer of pharmaceutical products, largely from the US. In 1987, Canadian exports of pharmaceutical and medicinal products

---

[77]   Neuschler (1990).

[78]   Rublee (1989).

[79]   *The Washington Post*, March 22, 1992.

[80]   Health and Welfare Canada (1993).

were C$140.4 million ($126m 1990) and imports were C$359.1 million ($323m 1990) leading to a trade deficit of C$218.7 million ($197m 1990).[81]

In most cases, pharmacists dispense medicines. However, in some remote areas where pharmacists are not available, doctors may dispense.

In general, expenditure on out-patient medicines are not covered by the provincial health plans, with exceptions made for the elderly (age 65 and over) and for the needy in some provinces. For these two exceptions, the provincial government provides a "formulary": a list of the medicines covered by the provincial plan. Most individuals other than those covered by the government have supplemental insurance to cover their expenditure on medicines; indeed, this coverage accounts for a large portion of private-sector insurance.

A firm with a new pharmaceutical product needs to obtain a Notice of Compliance (NoC) before it can market the product. The Health Protection Branch of Health and Welfare Canada processes new product applications. The branch examines the safety and efficacy data of new medicines and, upon approval, issues a NoC. On average, it takes about 10 years for a new product to receive a NoC: seven years for product development and three for the regulatory review.

After receiving a NoC, a new medicine can be marketed in Canada. However, to obtain maximum benefit from the sale of the product, manufacturers try to get their product onto the provincial formularies. The provinces often re-examine the data used for approval at the federal level, increasing the delay before the product can be sold in certain provinces.

4.3.6.2 Canadian Patent Law

For applications filed on or after October 1, 1989, patent protection lasts 20 years from the date of filing. For applications filed before this date, patent protection lasts only 17 years. Given that the development and regulatory approval processes can consume the first 10 years of patent protection, effective patent protection for medicines is more like 10 years. Moreover, from 1923 to 1993, Canada allowed some form of compulsory licensing for pharmaceutical products, which further reduced effective patent protection.[82]

---

[81]   Statistics Canada (1991).

[82]   Compulsory licensing requires that innovators grant a license to a competitor upon request.

284

In an effort to boost incentives for R&D spending in Canada, the Canadian Government placed severe limits on compulsory licensing in 1987 by amending the Canada Patent Act. The 1987 amendments provided patent holders varying periods of exemption, or market exclusivity, before a compulsory licence could be issued on their products. For products whose active ingredients are manufactured outside Canada, no compulsory licence can be issued until 10 years after the product has received a NoC. For products whose active ingredients are manufactured within Canada, no compulsory licence can be issued until seven years after NoC.[83] Thus, the 1987 amendments ceased "open" compulsory licensing and assured innovators of at least seven years of exclusive marketing before the compulsory licensing could be required.

In return for this improved patent protection, the Canadian pharmaceutical industry committed itself to doubling the ratio of its R&D expenditure to its sales revenue by 1991. In 1991, members of the Pharmaceutical Manufacturers Association of Canada had a ratio of R&D to sales of 9.6 percent, making the pharmaceutical industry second only to the Federal Government in the funding of health research.[84] Currently, the pharmaceutical industry funds 24 cents of every dollar spent on health research in Canada, representing a significant increase from 17 cents in 1987.[85]

The 1987 amendments also created the Patented Medicine Prices Review Board (PMPRB). The PMPRB sets maximum allowable price increases for existing products and monitors the price levels of new products. Permissible price increases for existing products are tied closely to increases in the consumer price index (CPI). In the event that a medicine's price rises at a faster rate than that allowed by the PMPRB, or a new medicine is priced excessively, the PMPRB has the authority to reduce that product's period of market exclusivity if firms do not lower prices to the level specified by the PMPRB. From 1987 to the end of 1990, the prices of patented medicines increased at an average annual rate of 3.1 percent compared with the 4.4 percent allowed under the

---

[83]   For products researched and discovered in Canada, there is no compulsory licensing unless the patentee fails to manufacture the product to supply substantially the Canadian market. In this case, a compulsory license to manufacture can be issued seven years after NoC.

[84]   PMPRB (1991).

[85]   PMAC (1992).

PMPRB's guidelines and with the average annual increase of 4.7 percent in the CPI over the same period.[86]

4.3.6.3 Recent Developments

Currently, the Canadian pharmaceutical approval process is under review. Due to insufficient manpower, the Health Protection Branch cannot maintain a "detail-oriented" approach, such as that used by the US FDA. Instead, Canadian regulators are looking more towards European approval processes as models to improve their current approach. They are now assessing whether it is possible to move towards a more cooperative approval process in which a lead country would conduct the actual review of clinical data and share information with other countries.

Canada is participating in the Pharmaceutical Evaluation Report (PER) project in which regulators from the EC, EFTA, Canada and Australia attempt to agree on a common format for submitting requests for marketing approval. Canada is also following and participating in international harmonisation discussions.

The Canadian government is continuing to strengthen its intellectual property laws. Recently, the Minister of Industry, Science and Technology, and International Trade announced that Canada has endorsed the intellectual property measures outlined in the draft text of the General Agreement on Tariffs and Trade (GATT), in an effort to make Canadian intellectual property protection consistent with that of its major trading partners (see Section 4.5.6). Canada's endorsement of the GATT proposals is expected to stimulate additional investment by the pharmaceutical industry.

In February 1993 Bill C-91 was signed into law in Canada.[87] Termed the Patent Act Amendment Act of 1992, this legislation eliminates compulsory licensing altogether. Thus, patented products will now receive the exclusivity granted them by the full term of the patent. Also, Bill C-91 eliminates the PMPRB's ability to reduce market exclusivity for products with excessive price increases. However, it gives the PMPRB significantly increased enforcement powers by allowing it to require firms to pay back revenues derived from "unfair" prices. Bill C-91 gives Canada significantly improved intellectual

---

[86]   PMAC (1992).

[87]   Pharmaceutical Manufacturers Association (PMA) Newsletter, February 8, 1993.

property protection. However, Canada still does not have any provision for patent term restoration, which exists in other G-7 countries.[88]

The North American Free Trade Agreement (NAFTA) between the US, Canada and Mexico establishes a minimum standard of intellectual property protection in each of these countries. NAFTA has been agreed in principle and, given ratification by the individual national legislative bodies, could come into force on January 1, 1994. Passage of Bill C-91, has been necessary for Canada to comply with the intellectual property provisions in NAFTA.

Despite the recent efforts to extend market exclusivity for patented products, Canada has a thriving generic pharmaceutical industry. Between 1987 and 1990, dollar sales by the two largest generic manufacturers "grew by 63 percent while the total market grew by 42 percent and their prescriptions grew 18 percent compared to total market growth of only 4 percent".[89] Generic substitution is allowed in most provinces and territories, except Prince Edward Island, Nova Scotia and the Northwest Territories, unless the physician specifies that no substitution may be made.

---

[88] Patent term restoration provides an extension in patent term for producers to compensate the patentee for time lost in the approval process.

[89] IMS data reported in PMAC (1992).

4.4   INTERSECTORAL ANALYSIS

4.4.1   Major Decision Makers

4.4.1.1   Financing

Government participation in health care is part of the culture in Canada. The two major decision makers on the financing side of the health care system are the Federal and provincial governments.

Ultimately, health care is a provincial responsibility. Therefore, many decisions regarding funding, the level of services, the existence of premiums, etc. are made at the provincial level. The Federal Government has been able to set and maintain national criteria for health care in Canada through the leverage provided by its financial contributions to the provinces. These criteria, which are outlined in the Canada Health Act, are: public administration, universality, comprehensiveness, portability and accessibility.

The growth in the Federal Government *per capita* contributions is linked to the rate of growth of nominal GNP. However, the general recession in Canada has caused the Federal Government to freeze its contributions to each province at the 1989-1990 level for the last two years. They are expected to remain frozen through 1994-1995. As a result, the federal contribution, as a percentage of total public spending on health care, has decreased from approximately 45 percent in 1979 to 33 percent in 1991 (Data Table 6). Meanwhile, per capita health expenditures have been steadily increasing. There has, therefore, been increasing pressure on the provinces and private sector to meet the financing needs of the health care system. The provinces, under pressure, have reduced the number of supplementary services covered and the private sector is slowly taking on a larger role (it increased from 24 percent of total health care expenditure in 1975 to an estimated 28 percent in 1991.

Currently, the Federal Government retains its considerable influence on the provincial health care plans and the federal contribution is still sufficient to ensure that provinces uphold the standards outlined in the Canada Health Act. However, if the Federal Government's share of total public spending on health care continues to decline, the provinces will bear more of the financing responsibility. The provincial Ministries of Health may then become more independent. If continued, this trend would cast doubt on the ability of the Federal Government to maintain national standards for health care in Canada.

4.4.1.2 Delivery

Physicians are the primary gatekeepers in the Canadian health care system. They determine the nature of the treatment that patients will receive as well as the place of treatment; that is, in a doctor's office, hospital, CHC, etc. Physicians also have a role in determining the timing of a patient's care. Since patients are free to choose their physicians,[90] they exercise some control over the health care that they receive. Indirectly, through their choice of physician, they choose the hospital at which they receive care.[91]

Since fee schedules are the result of bargaining between the provincial medical association and the provincial government, the fees for a procedure within a province are uniform across physicians.[92] Even if patients were sensitive to prices, price competition would not exist unless physicians wanted to discount from the agreed-upon schedule. Thus, price competition is virtually absent among Canadian physicians. During the period when specialist physicians were allowed to extra-bill, there was a mechanism for patient selection of physician services based on price. However, the ban on extra-billing removed this element of competition and contributed to the formation of queues. Currently, if there is any competition, it is over the quality of services provided.[93]

This absence of a price-rationing mechanism to allocate the amount of services consumed in Canada means that, when there is a supply shortage, health care services are rationed by queuing.[94] Patients are placed on a waiting list to receive certain hospital-based treatments. Their position on the waiting list is a function of the urgency with which the physician determines their need for

---

[90] Patients have the most control over their choice of primary care physician. In theory, they are free to choose a specialist. However, in practice, general practitioners refer patients to specialists, thereby controlling specialist selection.

[91] Most physicians have admitting privileges at one or more hospitals. Therefore, if a patient wants to receive treatment at a particular hospital, the patient must choose a physician with admitting privileges at that hospital.

[92] There may be some differences in fees between urban and rural areas.

[93] Competition based on quality would occur in those areas where the supply of physicians is plentiful.

[94] Carr and Mathewson show that "when extra-billing is banned, queues of patients will form for specialists" (Carr and Mathewson, 1992, p. 24). General practice physicians ration by time; that is, they reduce the length of a single visit, but increase the number of visits per patient.

treatment. Given that physicians assess a patient's need for treatment, they have a role in determining a patient's position in the queue and, therefore, the timing of treatment. A patient may select a physician based on the physician's ability to offer help in moving ahead in the queue.

In Canada, there is substantial debate regarding the problem of queuing for health care services. For example, waiting times for cataract/lens replacement and coronary bypass surgery have been highly publicized in Canada as examples of insufficient access to care within the health care system.[95] Lack of access to necessary treatments can manifest itself in a number of ways: most dramatically, patients suffer physically or die; or patients seek treatment out of the country. There are examples of both of these phenomena in Canada. The costs inherent in waiting lists include decreased productivity, lower quality of life and greater expenditure on substitutes for hospital care.

In Ontario, attention focused on waiting lists for open-heart surgery during 1988. In May 1988, a cardiovascular surgeon in Toronto announced that there had been twelve or thirteen deaths on his personal waiting list since 1987.[96] At the end of 1988, deaths of two cardiac surgery patients in Toronto attracted national media attention. Popular opinion was that long waits and multiple cancellations of scheduled surgery had been a major contributing factor to the deaths. In addition, Canadian patients travelling across the border to the US to receive timely treatment receive substantial media attention.[97]

Continuing publicity and political pressure led the Ontario government to mount a special investigation into cardiac surgery. At the time of the investigation, there were approximately 1,700 people in Ontario on cardiac surgery waiting lists. Total waiting times for elective cases of open-heart surgery ranged from as little as four to eight weeks to six months or more. The government and providers responded by increasing capacity (an increase of approximately 800 open-heart cases per year was attained) and enhancing efficiency at existing hospitals. Also, approximately 300 patients were allowed to seek treatment in the US and be reimbursed under the Ontario health plan. By January 1991, the cardiac surgery waiting list in Ontario was estimated to have fallen from 1,800 persons in 1990 to 1,000. Average waiting times for

---

[95]   Heritage Foundation (1992).

[96]   Naylor (1991).

[97]   Naylor (1991).

elective surgery were down to only a few weeks. With current capacity and waiting times, the Ontario Government has discontinued reimbursement for elective open-heart surgery performed in the United States. Therefore, the government targeted a specific amount of rationing and used the US as a safety valve.

The case of open heart surgery in Ontario illustrates that there are mechanisms in place, in the form of provincial government review and control, to address problems of queuing should it become a serious threat to the quality of health care. There are, however, other mechanisms for rationing that allow consumers choice rather than reliance on public outcry to spur government action in a timely manner. This example demonstrates the inefficiency inherent in a single-payer administered system to respond to a shortage. Patients died and the US health care system had to absorb Canadian patients before the Ontario policy makers could adjust. Furthermore, even after addressing the problem, a waiting list still exists.

4.4.1.3 Medical Technology

In recent testimony before the Standing Committee, the Canadian Federation of Biological Societies expressed their view that Canada has low levels of expenditure on R&D in general, including health research in particular. Health and Welfare Canada estimates that total expenditure on health research in Canada accounted for 0.8 percent of total health expenditure in 1975 and 0.9 percent in 1987. It is unclear, however, whether this level is above or below that which should be considered economically efficient.

The Medical Research Council (MRC) is the federal agency supporting most biomedical research in Canada. In 1990/91, MRC had a budget of C$241.5 million ($191m 1990). The MRC focuses on basic research. The National Health Research and Development Program (NHRDP) complements the MRC with research in public health and health care systems. In 1990/91, the NHRDP had a budget of C$28.1 million ($22.2m 1990).[98] For the year ending March 31, 1990, a total of C$1.17 billion was spent on medical research in Canada, up from the C$825 million spent in 1987.[99] In 1987, public spending

---

[98]   House of Commons Canada (1991).

[99]   PMAC Report (1992).

on biomedical research was about US$ 10 1990 per capita in Canada compared to US$ 38 1990 per capita in the US.[100]

In Canada, the introduction of major medical technologies is controlled by the provincial governments. The provincial government must provide the funds for the initial capital expenditure; however, the hospital is free to seek funding for capital investment from private sources. To implement a new medical technology, hospitals in Canada must have the associated operating expenses, which must be approved by the provincial government in the annual global budgeting process. Thus, through global budgets, provincial governments control the number of hospitals that can purchase high technology equipment; thereby controlling the rate of technological diffusion.[101]

Empirical evidence on the rate of technological diffusion in Canada compares the availability of six major technologies in Canada, Germany and the US;[102] and some information concerning France.[103] The six technologies are: open-heart surgery; cardiac catheterisation; organ transplantation; radiation therapy; extracorporeal shock-wave lithotripsy; and magnetic resonance imaging (MRI). Drawing on these sources:

- Canada has 65 percent more open-heart surgery units than Germany but less than the US;

- there are 70 percent more cardiac catheterisation units per capita in Germany than in Canada, and three times as many in the US;

- Canada has twice as many transplantation units as Germany per capita but less than the US;

- the number of radiation therapy units per capita in the US and in Germany are six to seven times the Canadian level;

- there are six times as many lithotripters per capita in the US than in Canada, and twice as many in Germany and in France; and,

---

[100]   OECD (1991).

[101]   Generally, regulations and price restrictions reduce diffusion of technology.

[102]   Rublee (1989).

[103]   French Hospital News (1987).

- there are eight times as many MRIs per capita in the US than in Canada, twice as many in Germany and around the same number in France.

These comparisons suggest that Canada has considerably fewer of these high technology facilities than the US, which spends more per capita on health care. Canada also seems to have marginally less access to technology than Germany or France, even though both of these nations have lower per capita health care expenditure.

With regard to medicines, new products must be on provincial formularies to be reimbursed for elderly and needy Canadians. For other Canadians, medicines must be either paid for out-of-pocket or covered through the purchase of supplemental private insurance. This creates a distortion in that medicines are often cost-effective forms of therapy, but consumers must pay relatively more (out-of-pocket or insurance premium) for a pharmaceutical therapy than a therapy covered by the provincial medical plan, which is available at zero price. Policies that create disincentives to use the most cost effective therapy create distortions and slow the diffusion of medical technology in Canada.[104]

4.4.2 Consistency of Objectives and Incentives

In any health care system, the primary goal of the patient is to receive quality care at the lowest possible price. In the Canadian system, the price of medically necessary services is set at zero at the point of delivery. Thus, it appears to patients that they are receiving "free" health care when, in fact, their health care system is quite costly. Using OECD data for 1987, the total health expenditures as a percentage of Gross Domestic Product (GDP) equalled 8.8 percent in Canada. Of the countries under study, Canada ranked third behind the US (11.2 percent) and Sweden (9.2 percent). Using the same database, per capita spending on health care in Canada was US$1,401. The comparable number for the US was US$2,051. While Canada ranked fourth of the countries in terms of per capita health expenditures in 1987, by 1990 Canada had moved to second at US$1,991 per capita behind only the US with health expenditures per capita of US$2,566.[105]

---

[104] Levy states that "cost sharing restricted to pharmaceuticals may encourage replacement of drug therapy with more expensive forms of treatment; therefore, cost sharing should apply to the full range of medical services to prevent service substitution" (Levy, 1992, p. iii).

[105] *New York Times*, 17 February, 1992.

Canadian patients cannot directly observe the costs of their individual treatments, nor do they share in many of the costs through copayments. Therefore, they lack incentives to restrict their health care consumption to cost-effective services. This lack of cost-consciousness on the part of Canadian patients creates an incentive to consume health care and decreases the incentive for patients to practice lifestyles that reduce the need for health interventions.

Moreover, patients often do not have sufficient information to make decisions regarding the amount or the type of treatments that they need.[106] Patients must rely on the advice of physicians. Therefore, physicians act as agents for patients in making their health care consumption decisions. Patients are often poorly informed about the quality of the agent or the availability of alternative treatments for a given problem.

In their role as gatekeepers to the Canadian health care system, physicians have incentives that combine to increase upward pressure on health care costs. First, physicians have an incentive to provide advice regarding necessary care as well as actual treatment in some cases. Since the patient does not pay directly for care, the physician has the incentive to recommend all treatments for which the marginal benefit to the patient is greater than zero, without necessarily considering the cost. Physicians wanting to keep patients will also have an incentive to respond to all requests by patients for treatment no matter how trivial, especially in the urban areas where the supply of physicians is plentiful. Second, physicians have an incentive to maximize their individual incomes. Since most Canadian physicians are paid on a fee-for-service basis, physician income is a function of the number of procedures performed. Therefore, physicians have an incentive to maximize their incomes by increasing the number of services performed. Of course, the first incentive ensures that the patient will receive medically necessary services, but it imposes a time-cost on patients. The second incentive is for physicians to perform services that will have health-neutral effects on the patient or provide treatments that are not necessarily the most cost effective.

One way for physicians to increase their incomes without affecting the health of their patients is to order more diagnostic tests than medically necessary. Although testing is not usually harmful to patients' health, it results in utilization of physician services and imposes time-costs on patients. Our

---

[106] "At the same time, 30 percent of Canadian doctors said they were frustrated by patients demanding services they do not need" (*Wall Street Journal*, June 9, 1992, p. B-5).

interviews with physicians confirm that this type of behaviour exists. Some physicians in Canada request that patients appear for repeat office visits for problems that have a high probability of being self-correcting. Another way this perverse incentive may manifest itself is in the physician's recommendation of treatment alternatives. Suppose a condition such as an ear infection in a child could be treated with an antibiotic or the surgical procedure of inserting tubes in the ears. Since the physician earns additional revenues by performing surgery, but not for prescribing an antibiotic, there may be a strong incentive for the physician to recommend surgery as opposed to prescribing a medicine.

There is evidence that over-utilization of physician services may be a problem in Canada. In some provinces, controls on real (inflation-adjusted) physician fees have been more than offset by increased activity by physicians. For example, in British Columbia, an index of real billings per physician increased by 8.4 percent despite the fact that real physician fees remained steady over the period.[107]

Unlike physicians in the Canadian system, hospitals have an incentive to control costs. Hospitals are funded by annual global operating budgets negotiated with the provincial health ministry. Since hospitals must fund all expenditures from the given prospective budget, they have an incentive to control costs. For the most part, the cost-cutting incentive provided by global budgeting has a positive effect on the goal of quality care at lowest possible cost. However, in some instances, this cost-minimizing incentive leads to undesirable hospital practices, such as bed blocking (see Section 4.3.5).

In an additional attempt to control hospital costs, provincial governments must approve capital expenditures for new medical technologies as well as the necessary increases in operating funds to use the technology. Such regulation is analogous to certificate-of-need regulation in the US, which has been, by and large, abandoned due to its cost-increasing effects. Artificially restricting the number of hospitals with particular equipment eliminates any possibility of price-reducing competition among hospitals for providing the services associated with the equipment.[108] An alternative theory holds that duplication of capital-intensive services (medical arms race) raises the costs of

---

[107]   Barer, Evans and Labelle (1988).

[108]   Competition could exist among hospitals with the same equipment.

care. However, it appears that this proposition does not stand up to scrutiny.[109]

4.4.3   Economic Implications for Efficiency and Equity

The Canadian health care system is based upon an equity principle; this is, that a patient's ability to pay should not affect the patient's access to health care. The five national standards set out in the Canada Health Act reflect this principle; public administration; universality; comprehensiveness; portability; and accessibility. Through the comprehensiveness and universality provisions, the Canadians achieve the goal of comprehensive insurance coverage for all residents for all medically necessary hospital and physician services. Further, the accessibility provision prohibits copayments on the grounds that such charges may impede access to necessary care. These provisions ensure that much health care is available to all Canadians at zero price at the point of delivery.

The Canadian system also prohibits supplemental, private insurance for services covered under the provincial plans.[110] This virtually eliminates the possibility of a two-tier health care system. Furthermore, it illustrates the Canadians' views on equity; namely, no one should have access to better health care as a result of greater ability to pay.

Even if public funding of health care is chosen on equity grounds, it is important to aim for efficiency in production. Several of the features of the current Canadian system, however, contribute to inefficiency:

- Combining fee-for-service with zero price at the point of delivery gives an incentive for excess utilization of physician services.

- Global budgets may prevent the efficient use of acute-care beds and, if tight, will create a queuing problem.

- Government control over the diffusion of technology may not take account fully of the benefits of technology relative to costs.

---

[109]   "[O]ur results undermine the importance of the MAR (medical arms race), and they cast doubt on claims that hospital mergers increase efficiency by reducing competition" (Dranove, Shanley and Simon, 1992, p. 261).

[110]   Private care is permitted for government-covered services; but patients must bear the full costs of such care. Therefore, this option is essentially unavailable to the great majority of Canadians.

4.5 ANALYSIS OF HEALTH CARE POLICY

4.5.1 Overview

In this section, we summarise the major issues regarding efficiency and equity arising in each sector of the Canadian health care system.

Given the overall enthusiasm for the Canadian system, within Canada and elsewhere and given its performance, evidenced by morbidity/mortality data, it would seem that the Canadian health care system is performing at a very satisfactory level in many respects. Nevertheless, we do not operate in a static environment. The Canadian system is not well-designed to make the tough choices associated with the increasing flow of new, high-cost medical technologies, which require that resources be rationed. This problem is exacerbated by general economy-wide problems (i.e. the recession), and new health problems (e.g. aging population).

Within each sector, we describe and assess the reforms recently implemented or proposed by the provincial and federal governments.

4.5.2 Patients

4.5.2.1 Information on Costs

Economic efficiency requires that a patient will not consume a particular health care service unless the expected benefit from consuming the service outweighs the cost of providing the service. (Equity concerns may require that health care expenditure is inefficient in this sense.) It is the market, and the information about costs and prices that a market situation produces, that generally allows an efficient allocation of resources.

A problem arises in the Canadian system, however, because there is little readily-available information regarding costs and Canadian patients receive health care at zero price at the point of delivery. Thus, patients are unaware of the actual costs of most health care services and have no incentive to become aware. Such uninformed consumers cannot make efficient decisions about the relative costs and benefits of consuming health care services. The illusion that health care is "free" in Canada is, of course, untrue. Canadians pay taxes to the Federal and provincial governments to fund the health care system.   However, Canadians do not know the exact portion of their individual tax dollars devoted to funding health care.[111]

4.5.2.2   User Charges

One solution to this problem that is currently under discussion is cost-sharing by patients at the point of service. Copayments make patients more aware of the cost of consuming care and deter the consumption of health care (given the standard relationship that the demand for health care is inversely related to the price).[112]   Of course, copayments may restrict access to care for some Canadians, so payments by patients in the low income group (those below the poverty level) could be zero and there could be an out-of-pocket maximum for all Canadians.   However, the introduction of copayments may violate the accessibility criterion described in the Canada Health Act. In the absence of amending legislation, a province introducing copayments for certain services into its system would no longer be eligible for the federal cash contribution.

In Québec, the Provincial Government proposed to introduce a user charge of C\$5 (\$3.71 1990), termed a reorientation fee, for "unnecessary" emergency room visits. An emergency room visit was deemed unnecessary if the patient could have received comparable care at a CHC. This measure was designed to increase efficiency in patients' choices of location for treatment. However, the Federal Government threatened to withdraw its funding since it viewed the proposal as violating the accessibility condition of the Canada Health Act. Thus, the Québec Government has not implemented this policy.

Survey evidence suggests that there is growing support in the provinces for the introduction of user charges. Eighty percent of the respondents in a recent survey found a C\$5 (\$3.71 1990) fee acceptable. Health ministers from the provinces recently met with Federal Government officials in Ottawa to discuss possible solutions to the increasing pressure on provinces to fund their health care plans. At this meeting, the participants discussed copayments as a means of controlling costs. Indeed, copayments already exist in some provinces for certain benefits not mandated by the Federal Government, primarily medicines, so Canadians already have some experience with copayments.

---

[111]   The Federal contribution for health care is known, and Canadians seem to be aware that health care accounts for approximately one-third of the provincial government budgets.

[112]   Using data from one randomized experiment, Manning et al. show that even with a cap on out-of-pocket expenditures, cost sharing affects the demand for medical services (Manning et al., 1987).

A problem could arise with copayments if they are selectively applied. That is, if copayments apply to some therapies such as antibiotics for ear infections (cost-effective therapies) but not ear tubes (surgery), patients may substitute the therapy available at zero price regardless of 'true' cost effectiveness.[113] Another problem arises because patient fees may reduce demand for necessary services. A patient may refrain from consuming a particular service because he/she cannot afford the fee and, as a result, the patient's condition may deteriorate. As well as the pain and discomfort (possibly death) that arises, the patient may also, ultimately, require more costly medical intervention.[114] Any policy requiring patient fees would need to be accompanied by patient education on cost-effectiveness and compliance with treatment schedules.

Another proposal to address the issue of patient insensitivity to costs is Ontario's proposal to tax patients' health care consumption if it is over a certain level. Specifically, if the annual limit on health care consumption is $5,000, but a patient consumes $7,000 of care, the patient pays a tax as if the $2,000 of care were additional income.[115] This is also a form of copayment. However, it could have an impact on those patients with severe medical problems, in addition to the frivolous consumer of health care. It is unclear whether this proposal would be acceptable to the Federal Government.

4.5.2.3 Information in Other Areas

Another policy aim is to improve information in areas other than prices, cost-effectiveness and compliance. Many of the provinces in Canada are already devoting resources to preventive care in an attempt to forestall the need for acute medical care later. Such efforts attempt to inform Canadians about the benefits and costs of particular lifestyles. Changing lifestyles to take account of known (i) adverse health consequences of tobacco use, alcohol and other drug abuse, and careless sexual practices; and (ii) improvements in health status through diet and exercise, will reduce the need for medical care later and help people lead more productive lives.

---

[113] One possibility is to have a lower copayment for the most cost-effective therapy.

[114] Manning et al. reject the hypothesis that less favourable coverage of out-patient services increases total expenditure (Manning et al., 1987, p. 251).

[115] The numbers used in this illustration are purely for exposition. They bear no relationship to the actual proposal. Note that this proposal is not consistent with standard economic models of optimal insurance.

Better information for patients could improve their choice of treatment. For example, video programs on particular diseases may help to educate patients on treatment options. One firm produced such videos that provide "viewers detailed descriptions of the risks and benefits of treatments ranging from monitoring symptoms to surgery. Early experience with the videos indicates that the results of such efforts can be profound. At Kaiser Permanente Medical Group in Denver, the rate of prostate surgery among its members plunged 44 percent in the first year after doctors began showing the prostates video in a pilot project involving more than 250 patients".[116]

4.5.2.4 The Elderly

Another issue in the patient sector is the potential impact of the aging Canadian population on the costs of providing health care services.[117] The proportion of elderly (age 65 and over) in the Canadian population has been steadily increasing and is expected to increase further into the next century. For example, in 1981, the percentage of the elderly in the total population was 9.7 percent. By 2011, this is expected to rise to 15.5 percent (see Data Table 1).[118] The rate of increase of this section of the population is higher in Canada than in the US, Germany, France, the UK, or Sweden. Of the countries we examined, only Japan has a higher rate of growth of the elderly population.

Although there is no doubt that the proportion of elderly in the Canadian population is increasing, there is some debate as to the likely effects of the aging population on the health care system. There are those that believe that the increase in health care costs associated with the aging population will necessitate major change or, possibly, a breakdown of the Canadian system. Others predict that much less dire consequences will result.[119]

A recent report of the House of Commons Standing Committee on Health and Welfare, Social Affairs, Seniors and the Status of Women acknowledged the opposing points of view; but, nevertheless, recommended reforms in the provision of services for the elderly in anticipation of the increase in their

---

[116]   *Wall Street Journal*, February 25, 1992, p. B-1.

[117]   "A person over 75 uses 10 times the medical care of a 40-year old" (*The Washington Post*, January 31, 1992).

[118]   Statistics Canada (1990).

[119]   For more information see Evans (1987).

relative numbers. The Standing Committee report emphasized the need for more community and home care alternatives to institutional care. Witnesses before the Standing Committee testified that many seniors receive services in relatively expensive, acute-care institutions when less costly home-care would be sufficient.

In addition, the Standing Committee addressed the problem of use of prescription medicines by senior citizens. Prescription medicines are generally included in the provincial health care coverage for the elderly and needy. The National Advisory Council on Aging reported that approximately 40 percent of emergency room visits and 10 to 20 percent of hospital admissions of seniors are directly or indirectly related to the over-use and/or improper use of medication. In Canada, the average senior citizen receives 33 prescriptions per year. By comparison, the average number of prescriptions per capita in the US is 7.[120] In addition to the obvious adverse effects on the health of seniors, such over-use is costly. Dealing with this problem would cut health care costs by reducing costs for provincial drug programs for the elderly and avoiding procedures and hospitalization related to the misuse of medicines.

4.5.2.5 Queuing

A further issue for patients is the costs imposed on them by the existence of queues for certain services. A recent survey by the Fraser Institute established that one percent of the Canadian population is waiting for some type of procedure. Many of these people seek care in the US. In so doing, they incur costs. Walker recounts the following example: "My next-door neighbours, Bill and Gloria Kelly, arise every morning at six o'clock to drive to Bellingham, Washington, where Bill, a retired engineer, goes to get radiation treatment for prostate gland cancer. They have been doing this for five weeks, and Gloria, a high school teacher, is beginning to feel the strain. The patients before and after Bill at the Bellingham clinic are also Canadians. The Kellys join hundreds of Canadians who travel to Seattle and Tacoma for heart bypass surgery, to get magnetic resonance imaging (MRI) scans, and to seek other treatments not available to them at home. (The costs and dislocations involved in this process are not included in the cost of Canadian health care. The Kellys' fatigue and travel-time figure in neither the provincial government's health care budget nor Barer and Evans's assessment)".[121]

---

[120]   Simonson (1991); and US Department of Commerce (1991).

[121]   Walker (1992), p. 233.

Generally, the process in Canada regarding provision of health care lacks information due to an absence of price signals. The government, then, assumes an administrative role to substitute for the market. In this regard, the provincial governments are aware of the problem of queues and occasionally institute measures to alleviate specific problems. However, the slow pace at which the Canadian health care bureaucracy addresses shortages is an administrative short-coming of the single-payer system that lacks appropriate signals.

4.5.3 Payers

4.5.3.1 Administrative Costs

There is evidence that a single-payer system, such as exists in Canada, requires relatively less expenditure on administrative and overhead costs than a multiple-payer system such as exists in the US. According to one estimate for 1985, the US system spent about 6 percent of all health care costs on prepayment and administration. The corresponding Canadian figure was just over 1 percent.[122] Other estimates of the overhead costs of private insurers in the US range from 12 to 34 percent of benefit payments compared with approximately 1 percent for overhead costs in Canada.[123] Woolhandler and Himmelstein estimated that overhead and billing expenses accounted for 25 to 48 percent of total expenditures on physician services in the US compared to 18 to 34 percent in Canada in 1987. For hospitals, the administrative costs were estimated at 20 percent and 9 percent of total costs in the US and Canada, respectively.[124] The argument is that "a single-payer system lowers the costs of insurance administration by streamlining reimbursement and eliminating expenses associated with selling multiple policies, billing and collecting premiums, and evaluating risk".[125]

---

[122]   Evans (1987).

[123]   Danzon (1992a).

[124]   Woolhandler and Himmelstein (1991).

[125]   US General Accounting Office (1991).

However, it has been suggested that, when properly measured, these cost advantages are substantially overstated.[126] Danzon points out that these estimates do not take into account "hidden" overhead costs in the Canadian system.[127] She says: "These hidden costs include excessive patient time-costs that result from proliferation of multiple short visits in response to controls on physicians' fees; diminished productivity and quality-of-life from delay or unavailability of surgical procedures; and loss of productivity due to under-use of some medical inputs." After adjusting the accounting measures of overhead costs for these and other hidden costs (e.g. risk), Danzon takes the view that the "true" overhead costs of the real-life single-payer system in Canada may be even higher than the overhead costs that might be associated with a well-designed competitive private health system.[128]

4.5.3.2 Decreasing Federal Contributions

As the federal share of the funding of the provincial health care plans decreases, the provinces are beginning to feel more pressure to control costs. In accordance with the Canada Health Act, all provincial plans must provide hospital and physician services. However, many provincial plans offer coverage for additional services such as free prescription medicines for the elderly or dental care for children.

Recent cost-cutting efforts by the provinces have resulted in decreased coverage for some of these additional services. For example, approximately five years ago, Ontario and Québec were paying for all medicines for senior citizens, while British Columbia covered 80 percent of the cost after a deductible of C$250 ($225 1990). New Brunswick used to reimburse all prescription medicines for the elderly after a C$7 ($6 1990) deductible. Currently, Ontario has restricted its formulary, offering coverage for approximately 75 percent of the products covered previously. As of May 15, 1992, Québec introduced a $2 ($1.48 1990) copayment per prescription, up to a maximum out-of-pocket cost of $100 ($74 1990) per year. British Columbia has increased its deductible to $400 ($297 1990) and as of July 1, 1992, New

---

[126] We do not mean to suggest that administrative costs are not, at least, a political issue in the U.S. U.S. insurers acknowledge that reducing administrative costs is an important issue. See Section 15.3.3.1.3.

[127] Danzon (1992a).

[128] Barer and Evans criticize Danzon. See Barer and Evans (1992); Danzon (1992b); and Walker (1992).

Brunswick has eliminated coverage of prescription medicines altogether, except for those in need. Nova Scotia and Saskatchewan have also cut reimbursement for medicines used by the elderly.

Another recent cost-control effort by the Québec government reduced the coverage of children's dental care. Previously, the government provided full coverage for children up to age 15. Recently, it eliminated coverage for 11 to 15 year olds, and now provides coverage for children up to age 10 only.

4.5.3.3 Preventive Health Care

The Federal Government is placing increasing emphasis on health promotion or preventive, as opposed to curative, health care. For example, in a 1991 report, the Federal Government made the following recommendations:[129]

- that a federal-provincial inter-departmental advisory committee be established to develop strategies to change health-threatening behaviour (e.g., avoiding use of tobacco products, alcohol and poor eating habits); thereby reducing risk factors associated with poor health in children and youth (e.g., low birth weight, fetal alcohol syndrome);

- that the promotion and advertising of tobacco products be phased out as soon as reasonably possible;

- that the advertising for alcoholic beverages reflect responsible use of the products; and

- that health warnings, directed towards pregnant women, be placed on alcoholic beverages.

Indeed, since the 1970s, the Canadian government at all levels has encouraged health promotion or a preventive approach to health care. The Federal Government will spend 1.2 percent (C$84.9 million) of the Health Program budget of Health and Welfare Canada on health and services promotion in 1991/92, while 83.8 percent (C$5.8 billion) meets health insurance claims.[130] Rhetoric in Canada suggests the share of the budget for health promotion will increase.

---

[129] Government of Canada (1991).

[130] House of Commons Canada (1991).

Based on a World Health Organization model, health promotion in Canada focuses on the physical and social environment as it relates to the health of the population; for example, environmental pollution, violence, highway accidents, stress, substance abuse, etc. "The 1974 federal document *A New Perspective on the Health of Canadians* recognized that the health care system was only one of four primary determinants of health, the other three being biology, environment and lifestyle. *Achieving Health for All*, published in 1986, outlined a health promotion framework for further improving the health of Canadians".[131] *The Ottawa Charter for Health Promotion* (1986) outlined five strategies to promote health: building health public policy; creating supportive environments; strengthening community action; developing personal skills; and reorienting health services.[132]

4.5.4 Primary Care Sector

Within the Canadian system, there are several issues regarding the primary care sector that merit attention.[133] These include: excess utilization of physician services, plentiful supply of physicians and geographic maldistribution of physicians.

Provincial health care plans reimburse Canadian physicians on a fee-for-service basis. Fee schedules are negotiated annually between the provincial governments and the provincial medical associations. This process is a bilateral monopoly; however, the relative bargaining strengths of the two parties are difficult to assess. The government, as the only payer for physician services, may be able to walk away from the bargaining table easier than the physicians, as happened recently in British Columbia;[134] but, the physicians can strike.

However, fee schedules alone have been less successful at controlling the overall level of expenditures on physician services. Although they control the

---

[131]   House of Commons Canada (1991), p. 13.

[132]   House of Commons Canada (1991).

[133]   See Barer and Stoddart (1991) for a complete discussion of physician resource policy in Canada. They make 53 recommendations for reform in the primary care sector.

[134]   Recently, in British Columbia, the government has enacted legislation (Bills 13 and 14) to allow it to withdraw from negotiating fees with the Provincial Medical Association. The physicians are spending C$3 million ($2.2m 1990) for advertising to generate support for repeal.

price of services, fee schedules cannot control the quantity of services provided and, thus, cannot control the overall level of resources consumed. For example, from 1971/1972 to 1983/1984, the rate of increase in physicians' fees lagged behind the CPI by an average of 1.7 percent per year, falling a total of 18 percent in real terms. However, over the same period, utilization per physician rose at an average rate of 1.4 percent per year, such that inflation-adjusted billings (price times utilization) per physician fell a total of only 3.4 percent.[135] Thus, it is clear that much of the benefit of the decreased growth in fees was offset by a corresponding increase in utilization of services.

Carr and Mathewson evaluated the Canadian system in terms of the impact on physicians. Their paper evaluates "the main caveats to those who would institute a Canadian-like health insurance scheme: The hidden and significant beneficiaries are physicians who operate within the system".[136] Their model suggests that the government-run system provided the opportunity for physicians to enhance their wealth through either extra-billing, which is now banned, or providing unnecessary services. Until 1984, the Canadian system permitted physicians to extra-bill giving them some control over their incomes even in the negotiated fee-for-service environment. With the elimination of extra-billing,[137] the only mechanism by which physicians can increase their incomes is to increase utilization. In the two years following Ontario's ban on extra-billing (1986-1987 and 1987-1988), services per physician increased by nearly 2.5 percent per year, contrasted with the average annual increase of 1.2 percent in the previous seven years.[138]

The problem of excess utilization of physician services has led individual provinces to try various methods to control use. Two approaches have been the "threshold approach" and the "capping approach." With the threshold approach, the provinces establish allowed increases in utilization. Beyond a threshold level, the cost of increases in the volume of services is at least partly borne by the medical profession. If a threshold has been exceeded, the

---

[135]   Barer, Evans and Labelle (1988).

[136]   Carr and Mathewson (1992), p. 35.

[137]   Extra-billing never accounted for more than 5 percent of total medical care costs nationwide; however, it provided physicians with a "safety valve", preserving their control over their incomes (Barer *et al.* 1988).

[138]   Lomas, Fooks, Rice and Labelle (1989).

provincial governments use one of three ways to recoup the resulting "excess" expenditures:[139]

- the following year's fee increase is adjusted downward accordingly;

- the profession temporarily works at reduced fees for a set period; or

- current fees are paid at a discounted rate.

The threshold approach does not target directly individual physician incomes; rather, it controls the total funds available for distribution across the entire profession. Four provinces have adopted this approach: British Columbia, Manitoba, Saskatchewan and Ontario.

Currently, only Québec uses the capping approach, which involves direct control of the income of general practitioners.[140] This approach establishes individual income ceilings for general practitioners as well as separate caps for overall expenditures on services of general practitioners and specialists. Unlike in other provinces, negotiations involve the income level of physicians, which is then translated into a particular fee increase. General practitioners' incomes are regulated through individual income ceilings and a total expenditure cap. The provincial government sets quarterly fee ceilings. Once the ceilings have been reached, the general practitioner is paid only 25 percent of the fee for additional services.[141] For specialists, the provincial government calculates an income target for a twelve month period. These target incomes are not applied at the individual level as in the case of general practitioners; however, they are used to calculate an overall expenditure cap for specialist services.[142]

At the national level, the Standing Committee proposed that research be undertaken to explore alternative methods of compensation for physicians such as capitation payments or salaries. Such forms represent a fundamental change in the manner in which physicians are paid. The current fee-for-service

---

[139]   Lomas et al. (1989).

[140]   Québec introduced individual income caps for general practitioners at the request of the profession.

[141]   "For example, once a general practitioner hits C$39,474 ($29,684 1990) in quarterly fees, the government pays only 25 percent of each bill submitted over that amount until the next quarter starts. The GP's association says about 20 percent of its members exceed the limit one or more times a year" (Wall Street Journal, December 31, 1991).

[142]   Lomas et al. (1989).

approach is retrospective payment. Capitation and salaries are forms of prospective payment schemes. The amount a physician receives is known before the patient receives any treatment. These schemes eliminate the incentive to over-treat patients, but may create an incentive to under-treat patients. Therefore, prospective payment schemes suggest the need for quality assurance programs.

The excess utilization problem inherent in the fee-for-service reimbursement system is exacerbated by the increasing supply of physicians. The pool of physicians has grown faster than the general population every year since 1965.[143] As observed by Barer, Evans and Labelle, "fee controls that are not backed up by some form of global payment caps will be at best only partially successful in controlling costs, in an environment of increasing physician supply".[144] This has led some provinces to take measures to control the supply of physicians. For example, Québec and Manitoba have taken steps to limit medical school enrolments. British Columbia tried to address this problem by restricting the number of physicians entitled to reimbursement by the provincial plan. However, this latter policy was subsequently overturned on constitutional grounds.[145]

In addition to the plentiful supply of physicians, Canada suffers from an inappropriate distribution of physicians on a geographic basis. There tend to be more than enough physicians in urban areas and corresponding shortages in rural areas. To address the imbalance, Québec has established incentives to attract physicians to areas with the greatest need. For example, the provincial government determines the regions with the least and greatest need of additional physicians. In areas with little or no need, newly-trained physicians will be reimbursed at a discount, say 70 percent, of the provincial fee schedule. Alternatively, in areas of great need, entering physicians will be reimbursed at a premium, such as, 120 percent of the provincial fee schedule. After five years a physician may move to an urban area with no penalty in terms of fees. This system of incentives has been in effect in Québec for the last ten years and seems to have the desired effect on the distribution of physicians. In July 1990, New Brunswick initiated a similar program.[146]

---

[143]   Iglehart (1990).

[144]   Barer et al. (1988), p. 44.

[145]   Barer (1991).

[146]   Health and Welfare Canada (1991).

4.5.5 Hospital Sector

A major issue arising in the provision of hospital services is the existence of bed-blockers (see Section 4.3.5). The existence of bed-blockers aggravates the problem of queuing. Queuing is the natural outcome of a non-price system of rationing health care services such as exists in Canada when funds are constrained. The degree to which queues affect health outcomes is a concern for policy makers.

There are factors in addition to bed-blockers that contribute to the queuing problem in Canada.[147] Another characteristic of the Canadian system that lengthens queues for certain hospital services is the slow rate of technological diffusion. In Canada, virtually all of the most sophisticated forms of technology are used in teaching hospitals only. This is due to a requirement that capital expenditures be approved by the provincial government. Non-teaching hospitals have difficulty gaining the appropriate approvals. One consequence of this is that capital-intensive new technologies are far less available in Canada than in the US.[148,149] The provinces will no doubt continue to control the use of technology as a means of containing costs. Physicians will have to decide patients' relative needs for these services, possibly lengthening queues.

The specific problem with cardiac surgery in Ontario has been addressed satisfactorily by the provincial government. However, queues persist. In testimony before the Standing Committee, Dr. Naylor acknowledged the existence of non-price rationing in the Canadian system and suggested as an alternative, better management and control of the supply of health care. For example, managed waiting lists, better informed consent for medical and surgical procedures and quality assurance mechanisms to determine whether the expected benefits of procedures outweigh the costs/risks.[150]

---

[147] Carr and Mathewson established that "when extra billing (by specialists) is banned, queues of patients will form for specialists" (Carr and Mathewson, 1992, p. 24).

[148] See the discussion of the Rublee study in Section 4.4.

[149] Iglehart (1990).

[150] House of Commons Canada (1991).

4.5.6   Pharmaceutical Sector

In Canada, the recent emphasis on strengthening intellectual property protection is consistent with efforts among countries generally to strengthen intellectual property protection schemes. In 1987, the Canadian government modified the compulsory licensing provisions in the Canada Patent Act in an effort to encourage pharmaceutical manufacturers to invest more in Canada. In return, pharmaceutical firms increased R&D spending in Canada from a bench-mark of 4.9 percent of sales, prior to the change in the law, to 9.7 percent of sales in 1991.[151] This represents a faster rate of growth in R&D spending than the industry had promised in 1987.[152]

In addition Bill C-91, passed in early 1993, eliminates compulsory licensing altogether. Bill C-91 strengthens intellectual property protection; however, it also further restricts firms' freedom in pricing. In addition to eliminating compulsory licensing, Bill C-91 strengthens the powers of the PMPRB. According to Consumer and Corporate Affairs Minister Pierre Blais, "entry prices (into Canada) of new patented drugs have been a concern".[153,154] Expanding the authority of the PMPRB to allow it to require firms to repay revenues derived from "unfair" prices of pharmaceutical products gives the Canadian government increased control over the pricing of pharmaceutical products.

Michael Wilson, Minister of Industry, Science and Technology and Minister for International Trade, announced that Canada has endorsed the intellectual property measures outlined in the GATT. "After months of consultation with the provinces and the private sector, and because of increased competition resulting from improved patent protection in other countries such as France, Italy, Japan, Mexico and the United States, to mention a few, it has become evident that if Canada is to remain competitive in research and development,

---

[151]   This represents the ratio of R&D to sales for the patented pharmaceuticals industry. The corresponding ratio for PMA firms is 9.6 per cent (PMPRB, 1991).

[152]   The industry committed to increasing its R&D to sales ratio to 8 percent by 1991 and 10 percent by 1996 (PMAC Report, 1992).

[153]   The entry price of a product is the initial price charged for a product following approval for marketing in Canada.

[154]   F-D-C Reports, July 13, 1992, p. 7.

we must provide investors with similar patent protection to that enjoyed by their competitors worldwide".[155]

4.5.7   Others

The Standing Committee hearings identified three areas in applied research that deserved further attention: utilization review or quality assurance; systems of delivering and managing services; and technology assessment.[156] Information gained through utilization review could help the payer educate physicians about cost-effective modes of therapy, and identify outliers.

Given the incentives in the Canadian health care system for excess utilization, there is an argument for utilization review comparable to that in the US.[157] If there is a change in the way in which physicians are paid from fee-for-service to capitation, there will be a concern about maintaining quality. This could be addressed through a quality assurance program. Both utilization review and quality assurance could be efficiently managed by the single payer. The single payer has access to a considerable amount of information to use in assessing the types of services provided and the ultimate effectiveness of these services.

With respect to technology assessment, Feeny and Stoddart proposed the creation of the National Health Technology Assessment Council to ensure a mechanism by which "rigorous evaluative evidence is available in a timely manner for use in initial adoption and subsequent utilization decisions".[158] They proposed the creation of a national-level agency to promote the production and dissemination of technology assessment in Canada. This proposal was in response to a perceived need to evaluate and disseminate centrally technological innovations. A single-payer system, such as the Canadian health care system, suppresses choice and, therefore, the signals that affect the flow of resources. As a result, the central administrator attempts to

---

[155]   PMAC Report (1992) p. 12.

[156]   House of Commons Canada (1991).

[157]   In the US, "a number of different services fall under the rubric of utilization review" (*Consumer Reports*, August 1992, p. 520). Included are: hospital pre-authorization; second opinion reviews; prospective procedure reviews; concurrent reviews; and overall case management.

[158]   Feeny and Stoddart (1988).

perform many of the functions that would come as a by-product of competition. Feeny and Stoddart envision that process in this case.

4.6   CONSTRAINTS ON REFORM

In discussing the prospects for reforming the Canadian health care system, it is necessary to address the constraints to reform operating within the actual cultural and political processes in Canada.   Based on our research and interviews with health policy makers in Canada, there are four distinct forces: popularity of the existing system; preference for the *status quo*; entrenched government policies; and laws or by-laws governing behaviour.

First, the existing health care system is extremely popular among Canadians. "Repeated polling shows that over 95 percent of Canadians are either 'satisfied' or 'very satisfied' with the Medicare system."   As a consequence of the popularity of the system, politicians and health policy makers appear to be reluctant to adjust the system, even in relatively minor ways.

Second, there is pervasive risk aversion or preference for the *status quo*.   The existing system seems to meet the needs of Canadians, and the resources have existed at the federal and provincial levels to fund the program.   Risk aversion dampens the incentive to change the system until a particular problem becomes severe.

Third, the existing system of financing health care is dominated by the Federal and provincial governments.   Members of this powerful bureaucracy seem to view consumers as poorly prepared to make the 'right' choices with regard to health care.   The entrenched position of the government regulatory agencies responsible for health care means that the typical response to a severe problem is to propose additional regulatory solutions.[159]   The policy process in Canada appears to consist of the following steps: (i) identify a problem; (ii) convene a committee of representatives of the appropriate government agencies; (iii) study the issue; (iv) propose solutions based on the existing regulatory structure; (v) select a solution; and finally, (vi) implement the solution.   Health care policy must be "played out in the public arena".   Therefore, the only alternative for those consumers who are dissatisfied with the health care system is to vote for a change in government.

Cost-containment reforms are now the focus of health policy in all developed countries.   "The Canadian approach, however, acknowledges the limited

---

[159]   "Attempts to control fees lead progressively into more extensive management of medical care—controls *do* beget further controls" (Barer *et al*. 1988).

effectiveness of market forces in health care and eschews such policies as managed competition and the creation of internal markets. Rather, Canada is managing the cost-containment reform process by using the monopsonistic control afforded to provincial governments as principal payers of health care and by focusing on quality assurance."[160]

Finally, the existing laws and by-laws in Canada may need to be changed to achieve significant reform. The Canada Health Act specifies the five criteria for provincial health plans to receive the full cash contribution from the Federal Government, which is estimated to be C$14.8 billion ($11 bn 1990) or C$536 ($398 1990) per capita in 1992-1993. The provincial and federal health ministers recently reaffirmed their commitment to the five principles of the Canada Health Act. This may make certain reforms difficult to implement. For example, reform such as allowing copayments for medically necessary services would require modifying or, at least, reinterpreting the principle of accessibility.[161] Copayment schemes introduced in the past violate the current interpretation of the accessibility criterion, i.e. uniform access without barriers. Similarly, any reform that entails binding patients to managed-care entities would violate the portability principle.

Professional associations may have long-established by-laws that inhibit competition among providers. For example, advertising by physicians is against the Code of Ethics of the Canadian Medical Association. In general, new institutional arrangements to inform consumers may be in conflict with established customs in the medical community.

---

[160]   Department of National Health and Welfare (1992).

[161]   Some provinces have introduced copayments for pharmaceuticals, which are not considered medically necessary services for the purposes of a province receiving the federal contribution to health care.

4.7   SHORT-TERM REFORM

There are several reform efforts currently underway that will increase the efficiency of the Canadian health care system.   These efforts could be expanded and additional reforms could be implemented without requiring major changes to existing Canadian legislation.   Such short-term reforms are politically feasible steps to bring Canada's system closer to the NERA Prototype.

4.7.1   Primary Care

In the context of the single-payer system, the method of physician reimbursement remains an important area for reform.   Fee-for-service reimbursement gives providers an incentive to provide services in excess of economically efficient levels.   Moreover, the negotiation process between the provincial government acting as a monopsonist and provincial medical associations representing collectively the physicians may keep fees above competitive levels.

Currently, physicians in Canada are actively evaluating alternatives to fee-for-service.   In a government commissioned study, Barer and Stoddart assert that "[a]lthough there is no single 'best' way to pay physicians in all circumstances, too little use is made of alternatives to fee-for-service as a payment method in Canada."[162]   The Canadian College of Family Practice realizes that fee-for-service is no longer appropriate.   Fee-for-service reimbursement does not encourage physicians to engage in health-promotion or counselling activities.   The Canadian Medical Association is participating in a project through Queen's University aimed at developing alternatives to fee-for-service.[163]

Under the current system, provincial medical associations and provincial health ministries negotiate 4,000-7,000 fees codes. One proposal under review in this project is moving to a salary basis for physician reimbursement as a means of reducing the administrative costs associated with such negotiations.

Another method of reimbursement under consideration by the Canadian Medical Association is capitation.   Barer and Stoddart recommend that

---

[162]   Barer and Stoddart (1991), p. 26.

[163]   Canadian Medical Association (1992a).

capitation replace fee-for-service for primary care.[164] If capitation emerges as a viable reimbursement scheme, utilization review methods will be necessary to ensure that the quality of care does not suffer.

A more dramatic and, possibly, more effective approach to lowering costs is to introduce competitive bidding by individual physicians or physician groups. Competitive bidding would enhance economic efficiency by encouraging competition among physicians or groups of physicians as opposed to maintaining the monopoly power of the provincial medical associations.

Physicians could bid, individually or as part of a group, on the fees they would charge for services in the Guaranteed Health Care Package (GHCP). The government would select the winning bids, which would determine the government reimbursement rate. No longer would physicians be allowed to meet as a single entity. They would be prohibited from discussing fees or bidding strategies under the auspices of the provincial medical associations. Although smaller groups could emerge as bidders, only by breaking this cartel can the government hope to achieve significant cost savings.

Patients using physicians from the winning bidder group would pay zero price. Patients choosing another physician would pay the price charged by that physician less the government contribution determined through bidding. This process would encourage physicians to innovate in organising health care. To be selected as a winning bidder, a physician or physician group would have to perform services more cost-effectively than other physicians. Successful bidders would structure new forms of delivery. For example, physicians and other providers (e.g. hospitals) may form capitated groups.[165]

In implementing such a scheme, however, care must be taken to avoid violating the federal accessibility principle. We believe the federal standard will not be violated if all residents have the option to use physicians from the group of winning bidders. Services obtained from this group would be paid in full by the government. Canadians seeking care outside of this group would be responsible for paying any additional cost.

---

[164] Muldoon and Stoddart estimate that providing a capitation alternative to Canadians such as the one in Sault Ste. Marie, Ontario would result in savings of approximately 11 percent over just a fee-for-service system. They assume that 50 percent of consumers choose the capitation alternative (Muldoon and Stoddart, 1989).

[165] Vigorous enforcement of Canadian antitrust laws must accompany a movement to this type of reform.

4.7.2 Hospitals

The current method of funding hospitals in Canada is to rely on global budgets. This can lead to quality reductions, the wrong mix of services being produced (bed-blockers) and queuing. These inefficiencies can be reduced by switching to cost-per-case funding, in which fees are set prospectively based on the type of care the patient will consume. At the outset, the hospital diagnoses the patient's condition, and then receives a lump sum with which to carry out the patient's treatment. In theory, cost-per-case funding creates the proper incentives to ensure economic efficiency.[166] Since hospitals receive different payments based on the type of care needed by the patient, this funding method eliminates the hospital's incentive to fill its beds with bed-blockers. However, there are some practical difficulties in implementing such a funding scheme. For example, it is very difficult to define a 'case' or 'episode' prior to patient treatment. It is entirely possible that a patient categorised by case 'x' upon admission to the hospital will later turn out to need a different type of care altogether.

Given the current emphasis on cost-containment in Canada, this type of hospital funding scheme will be difficult to implement without some type of overall cap on expenditures. Currently in Canada there is an ongoing experiment in Ontario to increase efficiency in hospital funding without removing the overall cap. Recognising the inequities and inefficiencies inherent in global budgets, the Ontario Ministry of Health undertook an extensive review of hospital funding in late 1988. This review has led to the ongoing transitional funding of hospitals, a collaborative process between the Ministry of Health and the hospitals, to modify Ontario's global budgeting system. "The goal of this initiative is to achieve greater equity and to improve allocation of resources within the given budget constraint."[167] This method relies on the classification of patients into case-mix groups, comparable to DRGs, so that annual growth in hospital budgets is based on weighted admissions. This experiment illustrates an acceptable interim step towards cost-per-case funding for hospitals.

---

[166] The US has implemented a cost-per-case type funding scheme for Medicare (not to be confused with Canadian Medicare) patients. Prior to treatment, patients are classified according to diagnosis related group (DRG). Hospitals receive funds based on DRG code. Although this method eliminates the hospital's incentive to fill its beds with low cost patients who would be appropriately treated in other settings, it creates an incentive to assign patients to a DRG with higher reimbursement than the problem that actually requires care. This is known as DRG creep.

[167] Lave, Jacobs and Markel (1992), p. 81.

Similarly, a capitation paid to the primary care physician that includes hospital care may be a practical payment arrangement. It preserves the incentives for the economic efficiency characteristic of cost-per-case funding.

In general, performing procedures or caring for patients in the most efficient location should be part of any reform package. In Canada, performing some surgery on an out-patient basis (surgi-centres) and getting patients requiring low-intensity care out of the hospital should be priorities. Global budgets discourage these trends.

4.7.3   Government

4.7.3.1   R&D and Technology

We recommend the elimination of the government approval process for capital expenditures by hospitals, to improve the diffusion of medical technology in Canada and stimulate competition among hospitals. Canadian health policy makers express concern that eliminating the government control of these decisions will result in an explosion of spending by hospitals as they all invest in the latest medical technologies. The current focus of health policy in Canada is one of cost-containment. There is a "fixed pie" for spending on health care. Therefore, increased expenditures by hospitals for equipment imply decreased expenditures in another sector. Since all sectors are under substantial cost pressure, it is unlikely that any one sector will be able to increase expenditure significantly. Thus, cost-containment forces make it unlikely that by increasing competition among hospitals the hospital sector will expand needlessly.

Reforms are needed in the area of technology assessment to improve the way in which decisions to adopt new technologies or replace equipment are made. However, policy makers should be careful that such reforms do not encourage adopting inefficient technologies. An increase in the use of cost-benefit and cost-effectiveness analysis in health care decision-making will help to focus on those technologies that improve the quality of health care and/or lower costs.

It appears that Canadian health policy makers have also recognized this need. They have proposed the introduction of a National Information Institute to act as a clearing house for this type of information. The mission of the Institute will be to increase the information available to health care consumers and providers to enable them to make more efficient health care consumption decisions.

4.7.3.2 Approval Time for Pharmaceuticals

Reforms regarding pharmaceutical innovation usually involve improving intellectual property protection to provide the incentive to devote resources to R&D. However, even the improved protection resulting from Bill C-91 will not solve all the problems. Another component of the R&D process for pharmaceuticals concerns the time required for approval of a new product for marketing by the Health Protection Branch.

As in other developed countries, the obtaining of a patent and the approval for marketing are conducted by two separate agencies in Canada. A patent is often granted prior to obtaining marketing approval in Canada. Therefore, the effective patent life for a product is less than the statutory patent term. Reducing the time required to obtain approval of a product for marketing in Canada will increase the incentive to conduct R&D, improve the diffusion of new pharmaceutical technologies and enhance competition among therapeutic alternatives.

In Canada, the pharmaceutical approval process is currently under review. Canadian regulators at the Health Protection Branch seem to be abandoning attempts to follow the same type of approval process as in the US. They are now assessing whether it is possible to move towards a more cooperative approval process in which a lead country would conduct the actual review of clinical data and share information (possibly for a fee) with other countries. Regulators in Canada would rely on opinions of regulators in other countries when deciding whether to approve some pharmaceutical products for sale in Canada.

Canada is participating in the Pharmaceutical Evaluation Report (PER) project in which regulators from the EC, EFTA, Canada and Australia attempt to agree on a common format for submitting requests for marketing approval. Canada is also monitoring and participating, when appropriate, in the international harmonisation discussions.

4.7.3.3 Utilisation Review

Another role for the government in Canadian health care reform is in the area of utilisation review. The government could encourage utilisation review and disseminate information about efficient providers and treatments.

When shifting to capitation payment methods of reimbursing providers, utilisation review can help to maintain the quality of services. It can also reduce overall health care costs. For example, in the US, Southern California Edison self-insures 55,000 employees, retirees and dependents. It spends nearly $100 million annually for health care. It now assigns case managers to its sickest beneficiaries. These managers evaluate treatment options and negotiate prices with providers for specific procedures. The company saved $16 million over three years by managing these catastrophic cases.[168]

---

[168]   Smith (1992).

4.8   LONG-TERM REFORM

In addition to the short-term reforms described in Section 4.7, we recommend several reforms that may require more fundamental changes to the Canadian system.   These reforms may require a reinterpretation of, or a change in, existing Canadian legislation such as the Canada Health Act. Thus, we refer to these as long-term reforms.

4.8.1   The Funding Side of the Health Care System

The funding side of NERA's Prototype health care system exhibits the following characteristics:

- competitive insurance market to provide coverage for GHCP and supplemental services;
- individual mandate for coverage of the GHCP, at a minimum;
- insurers may not deny coverage to any applicant;
- insurance premiums have income and risk components;
- central fund will provide reinsurance for risk adjustment.

Clearly, movement toward the NERA Prototype will require major structural changes to Canada's single-payer system.

Generally, single-payer insurance systems, such as the one in Canada, have weaknesses due to the administered nature of decisions on fees, budgets, caps and capital expenditures.   There are no self-correcting or self-monitoring (market) mechanisms for signalling potential problems with resource allocation. Relying, as in Canada, on the political process and monopsony is unreliable and inefficient. Therefore, we propose that the single-payer system be replaced with a multiple-payer, competitive insurance market.   The mechanism is already in place for moving to this alternative: private insurers exist to provide coverage for services not covered under the provincial plans. Their role could be expanded gradually to cover additional services.

As cost-containment pressures increase, the momentum for increasing the services covered by private insurers will exist. The primary benefit of this trend is enhanced patient choice with regards to coverage. This will increase economic efficiency by giving citizens more choice in designing optimal health care coverage, according to their individual preferences, and need not lead to excessive administrative costs or to inequity between patients.

It appears that the role of private insurers is already expanding, albeit slowly. In 1975, private sources accounted for 23.6 percent of total health care expenditures in Canada. By 1991, this percentage had risen to 27.8.[169] Given the general recession in Canada and the associated pressures on provincial government budgets, it is likely that this trend will continue. Current financial pressures are forcing the provinces to cut back or eliminate altogether coverage of some services,[170] thereby increasing opportunities for private insurers.

Recently, many provinces have had to cut drastically their coverage of health care services performed out of the country, largely in the US. The high costs of hospital care in the US have made it costly for provinces to continue to provide out-of-country hospital coverage. In October 1991, the Ontario Government instituted a ceiling of C$400 ($330 1990) per day on out-of-country care. Similarly, in the spring of 1992, Québec reduced its coverage to a maximum of only C$480 ($360 1990) per day. British Columbia covers C$75 ($56 1990) per day for care received outside of Canada. These cuts have prompted many private insurers to introduce new products designed to 'top-up' the provincial coverage. These private companies have acted quickly. Currently there are 55 companies in Canada offering such coverage, compared to only three, ten years ago.[171] This dramatic increase in suppliers shows the quick response of the market to an increase in demand for private health insurance.

This example suggests that it is possible to introduce more competition in the financing of health care in Canada. However, there are significant obstacles to expanding private insurers' roles to include coverage of medically necessary services (the GHCP).

- It violates the "public administration" criterion of the Canada Health Act, which requires that the health care insurance plan of a province must be administered and operated on a non-profit basis by a public

---

[169]   Health and Welfare Canada (1993).

[170]   Of course, provinces cannot eliminate coverage of services included in the GHCP without violating the Canada Health Act and losing their federal contributions. However, provinces can cut back on coverage of additional services such as: nursing home care; home care; dental services; pharmaceuticals; services of optometrists, chiropractors, osteopaths, chiropodists and physiotherapists; aids to independent living; and travel coverage.

[171]   MacDonald (1992).

authority appointed or designated by the government of a province.[172]

- Canadian health policy-makers seem convinced that a monopsony (government) buyer for health care services is necessary to protect consumers from the potential abuse of the monopoly power held by health care providers.

- Many Canadians are committed to a strict, egalitarian notion of equity. This equity notion will not permit alternative insurers for basic services, or the emergence of a 'two-tiered' health care system, such as exists in the UK.

We believe these concerns are sufficiently widespread to render movement to a competitive insurance market in the short-run unlikely. However, as the Canadian population ages and health care consumes a large share of national income into the next century, Canadians may be more willing to experiment with alternatives to government-provided insurance for some services. The greatest obstacles to change, however, may be the lack of any evidence that Canadians would prefer a radical change in this area, and the entrenched government bureaucracy at both the federal and provincial levels. The political power of these groups will likely mean significant opposition to change.

4.8.2   The Provider Side of the Health Care System

The provider sector of the NERA Prototype health care system has the following features:

- health care delivery rests with providers, who sell their services to insurers;
- providers negotiate reimbursement directly with insurance companies;
- potential providers are given unregulated entry into the health care market subject to meeting medical qualification requirements.

With the implementation of the short-term reforms outlined in Section 4.7, namely, improvements to provider reimbursement and removal of government control of hospital capital expenditures, the provider sector of the Canadian health care system will exhibit these characteristics.

---

[172]   Canada Health Act, p. 6.

4.8.3   The Responsibilities of Government

Within the NERA prototypical health care system, government has the following responsibilities:

- define a GHCP;
- establish a framework for the health care system;
- regulate where necessary to facilitate operation of competitive insurance market;
- act as agent for the mentally disabled and underprivileged;
- take responsibility for public health issues;
- maintain licensing agencies for providers;
- create a favourable environment for research;
- provide a mechanism for utilisation review.

4.8.3.1   *Definition of a GHCP*

In practice, Canada already has a GHCP, which is described in the Canada Health Act. The GHCP covers a broad range of services consisting of "hospital services, physician services and surgical-dental services," defined as follows.

- Hospital services means all medically necessary in-patient or out patient services, namely:
  - accommodation and meals at the standard level;
  - nursing services;
  - laboratory, radiological and other diagnostic procedures, together with the necessary interpretations;
  - drugs, biologicals and related preparations when administered in the hospital;
  - use of operating room, case room and anaesthetic facilities, including necessary equipment and supplies;
  - medical and surgical equipment and supplies;
  - use of radiotherapy facilities;
  - use of physiotherapy facilities; and,
  - services provided by persons who receive remuneration from the hospital.

- Physician services means any medically required services rendered by medical practitioners.

- Surgical-dental services means any medically or dentally required surgical-dental procedures performed by a dentist in a hospital.[173]

4.8.3.2 Health Care System Framework

The Canadian Constitution specifically states that health care is a provincial responsibility. Therefore, the powers of the Federal Government to shape the Canadian health care system are limited to establishing incentives and encouragement. The Canadian health care system actually consists of twelve individual provincial health care systems run by the provincial governments. By making federal financial contributions contingent upon compliance with the standards of the Canada Health Act, the Federal Government maintains some control over health care in Canada. However, health care in Canada remains a provincial responsibility.

Since health care in Canada is a provincial responsibility (as outlined in the Constitution), the Federal Government does not have the legal authority to require provincial health care plans to provide the services listed in the GHCP. However, the Federal Government uses the incentive provided by its cash contributions to the provinces to **encourage** all provincial health care plans to conform to a uniform set of standards: those described in the Canada Health Act. Thus, the Canada Health Act does not legally bind the provinces; it merely describes a set of five criteria that must be met in order for a province to be eligible for federal cash contributions to health care financing.[174] The federal contribution is approximately 30 percent of government health care spending in Canada.[175] To date, the incentive provided by these contributions has been sufficient to ensure compliance with the five federal criteria. Since the Canada Health Act was passed in 1984, the five criteria have been met by all provincial health care plans.[176]

---

[173] Canada Health Act, pp. 3-4.

[174] The "comprehensiveness" criterion delineates the services that are to be included in the GHCP.

[175] Farnsworth (1993).

[176] However, there have been some cases in which provinces proposed schemes that were determined to be in violation of the federal criteria, for example, copayments on medically necessary services. To remain eligible for federal contributions, the provinces abandoned such schemes.

Therefore, without a change in the Canadian Constitution, the Federal Government does not have the authority to pass the necessary legislation to establish a framework for health care. This responsibility belongs to the provincial governments. It is possible that the incentive provided by the federal cash contribution may become insufficient to ensure provincial compliance with the standards of the Canada Health Act. Without the incentive to adhere to a uniform set of standards, the Canadian health care system could splinter and become twelve distinct and, possibly, very different health care systems.

4.8.3.3 Other

We do not discuss the remaining responsibilities of government individually as they are either applicable only after major long-term reforms, already underway at federal or provincial levels in Canada, or discussed in Section 4.7.

For example, if Canada adopts a competitive insurance market to fund health care, there will be a role for government in the form of regulatory review. However, government responsibility will only follow major long term reform of the health care system.

Under the existing Canadian system the Federal or provincial governments have the responsibility to:

- act as agent for the mentally disabled and underprivileged;
- take responsibility for public health issues; and
- maintain licensing agencies for providers.

Finally, the remaining responsibilities of government according to the NERA prototype are to:

- create a favourable environment for research; and
- provide a mechanism for utilisation review.

We discuss these government responsibilities in detail in Section 4.7.

4.8.4 The Responsibilities of Patients

Under the NERA Prototype the primary responsibilities of patients are to:

- share the costs of specific treatments, whether part of the GHCP or not;
- form private organisations to ensure that the rights of consumers are upheld.

In the current Canadian system, zero price at the point of delivery creates incentives for patients to consume too much care; that is, consumption beyond the point where marginal benefit equals marginal cost. In general, Canadians need better information on the costs of providing health care. Health care costs should be transparent. Patients and taxpayers should be made more aware of the costs of particular services and the costs in terms of taxes to operate the health care system. Possible reforms include cost-sharing and providing patients with better information such as a list of the charges for services consumed[177] or the treatment options available for particular health problems. We will focus on copayments since improved information is already a policy goal in Canada.[178]

To increase patient price-sensitivity, we propose the introduction of cost-sharing arrangements such as copayments for all services. Of course, there would be exceptions for the needy, chronically ill and elderly as well as a cap on total payments for all.[179] Empirical evidence confirms that some health services are price sensitive. A 10 percent increase in prices leads to approximately a 2 percent reduction in the use of services.[180] Therefore, cost-sharing can be used to enhance price-responsiveness and control costs.[181]

Although cost-sharing reduces the total amount of services consumed, evidence shows that the total is reduced indiscriminately between 'necessary'

---

[177]   The American Medical Association recently approved a proposal to encourage physicians and other health care providers to disclose prices to patients (*U.S. News & World Report*, July 27, 1992). Some Canadian provinces have started to provide patients with itemized lists of charges they incur, even though the patient does not pay the charges.

[178]   Informed consumers are able to make better health care decisions. Some providers are using video programs to educate consumers about risks and benefits/costs of alternative treatments: "such patient education techniques have reduced demand for surgery for benign prostatic hyperplasia by up to 50 percent in one year" (Gross, 1992).

[179]   Establishing the criteria for need or other qualifying conditions for being exempt from copayments is an administrative problem that could be addressed in a number of ways.

[180]   Morrisey (1992).

[181]   See NERA (1992). NERA concludes:

- medical care consumers are moderately sensitive to price;
- the demand for optimal and essential medical care is as price-sensitive as the demand for less effective and less important medical care;
- the demand for marginal and discretionary pharmaceuticals is more price sensitive than the demand for essential pharmaceuticals;
- low-income groups are more price sensitive than high-income groups in their demand for both medical services and pharmaceuticals.

327

and 'unnecessary' services. Thus, it is not simply 'frivolous' utilisation that is being eliminated by increased cost-sharing. Also, low-income patients are more sensitive to cost-sharing than are patients with high incomes. So, unless carefully designed, cost-sharing programs can have regressive effects by reducing access to necessary health care services for the poor. Creese concludes that when establishing cost-sharing systems, it is essential to create carefully discriminating fee systems that ensure revenue is provided only by those who can afford to pay, and also to ensure that the revenue generated is collected and re-distributed in a way that improves the quality and accessibility of health care for the poor.[182]

With special reference to pharmaceuticals, Levy suggests four general principles for appropriate cost-sharing policies.[183]

- Consumers must be provided with the necessary information to make informed decisions, including the value of the medication, its importance in the treatment plan and the consequences of not having the prescription filled.

- Cost-sharing features must not distort patient incentives to consume optimal pharmaceutical therapy. Such distorting features include higher copayments for non-formulary pharmaceuticals, for brand-name products or for certain classes of pharmaceuticals.

- Copayments and coinsurance levels should be related to a patient's ability to pay.

- Cost-sharing should apply to the full range of medical services to prevent service substitution; for example, replacing pharmaceutical therapy with more expensive forms of treatment.

Canadians have had some experience with cost-sharing already. All but four provincial plans have some sort of cost-sharing arrangement (i.e. coinsurance, copayments or deductibles) in their coverage of pharmaceutical products.[184] Moreover, most private insurance plans involve cost-sharing. For example, in

---

[182]   Creese (1991).

[183]   Levy (1992).

[184]   Note, this cost-sharing does not apply to those receiving social assistance.

Ontario, Blue Cross indicated that, in 1988, the consumer paid 7 percent of the average prescription price of $23.13.[185]

Although the implementation of a cost-sharing scheme will increase economic efficiency, copayments may violate the conditions of the Canada Health Act. This accessibility criterion states that insured health services must be provided on a basis that does not impede or preclude access by charges or otherwise.[186] Some Canadian health policymakers interpret this to prohibit the introduction of patient cost-sharing as it will impede access to health care services. These policymakers are willing to tolerate some inefficiency in the system in order to maintain zero price for all medically necessary health care services. In addition, the Canada Health Act deals directly with user charges by stating that provinces permitting user charges will not be eligible for full cash contributions from the Federal Government.[187]

Furthermore, the view of some federal government administrators we interviewed seems to be that the effect of the zero price on consumption of health care services is small and there is a substantial down-side cost to user fees. The alternative is patient education combined with provider incentives. If this view is widespread, copayments schemes will be difficult to implement.

Because copayments for insured services may be in violation of the federal criterion, the provinces are more likely to implement selective copayment schemes for certain services not covered by the provincial plans, such as prescription pharmaceuticals. We encourage experimenting with copayment schemes. However, a selective copayment scheme will create distortions in health care consumption decisions by possibly making the more cost-effective mode of treatment more expensive to the patient. For example, if a copayment applies to pharmaceuticals, but not hospital care, prophylactic use of beta blockers to prevent heart attacks may not be selected by a patient. The patient may bear the heart attack risk.

---

[185]   Williams, *et al.* (1992).

[186]   Health and Welfare Canada (1989), p. 8.

[187]   The Act makes an exception with respect to "user charges for accommodation or meals provided to an in-patient who, in the opinion of the attending physician, requires chronic care and is more or less permanently resident in a hospital or other institution" (Canada Health Act, p. 11).

4.8.5   Long-Term Reforms

The long-term reforms outlined in the NERA Prototype may have significant effects on the pharmaceutical industry. The most radical reform, given the current Canadian system, is the replacement of the provincial government monopsony buyer with competitive insurers. This may have profound effects on providers, including the pharmaceutical industry.

Currently, each provincial plan has differing levels of coverage for pharmaceutical products; however, all plans cover pharmaceuticals for the elderly and needy. For these two consumer groups, each province has a formulary for determining reimbursement. The introduction of competitive insurers may eliminate the provincial formularies, leading to increased competition among pharmaceutical manufacturers for consumers in these two groups.

For patients other than the elderly and needy, the bulk of pharmaceutical coverage is already provided by private insurers. With respect to these two groups of consumers, then, the introduction of a competitive insurance market will have less significant effects.

ANNEX 4.1 DATA TABLES

List of Tables

TABLE 1
AGE STRUCTURE OF POPULATION ACCORDING TO THE
LOW-, MEDIUM- AND HIGH-GROWTH SCENARIOS

Year	0-17	18-64	65+	Total	0-17	18-64	65+
	in millions				in percent		
Low-growth scenario							
1981	6.8	15.1	2.4	24.3	28.1	62.2	9.7
1986	6.6	16.1	2.7	25.4	25.9	63.4	10.6
1991	6.6	17.0	3.2	26.8	24.7	63.5	11.8
1996	6.5	17.7	3.6	27.8	23.5	63.7	12.9
2001	6.2	18.4	3.9	28.6	21.6	64.6	13.8
2006	5.7	19.1	4.3	29.0	19.5	65.8	14.7
2011	5.1	19.5	4.8	29.3	17.3	66.3	16.4
2016	4.7	19.2	5.6	29.4	15.8	65.2	19.0
2021	4.4	18.6	6.4	29.4	14.9	63.3	21.7
2026	4.1	17.7	7.2	29.0	14.3	60.9	24.8
2031	3.9	16.8	7.8	28.4	13.7	58.9	27.4
2036	3.6	16.1	8.0	27.6	13.0	58.2	28.8
Medium-growth scenario							
1981	6.8	15.1	2.4	24.3	28.1	62.2	9.7
1986	6.6	16.1	2.7	25.4	25.9	63.4	10.6
1991	6.6	17.0	3.2	26.8	24.8	63.5	11.8
1996	6.7	17.9	3.6	28.2	23.8	63.4	12.8
2001	6.7	18.9	4.0	29.5	22.5	63.9	13.5
2006	6.5	19.8	4.4	30.7	21.3	64.5	14.2
2011	6.4	20.4	4.9	31.7	20.2	64.3	15.5
2016	6.4	20.5	5.7	32.6	19.5	62.9	17.6
2021	6.4	20.4	6.6	33.3	19.1	61.1	19.8
2026	6.4	20.0	7.5	33.8	18.8	59.2	22.0
2031	6.3	19.7	8.1	34.1	18.4	57.8	23.8
2036	6.2	19.6	8.4	34.2	18.1	57.4	24.5
High-growth scenario							
1981	6.8	15.1	2.4	24.3	28.1	62.2	9.7
1986	6.6	16.1	2.7	25.4	25.9	63.4	10.6
1991	6.6	17.0	3.2	26.8	24.8	63.5	11.8
1996	6.8	17.9	3.6	28.3	23.9	63.4	12.7
2001	6.8	18.9	4.0	29.7	22.9	63.6	13.4
2006	6.9	19.8	4.4	31.0	22.2	63.8	14.1
2011	7.1	20.4	4.9	32.4	21.9	62.9	15.2
2016	7.4	20.6	5.7	33.7	22.0	61.0	17.0
2021	7.8	20.5	6.6	34.9	22.3	58.9	18.9
2026	8.0	20.4	7.4	35.9	22.3	57.0	20.8
2031	8.1	20.5	8.1	36.7	22.0	55.9	22.1
2036	8.2	20.9	8.4	37.4	21.9	55.7	22.4

Source: *Statistics Canada (1990), p.33.*

TABLE 2

LIFE EXPECTANCY AT BIRTH, MALE AND FEMALE, PROVINCES AND TERRITORIES

Province	Observed				Projected		
	1971	1976	1981	1986	1989	1996	2011
FEMALE							
Canada	76.4	77.5	79.0	79.7	80.8	82.2	84.0
Newfoundland	75.7	77.4	78.7	79.4	80.2	81.8	83.7
Prince Edward Island	77.4	78.2	80.5	80.4	81.8	83.4	85.4
Nova Scotia	76.0	77.8	78.4	79.2	80.3	81.7	83.5
New Brunswick	76.4	77.7	79.2	80.0	80.9	82.3	84.2
Québec	75.3	76.5	78.7	79.4	80.6	82.0	83.8
Ontario	76.8	77.7	79.0	79.7	80.7	82.1	84.0
Manitoba	76.9	77.9	78.8	79.8	80.7	82.1	83.8
Saskatchewan	77.6	78.6	79.6	80.5	81.6	82.9	84.6
Alberta	77.3	77.9	79.1	80.0	81.2	82.4	84.1
British Columbia	76.7	78.4	79.6	80.3	81.4	82.7	84.6
Yukon	-	-	-	-	76.5	78.5	81.9
Northwest Territories	-	-	-	-	76.5	78.5	81.9
MALE							
Canada	69.3	70.2	71.9	73.0	73.7	75.1	77.2
Newfoundland	69.3	70.6	72.0	72.7	73.5	75.1	77.3
Prince Edward Island	69.3	69.2	72.8	72.6	74.1	75.7	77.9
Nova Scotia	68.7	69.5	71.0	72.3	72.9	74.3	76.3
New Brunswick	69.1	69.7	71.1	72.5	73.0	74.4	76.4
Québec	68.3	69.1	71.1	72.0	73.0	74.4	76.4
Ontario	69.6	70.6	72.3	73.5	74.0	75.4	77.6
Manitoba	70.2	70.7	72.2	73.0	74.1	75.5	77.5
Saskatchewan	71.1	71.1	72.4	73.7	74.4	75.7	77.6
Alberta	70.4	71.1	72.0	73.6	74.1	75.5	77.3
British Columbia	69.9	71.0	72.6	74.1	74.4	75.7	77.8
Yukon	-	-	-	-	70.1	72.1	75.0
Northwest Territories	-	-	-	-	70.1	72.1	75.0

Note: Official life tables are not available for two territories

Reproduced in: *Statistics Canada (1990), p.12.*

TABLE 3
ECONOMIC ENVIRONMENT

YEAR	Gross Domestic Product	Gross Domestic Product	Total Health Care Expenditure	Total Health Care Expenditure	Total Health Care Expenditure
	C$ mn	C$ per head	C$ mn	C$ per head	% of GDP
1981	353,454	14,506	26,650	1,094	7.5
1982	371,820	15,080	31,150	1,263	8.4
1983	402,229	16,151	34,512	1,386	8.6
1984	441,311	17,656	37,310	1,493	8.5
1985	474,339	18,837	40,408	1,605	8.5
1986	501,426	19,761	44,286	1,745	8.8
1987	546,517	21,312	47,935	1,869	8.8
1988	598,178	23,061	51,800	1,997	8.7
1989	645,894	24,602	56,100	2,137	8.7
1990	668,300	25,105	60,200	2,261	9.0

Source: *OECD (1991).*

TABLE 4
NATIONAL HEALTH EXPENDITURE BY SOURCE OF FUNDS, 1975 TO 1991

	1975	1980	1985	1987	1988*	1989*	1990*	1991*
	(in $ millions)							
National health expenditures	12267	22704	40408	48720	52933	57793	62706	66771
Public financing								
Federal direct	398	582	1153	1335	1416	1413	1350	1304
Federal Transfers to provinces	3391	6969	11199	12793	13504	14382	14789	14930
Provincial	5328	8942	16990	20500	22639	25258	27911	30700
Local	132	363	451	671	620	610	679	713
Workers' compensation	121	211	389	397	427	458	516	573
Private expense	2897	5737	10226	13025	14326	15671	17443	18550
Public financing								
Federal direct	3.2%	2.6%	2.9%	2.7%	2.7%	2.4%	2.2%	2.0%
Federal Transfers to provinces	27.6%	30.3%	27.7%	26.3%	25.5%	24.9%	23.6%	22.4%
Provincial	43.4%	39.4%	42.0%	42.1%	42.8%	43.7%	44.5%	46.0%
Local	1.1%	1.6%	1.1%	1.4%	1.2%	1.1%	1.1%	1.1%
Workers compensation	1.0%	0.9%	1.0%	0.8%	0.8%	0.8%	0.8%	0.9%
Private expense	23.6%	25.3%	25.3%	26.7%	27.1%	27.1%	27.8%	27.8%
National health expenditures ($ per capita)	540	944	1606	1902	2043	2202	2357	2474
National health expenditures/GDP	7.2%	7.3%	8.5%	8.8%	8.7%	8.9%	9.4%	9.9%
National health expenditures/GNP	7.3%	7.5%	8.7%	9.1%	9.0%	9.2%	9.7%	10.2%
Population (thousands)	22697	24043	25165	25617	25909	26240	26610	27000

* *Provisional estimates*
Source: *Health and Welfare Canada (1993)*

TABLE 5
NATIONAL HEALTH EXPENDITURE BY CATEGORY

	1975	1980	1985	1987	1988*	1989*	1990*	1991*
Hospitals	5443	9294	16228	19153	20679	22618	24686	26095
Other institutions	1194	2638	4259	4918	5410	5666	6127	6661
Physicians' services	1927	3448	6333	7679	8237	8759	9389	10141
Other health professionals	731	1578	2745	3255	3566	3917	4332	4614
Drugs	1091	2027	4230	5921	6712	7575	8352	9230
Capital	612	1234	1863	2232	2261	2511	2584	2393
Other	1269	2485	4751	5562	6069	6748	7237	7637
Total	12267	22704	40408	48720	52933	57793	62706	66771

* *Provisional estimates*
Source: *Health and Welfare Canada (1993)*

TABLE 6
FEDERAL GOVERNMENT CONTRIBUTION AS A PERCENT
OF TOTAL PROVINCIAL GOVERNMENT HEALTH EXPENDITURES

Year	Federal Government Contribution to Provinces	Total Provincial Government Spending	Federal Contribution as a Percent of Total Provincial Spending
	C$ Millions	C$ Millions	Percent
1979	6,104	13,711	44.5
1980	6,869	15,811	43.4
1981	7,720	18,682	41.3
1982	8,667	22,000	39.4
1983	9,607	24,493	39.2
1984	10,432	26,223	39.8
1985	11,199	28,189	39.7
1986	12,170	30,807	39.5
1987	12,861	33,288	38.6
1988	13,504	36,143	37.4
1989	14,382	39,640	36.3
1990	14,789	42,700	34.6
1991	14,930	45,630	32.7

Source: *Health and Welfare Canada (1990), p. 96 and Health and Welfare Canada (1993).*

TABLE 7
HOSPITALS AND RELATED INSTITUTIONS
Classified by status or licence and controlling body

	Hospitals	Total Beds Set Up	Distribution: Beds Set Up for Use								
			Med/Surg	General	Psyc.	Ment. Handi	Chronic Care	Rehab. Conv.	Ped.	Isol. Cont.	T.B. Resp.
PUBLIC GENERAL											
Lay	407	75,810	38,946	11,269	4,508	25	14,887	1,450	4,377	130	218
Religious	89	16,778	9,536	2,627	745	15	2,109	513	1,193	6	34
Municipal	297	20,181	11,906	2,551	837	22	2,606	285	1,963	10	1
Provincial	78	13,500	7,544	2,080	638	8	2,140	181	869	40	-
Total	871	126,269	67,932	18,527	6,728	70	21,742	2,429	8,402	186	253
PUBLIC SPECIAL											
Lay	106	20,371	413	362	5,607	599	9,904	2,329	754	25	378
Religious	34	5,471	-	120	820	-	3,691	840	-	-	-
Municipal	34	4,203	-	49	115	-	3,659	339	-	-	41
Provincial	76	18,974	-	301	10,192	5,472	1,860	1,014	114	-	21
Total	250	49,019	413	832	16,734	6,071	19,114	4,522	868	25	440
Total Public	1,121	175,288	68,345	19,359	23,462	6,141	40,856	6,951	9,270	211	693
PRIVATE											
Proprietary	57	3,516	393	12	330	-	2,574	207	-	-	-
Religious	3	297	-	-	40	-	257	-	-	-	-
Provincial	2	487	-	-	-	-	-	487	-	-	-
Total Private	62	4,300	393	12	370	-	2,831	694	-	-	-
FEDERAL											
DVA	1	1,084	-	-	294	-	790	-	-	-	-
HWC	9	311	170	72	2	2	7	-	56	2	-
Industrial	1	20	13	4	-	-	-	-	3	-	-
Sol. Gen	3	300	-	-	300	-	-	-	-	-	-
DND-Military	30	919	274	538	-	-	50	5	9	2	-
Total Federal	44	2,634	457	614	637	2	847	5	68	4	-
Grand Total	1,227	182,222	69,195	19,985	24,469	6,143	44,534	7,650	9,338	215	693

Source: *Canadian Hospital Association (1991)*

TABLE 8
PERCENTAGE OCCUPANCY (BASED ON APPROVED BED COMPLEMENT) FOR REPORTING PUBLIC HOSPITALS CLASSIFIED BY TYPE AND SIZE, CANADA AND PROVINCES, 1988-1989

Public Hospitals	Canada	Nfld.	P.E.I	N.S.	N.B.	Qué	Ont	Man.	Sask.	Alta.	B.C.	N.W.T T.N-O
Gen Non-Tch (No LTU) Beds												
1-24	60.64	58.05	-	74.44	71.58	44.69	-	57.61	65.72	49.86	41.24	29.92
25-49	58.10	46.91	78.43	64.31	72.05	-	49.05	58.37	60.08	55.87	50.69	-
50-99	65.41	52.00	69.88	58.20	73.41	85.59	72.46	59.27	68.29	52.63	69.50	-
100-199	71.04	59.65	78.44	68.75	65.18	83.19	80.04	67.36	64.28	68.65	70.67	-
200-299	78.21	-	-	69.67	76.08	83.06	82.87	-	59.45	71.08	-	-
300+	83.99	-	-	-	-	85.95	84.42	74.43	-	81.83	85.18	-
Subtotal	**72.03**	**56.24**	**75.77**	**67.26**	**71.06**	**83.65**	**82.38**	**63.15**	**63.79**	**61.03**	**68.78**	**29.92**
Gen Non-Tch LTU Beds												
1-49	69.68	73.16	64.13	60.59	-	73.38	69.33	-	67.16	76.10	66.79	43.56
50-99	75.15	58.48	-	72.10	69.41	76.53	79.26	67.22	69.56	73.21	74.68	49.00
100-199	80.64	-	-	83.50	-	83.68	83.24	67.12	71.38	78.96	76.13	29.75
200-299	85.98	75.28	-	-	82.47	83.88	88.65	81.94	85.25	81.75	89.52	-
300+	85.55	-	81.01	-	82.00	84.88	85.42	80.60	73.38	74.59	91.27	-
Subtotal	**82.95**	**70.53**	**79.98**	**77.83**	**81.65**	**83.86**	**83.93**	**77.05**	**73.67**	**75.10**	**86.77**	**38.95**
Non-Tch	**79.82**	**61.35**	**78.03**	**69.40**	**77.60**	**83.83**	**83.55**	**69.45**	**66.67**	**69.23**	**85.04**	**38.50**
Tch/Ens	80.75	83.33	-	82.82	-	83.75	80.71	74.80	80.47	74.01	85.36	-
Gen	**80.10**	**70.57**	**78.03**	**73.65**	**77.60**	**83.79**	**82.79**	**71.19**	**71.92**	**71.43**	**85.09**	**38.50**
Ped	63.62	51.30	-	48.38	-	67.96	62.31	-	-	68.64	80.03	-
ll Spec	90.61	9.90	86.45	83.19	81.89	94.43	86.60	85.85	89.20	93.14	87.65	-
Pub Grant Total:	**81.42**	**68.41**	**78.74**	**72.52**	**77.62**	**85.86**	**82.94**	**72.29**	**72.59**	**75.95**	**85.41**	**36.03**

Source: *Canadian Hospital Association (1991), p.236*

ANNEX 4.2 BIBLIOGRAPHY

Barer, M. (1988), "Regulating Physician Supply: The Evolution of British Columbia's Bill 41," *Journal of Health Politics, Policy and Law*, Vol. 13, No. 1, pp. 1-25.

Barer, M. (1991), "Controlling Medical Care Costs in Canada," *JAMA*, Vol. 265, No. 18, pp. 2393-2394.

Barer, M. and Evans, R. (1992), "Interpreting Canada: Models, Mind-Sets, And Myths," *Health Affairs*, Spring, pp. 44-61.

Barer, M. and Stoddart, G. (1991), "Toward Integrated Medical Resource Policies for Canada," Report prepared for the Federal/Provincial /Territorial Conference of Deputy Ministers of Health, June 1991.

Barer, M., Evans, R. and Labelle, R. (1988), "Fee Controls as Cost Control: Tales From the Frozen North," *The Milbank Quarterly*, Vol. 66, No. 1, pp. 1-64.

Blendon, R., Leitman, R., Morrison, I. and Donelan, K. (1990), "Satisfaction with Health Systems in Ten Nations", *Health Affairs* (Summer), pp. 185-92.

Brown, M. (1987), *Caring for Profit, Economic Dimensions of Canada's Health Industry*, The Fraser Institute.

Canadian Hospital Association (1991), *Canadian Hospital Directory*, Vol. 38.

Canadian Medical Association (1992a), "Toward a Revised CMA Policy on Physician Compensation: Digest of Consultation on Physician Payment Models," April 28, 1992.

Canadian Medical Association (1992b), "Report of the Advisory Panel on the Provision of Medical Services in Underserviced Regions," March 1992.

Carr, J. and Mathewson, F. (1992), "The Effects of Regulation: Incentives and Health Insurance," Mimeo, February 25, 1992.

Cohn, V. (1992), "Medical School Debt: You and I Pay," *The Washington Post*, May 21, 1992, Health Section, p. 9.

Consumer Reports (1992), "Health Care in Crisis: The Search for Solutions - Does Canada Have an Answer?" *Consumer Reports*, pp. 579-592.

Consumer Reports (1992), "Are HMO's The Answer", *Consumer Reports*, pp. 519-531.

Coyte, P. (1990), "Canada", *Advances in Health Economics and Health Services Research*, edited by R. Scheffler and L. Rossiter, Supplement 1, pp. 103-143.

Coyte, P., Dewees, D. and Trebilcock, M. (1991), "Medical Malpractice — The Canadian Experience," *The New England Journal of Medicine*, Vol. 324, No. 2, pp. 88-93.

Creese, A. (1991), "User Charges for Health Care: A Review of Recent Experience," *Health Policy and Planning*, December 1991.

Danzon, P. (1992a), "Administrative Costs: Answering The Critics," *Health Affairs*, Summer, pp. 231-233.

Danzon, P. (1992b), "Hidden Overhead Costs: Is Canada's System Really Less Expensive?", *Health Affairs*, Spring, pp. 21-43.

Department of National Health and Welfare (1992), "Health Context Paper," prepared for Joint Health and Finance Ministers Meeting, June 18, 1992, p. 3.

Department of National Health and Welfare (1983), *Task Force Reports on the Cost of Health Services in Canada*, 3 Volumes, 1983.

Dranove, D., Shanley, M. and Simon, C. (1992), "Is Hospital Competition Wasteful?", *The RAND Journal of Economics*, Vol. 23, No. 2, pp. 247-262.

Evans, R. (1987), "Hang Together, or Hang Separately: The Viability of a Universal Health Care System in an Aging Society," *Canadian Public Policy*, XIII:2, pp. 165-180.

Evans, R., Lomas, J., Barer, M., Labelle, R., Fooks, C., Stoddart, G., Anderson, G., Feeny, D., Gafni, A., Torrance, G. and Tholl, W. (1989), "Controlling Health Expenditures — The Canadian Reality," *The New England Journal of Medicine*, Vol. 320, No. 9, pp. 571-577.

F-D-C Reports (1992), "Canadian Patent Amendment Would Balance Longer Product Exclusivity with Increased Authority for Price Review Board; New Drugs Prices Emphasized," *F-D-C Reports, Inc.*, July 13, 1992.

Farnsworth, C. (1993), "Now Patients are Paying Amid Canadian Cutbacks," *New York Times*, March 7, 1993, A-1, 10.

Farnsworth, C. (1992), "Canadians Defend Care System Against Criticism," *New York Times*, February 17, 1992.

Federation Dentaire Internationale (1990), "Basic Facts 1990," pp. 35-36.

Feeny, D. and Stoddart, G. (1988), "Toward Improved Health Technology Policy in Canada: A Proposal for the National Health Technology Assessment Council," *Canadian Public Policy*, XIV:3, pp. 254-265.

French Hospital News, 1987 Edition.

Gladwell, M. (1992), "Why Canada's Health Plan Is No Remedy for America," *The Washington Post*, March 22, 1992, p. C-3.

Goad, G. (1991), "Canada Seems Satisfied With a Medical System That Covers Everyone," *Wall Street Journal*, December 3, 1991.

Government of Canada (1991), "Building Partnerships, Government Response to the Standing Committee Report entitled The Health Care System in Canada and its Funding: No Easy Solutions," November 1991, (Government Response to Committee Report).

Gross, P. (1992), "Health Goals and Targets, Health Care Meaningful Global Trends and Their Relevance for India," Health Group Strategies Pty. Limited, September 1, 1992, p. 9.

Hasting, J. and Vayda, E. (1989), "Health Services Organization and Delivery: Promise and Reality," *Medicare at Maturity*, edited by R. Evans and G. Stoddart, The Banff Centre School of Management, pp. 337-390.

Health and Welfare Canada (1989), *Canada Health Act*, Office Consolidation, R.S., 1985, c. C-6, January 1989 (Canada Health Act, 1985).

Health and Welfare Canada (1990), *National Health Expenditures in Canada 1975-1987*, Minister of Supply and Services Canada, September 1990.

Health and Welfare Canada (1991), *Canada Health Act Annual Report 1990-1991*, Minister of Supply and Services, 1991.

Health and Welfare Canada (1993), "Health Expenditures in Canada: Fact Sheets", March 1993.

Heritage Foundation, The, *Backgrounder* (1992), "Problems in Paradise: Canadians Complain about their Health Care System," No. 883, pp. 1-16.

House of Commons Canada (1991), *The Health Care System in Canada and its Funding: No Easy Solutions*, First Report of the Standing Committee on Health and Welfare, Social Affairs, Seniors and the Status of Women, Bob Porter, Chairman, June 1991.

Iglehart, J. (1990), "Health Policy Report: Canada's Health Care System Faces Its Problems," *The New England Journal of Medicine*, Vol. 322, No. 8, pp. 562-568.

Kaiser Commission on the Future of Medicaid (1992), "Medical Bills: Who Pays?", *The Washington Post*, July 21, 1992, Health Section, p. 5.

Krasny, J. and Ferrier, I. (1991), "A Closer Look At Health Care In Canada," *Health Affairs*, Summer, pp. 152-165.

Lave, J., Jacobs, P. and Markel, F. (1992), "Transitional Funding: Changing Ontario's Global Budgeting System," *Health Care Financing Review*, Vol. 13, No. 3, Spring 1992.

Levy, R. (1992), "Prescription Cost Sharing: Implications for the Pharmaceutical Industry," National Pharmaceutical Council.

Lomas, J., Fooks, C., Rice, T. and Labelle, R. (1989), "Paying Physicians in Canada: Minding Our Ps and Qs," *Health Affairs*, Spring, pp. 80-102.

Louis Harris & Associates (1992), "Most People Want More Medical Research," *The Washington Post Health*, July 14, 1992, Health Section, p. 5.

MacDonald, Gayle (1992), "Get Your Health Insurance to Go: Rising Hospital Costs Outside Canada Make it a Must," *The Financial Post*, November 21, 1992.

Manitoba Health (1992), *Quality Health for Manitobans: The Action Plan*, A strategy to assure the future of Manitoba's health services system, May 1992.

Manning, W., Newhouse, J., Duan, N., Keller, E., Leibowitz, A. and Marquis, S. (1987) "Health Insurance and the Demand for Medical Care: Evidence from a Randomized Equipment," *The American Economic Review*, Vol. 77, No. 3, June 1987, pp. 251-277.

Mannix, M. (1992), "Cost-shopping for Care," *US News & World Report*, July 27, 1992, p. 70.

Mathews, J. (1992), "Health Care: Drawing the Lines," *The Washington Post*, January 31, 1992.

McRae, J. and Tapon, F. (1985), "Some Empirical Evidence on Post-Patent Barriers to Entry in the Canadian Pharmaceutical Industry," *Journal of Health Economics*, 4, pp. 43-61.

Morrisey, M. (1992), *Price Sensitivity in Health Care: Implications for Health Care Policy*, The NFIB Foundation.

Muldoon, J. Stoddart, G. (1989), "Publicly Financed Competition in Health Care Delivery: A Canadian Simulation Model", *Journal of Health Economics*, No. 8, 1989.

Naylor, D. (1991), "A Different View of Queues in Ontario," *Health Affairs*, Fall, pp. 110-128.

NERA (1992), "The Impact of Cost Sharing for Medical Care and Pharmaceuticals: Evidence from the Literature," September 10, 1992, Unpublished.

Neuschler, E. (1990), "Canadian Health Care: The Implications of Public Health Insurance," Research Bulletin, Health Insurance Association of America, June.

Newhouse, J., Anderson, G. and Roos, L. (1988), "Hospital Spending in the United States and Canada: A Comparison," *Health Affairs*, Winter, pp. 6-16.

Ontario Ministry of Health (1991), *Annual Report 1990-1991.*

Organisation for Economic Co-Operation and Development, (1991), *OECD Health Data.* Comparative Analysis of Health Systems (Software Package), version 1.01, Paris.

Patented Medicine Prices Review Board (1989), *Bulletin*, Issue No. 4, September 1989.

Patented Medicine Prices Review Board (1991), *Fourth Annual Report*, December 31, 1991.

Pharmaceutical Manufacturers Association of Canada (1992), *Towards a Globally Competitive Research-Based Pharmaceutical Sector*, Report Submitted to the Steering Group on the Federal Government's Prosperity Initiative, April 1992, (PMAC Report).

Pharmaceutical Manufacturers Association, *PMA Newsletter*, February 8, 1993.

Poullier, J. (1989), "Health Data File: Overview and Methodology," *Health Care Financing Review*, Annual Supplement, pp. 111-194.

Rae, B. (1992), "Canadians Are Healthier," *The Washington Post*, April 3, 1992.

Roos, L., Fisher, E., Sharp, S., Newhouse, J., Anderson, G. and Bubolz, T. (1990), "Postsurgical Mortality in Manitoba and New England," *JAMA*, Vol. 263, No. 18, pp. 2453-2458.

Roos, L., Fisher, E., Brazauskas, R., Sharp, S. and Shapiro, E. (1992), "Health and Surgical Outcomes in Canada and the United States," *Health Affairs*, Summer, pp. 56-72.

Rublee, D. (1989), "Medical Technology In Canada, Germany, and the United States," *Health Affairs*, Fall, pp. 178-181.

Schieber, G. Poullier, J. and Greenwald, L. (1991), "Health Care Systems in Twenty-Four Countries," *Health Affairs*, Fall, pp. 22-38.

Shah, C. (1990), *Public Health and Preventive Medicine in Canada*, University of Toronto Press.

Simonsen, L. (1991), "What Are Pharmacists Dispensing Most Often?", *Pharmacy Times*, pp. 57-71.

Smith, L. (1992), "The Right Cure for Health Care," *Fortune*, October 19, 1992, pp. 88-89.

Statistics Canada (1990), *Population Projections for Canada Provinces and Territories 1989-2011*, Minister of Supply and Services Canada, March 1990.

Tholl, W. (1992), "Skating Faster on Thinner Ice: The Strengths and Weaknesses of Canada's Health System," Speech to the Medical Society of the County of Chemung, September 9, 1992.

US Department of Commerce (1991), *Statistical Abstract of the United States 1991*, The 111th Edition, National Data Book, Bureau of the Census.

US General Accounting Office (1991), "Canadian Health Insurance: Lessons for the United States," Report to the Chairman, Committee on Government Operations, House of Representatives, June 1991.

US News & World Report, July 27, 1992

Walker, M. (1992), "The Other Side of Canada," *Health Affairs*, Summer, pp. 233-235.

Walker, M., Miyake, J., Globerman, S. and Hoye, L. (1992), *Waiting Your Turn: Hospital Waiting Lists in Canada*, Fraser Institute, pp. 1-38.

Wall Street Journal (1992), "Canadian Drug Patent Bill Expected to Clear Commons," December 10, 1992, p. B-6.

Walsh, M. (1992), "A Big Dose of Family Medicine," *The Los Angeles Times*, July 16, 1992.

Williams, J., Lowy, F., Kennedy, W. and Chibba, M. (1992), "Report for the Pharmaceutical Inquiry of Ontario: An Overview," *Restructuring Canada's Health Services System: How Do We Get There From Here?*, pp. 63-72.

Winslow, R. (1992), "US Doctors Express Least Satisfaction in Three-Nation Survey of Health Care," *Wall Street Journal*, June 9, 1992, p. B-5.

Winslow, R. (1992), "Videos, Questionnaires Aim to Expand Role of Patients in Treatment Decisions," *Wall Street Journal*, February 25, 1992, pp. B1-3.

Winslow, R. and Stout, H. (1992), "Insurers Select McKesson Unit to Speed Claims," *Wall Street Journal*, July 22, 1992, pp. B1-6.

Woolhandler, S. and Himmelstein, D. (1991), "The Deteriorating Administrative Efficiency of the US Health Care System," *The New England Journal of Medicine*, Vol. 324, No. 18, pp. 1253-1258.

York, G. (1992), "Lankin Warns of Curbs on MDs," *The Globe and Mail*, June 23, 1992.

CHAPTER 5

THE HEALTH CARE SYSTEM IN FRANCE

Mike Burstall
Konrad Wallerstein

REMIT Consultants
London

5.1 SUMMARY

Structure

Health care in France is provided through the social security system. It is largely paid for by statutory sick funds which are financed by employers' and employees' contributions; 99.8 percent of the population is covered. More than 80 percent of the population has complementary insurance to cover patient copayments.

Aggregate Level of Expenditure

No single player has the power to decide how much shall be spent in total. The government has the largest influence.

Incentives

Primary Care Physicians: Primary care is provided by self-employed private sector practitioners. They are reimbursed on a fee-for-service basis. Hence, they have hence an incentive to expand the volume of treatments.

Hospitals: Hospital care is provided by a mixture of public and private hospitals. Public hospitals have global budgets. When these are tight they are under pressure to control costs. Private hospitals are paid on a fee-for-service or a *per diem* basis. They are therefore under less pressures to control costs.

Funders: Both the sick funds and private insurers want to control costs in order to avoid raising premia.

Medicines: Pharmaceutical prices are controlled, and are low in relation to income. The volume of pharmaceutical consumption is very high compared to other countries, despite some out-of-pocket patient copayments.

Issues

The level of service provided is high and people are generally satisfied with the health care system. The main problem is lack of control over expenditure in the out-of-hospital and private hospital sectors.

Current Reforms

Reforms under consideration include setting limits on the primary sector and new approaches to controlling pharmaceutical expenditure.

Political Environment

The health care system in France reflects two conflicting ideologies. Social solidarity ensures that all citizens are covered for medical treatment, and liberal-pluralism ensures that the suppliers of health care retain the maximum independence. The French consume health care of all kinds in unusually large amounts and have done so for many years.

NERA's Reform Recommendations

Any reform path which is to be acceptable to the French must satisfy the French belief in social solidarity coupled with the equally strong belief in freedom for patients to choose their supplier of medical care and in the freedom of those suppliers to practice as they see fit. French governments expect to exercise firm central control over many aspects of health care finance. Concern about the cost and efficiency of the French system, although rising, has not yet reached crisis point (see Section 5.6).

Current reform paths are largely concerned with controlling costs. They involve steps towards a more active role for government in financing and operating the existing system. It is suggested that the main driving force behind this strategy is the perceived success of earlier moves in this direction, most notably the introduction of global budgets for public hospitals. This approach is now being extended to private hospitals and to ambulatory care. It is further suggested that this path will be the preferred alternative unless and until it clearly fails (see Section 5.7).

Many elements of the NERA Prototype for reform are already present in the current French system. A guaranteed package of health care is in effect in existence; public insurance funds are obliged to accept all comers; transfer payments to maintain the stability of funds exist; copayments are a normal feature of health care finance. As far as providers are concerned, primary health care is provided by independent private practitioners working under contracts with the sick funds. Hospital care is similarly provided on a decentralised basis (see Section 5.8.1 - 5.8.4).

Nevertheless there are problems in following this path. A transition from the present occupationally-based sick funds to competing independent funds would be a major administrative task and would require a major effort of political will. Risk-based contributions might not be acceptable; nor might a ban on insuring against copayments. Above all, the recommended reform path would mean a much smaller role for central government; reforms recently introduced or currently contemplated are in the other direction. It is concluded that this last is the major obstacle to these proposals.

5.2   STRUCTURE OF THE HEALTH CARE SYSTEM

5.2.1   The Health Care System in Context

The French health care system is an attempt to reconcile two conflicting ideologies. The first is social solidarity: the duty of society to make sure that all its citizens are adequately covered against the risks of life, which include sickness and therefore medical treatment. The second is liberal-pluralism: the desire of those who supply health care - and those who consume it - to retain the maximum degree of independence. Both are deeply entrenched in French life and thought and have profoundly shaped the development and nature of health care in France.[1]

Public finance for health care is a part of the social security system. This is dominated by the concept of solidarity: between the young and the old, between the healthy and the sick and between the poor and the rich. It is provided through the *Sécurité Sociale*. Created in 1945, this is an organisation charged with the public duty to provide social security of all kinds for the French population. In 1990 it covered 99 percent of the population. However, it is not a unitary body, being composed of a large number of individual regimes for particular occupational groups. The main one - the *Régime Général* - covers 78 percent of the population; other important funds are those for farmers, the self-employed and agricultural workers. In turn, each fund is divided into several branches, providing pensions (*Assurance Vieillesse*) and family benefits (*Branche Famille*) as well as medical care (*Assurance Maladie*).[2]

In contrast the supply of health care is dominated by the concept of liberal-pluralism. It is highly decentralised. Patients have considerable freedom of choice. Primary care is largely provided by private practitioners who are subject to few controls. Most medicines are supplied by privately-owned retail pharmacies. Public, non-profit private and for-profit private hospitals coexist in large numbers. All three categories are subject to overall health planning but otherwise manage their own affairs to a considerable extent. Thus, financial provision for health care is in the hands of the sick funds and is in practice closely supervised by the Ministry of Health (*Ministère de la Santé*) and the Ministry of Social Affairs (*Ministère des Affaires Sociales*). It should be noted that the responsibilities are sometimes, as at present, split between two

---

[1]   de Kervasdoué, Rodwin and Stephan (1984); Zeldin (1980), (1981).

[2]   Rollet (1991); CNAMTS (1992).

Ministries and sometimes united in one (see Section 5.3.7). For the purpose of brevity both will normally be referred to as the Ministry of Health. The supply of health care is in the hands of a very large number of independent actors.

The ability of the central government to regulate expenditure on health care is therefore relatively restricted. The laws concerning the *Sécurité Sociale* are voted by Parliament and government agencies play a major part in deciding the payments for medical treatment through the sickness funds. However, the government has little influence over the volume of primary care supplied, although its powers over hospitals and their services are more substantial. By and large, the practice of medicine is outside official control. This circumstance gives rise to obvious problems; it has also conditioned the selection of possible remedies.

5.2.2   General Features of the Finance System

As with the other types of social security, public spending on health care is almost entirely financed by compulsory payroll taxes. Contribution rates are a percentage of salary, paid in part by the employee and in part by the employer. Employers pay more, which reduces the awareness of the population as to the real cost of health care. The rates fixed are the same for all individuals and employers within a regime but vary between regimes. Contribution rates are fixed by negotiation between the state, representatives of employees and employers, and the regimes themselves. The state provides little money directly but in effect underwrites the financial stability of the system. As will be seen, it also plays an active part in determining the rates of contribution and of payment to suppliers of health care.

Those who are not employed for one reason or another - children, the retired, the chronically sick, the unemployed - are in effect supported by those who are employed. Thus, pensioners pay sharply reduced rates, although they account for the majority of expenditure. Others pay nothing. The number of contributors to each fund is often substantially smaller than the number who benefit; in the case of railway workers beneficiaries outnumber contributors by 5:1. This is in accordance with the principle of social solidarity.

In 1990 French households paid about 23 percent of the health care bill themselves. Patient copayments - the *ticket modérateur* - for treatments payable by the sickness funds are normal. Such contribution rates averaged 30 percent for medicines, and 25 percent for primary care; in these cases the patient pays in full and recovers the balance from the funds. Copayments for hospital treatment are up to 20 percent of the total cost, although usually less; here the patient pays his or her contribution directly to the hospital, which then recovers the rest from the sickness funds.

Exemptions from copayments are granted largely on the basis of serious or long-lasting illness although they are also granted for social or economic reasons (see Section 5.3.2.3). In any year about 12 percent of the population qualify. Others usually insure themselves against copayments and other expenses mainly through cooperative non-profit schemes (*Mutuelles*) but also through private firms.

The state provides copayments for those whose income falls below a certain level. Those who have been members of a sick fund are automatically covered. They are exempt from contributions provided that their income does not exceed a certain level fixed by reference to the SMIC (minimum wage). If it does, then they pay 1.4 percent of their income for coverage against sickness, maternity, invalidity and death.

Those who are not covered in this way - for example because they have never worked long enough to qualify for any of the schemes - are covered by a personal insurance scheme for which the state pays the premiums under the *Revenue Minimum d'Insertion* scheme if the recipient's income is below a certain level, in 1990 FF 2,110 ($287 1990) per month for a single person.

5.2.3   General Features of the Delivery System

In France patients are free to consult any doctor they wish at any time. They have direct access to specialists as well as general practitioners. Primary care is very largely in the hands of doctors in private practice (*médécins libéraux*). They are paid by fee-for-service. Their density is high by European standards - 1.86 per 1,000 population - and there is a good deal of competition between them. Primary care is also provided by the out-patient clinics of hospitals and by municipal clinics (*dispensaires*) which are manned by salaried employees.

Hospital care is provided also on a generous scale. In 1990 there were 559,000 beds - 9.9 per 1,000 population - of which about two-thirds were in public and the balance in various kinds of private hospitals. Public hospitals receive a global budget from the *Sécurité Sociale*, as do most non-profit private hospitals. The bulk of their medical staff are salaried professionals. With-profit private hospitals rely on *ad hoc* agreements with the sickness funds based on fee-for-services performed and *per diem* charges for the stay. They are largely staffed by private doctors.

Approximately 90 percent of medicines by value were supplied through retail pharmacies. Qualified pharmacists have a legal monopoly for selling products and there is a legal restriction on the number of retail pharmacies in each area (one pharmacy for 2,500 inhabitants). Of this total, 80 percent were prescribed by doctors working in the primary sector and 7 percent were bought over the counter (OTC). The remaining 13 percent were prescribed in hospitals. Under pressure from patients, doctors may add what should be OTC products to their prescriptions. Medicine prices are strictly controlled and low by European standards. There are few restrictions on what may be prescribed and *per capita* consumption is high.

5.2.4 Inputs and Outputs of the System

In 1990 the population of France was 56 million. Of this total, 20 percent were under 15 years old and 14 percent 65 and over. As in the other countries in the study, those aged 75 and over are increasing rapidly in number, although they still make up only 6.9 percent of the whole.

Total health care expenditure in France in 1990 - including the costs of training, medical research and aid to the sick - was FF 603 bn ($82 bn 1990) or 9.3 percent of gross domestic product (GDP). Direct spending on the sick was FF 574 bn (8.9 percent of GDP). Of this latter total, 44 percent was spent on hospital care, 27 percent on primary care and 17 percent on medicines (see Chart 5.1). As a proportion of constant price GDP, the volume of spending on health care has continued to rise since 1985, but much more slowly than hitherto. The distribution of expenditure has also changed appreciably: the proportion spent on hospital care has fallen considerably, while that spent on primary care has risen. Medicines remained a roughly constant part of the whole during this period.[3]

---

[3] Unless otherwise specified, health care spending is taken to be that reported by the Ministry of Health as *Depenses Nationales pour les Malades* plus the cost of transport provided and subventions to the system. This total includes sick pay and other aid to the sick; it does *not* include spending on preventative medicine, on training or on medical R&D. This figure corresponds to that quoted in OECD (1991) as "total spending on health". There may be minor discrepancies between these figures and those quoted from other source, e.g. Eco Santé France du Credes.

Chart 5.1
Expenditure on Health Care in France, 1990

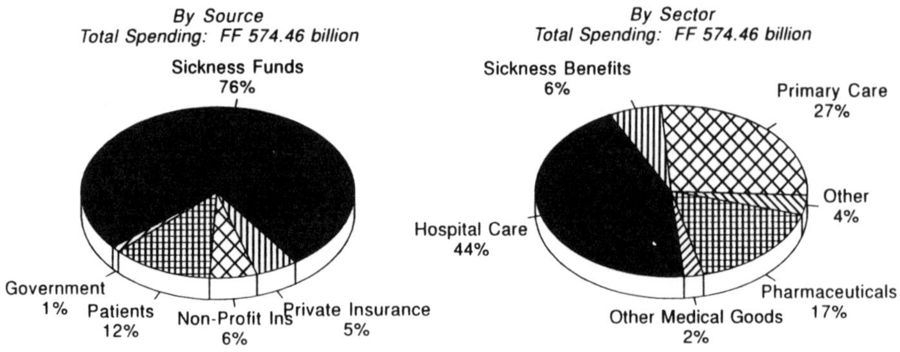

By Source
Total Spending: FF 574.46 billion

Sickness Funds 76%

Government 1%
Patients 12%
Non-Profit Ins 6%
Private Insurance 5%

By Sector
Total Spending: FF 574.46 billion

Sickness Benefits 6%
Primary Care 27%
Other 4%
Hospital Care 44%
Pharmaceuticals 17%
Other Medical Goods 2%

Source: National Accounts 1991

As elsewhere, health care spending is concentrated on the elderly. In 1987 those aged 60 and over accounted for 41 percent of total expenditure by the sick funds, although they made up only 19 percent of the population. *Per capita* expenditure rises sharply with age, those over 80 consuming 1.9 times as much as those aged 60-69 and 5.1 times as much as those aged 20-39. In all age groups, those suffering from serious and/or chronic sickness as opposed to milder and more transient conditions required much more expensive treatment: although only 11.6 percent of all patients they absorbed 46 percent of all sick fund spending.[4]

In terms of life expectancy France is broadly similar to the other countries in the study. In 1990 expectation of life at birth was 73 years for men and 81 for women; at the age of 60 these figures became 19 and 24 respectively; and at 80, 7 and 9. These figures suggest that people live somewhat longer than average in France. However, for men the expectation of life at birth is rather lower than might be expected, perhaps because of the larger than usual proportion of violent deaths. At 9.2 per thousand and 7.7 per thousand respectively, the perinatal and infant mortality rates are respectively slightly above and slightly below the 12-country averages.

[4]   Calculations based on CNAMTS (1990). This source divides reimbursement by the sick funds by age and by liability to copayment, from which the seriously and chronically ill are exempt.

Comparing inputs and outputs, it appears that France pays more for health care than most other countries, receives a more generous provision of services and may have marginally more favourable outcomes. Were the death rate from violence similar to that of other countries in the study, its showing would be better.

5.3   ANALYSIS OF INDIVIDUAL SECTORS

5.3.1   Key Participants in the Health Care System

Chart 5.2 shows the key participants in the French health care system and indicates the flow of funds and services in the system.

The key players are:

- patients;
- sickness funds;
- private insurance funds;
- primary care physicians;
- hospitals, both public and private;
- hospital clinicians;
- the pharmaceutical sector; and,
- the Ministry of Health.

In addition there are a variety of other participants, ranging from scientific institutions to agencies of the central and local governments, whose involvement is less continuous.

In a fragmented system it is possible for players to play different parts in different situations. Accordingly we consider how they do so in particular circumstances. There is a further point. The aims of the various players are usually implicit rather than explicit. Wherever possible we shall therefore deduce objectives from behaviour rather than from official statements of policy.

5.3.2   Patients

5.3.2.1 Behaviour of French Patients

The French health care system provides a large range of services, including not only medical and dental care of all kinds, but medicines, medical appliances, and home care and rehabilitation services. In addition a variety of cash benefits are available, notably sick pay, maternity benefit and death benefit.

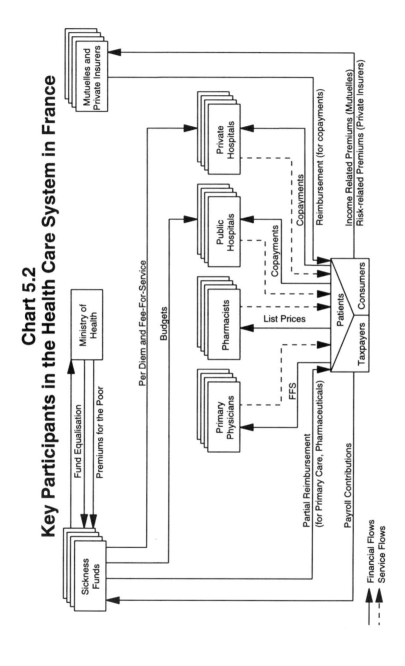

Chart 5.2
Key Participants in the Health Care System in France

French patients make a relatively frequent use of these facilities. In terms of the 11 countries in the study, France ranks fourth in *per capita* physician contacts, first in admissions to hospital as a proportion of the population, and an easy first in *per capita* consumption of medicines in terms of volume.[5]

Patient behaviour is more complex than might at first appear. In making contact with the health care system the initiative lies with the patient. The decision to see a doctor is generally prompted by need, but this is itself a flexible concept. Some illnesses are minor and self-limiting. Attitudes to the value of medical treatment must clearly condition the frequency of consultation. Moreover, while French doctors may have compelling reasons to maximise treatment (see Sections 5.3.4.5 and 5.3.6.1), French patients tend to expect to be given prescriptions. Thus there is a large element of covert agreement between all parties about the nature of illness and the appropriate forms of treatment.

The behaviour of French patients shows that they have an unusually positive attitude towards the benefits of medicine. Moreover, there is no doubt that the French approach to medicine - common to both doctors and patients - is appreciably different from that in the other countries in the study. There is more emphasis on maintaining the physical constitution than in the Anglo-Saxon countries or Scandinavia. Fringe therapies such as homeopathy and spa treatment are popular. This has an impact on the expectations of patients and therefore reinforces the behaviour of doctors - a significant factor when changes in the health care system are under consideration.[6]

5.3.2.2   Attitudes of Patients to the Health Care System

On the whole French patients are reasonably satisfied with the French health care system.

An international comparative study[7] carried out in 1989 found that 41 percent thought that it "works pretty well and that only a few changes were necessary to make it work better". However, 42 percent thought that although "there were some good things in [the system] fundamental changes are needed to make it better", and 10 percent thought that it needed complete rebuilding.

---

[5]   See, for example, the comparative data in Schieber *et al.* (1991).

[6]   Payer (1990), pp. 35-73.

[7]   Blendon *et al.* (1990).

Overall, satisfaction was lower than that in Canada, well above that in the UK and the USA, and comparable with that in Germany and the Netherlands. By the standards of the countries examined this was a favourable rating.

The comprehensive scope of French health care is clearly valued. Attempts to reduce its scope have been resisted. Thus, attempts to reduce reimbursement for minor operations or to introduce copayments for comfort medicines supplied to the chronically sick met with strong opposition and were eventually abandoned. The ambitious plan for privatising the ambulatory sector, put forward in 1979, met a similar fate and has never been revived. The principle that the patient should be free to choose the provider of health care commands general assent and none of the numerous projects for reform have proposed serious qualifications to this right. There are few complaints about waiting for consultations or treatment.[8]

There is, however, disquiet about the cost and volume of medical treatment. A very recent survey[9] carried out for the *Régime Général* found that 50 percent of French people thought that health care spending had risen "excessively" in recent years; 90 percent thought that the social security system faced great difficulties in the future. No less than 77 percent considered that people visited doctors too often, while 73 percent thought that doctors ordered too many tests and prescribed too many medicines. The doctors disagreed: 55 percent of them put the blame for excessive prescribing on patients.

When asked what should be done to control expenditure, 93 percent of patients and 58 percent of health care professionals favoured policies to promote cost awareness. Increases in health insurance contributions were opposed, as were reductions in the services offered under the national system. A large majority of patients were seriously concerned about possible future changes to reimbursement levels. They were willing to visit doctors less often and to become more aware of their levels of medicine consumption, though how much weight should be given to such statements is hard to know. The professionals endorsed some of these views, though less forcefully (see Section 5.3.4 below).

---

[8]   Nora and Naouri (1979).

[9]   CNAMTS (1991a).

5.3.2.3 Economic Incentives

These surveys suggest a certain awareness of the economic problems of the health care system on the part of the patients. However, they indicate diffuse anxiety rather than serious dissatisfaction. Patients want doctors to mend their ways; for what it is worth, they promise to mend their own. They dislike the idea that their own contributions should be raised. They think that cost-consciousness is a good idea, especially for other people. Despite the call for fundamental reforms, in reality there seems to be no real desire to move very far from the current arrangements for delivering health care. They may have defects but they also have virtues.

How do copayments impinge on patient behaviour? As Table 5.1 shows the rates charged are relatively high by European standards.

Table 5.1: Copayment Rates in the Health Care Insurance Scheme of the *Régime Général*

	Copayment level
Ambulatory services	25%
Doctors, midwives	25%
Auxiliaries	35%
Laboratory tests	35%
Hospital	30 FF day plus 20% of total cost for up 30 days stay
Medicines	0/30/60/100% of cost
Spectacles	30%
Dentures	25%
Hearing aids	100% after first 1300 FF.
Thermal cure	25-35%

Source: *CNAMTS (1992)*.

In spite of the high levels of copayment, the consumption of health care by French patients is high (and continues to rise). As was mentioned in Section 5.2.2, only 12 percent of the population is exempt from copayments, i.e. 88 percent is liable for payment. For that large majority of the population, the burden of copayment might seem substantial.[10] It is probable that in 1990 the

---

[10]   CNAMTS (1990).

value of such copayments was approximately 1360 FF ($185 1990) per capita. This is 2 percent of household consumption and most people are insured against these payments, either through the *mutuelles* or though private firms, so they have little effect on demand. The effect of copayment is to create a second tier of insurance, not to reduce demand. An attempt in 1980 to limit supplementary cover to 5 percent of the total paid met with strong opposition from the public and was dropped in 1982.[11,12]

The other main reason for the apparently modest, if any, impact of copayment on the level of usage is that the 12 percent who are exempt account for nearly half of spending by the sick funds. Exemptions are limited to those receiving special, prolonged or expensive treatment, war pensioners, chronic invalids, those unable to work, pregnant women and those living in certain kinds of residential homes. Age in itself is not enough to gain exemption. Almost half those patients over 80 still have to pay, as do almost all of children aged less than 15.

There is also provision of free health care, administered by local authorities (*municipalités*) for the benefit of the poorest. This provides many unemployed people with free health care. There are two other safety nets. The *aide humanitaire* is provided by voluntary organisations and now has direct support from the Ministry of Health. The other safety net is the legal obligation on doctors to provide their services free of charge if the patient cannot afford to pay.

Thus French patients have little reason to limit their consumption of health care. Indeed, there are strong indications that they are willing to spend more than is available through the sick fund system. If, as just suggested, the total value of copayments was FF 67,500 million in 1990 ($9.2 bn 1990), this figure should be compared with total spending by households - and their insurers - of FF 136,000 million ($18.5 bn 1990). The FF 68,500 million ($9.3 bn 1990) balance must represent expenditure on health care that is to some extent discretionary.

---

[11]   Taking the 1987 proportions (CNAMTS, 1990) as typical, spending by the sick funds in 1990 on those liable to copayment was FF 210 bn ($28.6 bn 1990) and the copayments were FF 68 bn ($9.1 bn 1990). Assuming that the proportion of those exempt from copayment - 11.6% - was the same in the population as in patients, the average annual copayment is FF 1,374 ($187 1990).

[12]   Steffin (1989).

5.3.2.4   Objectives of Patients

The objectives of patients are straightforward: to have their perceived needs - which are unusually large - met in the customary ways and at the customary costs. The present systems of finance and delivery are deemed essentially satisfactory. No compelling alternative presents itself.

5.3.3   Payers

5.3.3.1   Finance System in Context

The current health care system in France developed from the voluntary institutions of the late 19th and early 20th century and is still heavily marked by its past. The general nature of the arrangements for financing health care have been outlined in Section 5.2.2; this section is concerned with their operation.

Virtually all of the population is insured by the sickness funds. Membership of one of the occupational schemes is compulsory. They typically cover not only the subscribers but also their non-wage-earning dependents, children, unemployed and pensioners, although the exact details vary somewhat between schemes. Those who move from one occupation to another automatically change funds, but otherwise there is no choice. Some of the sickness funds, and their share of total benefits paid out, are shown in Table 5.2.

The only persons excluded from membership of the funds are small minorities such as those who live in France but work in another country. The duration of benefits under these schemes is unlimited.

As already mentioned in Section 5.3.2.3, patient copayments for medical treatment are relatively high in France and comparatively few people are exempt. It is therefore normal, though not compulsory, to insure against them. This is done through the *mutuelles*, co-operative non-profit societies, through the similar *Caisses de Prévoyance* or through commercial insurance companies offering sickness insurance policies. Broadly speaking, 55 percent of the population are insured through the *mutuelles*, 10 percent through *Caisses de Prévoyance* and 15 percent through commercial insurers. In 1989, some 17 percent of the population were without such complementary insurance.

Table 5.2: French Sickness Funds

Sickness Fund	Percentage of Total Benefits Paid Out
Caisse Nationale d'Assurance Maladie des Travilleurs Salariés (CNAMTS)[13]	80.4
Caisse Centrale des Secours Mutuels Agricoles (CCSMA)	9.5
Caisse National d'Assurance Maladie et Maternité des Travailleurs non Salariés des Professions non Agricoles (CANAM)	3.8
Caisse Autonome Nationale de la Sécurité Sociale dans les Mines	2.1
Société Nationale des Chemins de Fer Français (SCNF)	1.6
Caisse Nationale Militarie de Sécurité Sociale (CNMSS)	1.3
Etablissement National des Invalides de la Marine (ENIM)	0.5
Régie Autonome des Transports Parisiens (RATP)	0.2
Caisse de Retraite et de Prévoyance des Clercs et Employés de Notaires (CRPCEN)	0.1
CAMAC	0.1
Caisse de Prévoyance Maladie de la Banque de France	< 0.1
Régime Spécial de Sécurité Sociale du Personnel de la Compagnie Générale des Eaux	< 0.1
Caisse du Régime Spécial d'Assurance Maladie de la Chambre de Commerce et d'Industrie de Paris	< 0.1
Français de l'étranger	< 0.1

Source: *CNAMTS (1989)*

[13] The sickness fund of the Régime Général.

The basic benefits are the same for all members of all funds. These are as follows:

Table 5.3: Benefits Offered by French Sickness Funds

Benefits in kind	Benefits in cash
• Prevention	• Sickness benefit
• Regular check-ups	• Maternity benefit
• Immunisation	• Death benefit
• Ambulatory services	
• Medical care	
• Dental care	
• Midwives	
• Physiotherapy	
• Nursing	
• Hospital care	
• Medicines	
• Medical aids and appliances	
• Rehabilitation	

Source: *CNAMTS (1991b)*.

5.3.3.2 *Public Health Care Funding*

The breakdown of health care funding by sector of funding and by sector of provision in 1990 is shown in Chart 5.1, from which it is clear that the sick funds of the *Sécurité Sociale* accounted for 76 percent of the total, the *mutuelles* 6 percent and households, including their private insurance funds, 17 percent. The state itself accounted directly for less than 1 percent of the resources for the sick although it pays for part of the training and much of the medical research. The role of the sick funds is particularly marked in the provision of in-patient care, where it accounts for 89 percent of total spending, and in sick pay, of which it is the sole source. It is less overwhelming in the cases of primary care, medicines, and spectacles and other prostheses, in which it provides respectively 59 percent, 60 percent and 41 percent of expenditure.

As with the other types of social security, spending by the sick funds is financed by payroll deductions. The rates charged vary from fund to fund. In the case of the *Régime Général*, which covers 80 percent of the population, employees currently pay 6.8 percent of earnings in 1990 and employers paid 12.8 percent. Pensioners paid much reduced rates. These contributions cover maternity, invalidity and death benefits as well as purely medical insurance.

There is no upper limit on the earnings to which they apply and the rates are the same for all incomes. Contribution rates are fixed by negotiation between the state, representatives of employees and employers and the *régimes* themselves, with the state having the largest say because of its role as arbitrator when there is a disagreement between the parties. Each *régime* must be self-supporting (the *régimes* do not have reserves to draw on to prevent deficits occurring), but there is a system of compensation by which those *régimes* with a lower number of beneficiaries per contributor transfer funds to the others. In practice the *Régime Général*, which accounts for some 80 percent of total income, supports the other smaller funds.

The state itself is directly involved only to a limited extent. The little it provides is mainly in the form of medical aid (*Aide Médicale*) for particular groups of the disadvantaged. Some of the funds come from earmarked taxes on alcohol. However, the state is ultimately responsible for ensuring that the *Sécurité Sociale* remains solvent. This is by no means assured. The sickness, family and accident at work funds are normally in surplus but the pensions fund is usually in substantial deficit. In the past contribution rates have been raised to cover such eventualities, but, if necessary, the Ministry of Finance has to intervene.

In 1989 and 1990 the sick funds were in deficit and in 1991 the contribution rate for employees was raised by 0.9 percent; the circumstances under which this increase was imposed are discussed in Section 5.5.1 below.

5.3.3.3 *Private Health Care Funding*

The *mutuelles* are voluntary co-operative non-profit insurance organisations, broadly comparable to the friendly societies of the UK. Like them they are managed by their members, who decide what services to provide and what premiums to charge. Most of them are under public monitoring. Both premiums and services vary widely. There are currently about 6,500 *mutuelles*, organised by work-place, by occupational group or by geographical area. Like the sickness funds they must balance annual income and expenditure and adjust their premiums accordingly.

Before 1945 the *mutuelles* were the main force in health care insurance, but now they mainly concentrate on providing patient copayments, although they also support other health-related activities, including hospitals and public clinics. In most cases premiums are a flat rate or a proportion of earnings. There is no *overt* selection of members according to their health. Moreover, there is no discrimination against the elderly; the *mutuelles* provide cover for twice as many old people as the commercial insurance companies. Since 1981 they have significantly increased their share of health care spending, especially for medicines.

The commercial insurance companies play a less clear, but nevertheless significant role. Comprehensive data about their activities is lacking, although it is known that in 1990 there were 79 health insurance firms with perhaps 8 million customers. Estimates of the proportion of health care spending that they provide range from 2 percent to 6 percent but it is agreed that they are increasing in importance. Most of such insurance is arranged by firms for their employees and covers everyone without discrimination. In the case of private individuals, however, health status may be taken into consideration. Once again, the role of the commercial insurers is to supplement the provision of the sick funds rather than to provide a completely separate service. The profitability of private health insurance is apparently low.[14]

A possible problem for the French system of copayments is that the poor are less likely to carry private health insurance of any kind. In consequence copayments might more of a burden to them, while their health status is markedly below the norm. Medical aid is supposed to compensate but the take-up rate is uncertain.[15]

5.3.3.4 Economic Incentives and Competition

The sickness funds do not compete with one another, since they are organised along strictly occupational lines. They are, however, under considerable pressure to control their spending.

As we have seen, expenditure on health care has risen considerably in the last 10 years, both in absolute terms and, to a lesser extent, as a proportion of national income. Direct spending on the sick now stands at 8.9 percent of

---

[14] Arnold and Armann (1991), p. 47, give a figure of FF 13.8 bn for 1988, which they obtained from the Ministry of Health. Other figures quoted to us ranged from two to six percent of total spending.

[15] Persons below a certain income are entitled to *Aide Sociale*, most of which is disbursed locally. This includes the normal copayments for medical treatment; in these cases the doctor is paid 100 percent of his fee directly, rather than the patient having to pay and then recover from the sick fund. In 1989 spending on health care by the Departmental *Aides Sociale* was 1985 FF 2.9 bn, or 5 percent of all copayments. For the inferior health status of the less affluent, see Charraud, in Duru and Tachon (1988), pp. 33-48 and Fox (1990).

GDP. Sums of this magnitude must be of concern to national policy-makers. As has already been seen, the central government, via the Ministry of Health, plays the major part in deciding what the rates of contribution shall be. It is also involved in negotiating the fees for medical treatment (see Sections 5.3.4.3 and 5.3.5.2 below). In theory, this involves participation by both the payers and the providers; in practice, the will of the government is said to prevail.

The sickness funds therefore need to increase their income or to reduce their spending. Neither is easy. Some of the strategies which have been used are discussed in more detail in Section 5.5.1 below. At this point, it is enough to note that payroll deductions are increasingly seen as a significant burden, especially on employers. To raise them further may be difficult. In fact the rates charged by the *Régime Général* did not change during the 10 years before 1991, although the former income ceiling for contributions was abolished in 1983. Controls over spending have therefore attracted more attention: as will be seen, global budgets for public hospitals have been the principal move in this direction (see Section 5.3.5.2). Such policies have enabled the sick funds to reduce their proportionate contribution to the health care bill.

There is some competition in the private insurance sector, both between the *mutuelles* and the commercial companies and between each type of organisation. In principle the commercial companies could offer attractive rates to the fit and to provide very wide cover for them. However, as we have seen, much of their custom is in the form of company-wide agreements and to this extent they resemble the *mutuelles*. Both, therefore, have an interest in promoting economy in health care. The *mutuelles* have been particularly active in this respect. Thus, they favour the systematic evaluation of medical procedures, firm controls over rates of reimbursement and the use of generic equivalents to branded medicines. Some of them also limit the extent to which they will cover patient copayments (see Section 5.3.4).

5.3.3.5 Objectives of the Payers

To summarise, the payers have a strong interest in promoting economy in the use of health care. For political and economic reasons discussed in Section 5.5.1.3 below, the sick funds find it difficult to raise their incomes, while the state clearly has no wish to increase its direct role in funding. The *mutuelles* wish to avoid raising their contributions unduly, while the private insurers want to remain profitable. However, as we have seen, French patients expect to receive health care of the highest quality in large volumes and at very moderate prices at the point of service. Thus there is a direct conflict between the aims of payers and those of patients. The aims of providers will become apparent in the next two sections.

5.3.4   Primary Health Care Sector

5.3.4.1   Scope of Primary Health Care

In France, primary health care (*soins ambulatoires*) comprises all out-of-hospital treatment, including not only that supplied by doctors, dentists, and paramedical personnel, but also the services of biological and analytical laboratories and even some thermal cures. Although the services of doctors are clearly of central importance, they account for rather less than half of total expenditure on this account.

5.3.4.2   Primary Health Care in the French Context

Patients are not only free to consult any general practitioner (GP), or even several if they so wish, without restriction, but they are equally free to consult any specialist or hospital out-patient clinic. As a result, primary medical care has a wider meaning in France than in those countries where GPs act as gate-keepers who limit access to specialists. In practice, however, the first contact is with a GP in 80 percent of cases.

The bulk of primary health care is provided by private doctors (*médécins libéraux*), of whom there were 57,700 general practitioners (*généralistes*, GPs) and 48,000 specialists (*spécialistes*) in 1990. In descending order, the most commonly consulted specialisms are gynaecology, psychiatry, ophthalmology, radiology and surgery. These private doctors are not confined to primary health care; many of them, particularly the specialists, also work at least part-time in hospitals and other institutions. However, primary care is their major function. Most of them practise alone; in 1988 only 3 percent of GPs and 9 percent of specialists were members of group practices.[16]

GPs carry out only a limited range of procedures. They visit their patients; they receive them for consultations; they diagnose; they prescribe medicines and other forms of treatment, which may involve the participation of other medical or paramedical personnel or reference to hospitals. They do little else:

---

[16]   CNAMTS (1991c), pp. 20-23. In 1990, 74.7 percent of all such doctors had a purely private practice, 8.3 percent also had a salaried post, 13.5 percent worked part-time in hospitals and 3,5% full-time in hospitals. The figures for *omnipracticiens* include those who practice homeopathy, acupuncture etc.

in 1990 the average general practitioner was paid for 4500 consultations and visits and for only 250 other items of activity. Unlike their German counterparts, they do not do much minor surgery, as the tariffs for doing so are not attractive. Specialists receive fewer callers but carry out a wide range of more technical - and therefore higher-paid - activities, including the more elaborate forms of investigation, diagnosis and treatment.

Almost all dentists and most paramedical personnel working in primary care are also private practitioners, as are the ambulance services and many biological and analytical laboratories. Emergency medical services are publicly operated.

5.3.4.3 Financing Primary Health Care

Private doctors are paid by fee-for-service. In 1960 an agreement was signed between the government and most doctors. It was called *La Convention* and has been renegotiated and renewed at regular intervals ever since, most recently in 1989. As part of this, a set of reimbursable services (*la nomenclature*) is agreed together with an escalation clause. Standard fees (*tarifs conventionnels*) for each type of service are negotiated annually. Doctors who abide by these fees - those in the so-called sector 1 -then charge the patient according to the service performed and the patient then recovers a set proportion of the fee from the sick funds (see Section 5.3.2.3).[17]

However, higher fees, set by the doctor himself with the permission of the sickness funds, may be charged. Until 1980 this right was limited to physicians of exceptional professional standing. Subsequently it was extended to all doctors who are willing to pay higher taxes and social security contributions (whilst retaining the rights of those of exceptional professional standing). By 1990 32 percent of all primary care physicians had taken up this offer. This group of physicians were placed in sector 2. In such cases the patient pays the entire difference (*dépassement*) between the standard fee and that charged by the doctor, which, on average, is about 9 percent higher, with broad differences between poorer and richer regions in particular. In the same year, however, the right to join sector 2 was again confined to those with

---

[17]   Flat rates are set for consultations and visits; they are 25 percent higher for consultants than for GPs. In addition, each "act of specialism" carried out by the doctor carries a number of points, different values being assigned to each point depending on the nature of the speciality.

particular qualifications (though this time relatively junior ones) in spite of some opposition in the medical profession.[18]

Private dentists and paramedical personnel are in a similar position to doctors: reimbursement from the sick funds is normal for specified services, with standard fees being set by agreement between payers and suppliers and copayments imposed on patients. The scope of such agreements has been steadily extended over the years. In the case of dentists, however, there is more scope for providing services at a higher price than that reimbursed by the sickness funds.

5.3.4.4   Regulation of the Primary Health Care Sector

Thus, the supply of primary care is very largely in private hands.

There are indeed public clinics (dispensaires), of which the municipal health centres are the most significant. The clinics are operated by municipalities, voluntary bodies such as the mutuelles, or by humanitarian organisations. Their staff are salaried, but the clinics are remunerated on a fee-for-service basis. Hospital out-patient clinics also play a part in primary care. In addition there are specialised medical services for industry, for schools, and for the protection of infants and mothers (IMS). No pre-paid health maintenance organisations have developed in France, although there is some limited interest in this possibility.[19]

There are few controls over private doctors or other medical personnel working outside hospitals. Provided that they are properly qualified and registered with the self-regulated Medical Board (Ordre des Médécins), they are free to set up practices anywhere in France. There are no controls by the Sécurité Sociale over the kind of services that they may provide (so long as conventional medicine is used and not alternative therapies, most of which are not covered by the Sécurité Sociale) or over the frequency with which they provide them. If they subscribe to the national agreements (conventions) already mentioned, their patients will be reimbursed by the sick funds at the approved rate for the approved services that they provide. Virtually all private doctors do subscribe.

---

[18]   This limitation was not made retroactive. The necessary qualification is to have served as an assistant or chef de clinique in a regional or general hospital. These ranks are relatively junior.

[19]   Journal d'Economie Medicale, (special issue) (1986) 4 (3-4).

The density of private doctors in France is high: in 1990 there were 1.86 per 1,000 population. Even more to the point, it has risen unusually rapidly, with an increase of 144 percent since 1970. Spending on primary care by doctors rose by 225 percent in real terms during this period. There appears to be a relationship between the number of private doctors and the frequency with which they are consulted: thus, the *per capita* number of consultations in the private sector rose from 2.3 in 1970 to 3.4 in 1980 and 4.9 in 1990.

In an attempt to control rising health care expenditure a *numerus clausus* was imposed in 1972 on the supply of new doctors. It took the form of limiting the number allowed to pass from the first to the second year of medical studies. Despite opposition from medical students - and from the left-wing parties - it was put into effect and since that time the annual output of new doctors has fallen from 8,650 to 3,500. Given the structure of the medical profession, the main impact of this measure may be on the primary care sector,[20] though becoming a specialist has also become more difficult. The number of doctors, currently 150,000, is nevertheless expected to peak at about 200,000 in the year 2010 before falling to a stable level of 130,000 from 2050 onwards.

The geographical distribution of doctors is markedly uneven. Relative to population there are considerably more doctors in the south than in the north or east, with the south believed to have an excess in particular of private doctors. This regional imbalance is due to the concentration of medical schools in the south and possibly to the preference of French doctors to practice in the warmth of the south. The density of both specialists and of those who charge supplemental fees is highest in the major conurbations where *per capita* incomes are highest. Attempts have been made to encourage physicians to move to under-provided areas but without success.[21]

Thus official controls over the primary health care sector have hitherto been limited on the one hand to regulation of the kinds of services which may be paid for through the sick funds and the scale of reimbursement provided, and

---

[20]   There were approximately 150,000 practising doctors in France in 1990 - there is some uncertainty about the exact total - of which 108,000 are private doctors. Of the remainder, a majority work full-time in hospitals (CNAMTS, 1991b, p. 9). Trends in the population of doctors are discussed by Levy C. in Daru and Tachon (1988) pp. 23-32.

[21]   The highest densities of private doctors are in the regions of Marseilles (268/100,000 population), Montpelier (235) and Paris (216) and the lowest in those of Lille (146), Rouen (148) and Orleans (154) (CNAMTS, 1991a, pp. 238-41).

on the other to regulation of the number of doctors. This situation, however, is about to change (see Section 5.5 below).

5.3.4.5 Economic Incentives and Competition

Although the total consumption of primary health care by patients in France has risen quite considerably since 1981, the GPs are under some financial pressure.

Their numbers are still increasing quite rapidly. To an increasing extent their activity consists of less well-paid duties such as visits and consultations. Their *per capita* rates of activity actually fell by about 4 percent between 1980 and 1990 as their density rose and as specialists took an increasing part of the market. As a result their gross incomes have remained almost static in real terms: between 1980 and 1990 the annual average only increased from FF 522,500 to FF 537,400 in 1990 money ($71,000 to $73,000 1990), an increase of 2.9 percent. This is still below the level of 1970. In 1989 10 percent of them earned less than FF 200,000 ($28,000 1990).[22]

As a result competition is intense. As elsewhere, doctors in France are not allowed to advertise, and price competition has not been encouraged. Only since 1988 has it been permissable for doctors to display a list of fees in their waiting rooms. Doctors who charge standard fees are classified as sector 1. In principle, GPs dissatisfied with their incomes could change to sector 2 and charge higher fees. However, this is only practicable where, as in Paris, most of them have already done so. By 1990 only 22 percent of all general practitioners had taken this step.

Competition is therefore on the basis of quality of service and relationship with the patient. Factors such as the time spent waiting for an appointment and the time spent during the consultation are important. The patient is often in a buyers' market and may shop around for what he or she expects. Significantly, no less than 30 percent of the contacts between GPs and patients take the form of house calls. Equally significantly - and even more important from the financial standpoint - doctors prescribe freely and heavily (see Section 5.3.6.1 below).

Specialists in private practice are in a better position. Although their numbers increased even more rapidly than those of the general practitioners, they

---

[22]   CNAMTS (1991c).

benefit from the higher fees that they are allowed to charge. Moreover, in recent years patients have increasingly preferred to visit specialists rather than general practitioners. In consequence their *per capita* activity rates rose by 11.5 percent between 1980 and 1990. The average real income of specialists increased from FF 784,000 to FF 901,000 in 1990 money ($104,600 to $120,200 1990) during this period. An indication of their bargaining position is that 44 percent of them are now in sector 2 of the reimbursement system.

5.3.4.6   Objectives of Primary Care Physicians

GPs are suffering from static or declining incomes. In the absence of higher fees they can only improve their position by seeing patients as often as possible and offering them a high level of service. Alternatively they might benefit by performing a wider range of duties, such as minor surgery or preventative care. They might also work in groups so as to reduce their overheads and offer a more integrated service. Such strategies are being increasingly discussed.

Specialists are not so hard-pressed, but, as with GPs, the fee-for-service method of remuneration encourages them to see the largest number of patients as possible and, in their case, to treat them as intensively as possible. Since their numbers are increasing rapidly - by 58 percent in the 1980s - their position may also deteriorate.

Both groups remain, however, firmly attached to the principles of private medicine and have opposed any departure from it. So far no administration has felt itself able to challenge them on this point.

5.3.5   Hospital Sector

5.3.5.1   Hospital Care in the French Context

Hospital care in France is provided by both public and private institutions. Patients are admitted on reference from the primary health care physicians. They are free to choose between sectors. However, if they choose a public hospital they must go to the one in their catchment area.

Public hospitals (*hôpitaux publiques*) are attached to municipalities, departments or regions. Although legally distinct from the localities where they are sited, policy is decided by hospital boards containing representatives of the sick funds and of the medical and administrative staff of the hospital. Such hospitals are obliged to provide equality of treatment for all patients and round-the-clock care. Private hospitals (*cliniques privées*) may operate on a non-profit or for-profit basis. Some of them accept the same public service obligations as the public hospitals and complement the public hospital service. Others do not, but nevertheless are able to draw on public funds.[23]

In 1990 there were 558,700 beds available in French hospitals. Of these 65 percent were in public hospitals and a further 11 percent in non-profit private hospitals with public service obligations. Another 5 percent were in other non-profit and 19 percent in with-profit hospitals. Public sector hospitals are considerably larger (and generally better equipped) than those in the private sector; on average they contain 350 beds as opposed to 70 in both non-profit and with-profit private hospitals. They have a much higher proportion of medium-stay, long-stay and psychiatric patients, but also lower occupancy rates. They also carry out a larger proportion of major surgical interventions and high-technology treatments. This is reflected in their higher costs per patient-day. Private hospitals tend to specialise in minor and optional surgery.[24]

5.3.5.2 Financing the Hospital Sector

Until 1984 public hospitals were funded on the basis of a standard daily rate, which was the same regardless of the treatment given or the length of stay. Since then they have been granted annual prospective global budgets within which they are expected to stay. The Ministry of Health lays down the total to be spent on public hospitals after which the budget for each hospital is negotiated by the board of each hospital and the state with the sick funds being informed of the outcome. They are essentially based on 1985 expenditures with variable allowances for inflation and, less certainly, changes in activities. Capital requirements are met by the sick funds. The medical staff are usually salaried employees. Their salaries are set by the Ministry of Health and the medical associations. However, since 1988 they have been allowed to spend one day per week in private practice.

---

[23]   There are 29 regional hospitals, 332 *centres hôpitaliers* and 98 psychiatric hospitals in the public sector. *The Conseil d'Administration* of a general hospital (*Centre hôpitalier generale*) must by law contain 6 local and regional councillors, 8 representatives of the sick funds, 4 doctors and 4 other members of the staff and 3 persons nominated by the Prefect, of whom one must be a doctor and one a representative of the paramedical professions.

[24]   Up to 8 percent of beds in public hospitals may be reserved for private patients.

Private hospitals are in a different position. Those which have assumed the same responsibilities as the public hospitals also receive an overall budget. Those which have not done so may nevertheless be supported by the sick funds. Almost all of them have signed the national agreement (*Convention*) which allows their medical staff to be paid by fee-for-service in the same way as out-of-hospital practitioners (see Section 5.3.4 above). Other costs are reimbursed on a *per diem* basis, with fees which reflect the general standard of services and accommodation offered by the hospital. These also are set by the Ministry of Health and the medical associations. There is a national system of classification for this purpose but the actual rates charged vary considerably from area to area. Very few hospitals are totally outside this system.

From the standpoint of the patient, hospital treatment differs from primary care. Instead of paying the bill and then recovering most of it from the *Sécurité Sociale*, the latter reimburses the hospital directly (*tiers payant*), and the patient provides only the copayment. The reason is obvious: hospital bills come seldom but are large. In public hospitals patients pay FF 30 (about $4 1990) per day towards their hotel costs; in addition, for a stay of less than 30 days - the large majority - and for certain minor operations they are liable to a copayment of 20 percent of the total cost, from which the day payment is deducted. In private hospitals patients are also charged a copayment of 20 percent of the standard charges for medical treatment; in addition they have to find the balance of the other costs.

Due to the high proportion of hospital spending that is accounted for by people who are exempt (see Section 5.3.2), copayments account for only 9 percent of expenditure in public hospitals and 12 percent of that of private hospitals, a much lower proportion than in the case of primary care or medicines.

5.3.5.3 Regulation of the Hospital Sector

In contrast to the primary health care sector, hospitals are subject to a good deal of official regulation.

All hospitals require accreditation by the Ministry of Health, which places them in a particular category. This determines the types of reimbursable treatment that they may give. Their standards of care are periodically reviewed by the medical inspectorate (*Médécins Inspecteurs de Santé*). Another body of inspectors (*Practiciens-Conseil de la Sécurité Sociale*) maintains control over reimbursement for unusually costly or prolonged forms of treatment.

Public hospitals are also subject to the *Cour des Comptes*, which has a general oversight over the whole French administration, and which has, on occasion, taken a highly critical attitude. More importantly, they are controlled by the IGAS (*Inspection Général des Affaires Sociales*), the inspectors from the Ministry for Social Affairs.

Under a law of 1970 a national plan for hospitals (*carte sanitaire*) was introduced, accompanied by detailed regional plans. The object was to control the growth of hospital capacity without prejudice to the ability to deal adequately with health needs. Investment in new hospital beds and in new equipment, whether in the public or private sectors, was made subject to the permission of the Ministry of Health. However, these measures took some time to have an effect and the number of beds continued to increase until 1981. In part this was due to the standards adopted by the planners, which revealed that many parts of France were under- rather than over-supplied. In 1976, however, it was decided to stabilise the total number of beds, and in 1979 it was made possible for the Ministry to shut down beds in the public sector. This has been done in places, especially in psychiatric hospitals, although the total number of beds remains unusually high.[25]

The system of global budgets for hospitals in the public sector has had a considerable effect in restraining expenditure. Between 1970 and 1982, real expenditure was rising at between 6.5 and 9 percent annually; since then it has done so at no more than 3 percent per year. By one estimate, current spending is 9 percent lower than would otherwise be the case. Even allowing for the fall in the number of public beds this is an impressive achievement. No such change took place in the private sector during this period. However, problems have been reported. Owing to the basis on which budgets are decided, hospitals which have enjoyed disproportionately large budgets in the past continue to do so, while rewards for economy are lacking perhaps in part because of the commitment to quality.

There have also been allegations from time to time that budgeting has led to shortages of resources, to rationing and even to corruption, with influential patients getting preferential treatment. Such complaints are as yet scattered and opinions differ as to their severity. There is certainly a chronic shortage

---

[25]   Between 1980 and 1990 the number of psychiatric beds was reduced from 80,407 to 57,650, a drop of 28 percent. The number of beds in general hospitals rose slightly but showed a shift from short-stay to medium and long-stay beds.

of specialists and foreign doctors have had to be hired. The salaries offered are relatively unattractive.[26]

5.3.5.4   Economic Incentives and Competition

As with primary care, the French health care system provides hospital care on a relatively generous scale. There are approximately 10 beds per 1000 inhabitants. Much use is made of these facilities: in 1990 in-patient days *per capita* were 3.0, admissions to hospital were 22.8 percent of the population and the average stay lasted 13.1 days. Among the 11 countries in the study, France ranked 4th, 5th, 1st and 6th in these measures. Nevertheless, it is unusual to have to wait for more than a month for hospital treatment.

In private hospitals doctors have an excellent reason to offer the maximum amount of treatment: in a fee-for-service system their income depends on doing so. As salaried employees, the medical staff of public hospitals are not motivated in this way, but nor are they motivated towards economy. The practice of medical audit has developed only slowly, even though it is now officially encouraged. Cost-effectiveness and cost-benefit studies are few. By international standards, French hospitals carry out a large number of probably unnecessary operations: thus, the appendicectomy rate is five times higher than anywhere else in Europe. The number of X-rays and biological tests undertaken also seems very large.[27]

Competition within the hospital sector is largely between with-profit private hospitals and other kinds of institution. Since 1984 the former have gained a larger share of the market, whether this is measured by admissions or patient-days. Several reasons for this development have been suggested. They are often able to offer superior hotel facilities to those who can afford them, who now include a substantial proportion of the population (see Sections 5.3.2.3 and 5.3.3.3 above). Additional hotel costs for superior facilities are paid for either by patients or their insurers. Less certainly, they may offer better care and treatment. They can attract better staff by offering improved income prospects: potential earnings may be several times those available in public hospitals. However, they are not allowed to install new equipment without official permission.[28,29]

---

[26]   *L'Express* (9/3/1989); *Le Monde, passim*; Stevens, J. (1989) pp. 224-7.

[27]   Stevens, J. *op cit.*

[28]   The agreements between private hospitals and the sick funds expressly forbid this.

Nevertheless, the with-profit private hospitals face problems of their own. Despite the financial participation of several large companies from outside the health care field, notably the Compagnie Generale des Eaux, and the introduction of professional management, profits have been disappointing. Indeed, losses have been common in recent years and a number of such establishments have gone out of business. This means that more than ever private hospitals will wish to avoid difficult and expensive treatments and the unprofitable patient.

5.3.5.5 Objectives of the Hospital Sector

The public hospitals are under tight financial controls. Their aim is to maintain capacity - and equally important, public acceptability - with relatively limited resources. Their only serious hope of doing so without substantial changes in the financial system is to improve their efficiency, so as to avoid such untoward effects as the development of queues for treatment. Many of the private non-profit hospitals are in the same position. The sick funds and the *mutuelles* both favour increased efficiency.

The private with-profit hospitals are gaining at the expense of their competitors. They have a limited freedom in pricing and some in their choice of patients. However, they are in a symbiotic relationship with their public counterparts: if the latter were to deteriorate seriously, the private hospitals might find themselves under pressure to provide more of the output required from the sector. Without freedom to set prices this could reduce their profits which already are mediocre.

5.3.6 Pharmaceutical Sector

5.3.6.1 Role of the Patients

Only 7 percent of total medicine consumption by value is bought over-the-counter, although some OTC medicines may be and are prescribed. Of the balance, about 13 percent is prescribed within hospitals and 80 percent by doctors practising outside hospitals.[30]

---

[29] The career grade for a salaried hospital doctor is *practicien*, for which the salary in 1990 was FF 454 - 594,000 ($62 - $81,000 1990) after 21 years service or rather more than half that of a private specialist.

[30] *Scrip* (25/2/92) 1703, 6, quoting CNAMTS figures.

378

Qualitative evidence suggests that patients may play an active part in determining prescribing behaviour. In terms of volume, French consumption of medicines is high by European standards. Prescription items *per capita* were more than twice the European average. Attempts to restrict the reimbursement of "comfort" medicines have met with strong opposition from pharmacists and also patients, who consider them to be very useful. Patients are free to consult whichever doctor they please and it is widely believed that they expect a doctor to prescribe freely (see Section 5.3.4.5). Nevertheless, the age structure of the prescription medicine market is not unduly biassed to recent introductions. The demand is for medicines in general rather than the latest and most fashionable examples.

Generic products have only 2-3 percent of the market. Generic substitution is illegal in France. Because retail pharmacists are paid by a mark-up on wholesale prices, they have always strongly opposed generic products and have even boycotted them.

5.3.6.2 Financing the Pharmaceutical Sector

The sickness funds pay 71 percent of the overall bill for medicines prescribed outside hospitals and for all those used inside hospitals.

As with other forms of treatment the patient is charged a copayment, although the usual exemptions (Section 5.3.2) apply. Only medicines which are "irreplaceable and expensive" are free; the main categories are cytostatics and immunosuppressive products, serums and some vaccines, anti-anaemics, plasma substitutes, antifibrinolytics and thrombolytics and gonadotropics. In addition, however, certain illnesses qualify for 100 percent reimbursement of associated drug costs. A 30 percent copayment is imposed on medicines for other more or less serious conditions and one of 60 percent on those for "troubles and conditions usually not serious". Of all reimbursed medicines, 44 percent by value fell in the 100 percent reimbursement class, 45 percent in the 70 percent class and 11 percent in the 40 percent class. An increasing proportion of prescription medicines are not reimbursed (e.g. most vitamins). Medicines bought over the counter are also excluded.

As with other forms of medical treatment most patients insure against the possibility of copayment for medicines. The SNIP estimates that in 1990 21 percent of the out-of-hospital medicine bill was met in this way, 15 percent coming from the *mutuelles* and 6 percent from private insurance. Direct payments by patients amounted to 8 percent of the whole.[31]

5.3.6.3 Regulation of the Pharmaceutical Sector

Like all other countries in the study, France regulates the manufacture of medicines, the introduction of new products to the national market, the forms in which medicines are supplied to patients and the trade in medicines. In theory and to a large extent in practice France now follows the rules laid down by the European Community (see Chapter 16: The Role of the European Community).

The main exception is in the case of prices. In principle there are no controls over the prices of medicines but the state regulates admission to reimbursement, the extent of reimbursement and the permitted prices of individual products that are accepted. The Price Committee of the Ministry of Health is the responsible body. A "technical price" is set, based on the novelty, clinical efficiency and daily treatment cost of the product compared to others in the same therapeutic group. An "economic price" is then negotiated with the company in question, which takes into consideration the scale and nature of its activities in France.

It has been the practice of successive administrations to keep French medicine prices low, arguing that cultural factors make it difficult to restrain the volume of consumption. They are currently about 65 percent of the EC average. Companies are therefore willing to expand their operations in France in order to get a better price for a promising new medicine, even though such a concession is contingent on consumption not exceeding a certain maximum. If a company breaches that ceiling the permitted price is reduced; this has happened to both Merck and Glaxo in recent years. Policies of this kind arouse mixed feelings in the pharmaceutical industry. They are arguably illegal under the Treaty of Rome but have not been tested in the courts.

France also attempts to restrict marketing expenditure, currently about 18 percent of sales, by imposing a 7 percent tax on such spending.

---

[31] According to the SNIP, some 7 percent of all prescription medicines were either bought over the counter or by patients who did not claim reimbursement.

5.3.6.4   Pharmaceutical Distribution

Medicine distribution in France follows the usual European pattern: manufacturers sell to wholesalers who sell to retailers. The distributors charge mark-ups which are a proportion of the manufacturers' price and which are regulated by the Ministry of Health. The wholesaler's margin is 10.7 percent and the retailer's margin is between 8 and 45 percent, varying inversely with the price of the product. In 1990 the average distributor's mark-up was 63 percent of the manufacturer's price.

Retailers buy 90 percent of what they sell from wholesalers. The latter are increasingly concentrated: the three largest firms have 75 percent of the market. Formerly purely national in their operations, they are increasingly involved in pan-European alliances. The number of pharmacies is controlled; depending on the concentration of the local population, one is allowed for every 2-3000 inhabitants, although a significant number of derogations are given each year. Currently there are 22,150, virtually all of which are privately-owned. Pharmacists monopolise the sales of all kinds of medicines, including over-the-counter products; a recent attempt to legalise the sale of certain medicines in supermarkets was rejected. However, the pharmacists are in turn limited solely to the sale of health care products - admittedly generously interpreted.

Hospitals buy 90 cent of their medicines directly from the manufacturers. When several medicines are based on the same active substance, only the cheapest is available in hospitals.

5.3.6.5   Economic Incentives and Competition

The pharmaceutical industry competes by innovation on the one hand and by marketing on the other hand. Price is not a very important factor. Generic competition is limited in France, if only because prices of older products are too low to make it commercially attractive. The main customers for generic products are hospitals. The attitude of the international companies to French policies is equivocal; prices are low but volume is high, and in an industry where direct costs are a comparatively small proportion of the whole the contribution to overheads may be substantial. Significantly, despite many protests about price levels, no such company has withdrawn from France.

Arguably the main sufferers from low prices are the French-owned companies. Because they were slow to expand abroad - at least in part a reflection of the fragmented structure of the sector - they have remained tied to the French market. Their cash flow has been too small to permit the massive investment in R&D now required for successful innovation. The process of concentration is likely to bring about a two-tier industry, with an upper level of large research-oriented firms and a lower one of small niche players. The French Ministry of Industry has been concerned about the situation for a number of years, but until recently has done little about it (though see Section 5.3.6.3).

There are few elements of competition in the distribution system. Prices at the retail stage are in effect controlled but wholesalers often give discounts for volume and other reasons. In such circumstances retailers can raise their margins. The percentage cost-plus method of remunerating pharmacists makes them disinclined to supply cheaper products at the expense of more expensive ones. An attempt to promote generics in 1981 led to a strike of pharmacists, who saw it as threatening their livelihood.

Little has been done to sensitise either doctors or patients to the cost of medicines. The impact of copayments is diluted almost to vanishing point by the prevalence of complementary insurance. Doctors show little inclination to moderate their prescribing, for the reasons explored in Section 5.3.4.5 above. The Ministry of Health has done little to press them in this direction. Action has been left to the *mutuelles* who provide most of the copayments for medicines. They have actively promoted the use of medicines which are cheaper equivalents of popular branded products. This strategy seems to have had some effect.

5.3.7   Central Government

As has been seen repeatedly in this profile, the central government exercises a powerful, though not an overwhelming influence on the health care system of France.

It does so primarily through the Ministries of Health and of Social Affairs. At times these ministries have been combined; at times they have been under separate political heads, as at present; but their directorates endure. These directorates have separate responsibilities, dealing respectively with hospitals, medicines, public health and with the social security system as a whole. The last has the dominant influence as far as finance is concerned. It has close links with the Ministry of Finance where a senior official deals with health-related issues.

The social security directorate - and now the Ministry of Social Affairs - is primarily concerned with costs - "not cost-benefit, not cost-efficiency, just costs", as one of our informants remarked. The other directorates are more directly concerned with practical issues, such as the location of hospital facilities, the licensing of pharmaceutical products and so on. There is therefore some tension between the aims of the two ministries. For example, policies towards the pharmaceutical industry tend to place the Ministry of Social Affairs and the Ministry of Finance on one side and the Directorate of Medicines and the Ministry of Industry on the other.

The ministries exert their powers both directly and indirectly. In some cases they are - at least in principle - able to act freely. Thus, the Directorate of Hospitals decides where and what hospitals shall be built. The Directorate of Medicines decides what the price of a medicine shall be. Inevitably, political pressures of various kinds may enter into the final decisions, but the initiative lies with the government. In other cases the ministries exert their influence less directly. Thus the *conventions* between the sick funds and private doctors are in principle freely negotiated but must be approved by the government before they can come into force.

The *Sécurité Sociale* is nominally independent and its income and expenditure are not subject to parliamentary control and form no part of the national budget. However, the Ministry of Social Affairs exerts a powerful influence over such matters as the rates of contribution, partly through its legal powers of supervision, and partly through its role as arbitrator when there is disagreement between the negotiating parties. Our interviews suggest that the Ministry is and always has been the ultimate master over the financing of all aspects of social security, of which health care is only one aspect.

Nevertheless, there are limits to the role of government. There is no national health care budget as such. Where expenditure out of hospitals or in private hospitals are concerned, the ministries have limited powers. They can regulate such spending on a retrospective basis - by, for example, engineering an increase in payroll deductions - but they cannot do so on a prospective basis. Significantly, this is the main source of the financial problems of the French health care sector.

5.4   INTERSECTORAL ANALYSIS

5.4.1   Major Decision Makers

The main characteristic of the French health care system is decentralisation. There is no one single focus of decision making. Instead, there are many players in the game, each of whom exerts some influence even it is only negative (see Table 5.3). The boards of the *Sécurité Sociale* provide a national forum for the discussion of policy similar to that provided by the *Konzertierte Aktion* in Germany.

That said, some players are more important than others. On the financial side, the national government ranks first. The social security *régimes* are expected to be self-supporting; to the extent they are not, the state has an opportunity to intervene. In any case it is the central government, nominally in negotiation with representatives of the employers and employees, that decides the rates of the payroll deductions that pay for the sick funds (Section 5.3.3.3). Even more important, the Ministry of Health plays an active part in deciding which forms of treatment shall be reimbursable, what the reimbursement levels shall be and how much of the bill shall be left to the patient (Sections 5.3.4.3 and 5.3.5.2).

However, the effect of these controls is diluted by the availability of private finance for health care. This is a natural corollary of the relatively high patient copayments required. Moreover, in recent years doctors have been allowed to charge above-standard rates under certain conditions and many have chosen to do so. The *mutuelles* and the commercial health insurers therefore have an influence on health care spending. The former usually limit themselves to providing the standard copayment; the latter do not. The effect is to transfer a part of the financial responsibility for health care from the public to numerous private organisations and indeed to individuals.

As far as the delivery of health care is concerned, primary health care is extremely fragmented. The right of the patient to see any doctor that he or she wishes, and the right of doctors to practise anywhere in France means that most decisions about primary care are made by many thousands of physicians and allied personnel and many millions of patients. Other than the controls over reimbursement rates already mentioned, official action is confined to limiting the numbers of doctors qualifying (Section 5.3.4.4).

Table 5.4
The Decision Makers in Leading Sectors of the French
Health Care System

Subject of Decision	Participants						
	MoH	SF	O	M	P	Mut	I
Public finance							
- total spending	x	x					
- contribution rates	x	x	x[1]				
- benefits provided	x	x		x			
- reimbursement levels	x	x		x			
- patient copayments	x	x					
Private finance						x	x
Primary care							
- volume of care				x	x		
- cost of care	x	x		x			
Public hospital care							
- facilities provided	x						
- global budget	x		x[2]	x			
- utilisation				x	x		
Private hospital care							
- facilities provided	x		x[3]			x	
- charges	x	x	x[2]	x			
- utilisation				x	x		
Medicines							
- medicines reimbursed	x						
- prices charged	x						
- patient copayments	x						

[1] Employers and employees   [2] Local government   [3] Investors

MoH = Ministry of Health; SF = Sickness funds; O = other financially interested parties; M = medical personnel; P = patients; Mut = *mutuelles*; I = commercial insurance providers.

385

Hospital care is more firmly regulated. As Section 5.3.5.3 has shown, the central government is very much involved in decisions about how many hospitals there shall be, how many beds they shall contain and what types of high-technology equipment shall be provided. Public hospitals now operate under prospective global budgets and are obliged to ration the treatment provided. Private hospitals operate on a mixture of fee-for-service and *per diem* payments, with rather greater scope for individual initiative. Admission to hospital is controlled by the primary sector, although the patient has a choice of where to go.

Most medicines are available only on prescription and here the role of the primary care physician as gatekeeper is a real one. At the same time, however, patients expect doctors to prescribe freely. The state makes no attempt to restrain levels of prescribing but imposes firm controls over reimbursement by the sick funds and also regulates the processes by which medicines are distributed (Section 5.3.6.4).

5.4.2   Consistency of the Objectives and Incentives

The objectives and incentives of the major players under the present health care system have already been discussed in some detail in Section 5.3. There is a clear conflict of interests between the patients and the private doctors and hospitals on the one hand and the providers of public funds on the other. As has been seen at several points in this chapter, French private doctors are strongly attached to the principles of *médécine libre*: freedom to practice where they wish, freedom to prescribe treatment as they see fit, and payment by fee-for-service. They are strongly motivated to maximise treatment. On the whole, patients tend to agree. They are worried about present - and still more about future - levels of expenditure, but they value the freedom of choice in the French system and are used to receiving a high and rising level of service from the medical profession.

The providers of funds are in a very different position. In common with other parts of the social security system, the sickness funds find themselves under increasing financial pressure. As already indicated (see Section 5.3.3.4), they find it difficult to enlarge their incomes by raising contribution rates, and are therefore forced to consider ways in which to limit their commitments or to increase the efficiency of the delivery systems. Their major achievement of the last 10 years has been the imposition of cash limits on public hospitals. On the basis of recent interviews, it seems probable that this has not involved a reduced level of service (see Section 5.3.5.3).

The situation of the private insurance funds is also of interest. The *mutuelles* tend to take the same view as the sickness funds. Because they cover a large part of the population and do not discriminate between individuals, they see the promotion of economies as the best way to balance their books. The commercial funds aim to exploit a growing market without over-committing themselves. They need to draw off the cream while leaving the skimmed milk to the public sector. Thus, they have an interest in making sure that the public sector provides an acceptable basic service for those who cannot afford their services.

Finally, it is worth considering a conflict of objectives within the central government. It has been French official policy for many years both to restrain public expenditure on medicines and also to promote the growth of pharmaceutical capacity in France. On the one hand, positive lists and price controls are imposed; on the other, incentives are offered to encourage pharmaceutical companies to enlarge their operations in France (Section 5.3.6.3). Such measures have certainly distorted the market within and without France, without doing much to improve the competitive position of the French industry.

5.4.3   Economic Implications for Efficiency and Equity

The present French health care system is equitable but inefficient. Almost the entire population is covered by the sick funds, which provide most kinds of medical care. The differences between the sickness funds are marginal. They are organised on occupational rather than geographic lines and the *Régime Général* covers most of the population. The reimbursement rates apply nation-wide. In terms of equity a possible problem is the relatively high patient copayments, since they cannot but weigh more heavily on the poor. Although help is available through the *Aide Médicale*, this may not reach all who need it. The seriously ill, however, are exempt.

The delivery of health care is again reasonably equitable. The major problem is the uneven distribution of primary care doctors. For the reasons explained in Section 5.3.4 their density relative to population is disproportionately high in the south and in the major conurbations and low in the rural areas. This is particularly true of specialists. Access and choice are thereby reduced in some regions. As a result of the *carte sanitaire* (see Section 5.3.5.3) the spatial distribution of hospital beds and of high-technology equipment is more even, but is still far from perfect.

The finance system does not encourage efficiency. Membership of a sick fund is compulsory and decided by occupation. There is no choice: a patient cannot opt for a scheme that charges less for the same benefits. Accordingly he or she might as well consume as much health care as possible. The patient is, however, often able to choose between *mutuelles* and between commercial insurance plans. The former have a genuine interest in promoting efficiency but the latter may not.

In terms of efficient delivery the French system also leaves much to be desired. In the primary care sector physicians have good reason to over-treat and patients reinforce this because they appear to equate receiving prescriptions with the quality of the doctor's service. The fragmentation of primary care means that patient records are often erratic and treatments repeated unnecessarily. Public hospitals are under pressure to make good use of their resources but cost-benefit and cost-effectiveness studies are in their infancy. Like out-of-hospital doctors, private commercial hospitals are again motivated to maximise treatment.

5.5 ANALYSIS OF HEALTH CARE POLICY

5.5.1 Current Health Care Policies and Proposals

5.5.1.1 French Health Care Policies in Context

Expenditure on health in France is high by European standards and is continuing to rise. However, the problem should not be overstated. In real terms rates of growth are appreciably lower than in the 1970s. The proportion of spending borne by the public system is slowly falling.

Within the global total it is obvious that the rate of growth of spending on hospitals and especially public hospitals has been greatly reduced in the past decade. However, rates of growth in ambulatory care and spending on medicines have been rising. Only the predominance of hospital expenditure in the national health care budget has produced an apparently favourable outcome. Within these trends it is also possible to discern a shift in public spending on health, which is increasingly concentrated on hospital care. In 1975 the sick funds provided 81 percent of expenditure in public hospitals and 85 percent of that in private hospitals, 68 percent of that on ambulatory care and 63 percent of that on medicines. By 1990 these figures had become 90 percent, 88 percent, 59 percent and 60 percent.

These figures show that private spending is providing an increasing amount of the growth in the health care bill, especially in those areas where there may be an optional element. Nevertheless, expenditure on this account is again rising faster than GDP and, equally important, both official and public anxiety about its magnitude is also increasing (see Sections 5.3.2 and 5.3.3). Such anxieties have dominated the thoughts of policymakers since the 1970s.

5.5.1.2 Responses to Rising Health Care Costs

Faced with this situation, a government could take a number of steps:

- Public funding of health care could be increased.

- The burden could be shifted on to patients through increased copayments for treatment or by withdrawing reimbursement for particular therapies.

- Controls over expenditure could be imposed.

- The efficiency with which current forms of treatment is delivered could be improved.

- The forms of treatment could be changed, with, for example, a greater emphasis on preventative rather than curative medicine.

- The basic system could be changed. An example would be that a public primary health care sector could be created. A number of doctors (e.g., the 10 percent earning least) might be ready to join.

In practice successive French governments have preferred to maintain the basic system. They have, therefore, rejected the last option and have tried the other strategies with mixed results. These are summarised below.

5.5.1.3 Increasing Public Funding

Merely to increase public spending on health care would be to abandon all hope of controlling it. However, there have been a number of attempts to change the way in which the money is raised.

The current system of payroll deductions has a number of disadvantages. They discriminate against labour-intensive and in favour of capital-intensive sectors and may have untoward effects on the international competitive status of French industry. Their basis is narrow: only a minority of the population pays the full rate. Furthermore, income from investments is not taxed at all. The rates are not progressive and therefore weigh more heavily on the poor than on the rich; they also take no notice of family size or other responsibilities.

The possibility of extending the range of incomes on which payroll deductions could be charged or of subsidising health care from general taxation has been raised on several occasions. Most recently, a general tax of 1.1 percent on all incomes was proposed in 1991 to meet the anticipated deficit in the social security budget. This *Contribution Sociale Générale* met with considerable opposition, especially from pensioners, who would be liable, but was nevertheless imposed. However, when employee contributions to the sick funds were raised by 0.9 percent, this aroused little opposition.

There is general agreement that French public opinion is hostile to taxation *per se* and strongly attached to the independence of the social security system. Payroll deductions for the latter are seen as contributions rather than as taxes and arouse less hostility. In political terms, the difficulties of moving away from such a system are seen as overwhelming.

5.5.1.4 Increasing Copayments

More progress has been made here, especially where medicines are concerned, although the direct effects on consumption, due to the prevalence of complementary insurance, have been limited.

In 1976 a large number of less vital medicines were moved from the 70 percent to the 40 percent reimbursement category. In 1986 and again in 1991 a number of such products were removed altogether from reimbursement. Despite widespread protests, these measures were successfully imposed. In the hospital sector, a daily contribution to hotel costs for stays of up to 30 days has been in place since 1982. More generally, relatively high copayments for most forms of treatment are seen as normal in France (see Section 5.3.2.3).

Nevertheless there are limits to what is acceptable. Thus, the Seguin plan of 1987 proposed selective increases in copayments, notably in the field of medicines. Comfort medicines, hitherto free to the chronically sick (see Sections 5.3.2.3 and 5.3.6.2), would henceforth carry the usual charge. The plan was badly received and may have contributed to the downfall of the Chirac government at the subsequent election. The *mutuelles*, who are politically well-connected, are also opposed to increased copayments since they increase their costs.

However, as Section 5.3.2.3 has suggested, the French seem to be willing to spend appreciable sums on health care from their own pockets. Could this be translated into higher copayments? Probably not. Much optional spending must reflect the choice of superior facilities or of optional therapies. To argue that patients would be willing or able to spend more on urgent treatment would be unwise.

5.5.1.5 Controlling Costs

Controlling costs - or at least prices - has been the favoured strategy of French governments of both the right and the left.

The most successful initiative has been the system of global budgets for hospitals. Although crude in nature and not without disadvantages (Section 5.3.5) it has undoubtedly helped to reduce the growth of expenditure. In 1990-91 overall expenditure increased more slowly than the general price level. The planning system for beds and high-technology equipment has also had a positive effect in restraining the growth of hospital capacity. Under a new law most of the necessary decisions are to be made at the regional rather than the national level.

Elsewhere in the French health care system fee-for-service still prevails. The only way to control costs has been through the fees themselves which are negotiated each year (see Section 5.3.4.3). In 1991 a bill was introduced to limit the annual growth in all forms of primary care expenditure to a fixed percentage. If this was exceeded, then the increase in standard fees would be correspondingly reduced in the following year. This approach, possibly suggested by the German points system,[32] was also to apply to private hospitals. This bill was subsequently withdrawn, in part because of opposition from the medical profession and in part because of the deterioration in the standing of the present government.

However, a somewhat watered-down version was reintroduced in 1992 and has now become law. Although strict limits on reimbursement are not included, medical guidelines (*references medicales*) are to be laid down which will offer firm advice on diagnosis and treatment and will specify how much consulting and prescribing each doctor should generate each year. On the basis of these guidelines, annual forecasts of spending will be drawn up and will form part of the doctors' contracts with the sick funds. Sanctions will be imposed on doctors who do not adhere to the guidelines. A coding system will enable the sick funds to monitor the treatment given by individual doctors to individual patients.

Controls over medicine prices have been in place for many years, but with unhappy effects. The competitive position of the French pharmaceutical industry has been adversely affected, while medicine consumption has continued to rise rapidly (Section 5.3.6.3). After much discussion, a new approach was unveiled in 1991. The government would set a global limit on medicine spending by the sick funds and by negotiation a limit for each company. Innovative medicines would be allowed free prices but with a limit on sales; if the company exceeded its target, it would be obliged to refund a proportion of the overshoot. The prices of other products could be adjusted annually, provided that permitted total sales were not exceeded.

This bill aroused great opposition and was, like the global budget proposals for out-of-hospital doctors, shelved by the government.

---

[32]   See Chapter 6: The Health Care System in Germany.

5.5.1.6 Improving Efficiency

This approach has received less attention. As earlier sections have suggested, France is very well provided with both medical facilities and medical personnel. There is little doubt that treatment is provided on a lavish scale and that much of it is of doubtful utility. The scope for reform is considerable. Even obvious steps such as the use of day-surgery await a serious encouragement. Putting the necessary changes into effect, however, is far from easy. Cost-benefit and cost-effectiveness studies are thin on the ground and interest in them was slow to develop, although this is now changing. Basic information about inputs and outcomes is often lacking. The emphasis in the health care system in France still reflects the dominance of purely clinical considerations.

There are in any case formidable obstacles to be overcome before efficiency can be improved. Patients are used to a large element of choice, to prompt treatment and to a high level of service (Section 5.3.2). The medical profession is deeply attached to its freedom of action. Public hospitals are under more direct pressure to economise, but a public hospital may well be the largest single employer in a town. Thus, for example, to reduce the number of its beds, to lay off staff or to reduce the range of treatments provided may well be difficult.

Governments would like to improve efficiency but so far have taken few steps in this direction. The recent changes in the organisation of hospitals, which involve a considerable decentralisation of responsibilities, may, however, have some effect.

5.5.1.7 Changing the Treatments

There is an increasing emphasis on preventive medicine.

All persons aged under 60 are subject to health checks at regular intervals which are registered in a health insurance card (*carte de santé*). A law of 1988 created a state fund for preventive examinations. There are also programmes for immunisation, especially for tuberculosis, which still kills nearly 1,000 people per year. As yet, preventative medicine accounts for only 2.4 percent of health care expenditure, but this proportion, having fallen for most of the past decade, is now beginning to rise again. A new initiative aims at co-ordinating local efforts and diffusing knowledge of the best practices. A bill to restrict smoking in public places has been passed; 40 percent of the population in France smoke and the price of tobacco is kept low in the interests of the state monopoly and, mainly, of the tobacco companies.

Fringe medicine is popular in France. According to the official statistics some 4,500 GPs offered homeopathy, acupuncture and other less conventional forms of treatment in addition to their usual services. Their numbers have increased rapidly during the past decade: between 1980 and 1990, the number of acupuncturists rose by 2.8 times and those of homeopaths by 3.3 times. Homeopathic medicines are widely available and widely consumed; by one estimate more than one-third of the population take them, at least at times.

5.5.2 Assessment of Current Health Care Policies and Proposals

In France current health care policies centre on restraining expenditure through cost containment. As the previous section has shown, there has been and still is some interest in other solutions to the problem, but controlling costs appears to be the most effective approach, especially in political terms and in the short run.

There are no indications that any radical departure from the present system is envisaged. The aim is to modify the details in the hope that growth in spending will be brought down to an acceptable figure, which appears to be somewhere between the annual rate of inflation and the annual growth of the economy in current price terms. The political constraints on other forms of action are formidable. Some have already been mentioned. Others are inherent in French political life. Interest groups, both large and small, react quickly and very fiercely if they feel that their interests are in jeopardy. Governments are ready to back down when faced with serious opposition. The contrast with the UK, where health care reforms which had no popular support at all were imposed by a determined administration, is instructive.

This being the case, it is worth considering whether or not the various cost control measures of the recent past were the best that could be taken in terms of equity and efficiency. The system of global budgets for hospitals should have stimulated a more efficient use of resources and it clearly did so to some extent. However, the way in which it was put into effect largely maintained the national hospital structure as it was in 1985, with all the inequalities and maldistributions that had grown up over the preceding decades. Similarly, the hospital plan did something to prevent gross over-capacity developing in the hospital system, but nothing to remedy the problems already present. A policy of redistributing resources between hospitals would have been desirable but was presumably politically out of the question.

As far as ambulatory care is concerned, the measures taken prior to 1992 had obviously failed to restrain expenditure. The combination of fee-for-service payment with a rapidly increasing number of doctors caused a cost explosion in this sector. The latest measures, described in the previous section, have yet to be implemented and their impact is difficult to judge. They might represent the first step towards a system of cash limits for individual doctors, which would be a large departure from French traditions. However, this is far from certain. The problem of the rising number of doctors and of their markedly unequal distribution remains unsolved.

The Medicines Bill of 1991 represented an attempt to reconcile the interests of the pharmaceutical industry with those of the sickness funds. Prices of new products would have been allowed to rise but companies would have had to accept limits on how much they might sell in France. One set of controls would have replaced another. From the industry standpoint the balance of benefits and losses was by no means clear. The sickness funds would have gained in that they would to a large extent limit their commitments for the coming year. Patients would have neither gained nor lost from this measure.

It is sometimes argued that the French health care system seems to exemplify the reputation of France as a *société bloquée*, in which every course of action is vetoed by some powerful interested party. However, this is an exaggeration. As this chapter has shown, change is possible, if only within certain limits:

* Past experience suggests that in the short run some form of individual budgets for all forms of health care supplied through the sick funds would be both practicable and acceptable to all parties. This is not to say that such measures would be greeted with enthusiasm; rather that a consensus seems to be emerging that they are the least bad solution to a pressing problem.

* More speculatively, an opportunity for shifting expenditure may arise from the established willingness of the French to spend some of their own money on health care. In Section 5.3.2.3 we concluded that approximately one-eighth of total health care spending in France represented the free choice of consumers.

* It might be possible to increase the proportion of health care paid for in this way. Thus, the range of OTC medicines could be increased,

although doctors are very much opposed to this proposal. Reducing the number of therapies which qualify for reimbursement would be difficult politically, but it might be possible not to add new forms of treatment of less than major significance to the list, or alternatively, they might carry a large copayment. However, much would depend on the availability of insurance and especially of that provided through commercial companies (Section 5.3.3.3).

From a purely economic standpoint, reforms which to an increasing extent separate the provision of basic health care through the public system from optional private spending therefore appear to have potential in the French context. Politically they are less attractive since they would threaten the emergence of a two-tier system of medical care - something which has so far been rejected and which is at variance with the strong French belief in social solidarity.

5.6   CONSTRAINTS ON REFORM

The French health care system goes back to 1945 - and certain elements in it to the turn of the century - and by itself this conditions perceptions of what is desirable and what is possible. The present state of affairs is the norm by which alternatives are judged. Change for the sake of change will be rejected; even if seen as necessary, incremental changes will be more acceptable than radical ones. Moreover, they must not do violence to strongly held beliefs and attitudes which are expressed in the current system.

In the case of France what might such beliefs be? The most important is social solidarity, which is manifested by the transfer of resources from those who have to those who have not. In the case of health care this means primarily from the healthy to the sick, but also from the young to the old. Belief in social solidarity is extremely strong in France, as our respondents confirmed. Reform proposals have to take account of this feeling: any alternative scheme would have to provide universal and comprehensive health care. Exactly how comprehensive such coverage should be is open to discussion, as is the role of patient copayments.   Nevertheless, an overtly two-tier system would be unwelcome.

Other firmly held attitudes concern the delivery and financing of health care. The French consider that they should be free to choose who will supply it with the minimum of restrictions. Equally, they take it to be the right of doctors and paramedical staff to practice as they see fit and where they will. A mixture of public and private hospitals is seen as normal. As far as finance is concerned, they prefer to pay for health care by means of ear-marked contributions rather than from general taxation. This is seen as insulating health care spending from other financial pressures. Nevertheless, the current government has recently imposed a tax on incomes from *all* sources - the *Contribution Sociale Générale* (CSG) - in order to benefit the social security system as a whole, and this may prove to be the thin end of a very large wedge.

The traditions of French administration emphasise firm central control. This seems normal, both to the administrators and the administrated. As Section 5.3 has shown, such controls over health care spending as exist, from global budgets in public hospitals, through the permitted reimbursement rates to the *numerus clausus* in medical schools, have been imposed from the centre. That the French health care system is at the same time unusually fragmented in no way contradicts this fact.   It is what it is because of the innumerable compromises that have had to be made as funding has gradually moved from a predominantly private to a predominantly public basis. It remains true that initiatives in any direction are expected to come from above and from the centre in particular.

Finally, there is a further constraint to reform, less frequently articulated but equally important. The large majority of French people are broadly satisfied with their health service as it is. This is by no means an unreasonable position. The French health care system is good even if it is expensive and none too efficient. There is rising public disquiet about the cost and volume of treatment, but this has not yet reached an acute level. Insiders - professionals, health economists, administrators - take a less sanguine view, but this is by no means universally shared.[33] In sharp contrast to the UK, Germany or the USA, health care reform has not emerged as a major theme of political controversy in France.

Thus, in the eyes of the average French man or woman, the present system reconciles a variety of important but diverse objectives at a price which is high but so far bearable. This is a strength which must always be remembered when considering its weaknesses.

---

[33]   For a particularly scathing account of the current situation see Beraud (1992).

5.7   SHORT-TERM REFORM

Section 5.5 summarised recent initiatives in the field of health care policy.

Two general themes emerge - the emphasis on controls over costs and prices and the increasingly assertive role of central government. The central objective of the government is to limit the growth of public expenditure on health care, which it sees as a problem of increasing gravity. It is not necessarily to obtain maximum value for what it allows to be spent, although it is becoming interested in cost-benefit analysis as a means to its principle end. At least implicitly, it appears to believe that if it did not intervene in the health care process, health care spending would get completely out of hand, intolerable burdens would be imposed on the social security system, and the government would be left, at great financial and political cost, to pick up the pieces.

It also seems to be tacitly accepted that strategies other than cost control are either of limited utility or politically unattractive. To raise more money for health care by traditional means is increasingly difficult. Contribution rates are already high - especially for employers - and although the CSG was successfully imposed, it met with considerable opposition. Patient copayments are already substantial; to increase them further would place a serious burden on patients or on their insurers. Steps to improve efficiency with which current forms of treatment are delivered are desirable and clearly possible but are difficult to put into effect in the French context. To place a greater emphasis on prevention rather than cure means influencing life-styles, which in France as elsewhere, is a long-term process.

By elimination, then, cost control emerges as the favoured weapon. More than that, it has proved successful in the recent past. During the past decade government action in this direction has restrained has not only restrained health care expenditure but - up to the present - has done so without apparent loss of patient welfare. In real terms the total has grown between 3 and 4 percent per year as opposed to between 5 and 6 percent in the 1970s. Global budgets for public hospitals have played a leading part in this process. Given the deceleration in the growth of national income since 1990 and the perceived need for further economies in the health care system, what is more natural than to reach for the standard remedy?

The extension of official controls to spending in private hospitals and the ambulatory sector is now in progress. Global budgets are to be imposed on the former. As regards primary care, the negotiations of 1991-2 throw much light both on official thinking and on what is politically possible and what is not. Originally, it was intended to limit the annual growth of spending in this sector to a fixed percentage. If this was exceeded, then the increase in standard fees would be correspondingly reduced in the following year. This proposal was strongly opposed by primary care physicians, although it had been reluctantly accepted by their union. Subsequently it was withdrawn, in part because of this opposition and in part because of more general political factors.

More recently, however, a new set of proposals has been passed into law. Although no global budget for primary care will now be imposed, medical guidelines - *références medicales* - are to be introduced. These guidelines will be used to set consulting and prescribing targets for each doctor, on the basis of which annual spending forecasts will be drawn up. These forecasts will form part of the contract between the doctors and the sick funds. Sanctions will be imposed on those who do not adhere to the guidelines. Very significantly, a coding system which will enable the sick funds to determine how each individual patient has been treated by each doctor, will be introduced. These measures will come into effect later in 1993.

They represent a major step towards extending firm controls over public spending in all sectors of health care. At the same time they also represent a substantial extension of government power both over those who pay for and those who deliver health care. The potential disadvantages of government intervention need little emphasis. Many of the decisions that have to be made are open to political considerations. In the last analysis, all depends on the judgment of those who decide, and they must take into account irrational as well as rational factors and interested as well as disinterested arguments. Yet from the standpoint of government, official intervention has been successful in the past and may prove successful in the future.

In this scenario, the short- to medium-term future of health care in France is one in which the basic structure of the present system is preserved but in which control from the centre is gradually but steadily extended. The measures taken will be imposed according to circumstance and in an *ad hoc* manner. In form, they will be largely or entirely concerned with finance, but they will influence clinical judgement to an ever-increasing extent. Thus, the new agreements on primary care will for the first time enable the government to affect - admittedly at the margin - the scale and nature of the treatment given to patients. Ultimately, an exceptionally decentralised, not to say fragmented system could become a highly centralised one.

Moreover, such developments could well prove acceptable if put into effect over a period of years. They do little violence to the underlying constraints on reform which were discussed in Section 5.6 above. Most of the distinctive features of the French health care system would survive. From the patients' point of view there would be little change. The government could well claim that it was doing no more than eliminate incidental abuses in a fundamentally sound system and it would probably be believed. In any case, practice and tradition assigns a leading role to the central government, and by and large this is accepted by both the French political nation and French citizens.

The one factor that could create a willingness to envisage more radical changes, such as those implied by these recommendations, would be a failure of current approaches to restrain expenditure to what is seen as a reasonable level. Were this to happen, then administrations would be compelled to think again. They might conclude that they should withdraw from direct involvement in health care and assume a largely supervisory role. A certain disillusionment with the results of direct controls is already apparent in some circles.

5.8   LONG-TERM REFORM

We now turn to the recommendations of the NERA Prototype and consider them in the French context.

5.8.1   The Funding Side of the Health Care System

In a number of ways the funding of health care in France resembles that recommended:

- a guaranteed health care package (GHCP) already exists in the form of the *nomenclature*;[34]

- all citizens must belong to a sick fund which is obliged to accept all risks;

- sick funds charge premiums which are related to income;

- funds with a favourable income/expenditure balance support those that do not;

- special provision is made for those who are unemployed or chronically sick;

- private with-profit health care insurance provides for those who want facilities outside the existing guaranteed package.

Thus in general terms proposals consistent with the NERA Prototype are close to what is already in place.

That said, there remain a number of important and possibly critical differences between them. Currently, the sick funds are organised along occupational lines. There is no competition between them: engine-drivers are obliged to insure with the SNCF fund and notaries with that for notaries. A single scheme covers 80 percent of the population. Private insurance through the *mutuelles* and through private with-profit insurers is widely available but membership is often a benefit of employment and is not a matter of choice. It is an open question whether or not greater competition between funders would be welcome, given that it would require patients to exercise greater initiative in selecting their insurer for benefits that might initially seem less than compelling.

---

[34]   The current package of services available under the public system resembles very closely that outlined in the Prototype's definition of a GHCP.

Methods of funding would also have to change. At present the sick funds charge premiums related only to income from employment or pensions. Payments from employment are shared between employer and employee. The rates charged are fixed by law and there is again no competition between funds. Charges on other forms of income are unpopular, although, as previously noted (see Section 5.2 above), the CSG may have set a precedent. The idea of compulsory additional risk-related individual premiums, envisaged in these recommendations, is also relatively novel. The private with-profit insurers do so for individuals, but 70 percent of their business is arranged through companies, for whom risks are pooled. Again, it is uncertain whether or not the use of such premiums would be seen as a significant infringement of personal liberty and the principle of solidarity.[35]

If France were to adopt the methods of finance envisaged, it seems highly probable that the income-related part of the premium would have to be a large part of the whole, at least initially. At least initially, it might be wise to continue to base it on earned income, including pensions, and to make it a joint responsibility of employer and employee. Moves towards charging it on total income would have to be made with care. Individual risk-related premiums would perhaps be acceptable provided that they were a small part of the total.

5.8.2   The Provider Side of the Health Care System

Once again, we begin by summarising the points on which our recommendations concerning the delivery of health care are already similar to or are anticipated by current French practice.

The following elements of resemblance are present:

- ambulatory care is provided by independent professionals under contract to the sick funds; private hospitals are funded in a similar way;

- the services to be provided and the rates to be charged are the subject of negotiation between the interested parties;

- entry to the practice of medicine is unrestricted.

---

[35]   The consumption of alcohol and tobacco is very widespread in France and is falling only very slowly. The state is heavily involved in and benefits financially from both. Of course, to discriminate against smoking and drinking might well make them less popular, as British experience tends to suggest.

However, there are also sharp differences from our recommendations. The process of negotiation between funders and suppliers is highly centralised and much reduces the possibility of competition among the latter. Indeed, to a large extent the provision of health care is determined by non-economic forces. Thus, public hospitals, who are the backbone of in-patient care, receive global budgets which essentially depend on historical factors rather than the needs of their catchment area or the efficiency with which they operate. In so far as these latter considerations are taken into account it is by administrative fiat expressed through the *carte sanitaire*. Similarly, the sick funds contract with every out-of-hospital doctor who wishes to do so. The only controls over the number of doctors is the *numerus clausus* imposed on the medical schools, and, in the longer run, their ability to attract patients.

The NERA Prototype envisages a situation in which insurance funds would be able to pick and choose among suppliers. There would be no obligation on the former to contract with the latter if they did not wish to do so. This would represent a break with current practice. It seems unlikely that decentralised negotiations between groups of primary care physicians and insurers or between hospitals and insurers would be instantly acceptable to providers, who are conservative, powerful and politically volatile. To make health care contracts legally enforceable might also raise the question of clinical autonomy which has so far been essentially untouched in France. In both cases care would be needed to make any specific provisions acceptable to the French medical profession.

One problem would need immediate attention. The rapid growth of the French medical profession, which is set to continue for another 20 years, makes it probable that it will continue to be severely over-crowded for some considerable time to come. A 'sink or swim' approach to contracts could cause enough hardship to make the recommendations unacceptable. Transitional arrangements will probably be necessary. They might well centre on attractive financial packages for those willing to retire prematurely, coupled, for the time being, with continued restrictions on entry.

5.8.3   The Responsibilities of Government

Under these recommendations governments would have a number of responsibilities, most which already fall to the government of France or which would be acceptable in the French context.

Those which are effectively already in place are as follows:

- definition of the guaranteed health care package;

- general supervision of the insurers and the conditions of insurance;

- responsibility for issues of public health; and

- funding medical education and medical research.

Our proposals also envisage the government acquiring new roles in licensing participants in health care, in acting on behalf of the disabled and in monitoring quality and maintaining competition.

These last two functions would represent changes of considerable importance. Until now there has been little real competition in the French health care system.   Patients have been allocated to sick funds according to their occupation. Providers are paid standard rates for service or global budgets fixed centrally. This is not surprising. Apart from the special problems of health care, French official attitudes towards competition in general are equivocal. Mergers in areas seen as being of strategic importance tend to be waved through; active industrial policies in which government plays a leading part tend to be favoured. To move towards a more 'German' attitude to cartels might be difficult.

Monitoring the quality of health care has never been a major function of the French government. Hospitals, however, must be licensed and their standards of care are periodically reviewed by the medical inspectorate (*Médecins Inspecteurs de Santé*). In ambulatory care clinical freedom has hitherto been virtually unqualified. Nevertheless, informed sources consider that what is provided leaves a good deal to be desired and that much treatment is inappropriate, useless or even harmful. To impose outside monitoring of standards of care might well lead to strong opposition from doctors attached to the principles of *médecine libérale*. Equally, however, it could be argued that the medical guidelines just agreed are already a serious breach in these principles.

5.8.4   The Responsibilities of Patients

As elsewhere, the NERA Prototype recommends measures which already exist to an extent in the French health care system of today:

•   patient copayments for all forms of treatment;

•   supplementary insurance for services outside the GHCP.

French patients are used to the idea of copayments: they are general, charged as a percentage of the treatment cost and fairly high in percentage terms. The percentages charged depend to a limited extent on the type of treatment and are imposed regardless of the income of the patient. Exemptions are available only to those suffering from certain chronic diseases or who require particularly lengthy or expensive treatment. In many ways our proposal would represent a more equitable system of copayments than that which currently prevails in France. Copayments for heavy users of health care would be limited regardless of what kinds of care they consumed; similarly, those with limited incomes would benefit from the proposal to relate the magnitude of copayment to income.

However, at present most French people insure against copayments, which greatly dilutes their effect in reducing utilisation of health care facilities. Our recommendation would implicitly forbid this practice. If carried into effect French patients would then find themselves paying both income-related and risk-related contributions towards their health care costs *and* irrecoverable copayments when they made use of the system. Past efforts to forbid insurance against copayments have met with strong public opposition. Unless the rates were carefully adjusted, individuals might well feel that they were being asked to pay more for the same service. They might also feel uncertainty about the precise cost of any form of treatment and the precise amount of their personal liability. These factors could prejudice the acceptability of the recommendation.

5.8.5   An Overview: Problems and Opportunities

5.8.5.1   Would these Recommendations be Acceptable in France?

In some ways the answer is yes. Most of the proposals discussed already form part of the present system or are probably acceptable in principle.

In many ways our recommendations are congruent with French beliefs and values relating to health care (see Section 5.6 above). The preference for separating health care funding from general taxation, the freedom to choose one's provider of health care, and the right of providers to remain independent professionals would all be preserved. Equally important, the recommendations would build on a number of features already present in the French health care system.

That said, there are a number of problems. Some of these - the question of insurance against copayments, for example - are politically awkward, but clearly of secondary importance. Some, such as the transition to statutory insurance funds, or to contracts with individual providers, would be administratively complex but, equally clearly, would be soluble if there was a political will to do so. In the French context, to monitor the standards of health care provision would need considerable finesse but, again, could be established over time. As has been seen, the latest reforms include a step in this direction.

Yet the current thrust of health care reform is in a different direction (see Section 5.7 above), towards a greater role for government and an increased emphasis on central control. Some of the reasons for this development have already been explored: the French tradition that initiative comes from above; the lack of any feeling that a major crisis has emerged; and the encouraging results of earlier official policies. It has been suggested that in the short- to medium-term future policies are likely to involve more of the same, and that the only development that would lead to a re-evaluation of strategy would be the failure of such measures. That point has not yet been reached.

5.8.5.2   Is Compromise Possible?

Could the types of reform now favoured by the French Government lead ultimately towards the state of affairs favoured by the Prototype?

This cannot be excluded. For example, a rational system of global budgets for all providers could reveal a great deal about the real demand and the real budgetary needs of both hospital and out-of-hospital doctors. The devolution of authority to the regions, currently at an early stage, could eventually lead to their taking on policy-making roles; they might, for example, take over funding responsibilities and arrange their own contracts with local providers. Ultimately they might develop into organisations capable of functioning independently in a competitive manner. In this way conservative reforms might be a useful apprenticeship for more radical approaches.

Nevertheless there is no guarantee that this will happen. Indeed, the more successful are conservative reforms, the less likely are radical reforms to be considered. As has already been suggested more than once, there is plenty of room for incremental improvements in the present system. If one is to lead to the other, then continuous pressure will be necessary to maintain momentum in the desired direction, and that a major effort of persuasion will be necessary to convince all those involved - patients, professionals, government - that what is proposed represents an improvement on what exists already.

ANNEX 5.1 DATA TABLES

List of Tables

France

TABLE 1
POPULATION AGE STRUCTURE IN FRANCE, 1975 - 1990 (%)

	1975	1980	1985	1990
Male				
0-1	0.8	0.7	0.7	0.7
1-14	11.5	10.8	10.2	9.6
15-24	8.2	8.0	7.9	7.7
25-44	13.3	13.7	14.3	15.0
45-64	10.0	10.1	10.7	10.3
65-74	3.6	3.6	2.8	3.1
75-84	1.4	1.7	1.8	1.9
85+	0.2	0.3	0.3	0.4
Total	49.0	48.9	48.7	48.7
Female				
0-1	0.7	0.7	0.7	0.6
1-14	11.0	10.3	9.7	9.1
15-24	7.9	7.9	7.7	7.4
25-44	12.5	13.2	14.0	14.9
45-64	10.6	10.6	11.3	10.6
65-74	4.8	4.7	3.7	4.0
75-84	2.7	3.0	3.2	3.4
85+	0.7	0.8	0.9	1.1
Total	50.9	51.2	51.2	51.1
All				
0-1	1.5	1.4	1.3	1.3
1-14	22.6	21.1	20.0	18.8
15-24	16.1	15.9	15.6	15.1
25-44	25.8	26.9	28.3	30.0
45-64	20.6	20.7	22.0	20.9
65-74	8.4	8.3	6.5	7.2
75-84	4.1	4.7	5.0	5.3
85+	0.9	1.1	1.2	1.6
Total	100	100	100	100

Source: *CREDES (1991)*

410

TABLE 2

LIFE EXPECTANCY AT AGE X BY SEX, 1975 - 1990

At age X	1975	1980	1985	1990
Male				
0	69.0	70.2	71.3	72.7
1	69.1	70.0	70.9	72.4
15	55.5	56.4	57.3	58.7
25	46.3	47.2	47.9	49.3
45	28.0	28.9	29.6	31.1
65	13.2	13.9	14.4	15.5
75	7.8	8.3	8.5	9.4
85	4.2	4.5	4.4	5.1
Female				
0	76.9	78.4	79.4	80.9
1	76.8	78.1	79.0	80.4
15	63.1	64.4	65.3	66.7
25	53.5	54.7	55.6	57.0
45	34.4	35.6	36.4	37.7
65	17.2	18.2	18.8	19.9
75	10.0	10.7	11.1	12.1
85	5.1	5.4	5.5	6.1

Source: *CREDES (1991)*

411

TABLE 3
GROSS DOMESTIC PRODUCT AND HEALTH CARE EXPENDITURE
1975 - 1990 (FF MN 1990)

	GDP	GDP per Capita	Total Health Expenditure	Total Health Expenditure per Capita	Total Health Expenditure as % GDP
1975	4,413,384	83,746	332,270	6,304	7.5
1980	5,150,537	95,592	417,786	7,753	8.1
1981	5,210,404	96,165	430,952	7,954	8.4
1982	5,324,486	97,703	449,300	8,245	8.5
1983	5,279,279	96,385	460,978	8,416	8.7
1984	5,453,266	99,103	484,835	8,811	9.0
1985	5,554,298	100,468	493,087	8,918	9.0
1986	5,693,395	102,497	517,658	9,320	9.0
1987	5,822,579	104,301	525,681	9,416	9.0
1988	6,067,405	108,118	552,867	9,852	9.0
1989	6,304,662	111,738	580,512	10,086	9.1
1990	6,484,109	114,287	602,978	10,628	9.3

Source: *CREDES (1991)*

TABLE 4
EXPENDITURE ON PHYSICIANS, 1975 - 1990

Year	Total Expenditure on Doctors (FF mn 1990)	No of Doctors	Average Income (FF 1990)	% Change in Income
1975	36,483	58,205	626,802	
1980	42,019	73,899	568,604	(9.4)
1985	52,737	88,548	595,581	4.7
1986	56,813	91,836	618,636	3.9
1987	58,811	95,156	618,048	0.0
1988	63,490	99,340	639,118	3.4
1989	67,014	103,490	647,541	1.3
1990	70,546	106,547	662,112	2.3

Source: *CREDES (1991)*

TABLE 5
HEALTH CARE EXPENDITURE, 1975 - 1990
FF MILLION 1990

EXPENDITURE	1975	1980	1985	1986	1987	1988	1989	1990
Total health care expenditure	332,270	417,786	493,087	517,658	525,681	552,867	580,512	602,978
Primary health care	76,888	93,156	116,050	127,047	130,283	141,047	149,774	155,280
- doctors	36,483	42,019	52,737	56,813	58,811	63,490	67,014	70,546
- dentists	18,262	24,480	27,275	29,981	30,773	32,210	33,633	34,692
- medical auxiliaries	8,447	10,068	14,079	15,759	15,711	17,582	18,940	20,260
- private laboratories	7,238	8,815	11,834	13,320	13,546	15,673	17,133	16,308
Total hospital expenditure	129,569	187,720	215,202	221,790	224,991	230,751	240,806	248,055
- private	34,033	41,290	49,427	51,353	52,332	54,086	55,855	59,385
- public	95,536	146,430	165,775	170,437	172,659	176,665	184,951	188,670
Pharmaceuticals	61,329	62,012	74,798	79,629	81,008	87,962	92,884	96,125
Optical-orthopaedic	5,816	6,848	8,757	9,246	9,468	10,546	11,632	13,262
Sickness payments	33,651	35,532	34,946	34,869	32,724	32,997	34,437	36,480
Other	25,017	32,518	43,334	45,077	47,207	49,564	50,979	53,776

Source: *CREDES (1991)*

TABLE 6

HEALTH CARE EXPENDITURE BY TYPE OF FINANCE, 1975 - 1990

FF MILLION 1990

EXPENDITURE	1975	1980	1985	1986	1987	1988	1989	1990
Total Health Care								
FF Million 1990	332,270	417,786	493,087	517,658	525,681	555,867	580,512	602,978
% total	100.0	100.0	100.0	100.0	100.0	100.0	100.0	100.0
Private Finance								
FF Million 1990	49,840	55,566	72,977	78,166	83,058	88,939	91,140	98,897
% total	15.0	13.3	14.8	15.1	15.8	16.0	15.7	16.4
Mutuelle Finance								
FF Million 1990	15,949	21,307	27,120	30,024	33,117	37,243	38,314	39,257
% total	4.8	5.1	5.5	5.8	6.3	6.7	6.6	6.5
Social Security								
FF Million	237,905	310,415	360,940	379,961	379,016	398,557	420,290	433,305
% total	71.6	74.3	73.2	73.4	72.1	71.7	72.4	71.9
Public Finance								
FF Million	23,923	24,649	25,641	22,776	23,130	23,346	22,640	23,135
% total	7.2	5.9	5.2	4.4	4.4	4.2	3.9	3.8

Source: *CREDES (1991)*

TABLE 7
THE HOSPITAL SECTOR, 1975 - 1990

	1975	1980	1985	1986	1987	1988	1989	1990
All Hospitals								
Total no. of beds	548,543	594,084	588,377	579,990	574,612	568,905	563,714	558,693
No. of beds/1000 pop.	10.4	11.0	10.6	10.4	10.3	10.1	10.0	9.8
Average length of stay (days)	19.8	16.7	15.5	14.9	14.3	13.8	13.4	12.8
Total hospital expenditure								
FF million 1990	129,569	187,720	215,202	221,790	224,991	230,751	240,806	248,055
Average cost/bed (FF 1990)	236,206	315,982	365,755	382,403	391,553	405,606	427,178	443,992
Public hospitals								
Total no. of beds	336,628	377,499	384,761	378,002	374,002	370,059	366,781	363,115
No. of beds/1000 pop.	6.4	7.0	7.0	6.8	6.7	6.6	6.5	6.4
Average length of stay (days)	20.1	16.5	16.1	15.6	15.0	14.7	14.3	13.7
Public hospital expenditure								
FF million 1990	95,536	146,430	165,775	170,437	172,659	176,665	184,951	188,670
Average cost/bed (FF 1990)	283,803	387,957	430,852	450,889	461,653	477,370	504,255	519,587
Private hospitals								
Total no. of beds	211,915	216,585	203,616	201,988	200,610	198,846	196,933	195,578
No of beds/1000 pop.	4.0	4.0	3.7	3.6	3.6	3.5	3.5	3.4
Average length of stay (days)	19.4	17.1	14.6	13.9	13.4	12.6	12.1	11.6
Private hospital expenditure								
FF million 1990	34,033	41,290	49,427	51,353	52,332	54,086	55,855	59,385
Average cost/bed (FF 1990)	160,597	190,641	242,746	254,238	260,864	271,999	283,624	303,638

Source: *CREDES (1991)*

TABLE 8
CHANGES IN SUPPLY AND UTILISATION OF HOSPITAL FACILITIES
1984 - 1990

	1984	1986	1988	1990
Beds, 000				
- public	388	378	371	363
- private, non-profit	112	95	91	88
- private, with profit	94	107	108	108
Admissions, 000				
- public	6,418	6,953	7,120	7,534
- private, non-profit	1,754	1,335	1,295	1,353
- private, with profit	2,709	3,332	3,655	3,972
Patient days, m				
- public	110	109	105	103
- private, non-profit	31	29	27	26
- private, with profit	33	36	36	36
Expenditure, 1990 FF				
- public	165,411	170,437	176,665	188,670
- all private	49,425	51,353	54,086	59,385
Cost/patient day, 1990 FF				
- public	1,504	1,564	1,683	1,832
- all private	741	790	859	973

Source: *CREDES (1991)*

ANNEX 5.2 BIBLIOGRAPHY

Arnold, M. and Armann W. (1991), *Die Gesundheitsversorgung in Frankreich*, Köln: Deutscher Ärzte-Verlag.

Berger, P., Carrere, M., Duru, G., Geffroy, L., Rochaix, L. and Roche, L., in Casparie, A. F., Hermans, H. E. G. M. and Paelinck, J. H. P. (1991), *Competitive Health Care in Europe*, Aldershot: Dartmouth, pp. 119 - 146.

Blendon, R., Leitman, R., Morrison, I. and Donelan, K. (1990), "Satisfaction with Health Systems in Ten Nations", *Health Affairs*, (Summer), pp. 185-92.

Beraud, C. (1992), *Le Secu c'est bien, en abuser ca craint*, Paris: CNAMTS.

Centre de Récherche pour l'Etude de Santé - see *CREDES*.

CNAMTS (1989), *Carnet Statistique No. 52 - Statistique des Régimes d'Assurance Maladie en 1988*, Paris: CNAMTS.

CNAMTS (1990), Bloc-Notes Statistique no. 46 - Les remboursements d'Assurance Maladie repartis selon l'age et le sexe des beneficaires 1987, Paris: CNAMTS.

CNAMTS (1991a), Sofres for the Caisse Nationale d'Assurances Maladie, reported in *Scrip*, 11/12/1991, 1676, 3.

CNAMTS (1991b), *Carnets Statistique 1991 - Le Secteur Liberal des Professions de Sante en 1990*, vol. 1 - Médécins, Paris: CNAMTS.

CNAMTS (1991c), *Les Omnipracticiens a faibles recettes*, Paris: CNAMTS.

CNAMTS (1992), Caisse Nationale de l'Assurance Maladie des Travailleurs Salaries: *Le Régime Général en 1990*, pp. 39-55.

CREDES (1991) "Eco santé France", version 3.0, Paris.

Daru, G. and Tachon, M. (1988), *La Société Inquiet de la Sante*, Lyon: Edition Eres.

de Kervasdoué, J., Rodwin, V. G. and Stephan, J-C (1989), in de Kervasdoué, J., Kimberly, J. R. and Rodwin, V. G. (eds), *The End of an Illusion*, Berkeley: University of California Press, pp. 137-167.

Fox, J. (ed.) (1990), *Health Inequalities in European Countries*, Aldershot: Gower.

GAO (1991), "Health Care Spending Control - The experience of France, Germany and Japan", General Accounting Office of the USA, Washington DC.

Nora, S. and Naouri, J. C. (1979), *Note sur le financement des depenses de sante*, unpublished, cited in Steffin [qv].

Organisation for Economic Co-Operation and Development (1991), *OECD Health Data* Comparative Analysis of Health Systems (Software Package), Paris

Payer, L. (1990), *Medicine and Culture*, London: Gollancz

Rollet, C. (1991), *Social Policy and Administration*, 1991, 25, pp. 193-201.

Schieber, G. J., Poullier, J-P. and Greenwald, L. M. (1991), *Health Affairs*, 10 [3], pp. 22-38.

SNIP, (1991), "L'Industrie Pharmaceutique - Ses Réalités 1991", Societe Nationale de l'Industrie Pharmaceutique, Paris.

Steffin, M. (1989), *Int. J. Health Services*, 19 [4], pp. 651-661.
Stevens, J. (1989), *Health Services Management*, October 1989, pp. 224-7.
Zeldin, T. (1980), *The French*.
Zeldin, T. (1981), *France 1848-1945*, 1981, Oxford University Press.

CHAPTER 6

THE HEALTH CARE SYSTEM IN GERMANY

Ullrich Hoffmeyer

National Economic Research Associates
London

6.1   SUMMARY

Structure

The health care system of the Federal Republic of Germany is based on a comprehensive statutory health insurance scheme. Health insurance with an insurance (or sickness) fund is mandatory for the majority of the population. There are more than 1,000 such funds. In general, all individuals are at present eligible to join the local fund whose boundaries include their place of work. A segment of the population has choice of becoming a member of one or several other funds subject to meeting the membership qualifications of those funds. According to legislation passed in December 1992, these membership restrictions will be lifted in the near future.

Aggregate Level of Expenditure

Sickness funds and primary care physicians, through their regional and national organisations, negotiate the level of global budgets from which fee-for-service payments are made. Flexible hospital budgets, based largely on *per diem* rates, are usually determined in negotiations between hospitals and sickness funds at the local level. The federal government can set national guidelines for the annual round of negotiations through the so-called 'Concerted Action'. This is a national forum which brings together the key participants of the health care sector.

Incentives

Office-Based Physicians: fee-for-service reimbursement provides doctors with a financial incentive to treat as many patients as possible, and to expand the volume of services. Policies designed to cap overall expenditure of physicians lead to strong competition amongst physicians that often takes the form of volume increases.

Hospitals: prior to legislation enacted in 1992, hospitals were reimbursed through flexible budgets, based largely on *per diem* rates. Hence hospitals had an incentive to treat all patients as long as capacity was available, and to provide treatment for longer than may have been necessary. According to the new legislation *per diem* rates will be replaced by prospective payments made on a cost-per-case basis. Furthermore, flexible budgets have been abolished.

Medicines: Pricing of medicines is free from direct control at manufacturers' level. 'Reference prices', introduced in 1989, specify the levels at which sickness funds reimburse prescription medicines. Patients pay the difference between price and reimbursement level. As a consequence manufacturers' prices have generally converged towards reference prices. Changes introduced in the 1993 Health Care Act included a price freeze and price roll-back on non-reference priced medicines during 1993/94 and copayments on all prescription medicines. A global pharmaceuticals budget was introduced; this will be replaced by regional budgets and prescription limits in 1994.

Issues

The fact that some people have a choice of which fund they wish to join means that there is scope for risk-selection. As a result, there is premium differentiation across funds. The 'hidden competition' between funds takes other forms as well, such as generous interpretations of health care service entitlements.

There still is a lack of integration between primary and secondary care; this lack of coordination leads to some duplication of work and hence costs.

Current Reforms

Several health care cost containment acts have been passed in the last fifteen years, to restrain the costs of the health care system. The 1993 Health Care Act introduces some far-reaching structural and organisational reforms to the health care system over the coming years. The Act also proposes short-term cost containment measures. These measures take the form of revenue-linked expenditure ceilings or capped budgets for specific health care services.

Major structural changes to the health care system foreshadowed by the 1993 Health Care Act include:

- A comprehensive reorganisation of the sickness funds by allowing free choice of fund for most people in most funds; and the introduction of a global risk adjustment mechanism across all funds.

- Greater emphasis on prospective cost-per-case payment methods of reimbursing hospitals, replacing the current system of full reimbursement for operating costs.

Expenditure ceilings have been set for office-based physicians and for hospitals for the years 1993 to 1995. A global budget has been set for medicines prescribed by office-based physicians for 1993.

Political Environment

The German health care system is embedded in the so-called 'social market economy' which constitutes the framework for German social and economic policy making. Social market economy principles which affect the health care system are those of self-governance, social partnership, and social solidarity. It is difficult to imagine circumstances under which attempts to abandon these principles would be politically acceptable.

NERA's Reform Proposals

The 1993 Health Care Act introduces various reform measures that are in line with our proposals for long-term structural reform. At the same time, the Act introduces cost containment measures that are generally incompatible with a market-led approach to health care reform. The main need for the interim period is therefore to speed up the implementation of the structural changes to the health care system, so that transitory budgetary controls can be eliminated as soon as possible.

To counter the tendency to short-term cost containment measures, we recommend:

- a re-evaluation of Germany's list of health service entitlements with the aim of reducing it to a less fulsome benefits package;

- the introduction of a two-source funding mechanism for sickness funds to allow greater scope for competition.

- the transformation of sickness funds into nationwide commercially oriented businesses;

- the decentralisation of reimbursement negotiations between insurance funds and providers, by re-defining the role of associations of funders and providers;

- the establishment of contracts between hospitals and insurance funds that cover both operating costs and investment expenditure;

- the introduction of copayments for office-based physicians visits; and,

- changes to the role of the government.

The consequences of the our long-term reform recommendations are:

- Patients would be given a free choice in selecting their insurance fund. Each patient would purchase an insurance policy with an insurance fund that would contain, as a minimum, a nationally-defined guaranteed benefits package.

- Sickness Funds would be encouraged to be more competitive. Insurance fund members would pay an income-related fee that would be risk adjusted by the funds; plus a direct premium that would reflect the efficiency of the fund.

- Providers would compete for contracts with individual insurance funds. Providers would not receive automatic accreditation with insurance funds.

- The Government would supervise, but not actively participate, in the health care system. In particular, it would ensure that existing competition legislation is adapted to apply to health insurance funds and health care providers.

6.2 STRUCTURE OF THE HEALTH CARE SYSTEM

6.2.1 The Health Care System in Context

The Federal Republic of Germany[1] has a comprehensive health care system which covers everything except long-term or permanent care. It is based on a compulsory insurance scheme. The insurance scheme is highly decentralised and comprises more than 1,000 *insurance funds* (or *sickness funds*; the terms are used synonymously throughout this chapter). Approximately 90 percent of the population are insured with one of the compulsory insurance funds. (Four percent have additional insurance with private insurers). Eight percent of the population are fully covered by private insurance. The remaining 2 percent are mainly civil servants for whom the Government administers health care.

Health insurance is one of the four branches of social insurance in Germany. The other three branches are work-related accident insurance (paid exclusively by the employers), pensions insurance and unemployment insurance.

Entitlements of the health system are generous by international standards and several health care services are free at the point of delivery. Benefits in kind include primary care, in-patient hospital care, dental care and even rehabilitation and preventative care stays in health resorts (*Kuren*), but not long-term care; benefits in cash include sickness payments, and burial allowances.

At the national level the Federal Government passes health care act amendments which apply nationwide. The health care legislation lists the health care benefits to which all Germans are entitled and specifies the regulatory regime which governs the health care system. Through the so-called 'Concerted Action' (*Konzertierte Aktion*), a national forum which brings together representatives of insurance funds, physicians and other organisations, the Federal Government sets national priorities for the annual round of negotiations between health care providers and purchasers.

---

[1]   This chapter describes the health care system in the western *Länder* of the Federal Republic of Germany. At present the former German Democratic Republic is in the process of adopting the laws and regulations of western Germany. This includes all matters relating to health care. This means that the analysis of the health care system described in this chapter applies to both western Germany and - allowing for a transitional phase - eastern Germany. The data sets, however, refer exclusively to western Germany. Annex 1 briefly describes the process of integrating eastern German health care into the western German system.

Several amendments to the existing health care legislation, so-called cost containment acts, have been passed in the last fifteen years. The latest reforms came into effect in January 1993. Throughout this chapter this act will be referred to as the '1993 Health Care Act' (*Gesundheits-Strukturgesetz*).

The responsibility for providing ambulatory health care rests mainly with office-based (primary) physicians (*Sicherstellungsauftrag*); this responsibility may be transferred to sickness funds if physicians fail to fulfil this obligation.[2] Regulation and supervision of the provision of health care, however, is largely the responsibility of the eleven (since 1990: sixteen) states (*Länder*) which constitute the Federal Republic of Germany. They are also largely responsible for financing hospitals' capital expenditure and for the supervision of the health care system. The ministries in charge of this duty are the *Länder* Ministries of Labour and Social Affairs.[3] Regulation of the financing side of the health care system is largely a matter for the federal authorities. Thus health care in Germany is regulated and supervised by both federal and *Länder* ministries (as well as other organisations such as the Federal Insurance Office).

After the last federal elections in December 1990, the Government reorganised the Ministry of Youth, Family and Health as three separate ministries. In this process, the Federal Ministry of Health was created.[4] At the same time, the responsibility for social health insurance, which previously lay with the Federal Ministry of Labour and Social Affairs, was transferred to the newly created Ministry of Health.

6.2.2 General Features of the Finance System

The foundations of a statutory health insurance system were laid by Chancellor Bismarck in 1883, although several health insurance schemes

---

[2] This means that in case of a collective boycott of physicians the responsibility for providing health care is passed on to sickness funds. In order to fulfil this obligation sickness funds may contract directly with individual doctors, or they may establish their own provider organisations. Physicians who have participated in a boycott may re-apply for accreditation with a sickness fund after a period of six years.

[3] The *Länder* Ministries of Labour and Social Affairs have different names in different *Länder*. Some specifically mention 'health' in their title, while others do not. The exception is Bavaria where health care is largely supervised by the *Land* Interior Ministry.

[4] The other two ministries created in the process are the Ministry for the Family and the Elderly, and the Ministry for Women and Youth.

already existed at that time.[5] The financing side of the German health care system is characterised by self-governing statutory insurance funds. In 1911, 18 percent of the population was insured; by 1990 this figure had risen to approximately 90 percent.

Insurance funds are organised on a local, company, or national basis. Sickness funds reimburse health care providers for a broad range of services. An exception is long-term residential care which is not covered. Sickness funds are largely financed through a proportional[6] payroll tax which is levied on income earned in regular employment.   Both employer and employee contribute equally to health insurance payments. Other sources of sickness funds' revenues include transfers by pension funds, local unemployment offices and welfare organisations.

Sickness funds are required to accept all persons who qualify for membership. In particular, the local funds must accept all comers whose place of *work* falls within their geographical boundaries (the 1993 Health Care Act extends the membership option to place of *residence*). They must also set premiums which do not discriminate on grounds of age, sex or risk factors.   Furthermore, premiums are set and reviewed regularly to ensure that neither excessive reserves nor deficits accumulate. Thus there is general risk-sharing (solidarity) across all members of a particular sickness fund and funds operate on a pay-as-you go basis.

Each individual's contribution to a sickness fund is linked to income.   The contribution is deducted directly from the individual's pay-cheque and transferred to the individual's sickness fund. Sickness funds also act as first recipient of the individual's pension and unemployment contributions. These payments are then transferred to the individual's pension and unemployment fund.

People above a certain income level (in 1992: DM 61,200 or $24,000 1990) may choose to become voluntary members of the social insurance system, or to opt out of the system and seek private health care insurance instead.   Such a decision is usually irreversible. On the other hand, private health insurance companies may link their premiums to the perceived risk of the individual.

---

[5] Compulsory accident insurance followed in 1884. Pension funds were established in 1889.

[6] Contributions only start after a minimum threshold, so they are not strictly proportional.

427

However, in practice, most private health insurers charge community-rated premiums that are based on gender and age only.

The 1993 Health Care Act has relaxed membership restrictions of sickness funds. It is envisaged that a large part of the population may eventually choose the sickness fund they wish to join. The new system will be introduced in 1997 (see Section 6.3.3).

6.2.3 General Features of the Delivery System

Patients have the right to seek treatment from any office-based and sickness fund accredited physician. Physicians act as gatekeepers to hospital services. Within limits, physicians and patients also have free choice with respect to the hospital to which patients are referred.

In 1990 there were 195,254 doctors in (western) Germany. This amounts to 3.1 doctors per thousand population, compared with an average of 2.3 per thousand over our study countries. Of these 75,251 were office-based physicians; 96,203 were clinicians; 8,356 were in public office; and 15,444 were in other forms of employment.[7] The number of doctors has risen steadily during recent decades.

At the beginning of 1990 there were 3,046 hospitals in (western) Germany with 670,000 beds (10.8 per thousand population, compared with an average of 9.1 per thousand over our study countries). Most hospitals are owned by public authorities or private non-profit organisations; some are in private ownership. Less than 10 percent of hospitals own more than 30 percent of all beds. The number of acute hospitals has been decreasing, while the number of hospitals for the chronically ill has increased slightly in recent years. The number of hospital beds rose from approximately 580,000 (in 1960) to 760,000 (in 1974), and has since decreased to 670,000 (in 1989).

6.2.4 Inputs and Outputs of the System

In 1989 total health care expenditure was DM 277 billion ($119 bn 1990). In comparison to 1970 when health care expenditure stood at DM 71 billion ($62.9 bn 1990), this is an increase of approximately 90 percent in real terms.

---

[7]   *Sachverständigenrat für die Konzertierte Aktion im Gesundheitswesen* (1992).

Of the DM 277 billion total health care expenditure in 1989, DM 50 billion (18 percent) was spent on ambulatory (primary) care, DM 60 billion (22 percent) on in-patient care, DM 37 billion (13 percent) on pharmaceutical and medical aids, DM 77 billion (28 percent) on rehabilitation and benefits in cash, and DM 18 billion (6 percent) on preventative and maternity care. The remaining DM 35 billion (13 percent) was spent on dentures, education and research.

These data are shown in Chart 6.1, along with the breakdown of total expenditure on health care by different payers. Sickness funds account for approximately 50 percent of overall health care expenditure. The other half comes from pension funds, accident insurance, employers, government expenditure, private health insurers and patient copayments. Pension funds are responsible for the finance of rehabilitation care for people who are in employment or are potentially able to work. Statutory accident insurance is usually responsible for financing all acute or non-acute treatments as a result of injuries inflicted on people during work. (The accident insurance, financed by employers, generally reimburses the sickness funds which, in the first instance, reimburse providers). Contributions by employers in Chart 6.1 mainly relate to benefits in cash during absence of work because of illness. The federal and *Länder* governments are responsible for public health and capital investment programmes, e.g. hospital facilities.

Expenditure by statutory insurance funds has increased steadily in recent years. In 1970 it was DM 24 billion ($21 bn 1990), in 1980 it was DM 86 billion ($47 bn 1990), and by 1990 it had risen to DM 134 billion[8] ($56 bn 1990). Insurance funds pay the majority of health care costs related to primary care, hospital care and medicines.

At the end of 1989 the size of the population of West Germany was around 62 million. That of East Germany was 16.4 million. From 1970 to 1988, the size of the population in West Germany has changed very little.[9]

Life expectancy at birth has steadily increased and stands now at 72 years for males and 79 years for females, slightly below the averages for our study countries which are 73 and 80 respectively. On other measures of health status, Germany is close to the average for our study countries with an infant

---

8   *Sachverständigenrat für die Konzertierte Aktion im Gesundheitswesen* (1992), Table T465.

9   OECD (1991).

mortality of 7.5 per thousand (average 7.6), and 'potential life years lost'[10] of 29 per thousand for females and 52 per thousand for males (average 30 and 52). By international standards, Germany does well on perinatal mortality (6.4 per thousand, average 8.6).

Chart 6.1 A
Expenditure on Health Care in Germany, 1989

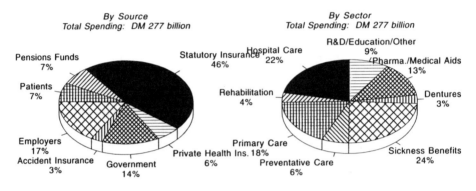

Source: Der Bundesminister fur Gesundheit (1991)

Chart 6.1 B
Expenditure on Health Care in Germany, 1989

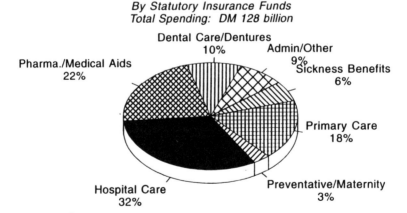

Source: Der Bundesminister fur Gesundheit (1991)

---

[10] Potential Life Years Lost: this is a WHO estimate of years of life to deaths which could have been prevented by the use of currently available technology, improved public health, or less risky behaviour.

430

6.3 ANALYSIS OF INDIVIDUAL SECTORS

6.3.1 Key Participants in the Health Care System

Chart 6.2 provides an overview of the key participants of the German health care system, and the flow of funding and delivery of services in the system. Other relationships which are not linked to the funding and delivery of services, such as membership associations, are also indicated in the chart.

In Section 6.3 we describe the role of the key participants of the German health care system. The key players are:

- The patients, who are also members of insurance funds;
- the statutory insurance funds, as well as their *Land* and federal associations;
- the primary sector (i.e. office-based physicians and specialists), as well as their *Land* and federal associations;
- hospital clinicians;
- the hospitals, as well as their *Land* and federal associations;
- the pharmaceutical sector;
- the Ministries of Labour and Social Affairs in the *Länder*; and the Ministry of Health of the Federal Government.

In addition, there are numerous scientific and medical research-based institutions in Germany, as well as professional associations and self help groups such as the German Multiple Sclerosis Society or the German Aids Help. There are no patient rights groups with significant influence in Germany.

In the remainder of this chapter *office-based physicians* (*Kassenärzte*) will sometimes be identified as 'primary physicians', as opposed to *hospital-based physicians* for which the term 'clinicians' is used.

6.3.2 Patients

6.3.2.1 Attitudes Towards the Health Care System

Germany's statutory health insurance system is based on the principle of solidarity. That principle states that citizens should receive health care benefits according to their needs and should pay according to their ability. Consequently, the general view that appears to prevail in Germany is that health care should largely be free at the point of delivery and should be comprehensive.

431

Chart 6.2
Key Participants in the Health Care System in Germany

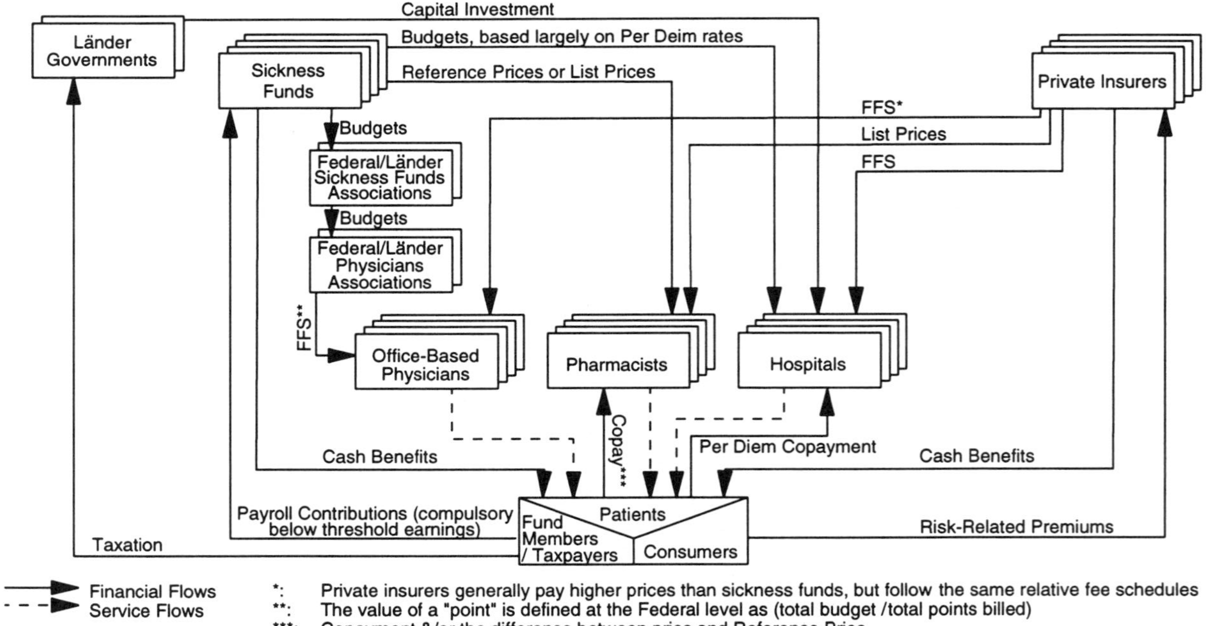

Länder Governments

Sickness Funds

Federal/Länder Sickness Funds Associations

Federal/Länder Physicians Associations

Office-Based Physicians

Pharmacists

Hospitals

Private Insurers

Patients / Consumers

Fund Members / Taxpayers

Capital Investment

Budgets, based largely on Per Deim rates

Reference Prices or List Prices

Budgets

Budgets

FFS**

Cash Benefits

Cash Benefits

Taxation

Payroll Contributions (compulsory below threshold earnings)

Copay***

Per Diem Copayment

FFS*

List Prices

FFS

Risk-Related Premiums

*: Private insurers generally pay higher prices than sickness funds, but follow the same relative fee schedules
**: The value of a "point" is defined at the Federal level as (total budget /total points billed)
***: Copayment &/or the difference between price and Reference Price
FFS: Fee For Service

Financial Flows
Service Flows

Legislation enacted over the past decades has seen a gradual extension of health care benefits. Today they even include rehabilitation and preventative care in health care resorts. It is generally felt that the entitlement mentality of the population coupled with the fact that reimbursement methods for health care services are largely based on a fee-for-service regime have led to a generous provision of services and facilities to deliver these services. Queues for health care services are virtually unheard of.

However, there is a continuing debate on health care reform, and health care policy is an important political topic in Germany. In surveys conducted periodically by the research organisation *Infas*, health care reform policies were considered to be an 'important topic' by 50 percent of all Germans in 1989.[11] In 1987, the figure was 24 percent. When asked to compare the importance of health care reform with other political topics, health care reform came fourth in the ranking order (with 50 percent) in the survey in 1989, after 'unemployment' (62 percent), 'maintaining social security' (61 percent) and 'environmental protection' (59 percent). But it came before 'disarmament and peace' (37 percent), 'pensions' (33 percent) and 'economic growth' (33 percent). Two years earlier, health care reform ranked only eighth.

The same survey suggests that Germans in general are satisfied with the health care provision in their country. In 1988, 29 percent of interviewees were said to be 'very satisfied' with the health care service, while 61 percent said that they were 'satisfied'. However, 45 percent of those being asked thought that the Health Care Cost Containment Act of 1989 would make the quality of health care worse. Only 3 percent thought that it would get better, while 45 percent thought that quality would not change.[12]

6.3.2.2   Roles and Objectives of the Individual Patient/Insuree

Besides having their health restored, patients have few objectives other than receiving prompt treatment at no or little cost whenever the need arises. This includes free choice of physician, and, to a lesser extent, free choice of hospital (both subject to transport costs).

In the role as payer, the insuree's objective is to keep the annual increase of their insurance fund contributions low, while receiving high quality health care

---

[11]   Infas (1988 and 1989).

[12]   *Ibid.*

services. There is little evidence that Germans think of the health care system to be seriously underfunded. There is, however, no direct link between insurance contributions and benefits. As a result, patients demonstrate little cost-consciousness.

According to an international survey, patients in Germany appear to trust their doctor's medical judgement. There is little evidence that patients question a doctor's diagnosis or choice of treatment. Physicians are self-employed professionals and enjoy a high status in German society. The same applies to clinicians, although they are generally employed by hospitals. Trust in doctors' behaviour is also reinforced by the fact that relatively few cases of malpractice or incorrect diagnosis are dealt with by courts. Instead, malpractice cases are usually settled by mediation involving physicians' organisations.

6.3.2.3 Objectives of the Insured Population

The German health care system is embedded in the German social and economic system, the so-called 'social market economy' (*Soziale Marktwirtschaft*). The values underlying the health care system can be characterised by several basic principles, which in turn stem from the values relating to a social market economy. The most relevant of these are the principles of self-governance, social partnership, and social solidarity. Self-governance means that purchasers and providers of health care should operate as self-managing private organisations (under public law) with as little interference from the government as possible. Social partnership rests on the assumption that both employers and employees should share the burden of financing health care. Social solidarity means that the economically stronger members of society should support the weaker members to ensure equality in the provision of health care. Specifically, this means that:

- the younger and healthier subsidise the older and less healthy;
- those with higher incomes subsidise those with lower incomes;
- those who are single and childless subsidise families and those with children; and,
- those who are employed subsidise those who are unemployed.

It is difficult to imagine circumstances under which it would be politically acceptable to abandon these general principles as part of health care reform policies.

6.3.3   Payers

6.3.3.1   *Structure of the Insurance Sector*

In 1990, approximately 90 percent of the population of (western) Germany, 55 million people, belonged to a statutory insurance fund (*Krankenkasse*). In 1991, 1,135 such insurance funds existed, a number that had gradually decreased from approximately 22,000 in 1911. About 8 percent of the population is covered exclusively by private health insurance schemes (although many people have supplementary private insurance). Approximately 2 percent are covered by special arrangements for civil servants (e.g. police and military forces). The government administers health care coverage for these groups. Less than 0.5 percent of the population has no coverage at all. This includes persons with high incomes as well as non-registered individuals such as illegal immigrants.

Sickness funds are established as 'private corporations under public law' (*Körperschaften des öffentlichen Rechts*). The sickness fund system is highly decentralised. It consists of a number of different types of funds. This diversity is largely the result of historical developments. In 1991, the following insurance funds existed in (western) Germany:

Table 6.1: Number and Type of Sickness Fund[13]

264	**Local Sickness funds** (*Allgemeine Ortskrankenkassen*), which geographically cover the entire country;
684	**Company-Based Funds** (*Betriebskassen*), which are set up by large companies;
151	**Crafts' Funds** (*Innungskassen*), which are set up by crafts' organisations[14];
19	**Agricultural Funds** (*Landwirtschaftliche Krankenkassen*), which are responsible mainly for farmers and their families;
7	**White Collar Workers Substitute Funds** (*Ersatzkassen für Angestellte*), which operate nationwide;
8	**Blue Collar Workers Substitute Funds** (*Ersatzkassen für Arbeiter*), which operate nationwide, or on a regional basis;
1	**Sailors' Fund** (*See-Krankenkasse*), for seamen; and,
1	**Miners' Fund** (*Bundesknappschaft*), for miners.

Total 1,135 Funds

---

[13]   *Der Bundesminister für Gesundheit* (1991), p. 171. In 1990, there were 1,147 sickness funds.

[14]   Crafts' funds in Germany serve legally defined occupational groups, as opposed to company-based funds which serve the employees of a single organisation.

Sickness funds fall into two basic categories. The first category mainly comprises funds which cover individuals within their geographical boundaries (local funds), crafts' funds, company-based funds, and some small special funds. These are the so-called primary funds (*RVO-Kassen*). The second category comprises all other funds which cover people in particular classes of occupation. These are the so-called substitute funds (*Ersatzkassen*). Of particular importance are the white collar substitute funds. This group comprises nationwide operating funds for certain professional groups that are open to all who qualify for membership, mainly *all* white collar workers.[15] An exception is the 'technician substitute fund' which restricts membership to technicians. By contrast, all blue collar substitute funds are strictly trade-specific. This automatically restricts membership.

Under the statutory insurance fund system, all insured people receive the following benefits:[16]

Table 6.2: Benefits in Kind and in Cash

Benefits in Kind	Benefits in Cash
Preventive Care (Health Counselling, Annual Check-Ups etc.)	Sickness Benefits
	Maternity Allowances
Primary (Ambulatory) Care	Travel Costs
Hospital Care	Burial Allowances
Dental Care	
Maternity Care	
Family Planning Advice	
Physiotherapy	
Rehabilitation	
Eyeglasses	
Medical Appliances	
Rehabilitation/Preventative Care Stays in Health Care Resorts	
Medicines	

Many of the benefits in kind are free at the point of delivery, although there are exceptions. Copayments exist for in-patient care in hospitals, for

---

[15] Approximately 50 percent of those within the statutory insurance fund system have a choice of which fund they belong to.

[16] Health Care Act, para. 11, pp. 20-62; also *Der Bundesminister für Arbeit und Sozialordnung* (1990) p. 31; and Henke, 1990, p. 150.

medicines, and for some specialist primary services such as dentures and orthodontics treatments. Copayments tend to be small, with the exception of those for dental services. Upper reimbursement limits for prescription medicines also exist.

All benefits are listed in the Health Care Act (*Sozialgesetzbuch, 5. Buch: Die Krankenversicherung*), mainly in paragraphs 11 to 68. They are available to all insured and apply to all sickness funds. It is thus not possible for insurance funds to deny coverage of any of these services to their members. Germany thus has a well-defined guaranteed health care package. The 1993 Health Care Act slightly changed the composition of this package. Some additional services, such as transport costs and (under certain circumstances) treatment abroad, have been included in the package. Other services, such as special orthodontic treatments and vaccinations for holiday travel abroad, have been excluded from reimbursement.

Patients do not pay for physicians' services at the point of delivery. Instead, the patient hands over a form (*Krankenschein*) to the physician which forms the basis of an invoice by the physician to the sickness fund. Forms are to be replaced by a so-called sickness insurance card (*Krankenversicherungskarte*) by January 1995.

The guaranteed health care package includes not only benefits in kind, but also benefits in cash. The most important of the latter are sickness benefits. Under German social legislation, employers must continue to pay the wages of employees who have fallen ill for the first six weeks of illness. After six weeks sickness funds assume responsibility for the payment of sickness benefits. These usually amount to 80 percent of the last wage the insured earned prior to becoming ill. The fund's commitment is for a maximum length of 78 weeks at which time the insured person qualifies as a permanently disabled person, or as a person requiring long-term care. In either case the insurance fund ceases to be responsible.

Residential long-term care is not covered by the statutory sickness funds.[17] The burden of care for these people falls either on their families, or, if this is

---

[17]   The responsibility of the insurance fund ceases when a doctor decides that in-patient care cannot improve the health status of the patient. In many cases, the decision as to when in-patient care stops and long-term care starts is a difficult one.

not possible, on local government and voluntary organisations.[18]   The financial burden, especially for in-patient long-term care, may be met out of the individual's pension or savings, as well as out of support from the family. Since this generally does not cover the costs of care, patients usually receive so-called welfare assistance (*Sozialhilfe*).   Eighty percent of those receiving institutional (long-term) care depend on welfare payments.

The fact that no adequate cover for long-term care exists is considered a weakness of the German social security system.   The Federal Government is at present debating introducing a statutory long-term care insurance, possibly on similar lines as the health insurance.

On 1 January 1990, there were 44 private health insurers covering in full or in part 11 million people in all.   Of these 6.5 million had exclusively private sector coverage (approximately 10 percent of the population), while 4.5 million had supplementary coverage in addition to that guaranteed to them by the statutory sickness funds.   In 1989 private insurers' expenditure on health care was DM 17 billion ($7.3 bn 1990).

6.3.3.2   Degree of Choice for the Insured

According to the Health Care Act the following groups are subject to mandatory insurance and are insured automatically, i.e. without application for admission, other than self-registration or registration by their employers:[19]

- salaried workers;
- unemployed persons (if they receive unemployment benefits);
- students (up to age 30);
- pensioners;
- farmers;
- artists; and,
- disabled persons.

Persons whose regular annual salary exceeds a certain amount (*Versicherungspflicht-grenze*; in 1992:   DM 61,200 or $24,000 1990) are not required to belong to an insurance fund; instead they may remain voluntary

---

[18]   Since 1989 sickness funds have provided financial support to help cover the costs of home care.   New proposals (June 1993) would bring long-term care within the social insurance system.

[19]   Health Care Act, para. 5. The Health Care Act usually specifies exactly the conditions which determine to which category a person belongs.

members of their sickness fund, or, alternatively, opt out of statutory health insurance and buy private insurance.[20] The latter decision is in general irreversible: people cannot revert back to statutory insurance fund membership once they have left their fund unless their income drops below the specified threshold and is expected to remain there permanently. Special rules apply if the annual income of an individual is occasionally below and occasionally above the threshold. In the past, few of those who were entitled made use of the option of leaving an insurance fund.[21] There are various additional regulations on voluntary membership in statutory insurance funds.[22]

Spouses of insurance fund members are automatically covered if they earn less than a minimum threshold (in 1992: DM 500 or $195 1990 per month).[23] Dependents are automatically covered until the age of 18, or 25 for children attending university or vocational training courses. Civil servants are usually covered against sickness through the *Land* or federal government which pay part of their health expenses directly. The remainder may be covered by private insurance.

The health care legislation determines the insurance fund to which the insured belongs. For employed persons this is usually their local sickness fund. The location of their workplace, rather than their residence, determines membership of the local fund (although the 1993 Health Care Act changes this). For craftsmen the craft's fund of the employer determines membership of crafts people. Special rules apply for company-based funds. If a firm has more than 450 (since January 1993: 1,000) employees and if the existence of the local sickness fund is not endangered by the establishment of a company-based fund, a company-based fund can be founded. The foundation requires the approval of a majority of employees. Workers who enter a firm which has a company-based fund are eligible for membership of this fund.

Due to the rules of selective enrolment a large part of the population is restricted in its choice of an insurance fund. However, a segment of the

---

[20]   Health Care Act, para. 6.

[21]   This is apparently changing, with more and more young and healthy people making use of the option.

[22]   Health Care Act, para. 9.

[23]   Health Care Act, para. 10.

population, notably white collar workers, some blue collar workers, crafts people and employees of a company which has its own fund, have a choice of which fund they wish to join.

This situation creates imbalances. Funds for white collar workers and funds for blue collar workers are known as 'substitute funds' (*Ersatzkassen*) because they offer a choice for those eligible for membership. These substitute funds therefore provide some competition for the local funds. People who qualify for membership of a substitute fund have a choice between the substitute fund and their local insurance fund. White collar workers in particular almost always have a choice of belonging to one of several substitute funds (the exception is the technicians substitute fund which restricts membership to technicians). Blue collar workers, on the other hand, usually only have a choice of one substitute fund only, based on their blue collar profession. The criteria for membership are becoming increasingly questionable, not least because there is no legally binding definition of what constitutes a white collar worker.

The 1993 Health Care Act mandates that all members of local funds, company-based funds and crafts' funds may chose their sickness fund in the same say as most white collar workers do at present. This new regulation will come into effect in 1996. Insurance fund members can then terminate their membership of one fund and seek membership of another. Terminations will become effective at year-end. This means that switching insurance funds will become possible from January 1997 onwards. The aim of this reform is to provide most funds with the same competitive framework. This is expected to lead to a reduction in the differences in contribution rates that are currently manifest. Premium differentiation is expected to continue, but will depend much more on the efficiency with which sickness funds conclude contracts with providers, and much less on risk differentials in the insured population.

This organisational reform of the sickness fund will have major implications for the German health care system. It means that the overwhelming majority of people will for the first time have a choice as to which fund they wish to belong.

The 1993 Health Care Act also proposes the establishment of an overall risk adjustment mechanism (*Risikostrukturausgleich*) across funds. All funds will participate in this global risk adjustment mechanism, which will be gradually implemented beginning in January 1994 (i.e. two years prior to the lifting of membership restrictions). By 1995, the risk adjustment mechanism of pensioners will be integrated in the general mechanism.

The risk adjustment mechanism will be administered by the Federal Insurance Office (*Bundesversicherungsamt*) and will be based on revenue sharing involving all sickness funds (except the agricultural funds). Risk factors to be included in the risk adjustment mechanism will initially be limited to a small number of factors and will include income, number of dependents, gender and age.

The latter regulation takes account of the fact that a comprehensive compensation scheme across insurance funds is in place which ensures an equal share for all funds for the financing of services for pensioners, albeit retrospectively. The compensation scheme eliminates undesirable differences resulting from different numbers of pensioners in individual funds. Pensioners pay approximately 17 percent of total insurance fund contributions, but account for 40 percent of their expenditure. This mechanism thus already acts as a safeguard for those funds which have a high proportion of pensioners.

To phase in the new organisational structure of sickness funds, the following regulations have also been included in the 1993 Health Care Act:

- Current membership restrictions of substitute funds will be abolished; instead, there will be open enrolment for all comers.

- Substitute funds which currently only operate region-wide will be allowed to expand to cover the entire country.

- Open enrolment will also be extended to company-based funds where currently membership is restricted to employees of the company. These funds may open up membership if they wish to do so, but do not have to introduce open enrolment. The miners' fund, the sailors' fund and the agricultural funds have been excluded from mandatory or voluntary open enrolment.

- Small (local) funds will be encouraged to merge. This process is already underway but is likely to accelerate once membership restrictions are lifted.

6.3.3.3 *Funding of the Payers*

The contributions which members pay to their insurance funds depend solely on their ability to pay and are calculated as a percentage of their income. The

441

premiums are calculated as a percentage of the gross salaries up to an upper limit (in 1992: DM 61,200 or $24,000 1990) after which the premium is fixed at the maximum. This upper limit (*Beitragsbemessungsgrenze*) is set at 75 percent of the upper limit for the statutory pension insurance and is adjusted annually to coincide with the growth rate of the average income of the insured population. At present, i.e. prior to the changes mandated by the 1993 Health Care Act, the percentage charged by insurance funds differs across funds. This is due to differences in the risk structures of the funds, in the revenue bases, and in the regional distribution of facilities.

For example, in 1989 the average insurance fund contribution rate was 12.9 percent. By 1990 that rate had decreased slightly to 12.5 percent (the first decrease since 1984), and decreased again in 1991 to 12.1 percent. However, average premiums charged by different types of funds in 1991 varied in the range of 11.1 to 13.3 percent. Charges made by individual funds differed even more. Contribution rates varied between 10.8 percent (for the city of Böblingen, a suburb of Stuttgart) and 16.4 percent (for the city of Kiel in northern Germany).

The variations in the contribution rates can also be seen from the following table, which lists the annual average contribution amounts in 1988 (in DM) for various types of sickness funds:[24]

Table 6.3: Contribution Rates of Sickness Funds in 1988

	DM	$1990
Local sickness funds	4,111	1,817
Company-based funds	4,372	1,932
Crafts' funds	3,365	1,487
Agricultural funds	3,098	1,369
White collar workers' funds	4,067	1,798
Blue collar workers' funds	4,230	1,870
Sailors' fund	5,659	2,501
Miners' fund	5,439	2,404

---

[24]   Schulenburg (1991a).

Sickness funds finance health expenditure on a pay-as-you-go basis from contributions. They do not receive additional funding from the government.[25] Sickness funds are not for-profit organisations. They do not accumulate capital reserves. Changes in premiums are decided upon at irregular intervals rather than on an annual basis. The executive board of an insurance fund takes the necessary decisions, which then have to be passed by the general assembly of the insurance fund (see Section 6.3.3.4 below) and approved by the supervisory authority, which is usually the Ministry for Labour and Social Affairs of the respective *Land*.

Employers and employees each pay 50 percent of the premium. Pensioners pay 50 percent of the contribution out of their pension; the remaining 50 percent is paid by their pension fund. For the unemployed the Federal Labour Agency pays the contributions, while for other groups (e.g. students, those in military service) special regulations are in place.

People with an income above the opt-out level, who nevertheless decide to remain members of the statutory insurance funds and are employed, also pay only part of their premium, with a maximum of 50 percent being paid by the employer. In contrast to non-voluntary members whose contributions are deducted directly from their pay cheques, voluntary members (rather than the employers) are themselves responsible for the regular payments of their premiums.

6.3.3.4 Regulation of the Payers

Sickness funds are autonomous, self-managing bodies, regulated by the government as set out in the health care legislation. Judicial cases are dealt with by a system of special courts (*Sozialgerichte*). They are generally inclined towards a generous interpretation of the rights of the insured.

Insurance funds are required to have the following decision making bodies:[26]

- A general assembly (*Vertreterversammlung*) which decides on the statutes of the fund and decides on such matters as the annual administrative budget, or cooperation with other sickness funds. The

---

[25] There are exceptions. Sickness funds which grant maternity payments are reimbursed by the federal government with a fixed fee (in 1990: DM 400).

[26] *Sozialgesetzbuch IV - Gemeinsame Vorschriften für die Sozialversicherung* (Common Regulations of the Social Insurance Legislation), para. 29-47.

general assembly is elected every six years in so-called 'social elections' by the insured and their employers.

- An executive committee (*Vorstand*) which carries out day-to-day business. The executive board is elected by the general assembly.

Half the members of both the general assembly and the executive board come from the insured, the other half from employers. The general assembly and the executive board of substitute funds consist exclusively of the insured. Special rules apply to the miners' fund. The 1993 Health Care Act introduces changes to the internal organisation of sickness funds. In particular, it plans to phase out the general assembly and replace it with administration boards (*Verwaltungsrat*) which will consist of approximately 30 people. The executive committee will be replaced by a Chief Executive Officer (*Geschäftsführender Vorstand*).

The government supervises the insurance funds and ensures that all actions taken by the funds are in accordance with the law.[27] Supervising authorities for insurance funds whose areas of competence fall within one *Land* only are the Ministers for Labour and Social Affairs of the respective *Land*. For those funds whose area of competence falls within several *Länder*, the supervising authorities are the Federal Minister for Health and the Federal Insurance Office. The Federal Insurance Office must also approve the premiums of private health insurers.

Local sickness funds cooperate on several levels. On the *Land* level the local sickness funds based in one *Land* form a regional association (*Landesverband*). There are presently 264 local insurance funds in (western) Germany.[28] They form 12 *Länder* associations.[29] The number of insured members per local fund varies between 800 members (on the island of Helgoland) to more than a million. Each local fund appoints members to the *Land* general assembly and the *Land* executive committee. They, in turn, appoint members for the federal assembly and the federal executive committee.

---

[27]   The government and its institutions are not allowed to impose their views on the funds with respect to abstract legal terms such as the directive for funds to "be economical".

[28]   There are 13 local funds in the ex-GDR (German Democratic Republic).

[29]   There are 5 *Länder* associations in the ex-GDR.

All *Länder* associations form one federal association (*Bundesverband*). Some funds, in particular the substitute funds, form only federal associations. These associations are also self-governing bodies whose governing institutions are similar to those of the local funds. The federal associations of substitute funds and the regional associations of other funds conclude contracts with their counterpart providers, in particular with the federal and regional associations of physicians.

6.3.3.5 Economic Incentives

Until the changes introduced by the 1993 Health Care Act come into effect, different sickness funds continue to be in different competitive situations. These differences can be described as follows: fund membership is compulsory for most people, and funds are not allowed to refuse membership to anyone who fulfils membership conditions. This means that funds cannot generally engage in *open risk selection*. However, the potential membership of some funds includes a wider segment of the population than that of other funds; these funds are therefore able to attract better risks. For example, people who are eligible for membership in white collar funds are often younger and healthier than those in the local funds. White collar funds therefore have an incentive to attract (qualifying) members, and indeed seek to do so. This behaviour can be described as a *concealed form of (positive) risk selection*.[30]

Competition is much less typical for blue collar funds. This is because they are usually small in terms of membership, as the number of blue collar workers has declined in recent years, in Germany as elsewhere. Furthermore, all blue collar funds restrict membership to workers of a specific economic sector.[31]

Company-based funds also play a less significant competitive role than white collar funds, although their contribution rates are usually comparatively low. It is therefore usually advantageous for an employee to switch to a company-based fund. Company-based funds cannot demand a health check of an

---

[30]   For example, while sickness funds are not allowed to advertise openly for members, they can in fact provide the general public with information on health care issues. This is sometimes mixed with concealed forms of advertisement.

[31]   Similar membership restrictions apply to individual funds within the group of white collar funds. However, since it is much more difficult to differentiate white collar (service) workers than blue collar (industrial) workers, the restrictions are less binding.

applicant, but employers sometimes do so as part of the recruitment of new employees.

To summarise, the risk structure of some funds, notably nationwide operating white collar substitute funds and company-based funds, is better than that of other funds. Consequently, such funds have been able in the past to offer lower premiums to their members. At the same time, substitute funds have been able to pay slightly higher reimbursement fees to physicians.

With the passing of the 1993 Health Care Act the Government signalled its intention to abolish the unequal competitive standing of sickness funds, and instead to put them on an equal footing. It remains to be seen whether or not the organisational reform of sickness funds will be implemented as prescribed by the 1993 Act. If the changes are implemented, and if furthermore the global risk adjustment mechanism between funds operates in a satisfactory manner, then the reforms will have succeeded in removing the incentive for some funds to pick and choose. Ideally, any remaining discrepancies in the income-related premiums between funds should then reflect efficiency differences between funds rather than variations in the risk structure of funds.

6.3.4   Primary Health Care Sector

6.3.4.1   Roles and Objectives

The primary health care sector in Germany comprises all office-based physicians and specialists (including dentists) who deliver ambulatory care. In 1990, there were 75,251 office-based physicians providing services in Germany, or 1.19 per thousand of the population. As gatekeepers to the hospital sector, they are of central importance in determining the amount of care that is to be provided to the insured.[32]

Apart from treating patients, office-based physicians provide health advice, refer patients to hospitals, prescribe medicines, and determine whether or not a patient is able to work (and thus becomes eligible for sickness benefits).

---

[32] There are approximately 37,000 practising dentists in Germany. They are organised in a similar way as physicians. The Federal Association of Dentists (*Kassenzahnärztliche Bundesvereinigung*) negotiates contracts with the sickness funds, while the Federal Chamber of Dentists (*Bundeszahnärztekammer*) acts as an interest group for dentists. The oral health care system is organised and financed in similar ways as the primary physician sector. Patient co-payments, for example for dentures, are in place. Per capita expenditure for dental care are the highest in the world.

In principle, each doctor who has achieved the required educational and training qualifications has the right to set up a practice and be accredited as a physician with the sickness funds. An exception is made for doctors of 55 years of age or more, who have no such right. Doctors do not have to ask for accreditation with sickness funds, unless they wish to be reimbursed by them. Sickness funds, on the other hand, must accept all applicants. Once a doctor is accredited with a fund, he or she is accredited with all funds. Thus accreditation with selected funds is not possible.

According to the 1993 Health Care Act, physicians' right to establish practices will be subject to stricter control by the physicians' associations. Beginning in 1999, quotas will be used to determine the number of doctors allowed in any one region. The aim of this regulation is to reduce the expected surplus of doctors by curtailing their right to automatic accreditation with sickness funds.

The availability of technological equipment in the German ambulatory sector is, by international standards, high. On average each physician has approximately five assistants, which means that many diagnostic and therapeutic treatments involving high-tech machinery can be provided. This will often include ECGs, X-rays and endoscopy facilities, or even computer-tomography, as well as a range of laboratory services.

Office-based physicians are organised in regional Associations of Accredited Physicians (*Kassenärztliche Vereinigungen*) for their dealings with statutory sickness funds. Each *Land* has one or more *Land* Associations of Accredited Physicians (*Kassenärztliche Landesvereinigung*), and there is also one at the federal level (*Kassenärztliche Bundes-vereinigung*). One legal obligation of these associations is to set up a system of contracts with the insurance funds which will determine the level of reimbursement for physicians. The 1993 Health Care Act requires all contracts to be negotiated on a regional basis (usually a *Land*). Prior to the 1993 Health Care Act, the Federal Association of Primary Physicians was responsible for the contracts with insurance funds which operate in more than one *Land*.

Contracts between associations of sickness funds and associations of physicians covering reimbursement levels of the latter have to be in place at all times. This means that physicians are not allowed to strike. If the two parties cannot agree, the issue is resolved by an arbitration committee. Its non-partial chairman is appointed either by agreement or, failing that, by casting lots.

6.3.4.2 Patient's Choice within the Primary Health Care Sector

All insured persons have a free choice of physician. Patients usually see their family doctor in the first instance, who may refer them to a specialist. Patients may also seek treatment directly from a specialist.[33] Unless there is a compelling reason, a patient who sees a doctor who is not accredited with an insurance fund may have to pay the additional costs, i.e. the extra cost over and above the agreed fee of an accredited physician.

Hitherto primary and hospital care has not been well integrated in Germany. The 1993 Health Care Act appears to encourage the establishment of 'out-patient clinics' in hospitals. These would be hospital departments where people undergo minor surgery on a day-basis. The Act stipulates that free choice of physician be extended to out-patient clinics where these are established.

Certain specialties are not included in the list of treatments offered by office-based physicians. Examples of such treatments are the services of psychologists and natural (alternative) therapists. The insurance funds will only pay the costs of such treatments if the physician specifically requests that such treatment be provided and gives reasons for his or her request.

6.3.4.3 Funding of the Primary Health Care Sector

Primary physicians are usually paid on a fee-for-service basis, although the health care legislation also allows other forms of payment. In practice, funding of physicians is based on a relationship between a budget set at the *Land* level and the amount of work undertaken by physicians as expressed in volume terms. In detail the procedure is as follows.

On the *Land* level, the *Länder* Sickness Fund Associations negotiate a budget for the following year with the *Länder* Physician Associations. Thus physicians submit their bills to the respective *Land* association which is responsible for distributing the payments for services rendered. There are 18 *Länder* Physician Associations.[34]

---

[33] Health Care Act, para. 76.

[34] There are 5 *Länder* Physician Associations in the ex-GDR.

On the federal level, the Federal Association of Physicians and the Federal Association of Sickness Funds negotiate a fee schedule for the services provided by physicians.[35] These fee schedules are relative value scales, expressed in points per service provided. For example, a telephone conversation with a patient may be worth 80 points, a home visit 360 points, and a radiology test up to 900 points. Detailed listings are published covering numerous services and their respective point values.

To translate the points into German Marks the following formula is applied:[36]

$$\text{Monetary Conversion Factor (Point Value)} = \frac{\text{Budget}}{\text{Points Billed By All Physicians}}$$

Monetary conversion factors may differ across groups of sickness funds, but not within groups of funds in the same *Land*. Monetary conversion factors for substitute funds have traditionally been marginally higher than those of the local sickness funds. At present, the value of a point is approximately 9 Pfennig ($0.038 1990) for local insurance funds, and 11 Pfennig ($0.046 1990) for substitute funds. For private patients the same relative value scheme is used. Physicians treating private patients are allowed to charge fees that are between 1.7 to 3.5 times the level of those paid by statutory sickness funds.

The reimbursement scheme has led to a decrease in the relative income of German doctors, not least because the number of doctors has risen steadily. According to one estimate the average income earned by German physicians was 6.5 times the average income of all German employees in 1971, but it was only 3.5 times the German average income in 1991.[37]

---

[35]   Health Care Act, para. 82-87.

[36]   This section describes the reimbursement process as it was until the beginning of 1992. In January 1992, a new contract was negotiated by sickness funds and physicians in which the capping of the overall physicians' budget was abandoned. As a result, physicians responded with a significant increase in the volume of treatments in the first half year of 1992, thus putting in doubt whether the new contract will actually come into effect. Meanwhile the 1993 Health Care Act reintroduced capped budgets for physicians. This means that the situation will remain as it is described in this Section.

[37]   Schulenburg (1991b).

The 1993 Health Care Act limits the increase of the overall physicians' budget for the years 1993 to 1995 to the increase in the revenue base of members of the statutory insurance system. Several treatment items, such as minor ambulatory surgery and preventative care (check ups, ante-natal care) will receive their own budgets. These budgets will also be linked to the revenue base of insurance contributions but will also receive additional funding. A separate budget for medicines prescribed by physicians has been introduced for the first time (see Section 6.3.6).

Plans to change the reimbursement method of physicians have also been introduced by the 1993 Health Care Act. Instead of reimbursing each single act which a physician performs, individual acts of services may be grouped together to form so-called service-groups (Leistungskomplexe). Physicians may therefore increasingly be reimbursed for service groups rather than fee-for-service. Furthermore, office-based specialist physicians (e.g. paediatricians) will have to decide by the end of 1995 whether they wish to be known as family doctors (*Hausärzte*) or specialists (*Facharzte*). The aim of the latter reform is to financially upgrade service groups predominantly performed by family doctors.

6.3.4.4 Regulation of the Primary Health Care Sector

Apart from malpractice issues, regulation of the primary health care sector takes the form of checks on whether physicians provide treatment in a way which is both economic and cost-effective. To do this, sickness funds' associations and physicians' associations form regulatory committees. Membership on these committees is allocated on a bipartisan basis, with representatives from either group alternating as chairman for one year. Either party can initiate proceedings against a doctor who is considered to have provided treatment that is not economic or not cost-effective. Before any action is taken advice and counselling are offered.

The two associations also jointly audit referral patterns of individual doctors and check on the number of people taking sick-leave on the doctor's advice. This control is mainly performed on the basis of detecting significant discrepancies between the average cost of an individual doctor's services (*Arztkostendurchschnitt*) and the average cost of services of all doctors of the same specialty (e.g. all gynaecologists). In addition, more detailed checks are undertaken on a random sample basis and involve investigations of 2 percent of all doctors per quarter. This form of random checks is specifically designed to complement the average-based procedure control technique. The 1993

Health Care Act specifies auditing procedures in more detail including controls based on prescription limits.

6.3.4.5 Economic Incentives

The method of reimbursing physicians described above was intended to combine two things: fee-for-service reimbursement, and an attempt to contain costs. The fee-for-service reimbursement provides doctors with an incentive to treat all patients (and, indeed, to overtreat them). On the other hand, the reimbursement system also resembles a zero sum game. If one doctor generates 10 percent more services, his or her income might rise by 10 percent. However, if all doctors generate an additional 10 percent of service the monetary value per point must fall by 10 percent to keep expenditure within budget limits. The result is strong competition amongst physicians to expand the volume of treatment.

The introduction of service group payments, to replace fee-for-service payments, may eventually reduce somewhat the incentive for doctors to provide extra treatments beyond what would appear reasonable on medical grounds. Instead, this will give doctors incentives to choose the most cost-effective course of therapy for a treatment covered by a service group arrangement.

6.3.5   Hospital Sector

6.3.5.1   Roles and Objectives

In 1989 there were 3,046 hospitals in (western) Germany. These are divided into hospitals for the acutely ill, special hospitals, and hospitals which care for patients with long-term illnesses. Three different types of ownership of hospitals exist. They are public, private voluntary and private proprietary ownership. Each group owns approximately one third of all hospitals.

Public hospitals are owned by cities and municipalities, by counties, by *Länder*, or, in the case of special (e.g. military) hospitals, by federal authorities, or combinations of these. University clinics are always owned by *Länder* governments. Public hospitals account for 51 percent of beds; private voluntary hospitals, often owned by religious organisations, account for 35 percent of beds; while private proprietary hospitals, often owned by doctors, account for 14 percent of beds.[38]

On the lower level of city or county hospitals there is a trend amongst local authorities to establish a private company with limited liability as direct owner of the hospital. In so doing, local authorities create an institution governed by private, rather than public, law. This allows more flexibility with respect to wage setting for managers and some clinicians. It is the owner of the hospital (i.e. the municipal authorities or the local parliament) which appoints hospital managers. In the last few years these appointments have increasingly taken the form of temporary, rather than unlimited, appointments.

Hospitals can also be classified according to categories. Categories range from I to IX, depending on the number of medical departments. Thus, category I hospitals are university clinics with at least twelve medical departments, while category IX hospitals are small local hospitals.

Several *Länder* associations of hospitals (*Landeskrankenhausgesellschaften*) exist, as well as a national organisation (*Deutsche Krankenhausgesellschaft*), but because of the heterogeneity of their members they are rather less powerful organisations than, say, the physicians' associations. One of their functions is to negotiate the annual wage increases for clinicians and nurses with their respective trade unions. In 1990 there were 96,203 clinicians working in German hospitals. They are represented in wage negotiations by their one and only trade union, the *Marburger Bund*. The *Marburger Bund* is affiliated to the German Trade Union for White Collar Workers (*Deutsche Angestelltengewerkschaft*). Unlike physicians, clinicians have the right to strike for their wage demands as long as an emergency service is in place. This, however, rarely happens. Clinicians are also organised in the *Hartmann Bund*, a political pressure group, which is also open to physicians. Participants in the wage negotiations for nurses and other hospital staff include trade unions, such as the Trade Union for Public Services and Transport (*Gewerkschaft Öffentliche Dienste, Transport und Verkehr*), churches (as owners of hospitals), the Red Cross as well as other organisations.

The internal organisation of hospitals varies, not least because of the diversity of their legal form. For public local hospitals the organisation is usually as follows: central management consists of three people; these are a clinical

---

[38]   Private hospitals need licences which are granted to the owners personally.

director, a director of nursing and a director of administration. All three directors are usually appointed by the owner of the hospital, to whom they are accountable. They are paid a salary which is usually agreed in negotiation with the owner. In the case of university clinics, the clinical director is often elected by the medical staff. Directors of administration are increasingly being recruited from the private sector, and have a background as managers, economists or lawyers. Some come from the civil service. This reflects the growing awareness that hospitals need to be run on business-type lines. It is also mirrored in the fact that salaries for these positions are now more in line with salaries of equivalent positions in the private sector, and that contracts are being reviewed regularly.

The three directors usually run the affairs of the hospital as a team, with the clinical director possibly having the final say in case of disputes. In private proprietary hospitals, the organisation may be quite different. The same holds for university clinics, where universities and research organisations often have considerable influence.

Efforts are being made to introduce clinical budgeting in German hospitals, but these attempts have not yet reached a sophisticated stage in all hospitals. The purpose of clinical budgeting is mostly directed towards improving resource allocation among hospital departments. It is generally not intended to involve doctors and nurses in the establishment of contracts with sickness funds in a systematic way. It is generally felt that hospital doctors and nurses lack the necessary skills and experience to be involved in contracting.

Incentive-based methods are increasingly being introduced in hospitals to encourage doctors to economise on resources. For example, doctors who spend less than the allocated internal budget on health care, may be permitted to spend the savings on research.

6.3.5.2 *Patient's Choice within the Hospital Sector*

Insured persons have a say in the choice of the hospital to which they are referred by their physician. However, the physician has to take account of two criteria:

- the hospital should offer suitable treatment for the patient; and,
- it should be cost-effective.

Thus, if the doctor refers a patient to a hospital, he or she has to give reasons why this is necessary. Usually this involves referring patients to either of the two nearest hospitals, taking into account medical suitability and costs of service. To help doctors with their choice, a price list, giving *per diem* or cost-per-case rates, of nearby hospitals is usually available. If an insured person chooses another hospital without compelling reason, then the insurance fund can claim back from the patient a percentage (which may be 100 percent) of the additional costs that have arisen in the course of the treatment at that hospital compared to the cost of the recommended hospital.

6.3.5.3   Funding of the Hospital Sector

Only the following types of hospitals provide treatment to patients and are reimbursed by sickness funds:

- university clinics;
- hospitals which are part of the 'Hospital (Need) Plan' of a *Land*; and
- hospitals which have a contract with a *Land* Association of Sickness Funds.

Sickness funds may contract with public, voluntary and private (for-profit) hospitals. A flexible prospective annual budget is calculated on the basis of anticipated occupancy rates in the forthcoming year and the costs per day. This means that budgets are mainly based on *per diem* rates. A *per diem* rate is a uniform sum which the hospital receives for each day for the entire duration of the hospital in-patient stay of each of its patients. The *per diem* rate can vary for some specialties. Other treatments are priced on a cost-per-case basis. All patients, whether privately or socially insured, are charged directly for additional service, such as a single room, television, or treatment by doctor of their choice. Costing and pricing rules are listed in the Federal Care Ordinance (*Bundespflegesatzverordnung*). A twenty page formula (*Selbstkostenblatt*), detailing calculations and cost allocations must be filled out once a year by the hospital administration.

Hospitals and sickness funds must agree on the following rates (if they fail, a neutral non-governmental arbitration office is called in):

- General rates; these are *per diem* rates irrespective of patient categories and specialty. They inevitably lead to cross-subsidisation across specialties.

454

- Special rates; these are *per diem* rates for special patient groups such as obstetrics patients, burn victims, infants in neonatal care, mental patients, etc.

- Cost-per-case payments; these are for specialised treatment and surgery (*Sonderentgelte*) including cancer treatment, thorax surgery, dialysis, heart and other transplants, lithotripsy and medical innovations. Rates for specialised services are cost-per-case payments outside the budget.

For example, at the University Hospital of Hannover in Northern Germany, one of the most expensive hospitals in Germany, the rates for selected procedures are as follows (as of February 1992):

Table 6.4: Rates of Selected Procedures

	DM	$1990
General *Per Diem* Rate	727	283
Special *Per Diem* Rate		
Haemodialysis	791	308
Paediatric Oncology	990	385
Intensive Care	1,728	673
Cost-per-Case Payments		
Kidney Transplant	50,111	19,509
Liver Transplant	163,206	64,540
Heart Transplant	129,310	50,343
Cardiothoracic Surgery	20,035	7,800
Bone Marrow Transplant	194,057	75,550
Lung Transplant	175,043	68,148
Heart-Lung Transplant	175,043	68,148

Under the global budget, if actual bed days *(ex post)* exceed the expected bed days *(ex ante)*, hospitals receive only 25 percent of the *per diem* rate on the excess number. If the actual bed days fall short of the expected bed days the hospital receives 75 percent of the per diem rate for the shortfall. The rationale for these figures is the assumption that 75 percent of hospital's cost are fixed, and 25 percent are variable. Therefore, if a hospital does not achieve its target, it can still honour its employment contracts and other fixed cost obligations.

At present, sickness funds are obliged to meet the expected operating costs of hospitals (*Selbstkostendeckung*). The 1993 Health Care Act has changed this. Hospitals now carry the risk of not covering their costs. Hospitals can carry surpluses over into subsequent years. Deficits are usually paid by the (public) owners. If the owner is a voluntary organisation without sufficient funding, the deficit is financed by banks. Consequently, such hospitals accumulate debt over the years.

The negotiations between hospitals and insurance funds usually take place on a local level, not, as with the negotiations for reimbursement levels of physicians, on a national or *Land* level. It is the local sickness funds that usually take the lead in negotiations with local hospitals, often with a representative of a nationwide operating substitute funds being present at these negotiations. Often, several local insurance funds will negotiate jointly with a hospital. In practice, the negotiations concentrate on a percentage increase on the previous budget.

The substitute funds have much less of an incentive for tough negotiating with hospitals. Since their expenditure is distributed across hospitals nationwide, rather than concentrating on a few in a municipality, they have more opportunities to compensate cost differences among hospitals.

Hospitals always bill the local insurance fund of a patient's residence. For most funds, such 'cross-boundary' referrals and payments usually account for only a small amount of a local fund's budget. For nationwide operating funds cross-boundary payments do not apply.

Since January 1993, insured persons of age 18 or above pay a copayment of DM 11 ($4.51 1990) per day in hospital up to a maximum of 14 days. From January 1994 the copayment will increase to DM 12 ($4.92 1990). In eastern Germany copayments have been lowered from DM 10 to DM 8 ($3.28 1990) per day. As of January 1994 they will be increased to DM 9 ($3.69 1990).

Investments (including expenditure for medical technology) are financed by the *Länder* governments. This can include investments for private for-profit hospitals. Investments which lead to a rationalisation of services, and hence to a reduction of operating costs, may be financed through *per diem* or cost-per-case rates by insurance funds, rather than by *Länder* Governments through separate funds.

Prior to 1993, investment funds were allocated solely on the basis of the number of beds in hospitals for each hospital category I to IX. For university clinics, the Federal Government (which is responsible for research) usually has to be consulted. The Ministry for Labour and Social Affairs of the respective *Land* draws up the investment plan, with the *Land* Ministry of Finance deciding on the level of funds available. Thus, *Länder* funds for capital expenditures are made available to those hospitals which have received accreditation under the Hospital (Need) Plan. Every *Land* must have such a Hospital Plan. Hospital accreditation is intended to achieve an equitable distribution of hospital facilities and available hospital beds within a *Land*, as well as a well balanced structure of hospitals. Small local hospitals are responsible for basic care while university clinics are responsible for highly specialised care. Private hospitals find it increasingly difficult to receive accreditation and thus become eligible for capital expenditure funds.

The 1993 Health Care Act introduces several changes to the hospital sector. Most notably the Act states that for the years 1993 to 1995 budgets for hospitals are linked to the growth of income of members of sickness funds. Also more *per diem* rates will eventually be replaced by cost-per-case payments. A list of treatments for which cost-per-case payments is feasible will be drawn up by 1996. Treatments for which cost-per-case payment is not feasible will be reimbursed by a tariff which separates direct medical expenses from hotel costs.

The new regulation abolishes the long-standing principle of hospital finance whereby hospitals' operating costs were reimbursed in full (*Selbstkostendeckungsprinzip*) or almost in full (flexible budget). The aim of the new regulation is to create incentives for improved hospital efficiency by basing hospital funding increasingly on prospective cost-per-case payments (*Leistungsentgelte und Fallpauschalen*).

Other changes envisaged by the 1993 Health Care Act include the following:

- The conditions under which capital investment funds may be attracted from private sector sources will be simplified and private sector finance promoted.

- Hospitals will be obliged to make better use of 'large' technical equipment facilities, such as MRI units, by sharing such facilities with other providers. Planning for new large equipment facilities will be improved and will involve better consultation among providers of a *Land*.

- The integration of primary and secondary care will be improved. This may lead to the establishment of out-patient clinics in hospitals.

6.3.5.4 Regulation of the Hospital Sector

It is possible for the *Land* associations of the sickness funds to withdraw funding from hospitals, or hospital departments, which are deemed to work inefficiently. To begin the proceedings, the *Land* association of sickness funds together with the association of private insurers and the hospital in question jointly appoint a controller to evaluate efficiency, cost-effectiveness and quality of the hospital. If no agreement is reached concerning the choice of an auditor a neutral arbitrator is called in to make this decision. The recommendations of the evaluation are taken into account at the next year's negotiations of *per diem* rates, and may eventually lead to the closure of the hospital or parts of the hospital. Under the 1993 Health Care Act these proceedings are further simplified.

There are some differences between hospitals and rehabilitation institutions. The latter do not have to be included in the hospital need plan of the *Länder*, but can contract directly with the sickness funds. Rehabilitation institutions also generally have more freedom in the setting of prices for services which they provide. Consequently, they are largely exempt from cost-effectiveness controls, but not from quality controls.

Formalised quality control has only recently been introduced into the German health system. At present it is envisaged that a committee made up of the physicians' associations, the hospital associations, and the sickness funds will formulate recommendations and guidelines for quality control.

6.3.5.5 Economic Incentives of the Hospital Sector

There are few for-profit hospitals, and most hospital managers are paid a salary. Nevertheless, the incentives of hospital managers are largely dependent upon the way the hospitals are reimbursed for the services which they provide. The incentive structure can therefore be described in four ways:

- Because payment is based on daily rates, the hospital's income is directly related to the number of patients and the average length of stay per patient. Hence a hospital has an incentive to treat all patients, as long as beds are available. It also has an incentive to provide treatment for as long as is necessary for medical reasons. But when beds are empty, there is a financial incentive to extend the hospital stay

458

beyond the point at which hospitalised treatment is no longer strictly required. The introduction of cost-per-case payments for some services, as envisaged by the 1993 Health Care Act, will lessen this incentive.

* The incentive to keep as many patients as long as possible is compounded by the fact that if marginal costs make up less than 25 percent of the *per diem* rate, a higher than projected occupancy rate yields extra income. Furthermore, the surplus can be carried over into the next year.

* In fact, given that the bulk of a hospital's care is often concentrated in the first days of a patient's treatment with little other than hotel care required towards the end of a patient's hospital stay, a hospital may decrease its average cost per day by keeping patients longer in the hospital than necessary. Thus, hospitals with a low turnover and long in-patient stays may compare favourably in terms of cost-per-day to hospitals with a high turnover and short in-patient stays.

* While some hospitals are run by a team of relatively independent managers, others are more closely associated with their owners (e.g. towns, municipalities or regions). In the latter case they are more likely to operate under the political influence of their owners which may affect their efficiency.

* Under the conditions of fixed budgets during 1993 to 1995, hospitals are forced to balance revenues and expenditure. Since increases in revenues are unlikely, they therefore have an incentive to reduce their costs, either by shortening the length of stay of their in-patients, or by referring (expensive) patients to other hospitals.

6.3.6   Pharmaceutical Sector

6.3.6.1   *Structure of the Pharmaceutical Sector*

In 1990 there were 18,500 pharmacies in Germany, of which the great majority (18,000) were retail pharmacies and the rest hospital pharmacies. These pharmacies employed 36,500 pharmacists. Any pharmacist who has acquired the necessary qualification has the right to set up a pharmacy. Each pharmacist can operate only one pharmacy. Expenditure on medicines as a percentage of overall spending on health care has remained fairly constant in recent years at around 14 to 16 percent.

Like physicians, pharmacists are organised in *Land* councils and a federal council. Councils decide mainly issues relating to education and professional standards. In addition, the Economic Associations of Pharmacies (*Wirtschaftsverbände der Apotheker*) establish agreements with the insurance funds on drug labelling, prescription rules, inventory standards, etc., but not on reimbursement levels.

In 1990, there were approximately 1,000 pharmaceutical manufacturers.[39] Less than 500 manufacturers produce 95 percent of all drugs. The industry is mainly organised in the Federal Association of the Pharmaceutical Industry (*Bundesverband der Pharmazeutischen Industrie*), which is also represented at the meetings of the Concerted Action.

A survey of its members conducted by the Federal Association of the Pharmaceutical Industry revealed the following cost structure of the pharmaceutical industry in 1989 (in percent):[40]

Table 6.5: Cost Structure of the Pharmaceutical Industry in 1989

	Percentage of Total Costs
Production	41.7
Scientific Information	13.2
Advertising	4.5
Research and Development	15.0
Licences	1.6
Distribution	8.8
Administration	7.5
Other	7.7
Total	**100.0**

Patent duration in Germany is 20 years. However, given the time lag between patent application and market introduction, the effective patent protection period for medicines is very much less, on one estimate 7 to 8 years.[41] A regularly updated list, published by the Federal Association of the Pharmaceutical Industry, lists 8,429 medicines in 1991. This number is likely to constitute a lower bound for the actual number of medicines, due to difficulties in distinguishing substance combinations and ingredients.

---

[39] *Bundesverband der Pharmazeutischen Industrie* (1990 and 1991).

[40] *Bundesverband der Pharmazeutischen Industrie* (1990), p. 28.

[41] *Bundesverband der Pharmazeutischen Industrie* (1991), p. 51.

6.3.6.2   Funding of the Pharmaceutical Sector.

The funding of the pharmaceutical sector in Germany is shown in Chart 6.3. Medicines are distributed from the manufacturers to retailers via wholesalers and are distributed directly to hospital pharmacies. Manufacturers are free to choose the price of their products. Wholesalers can add a percentage mark-up to the price, up to a maximum which is determined by federal law in the Medicines Price Ordinance (*Arzneimittel-preisverordnung*). The maximum mark-up varies inversely with the manufacturer's price.   Currently, the rate decreases in several steps from 21 percent for a manufacturer's price of up to DM 2.65 ($1.03 1990), to 12 percent for a price of DM 108.71 ($42.32 1990) and above.

The retail pharmacist is required to add a fixed mark-up to the 'hypothetical' wholesalers price; this is the manufacturer's price with the maximum wholesaler's mark-up added.   This regulation ensures that prices for drugs in retail pharmacies are uniform throughout Germany.   Again, the fixed mark-up decreases in inverse relation to the hypothetical wholesaler's price, this time in several steps from 68 percent for a hypothetical price of up to DM 2.40 ($0.93 1990), to 30 percent, for a price of DM 170.30 ($66.30 1990) and above.

However, retail pharmacies generally receive medicines from one to three wholesalers, and these provide quantity discounts to retailers in order to ensure long-term business relationships.   The federal authorities decreed that these discounts should be passed on to the sickness funds. They estimated the average discount at 5 percent.[42]   As a result, all retail pharmacists have to pay 5 percent of the hypothetical wholesaler's price to insurance funds.

Retail pharmacies are reimbursed partly by Pharmacy Data Centres (*Apotheken-rechenzentren*), which they have set up themselves and partly by patients (see Chart 6.3).   There are four such data centres in Germany.   These centres are then reimbursed by the insurance funds.

Manufacturers of medicines generally compete on the basis of the prices and benefits of their products.   Wholesalers of medicines also compete in the setting of prices to the extent that they set margins below the maximum

---

[42]   In the five new *Länder* of the ex-GDR a so-called deficit reimbursement scheme was set up, whereby the pharmaceutical industry, wholesalers and retailers would reimburse the sickness funds for any occurring deficit on pharmaceutical spending in these five *Länder*. A deficit was defined as an expenditure level on drugs which exceeds 15.6 percent of the insurance fund premiums. In 1991, the deficit was approximately DM 1 billion.

461

Chart 6.3
The Pharmaceutical Sector in Germany

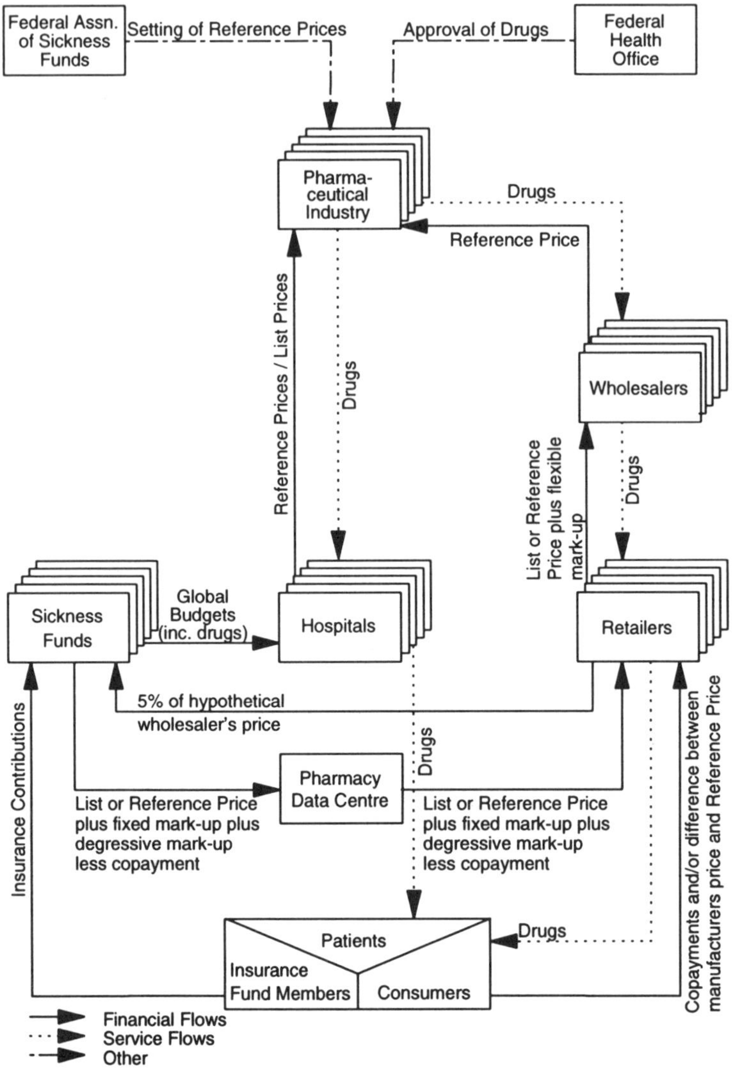

| Federal Assn. of Sickness Funds | Setting of Reference Prices | Approval of Drugs | Federal Health Office |

Pharma-ceutical Industry

Drugs

Reference Price

Reference Prices / List Prices

Drugs

Wholesalers

List or Reference Price plus flexible mark-up

Drugs

Sickness Funds

Global Budgets (inc. drugs)

Hospitals

Retailers

Insurance Contributions

5% of hypothetical wholesaler's price

Pharmacy Data Centre

Drugs

List or Reference Price plus fixed mark-up plus degressive mark-up less copayment

List or Reference Price plus fixed mark-up plus degressive mark-up less copayment

Copayments and/or difference between manufacturers price and Reference Price

Patients

Insurance Fund Members | Consumers

Drugs

→ Financial Flows
···▶ Service Flows
--▶ Other

462

allowable margin. Retail pharmacists do not compete as far as prices are concerned.

Even though mark-ups on prices are degressive, the absolute difference between retail price and manufacturer's price is significantly higher for more expensive medicines. The actual wholesale price is determined in negotiation (the hypothetical wholesale price being very much an upper limit), so wholesalers and retailers divide this total margin between them. Neither, therefore, has any financial incentive to keep medicine prices low.

6.3.6.3 Reference Prices

Insurance funds are required to reimburse the retailers for part of the cost of medicines. The level at which this reimbursement is set is determined by the so-called reference pricing system. This was introduced in the 1989 Health Reform Act.

Reference prices (or more correctly: fixed level reimbursement schemes; *Arzneimittel-Festbeträge*) are administratively set reimbursement levels for medicines with similar properties (see below). They are set by a federal commission comprising representatives of sickness funds and physicians, but not including representatives of the pharmaceutical industry. This constitutes the reimbursement level for insurance funds.

If an insured person wishes to obtain a medicine whose price is above the reference price, then he or she has to pay the difference between the actual price and the reference price. Furthermore, doctors have to indicate on the prescription form whether the pharmacist is allowed to hand out an equally efficacious but more cost-effective drug.[43]

The system of reference prices was to be developed in three groups:[44]

1. Group 1 contains medicines with therapeutically equivalent active substances.

2. Group 2 includes medicines with pharmacologically comparable active substances, especially chemically related ingredients.

---

[43] Patients can choose the retail pharmacy, i.e. the non-hospital based pharmacy, at which they obtain prescribed medicines. Hospital-based pharmacies are only accessible to clinicians.

[44] Health Care Act, para. 35.

3.   Finally, Group 3 includes those with comparable therapeutic effects, particularly drug combinations. Originally the Health Care Act of 1989 specified that drugs with comparable pharmacological-therapeutic effects be included, but the 1993 Health Care Act changed this to comparable therapeutic effects.

The Ministry of Health originally hoped that progress would be such that by the end of 1992 80 percent of all drugs would be covered by reference prices. Patented drugs were supposed to be excluded from reference pricing, but, prior to the 1993 Health Care Act, it appeared that the distinction between patented and non-patented drugs was not always observed. Under the 1993 Act the conditions for including out-of-patent drugs in Group 1 have been relaxed, whereas inclusion of drugs into Groups 2 and 3 appear to have been tightened by clarifying the term 'innovative': an active ingredient is now considered innovative "so long as that active ingredient of this group which was first marketed is protected by patent".[45]

The first reference prices were introduced on 1 September 1989. By 1 January 1993 reference prices had been fixed for:

- 86 substances of Group 1 (of an estimated potential of 130 substances);

- 12 substance groups of Group 2, comprising 108 substances; and,

- 3 substance combinations of Group 3.[46]

This amounts to 45 percent of the total expenditure of sickness funds on medicines.

The administration of reference prices is complex. The Federal Association of Company-Based Insurance Funds (*Bundesverband der Betriebskrankenkassen*) is responsible for the calculation of reference prices. The basis for this calculation is an econometric model which aims to determine relative standard prices by regressing manufacturers' prices of drugs of the same therapeutic group on the variables 'dosage strength' and 'package size'. Standard prices are then converted into reference prices by multiplying the chosen price of a standard unit with the relative standard prices.

---

[45]   *MPS Intern* (1992b), p. 2.

[46]   *Bundesverband der Betriebskrankenkassen* (1993).

The reference price system is controversial not least because it is difficult to decide what exactly a therapeutically comparable effect is. Its effects on pricing of drugs are significant. Although pricing of new drugs is free upon market introduction, prices for many medicines did in fact converge to their reference price after the introduction of the new system. Since reference prices were calculated on an average basis, the prices of some medicines actually increased. Furthermore, generic drug competition almost collapsed as their prices were also brought into line with reference prices.

6.3.6.4 Copayments

Prescription fees were introduced in 1970. The copayment structure has changed frequently in recent years. Initially, when reference prices were introduced, medicines covered by these were free of charges other than the difference between sales price and reimbursement level. This has changed with the passing of the 1993 Health Care Act. Patients now have to pay copayments for all medicines irrespective of whether or not they are covered by reference prices. The new structure is as follows:

- DM 3 ($1.2 1990) for medicines priced DM 30 ($11.6 1990) or less (or the full price if less than DM 3);

- DM 5 ($1.9 1990) for medicines priced between DM 30 and DM 50 ($19.4 1990); and,

- DM 7 ($2.7 1990) for medicines priced over and above DM 50.

However, according to the 1993 Health Care Act the current structure of copayments is to be replaced by yet another structure. From January 1994 the level of copayments will depend of the package size of medicines. Thus 'small' packages will have a copayment of DM 3, 'medium-size' packages will cost DM 5, while 'large' packages will cost DM 7.

In order to protect chronically ill people, or those on low incomes, the annual sum of copayments to be paid by individuals is capped at an upper limit. That upper limit is dependent upon the income of the individual, marital status and the number of children. Different limits also apply to people living in the former East Germany; this regulation takes account of the fact that income levels in eastern Germany are below those of western Germany.

Copayment limits usually apply to copayments on most services, e.g. medicines, medical appliances, medical aids and transport costs. In-patient stays in hospitals are excluded. Thus, for example, people with a monthly gross income of DM 1,484 ($590 1990) do not have to pay any copayment at all. For married couples the limit is lifted by DM 556.50 ($225 1990), and for each additional child the limit is further lifted by DM 273.00 ($109 1990). For people on lower incomes, the upper ceiling of copayments is limited to 2 percent of gross income. For income levels over and above the threshold at which people can opt out of the social insurance scheme the copayment ceiling is limited to 4 percent of gross income. These figure are adjusted for family members. For people living in eastern Germany copayment limits are approximately 25 percent below that of western Germany. Several additional regulations specifying exemption categories (e.g. chronically sick people) exist.

In practice the system of copayment ceilings is operated in a flexible manner. Chronically ill people who are unlikely to pay any copayments may receive a form from their insurance funds that serves as evidence that they are exempt from payment. Others who have paid more than their annual copayment limit can ask their insurance fund for a refund.

6.3.6.5 *Regulation of the Pharmaceutical Sector*

The Medicines Act (*Arzneimittelgesetz*) describes the conditions under which drugs may be produced. New medicines have to be approved by the Federal Health Office (*Bundesgesundheitsamt*) which has a medicines commission responsible for the approval. At present there is a backlog of approval admissions and the average procedure may take several years, depending on the type of drug. Approval procedures can be shortened if a pharmaceutical company applies for approval of a medicine which is the equivalent of an approved medicine whose patent has expired.

Some medicines, notably high-tech and biotechnological drugs, must be approved by the European Commission; once this has been secured, the drug can then be put on the market in all member states of the Community. By 1995 it is envisaged that European Community-wide approval procedures will be in place for most medicines. The details of the approval procedure are listed in the Medicines Act. There are several other ordinances which regulate the market for medicines. The Federal Health Office also decides whether or not a medicine needs to be prescribed by a doctor.

Advertising of drugs is highly regulated, even for over-the-counter medicines. For prescribed medicines, advertising is usually restricted to scientific journals and to publications for doctors, visits to hospital personnel, or seminars for health care professionals. Cost effectiveness studies or cost benefit studies are not required as part of the registration procedure.

Since 1983, there has been a list of medicines which the patient has to pay for in full (i.e. a negative list). It covers mainly OTC medicines. The negative list is to be replaced by a 'List of Reimbursable Drugs' by January 1996. To this effect, the 1993 Health Care Act plans the establishment of an 'Institute For Medicines' (*Arzneimittel-institut*). A board with eleven independent experts will be set up and will draw up the initial list of reimbursable medicines. A decision on whether or not a new medicine will be included on the list has to be made within three months of the application. If no decision is made within this time limit, the drug may be prescribed by physicians until a decision to the contrary has been made. Drugs with little therapeutic value will not be included in the list. In exceptional cases physicians may prescribe medicines which are not listed, if they give reason for their choice.

The 1993 Health Care Act introduced two severe cost containment measures targeted at the pharmaceutical sector:

1.   A price freeze on medicines not covered by reference prices was introduced. Specifically, the industry has been asked to lower prices by 2 to 5 percent from January 1993 onwards until 1994, based on price levels as at 1 May 1992.

2.   A budget for medicines prescribed by office-based physicians was also introduced. This budget was set at DM 24 billion ($9.3 bn 1990) for the year 1993. The Act states that indicative budgets may also be set for 1994 and beyond, thus introducing the possibility of firmly establishing capped medicines budgets into the German health care system.

The Act rules that if the medicines budget for 1993 is exceeded by up to DM 280 million ($109 mn 1990), physicians must pay for the overrun in the following year by reducing their collective budget. The 1993 Act does not introduce individual physicians' budgets. If the budget is exceeded by between DM 280 million and DM 560 million ($217 mn 1990), it is the pharmaceutical industry which will pay for the overrun, mainly through a continuation of the price freezes agreed for 1993 and 1994.

First effects of the medicines budget appear to be significant. In January 1993, the level of prescriptions by office-based physicians dropped by some 30 percent. At present, it is not clear what the long-term effects of the new regulations will be.

6.4   INTERSECTORAL ANALYSIS

6.4.1   Major Decision Makers

The German health care system appears to be characterised by an extremely heterogenous decision making process in which numerous participants have vested interests and are often well organised in pressure groups to lobby for their interests. Physicians, clinicians and sickness funds, as well as the federal and *Länder* governments, all have varying degrees of influence. The sickness funds themselves are a heterogenous groups comprising local funds, company funds, and large nationwide operating substitute funds. Their interests partly overlap and partly diverge.   Physician associations also comprise various interest groups which may not always agree on issues such as the re-evaluation of relative point values for different services (e.g. laboratory testings versus patient counselling).

However, despite the heterogeneity and multiplicity of the participants in the German health care system, the actual decision making process in the system is much less decentralised than might be expected. Two features of the system can be identified as being largely responsible for this.   These are (1) the federalist nature of the key decision makers' interactions, and (2) the indirect, but strong, influence of the Federal Government on health care policies. We will briefly turn to both features.

Characteristic of the federalist nature of the German health care system is the fact that almost all key participants in it form *Land* and federal associations. It is these associations that are largely responsible for the financing decisions in the health care system. In fact, their responsibility for negotiating budgets or fee schedules is often the primary reason for their existence. The decisions which provider and purchasing associations reach are always binding for their constituency; where federal associations are involved, this is for Germany as a whole; where *Länder* associations are involved, it is for the respective *Länder*. For the negotiations on reimbursement levels, each side agrees to be represented by their association; hence, the negotiations between the associations often take the form of bilateral bargaining.

The most important decision making processes are the following:

- Reimbursement levels for primary physicians are negotiated between the federal and *Länder* associations of the sickness funds, and the federal and *Länder* associations of the primary physicians.

- Reimbursement levels for clinicians and nurses are negotiated between Trade Unions representing clinicians and nurses, and the German Hospital Association, representing hospitals.

- Budgets for hospitals are negotiated between hospitals and sickness funds on the local level. Representatives of national sickness funds may also be present.

The exception to this rule concerns pharmaceuticals. Reimbursement levels for medicines are increasingly fixed unilaterally by the National Association of Sickness Funds.

Health care is no longer the responsibility of the Ministry of Labour and Social Affairs, but rather the responsibility of the newly created Ministry of Health. As a result the influence over general policy issues that was exerted in the past by employers and employees is vanishing.

In order to guide the bargaining process of the key decision makers of the health care system, the Federal Government convenes meetings of the so-called Concerted Action (*Konzertierte Aktion*).[47] The Concerted Action has no regulatory powers; rather it exerts its influence on the basis of 'moral suasion'. Established in 1977 the Concerted Action is a national forum which meets twice annually. This top level meeting is convened by the Minister of Health and attended by representatives of the major sectors of health care. Over the years it has grown considerably, and now has approximately ninety members from various organisations (see Table 6.6).

In meetings of the Concerted Action, guidelines are agreed for the rates of increase in different types of health care expenditure (such as primary care, hospital care, dental services or prescription drugs). In general, these guidelines aim to align health care expenditure with the growth of the revenue base of the statutory sickness funds. This principle of 'contribution rate stability' (*Beitragssatzstabilität*) is actually written into health care legislation.[48] This policy of revenue-based expenditure levels has often been criticized as not being an adequate basis for health care financing decisions, because it fixes health care expenditure as a constant share of income and thus links health care budgets to overall economic activity: in times of increasing growth, more

---

[47]   Health Care Act, para. 141-142.

[48]   Health Care Act, para. 71, and para. 141.

money is available for health, while in times of recession, when health care need may be greater, less money is available.

Table 6.6: Membership of the Concerted Action

Insurance Funds
1.   the Federal Association of the Local Sickness Funds;
2.   the Federal Association of the Company-Based Sickness Funds;
3.   the Federal Association of the Crafts' Sickness Funds;
4.   the Federal Association of the Agricultural Sickness Funds;
5.   the Miners' Sickness Fund;
6.   the Sailors' Sickness Fund;
7.   the Association of White Collar Sickness Funds;
8.   the Association of Blue Collar Sickness Funds; and,
9.   the Association of Private Insurance Companies.

Doctors and Dentists
10.   Federal Association of Physicians;
11.   Federal Association of Dentists;
12.   Federal Medical Chamber;
13.   Federal Dental Chamber;

Hospitals
14.   German Hospital Association

Pharmaceutical Sector
15.   Federal Association of German Pharmacists; and,
16.   Federal Association of the German Pharmaceutical Industry.

Trade Unions and Employer Organisations
17.   German Trade Union Association;
18.   German White Collar Trade Union;
19.   German Civil Servant Association; and,
20.   Federal Association of German Employers.

Government
21.   Federal Association of Municipalities;
22.   the *Länder* Ministries for Labour and Social Affairs;
23.   the Federal Ministry for Labour and Social Affairs;
24.   the Federal Ministry for Economic Affairs; and,
25.   the Federal Ministry of Health.

The Concerted Action also seeks to regulate the bargaining process of the federal and *Land* associations of purchasers and providers by acting as a mediator. The recommendations of the Concerted Action conference are sometimes based on expert advice commissioned by the Concerted Action from an expert council (*Sachverständigenrat*). Members of the expert council are usually academics with a background in health care and economics. They are appointed by the Minister of Health. Some economic advisors have recently pointed out that payroll deduction rate stability over the next few years can only be achieved by reducing services.

6.4.2 Consistency of Objectives and Incentives

The main problems areas, prior to the passing of the 1993 Health Care Act, are listed below. Since the 1993 Act envisages changes to be implemented over a period of several years, these shortcomings can be expected to persist for a number of years.

Patients, Physicians and Insurance Funds

Although the total reimbursement level for primary physicians is limited by an agreed overall budget, neither the associations of physicians nor the associations of sickness funds have any control over the volume of services provided by physicians. That volume is determined by patients and their individual physicians. Because physicians compete with each other in this way, they have an incentive to expand volume. Patients who are fully covered against expenses are more likely to accept additional services from their physicians than would be the case if they were billed for these services.

The result has been a continuous expansion of services provided by physicians. This situation is exacerbated by the fact that the number of young physicians setting up practices has increased steadily in recent years. The increase of services generated by physicians is usually translated into an increase of the overall budget for office-based physicians in the next year, rather than a continuous devaluation of the point values for individual services.

Physicians and Hospitals

A significant feature of the German health care system is the strict division between in-patient care and ambulatory, or primary care. Prior to the 1993 Health Care Act hospitals were not allowed to provide ambulatory care. However, since in-patient treatment usually follows ambulatory treatment, procedures (such as X-rays or blood tests) are often performed twice. This lack of integration of primary and hospital services tends to duplicate effort and increase costs. The problem is exacerbated if the patient is referred from an office-based physician to a specialist physician, referred from there to a hospital and then referred back to the primary care sector. The 1993 Health Care Act introduces a number of provisions designed to improve the integration of ambulatory and hospital services.

Hospitals and Insurance Funds

Hospitals generally have their operating costs reimbursed by sickness funds. This means that hospitals are relatively free to decide what services to provide as part of medical care. This system gives the payer i.e. the sickness funds, little authority to co-determine how resources are spent, and in particular whether resources are allocated in a cost-efficient and economic way. Local insurance funds are often not in a position to evaluate whether a hospital works efficiently or not. The dual finance system of hospitals leads to a lack of coordination: *Länder* governments, which finance investment expenditure of hospitals, are not responsible for the follow-up operating costs; while insurance funds, which fund operating costs of hospitals, are usually not involved in the investment decision.

Different Groups of Insurance Funds

The selective enrolment rules of the statutory health insurance system have led to concealed positive risk-selection by some funds ('cream-skimming'), and to premium differences. Some funds could thus afford to be more inclined towards a generous interpretation of members' entitlements than others. The resulting increase in health care expenditure was passed on to fund members in increased contributions.

6.4.3 Economic Implications for Efficiency and Equity

The German health care system is equitable as far as access to services and provision of services is concerned. Equity in the provision of services is virtually guaranteed to all Germans, regardless of age, income or status in society. The main reason for this is that most people are covered by the statutory insurance system or by private insurance schemes. Even those who, for whatever reason, fall through that net and have no coverage are usually entitled to welfare assistance payments. Despite the decentralised structure of health care provision, there are few regional imbalances in western Germany as far as service availability is concerned.

The system is, however, inequitable as far as the level of insurance contributions is concerned. Because each insurance fund is a separate self-governing organisation, it sets its own contribution level. Factors influencing the variability in insurance fund contributions include differences in the risk structure of the insured population and differences in the wage base (*Grundlohnsumme*). This has led to considerable differences in insurance fund contributions for the same level of health care services.

Under the former legislation, efficiency losses were generated in the following areas:

- Physicians were likely to provide too much treatment and patients likely to accept this over-provision. (The 1993 legislation counters this with revenue-based budgets for physician services.)

- Physicians could provide services, especially high-tech services, which were then duplicated by hospitals. Medical records often do not accompany patients who are referred to the hospital by their physician; hence patients may undergo the same procedures several times. (The new legislation remedies this situation through the introduction of provisions for improving the integration of institutional and ambulatory services.)

- Hospitals had few incentives to use resources as efficiently as possible. Sickness funds were not usually in a position to check whether the hospital provided cost effective treatment. (Hospital efficiency should improve as the result of the transition to a hospital finance system based on cost-per-case payments.)

- The relatively long length of stay in hospitals (compared to other countries) is partly due to a reimbursement method based on flat daily rates. This gives hospitals an incentive to keep patients longer than is strictly necessary on medical grounds. (This incentive will be removed under the future system for hospital reimbursement.)

- Several sickness funds are in a position to risk-select their members and do so. Sickness funds compete on the basis of generous interpretations of health care entitlements (for example with respect to the duration of rehabilitation stays in health resorts), rather than on the basis of premium reductions. Sickness funds often simply pass on the additional expenditure to their members. (Risk-selection will still be possible, but will have little effect on contribution rates due to revenue sharing.)

6.5   ANALYSIS OF HEALTH CARE POLICY

In the early seventies, health care expenditure increased rapidly as a percentage of GDP causing politicians to speak of a 'health care cost explosion'. In the late 1970s, when economic recession started to erode the financial basis of the sickness funds, the Federal Government passed several health care reform acts, designed to bring expenditure under control.

Most of these reform acts were in fact cost containment acts, and introduced little structural or organisational reform. The 1977 Health Care Act, for example, focused on improving the cooperation among the participants of the health care sector by introducing the Concerted Action. Cost sharing was extended, as was the risk adjustment mechanism between funds for pensioners.

The main aim of the 1989 Health Care Act was to improve the financial performance of the system by strengthening cost-consciousness on both the supply and the demand side. Reference prices for drugs were introduced, and copayments for services were either introduced or increased. Some of the benefits in cash, such as the reimbursement for transportation to hospitals, were reduced. Sickness funds were given the right to terminate contracts with inefficient hospitals. Quality assurance and efficiency audits were also introduced.

The effects of the Health Care Reform Act of 1989 were dramatic, but short-lived. In 1989, health care expenditure as a percent of gross domestic product dropped to 8.2 percent, from 8.9 percent in the previous year.[49] In 1990 it dropped further to 8.1 percent. Since then, however, the share of GDP allocated to health care has increased sharply, and, prior to the introduction of the 1993 Health Care Act, had increased further. Similarly, the average health insurance premium, which had dropped from 12.9 percent in 1989 to 12.2 percent in 1991 had by 1992 risen to a record high of 13.3 percent.[50]

This renewed rise in health care expenditure led the coalition government of Chancellor Helmut Kohl to look yet again at health care reform. The newly appointed Minister for Health, Horst Seehofer, a member of the Christian Social Union (CSU), the Bavarian branch of the Christian Democratic Union

---

[49]   OECD (1991). The OECD data does not include all health care related costs.

[50]   Zipperer (1993), p. 25.

(CDU), was given the task of proposing new reform measures. After many discussions, which involved the opposition Social Democratic Party as well as the key participants of the health care system, the 1993 Health Care Act was passed in December 1992. It came into effect in January 1993. Table 6.7 lists some of the events during the negotiation process. This serves to show how important it had become to forge a coalition among decision makers in order to put together the reform package.

Table 6.7: Events Surrounding the Negotiations of the 1993 Health Care Act

24-31 May 1992	Closed session of a working group of members of the Christian Democratic Union (CDU) and the Free Democratic Party (FDP) to prepare a reform package.
2 June 1992	Coalition agreement on the health care reform package.
12 August 1992	Federal Government announces plans for structural health care reform.
8 September 1992	Social Democratic Party (SPD) introduces a reform programme in the Lower House of the Federal Parliament (*Bundestag*).
11 September 1992	*Bundestag* debates the reform packages of both the Government (CDU/FDP) and the SPD. SPD agrees to participate in consensus talks with the Government.
23-25 September 1992	Hearings for both reform packages.
25 September 1992	Upper House of the Federal Parliament (*Bundesrat*) rejects Government proposals.
27-30 September 1992	Closed session of a working group of members of the CDU, FDP and SPD to reach agreement on a joint reform package.
1-4 October 1992	Closed session of CDU, FDP and SPD and agreement to a joint concept for health care reform.
5 November 1992	CDU, FDP and SPD introduce package for structural health care reform in the *Bundestag*.
6 November 1992	Hearings.
6-25 November 1992	Consultations in various committees of the *Bundestag*.
9 December 1992	Second and third debate in the *Bundestag*. *Bundestag* accepts the reform proposals.
18 December 1992	*Bundesrat* accepts the proposals.
1 January 1993	Health Care Act becomes law.

Source: *Zipperer (1993), p. 28.*

The government hopes that this package will lead to annual savings of DM 10.7 billion ($4.2 bn 1990), of which DM 8.2 billion ($3.2 bn 1990) are due to savings made by hospitals, physicians and the pharmaceutical sector. Increases in copayments are expected to yield an additional DM 2.5 billion ($1.0 bn 1990). Table 6.8 shows the breakdown of these figures.

Table 6.8: Expected Financial Savings of the 1993 Health Care Act

	Billion DM	Billion $ 1990
Hospital Sector		
Revenue-Based Expenditure Ceilings	2.50	0.98
Increase in Copayments	0.07	0.03
Other	0.72	0.28
Office-Based Physicians		
Revenue-Based Expenditure Ceilings	0.75	0.29
Office-Based Dentists		
Revenue-Based Expenditure Ceilings	0.40	0.16
Other (incl. GHCP exclusions)	1.70	0.67
Medicines		
Price Freezes	1.50	0.59
Global Budget	0.56	0.22
Increase in Copayments	1.30	0.51
Medical Aids/Preventative Care		
Revenue-Based Expenditure Ceilings	0.35	0.14
Global Budget	0.20	0.08
Increase in Copayments	0.01	0.004
Sickness Funds		
Revenue-Based Expenditure Ceilings on Administrative Expenditure	0.24	0.09
Increased Revenues[51]	0.35	0.14
TOTAL SAVINGS	**10.65**	**4.18**
Increase in Expenditure (GHCP additions)	0.65	0.25
NET SAVINGS	**10.00**	**3.92**

Source: *Zipperer (1993), p. 30.*

---

[51] Increased revenues are due mainly because of changes with respect to the treatment of those who seek voluntary insurance with sickness funds, and whose income levels were above the threshold (*Beitragsbemessungsgrenze*) during their working life.

The 1993 Health Care Act introduces a mixture of radical organisational reforms and stringent cost containment measures, targeted at specific sectors of the health care system.[52] Perhaps the most radical step is the introduction of open enrolment for the majority of the population with all funds, coupled with a global risk adjustment mechanism between funds. If implemented, it will mean that premium differentials between funds reflect differences in efficiency with which funds conclude contracts with providers, rather than differences in the risk structure and the income base of their members. The current feature of the health care system whereby some funds can engage in risk-selection but other cannot will be abolished by the new system. Instead, competition between funds may take the form of premium reduction.

Structural reform policies have also been introduced on the provider side of the health care system. This is most clearly the case as far as the financing of hospitals is concerned. The *per diem* rates are to be replaced by cost-per-case or other payments which form a closer link between the costs of services and the resource utilisation. Under the *per diem* rates, hospitals have a statutory right to see their operating costs reimbursed, using past cost data and anticipated utilization rates. Hence, hospitals had little incentive to reduce costs or to allocate resources efficiently. In the future, hospitals will find that in some cases their costs are not covered, while in other cases they are left with surplus funds. Also, purchasers will be able to make cost comparisons for similar services offered at various hospitals. (Cost comparisons of daily rates are often not meaningful because of the heterogeneity of services.)

The fact that insurance funds can more easily put pressure on inefficient hospitals, and eventually have them closed, strengthens their negotiating position. There is already an overcapacity of hospitals in Germany. One way of reducing their numbers is through the contracting process whereby inefficient hospitals do not have their contracts renewed.

The government has also taken a first step towards reducing the growth in the number of primary physicians. Their number has increased by almost 50 percent between 1977 and 1988. Although it is not clear how the Government intends to do this,[53] it is widely recognised that the number of physicians needs to be reduced. One method would be to discourage young people from

---

[52]   See for example Der Spiegel (24, 1992): *Kranker Medizin Betrieb - Der ausgebeutete Patient.*

[53]   In 1960 the Constitutional Court declared any restriction to the right of free choice of profession as unconstitutional.

studying medicine; another is to give funds the right to hold examinations to decide who is going to become accredited with the fund.

The 1993 Health Care Act also introduces new regulations which are clearly designed to cut expenditure in the short term, rather than to implement structural and market-oriented reforms that would generate greater efficiency. Most notably these cost containment policies target the pharmaceutical sector in several ways. A price freeze for manufacturers' prices for drugs has been implemented for 1993 and 1994. The Government has also introduced a budget for medicines to be prescribed by office-based physicians for 1993. First indications are that the likely effect of this regulation is that doctors will reduce the value of their prescription levels by prescribing less or by increasingly prescribing generics.

6.6   CONSTRAINTS ON REFORM

6.6.1   Satisfaction with the Existing System

The German health care system performs well in many respects. The range of benefits to which Germans are entitled is considerable (see Section 6.3.3). There is an extensive network of health care facilities, so that access to care is easy and relatively uniform throughout (western) Germany. The quality of care is considered to be high by international standards. Waiting lists exist for few, if any, treatments. Seen from this perspective, it may be difficult to implement a reform programme that is *perceived* to limit health service entitlements, or is *perceived* to restrict access to doctors and hospitals.

6.6.2   Emphasis on Social Solidarity

The concept of social solidarity, namely to provide health care for all irrespective of their ability to pay, is a central feature of the German health care system and dates back to last century when sickness funds were established. The emphasis on social solidarity has been strengthened over decades, not least because of a broadening of the health care service entitlements in the 60s and 70s. Policies which seek to re-balance the concept of social solidarity are relatively new; for example, copayments are still limited to some services and tend to be 'small'. Any reform which is perceived as abandoning the concept of social solidarity in favour of unregulated competition is unlikely to be acceptable to the German population.

However, the original intention of social solidarity has gradually been eroded. Today, there is a growing expectation that the costs of ever more services should be shared by society. Such expectations sometimes encourage abuse: instead of redistributing funds from the healthy to the sick, it is increasingly the healthy themselves who make use of entitlements, for reasons of availability, rather than for reasons of need.[54]

---

[54]   See Arnold (1992).

6.6.3   Decentralisation

Germany is a federal republic with tiers of government existing on the local, on the state (i.e. *Länder*), and on the national level. Elections take place on all three levels. The *Länder* governments form the upper house of Parliament, and must therefore usually be consulted before legislation is passed by Parliament. *Länder* governments are unlikely to agree to changes that diminish their powers; hence consensus between the Federal Government and a majority of the sixteen *Länder* Governments is essential for passing legislation.

6.6.4   Compatibility with the 'Social Market Economy'

Any change to the health care system is likely to meet opposition if it is perceived by politicians and other decision makers to be incompatible with the general economic and social framework of Germany, the so-called 'Social Market Economy' (*Soziale Marktwirtschaft*).   The social market economy supports private ownership and competitive markets as means of exchange of goods and services, but at the same time approves of government intervention whenever the market mechanism is perceived to yield unacceptable outcomes. This in particular concerns the weaker members of society whose welfare would be at risk if the government did not intervene.

In health care, compatibility with the social market economy finds its expression in the fact that sickness funds are largely self-governing organisations with decision-making bodies that are elected by the members of these funds.   It is unlikely that a reformed health care system which is not perceived as being compatible with this framework will find general acceptance.

6.6.5   Corporatism

In theory the social market economy is intended to introduce elements of democracy into commercial and social relationships; in practice it has led to the development of a 'corporatist' society in Germany, where powerful interest groups (such as political parties, employer federations, trade unions, federal and *Länder* authorities) settle disputes in highly centralised negotiations which have the aim of finding mutually agreeable outcomes.   Again, in health care, this finds its expression in the existence of federal and *Länder* associations (of sickness funds, physicians and hospitals) who have the right to conclude collectively binding contracts.   In general, a consensual approach appears to be a more promising way to achieve the successful implementation of reforms, rather than an adversarial approach.

6.7   SHORT-TERM REFORM

6.7.1   The Need for Reform

On 1 January 1993 the new (1993) Health Care Act (*Gesundheits-Strukturgesetz*) came into effect. It has been described as a piece of legislation that "may lead to a thorough re-structuring of the health care system".[55] Whereas previous health care acts concentrated on amending the existing legislation without changing the *structure* of the health system, the 1993 Health Care Act aims to establish a complete overhaul of the existing system.

Although the latest health care reform measures had only been passed in 1989, they were widely considered to be a failure. The main reason for this was the fact that, since summer 1990, health care expenditure of the sickness funds again increased at a faster rate than their income. This development accelerated in 1991: expenditure per sickness fund member increased by 10.6 percent, whereas premiums increased only by 5 percent. By 1992 the gap had further increased. In western Germany the sickness fund system accumulated a deficit of DM 5.6 billion in 1991 ($2.5 bn 1990), and approximately DM 10 billion in 1992 ($3.9 bn 1990). As a result, the average premium, which had decreased from 12.9 percent in 1989 to 12.2 percent in 1991 increased to a record high of 13.3 percent in 1992. The situation in eastern Germany was similar: the surplus accumulated in 1991 had by 1992 changed into a deficit of DM 230 million ($90 mn 1990) for the first six months.[56]

This development had political implications, for example with respect to pensioners whose pensions adjustments are inversely linked to health care premium increases. The need for further health care reform thus became eminent. After much debate, the Minister of Health, Horst Seehofer, was able to strike a consensus among the main political parties of the federal parliament, as well as with the *Länder* governments. As a result new legislation was accepted by the Lower House of Parliament, where the ruling Christian Democrats and Free Democrats have a majority, as well as by the Upper House of Parliament, where the opposition Social Democrats currently hold the majority. Since most changes of the 1993 Health Care Act affect the *Länder*, approval of these changes by the *Länder*, through the Upper House, was essential.

---

[55]   Knieps (1993), p.152.

[56]   Zipperer (1993), p.25.

6.7.2   The Changes of the 1993 Health Care Act

In summary the most important of the reforms of the 1993 Health Care Act are as follows (details have been described in Sections 6.3 and 6.5):

Table 6.9: Major Reforms of the 1993 Health Care Act

Sickness Funds

Comprehensive reorganisation of the sickness funds by allowing free choice of fund for most people with most funds; the introduction of a global risk adjustment mechanism across all funds, and the reorganisation of the sickness funds' self-administration bodies.

Revenue-based expenditure ceilings for the administration expenditure for sickness funds for the years 1993 to 1995.

Additions and deletions to the health care service entitlements.

Office-Based Physicians

Revenue-based expenditure ceilings for office-based physicians for the years 1993 to 1995.

Restrictions of accreditation of physicians with sickness funds to reduce the oversupply of physicians in some areas.

Improvements in the reimbursement methods of physicians by replacing fee-for-service reimbursement with service-group payments, and by re-evaluating services typically performed by family doctors.

Hospitals

Revenue-based expenditure ceilings for hospitals for the years 1993 to 1995.

Greater emphasis on prospective cost-per-case payments to reimburse hospitals. This will eventually replace the current system which guarantees hospitals the reimbursement of their operating costs.

Better integration of ambulatory and hospital care.

Increase of copayments for in-patient stays in hospitals.

Medicines

Global budget in 1993 for medicines prescribed by office-based physicians.

Price-freezes and price decreases for medicines.

Establishment of an 'Institute for Medicines' that will set up a list of reimbursable drugs.

Introduction of new copayments for medicines based on prices for drugs, and in 1994, based on package size. Introduction of copayments for reference-priced medicines.

Several of the reform steps listed above in Table 6.9 are similar, or indeed identical, to our recommendations for long-term reform, as identified by the Prototype. This applies in particular to the planned reorganisation of the German sickness fund system which eventually, by 1996, will allow most people free choice of sickness funds, and the switching from one sickness fund to another. This reform proposal is endorsed on the ground that it will stimulate premium competition between funds. Premium competition between funds means that people will begin to shop for health insurance and will seek insurance with funds that offer lower premiums while guaranteeing access to those services covered by the Guaranteed Health Care Package (GHCP). Open enrolment with most funds will ensure that neither positive nor negative risk-selection will be possible. The global risk adjustment mechanism will ensure a level playing field for sickness funds.

Several other reform policies are also endorsed. This includes a larger reliance on copayments, as well as the move towards prospective cost-per-case payments for hospitals and also for physicians. Prospective reimbursement methods lead to better incentives for providers and insurance funds, in contrast to retrospective funding arrangements which generate incentives for volume expansion, and thus inefficiencies.

On the other hand expenditure ceilings for office-based physicians services, hospital services, and, most notably, budgets for medicines prescribed by office-based physicians, are regulatory instruments that are incompatible with greater reliance on market forces to contain costs. The use of ceilings or budgets can only be justified during a transitional period when market instruments have not yet been developed. It appears that the 1993 Health Care Act recognises this fact. By limiting physicians' and hospitals' expenditure ceilings to three years it signals its intention to use administrative measures to control costs in the short term, but to strengthen market forces to do so in the longer term.

Unfortunately it is not clear that this is so in the case of budgets for medicines prescribed by office-based physicians. In accordance with the 1993 Health Care Act regional budgets and/or prescription limits for medicines prescribed by office-based physicians will be introduced on a permanent basis. Efforts should be made to replace these by other means of cost-control, including reviews of prescribing behaviour by doctors. The planned establishment of a list of reimbursable drugs may also assist in avoiding further budgeting of medicines.

483

Similarly, mandatory price freezes are generally incompatible with market-led reforms. They should thus be repealed as soon as possible. The establishment of an Institute for Medicines that will eventually draw up a list of reimbursable drugs may lead to a more rational prescribing by physicians. However, steps should be taken to avoid the list of reimbursable drugs leading to a positive list, which would exclude some medicines from reimbursement altogether. That would restrict doctors' and patients' choice. An alternative method could involve a list of reimbursable medicines that is reviewed at regular intervals, such that new medicines are added and 'old' medicines are deleted (a so-called 'bathtub' model). Old medicines are medicines that are no longer needed, primarily because alternative medicines have become available that either have additional benefits or are more cost-effective.

6.7.3   Interim Reform Steps

It is necessary to make significant progress over the coming years and develop a health care system that relies on market forces, rather than a continuation of administrative measures, such as budgetary ceilings. This means, in particular, that progress should be made on the organisational reform of the sickness fund system, the global risk adjustment mechanism and the development of prospective payment methods for providers.

It is our view that over the next three years there exists a 'window of opportunity' for the pharmaceutical industry to persuade office-based physicians and hospital administrators of the need for further far-reaching structural reforms of the health care sector. This opportunity arises because all providers are faced with budgetary ceilings over the coming years. In the absence of structural reforms such transitional ceilings may become a permanent feature of the health care system. This is so, because from a pure cost containment point of view ceilings are likely to be successful. During the same time period (i.e. the next thee years) the industry should aim to engage in a dialogue with sickness funds and point out that it is them that stand to gain most from a shift towards structural reforms.

Further measures then those envisaged by the 1993 Health Care Act are required to strengthen market-based reform of the health care system. Some of these changes are listed in the next section. Most of these additional measures could be implemented in a relatively straightforward way, given that Germany is already embarking on a far-reaching structural reform programme. However, the fact that these measures have been excluded from the 1993

Health Care Act suggests that some are politically difficult to implement in the short term. We therefore list them as suggestions for the long-term reform.

6.8   LONG-TERM REFORM

6.8.1   The Funding Side of the Health Care System

6.8.1.1   Re-evaluation of the GHCP

Germany is one of the few countries that have a specifically defined Guaranteed Health Care Package (GHCP). The GHCP lists the health care goods and health care services, in kind or in cash, to which each member of each sickness fund is entitled. The entitlements are listed in the health care legislation (*Sozialgesetzbuch V - Gesetzliche Krankenversicherung*), Chapter 3, Paragraphs 11 to 68. They cover preventative care services, early diagnosis services, ambulatory services, some dental services, hospital services, medicines, some aspects of long-term care, monetary sickness benefits, and burial allowances.

A thorough re-evaluation of the entitlements listed in the GHCP is required. The aim should be to assess which services are essential to the health status of the individual, so that they should be covered by the social insurance system; and which services are not essential to the health status of the individual and thus should not be covered, in part or in total. In short, what appears to be required is a re-balancing of social solidarity and individual responsibility. The aim of the re-evaluation should therefore be to reduce the GHCP to a benefits package that only includes essential services (*Regelleistungen*).   Distinct from these should be additional services (*Wahlleistungen*) that can be bought as supplementary insurance by individuals.

The NERA Prototype provides guidance on how essential benefits can be distinguished from optional benefits. The aim is to define a GHCP that lists those services to which everybody is entitled irrespective of ability to pay; and to distinguish these form non-GHCP services that individuals may purchase in addition to the GHCP. The NERA Prototype recommends that the GHCP should be defined in terms of *medical conditions*, rather than treatments. The following three criteria might be used to determine whether or not a condition is within the GHCP. A condition is within the GHCP if all of the following criteria are *simultaneously* fulfilled:

1.   The inclusion of any treatment for the condition prevents an irreversible decline in the health status of the individual, or the public at large.

2.   The treatment for the condition is catastrophically expensive compared with normal income levels, so that the individual would find it difficult to finance the service.

3.   It is unreasonable to expect individuals to fund any treatment for the condition by saving up over their working lives, either because the need for treatment may arise before retirement, or because it is an uncommon occurrence, even in old age.

These three conditions are meant to serve as guidelines only when defining a GHCP. However, when assessing the list of entitlements in Germany, it becomes clear that the current GHCP is over-generous. This over-generosity of entitlements may lead people to use services because they are available, not because they need them. A generous GHCP means that individuals consume more health care than they would if they were given the choice of funding some of the services themselves (and not suffering bankruptcy and an irreversible decline in their health status). This leads to allocative inefficiencies and a higher health care expenditure than would be the case in a more efficient system.

Considering the list of entitlements under the current GHCP, and applying the conditions specified by the NERA Prototype to re-define it, would mean that several services would be excluded from the present GHCP. These include preventative care services such as immunisations (on grounds that informed consumers will purchase these themselves), several types of dental care, medical aids, glasses, types of support services (e.g. physiotherapy), categories of medicines (on grounds that these are usually not catastrophically expensive), visits to health care resorts (unless they prevent an irreversible decline in the health status), as well as most monetary benefits such as sickness money (these could be paid by the employer), and burial allowances. This list is not meant to be prescriptive; rather the list intends to make suggestions on how a GHCP might be defined. Any re-evaluation of the existing GHCP will require great care; this means in particular that consideration must be given to exemptions and entitlements.

487

6.8.1.2   Direct Payments to Sickness Funds

The 1993 Health Care Act envisages that, by 1996, most people will have a choice of which sickness fund they wish to join. Sickness funds must accept all comers, and a global risk adjustment mechanism will be in place. The current level of the GHCP remains unaltered for the time being.

While we generally endorse these reform policies, some concern about the workings of the system remain. To deal with these concerns may require further long-term reform. The issue is this: Freedom of choice of sickness funds, combined with open enrolment, can be expected to lead to a reduction of the premium differences that characterise the current system. In the new system individuals will 'shop around' for a sickness fund that offers low premiums, and they will have an incentive to do so until the premiums of all sickness funds are roughly equal (i.e. the 'sick' following the 'healthy'). This process, at least in theory, can be expected to take place irrespective of whether or not a global risk adjustment is in place. The fact that a risk adjustment mechanism will be in place is likely to speed up the equalisation of premiums across funds.

However, once premiums are (fairly) equalised across funds, funds may have fewer incentives to compete. This is the case for two reasons:

• First, funds cannot compete by offering different products. They must all offer a GHCP that is already over-generous and includes too many services.

• Second, funds' incentives to compete by offering lower premiums are undermined because:

    - they are not commercial organisations allowed to make a profit;

    - reimbursement negotiations with providers are still relatively centralised, thus making it unlikely that significant differences in the reimbursement levels for providers paid by different sickness funds will emerge; and,

    - the insured make no direct payments to their sickness funds that relate to the efficiency of the fund.

It is the latter point that matters most. The NERA Prototype recommends direct payments by the insured to sickness funds that are related to the efficiency with which sickness funds purchase health care on their behalf. These direct payments should in general be related not to risk (unless they have specifically been excluded from the general risk adjustment mechanism), but to the efficiency of the fund. Under the NERA Prototype, insurance funds have a strong incentive to negotiate directly with providers, and to slim down their reimbursement levels, since any efficiency gains made in this way feeds through in lower direct payments by the insured to their funds. Funds therefore have a much stronger incentive to compete on efficiency. This emphasis on *premium competition* is absent in the system envisaged by the German reforms, because there is too much emphasis on *cooperation* between funds. This cooperation takes the form of arriving at an acceptable global risk adjustment formula to distribute the total sum of premiums to funds. Direct residual payments from the insured to the insurance funds are the essential motivating force for competition in the system. Without direct payments, sickness funds have fewer incentives to become prudent buyers of health care services since all of their income is risk-adjusted anyway (albeit prospectively, not retrospectively). Direct payments reinforce the incentives for efficiency, provided that the direct payments are large enough to induce people to switch membership, and small enough to protect them from bankruptcy.

Whereas under the NERA Prototype a commercialisation of funds is desirable, it is not essential. Funds may be organised as for-profit, or not-for-profit organisations, but should at the very least be allowed to determine the salaries for those who act as managers. They should be encouraged to become customer-oriented in a competitive market. The best way to achieve this may be to transform them into commercial businesses, should that become politically acceptable.

6.8.1.3 *Lifting Remaining Membership Restrictions of Funds*

Company-based sickness funds, and to a lesser extent crafts' funds, may constitute a special problem in the new system. Under the 1993 Health Care Act, both groups of sickness funds can decide whether or not they wish to establish open enrolment. This means, unlike substitute funds, they do not have to introduce open enrolment. Few of the company-based funds will have an incentive to do so. Companies usually found their own sickness funds because the premiums paid by employees and employers are less than under any alternative.

This means that under the new system, some privileges remain. Currently approximately 12 percent of people in (western) Germany are enrolled with a company-based insurance fund (in eastern Germany the figure is approximately 8 percent). These funds may be able to continue to charge lower premiums because of the advantageous risk-structure of their members. In essence this means that they may continue to risk-select.

In order to establish a competitive insurance system it is essential that no such privileges should exist. NERA therefore proposes that a mandatory, rather than voluntary, opening of company-based funds should be introduced. This means that any remaining membership restrictions should be lifted. During a transitional stage, membership restrictions should be lifted only for that region from which a company largely recruits its employees.

6.8.2   The Provider Side of the Health Care System

6.8.2.1   Decentralisation and Competition

Our recommendations for long-term reform include the creation of a competitive market for health care services. In that market, competing sickness funds would purchase health care services from providers, either through open-market sales, or through long-term contracts. In the past the health care system was characterised by highly centralised negotiations that took place between sickness fund associations and provider associations, in particular the office-based physician associations. Under the new legislation most negotiations are to occur on a regional level. While endorsing this decentralisation, we also recommend that measures be taken to ensure that a truly competitive framework is established. This means that participants in the health care system should have freedom to conclude binding contracts (*Vertragsfreiheit*) on an individual, rather than a collective, basis.

To some extent decentralised, i.e. local, negotiations already take place in the hospital sector. For the ambulatory sector this is not the case. A system of negotiations between regional groups of office-based physicians and individual large sickness funds is therefore recommended. Sickness funds must also have the right to discontinue the accreditation of individual doctors to reduce any emerging over-supply of physicians. (The 1993 Health Care Act enables them to do so in the long run.)

Since sickness funds are expected to compete in the new system, it is essential that sickness funds do not join forces when negotiating reimbursement levels with providers. This means that there should be no *Länder* or federal association of sickness funds, other than for the purpose of risk-adjusting their members' premiums. Methods of reimbursement of providers should be left to the market participants. For physicians, these may include fee-for-service payments, capitation payments, or combinations of these. For hospitals, these are likely to be based on prospective cost-per-case payments.

6.8.2.2 Operating Costs And Investment Expenditure

At present, the investment expenditure of hospitals is funded mainly by federal and *Länder* authorities in Germany, whereas operating costs of hospitals are overwhelmingly reimbursed by the sickness funds. This means that the *Länder* governments make decisions about hospital investment projects with disregard to consequential operating costs, which they do not have to fund. Sickness funds, on the other hand, are obliged to pay the additional operating costs of new facilities of accredited hospitals, but are generally not able to influence the allocation of investment resources through the *per diem* payments they make.

It is proposed that individual providers are given more freedom and authority to decide about capital investment programs, and, if necessary, to raise funds through contractual income or through the capital markets. This means that hospitals should operate as business-like institutions that are independent from their owners as far as managerial control is concerned. Sickness funds, on the other hand, should become responsible to reimburse not only operating costs of hospitals, but also to remunerate their investment. This would provide the sickness funds with a much larger role in determining the allocation of investment funds. It would also mean that hospital investment would be financed by the insured through their premiums, rather than by the federal and *Länder* governments through taxation.

6.8.3   The Responsibilities of Government

6.8.3.1 Regulation

Under the these proposals for long-term reform, the role of the government would change considerably. From being an influential participant of the health care system, the government would step aside and cease to be a key player. Instead, it would supervise and regulate a largely competitive health care market. The main roles of the government would include:

*   to enforce and oversee competition among insurance funds, and among providers;

*   to set up an agency that would act as an agent for the mentally disabled and others who are unable fully to participate in the health care system;

- to grant licenses to sickness funds and providers; and,

- to assist in the collection of income-related health insurance fees.

The government would furthermore perform several functions for which it is currently responsible. These include the financing of teaching and public research facilities, and the approval of medicines.

A more immediate role of the government is to act as a facilitator in the setting up of the new health care system. This comprises several tasks, including the re-evaluation of the GHCP and the commercialisation of sickness funds.

6.8.3.2 Information

The government should also pass the necessary legislation to allow insurance funds, as well as providers of health care goods and services, to have unhindered access to the consumer by advertising their services, subject to ethical guidelines. Such a flow of information is essential in order to strengthen the individual responsibility of consumers and enable them to make better choices relating to health care.

6.8.4   The Responsibilities of Patients

6.8.4.1 Copayments

At present, German patients pay no copayments for visits to office-based physicians. Because the reimbursement system for physicians encourages strong competition and expansion of service volumes by doctors, the number of visits to physicians may be higher than would be necessary on medical grounds. These long-term reform proposals therefore include the introduction of copayments for physician services. Direct payments at the point of delivery may reduce the level of physicians' services without reducing quality or access. Direct payments may also lead to more cost-consciousness among patients, and may therefore increase efficiency.

Copayments for physicians and copayments for hospitals (which already exist) should be grouped together with copayments for medicines, medical aids and transport costs to determine an upper ceiling of copayments for patients. The ceiling sets an upper limit for copayments, and should be dependent upon the individual's income.

6.8.4.2   Patient and Consumer Groups

Patients, as well as insurance fund members, should be encouraged to form private consumer groups that monitor the health care system. In a competitive funding system it is particularly important that consumer groups scrutinize individual sickness funds and make recommendations to potential members. Consumer organisations may also be involved in setting up ethical codes relating to such issues as: the quality of services provided by physicians and hospitals; the inclusion of services in, or their exclusion from, the GHCP; or the procedures of sickness funds for handling complaints.

ANNEX 6.1 HEALTH CARE IN THE FORMER EAST GERMANY

6.1.1 Introduction

Unification of the Federal Republic of Germany and the former German Democratic (GDR) Republic took effect on 3 October 1990. Prior to unification, the GDR had a centralized and integrated, publicly financed and provided health service. With the exception of copayments for medicines, all other health care was provided free of charge. Services were funded mainly through general taxes and payroll taxes. Primary care physicians as well as clinicians were salaried and were under direct control of the government. A significant private health care sector did not exist. The life expectancy of east Germans was two to three years below that of western Germans.

Of special importance in the ex-GDR was the integration of ambulatory care and in-patient care. A range of different types of providers co-existed, such as medical practices, ambulatory clinics, so-called polyclinics, factory based clinics, and public hospitals. Polyclinics can be described as day care centres offering a range of ambulatory services to patients. Although patients had no guarantee of being treated by the same doctor at each visit, they nevertheless were rather popular with a majority of east Germans, as well as doctors. In 1989, there were 539 hospitals with 163,000 beds. Of these, 462 hospitals were owned by the government, 75 were owned by voluntary organisation, and 2 were in private ownership.

In the negotiations leading to the reunification of Germany, it was decided to bring the eastern system in line with the system in the Federal Republic. This involved a rapid and profound change of the organisation and financing of health care in the ex-GDR. The major changes are as follows:[57]

6.1.2 Sickness Funds

By 1991 a complete network of local sickness funds came into operation in eastern Germany. Substitute funds may also set up offices, and compete for members, if they wish. By June 1991, approximately 11.6 million people out of a population of 16.4 million people were statutory members of the following insurance funds:

---

[57] This section is largely based on Hurst (1991).

Table 6.10: Sickness Funds in Eastern Germany

13	Local Insurance Funds;
112	Company-based Funds;
37	Crafts' Funds;
2	Agricultural Funds;
1	Sailors' Fund;
1	Miners' Fund;
5	Blue Collar Funds; and,
6	White Collar Funds.

Total   177   Funds

The relatively small number of local insurance funds (which must cover the entire area of the ex-GDR) may seem surprising. This reflects the growing tendencies of local insurance funds to consolidate their basis by establishing geographically larger districts in order to become more competitive. In January 1992, the upper limit for insurance contributions (*Beitragsbemessungsgrenze*) was set at DM 43,200 ($17,000 1990). This is markedly lower than in western Germany, and reflects the lower living standards in eastern Germany.

Most people are insured compulsorily because of their low incomes. The setting up of sickness funds in eastern Germany is facilitated by the fact that their finances are relatively unaffected by unemployment which is much higher in the east. This is because the Federal Labour Office pays the health insurance contributions for the unemployed on the basis of their former earnings.

The insurance contribution rate to all sickness funds was set at 12.8 percent, the average rate for western Germany, for one year initially. From 1992, the setting of the contribution rate will be left to individual funds.

6.1.3   Office-Based Physicians

For medical and dental services, the statutory health insurers have agreed with the physicians and dentists on fees which are on average 45 percent below those prevailing in western Germany, reflecting the difference in living standards. The 1993 Health Care Act states that growth in physicians' budget should coincide with growth in the income levels of members for the years 1993 to 1995.

495

6.1.4 Hospitals

East Germany had an extensive system of polyclinics with multi-specialty out-patient departments which often affiliated to hospitals or university clinics. Because these polyclinics are not hospitals and because the physicians worked on a salaried basis, comparable to group practices that are in existence in western Germany, it was originally thought that it would be unlikely that they would survive in the new system. The 1993 Health Care Act appears to guarantee polyclinics a continued existence. Under current agreements reached in the unification treaty between the two Germanies, they are granted a five year period during which they act as providers and contract with the sickness funds. Many of the doctors in polyclinics are not young any longer, and hence will find it difficult to set up a private practise under new regulations. Therefore, polyclinics, one of the few achievements of the ex-GDR in the health care sector, are set to be gradually abolished. The 1993 Health Care Act effectively caps hospital budgets at their 1992 levels. Copayments for in-patient stays are lower than in western Germany: in 1993 they are set at DM 8 ($3.1 1990) for the first fourteen days; in 1994 this will increase to DM 9 ($3.5 1990).

Investment in buildings and equipment will be required in eastern Germany of approximately DM 20 billion ($7.7 bn 1990) to bring the standard up to that in western Germany. The majority of these funds will go to hospitals. The Federal Government is expected to provide annual funding of DM 700 million ($271 mn 1990) for the years 1995 to 2000. This sum is expected to be matched by the governments of the five eastern German *Länder*.

6.1.5 Pharmaceuticals

The pharmaceutical industry in the ex-GDR consisted of one *combinate* which had production facilities at various sites. On 1 July, these facilities were re-organised as private companies and were placed under the ownership of the *Treunhandanstalt*, which will seek to privatise them. The number of people working in the industry has decreased from 16,000 in 1990 to below 10,000 in 1991. In 1990, the estimated value of all sales was DM 2 billion ($0.8 bn 1990), of which 30 percent were exported, mainly to Eastern European countries.

In the first year following unification, the industry maintained its market share in eastern Germany, 80 percent, but this is unlikely to last as competitive pressure starts to build up. Production and quality standards are in general below west German standards.

In order to contain costs in the ex-GDR, the government demanded that manufacturers' prices for medicines supplied to eastern Germany should be 55 percent below prices in western Germany. This new rule, which came into effect in January 1991, was replaced in April by new regulations which stated that any deficit in expenditure on drugs incurred by insurance funds in eastern Germany should be financed by the pharmaceutical industry and the wholesale and retail pharmacists through price discounts. This new method has led to an effective price mark-down of approximately 25 percent (by March 1992). The major difference to the replaced regulation is that the new rule applies to the reimbursement levels which sickness funds pay rather than to manufacturers' prices. This is advantageous from the industry's point of view as it avoids re-imports to western Germany.

ANNEX 6.2 DATA TABLES

List of Tables

TABLE 1
POPULATION ACCORDING TO AGE GROUPS
(PERCENT)

	1950	1970	1985	1988
Male				
0-6	8.9	10.2	6.3	6.5
6-14	16.6	14.8	9.7	9.3
15-17	4.9	4.2	4.8	3.5
18-20	4.6	4.3	5.5	4.8
21-44	32.4	35.7	37.4	38.1
45-64	23.6	20.1	25.6	26.8
65 and above	9.0	10.7	10.7	10.9
Total	100	100	100	100
Female				
0-6	7.4	8.8	5.5	5.7
6-14	14.0	12.8	8.5	8.2
15-17	4.1	3.7	4.1	3.2
18-20	3.9	3.7	4.8	4.2
21-44	35.6	30.5	32.6	33.8
45-64	25.3	25.1	25.5	25.4
65 and above	9.7	15.4	18.9	19.5
Total	100	100	100	100
All				
0-6	8.1	9.5	5.9	6.1
6-14	15.2	13.7	9.1	8.7
15-17	4.5	3.9	4.4	3.4
18-20	4.2	4.0	5.2	4.5
21-44	34.1	33.0	34.9	35.8
45-64	24.5	22.7	25.6	25.1
65 and above	9.4	13.2	15.0	15.4
Total	100	100	100	100

Source: *Der Bundesminister für Geshundheit (1991), p.18.*

TABLE 2
LIFE EXPECTANCY AT AGE X

Completed Age X	1901/10	1924/26	1932/34	1949/51	1960/62	1970/72	1979/81	1986/88
Male								
0	44.82	55.97	59.86	64.56	66.86	67.41	69.90	72.21
1	55.12	62.24	64.43	67.80	68.31	68.20	69.91	71.88
5	55.15	60.09	61.70	64.47	64.68	64.49	66.09	68.02
10	51.16	55.63	57.28	59.76	59.88	59.68	61.22	63.10
20	42.56	46.70	48.16	50.34	50.34	50.21	51.63	53.37
30	34.55	38.56	39.47	41.32	41.14	41.00	42.28	43.88
40	26.64	30.05	30.83	32.32	31.91	31.77	32.94	34.46
50	19.43	21.89	22.54	23.75	23.10	23.05	24.19	25.50
60	13.14	14.60	15.11	16.20	15.49	15.31	16.41	17.55
65	10.40	11.46	11.87	12.84	12.36	12.06	13.00	14.05
70	7.99	8.74	9.05	9.84	9.60	9.35	10.01	10.90
75	5.97	6.50	6.68	7.28	7.20	7.17	7.59	8.21
80	4.38	4.77	4.84	5.24	5.24	5.36	5.70	6.06
85	3.18	3.50	3.52	3.72	3.76	3.92	4.32	4.43
90	2.35	2.68	2.63	2.66	2.69	2.81	3.36	3.25
Female								
0	48.33	58.82	62.81	68.48	72.39	73.83	76.59	78.68
1	57.20	63.89	66.41	71.01	73.46	74.32	76.44	78.23
5	57.27	61.62	63.56	67.61	69.78	70.56	72.61	74.35
10	53.35	57.11	59.09	62.84	64.93	65.70	67.70	69.40
20	44.84	48.09	49.84	53.24	55.17	55.97	57.91	59.55
30	36.94	39.76	41.05	43.89	45.53	46.30	48.20	49.77
40	29.16	31.37	32.33	34.67	36.09	36.77	38.60	40.11
50	21.35	23.12	23.85	25.75	27.00	27.65	29.36	30.78
60	14.17	15.51	16.07	17.46	18.48	19.12	20.69	21.95
65	11.09	12.17	12.60	13.72	14.60	15.18	16.63	17.82
70	8.45	9.27	9.58	10.42	11.12	11.63	12.87	13.96
75	6.30	6.87	7.09	7.68	8.16	8.59	9.58	10.48
80	4.65	5.06	5.15	5.57	5.85	6.16	6.91	7.57
85	3.40	3.76	3.70	4.02	4.17	4.37	4.90	5.34
90	2.59	2.92	2.72	2.89	3.03	3.16	3.59	3.74

Source: Der Bundesminister für Geshundheit (1991), p.23.

TABLE 3
GROSS DOMESTIC PRODUCT AND HEALTH CARE EXPENDITURE

Year	Gross Domestic Product (DM bn 1985)	Gross Domestic Product / Head (DM '000 1985)	Total Health Expenditure (DM bn 1985)	Total Health Expend / Head (DM 1985)	Total Health Expenditure As % of GDP
1981	1,740	28.2	151.4	2,455	8.7
1982	1,715	27.8	146.7	2,380	8.6
1983	1,742	28.4	148.0	2,410	8.5
1984	1,790	29.3	155.0	2,535	8.7
1985	1,825	29.9	158.5	2,597	8.7
1986	1,864	30.5	162.1	2,654	8.7
1987	1,890	30.1	163.5	2,678	8.7
1988	1,960	31.9	174.5	2,837	8.9
1989	2,023	32.6	166.8	2,688	8.2
1990	2,119	33.6	171.1	2,712	8.1

Source: *OECD (1991).*

TABLE 4
EXPENDITURE ON PRIMARY CARE

Year	Total Expenditure on Primary Care (Billion DM 1985)	Total Expenditure on Primary Care as a % of total Health Expenditure	Total Expenditure on Primary Care Physicians (Billion DM 1985)
1981	40	26.5	24
1982	39	26.7	24
1983	39	27.0	24
1984	41	26.8	25
1985	42	26.7	25
1986	42	26.5	25
1987	43	26.8	26
1988	45	26.0	27
1989	n.a.	n.a.	27
1990	n.a.	n.a.	29

Source: *OECD (1991).*

TABLE 5
NUMBER, TYPE AND MEMBERS OF INSURANCE FUNDS, FORMER AND NEW STATES OF GERMANY, 1991

Type of Fund	All Germany			Western Germany			Former East Germany		
	No. of Funds	No. of Members	% of all Members	No. of Funds	No. of Members	% of all Members	No. of Funds	No. of Members	% of Members
Local Sick Funds	277	23,615,146	47.3	264	16,470,312	43.0	13	7,144,834	61.7
Industrial Funds	796	5,427,565	10.9	684	4,523,679	11.8	112	903,886	7.8
Crafts Funds	188	2,239,270	4.5	151	1,997,018	5.2	37	242,252	2.1
Miners' Fund	1	1,350,619	2.7	1	930,647	2.4	1	419,972	3.6
Sailors' Fund	1	58,929	0.1	1	47,153	0.1	1	11,776	0.1
Agricultural Funds	21	721,666	1.4	19	715,015	1.9	2	6,651	0.0
White Collar Workers' Fund	13	15,767,367	31.6	7	12,952,188	33.8	6	2,815,179	24.3
Blue Collar Workers' Fund	13	733,871	1.5	8	692,339	1.8	5	41,532	0.4
Total	1,310	49,914,433	100	1,135	38,328,351	100	177	11,586,082	100

Source: *Bundesminister fur Arbeits - und Sozialordnung, Bundesarbeitsblatt, Nr. 4, Bonn 1991, p. 102.*

TABLE 6
EXPENDITURE OF INSURANCE FUNDS ACCORDING TO BENEFITS (DM million)

Year	Primary Care	Dental Care	Dent-ures	Pharm aceut icals	Aids & Remedies	In-patient Care	Sickness Money	Preven-tative Care	Mater-nity Care	Other	Total	In kind	In cash	Admin	Grand Total
1960	1,874	467	268	1,093	212	1,565	2,688	78	392	324	8,965	5,849	3,115	547	9,512
1965	3,194	953	401	2,020	372	2,947	3,698	146	680	499	14,914	10,545	4,368	871	15,785
1970	5,457	1,708	828	4,223	667	6,009	2,467	248	1,101	1,137	23,849	20,266	3,582	1,329	25,179
1975	11,258	4,129	4,180	8,901	2,581	17,534	4,664	1,009	1,689	2,172	58,170	51,704	6,446	2,819	60,989
1980	15,357	5,517	7,351	12,572	4,880	25,465	6,653	874	3,036	4,246	85,955	76,193	9,762	3,878	89,833
1981	16,490	5,936	8,109	13,630	5,272	27,321	6,439	906	3,248	4,727	92,203	82,456	9,746	4,187	86,390
1982	16,917	6,072	6,988	13,776	5,045	29,596	5,896	729	3,067	4,458	92,676	83,422	9,254	4,455	97,224
1983	17,763	6,280	6,664	14,449	5,234	30,969	5,781	725	2,955	5,073	95,897	86,593	9,303	4,699	100,692
1984	18,924	6,562	7,33	15,544	6,063	33,215	6,301	875	2,656	6,079	103,561	94,011	9,549	5,118	108,679
1985	19,660	6,656	7,666	16,602	6,512	35,049	6,378	955	2,736	6,486	108,703	98,891	9,722	5,404	114,107
1986	20,295	7,164	6,897	17,625	7,220	37,489	6,874	1,036	2,516	6,940	114,061	104,081	9,980	5,806	119,867
1987	20,965	7,370	6,283	18,888	7,848	39,211	7,391	1,167	2,383	7,418	118,930	108,545	10,384	5,966	124,996
1988	21,649	7,692	9,650	20,435	8,905	39,488	7,781	1,223	2,686	7,365	128,059	117,145	10,913	6,202	134,376
1989	22,652	7,693	4,861	20,216	7,825	40,814	7,779	1,279	2,773	7,344	123,241	111,943	11,298	6,572	129,926
1990	24,370	8,172	4,839	21,840	8,424	44,595	8,777	1,218	3,161	8,837	134,237	122,010	12,227	7,275	141,654

Source: *Der Bundesminister für Geshundheit (1991), p.176.*

TABLE 7
EXPENDITURE OF INSURANCE FUNDS PER MEMBER (DM)

Year	Primary Care	Dental Care	Dentures	Pharmaceuticals	Aids & Remedies	In-patient Care	Sickness Money	Preventative Care	Maternity Care	Other	Total	In kind	In cash	Admin	Grand Total
1960	69	17	10	40	8	58	125	3	15	12	331	216	115	20	352
1965	111	33	14	70	13	103	162	5	24	17	519	367	152	30	549
1970	178	56	27	138	22	196	109	8	36	37	778	661	117	43	822
1975	336	123	125	266	77	524	195	30	50	65	1,737	1,544	193	84	1,821
1980	433	155	207	355	137	719	265	22	86	120	2,432	2,152	276	109	2,542
1981	462	166	227	382	148	765	254	25	101	132	2,582	2,309	273	117	2,700
1982	472	170	195	385	141	826	232	20	84	124	2,587	2,329	258	124	2,714
1983	496	175	186	404	146	865	228	20	83	138	2,678	2,418	260	134	2,812
1984	525	182	204	432	168	922	245	24	74	169	2,876	2,610	265	142	3,018
1985	543	184	212	459	180	968	244	26	76	178	3,002	2,733	269	149	3,151
1986	557	197	189	483	198	1,029	261	28	69	185	3,129	2,856	273	159	3,289
1987	571	201	171	514	214	1,068	279	32	65	192	3,239	2,956	283	163	3,404
1988	585	208	261	552	241	1,067	290	37	73	115	3,461	3,166	295	168	3,632
1989	608	207	131	543	210	1,096	296	38	75	106	3,310	3,012	298	177	3,490
1990	642	215	128	576	222	1,175	362	32	83	139	3,538	3,177	361	192	3,734

Source: *Der Bundesminister für Geshundheit (1991), p.175.*

TABLE 8
ANNUAL AVERAGE OF MEMBERS' CONTRIBUTIONS ACCORDING TO INSURANCE FUNDS
(PERCENT OF WAGE)

Year	Total	Local Sickness Funds	Industrial Funds	Crafts Funds	Sailors Fund	Miners' Fund	Blue Collar Substitute Funds	White Collar Substitute Funds
1970	8.20	8.15	7.51	7.82	6.60	9.60	8.07	8.89
1975	10.47	10.64	9.43	10.38	9.00	11.90	10.17	10.70
1980	11.38	11.70	10.49	11.21	9.90	12.60	11.01	11.22
1985	11.80	12.09	10.29	11.26	10.50	11.60	11.33	12.10
1986	12.20	12.69	10.76	12.01	11.70	11.60	11.49	12.10
1987	12.62	13.16	11.18	12.66	12.30	12.36	11.62	12.42
1988	12.90	13.46	11.45	12.79	12.80	13.13	11.96	12.69
1989	12.90	13.48	11.47	12.74	12.80	13.30	11.96	12.68
1990	12.53	13.13	11.10	12.28	12.52	13.30	11.23	12.32
1991	12.20	12.74	10.85	11.94	11.90	12.70	11.01	12.04

Source: *Der Bundesminister für Geshundheit (1991), p.177.*

505

TABLE 9
HOSPITALS

Year End	Total			Public			Voluntary			Private		
	Hospitals Number	Beds Number	Beds per 10,000 People	Hospitals Number	Beds Number	% of beds	Hospital Number	Beds Number	% of Beds	Hospitals Number	Bed Number	% of Beds
1960	3,604	583,513	104.6	1,385	326,413	55.9	1,307	215,120	36.9	912	41,980	7.2
1965	3,639	631,447	106.5	1,365	348,364	55.2	1,291	230,787	36.5	983	52,296	8.3
1970	3,587	683,254	112.0	1,337	373,137	54.6	1,270	249,357	36.5	980	60,760	8.9
1971	3,545	690,236	112.2	1,340	377,477	54.7	1,248	251,780	36.5	957	60,790	8.8
1972	3,519	701,263	113.5	1,322	381,315	54.4	1,239	255,002	36.4	958	64,946	9.3
1973	3,494	707,460	113.9	1,330	386,489	54.6	1,217	253,252	35.8	947	67,919	9.6
1974	3,483	761,530	115.6	1,309	387,590	54.1	1,200	253,949	35.4	974	74,991	10.5
1975	3,481	729,791	118.4	1,297	389,429	53.4	1,187	257,365	35.3	997	82,997	11.4
1976	3,436	726,846	118.3	1,271	383,674	52.8	1,159	256,371	35.3	1,006	86,801	11.9
1977	3,416	722,953	117.8	1,258	380,083	52.6	1,141	255,003	35.3	1,017	87,867	12.2
1978	3,328	714,879	116.6	1,215	373,675	52.3	1,128	253,239	35.4	985	87,965	12.3
1980	3,234	707,710	114.8	1,190	370,714	52.4	1,097	248,717	35.1	947	88,279	12.5
1982	3,130	683,624	111.1	1,143	351,673	51.4	1,070	244,068	35.7	917	87,883	12.9
1983	3,119	682,747	111.4	1,133	351,885	51.5	1,069	242,570	35.5	917	88,292	12.9
1984	3,106	678,708	111.2	1,119	347,457	51.2	1,054	240,137	35.4	933	91,114	13.4
1985	3,098	674,742	110.6	1,104	343,044	50.8	1,049	237,565	35.2	945	94,133	14.0
1986	3,071	674,384	110.3	1,086	340,877	50.5	1,044	237,186	35.2	941	96,321	14.3
1987	3,071	673,687	110.2	1,073	339,365	50.4	1,044	235,671	35.0	954	98,651	14.6
1988	3,069	672,834	109.0	1,059	336,447	50.0	1,035	233,694	34.7	975	102,693	15.3
1989	3,046	669,750	106.9	1,046	333,239	49.8	1,021	230,728	34.4	979	105,783	15.8

Source: *Der Bundesminister für Geshundheit (1991), p.209.*

TABLE 10
COSTS PER HOSPITAL IN-PATIENT DAY (DM)

	1978	1979	1980	1981	1982	1983	1984	1985	1986	1987	1988	1989	1978-1989 +/-%
Doctors	23.67	25.93	28.22	31.76	33.99	35.68	36.20	37.34	38.86	41.22	42.49	45.04	90.3
Nursing	39.60	42.57	46.29	50.82	53.50	56.14	57.43	60.22	63.11	66.20	68.30	73.95	86.7
Medical/Technical	12.60	13.62	14.72	16.69	17.88	18.69	19.18	19.74	20.60	21.60	22.08	23.71	88.2
Functional	8.70	9.56	10.53	12.02	12.86	13.66	14.11	14.82	15.70	16.69	17.31	18.83	116.4
Clinical	7.0	7.44	7.78	8.32	8.08	8.17	7.68	7.42	7.33	7.43	7.29	7.33	4.6
Hotel	13.40	14.56	15.51	16.66	17.24	17.53	17.75	17.11	16.98	17.58	17.82	18.70	39.6
Technical	1.31	1.38	1.40	1.66	1.69	1.79	1.82	2.86	3.91	4.29	4.42	4.75	262.9
Administration	6.97	7.59	8.12	8.94	9.49	9.78	9.90	10.34	10.79	11.19	11.46	12.28	76.2
Other	3.64	4.10	4.21	4.83	4.56	4.59	4.44	5.10	5.28	5.77	5.98	6.77	85.99
Personnel Costs	116.88	126.75	136.78	151.70	159.29	166.03	168.51	174.94	182.56	191.97	197.14	211.36	80.8
Catering	6.97	7.11	7.50	7.87	8.08	8.21	8.38	8.46	8.50	8.38	8.48	8.87	27.3
Medical Supplies	23.54	24.91	27.57	30.40	32.49	35.78	38.15	40.44	43.26	45.64	47.81	51.26	117.8
Utilities	5.22	6.26	7.11	8.33	9.23	9.13	9.44	10.49	9.92	8.98	8.53	9.21	76.4
Non Medical Supplies	4.25	4.80	5.45	6.16	6.72	7.16	7.59	8.36	9.60	9.91	10.35	11.05	160.0
Administration	2.25	2.46	2.73	2.91	3.15	3.33	3.50	3.76	4.14	4.43	4.71	5.07	125.2
Central Administration	1.19	1.23	1.26	1.53	1.38	1.60	1.66	1.50	1.55	1.74	1.76	1.86	56.7
Overheads	0.39	0.48	0.54	0.63	0.70	0.71	0.83	0.80	0.72	0.96	1.01	1.06	170.5
Taxes, Insurances	1.13	1.22	1.35	1.53	1.80	1.99	2.09	2.01	1.83	1.91	2.05	2.28	102.0
Works	3.09	3.46	3.88	4.43	4.95	5.26	5.92	6.39	8.16	9.19	9.80	10.83	250.5
Consumers Goods	1.69	1.94	2.21	2.46	2.54	2.72	2.98	2.89	0.88	0.75	0.74	0.74	-56.4
Other	0.25	0.31	0.38	0.44	0.49	0.62	0.92	0.83	0.88	1.11	1.15	1.40	461.8
Non-Personnel Costs	49.97	54.18	59.98	66.69	71.53	76.51	81.46	85.95	89.44	92.98	96.40	103.64	107.4
Interest	0.27	0.34	0.64	0.99	1.00	0.67	0.60	0.56	0.46	0.41	0.40	0.58	114.0
Teaching Costs	1.16	1.31	1.32	1.51	1.59	1.77	1.89	1.83	1.99	2.05	2.10	2.24	93.5
Total	168.28	182.58	198.72	220.89	233.41	244.98	252.46	263.28	274.44	287.40	296.04	317.82	88.9
Deductions	13.35	13.91	14.44	17.46	19.12	18.73	19.92	18.04	18.24	18.81	17.51	21.19	58.8
Expenditure Costs	154.93	168.67	184.28	203.89	214.29	226.25	232.46	245.25	256.20	268.59	278.53	296.62	91.5
of which: Medical Services	64.83	70.82	78.34	86.79	92.55	100.30	104.72	111.00	117.01	123.62	129.41	136.56	110.6
of which: Nursing Services	43.42	46.73	50.45	55.52	58.52	61.32	62.79	65.70	69.09	72.34	74.44	80.73	85.9
of which: Hotel Services	46.67	50.12	55.48	61.13	63.22	64.64	65.03	68.54	70.10	72.63	74.68	79.33	70.0

Source: *Der Bundesminister für Gesundheit (1991), p.230.*

ANNEX 6.3 BIBLIOGRAPHY

Altenstetter, C. (1986), "Reimbursement Policy of Hospitals in the Federal Republic of Germany",4 *International Journal of Health Planning and Management*, 1, pp. 189-211.

Altenstetter, C. (1987), "An End to a Consensus on Health Care in the Federal Republic of Germany", *Journal of Health Politics, Policy and Law*, 12, pp. 505-536.

AOK-Bundesverband (1992a), "Fakten und Argumente zum Risikostruktur-ausgleich", *Intern*, 1.

AOK-Bundesverband (1992b), "Risikoausgleich ab 1993 machbar: AOK legt Modell zur praktischen Realisierung vor", *Intern*, 3.

Arnold, M. (1990), *Das medizinische Versorgungssystem in der Bundesrepublik Deutschland*, Deutscher Ärzte-Verlag, Köln.

Arnold, M. (1992), *Von der Urhorde zur Solidargemeinschaft - und zurück?*, unpublished manuscript.

Bayerische Rückversicherung (1991), "Social Security and Private Insurance: Long-term Care - The No. 1 Topic in the Future?" *Experts' Discussion No 11*.

Blendon, R., Leitman, R., Morrison, I. and Donelan, K. (1990), "Satisfaction with Health Systems in Ten Nations", *Health Affairs*, (Summer), pp. 185-92.

Bölke, G. (1990), "Auswirkungen der derzeitigen Finanzierung der Krankenhäuser in der Bundesrepublik Deutschland", *Das Krankenhaus*, pp. 303-310.

Brenner, G. (1990), *Die Reform des Einheitlichen Bewertungsmasstabes für ärztliche Leistungen in der Bundesrepublik Deutschland in den Jahren 1985-1988*, Deutscher Ärzte-Verlag, Köln.

Bundesministerium für Gesundheit (1992), *Info-Papiere zum Gesundheits-Strukturgesetz*, Bonn.

Bundesverband der Betriebskrankenkassen (1993), *Festbeträge für Arzneimittel, Preisinformationen zum 01. Januar 1993* (leaflet).

Bundesverband der Pharmazeutischen Industrie e.V. (1990), *Pharma Jahresbericht 1990*, Frankfurt.

Bundesverband der Pharmazeutischen Industrie e.V. (1991), Pharma Daten '91, Frankfurt.

Der Bundesminister für Arbeit und Sozialordnung (1990), *Soziale Sicherheit-Krankenversicherung*, Bonn.

Der Bundesminister für Gesundheit (1991), *Das Gesundheitswesen im vereinten Deutschland: Zusammenfassung und Empfehlungen*. Auszug aus dem Jahresgutachten 1991 des Sachverständigenrates für die Konzertierte Aktion im Gesundheitswesen, Bonn.

Der Bundesminister für Gesundheit (1991), *Daten des Gesundheitswesens, Ausgabe 1991, Nomos Verlagsgesellschaft*, Baden-Baden.

Deutsche Bundesbank (1991), "Recent Trends in the Finances of the Statutory Health Insurance Institutions", *Monthly Report of the Deutsche Bundesbank*, Frankfurt, pp. 24-36.

Deutscher Bundestag (1990), *Strukturreform der gesetzlichen Krankenversicherung - Endbericht der Enquete-Kommission des 11. Deutschen Bundestages, Band 1 und Band 2*, Bonn.

Dietz, O. (1989), "Die Zustimmung der Kassenverbände zur Pflegesatzvereinbarung", *Das Krankenhaus*, 1, pp. 8-11.

Dopson, L. (1988), "Health Care in Germany", *Nursing Times*, 84, pp. 33-34.

Eichhorn, S.(1989), "Health Services in the Federal Republic of Germany", in Raffel, M. W. (ed.), *Comparative Health Systems*, Pennsylvania State University Press, University Park and London.

Finsinger, J. and Mühlenkamp, H. (1989), "Einige Aspekte der Krankenhausfinanzierung in der Bundesrepublik Deutschland", in Duru, G., Launois, R., Schneider, F., Schulenburg, J. M., (eds), *Ökonomische Probleme der Gesundheitsversorgung in Deutschland und Frankreich*, Campus Verlag, Frankfurt, New York; Edition de la Maison des Sciences de l'Homme, Paris, pp. 157-176.

Gläske, G. (1990), "Festbeträge fuer Arzneimittel - Preiswettbewerb, wo aber bleibt die Qualität?", *WSI Mitteilungen*, 2, pp. 97-109.

Göbel, W., Reform of Health Services in the Federal Republic of Germany, pp. 462-478.

Henke, K.D. (1988), "Funktionsweise und Steuerungswirksamkeit der Konzertierten Aktion im Gesundheitswesen (KAiG)", in Gaefgen, G. (ed.), *Neokorporatismus und Gesundheitswesen*, Nomos Verlagsgesellschaft, Baden-Baden, pp. 113-157.

Henke, K.D. (1990), "The Federal Republic of Germany", in *Advances in Health Economics and Health Services Research, Supplement 1: Comparative Health Systems*, pp. 145-168.

Henke, K.D. (1991), "Alternativen zur Weiterentwicklung der Sicherung im Krankheitsfall", in Brümmerhoff, D., Henke, K.D., Ulrich, V., Wille, E. (eds.), *Finanzierungsprobleme der sozialen Sicherung II*, Duncker & Humblot, Berlin.

Henke, K.D. (1992), "Cost Containment in Health Care: Justification and Consequences", in Zweifel, P. and French, H.E. (eds.), *Health Economics Worldwide*, Kluwer, pp. 245-265.

Hurst, J. (1991), "Reform of Health Care in Germany", *Health Care Financing Review*, 12, pp. 73-86.

Iglehart, J.K. (1991), "Health Policy Report - Germany's Health Care System", *The New England Journal of Medicine*, Part I, pp. 503-508; Part II, pp. 1750-1756.

Infas (1988), *Aktuell - Infas Politogramm der Woche* (Nr 50).

Infas (1989), *Aktuell - Infas Politogramm der Woche* (Nr 3).

Kehr, H. (1985), "Inhalte und Probleme der neuen Bundespflegesatz-verordnung", *Die Ortskrankenkasse*, 23-24, pp. 831-836.

Kirkman-Liff, B.L. (1991), "Health Insurance Values and Implementation in the Netherlands and the Federal Republic of Germany", *Journal of the American Medical Association*, 265, pp. 2496-2502.

Knieps, F. (1992), "Organisationsreform", *Deutsche Ortskrankenkassen*, 18, pp. 625-633.

Knieps, F. (1993), "Die AOK im neuen Ordnungssystem der GKV", *Deutsche Ortskrankenkassen*, 4/5, pp. 152-162.

Krause, P. (1988), "Selbstverwaltung als mittelbare Staatsverwaltung: Ihre verfassungsrechtliche Problematik", in Gaefgen, G. (ed.), *Neokorporatismus und Gesundheitswesen*, Nomos Verlagsgesellschaft, Baden-Baden.

Leidl, R. (1988), "Training Health Services Managers: Improving Health by More Health Economics", *Health Policy*, pp. 25-37.

Lieber, M. (1988), "Gebührenordnung für Ärzte (GOÄ)", Textausgabe nach dem Stand vom 1. Juli 1988, Bundesanzeiger.

Loytved, H. (1980), "Der Wettbewerb in der Krankenversicherung", Dissertation, Universität Bayreuth.

Medizinisch-Pharmazeutische Studiengesellschaft e.V. (MPS) (1992a), "Pharmaceutical sector: Results of the Lahnstein meeting", *MPS Intern*, 5.

Medizinisch-Pharmazeutische Studiengesellschaft e.V. (MPS) (1992b), "The Health Sector Act has been passed - Industry must now draw the right conclusions", *MPS Intern*, 6.

Meyer, H. J. (1990), "Arzneimittelfestbeträge", *Pharmazeutische Industrie*, 52, pp. 391-398.

Meyer, H. J. (1991), "Arzneimittelfestbeträge", *Pharmazeutische Industrie*, 53, pp. 1-8.

Moran, M. (1992), "Between the Lines - Healthcare in Germany", *Health Service Journal*, pp. 20-23.

Neubauer, G. (1985), "Wahlen as Steuerungs- und Kontrollinstrument der gemeinsamen Selbstverwaltung", in Gaefgen, G. (ed.) *Ökonomie des Gesundheitswesens, Schriften des Vereins für Socialpolitik*, Duncker & Humblot, Berlin.

Neubauer, G. (1988), "Staat, Verwaltung und Verbände - Entwicklung der Ordnungs- und Steuerungsstrukturen in der gesetzlichen Krankenversicherung", in Gaefgen, G. (ed.) *Neokorporatismus und Gesundheitswesen*, Nomos Verlagsgesellschaft, Baden-Baden.

Organisation for Economic Co-operation and Development (1991), *OECD Health Data. Comparative Analysis of Health Systems* (Software Package), version 1.01, Paris.

Orth, G. (1985), "Grundzüge der neuen Bundespflegesatzverordnung", *Krankenhaus-Umschau* 12, pp. 905-911.

Pfaff, M. (1990), "Market Elements and Competition in the Health Care System of the Federal Republic of Germany", in Casparie, A.F., Hermans, H., Paelinck, J. (eds.) *Competitive Health Care in Europe - Future Prospects*, Dartmouth, Aldershot.

Piggin, J. B. (1987), "West German Healthcare: Gearing Up for 'Reform or Ruin'", *The Health Service Journal*, p. 1467.

Postina, T. (1992), Steigende Kosten im Visier, Pharma Verlagsbeilage, *Deutsches Allgemeines Sonntagsblatt*.

Sachverständigenrat für die Konzertierte Aktion im Gesundheitswesen (1991), *Stabilität ohne Stagnation? Sondergutachten 1991*, mimeo.

Sachverständigenrat für die Konzertierte Aktion im Gesundheitswesen (1992), *Ausbau in Deutschland und Aufbruch in Europa, Jahresgutachten 1992*, Nomos Verlagsgesellscahft, Baden-Baden.

Schlesinger, H. and Schulenburg, J. M. (1988), "Mehr Markt im Gesundheitswesen", *Journal of Institutional and Theoretical Economics*, pp. 396-402.

Schneider, M. (1991), "Health Care Cost Containment in the Federal Republic of Germany", *Health Care Financing Review*, 12, pp. 87-101.

Schulenburg, J. M., "Konkurrenz und Kollegialität - Der sich verschärfende Wettbewerb auf dem Arztleistungsmarkt: Erste empirische Ergebnisse", in Gaefgen, G. (ed.), *Systeme der Gesundheitssicherung im Wandel*, Nomos Verlagsgesellschaft, Baden-Baden.

Schulenburg, J. M., "Thesen zur Ordnungspolitischen Neugestaltung des Gesundheitswesens", in Farny, D., Felderer, B. (eds.) *Ordnungspolitik der Lebens- und Krankenversicherung*, VVW, Karlsruhe.

Schulenburg, J. M. (1982), "Die Arzthonorierung aus ökonomischer Sicht", *Wirtschaftswissenschaftliches Studium*, 5, pp. 235-237.

Schulenburg, J. M. (1983), "Report from Germany: Current Conditions and Controversies in the Health Care System", *Journal of Health Politics, Policy and Law*, 8, pp. 320-348.

Schulenburg, J. M. (1985), "'Pro-Competitive-Strategy' im Gesundheitswesen: Eine kritische Stellungnahme aus deutscher Sicht", in Hamm, W., Neubauer, G. (eds.), *Wettbewerb im Gesundheitswesen*, Bleicher, Gerlingen.

Schulenburg, J. M. (1988), "The Health Care System of the Federal Republic of Germany: Moral Issues and Public Policy", in Sass, H. M., Massey, R. (eds.), *Health Care Systems*, Kluwer, pp. 59-74.

Schulenburg, J. M. (1991a), *Health Care in the '90s: A Report from Germany*, pp. 95-105.

Schulenburg, J. M. (1991b), "The German Health Care System: A Close-Up View", *The Internist*, pp.10-12.

Schulenburg, J. M. (1992), *Weiterentwicklung des gegliederten Krankenversicherungssystems durch eine Organisationsreform, Verband der privaten Krankenversicherung*, Köln.

Shephard, G. (1988), "The West German Health Service", *The Health Service*, p. 9.

Southby, R., Hurley, B. (1991), "Healthcare for a New Germany", *Hospital Topics*, 69, pp. 20-24.

Sozialgesetze der Krankenversicherung '92 (1992), Verlag W Kohlhammer, Stuttgart, Berlin.

Der Spiegel (1992), "Kranker Medizin Betrieb - Der Ausgebeutete Patient", Hamburg, pp. 112-119.

Stone, D. A. (1991), "German Unification: East Meets West in the Doctor's Office", *Journal of Health Politics, Policy and Law*, 16, pp. 401-412.

Verband der Angestellten-Krankenkassen e.V., *Krankenhausrecht*.

Verband der privaten Krankenversicherung e.V (1990), *Die private Krankenversicherung im Jahre 1989*, Köln.

Zipperer, M (1993), "Gesundheitsstrukturgesetz stellt neue Weichen in der Gesundheitspolitik", *Deutsche Ortskrankenkassen*, 1/2, pp. 25-69.

CHAPTER 7

THE HEALTH CARE SYSTEM IN ITALY

Daniel Whitaker

National Economic Research Associates
Madrid

7.1   SUMMARY

Structure

Italy has a national health service. Nevertheless, health care services are provided by the public and private sectors in roughly equal proportions since much of the private provision is contracted by the public sector. Public funds are channelled through 21 regional authorities to over 600 local health care units. A significant number of people have additional private health insurance.

Aggregate Level of Expenditure

Two thirds of Italy's health care services are financed from public funds. Virtually all of this is raised by the central government. The health care budget is determined at the national level through negotiations between the Ministry of Health and the Treasury and Budget Ministries. However, it is the 600 local health care units that ultimately make expenditure decisions. They regularly overspend their budgets. The deficits are passed back through the regions to the central government.

Incentives

Primary Care Physicians: General Practitioners (GPs) are paid on a capitation basis. This, combined with a substantial surplus of qualified doctors, creates a financial incentive for GPs to minimise the care they themselves provide while catering to their patients' needs and wishes in terms of prescriptions and referrals. One way in which GPs do this is by referring patients to private specialists and hospitals. Primary care providers have no incentive to control costs.

Hospitals: Public hospitals are allocated a global budget. However, since these budgets can be overspent, the hospitals are not under much pressure to control costs. Public hospitals have no financial incentive to ensure patient satisfaction. *Private hospitals* charge the public sector on a *per diem* basis, and thus have a financial incentive to maximise the number of low-cost patient-days. When treating private insurance policyholders, they have a financial incentive to maximise the charge, subject to not being removed from insurers' lists. Private hospitals do have an incentive to control costs, but always subject to providing patient satisfaction.

Funders: The private medical insurance market is relatively under-developed. Private insurance organisations have an incentive to minimise their outlays on health care expenditure. One way in which they do this is by operating a positive list of acceptable private providers.

Medicines: Pharmaceuticals must be approved by central government, which also sets the prices that may be charged. A positive list of prescribable medicines is drawn up from those that have been approved. There is a national 50 percent copayment for most publicly prescribed medicines, and the number of exemptions to this charge has recently been reduced. Some regional governments have recently raised the copayment level within their region.

Issues

- Because of the almost total lack of any incentive to control costs, public health care expenditure in Italy is very difficult to control.

- The ease with which patients may obtain private treatment at public expense adds to the costs. When public facilities are unable to buy high technology equipment, for example, the same equipment is purchased by the private sector and offered under contract to public patients.

- Waiting lists exist in some areas of the public sector, but the ready availability of private provision makes them comparatively rare.

Current Reforms

Various proposals for reform are currently before parliament. These include:

- charging individuals from households whose annual income exceeds L40mn ($23,300 1990) either higher copayments or the full cost of SSN services.

- allowing Italian citizens to opt out of the public health care sector;

- making Italy's regions responsible for meeting deficits and giving them greater power over copayments; and

- increasing the autonomy and professionalism of management in public hospitals.

Political Environment

The central government has recently been given a strong incentive to contain costs by its agreement to the Maastricht conditions for fiscal convergence. The current government deficit must be substantially reduced. Pressure is also growing in Italy's northern regions for greater political decentralization.

7.2   STRUCTURE OF THE HEALTH CARE SYSTEM

7.2.1   The Health Care System in Context

Italy's constitution "considers health a fundamental right of the individual" and "guarantees the free provision of health care to the poor".

Since 1948, Italy has been a parliamentary democracy. Strict proportional representation has meant that coalitions have been necessary in all of the 51 governments since the war. To date these have all included Italy's largest party, the Christian Democrats, and excluded the second largest, which recently changed its name from "the Communist Party" to "the Party of the Democratic Left" (PDS). The 1948 constitution calls for decentralisation of power, and authority has increasingly been transferred to the 21 regions and their constituent communes.[1]

The economy is mixed, and the large public sector has so far been less affected by privatisation policies than in some other EC countries. However, important changes in this regard are included in the government's programme to reduce drastically the budget deficit, announced in early July. One of the original EC members, Italy in fact faces greater pressure than most other large member states upon its public finances as a result of the convergence conditions agreed at Maastricht. Substantial inequalities remain between the more developed north of the country and the poorer south.

Italy's national health service, the *Servizio Sanitario Nazionale* (SSN) was effectively founded by Law No. 833, also known as the Health Reform Law (*legge di reforma sanitaria*), on December 28 1978. Law No. 833 begins by stating that "The Republic will protect health as a fundamental right of the individual and interest of the community through the national health service" - an almost direct quote from Article 32 of the Constitution. The Act followed earlier legislation that had unified health insurance contributions, placed hospitals under public boards and passed responsibility for hospital financing to the country's regions, in 1958, 1968 and 1974, respectively. Prior to the SSN, the health system was made up of numerous health funds offering varying coverage, with a bias toward labour market participation and characterised by pluralism in provision.

---

[1]   King (1987), pp. 330-345.

Italy's SSN provides for comprehensive health insurance coverage and uniform health benefits for all citizens, subject to copayments for certain services. It is organized on three levels: national, regional and local. The Ministry of Health is responsible for national health planning, the establishing and enforcement of standards and the overall administration of the SSN. More importantly, it is also responsible for the SSN's finance. The public health budget is set in the annual Finance Act and distributed among Italy's 21 regions by the Health Ministry according to prearranged parameters.

There is constant conflict between the central and regional government over public health expenditure needs, with central government's estimates always falling significantly below those of the regional governments and the local health units (*unite sanitarie locali* - USL). Regional governments are then responsible for using these resources to ensure the provision of health care to all citizens within their jurisdiction. The operational side of this responsibility is delegated by the regions to the USLs. Regional health plans are drawn up to specify goals, guidelines, investment programmes, staffing levels and priorities, but the efficacy of this varies across regions.

The USLs are the key element of the SSN. In 1992 there were 659, though their number often varies, with regional governments combining or splitting USLs in search of greater efficiency. The USL provides a broad range of health services - including hospital administration, diagnosis and treatment of illness at general and specialist levels on an out-patient, day-patient and in-patient basis, provision of medicines, rehabilitation and preventative care. Each is responsible for the health of populations of between 50,000 and 200,000. USLs are supervised and reviewed by a board nominated by local councils, and are managed by professional administrators on a fixed term contract.

Law 833 allows the SSN to contract out the delivery of medical health services to the private sector and this has come to represent an important aspect of the SSN. Subsequent legislation and decisions by the Constitutional Court give patients the right to go to uncontracted providers when services are not readily available in public or contracted facilities.

In common with much of Italy's public sector, constitutionally-mandated decentralisation of (expenditure but not revenue-raising) powers combines with a lack of decisive national political leadership to create weak vertical lines of control. Parliament has so far failed to approve any of the government's national health plans, though their innocuous nature makes indifference a more plausible explanation than political opposition. The importance of patronage in Italian politics has led to power-holders doing their best to incorporate in legislation as many opportunities as possible for the exercise of discretionary administrative decisions. Political interference in the USLs is also a problem, as is corruption - unsurprisingly given that health is the largest expenditure item in the regional governments' budgets. Total expenditure has been steadily rising (at an annual rate of 5.3 percent between 1984 and 1989).

7.2.2   General Features of the Finance System

The SSN is funded from three main sources: a dedicated payroll tax in the form of insurance contributions, a grant from general national taxation, and copayments. Health care services provided by the private sector, where not purchased by the SSN, are paid for by private medical insurance (subscribed to by an estimated 16 percent of the population) and from out-of-pocket funds.

The payroll tax combines health insurance, social security insurance and pension contributions, and is levied on both employers and employees. All employed workers have to pay a contribution currently rated at 10.95 percent of their salary. Tradesmen, businessmen, farmers and the self-employed pay a lower rate. Self-employed income, and income earned by self-employed workers outside their principal employment, is subject to a lower rate than national insurance and is paid entirely by the employee. To a marginal extent, the SSN is also supported by contributions from regions and communes, though this is limited by these entities' weak revenue-raising powers. A 1972 tax reform abolished almost all regional and local taxing powers.[2]

Copayments and coinsurance are required from SSN patients for medicines, specialist ambulatory treatment, diagnostic and laboratory tests, medical appliances and glasses. A copayment for hospital treatment had to be withdrawn following protests from patients and trade unions.

In 1990 it is estimated that 28 percent of total health sector funding came from general taxation, 35 percent from national health insurance, and 34 percent from private health insurance and copayments (the estimate of the tax component is likely to be increased because deficits are belatedly covered). The SSN budget is set by central government in the annual Finance Act. This contains two important items: the National Health Fund (*Fondo Sanitario Nazionale - FSN*) into which payroll health contributions are paid, and the

---

[2]   France (1991c) p. 3.

amount by which this will be supplemented from general taxation in order to meet the Ministry of Health's budget for health care expenditure.

The national health budget is divided into capital (generally around 5 percent of the total) and current spending. The capital component is based on the cost of those capital projects proposed by the regions which are approved by the Ministry of Health (and the Inter-ministerial Committee on Economic Planning).[3] Legislation mandates that a portion of capital purchases is made from suppliers based in the south of the country, though this law is rarely adhered to. The capital component of the national health budget has been falling in recent years,[4] both in absolute and relative terms, probably because it is easier for the central administration to control such spending.

The regional governments each receive a share of the national current expenditure budget and distribute this between their USLs. Previously, this distribution was based on a complex formula involving population size, average age and mortality levels and other characteristics, including historical spending levels (which favoured central and north-eastern regions).[5]

However, from 1992 onwards, the distribution is almost exclusively based on population.[6] There is also lagged compensation for in-patient transfers between regions, which is likely to be developed further in the future. A small portion of the health budget is retained by the Ministry of Health, for administration and national campaigns such as that against AIDS. While the capital funds are earmarked, current funds may be allocated as regions and USLs see fit, though they are subject to centrally fixed levels of minimum provision.

Within total state health expenditure, the tax-financed component has recently been growing at the expense of the contribution component. Total public health expenditure in 1990 was budgeted at L61.2 tn ($39.8 bn 1990), and 1991's budget was increased to L78.8 tn ($48.2 bn 1990), but actual expenditure is generally well over the budget estimate, and this deficit is normally carried over into the next year's budget. In 1990, it was estimated that the regions

---

[3]   Garattini (1992), p. 62.

[4]   France (1988a), p. 214.

[5]   Arcangeli *et al.* (1988), p.111, also Camara dei Diputati (1992b).

[6]   Ministero della Sanità (1987), pp. 1-5.

overspent their FSN allocations by 19 percent, with the Marche region managing a 34 percent overspend.[7] The regions accuse the government of inadequate funding of the SSN, and ignoring health care needs.

7.2.3   General Features of the Delivery System

Of 1989's total SSN current expenditure of L67,172 bn ($46.6 bn 1990), it is estimated that 52 percent went on hospitals (45 percent public; 7 percent contracted); 18 percent on pharmaceuticals; 11 percent on GPs and specialists; and 4 percent on preventive care.[8]   Altogether, if payments to GPs and pharmacies are excluded, around 13 percent of the total went to the private sector, and this share has remained relatively constant over time.   There has been some change in the composition of other elements of SSN spending in recent years, with a declining share going to both public and contracted hospitals.   The fastest growing items have been contracted specialists; medicines dispensed through pharmacies; and preventive care, all of which more than doubled in terms of real cost between 1984 and 1989.   Provision of private specialist and hospital care for patients who pay either through insurance or out-of-pocket has also been increasing and accounted for around 20 percent of total health care expenditure in 1989.

Neither the regions nor USLs (who in 1989 received 93 percent of their income from transfers) have any significant own-source revenue.   Nevertheless they enjoy considerable autonomy over spending the funds allocated to them by central government.   Once they have allocated the funds from the SSN, regions are supposed to regulate the organization and administration of the USLs to ensure effectiveness and efficiency.   The main responsibility for primary health care and the provision of medicines lies with the USLs, although some regions retain important powers regarding the financing of medicines.

Public hospitals are in theory regulated by the Health Ministry but in most cases are directly administered by the USLs.   The USLs also enter into contracts with private providers to cover treatment of patients under the SSN, although conditions are set by the regions and the Ministry of Health. Regions are responsible for the training of auxiliary personnel (nurses, technicians) and for keeping health care personnel up to date on new techniques.   Patients may

---

[7]   ISIS (1991b), p. 5.

[8]   Garattini (1992), p. 75.

move between GPs and GPs may refer patients to private specialists and hospitals when public ones are unavailable.

Governance of the USLs is in the process of moving from a political-administrative model to a medical-managerial one. Until recently USLs were governed by a Management Committee (*Comitato di Gestione*), whose members are appointed by the commune(s) in whose jurisdiction the USL operated. Criticism of politically-inspired mismanagement were common. In March 1991, legislation transferred executive management power within the USLs to a technical commissioner selected by the region. A Trust Committee (*Comitato di Garanti*) replaces the Management Committee. While its members are still appointed by the commune, the legislation establishes criteria aimed at guaranteeing they are primarily of a technical-professional background and the new body as a whole has reduced powers.

Although some USLs are well run, problems in USL management have included irregularities in contracts with suppliers and employees, excessive absenteeism, under-usage of expensive equipment, hidden deficits and generally inadequate auditing arrangements. The recent introduction of Treasury officials to regional USL audit commissions, and the extension of such commissions' responsibilities, may help. In some regions, the USLs have considerable autonomy from the commune, and are often seen as a level of local government, if only because of their spending power (in 1989 they accounted for around 25 percent of sub-central government public expenditure). Generally, vertical lines of control are weak, and the relationship between regions, communes and USLs is still not yet well-defined.

USLs are nominally divided into districts (*distretto sanitario di base*) with populations of about 10,000, although most decisions are taken at the USL level. Administrative arrangements vary between regions, but many USLs have the following divisions: hospitals; GP and pharmacies; maternal and child health; occupational health; public health; and mental health and psychiatry.

USL professional health staff may be employed full-time on salary, or they may be in full-time private practice, receiving a capitation allowance for each patient, or some combination of these. Non-medical personnel are normally on salary, as are a substantial proportion of hospital medical staff, though this varies according to the region. Contracts may be full-time or part-time. SSN contracts with health personnel must be established on a national basis after triennial negotiations between representatives of central and local government and the trade unions or professional associations (*organizzazioni sindacali*) of each occupational category. For SSN doctors (and other hospital employees) in regions with a substantial private presence it has been common practice also to work in a private facility. Recent regulations prohibit this.

7.2.4 Inputs and Outputs of the System

According to official Italian sources, total health care expenditure in Italy amounted to 7.2 percent of GDP in 1989, of which 5.5 percent was publicly-funded. This compares with figures of 6.6 percent and 5.2 percent respectively in 1984. The OECD estimated per capita health expenditure in 1990 to be $1,113 (1990 dollars), marginally below the median for all OECD countries. As elsewhere in the OECD, there has been an upward trend in real health expenditure in Italy for some time. Between 1984 and 1989, for example, public real current expenditure rose 28.3 percent. Chart 7.1 illustrates the sources of funding and the proportion of spending by sector.

Chart 7.1
Expenditure on Health Care in Italy, 1989

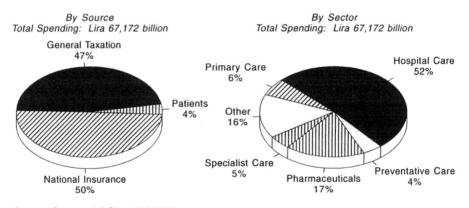

Source: Camara dei Diputati (1992)

Infant mortality in 1988 was 9.3 per 1,000 live births; perinatal mortality was 12.3 per 1,000 (1988); life expectancy was 73 (1987) for men and 79 (1987) for women. At age 80, life expectancy was 6 (1987) for men and 8 (1987) for women. Some 14 percent of the population were aged over 65 in 1989, while the dependency ratio (the number of people aged 0-15 or 65 and older, divided by the number aged 16-64) was 0.49 in 1991. A relatively low 39 percent of Italian mortalities occur in hospitals. This is due, in part, to a shortage of long-term care beds.

Italy's health system is very well-endowed with high technology equipment. This includes: lithotripters, of which Italy was recently estimated to have 111 compared to 15 in the UK, CT scanners, magnetic nuclear resonance (MNR) and therapies such as dialysis.[9] Rapid diffusion has generally followed early introduction, with the private sector playing an important role. The opportunity cost has been less activity in other areas, such as transplants, although Italy was, in fact, something of a pioneer of transplant technology. Kidney transplantation in Italy began in the 1950s. Some 658 kidney transplant operations were carried out at 24 centres in 1988, and a waiting list of 4,000 patients was reported. Heart transplants have taken place since 1985 (with around 200 in 9 centres in 1988), and liver transplants since 1981 (less than 100 being carried out in 6 centres in 1988).[10] Around 60 percent of lithotripters are located in private health care facilities.

[9]   Kirchberger (1991).

[10]   Bos (1991).

7.3   ANALYSIS OF INDIVIDUAL SECTORS

7.3.1   Key Participants in the Health Care System

The key participants of the Italian health care sector are as follows:

- patients;
- payers;
- the primary health care sector;
- the hospital sector (acute, out-patient, day-patient, community care, long term, mental health);
- the pharmaceutical sector; as well as
- other participants;

The main relationships between these participants, and the flows of finance and services between them, are shown in Chart 7.2.

7.3.2   Patients

The Italian population was 57.65 million in 1990, all of whom are eligible for SSN treatment. Though there has been a measure of convergence, marked regional differences remain. Northern Italians are, on average, older than southern ones, due to both greater life expectancy and a lower birth rate. 14.3 percent of the national population were over 65 years of age in 1989, though more than 20 percent of the inhabitants of Liguria (a popular retirement destination) and only 10 percent of Campania's population are over 65. Around 6 percent of the national population were over 75 in 1989. With the birth rate one of the lowest in the world, the Italian population profile will continue to age. The increase in older citizens is likely to be balanced by decreasing numbers of children, leaving the dependency ratio overall, broadly constant. Italy is expected to be the first OECD country to have more dependants than workers.

A national survey[11] revealed that the average number of days in 1987 for which an Italian was inactive due to illness was 6.5, with higher incidence in northern regions (Liguria's average was 8.2, while Puglia's was 5.9). The average number of days confined to bed in the same year was 4.7, with marginally higher incidence in the south. In-patient days per capita were 1.9 in 1989, well below the OECD average of 2.8. However, hospital admissions

---

[11]   ISIS (1991a).

Chart 7.2
Key Participants in the Health Care System in Italy

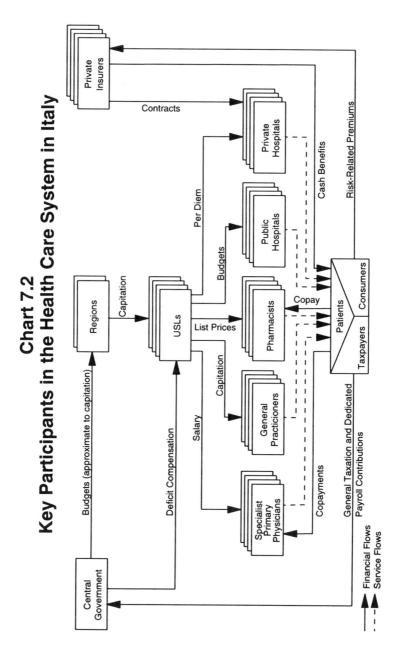

as a percentage of the total population were 16.6 in 1989, above the OECD average of 16.1. The average length of stay in hospital has fallen from 27.0 days in 1960 to 11.7 days in 1989 (equal to the OECD average), though this remains above the goal of 9 days set in the original national health plan of 1978.

There is little geographical variation of causes of death, although respiratory system-based disease is somewhat more prominent in the south, while attacks on the nervous system are more common in the north. Of Italians between 15 and 64 years of age, 32 percent described themselves as smokers and 8 percent as ex-smokers.

Some evidence suggests that consumption of health care services is related to educational level rather than income, with better-paid but similarly-educated self-employed Italians consuming an amount close to that of industrial workers. However, recent studies suggest that better-educated Italians' consumption of health care is similar to the rest of the population in terms of volume (number of consultations, days in hospital), but somewhat biased towards costlier procedures.

In principle, the SSN enjoys substantial popular support. However, there is frequent media criticism of waiting lists and of the overcrowding that occurs in some hospitals. A 1991 survey[12] of seven European nations revealed that Italians were the most dissatisfied with their health service, although some observers have attributed this to a generalised Italian feeling of frustration with state services. A growing awareness of the financial difficulties within the health care sector does appear to be leading to greater acceptance of the need to contain expenditure.

Beyond the health care system, Italian public services in general attract widespread criticism for their perceived inefficiency and quality problems. Rather than there being a negative attitude towards profits being made from the provision of health care, there tends to be criticism of particular private sector strategies, such as doctors employed in both the SSN and the private sector who direct patients toward the latter in order to increase their earnings. However, in general, the existence of the private sector is seen as beneficial since, given SSN-financed access, it serves to widen patient choice.

---

[12]   Schieber *et al.* (1991).

Support for the principle of public provision does not prevent a large number of patients from evading charges whenever possible, particularly, according to most observers, in the south, and often with the collusion of GPs. Favoured techniques include using old-age relatives to buy medicines, thus avoiding the copayment which all but pensioners and low-income households must pay.

Tax evasion by potential patients remains a serious problem in Italy, and reduces the number of contributors to the national health fund (FSN) and central government revenues in general. Amongst the majority who do pay their taxes, contribution levels to the FSN have not yet become a controversial political issue, though the prospect of regions being allowed to levy new taxes in order to support health spending has met with objections. Uncertainty about true levels of individual's income results in abuses of means-testing when it is applied to copayment exemptions, thus acting as a constraint on selective policies.

Patients have an increasing demand for, and expectation of, health care provision in private health care facilities (especially when it is at the SSN's expense). The preference for private provision is particularly strong regarding gynaecology and obstetrics (which together had 65 percent of their consultations in the private sector), and weakest for paediatrics and cardiology (where the private sector attracted 44 percent and 39 percent of consultations, respectively). Private care is becoming increasingly used for certain types of major general surgery, for which the public sector used to be preferred. Private health care providers are proportionately more important in the south. This is primarily due to the historical lack of public provision there, and most private providers are contracted to the SSN.[13]

Patients reportedly often feel aggrieved if refused USL authorization to go to contracted (private) hospital providers, particularly where they perceive private services to be significantly superior. Where they exist (more often in northern regions), restrictions on choice in the private hospital sector are more difficult for patients to accept when contrasted with the relative freedom of choice they have in choosing GPs and paediatricians, and in choice of contracted not-for-profit hospitals.

Doctors are generally respected by patients in Italy, though, especially in the case of GPs, they command a somewhat lower reputation than in some other

---

[13]   France (1991b), p. 11.

countries. This may be due both to their oversupply and to their relative lack of training. A recent survey[14] carried out by the *Istituto Nazionale di Statistica* (the official national statistical office) indicated substantial support for hospitals. According to this survey, 38 percent of Italian hospital patients were "very satisfied" with their doctor, and 52 percent were "reasonably satisfied". However, the proportion who were "very satisfied" ranged from 48 percent in the northwest to 25 percent in the south and islands. Nurses received marginally lower approval ratings in all regions, while hygiene and meal standards were generally still less appreciated. However, faith in hospitals may, together with social change, explain the continuing increase the proportion of births taking place in hospitals, and the increase in institutionalisation of the elderly.

There is a substantial demand for financial protection against the risk of illness. Large scale medical insurance (often work-based) has a reasonably long history prior to the founding of the SSN. In the 1970s and early 1980s there was a rapid expansion in individual private health insurance. Growth rates have been lower during the last few years, but company health insurance plans (to complement or even substitute for SSN care) are becoming increasingly common.

Patient organisations have been a recent feature of the Italian health care sector. Aggrieved patients may now go to their local *tribunal per i diritti del malato*, which will publicise doctors and USLs they believe to be at fault, and in some cases seek prosecution. Health care issues, particularly concerning copayments, can be important electorally. Old people have influence over government policy through membership of pensioner organisations, and these in turn, are represented in trade union federations.

7.3.3 Payers

7.3.3.1 Overview

The main payers in the Italian health care system, apart from taxpayers, are those whose employment and employees are officially registered. SSN copayments and private health insurance contributions represent smaller, but still important sources of funds for the system. The part of this revenue that represents public expenditure is channelled through the central government to the regional governments, and then to the USLs. The USLs spend their

---

[14]   ISIS (1991b).

revenues (and more, expecting additional central government funds to cover the deficit) on the health care services of public and private contracted providers.

Private medical insurance companies also use premium income to purchase private health care services. Copayments are retained by pharmacists and ambulatory providers; the corresponding reduction in USLs' reimbursement obligations is then deducted from the central administration's funding of the region but only ex-post (thus allowing an improvement of USLs' cash-flow).

7.3.3.2 Employers, Employees and Other Taxpayers

Taxpayers, who generally pay in two ways - once in dedicated payroll taxes, and once through general taxation - and employers, who must also pay a payroll tax, are the ultimate funders of the SSN. Those active, as either employers or employees, in Italy's large informal economy make no contribution to the SSN based on such activity. The problem of widespread tax evasion is thought to substantially reduce government income.

The payroll tax combines health insurance, social security insurance and pension contributions (though these are clearly differentiated), and is levied on both employers and employees. The payroll tax is paid, via ENPAS (*Enti Nazionale Previdenza Assistenza Dipendenti Statali*) in the case of public employees and INPS (*Istituto Nazionale Previdenza Sociale*) in the case of other employees, into general central revenue. The current contribution currently rate is 10.95 percent of salary. Of this amount, the employee pays 1.3 percent and the employer 9.65 percent.

Tradesmen, businessmen, farmers and the self-employed pay a lower rate, equivalent to 7.5 percent of their taxable income, plus a nominal flat fee (irrespective of income). However, in 1988 the self-employed, who represented over 30 percent of the total labour force, were estimated to contribute only 13 percent of the FSN. There is an assessment annual income threshold for contributions which is currently L40 mn ($23,300 1990). Any amount over this elicits a contribution rate of 4 percent on earnings. For salaried workers, the employee pays 0.2 percent and the employer 3.8 percent of such income. No contribution is levied on income above a second assessment ceiling, currently 100 mn Lire ($58,300 1990). The same contribution rates (called the *tassa sulla salute*) apply to any income an employee or pensioner earns from an independent activity or part-time occupation. Pensioners must pay 0.9 percent of their income if it exceeds a threshold which is currently set at L18 mn

($10,500 1990) p.a.[15]   Until recently, there was also a minimum annual contribution payable by tradesmen, businessmen and the self-employed equal to L648,000 ($378 1990), and equal to L324,000 ($189 1990) for farmers. This measure was aimed at generating guaranteed income from those who declare (possibly fraudulently) low incomes, but was overturned by the Constitutional Court.

General income taxation is on a progressive scale, with a top marginal rate of 50 percent for incomes over L359.7 mn ($220,000 1990) in 1991.

7.3.3.3   Copayments

Increasingly, SSN patients are becoming important direct contributors to the SSN's revenues via the expanding list of products and services on which they must make copayments.   At present, the following copayments and coinsurance is required from SSN patients:

- *Drugs*: L3,000 ($1.75 1990) minimum per prescription L1,500 ($0.88 1990) for antibiotics) with maximum of two drugs per prescription; 50 percent of retail price (30 percent on a limited number of traditional, unbranded drugs for historical reasons) with maximum of L50,000 ($29.15 1990) per prescription; positive list of which drugs qualify. Note: In 1992 at least one region (LN210) had unilaterally raised its main copayment rate from 50 percent to 60 percent.

- *Ambulatory Medical Services*: Ambulatory medical services are free but with a L15,000 ($8.75 1990) copayment for specialists.

- *Diagnostic and Laboratory Costs*: For diagnostic and laboratory costs there is a 30 percent copayment, with a L1,000 ($0.58 1990) minimum and an L80,000 ($46.64 1990) maximum.

- *Medical Appliances*: Reference prices for prostheses, hearing aids and glasses exist. Coinsurance is available up to a maximum of 50 percent.

- *Dental Treatment*: Dental treatment is free, though dentures are not covered as part of SSN benefits.

- *Hospital Treatment*:   For hospital treatments, a copayment was introduced but was withdrawn after protests from trade unions and patients.

---

[15]   Dirindin (1992), p. 5.

- *Transport*: Generally there is no entitlement for transport available within Italy, though there may be some reimbursement of foreign travel for treatment unavailable domestically.

Pensioners and low-income families are in theory excused copayment obligations. However, since 1991, this has only been the case if local authorities can pay their copayments. This is because other SSN patients have proved adept at avoiding copayments. This can be done by arranging for people who qualify for exemptions to collect the drugs, or by ruses such as persuading GPs to have them admitted to hospital, where medicines and diagnostic tests are free. Local authorities were considered best able to detect such fraud, though since they were offered no extra funds to meet the cost of copayments, in much of the country the effect has been to abolish copayment exemptions.

7.3.3.4 Private Health Insurance

Some 16 percent of the population have their own private health insurance.[16] There was strong growth in private insurance coverage growth during the early 1980s but recently it has remained broadly stable. A 1988 survey of private hospital patients with insurance showed that only a third were covered for all hospital expenses and over half had first taken out a policy between 1980 and 1985. Within private health insurance a distinction has to be made between company schemes, which offer employees additional benefits in the event of sickness, and private complementary or comprehensive health insurance schemes offered by for-profit commercial insurance companies. Private medical insurance in Italy tends to be relatively unsophisticated,[17] and several of the commercial insurance schemes are known to be experiencing difficulties.[18] According to Marsh & McLennan Italia, the costs to Italian insurance companies of meeting their obligations exceeded their income by around L74 bn ($51 mn 1990) in 1989.

The company-based health plans are quite extensive in some sectors (heavy industry, the chemical industry, financial companies, the energy sector and the transport sector), and represented an estimated 58 percent of the private insurance market by health care expenditure in 1988. The benefits offered by

---

[16]   Bevan, France and Taroni (1992), p. 22.

[17]   Borgonovi and Meneguzzo (1990), pp. 225-226.

[18]   Schneider *et al.* (1991), p. 189.

both types of private insurance schemes are designed specifically to fill the gaps not covered by the SSN benefits. These may include private hospital and out-patient treatment, dental treatment, daily sickness benefit (to compensate for loss of earnings), and daily hospital benefit. Policies generally tend not to cover SSN copayments, though some company-based schemes may do so. Risk coverage varies between schemes, but there may be no choice within them, and some risks (such as AIDS) are always excluded. Coverage for family members is common. Premia for company complementary insurance schemes tend to be between 0.5 percent and 1 percent of earnings, and portability of schemes between jobs is not usual.

Some private health insurance schemes operate preferred provider lists, with copayments required for treatment from other providers. In the commercial private insurance plans (which represent an estimated 42 percent of the private insurance market) the premium depends on the policyholder's current age, age on entry to the plan, and the scope of benefits. Premiums are then calculated according to an index scheme that takes into account current costs in the SSN.

Private medical payments are tax deductible. Due to the SSN's perennial financing problems, proposals are currently being considered for encouraging more health insurances (*mutualità*) for individual professional groups, offering services that are not merely complementary to those of the SSN.

Several foreign insurers have been attracted to the Italian medical insurance market, such as the French company *UPA*, *Allianz Pace* of Germany, *Zurigo Assicurazioni* of Switzerland and several Austrian insurers. Total premia collected in 1991 were L1,100 bn ($673 mn 1990), a rise of 20.1 percent in nominal terms on 1990, though it is unclear from the data what change in the volume of policies this implied.[19] The share of total insurance premia taken by medical insurance rose from 2.1 percent in 1985 to 3.6 percent in 1990.

7.3.3.5 Government and the USLs

The central government attempts to govern expenditure on health care by setting the national health annual budget. The budgetary process involves a national health plan, normally for a term of three years, which establishes the criteria (currently based mainly on population size) for the regional distribution of the FSN's funds.

---

[19]   Fausto (1990), p. 233.

The arm of central government most concerned with health spending is the Ministry of Health, which has responsibility for national health planning, the establishing and enforcement of standards and the overall administration and financing of the SSN. The Treasury and Budget Ministry also have a strong influence on health spending and this may be expected to increase in the light of growing alarm about the public deficit. USLs are already required to send quarterly accounts to the Treasury as well as to the Ministry of Health, and USLs' three-member auditing committee must include one Treasury member.

The Health Ministry is advised by three important bodies. The National Health Council (*Consiglio Sanitario Nazionale* - CSN, containing 40 members) gives its opinion on most measures concerning the SSN and publishes a detailed report on national health conditions. It is composed of representatives of the Ministry of Health and the Treasury, the Ministry of Social Security and Employment, the regions, local government associations, medical organisations and technical experts. This varied composition means that the CSN's views may often differ from those of the Health Ministry. The Health Institute (*Istituto Superiore di Sanità* - ISS, with a staff of 2,500), a technical research and advisory body, has special responsibility for approving and classifying medicines. The ISS is accountable to the Ministry of Health, though it may offer advice to all sectors of the SSN. Finally, the Health Council (*Consiglio Superiore Sanità*), is made of academic experts and advises the Minister of Health.

The regional governments' primary responsibilities consist of producing regional health plans every three years (which must be consistent with national health plans); allocating financial resources between USLs; defining USLs' territories and organisational structure; setting guidelines particularly in the area of capital investment; and indicating what use should be made of contracted private providers. A legal requirement for regions to cover USL deficits has been on the statute books for some time, but it has yet to be enforced.[20]

USLs, over which the local communes have what was a strong but is now a declining influence, are allocated resources by their regions, divided into capital and current spending. Actual expenditure for many USLs is often over the budget, eventually being covered by supplementary funds from central government. Although the USLs are responsible for health care provision

---

[20]   Schenkluhn (undated), p. 8.

within their own territory, it is the national government that sets the patient contributions to the SSN, sets pharmaceutical prices and copayments, sets doctors' fees and decides which medicines will be eligible for reimbursement.

The attitude of regions and USLs towards health care policy and reforms, and towards the role of the private health care sector, depends to some extent on the political colour of their administrations. Regional laws are subject to central scrutiny before they acquire force. The final arbiter of the legitimacy of disputed regional legislation is the Constitutional Court.

7.3.3.6   Economic Incentives

The link between health care spending and taxes is not such as to provide individual taxpayers with an incentive to economise on the use of SSN facilities. In general their incentive is to get as much as possible for their, already spent, contributions. In the Italian context that may mean two things: persuading the SSN to pay for superior treatment from private sector providers; and avoiding copayments if possible.

Central government seeks to control expenditure but, in the end, has to cover the expenditure decisions of more than 600 separate USLs. The USLs have no direct economic incentives to economise on expenditure. Efforts are being made to tighten the supervision of their activities. However, other than price-setting, the only effective control on their spending relates to capital expenditure. This might be expected to exert a longer term constraint on their capacity to deliver increasing quantities of services, but the effect is rather to divert their expenditure towards private facilities which are not subject to the same restraints.

Private health insurers tend not to reimburse the copayments required from individuals. This avoids the dilution of the disincentive effect of copayments. In practice private insurers concentrate largely on supplementing the core services provided by the SSN. In doing so, they are permitted to, and do, select risks, notably by differential premia.

7.3.4   Primary Health Care Sector

7.3.4.1   General Practitioners and Paediatricians

Within the primary health care sector, which accounted for an estimated 30 percent of total health care expenditure in 1989, a distinction should be drawn between general practice and ambulatory treatment by specialists. Specialist treatment, which need not require referral, is provided by hospitals' out-patient departments, public health centres and contracted private surgeries. Primary health care absorbed close to 31 percent of the budget for SSN health care in 1989 - of which payments to general practitioners contributed almost 7 percent, specialists 6 percent, primary care prescriptions an estimated 16 percent, the *Guardia Medica* 1 percent, with the remainder being used to fund community health services.

The central figure in the primary care health sector is the general practitioner (GP), who acts as a gatekeeper to the health care system, judging his patients' need for specialised treatment and curing less complicated ailments himself. GPs are usually doctors working under contract to the USL and treating patients at the expense of the SSN. Patients register with a GP (*medico di fiducia*) or, if under 14, paediatrician (*pediatra di fiducia*) who are also usually contracted by the USL. The paediatricians were established because GPs were considered inadequately trained to deal with children's problems (and also to provide more employment for doctors), but many parents take their children to the GP anyway.[21]

In 1988 there were 59,129 GPs and 4,679 paediatricians practising, two thirds of whom are in the provincial capitals, where one third of the country's 57 million population lives. There is also an unbalanced regional distribution of physicians, with 0.98 GPs per 1,000 adults in north eastern regions and 1.39 in southern ones. Every Italian resident is supposed to be registered with a general practitioner or paediatrician. The maximum list size is 1,500 for a GP (1,800 for a doctor who began practice before 1979) and 800 for a paediatrician, though a 1990 study found the average GP's list to be under 900.

In 1989, a further 13,000 doctors worked for the *Guardia Medica*, an arrangement that covers all general practitioners' work at night and weekends. The *Guardia Medica* was created in 1982 mainly, according to many observers, to boost young doctors' employment. The rate of unemployment and

---

[21]   *Ibid*, p. 16.

underemployment among qualified doctors is currently estimated at 17 percent. This oversupply is an important part of the explanation for the relatively large numbers of doctors employed by the SSN, since the Italian state feels to some extent responsible for the provision of work and employment for these doctors.

Italy's 25 medical schools substantially oversupply the labour market for doctors, though student numbers are now falling and it is predicted that the supply of doctors will equal demand by 2010. Upon graduating and taking a further exam, any doctor can set him/herself up as an unsupervised general practitioner. In fact, most work in hospitals, as locums in general practice or hold posts in the *Guardia Medica* before entering general practice. When retirements, deaths and resignations of doctors increase the average number of patients in a geographical zone to over 1,000 per doctor, the doctor highest on the waiting list is offered recruitment to that zone. Often such a doctor starts with no patients on his list, and many young doctors struggle for years with only a few hundred patients and a correspondingly low income. Indeed, 40 percent of general practitioners have list sizes of under 500 patients.[22] Many doctors do not succeed in attracting a viable number of patients and, after several years, abandon general practice.

Compared to other OECD countries, there is an unusually large number of general practitioners in Italy. In 1988, the national ratio of GPs was 1.17 per 1,000 adults, substantially higher than the World Health Organisation's recommended target. There were only 0.56 paediatricians per 1,000 children, however, well below the official target of 1.4 per 1000. Physician contacts (including specialists and hospital doctors) were 11 *per capita* in 1988, almost double the OECD average of 6 *per capita*. Public expenditures per physician were $72,926 in 1988.

7.3.4.2 Payment Arrangements

Since 1978 GPs and paediatricians have been paid a capitation fee by the USL. Prior to this, payment was on a fee-for-service basis. The capitation rates vary somewhat according to the length of experience of the doctor (GPs with 20 years of experience, for example, receive a 30 percent higher rate than the fee for doctors who have practised less than 6 years), the age of patients and the region. In addition, there are series of further payments, comprising a small office allowance; a computer allowance (L1.2 mn per year and only available

---

[22]   Pringle (1991), p. 473.

to 15 percent of general practitioners in 1991); a staff allowance (approximately 20 percent reimbursement); a paper records allowance (around L40 mn per year); an allowance for working in sparsely populated or unpopular areas; and a subsidy in the form of waivers of doctors' national insurance contribution payments.

While a general practitioner with an above average list size has an income comparable to that of a GP in the UK, the income of one with a small list size is dramatically less. One indication that surgeries may be under-equipped was that in April 1990 GPs were awarded an extra sum for the purchase of answering machines, instruments for performing minor surgery and a refrigerator to preserve serum. The *Guardia Medica* are paid on an hourly basis.

Italian GPs wanted to extend payment structures beyond capitation fees and fixed allowances. They seemed to have succeeded when the 1987 contract specified 31 qualified services which would be remunerated on a fee-for-service basis. But several months later these payments were discontinued because more extensive use was made of this itemised billing than had been anticipated. The method of remuneration and the amount of payment are set at the national level by the central government after consultation with representatives of the doctors. USLs have to pay for GP's services but have no influence over the economic incentives influencing GP's performance.

7.3.4.3 *Practice Organization*

Almost all Italian general practitioners work alone, rather than in partnerships. This is the result of both the culture of general practice[23] and the contract GPs have with the USL. Since capitation forms such a high proportion of a doctor's income and overhead costs are low, group practice offers little financial advantage. Since all practices are covered by the *Guardia Medica*, the benefit of an after hours rota also is absent, and those few doctors in group practice still feel the need to employ locums for holiday cover. Employed staff - secretaries, receptionists and practice nurses are extremely rare. A recent survey found that only 5,000 practitioners use any medical computer system, with some 70 varieties of system in use.[24]

---

[23]   Passerini (1990), pp. 16-18.

[24]   Sanesi (1990), pp. 43-44.

Attempts to encourage group practices were made with the 1987 contract for GP's remuneration. If three doctors join together they receive a 4.7 percent higher capitation fee, higher practice allowances and higher risk compensations. So far, these incentives have not had much effect and the number of GPs working in group practices is thought to be only around 1 percent.

The Italian GP has traditionally worked in two or three jobs at the same time, either in another ambulatory institution or in a private or public hospital. This means that "clinical drift" (of patients towards hospital doctors) has not mobilised Italian GPs to combine general practices into health centres as it has done their counterparts in other European countries. There is also no well developed community care sector that GPs might wish to gain control over. Thus primary care in Italy is fragmented between GPs and community health care. There is also gives an incentive for GPs to refer SSN patients to their second (and possibly more lucrative) place of work. However, the 1991 Finance Act prohibited GPs and hospital doctors from holding more than one contract with a public or contracted institution.

7.3.4.4 Patient Choice

The local USL has a list of practising doctors from which prospective patients may select. The USL issues each registered patient with a medical card called the *Libretto Sanitario Personale*, used to record the main details of the patient's medical history. Officially patients are then expected to seek treatment with the GP with whom they are registered. However, a patient can change doctors without giving a reason, whereas the GP must give a justification for removing the patient from his list.[25]

Referral to specialists is usually done by the GP, with the USL playing a co-ordinating role, though gynaecologists, opticians and dentists can be consulted without prior referral. GPs also refer patients in the case of laboratory tests and medical diagnostic establishments. A four day rule applies, which means that if the public laboratory (or any other ambulatory facility) cannot provide a service within four days, patients have the right to go to private contracted facilities with the bill met by the SSN.

Residents in southern regions depend on ambulatory care to a considerably greater extent than do those in the northern and central regions. This

---

[25]   Quaranta (1985), p. 130.

tendency is reflected in the budgets of USLs, with northern and central USLs spending considerably less of their current expenditure budgets on private contracted and extra-contractual hospital care.

7.3.4.5   Specialists, Health Centres and Diagnostic Facilities

Before the creation of the SSN, the largest sickness fund, INAM, had created its own network of health centres, staffed by contracted specialists. With the formation of the SSN, out-patient departments were created in all public hospitals and became a new feature of the health care sector, but the health centres (*assistenza specialistica ambulatoriale convenzionata interna*) continued to exist, and have been augmented by growing numbers of both public and private facilities. The role of specialists is limited to diagnosis, since they are not permitted to perform minor operations and they do not follow up patients in hospital. However, specialists may also have part-time contracts within hospitals. In the north, specialist clinics are more common, while in southern Italy, specialists are more likely to work single-handed.

Reimbursement of specialist ambulatory care is difficult to analyse since each facility tends to develop its own arrangements and little data is compiled. Specialists that work in public facilities (numbering 18 to 20 per 1000) are either salaried USL employees or, if contracted on a part-time basis, tend to be paid on an hourly basis (*plus orario*). In private facilities, specialists contracted to the SSN are likely to receive a set fee-per-service. The fees are determined by national contracts, infrequently renewed by the Ministry of Health. If private medical treatment is given within the out-patient clinic of a public hospital, 5 percent of the doctor's fee is payable to the hospital, though it is unlikely that this will cover overheads. There are frequent complaints that GPs do not do enough to try and solve patients' health problems, preferring to refer them to specialists. In 1990, expenditure on contracted specialist care was 3.3 percent of total USL expenditures.

Some specialist services come out of the hospital component of the USL's budget, and some come from the primary care component. Thus it is difficult to determine total expenditure on specialist care. Copayments currently exist, but have been introduced and withdrawn several times in the past. The 1991 Finance Act allowed the SSN to contract for the first time with limited liability companies and partnerships in the ambulatory sector, whereas previously contracting was only possible with individual specialists.

7.3.4.6   Physicians' Associations

The most professionally and politically important organisation is the *Ordine di Medici*, to which all practising doctors must belong. The *Ordine* is capable of having physicians either de-contracted from the SSN, or banned from practising altogether. It is represented in the official organs that monitor prescriptions, as well as in other institutions.

The *Societa Italiana di Medicina Generale* was formed in 1982, and, with 8,000 members, is the largest physician association organised on a voluntary membership basis.[26] The society publishes a journal, *Medicina Generale*. There are other voluntary professional groupings according to specialisation, the largest of which are: SUMAI (specialist doctors), ANPO (hospital doctors), ANAAO (hospital assistants) and AMC (physicians with public functions). The only non-commercial bulletin received by all members of the medical profession is the *Bolletino d'Informazione sui Farmaci* (Pharmaceutical Information Bulletin), published by the Ministry of Health.

7.3.4.7   Economic Incentives

GPs are the "gatekeepers" of the specialist and hospital services. They are paid on a capitation basis and so have an incentive to hold down the costs that they incur in treating their patients. They also typically work alone, with few support services or facilities. Hence they have an incentive to refer patients on to some other part of the system whenever possible. This is reflected in comparatively high referral rates to specialists and to testing facilities.

On the other hand there is no disincentive to Gps prescribing expensive drugs or specialist treatments, and this may be a way of retaining the loyalty (and capitation fee) of patients who are free to move to another GP if they wish.

Unlike many other countries, Italian specialists do a significant amount of publicly funded work outside the hospitals. Their remuneration arrangements are varied, but consist largely of either time payments or fee-per-service. Such arrangements, in general, tend to encourage over-provision of treatment.

---

[26]   Pringle (1991), p. 472.

There appears to be no incentive for primary care doctors to work with, or encourage, potentially cost-saving community health or preventive care activities.[27]

7.3.5 Hospital Sector

7.3.5.1 Hospitals

For the purposes of this study a distinction is drawn between hospital in-patient and day-patient treatment (discussed here) and ambulatory treatment (see Section 7.3.4). All public and many private hospitals have out-patient departments providing ambulatory specialist treatment, but these have a function similar to non-hospital specialist facilities. Expenditure on hospital care is believed to have represented almost 55 percent of total public spending on health care in 1990.

Based on contracting arrangements there are five types of hospital in the Italian health care system:

- *Pure Public Facilities*: Pure public facilities are financed and managed by the USL and constitute hospitals, day hospitals, ambulatory services, clinical laboratories, rehabilitation centres.

- *Not-for-profit Providers*: Not-for-profit providers are university teaching hospitals, public research hospitals, ecclesiastical hospitals, which may also deliver ambulatory care. These are self-managed, though their compensation for SSN treatments comes from the USLs.

- *For-profit Providers under Contract with the SSN*: These include hospitals, ambulatory clinics, diagnostic centres, rehabilitation and nursing homes;

- *For-profit Providers*: For-profit providers deliver care to SSN patients on an extra-contractual basis;

- *"Pure" for-profit Providers*: These institutions rely entirely on private patients who pay out of their own pockets or through private health insurance;

Official statistics group the pure public and the not-for-profit institutions together, treating both as being in the public sector. This means that the private sector is restricted to for-profit providers, each of which may provide

---

[27]   Schenkluhn (undated), p. 14.

service on more than one contractual basis. In 1989, 90 percent of private facilities had some contract with the SSN.

At present, hospital care under the SSN is delivered in 1,074 pure public hospitals, which in 1988 had almost 77 percent of the national stock of beds and 81 percent of SSN patients; by 84 not-for-profit hospitals, with 6.5 percent of the bed stock and 8 percent of SSN patients; and by 616 for-profit hospitals, with 26 percent of the bed stock and 11 percent of SSN patients. There are a small number of private beds in public hospitals.[28] The total number of public hospital beds in 1989 was around 369,000. It is widely agreed that this represents an excess of hospital beds. In 1989 there were 7.5 public hospital beds per 1,000 persons, compared to the figure of 6.0 established as optimal in the initial national health plan. As a result, the in-patient occupancy rate, was only 70 percent in 1989 (compared to an OECD average of 80.2 percent for the same year). This is low, representing a significant inefficiency in the hospital sector. Day hospitals represent a small but expanding part of the hospital sector.

Under-utilisation of beds is significantly worse in the public sector. For instance, an official report in 1991 showed that general surgery beds achieved a 69 percent occupancy rate in public hospitals and a 83 percent rate in contracted private hospitals. Under greater central pressure in recent years, however, numbers of public beds are being cut and hospitals being closed. In contrast to the excess of hospital beds, there is a shortage of nursing home beds, though this represents a more efficient form of long-term care for the elderly.[29]

As with other aspects of health care, there is significant geographical variation of provision in the hospital sector. Due to regional differences in hospital treatment quality, there is a certain amount of movement by patients from one USL area to hospitals in another. Pronounced variations also exist in the public-private mix within the hospital supply structure. While just under 37 percent of hospitals in Italy as a whole are private, this figure varies from 13 percent to 54 percent between regions. Private hospitals have tended to play a greater role in the supply of hospital care in the southern regions than in the northern regions. Nationally, some 87 percent of private hospitals' income came from the SSN in 1989.

---

[28]   Borgonovi and Meneguzzo (1990), p. 228.

[29]   Schneider *et al.* (1991), p. 187.

However, private hospitals have in general tended to offer only a limited range of clinical procedures, together with long-term care for the aged and mentally and physically disabled. In 1991, 66 percent of all beds for mental illness were in the private sector, 57 percent for long-stay, 57 percent for rehabilitative care and 88 percent for physiotherapy. Although some private (generally non-contracted) institutions are now starting to offer increasingly complex procedures with a relatively high content of advanced technology, the continuing regular migration of southern residents to northern and central public hospitals suggests that private hospitals in the south are not seen as good substitutes for public hospitals.

7.3.5.2 Public and Private Provision

The SSN uses mainly publicly-owned and contracted private hospitals, clinics and laboratories, though non-contracted private facilities are increasingly being used. If not-for-profit providers meet certain requirements, the SSN is statutorily obliged to contract with them. A prerequisite for admission to any hospital under the SSN is an application for admission from the patient's doctor and an admission certificate (*documento d'assistenza*) from the patient. These formalities may be postponed in cases of emergency. Copayments for SSN hospital treatment were introduced in 1989, with pensioners and low-income families exempted. But this was abandoned after a trial period due to its unpopularity.

If public institutions cannot satisfy a patient's demand within four days, access to private provision must be granted. Once the patient has obtained an authorization from the USL to use contracted services, this will not specify which provider to use, and the patient may choose (since reimbursement rules are nationally fixed). However, some high-cost services (such as magnetic nuclear resonance) are deliberately excluded from the national list of reimbursement. In such cases, the region in question decides its own reimbursement policy.

Under the original reform design, the SSN was to contract out medical services only if public providers are being utilised to the full. This was therefore intended to represent an interim solution, persisting only until public provision could be expanded. But the private sector has come to be an indispensable part of SSN in-patient health care provision, especially in the south and in some central areas. The share of SSN services met by private contracted providers has been broadly constant since 1982. The reason for this continued reliance on private provision is debateable. It may be that private services remain complementary, or it may be that there is some public-private collusion to maintain the contracted private sector's share of the SSN market. In areas of non-provision of certain services by the public sector (such as some parts of the south), contracted hospitals may effectively be operating monopoly franchises.

Initially, there was a clear division between the SSN (including services provided by contracted private hospitals) and the private sector. However, this distinction has become increasingly blurred, because of the growth of extra-contractual hospital services. This involves the reimbursement by the SSN of part or all of the medical costs incurred by patients when they are authorised to go to private providers.

7.3.5.3 Payment for Hospital Services

Though bench-mark hospital tariffs are set at the national level (with small adjustments at the regional level), it is the USLs that must settle accounts with contracted and extra-contractual private clinics. Payment for private hospital services is done on a *per diem* basis. These are renegotiated every year. It is only through the National Association of Communities (ANCI - *Assemblea Nazionale dei comuni Italiani*) that USLs are represented at these negotiations. Services provided by public and contracted hospitals are free at the point of delivery. Only for uncontracted hospitals are patients required first to pay, applying later for reimbursement (up to regionally agreed maxima).

Several observers describe the daily rates that private hospitals are paid as being below the daily costs of public hospitals (measured by estimated total costs divided by patient days), even though the average length of in-patient stay is longer for private hospitals.[30] In fact, due to the inherent differences between the two sectors, comparisons should be treated with extreme caution. Public hospitals must provide an almost complete range of services, under more inflexible working arrangements than private hospitals. The private sector can pick the most profitable services. There are also important differences in the treatment of amortisation,[31] and if the shift to private provision leaves public capacity unused there is an argument for including this as a cost of private provision.

---

[30] Grattini (1992), p. 51; Schenkluhn (undated), p. 30.

[31] Desideri and France (1991), p. 11.

Apart from an intentional policy by private providers to prolong stays in the private sector, estimated cost differences may also reflect a different treatment profile, with private hospitals providing more long-term care, geriatrics and rehabilitation. The different profile probably reduces the possibility of competition and substitution between the public and private sectors and may also help to explain the stable share of private hospital expenditure. Further, private hospital costs may be lower partly because of lower staffing ratios. Private providers, on the other hand, are allowed by Italian tax legislation to write off investment expenditure and can raise investment capital on the financial markets. Furthermore, SSN reimbursements to contracted providers include an allowance for capital expenditure.

7.3.5.4 Competition

The majority of private hospitals deny that they seek to compete with the public sector, though this is disputed. Non-contracted private institutions are more likely to admit to such competition. Many contracted and non-contracted private hospitals buy advertising space (television, radio and open air) in order to publicise their services.[32]

Within the contracted sector there is a separation between price-setting at the national level, and delivery decisions (often in the form of GP referrals) at the local level. Hence contracted providers do not compete on the basis of price. Since patients are often reimbursed in part or wholly by their USLs or by private health insurance, even with non-contracted private providers these are unlikely to compete on the basis of price. Growth in insurance companies' use of positive lists may change this. Moreover, as much of the professional literature argues, health care is intrinsically inelastic with respect to price.

Until recently, quality-based competition meant trying to offer superior hotel amenities, more flexible visiting and appointment hours, shorter waiting lists and faster delivery of diagnostic tests than public or other private providers. However, for certain categories of private providers, competition is increasingly becoming technology-based, particularly in the diagnostic field.[33] For the reasons already noted, private providers are freer to invest in the latest in medical technology and there is a clear commercial advantage to being first in the market with any new process. Inadequate capital spending is frequently

---

[32] France (1991b), p. 17.

[33] Desideri and France (1991), p. 12.

cited as a problem in public hospitals. To ameliorate this situation, the SSN has embarked on a major capital expenditure programme since 1988, although this has conflicted with the objective of limiting expenditure in the hospital sector.

Private hospital behaviour sometimes displays distinct opportunism. If patients develop serious symptoms (e.g. complications during labour) which require more physician time and equipment than had been expected, they may be transferred by ambulance to a public facility. However, a new type of large and well-equipped private hospital is beginning to emerge. Since this kind of hospital has no captive SSN patients, it relies solely on its reputation amongst private patients (and their insurance schemes), thus creating a different, more consumer-oriented incentive structure. The market for such hospitals is currently limited to that of non-SSN expenditure, but each extension of the principle of patient choice (beyond the contracted private sector) augments it.

7.3.5.5 Regulation

Under Law No. 833, the state exercises certain regulatory powers with regard to all public and private providers. These include setting standards and authorising the operation of hospitals, ambulatory clinics and diagnostic centres and other health care facilities. Regional legislation, central government directives and health jurisprudence are not completely clear regarding the form that public regulation of pure private providers can take. However, it is generally agreed that such regulation should only relate to hygiene and safety standards and cannot be used to limit private sector activity nor to direct it towards specific geographical areas or health fields.

Although national standards are established by the Ministry of Health, operational regulation and inspections of hospitals are carried out by the USLs. The substance of this varies between regions, but can be strict. On-site inspections may occur (though law requires that these must be announced in advance) and the threat of contract termination has been realised on some occasions. The situation could sometimes be described as one of "relationship contracting", whereby the contractees prefer non-legal settlement of disputes, due to the high costs of legal action and the difficulties involved in the search for new contractors. However, this tends to raise the likelihood of collusive behaviour.

7.3.5.6   Hospital Management

In general, public hospitals have followed USLs in resisting rigid hierarchies and clear chains of command in favour of a more horizontal collegialism (often characterised as *deresponsibilizazzione*). This is visible in the fact that public hospitals tend to be run jointly by a health director (usually a doctor), and an administrative director. Public hospitals are administered by the USLs; but day-to-day decision making in both public and contracted private hospitals tend to be made by doctors and internal administrators.

The newest, large private un-contracted hospitals tend to have professional managerial expertise, due both to the large amounts of capital they manage and to the rigours of corporate ownership. Comprehensive data are not available, but there is evidence to suggest that increasing numbers of private hospitals are moving from single proprietorship or partnership status to investor-owned status in order to increase their capacity to obtain capital. By international standards, management salaries are considered fairly low.

Since 1978, the SSN has pursued a strategy of attempting to reduce the dominance of hospitals and doctors within USLs. This is one of the reasons that hospitals do not even have their own separate accounts within the USL budget and has led to many problems. Within public hospitals, there have been attempts to get clinicians involved in budgeting, but these tend to be resisted.

7.3.5.7   Hospital Doctors

In 1991 over 82,000 doctors were employed in public hospitals in Italy. Law 595/1985 calls for this number to be increased to 95,000. However, it is unlikely that this policy will ever be implemented and it is contradicted by a SSN hiring freeze, operative since 1983. The number of hospital physicians per 1,000 population, at 1.3 in 1988, is very high. In 1984, since when doctor numbers have changed little, though bed numbers have been somewhat reduced, for every 100 beds, there were 18.2 physicians in public hospitals and 11.4 in private clinics. The greatest ratio of hospital physicians to beds is in central and southern regions (e.g. Lazio 26.6 per 100 in 1984, Campania 25.5 per 100).

Hospital consultants (*primari*) have a higher reputation than GPs and this, according to some writers, has led to their having greater influence over medical policy at the USL and national level. SSN doctors may work part-time in private hospitals (though since 1991 no longer in the contracted sector). In 1987, an estimated 36 percent of public hospital doctors were doing this. When this occurs, it offers the private sector a labour cost advantage, since the SSN will have paid the doctor's national insurance contributions. In the evenings, in order to reduce labour costs further, private hospitals generally employ young doctors, to whom they can offer a much lower salary. In 1988, private hospitals employed only 13.5 percent of their doctors on a full-time basis.

7.3.5.8   Nurses and Other Hospital Employees

In 1990, there were an estimated 232,000 professional nurses employed by the SSN. There is widely acknowledged to be a shortage of nursing personnel, and to meet Ministry of Health standards, a further 68,000 would have to be employed. However, as with doctors, a hiring freeze makes any such expansion in numbers unlikely. Professional nurses are supplemented by a substantial number of untrained nursing assistants. In 1984, there were 44.7 nurses per 100 beds in public hospitals, well above the figure of 27 in private clinics. The low bed occupancy rate in Italian public hospitals, means that the number of nurses per 100 occupied beds was around 60 in 1987. This is lower than the averages of 69 in the UK and 68 in Canada, but high compared to Germany's average of 45. The shortage of nurses (and of other hospital non-doctor staff) to some extent offsets the large number of hospital doctors and this keeps the overall hospital staff:bed ratios low.

Schools of nursing are few and lack resources, although a new nursing course has been established within medical schools (which will create two parallel systems of nursing qualification). Nursing pay is not high and the result is that nursing recruitment in most areas is low. In May 1991, the average total remuneration of a professional nurse with ten years experience was L3.2 mn ($1,970 1990) per month. Nursing at home is provided by nurses working for the USLs and by private charitable organizations, and is an important activity due to a shortage of beds at nursing homes. Unlike doctors, nurses have little involvement in managerial functions. The other major group of professional hospital workers is technicians, who are gradually replacing doctors in the operation of some of the more complex medical technologies.

The right to strike, including striking in sympathy with other workers, is guaranteed by Article 40 of the Constitution. Hospital unionisation is high and encompasses a large number of labour federations, organised on both functional and regional bases. Strike action was previously quite high, but political pressure is building against striking in the public sector, with legislation being gradually introduced to guarantee minimum services, advance notice of strikes and individual fines for non-compliance.

7.3.5.9 Economic Incentives

The economic incentives which hospitals face depend on their contractual status. In the public sector, hospitals are financed from the USLs' lump sum budget, which is unrelated to any performance criteria but simply has the aim of covering incurred expenditure.[34] This means that there are no economic incentives to attract patients or improve performance. As far as central government's distribution of hospital funds across regions is concerned, adjustments have recently been made to take account of patient movements between regions, with deductions from funding entitlements for those regions that "export" their patients. This may encourage those regions to improve their local services.

Private contracted hospitals receive *per diem* reimbursement irrespective of the surgery performed, and so have an incentive to attract patients and keep them in hospital for as long as possible. Ecclesiastical (not-for-profit) hospitals have always had the possibility of being reimbursed via lump-sum fees (cost-per-case) for certain surgeries (e.g. tonsillectomy). However, they declined to adopt this system, fearful of the financial risk from possible medical complications. Up until now, therefore, the state has borne such risks. But the Ministry of Health is known to want to establish this form of payment to all contracted hospitals, in order to change economic incentives. Indeed the extension of such a system was included in the 1990 Finance Act but resistance by the hospitals involved has prevented its implementation.

Law No. 833 lays down only general rules for contracting out to the private sector; the details of the contracting arrangements are left to Ministry of Health decrees and regional legislation. Although in theory, SSN costs should act as a bench-mark, there is no evidence of this ever having been done, and the rates appear to be set by a process of pure negotiation. The state has monopsony power within these negotiations, but to an extent it depends on private provision. In addition, the private hospitals know they may be able to boost revenues substantially if they can effect longer patient stays per visit, since marginal costs fall rapidly after surgery (being essentially little more than hotel costs).

---

[34]   France (1991b), p. 9.

Not-for-profit hospitals are generally classed as public facilities due to the close link they have with the public sector. However, some of the more recent literature offers a dissenting view with not-for-profits being described as acting just like for-profit facilities, but with profits going to salary increases and extra investment rather than dividends. Unlike pure public hospitals, with whom they compete, SSN payments for services provided by non-profit hospitals include a capital component and amortisation. Yet at the same time such facilities have an advantage over for-profit hospitals in their stronger grip on captive customers, since certain types of not-for-profit providers are automatically eligible for contracted status.

Salaried hospital doctors are likely to earn substantially less than doctors in large private practice and obtain relatively small increments for seniority. On various occasions, this has combined with general resentment at the transfer of decision-making powers since 1978 from physicians to the USLs to result in strike action among hospital doctors. Though they enjoy less general management powers, head doctors (*primari*) may still be able to block ward closures, since "hospital empires" tend to continue to be based on the number of beds controlled.

7.3.6   Pharmaceutical Sector

7.3.6.1   Pharmaceutical Treatment Under the SSN

Spending on pharmaceuticals, at ECU7,330m, represented 14.0 percent of total health expenditures in 1989, significantly above the EC average of 10.2 percent. Some 66 percent of 1989's spending was publicly-financed. In the same year, expenditures on medicines per capita (measured at manufacturer's prices) was ECU128, compared to an EC average of ECU109, while per capita consumption by volume was 35 percent above the EC average.[35] In 1991 pharmaceutical expenditure had risen to a reported 15.2 percent of total health care expenditures. Copayments were introduced by the government soon after the start of the SSN in an attempt to stem the growth of expenditure on medicines.[36]

The vast majority of medicines are dispensed by public and private pharmacies, since physicians are prohibited from dispensing medicines and

---

[35]   Burstall (1992), p. 22.

[36]   Lucioni and Rossi (1991), p. 225.

hospital dispensaries do not issue drugs to patients receiving out-patient treatment. "Part packages" (manufacturers' packages that have been sub-divided) may not be prescribed either. In theory, generics may be prescribed. However, lack of information and incentives for GPs to do this means that it rarely happens. Under the SSN, obtaining drugs requires a doctor's prescription, with a maximum of two products allowed for each prescription sheet (except for antibiotics). Repeat dispensing of prescriptions is allowed for certain medicines.

Those medicines that are reimbursable under the SSN are listed positively in the *Prontuario Terapeutico Nazionale*. This list contains about 4,210 drugs, corresponding to 8,906 different dosage forms. Group A of the *Prontuario* covers life-supporting drugs (including for drugs of vital necessity to the treatment of rheumatic disorders, glaucoma, epilepsy, diabetes, Parkinson's disease, tuberculosis, etc.) and those used in emergencies, the costs of which are fully covered by the SSN. This category accounts for about 2 percent of total drug expenditure.[37] Group B consists of prescribed medicines for which the patient must make a copayment and the pharmacy is reimbursed the difference. Group C medicines are over the counter (OTC) medicines for which the patient must pay the full price.

The remit of the SSN when drawing up the *Prontuario* is to bear in mind the principles of efficacy, cost effectiveness and the promotion of innovation. New medicines introduced by Italian companies are, apparently, given preference. The list should be revised every four months, though in practice this happens about once a year.

7.3.6.2 *Copayments and Pricing*

In January 1992, the general copayment rate was raised from 40 percent to 50 percent, with the minimum payment rising from L1,000 to L1,500 ($0.59 - $0.89 1990) for antibiotics and L1,500 to L3,000 ($0.89 - $1.78 1990) for other drugs. For historical reasons, there is a lower copayment of 30 percent for some traditional, unbranded medicines, though these are rarely prescribed. The maximum copayment level is L50,000 ($29.71 1990), and low-income families with a poverty certificate may be exempted from the copayments if their commune agrees to meet this cost. There are no copayments for medicines issued during hospital treatment. While these are national conditions, regional

---

[37]   Garattini (1992), p. 25.

governments have recently been allowed discretion over levels within their region and Lazio raised its general rate from 50 percent to 60 percent in 1992.

Since the copayment system was introduced in 1979, overall expenditure on medicines has risen substantially. Prescription quantities of drugs requiring copayments suffered initial falls followed by stability. The higher copayments led to changes in the type and quality of medicines prescribed by physicians, with prescriptions shifting towards copayment-free medicines. These tended to be of higher therapeutic value, but also of higher cost.[38] Thus legislation was introduced in 1984, setting a ceiling for total SSN pharmaceutical expenditure, based on a reduction in the number of copayment-exempt medicines. However, this was reversed after consideration of the adverse effects on the Italian pharmaceutical industry. Since then, the number of categories and the copayment amounts have continued to be regularly adjusted.

Generics have been virtually absent from the Italian prescription market. GPs have no incentive to prescribe them and manufacturers, wholesalers and pharmacists all enjoy superior profit margins in their absence. Despite increasing copayment rates, patients' behaviour exhibits pronounced inelasticity of demand and they have not developed a preference for cheaper generics. In this regard, the central administration has so far been more mindful of the pharmaceutical sector's existing interests than of potential cost savings to the SSN.

Prices for both new and existing medicines on the *Prontuario* are set by the Inter-ministry Committee on Prices (*Comitato interministeriale prezzi* - CIP). Previously, the CIP employed a rigid cost-plus formula to set the price of new medicines, taking no account of therapeutic benefits or of the likely economic effects on the SSN. Since January 1991, however, a more flexible approach has been adopted, taking into account five factors: incidence of illness, dosage, therapeutic innovation, production technology and economic importance. These factors are balanced by negotiation and, to date, the new approach has led to Italian prices for recent products converging towards average EC levels, though older products remain substantially below EC levels. Manufacturers may price OTC medicines at their own discretion, but these products are subject to a value added tax of 19 percent.

---

[38]   Fausto (1990), p. 218.

In 1991, Italian retail medicine prices were estimated to be 94 percent of average EC retail prices.[39] This represents a continuation of a trend to convergence that has characterised the last few years. In 1989 the figure was 80 percent; while in 1988 it was only 72 percent.

January 1992 saw a reduction in the price of existing medicines listed in the *Prontuario*. The prices of products costing up to L15,000 ($8.91 1990) were lowered by 1 percent; those costing between L15,000 and L50,000 ($8.91 - $29.71 1990), by 2 percent; and those costing over L50,000 ($29.71 1990) by 4 percent. Analysts predict that these reductions (which do not apply to biotechnological drugs) will lower total profits in the Italian pharmaceutical market by 1.9-2.0 percent. However, the continuing introduction of new, more expensive medicines (which may differ only slightly from existing ones in therapeutic effects) is expected to raise the average price of *Prontuario* drugs by between 10 and 20 percent, similar to the average price increase in 1991. Following price rises for existing *Prontuario* medicines in 1990 and 1991, the recent cuts indicate the central administration's lack of success in finding any other effective policies to cut the costs of medicines. Despite policy statements to the contrary, critics claim that there has only been a marginal reduction of the number of medicines on the *Prontuario*, which remains at around 700.

7.3.6.3   Other Regulations

The Ministry of Health is responsible for overall regulation of the pharmaceutical sector. Manufacturers must hold a licence issued by the Ministry's *Direzione-Generale dei Servizi Farmaceutici* (DGSF). The licence covers specific categories of products - medical specialities, generics, raw materials, sera, vaccines and biological products. Italian Good Manufacturing Practice standards must also be met.

Until recently, authorization for new chemical entities could take up to two years, and averaged an estimated 8-10 months. There was some suspicion that this delay was a cost-cutting device to slow the entry of expensive new medicines onto the market, and into the *Prontuario*. However, since the issue of the EC Transparency Directive (which allows only a period of 90 days), the average authorization delay has started to fall. Patents and trademarks both last for 20 years, though trademarks can be renewed for a fee.

---

[39]   Burstall (1992), p. 26.

7.3.6.4   Manufacturers

Private pharmaceutical companies carry out around 90 percent of total pharmaceutical R&D expenditure in Italy, though some of this (around 7 percent of it) is supported by grants from the Ministry for the Co-ordination of Scientific and Technological Research. Some 15 companies can be described as running significant research facilities, though these are all on a smaller scale than those of the large German, Swiss, French and British pharmaceutical manufacturers.   The   pharmaceutical   industry's   trade   association   is *Farmindustria*.

Previously, since prices for medicines were considerably lower than in most of its trading partners Italy was a major source of parallel exports. This is less true now, and indeed Italy currently receives some parallel imports from France and Spain. Also, according to some manufacturers, the country was alleged to be a major international producer of counterfeit pharmaceuticals, though such production is now thought to be shifting towards lower-cost areas such as Greece.

7.3.6.5   Wholesalers and Distributors

As in other areas of distribution in Italy, the pharmaceutical distribution channels are rather undeveloped.   Most networks are localised and few wholesalers distribute in both the north and the south of the country. Distribution in the south is comparatively sparse.   According to the pharmaceutical trade association *Farmindustria*, there were 291 wholesalers in 1990. In order to reduce costs, the government reduced the nationally-agreed wholesale mark-up over the manufacturer's price in January 1992 from 8 percent to 7.5 percent.

The IMS Pharmaceutical Index for 1990 estimated distribution channels as follows: 87 percent of sales went to retail pharmacies (1 percent of which then went to hospitals), 77 percent were sold via wholesalers and 10 percent directly; 13 percent went to hospitals, 1 percent each from wholesalers and pharmacies, and 11 percent direct; and 1 percent went to public organisations (e.g. the armed forces). Overall, 22 percent of sales were direct, and 78 percent via wholesalers.

7.3.6.6   Retail and Hospital Pharmacists

Most pharmacies are privately-owned and contracted to the SSN, but in some areas, particularly those with leftist local governments which feel that the locality is poorly-served by private pharmacies, communes operate their own pharmacies. These charge lower prices than private pharmacies, though they are still profitable.

In 1990 and 1991, chronic cash shortages among USLs slowed reimbursements to such an extent that some private pharmacists refused to co-operate with the SSN any longer. Such pharmacies required patients to pay for all medicines in full and then claim reimbursement from their USL. The national average waiting period for payment is now estimated to be 8-10 months.

Pharmacists charge a retail mark-up on the wholesale price which the government reduced in 1992 from 25.5 percent to 23 percent and IVA (value-added tax) is charged at 8.25 percent on both prescription and non-prescription medicines. Established practice is that pharmacies sell many medicines, such as antibiotics, which would require a doctor's prescription in several other developed countries. By law, pharmacies cannot stock products which are not labelled in Italian.

The total number of retail pharmacies in 1990 was 15,754. The number of pharmacists (52,698 in 1986, or 9.2 per 10,000 persons) in Italy is not particularly high relative to other OECD countries. There are a number of professional associations to which pharmacists may belong. *Federfarma* is the association of pharmacy owners; FOFI is the association of professional pharmacists; and *Fiamclaf* is the association of public sector pharmacists.

In 1991, an investigation by the Ministry revealed a high level of infringements of its regulations being carried out by retailers. Offenses identified included the sale of unregistered pharmaceuticals, the stocking and sale of medicines beyond their expiry date, the sale of herbal medicines as pharmaceutical products; and the sale of reimbursable products with inappropriate labelling. Fraud undoubtedly still exists, but its extent is probably exaggerated by the media (for whom it is good copy). Electronic label reading devices have been widely installed and are considered to have substantially reduced opportunities for fraudulent behaviour.

7.3.6.7   Consumers

The Italian media devotes substantial attention to the medicinal product market, offering patients considerable information on innovations. GPs, meanwhile, have an incentive to cater to patients' wishes, and tend to decline the responsibility for rationing the SSN's scarce resources. Numerous publications keep GPs informed of new medicines and therapies. Most of these journals depend on advertising revenue from pharmaceutical companies. The largest circulation journal without advertising is *The Medical Letter*, with around 35,000 GP subscribers.

7.3.7   Other Participants

In recent years, the Italian university system has been experiencing great difficulties. Once narrowly selective, by 1969 admission had been broadened to such an extent that all those completing any type of senior secondary school were eligible for university entry.   However, the resulting expansion of numbers (a quadrupling between 1960 and 1975) was not met with an equivalent expansion of resources. Post-graduate courses have also remained limited, and until 1982 there was virtually no provision for the award of a degree comparable with the Ph.D. As a result of the overcrowding and lack of resources, attendance even in professional and laboratory courses tends to be low.

By 1986, there were 133,000 students enrolled in medical courses in Italy, almost double the number enrolled in all the medical schools in the US, resulting in a massive over-supply of doctors.

Italian medical students can graduate with what, compared to other countries, is a remarkably small amount of supervised practical experience. Medical qualification in Italy only involves around six months of clinical training, and during this period the medical student has relatively little contact with patients due to the large number of students and inadequate number of hospital beds available for training. It was calculated by a committee at the University of Rome during the 1970s, that in accordance with EC directives prescribing a student-bed relation of 1:4, the number of hospital beds and patients needed for clinical training would have been 8,000; but only 2,000 were available. Thus, to an extent, the completion of health care reform requires reform of the universities.

Upon receiving their undergraduate diploma (*laurea*), students must then sit two additional exams, neither of which contains any practical component. Next, candidates compete for the limited number of GP (and hospital) positions in a competitive selection (*concorso*) by the USL, whereby they are ranked according to exam results, professional experience within the SSN and the time that has passed since their university graduation.

Paediatrics remains the most popular medical specialisation, accounting for 18.8 percent of qualified doctors in 1989. Second was cardiology with 13 percent of doctors, and third was surgery with 12.5 percent.

The problem is the opposite in the field of nursing training. The occupation still has connotations of the church, and, as recently as 1967, approximately half of all registered nurses (*infermieri proffesionali*) belonged to religious orders.[40] Schools of nursing are few and lack resources, although nursing training is now provided at some universities.

Increasingly, technicians (often referred to as the "new health professionals") are required in order to operate health care equipment. Particularly in diagnostics, but to some extent in therapy as well, doctors are reluctantly ceding responsibility as operating requirements become more technical and specialised (and as the lower labour cost of technicians is recognised). Apart from diagnostic processes like CT and MR scanners and lithotripters, this process is noticeable in chemotherapy, neonatology and in transplant technology.

Medical equipment suppliers act as a significant, if not formally organised, pressure group for increased capital expenditure by the SSN. They may often be small-scale and lobby government at the local or regional level. Suppliers of higher price capital goods may also have an interest in extending the role of the private sector, with its propensity to make large investments in new medical technologies.

The market for high margin products tends to be less concentrated than in some other countries. In the market for lithotripters, for example, the three largest companies (Dornier, Technomed and Siemens) accounted for only 66 percent of total sales as of March 1992. In comparison, in 1989, a single

---

[40]   Robb (1986), p. 623.

company (EDAP) held 60 percent of the French market; and another (Wolf) accounted for around 50 percent of the UK market.

The Italian confederation of industry (*Confindustria*) has begun to take a significant interest in health care policy, mindful of the rapid growth of both employers' national insurance contributions and the cost of company health plans, as well as its overall concern with the need to contain public expenditure. To date, suggestions have focused on developing greater competition between the public and private sectors.

The private health care sector itself has a vocal and well-organised lobby, through such organisations as the national association of hospitals, though it has not achieved influence over all of Italy's political parties. Of the larger parties, the PDS is the staunch supporter of public provision, but even this party is becoming more flexible in the face of the need to contain public spending.

7.4   INTERSECTORAL ANALYSIS

7.4.1   Major Decision Makers

In the Italian system, despite the formal distinction, it is difficult fully to separate financing from delivery decision making.   In theory, central government is the sole decider of health care funding.   However, since expenditure is demand-led and the Health Ministry at present covers deficits, patients, their GPs and those private providers used by the SSN have so far had decisive decision making power regarding expenditure levels. The central administration does, however, have an important influence over expenditure levels in its setting of national health provision standards and in its agreement of copayments and of national contracts for salaries and for payments to the private sector.

In the pharmaceutical sector, the CIP has the power to set prices, while GPs and hospital doctors determine quantities of drugs used.   Given the Italian political system's characteristic coalition governments, which must constantly keep a wide range of constituents satisfied, the various lobbies associated with health care policy (e.g. the *ordine de medici* and the domestic pharmaceutical industry) may be considered to have particular influence.

The central government does retain discretion over how the total funding level should be financed.   Since 1978 a policy (known as *fiscalizazzione*) has been pursued,[41] involving the transfer of financial obligations from employer national insurance contributions, which directly affect industry competitiveness and employment, to general taxation.

However, in exercising the planning function which Law No. 833 assigned it, the Ministry of Health has encountered many obstacles. Getting a national health plan through Parliament - as Law No. 833 requires - has proved to be extremely arduous; in fact, as of 1992, not one national health plan had ever been approved.   Regional planning has similarly offered little concrete guidance, leaving decisions to be made on the basis of regional legislation and directives.   With specific reference to contracting, the tendency has been automatically to confirm existing contracts with private providers when they expire, making health planning redundant. This also means that USLs are unable to choose between providers on the basis of their relative performance. The courts have also played an important role in determining health care

---

[41]   Paci and Wagstaff (1991), p. 2.

delivery by extending the rights of patients to access, largely at the SSN's expense, health care technologies which the SSN possesses in fewer numbers than the private sector.

There is a lot of talk about a switch to preventive measures, but little action. Law No. 833 is worded and arranged to stress preventive health activities. For example, Articles 20 to 24, which deal with preventive measures, occupy about eight times as much space in the law as Article 25, which covers the curative services.[42] However, the perceptions and behaviour of health operators, and the general population, have clearly not adapted to match this rhetoric. GPs place little emphasis on preventive medicine. According to one critic, preventive services were better provided by the community doctors (*medico condotto*) that existed before the SSN was formed in 1978.

The "gatekeepers" to the system of health care provision are the physicians: GPs who prescribe medicines and refer to specialists and hospitals; and hospital doctors who decide on length of hospitalisation, laboratory tests, and further provision of medicines. The USLs to some extent also serve as gatekeepers in that it is they who authorise treatment in private facilities, though legislation and the courts law have limited their discretion here.

Rationing devices can be seen in the waiting lists that exist for certain SSN services in some areas, and in copayments. But waiting may be more indicative of weak planning than an attempt to manage resource shortages;[43] the relative ease of access to private provision (at little or no expense to patients) means that rationing is far less used in the Italian health care system than in some other countries.

The USLs have a fair degree of discretion in deciding which medical technologies to adopt in their facilities, subject to their capital allocation from the region and regional directives on technology policy. However, private sector investment decisions and the referrals of GPs seem to be exerting an increasing influence on technology adoption throughout the health care sector. This is because once the private sector has purchased a new technology, demand for it among SSN patients tends to be generated and the SSN is forced either to continue to contract for it with private providers or follow suit by purchasing the technology themselves. The private sector tends now to be the

---

[42]   Robb (1986), p. 621.

[43]   Schenkluhn (undated), p. 29.

first purchaser of any new technological process because of its greater access to capital, given that an adequate return is virtually guaranteed by SSN patient usage. Some examples of areas in which private providers have played a leading role in the introduction and diffusion of advanced medical technologies are ultrasonics, CT and MR scanners and lithotripters.

The Italian constitution explicitly establishes the right to engage in free enterprise and this prevents the Ministry of Health from taking action to limit the supply offered by private health operators.

The result of this unplanned growth in medical technology has been substantial overcapacity in some areas. A 1991 study showed excessive numbers of NMR scanners (110 instead of the 11 prescribed by official standards, lithotripters (97 instead of 11), CT scanners and, possibly, ultrasonics.[44]

7.4.2 Consistency of Objectives and Incentives

As with any other part of the public sector there are substantial conflicts over resource allocation, as government decisions include consideration not only of health sector objectives, but also of macroeconomic issues. Remuneration disputes regularly develop and have led in the past to industrial action, particularly in hospitals.

There is also significant conflict over funding between the USLs and regions, who both try to maximise funding levels, on the one hand and the Ministry of Health trying to minimise them on the other. USLs complain that they are at the mercy of exogenous factors influencing expenditure, such as centrally-determined prices for medicines, but to some extent this is merely an alibi.

Another problem is the optimism of Ministry of Health spending forecasts, given national health provision standards, and the regular omission of any allowance for upcoming labour contract revisions. One ex-Minister of Health admitted that his Ministry pursued a policy of "planned under-funding". USLs reply by automatically demanding increased funds and threatening politically unpopular service cuts almost as a matter of course. Legally, USLs are not allowed to have deficits, but they frequently do and these are the basis of the regional health expenditure deficits. Since 1984 the regions have been supposed to replace the board of any USL that overspends its ceiling, or ask

---

[44]   France (1991b), p. 25.

the government for the USL's dissolution, but this has rarely been done. The Ministry of Health only covers these deficits at the end of the financial year (or later), leaving USLs with perennial cash flow difficulties in the meantime. These result in management and quality problems.

Although the commitment of many USLs to containing costs may be doubted, a problem of incentives clearly exists in the decentralisation of expenditure decisions. Patients generally prefer private treatment (for which they do not have to pay) and high consumption of medicines (for which they need only pay copayments); GPs are happy to oblige since they are not charged, and have an incentive to keep their patients content; and the USL has little control over the process, though it has to pay.

Within the hospital sector, central government has made an array of attempts to promote cost control, certainly since 1985, with mixed success. Due to the constraints upon the central administration's role, these have mainly consisted of trying to persuade the regions to reduce bed numbers and merge departments. Increases in day rates for contracted care have also been held slightly below the overall rate of increase in public hospital expenditure. However, there has been little attempt to reform the *structure* of the health care sector in any way that might control hospital expenditure (e.g. by promoting preventive and community care), in spite of the hospital sector's relative inefficiency.

One problem in attempts at raising the occupancy rate has been that hospitals represent a source of patronage power and popular support for local politicians.[45] This, together with opposition from doctors, staff and local suppliers, has acted to frustrate attempts by the regions to rationalise the sector.

Perhaps the most far reaching conflict, even if it never exhibits the acrimony of wage and funding disputes, lies in the structural relationship between the public and private sectors. Far from the interim solution to the public sector's shortcomings which it was originally seen as, private provision has come to represent an indispensable source of supply for the SSN. The tendency towards automatic renewal of contracts and divorce of payment negotiations from expenditure decisions (which means that USLs can affect neither price

---

[45]   Robb (1986), p. 620.

nor quantity of private provision) protects private contractors from competitive forces.

The economic incentive that private hospitals have to prolong in-patient stays also appears to produce inefficient over-treatment. According to the Ministry of Health, in 1989, for example, the average length of stay for beds contracted for cardiology was 14.9 days compared with 8.8 days in public hospitals; for general medicine it was 18 days compared to 11.6 days; and for orthopaedics, 11.3 days and 8.2 days.

Formally, the role assigned to the private sector is one of integration (in the case of non-profit providers) and complementarity (in the case of for-profit providers).[46] Since competition for patients was not envisaged, the SSN has been given no significant regulatory power in this regard. However, available data suggest that for certain types of care both contracted and uncontracted private providers compete with the public sector for patients.

Public health planning is thus made much more difficult, with the impossibility of restricting growth of usage in any medical field, and public decision making becomes inevitably reactive to private decision making.[47] This creates what may be described as a vicious circle of decline for public provision: poor public infrastructure causes a higher consumption of contracted private services and leaves a reduced share of the limited USL budget for public services.

The problem of physicians being allowed to offer their services in the same field in both the public and the private sector also made efficient use of public resources unlikely. Until recently, a GP could certify certain treatment was needed which could not easily be obtained from a public hospital, thus obliging the USL to send the patient to a private (usually contracted) institution where the same GP might work, for more lucrative remuneration. Doctors are now no longer allowed to have more than one contract with the SSN (including the contracted private sector). There may be some possibility for this practice to continue with SSN doctors working in the non-contracted sector, but this offers substantially less scope for such behaviour.

---

[46]   France (1991b), p. 2.

[47]   Desideri and France (1991), p. 13.

565

On the benefit side of the increasing use of private provision by the SSN is the fact that it does provide greater responsiveness to patients' demands, if not greater efficiency in meeting them. This expansion of choice, since it may unduly benefit higher income, higher educated households, may however have negative equity implications.

There has been some criticism that the extent of private provision may run counter to the constitutional requirement for the centrality of public provision. In the Constitution the state is assigned a regulatory competence (to protect health) and a welfare competence (to ensure the provision of free health care to the poor). However, the Constitution does not require that the state assume responsibility for actually delivering health care, nor that it be the sole provider of health care.

Attempts by the government to prohibit the contracting with private facilities for certain high-cost technological care have been undermined by judicial decisions. These oblige the SSN to pay for patients to have such private care on an (even more costly) extra-contractual basis. Moreover, the private providers' right to introduce any new medical technology they wish is guaranteed under the constitution. Central authorities are thus finding it increasingly difficult to control technology-related expenditure. Constraints placed on public providers in the acquisition of those technologies may tend to have only the effect of placing them at a competitive disadvantage *vis-a-vis* independent providers.

As a result of several Constitutional Court decisions, there has also been increasing recognition of the right of the patient to be reimbursed, at least in part, for medical expenses incurred using specialised uncontracted facilities in Italy and in foreign hospitals when these services are not available in SSN public or contracted facilities.[48] This represents a substantial increase in patients' freedom of choice, and, to some extent, to the SSN's costs.

7.4.3 Economic Implications for Efficiency and Equity

The fact that SSN employees and contracted workers are also state employees means that their wage bargaining is subject to extra pressures unrelated to the efficiency of the health service, as governmental attempts to control public spending and inflation are brought to bear. The perennial disequilibrium between central versus regional and USL expenditure forecasts, and the delay

---

[48]   France (1991b), p. 25.

and uncertainty over coverage of the deficits also makes effective management difficult and adds further inefficiency.

SSN capital allocations are one example of this. Since the central government has more control over the SSN's capital spending than over its current expenditure, capital allocations have fallen as a share of the total national health budget. As a result, USLs have increasingly leased capital goods using current expenditure funds, in order to beat this restriction. Suppliers also have been increasing their practice of offering USLs *comodato d'uzo* agreements, whereby capital equipment is donated free in exchange for the USL agreeing to purchase that suppliers' spare parts, raw materials, etc., at above market prices. This results in a cost which is probably substantially greater than any savings to the government from lower official capital spending.

But perhaps most importantly, it is the unequal nature of competition between the public sectors providers and the private sector within the SSN that the greatest potential inefficiency. The problems discussed in the previous section all lead to inefficiencies which are difficult to measure but certainly exist.

The equity problems created by the role of the private sector are less obvious. The extension of patients' right to treatment within the non-contracted private sector is apparently an amplification of choice available to all. However, some patients are denied access to those services for want of sufficient cash to pay for private care and then be able to afford to wait for reimbursement, and reimbursement maxima also vary according to region.

It has also been suggested that there is a correlation between income level and the capacity to obtain information about the choices which are available.[49] Increasing ability to avoid using the public service may also result in decreasing pressure from wealthier patients to improve that service. Thus, contrary to widely held belief, expansion of SSN patient choice may lead also to negative equity effects.

Copayments can encourage abuses and do not necessarily work equitably. For example, there have been problems with means-testing, with the result that a considerable number of households with income above eligibility levels have been granted exempt status. Copayment increases represent an additional

---

[49]   Desideri and France (1991), p. 14.

mitigation of the SSN principles of "gratuity" and "equality", as does the recent effective curtailment of exemptions for pensioners and low-income families.

Regional disparities still exist in health as in most other features of Italian life, but according to measurements based on health expenditure there has been some convergence.[50] Where inequalities continue to exist, these are often due to differences in regional and local interpretation of enabling health reform legislation.

The essential problem of the Italian health care system lies in the incompatibility of SSN principles (freedom of choice and provision, equity and economic efficiency),[51] both with each other and with the existing uncoordinated system of financing and expenditure. Italy has a generalised problem of budgetary and expenditure control and health is no exception. It may be that there has been an implicit diminution in the importance attached to the equity goal and that this is reflected in government policy. The political constituency pushing for greater patient freedom of choice (including patients, GPs, the private medical sector and the judiciary) seems more powerful.

---

[50] Brenna *et al.* (1988).

[51] France (1991b), p. 23.

7.5   ANALYSIS OF HEALTH CARE POLICY

7.5.1   Current Health Care Policies and Proposals

The central government has launched a large number of policies designed to contain health care expenditure. These measures have tended to be most effective in the hospital sector, and probably least effective in the field of spending on medicines. Within the hospital sector, cost cutting has tended to concentrate on reducing existing over-supply of beds, rather than on any attempt to shift services from hospitals to the cheaper primary care sector. A problem facing the government is the lack of statistical information (e.g. about the real needs of each region and about hospital expenditure) available to inform decision making. There have been various announcements by the Ministry of Health that medicines were to be cut from the *Prontuario*, but there has been little if any real headway made against the rising average price of medicines or against GPs' willingness to prescribe them.

It is proposed that copayments (which were raised in January 1992) be extended and possibly increased further. However, copayment policy suffers from the familiar problem that charges are either too small to deter patients (or to pay for their own collection), or they are large enough to threaten the state's constitutional commitment to free health care. Due to the SSN's perennial financing problems, proposals are currently being considered for allowing more complementary health insurances (*mutualità*) for individual professional groups. Government proposals also encompass levying higher charges on patients from households whose annual income exceeds L40mn ($23,300 1990), and allowing regional governments to vary levels of copayments. In 1992, Lazio region became one of the first to take advantage of this policy, raising its general copayment for drugs from 50 percent to 60 percent.

There has been scant evidence so far of policies designed to shift the emphasis of health care from curative to preventive measures. One exception to this is an increased vaccination campaign. Italy is shortly due to become the first country to introduce wide-scale hepatitis B vaccination. The groups to be approached will be children, the elderly, drug addicts, homosexuals, prostitutes and those employed in the health care services. Demand for so-called fringe medicine is expanding, but so far remains within the private sector.[52] While the share of hospital expenditure relative to total expenditure

---

[52]   Borgonovi and Meneguzzu (1990), pp. 230-231.

on health has declined, this is more attributable to cost-cutting in hospitals than to a policy of service shifting. There is also an increase in day-care surgery, often at contracted private hospitals, though the total amount of such care remains small relative to total hospital provision.

As many writers have pointed out, centralised public organisation of health care tends to slow the diffusion of expensive new technologies, while more decentralised and private systems encourage faster diffusion. In Italy it is certainly the case that advanced medical technologies, such as CT and NMR scanners, ultrasonics and lithotripters, are increasingly being more rapidly introduced and diffused in the private sector.

Italy's attempts to meet EC fiscal convergence criteria may prove to be a major indirect impetus to health care sector reform in forcing through new policies to contain costs. But beyond a few examples such as the effect of the EC's Transparency Directive on the pharmaceutical approval process, there have been few noticeable direct effects on the Italian health care sector emanating from abroad.

Current reforms being debated in parliament are:

- Allowing citizens to opt out of SSN and pay reduced national insurance contributions (i.e. movement further along the public-private continuum), and promoting competition between the public and private sectors. A significant increase is proposed in the allowance for private extra-contractual care to be paid for out of public funds. It is also proposed that patients be given the choice once every three years to opt either for SSN providers (including private contracted providers) or for extra-contractual providers.

- Transferring the FSN into an inter-regional health fund, and making regions responsible for covering deficits with their own resources. Regions also to be given more independence in negotiating wages and in setting copayments.

- The administration of hospital services to be partly separated from the other health services and set up as autonomous hospital agencies (*aziende ospedialiere*) subject to regional control. These agencies would be run by a general manager with the hospitals being given more autonomy in decisions such as staffing levels, contracting and general management. Control of more specialised hospitals, and those delivering services within more than one USL area, may be handed over to the regions.

- Reintroduction of copayments for hospital treatment.

- Professional managers to be hired by regions to run USLs with five-year renewable contracts. The number of USLs to be reduced to around 400 (i.e. each containing between 150,000 and 400,000 patients).

7.5.2 Assessment of Current Health Care Policies and Proposals

Copayment requirements and contracting out to private providers both continue to be extended. Critics claim that the first of these policies reduce equity while the second reduces efficiency. However, while implicitly accepting the first charge, the government sees both as improving efficiency. Contracting out is certainly popular with patients, who tend to view it as an extension of choice. Additional problems relate to education and training and a surplus of doctors is slowly abating, though there has been less progress with the shortage of nurses. Copayment fraud is declining as the number of exemptions is reduced, but instances of corruption continue to surface.

The current reform proposals indicate that promoters of the private sector have expanded their argument somewhat beyond the issue of consumer choice. The government now argues that the private sector can act as an essential spur to the public sector.[53] However that would require the public sector to become more responsive than hitherto to competitive pressure from the private sector - e.g. on surplus capacity, over-staffing and the introduction of new technologies. Consequently some other observers argue for much greater control over the private sector, so that Italy does not develop a two-tier health system.[54] If the proposed increases in copayments are introduced this will already lead to less equal access to health care for poorer Italians.

Proposals to curb spending on medicines are conspicuous by their absence. For the SSN to contain its spending on medicines will require a major change in the central government's attitude towards the domestic pharmaceutical industry. The current policy of cutting the price of established prescription drugs while allowing vastly more expensive new drugs to enter the *prontuario* will result in continued growth in pharmaceutical expenditure.

---

[53]   France (1991b), p. 2.

[54]   *Ibid*, p. 3.

As regards private sector payments, a reduction of potential conflicts of interest involving doctors working in both the public and private sectors was brought about by the 1991 change in SSN contract regulations. But GPs still have no incentive to block patients' wishes - the real dynamic behind large scale referrals to private treatment.

The success of many health care policy proposals will depend on reforms elsewhere in the political system, none of which are impossible, but none of which will be easy in the Italian political context. The proposed transfer of fiscal responsibility from central to regional government, for example, will depend on the regional governments being given greater revenue-raising powers. Meanwhile, regions will almost certainly be forced into using discretionary powers which they have possessed since 1984 allowing regional surcharges on copayments. This could lead to equity problems, due to disparities in the sizes of regional "tax-bases".

At the national level, copayments have been applied very erratically and ambivalently over the lifetime of the SSN. The government has never made it explicit whether copayments are seen primarily as revenue-raisers or as demand curtailers. They are probably seen as useful in both functions, but the fact that no studies have been carried out by either the Ministry of Health or the Treasury to assess copayments' efficacy as demand curtailers, suggests that revenue-raising may be uppermost in administrators' minds.

ANNEX 7.1 DATA TABLES

List of Tables

TABLE 1
POPULATION ACCORDING TO AGE GROUPS

	1988	1989	1990	1991
All				
<1	554,626	572,043	562,427	576,607
1-4	2,332,317	2,285,058	2,267,457	2,252,748
5-9	3,242,440	3,143,098	3,064,503	3,019,669
10-14	4,089,239	3,923,803	3,725,683	3,535,739
15-24	9,437,228	9,370,886	9,235,477	9,099,985
25-44	15,894,915	16,161,657	16,489,304	16,860,616
45-64	13,961,128	13,935,139	13,895,948	13,843,431
>65	7,887,215	8,112,987	8,335,630	8,557,368
Total	57,399,108	57,504,691	57,576,429	57,746,163
Male				
<1	285,807	294,636	289,062	296,976
1-4	1,198,443	1,175,143	1,166,949	1,161,063
5-9	1,664,729	1,613,797	1,573,812	1,551,690
10-14	2,096,444	2,013,070	1,911,556	1,815,687
15-24	4,806,703	4,775,146	4,708,819	4,648,262
25-44	7,958,727	8,099,158	8,268,594	8,468,851
45-64	6,716,897	6,712,391	6,700,686	6,684,943
>65	3,162,161	3,255,465	3,349,052	3,445,026
Total	27,889,911	27,938,806	27,968,530	28,072,498
Female				
<1	268,819	277,407	273,365	279,631
1-4	1,133,874	1,109,915	1,100,508	1,091,685
5-9	1,577,711	1,529,301	1,490,691	1,467,979
10-14	1,992,795	1,910,733	1,814,127	1,720,052
15-24	4,630,525	4,595,740	4,526,658	4,451,723
25-44	7,936,188	8,062,499	8,220,710	8,391,765
45-64	7,244,231	7,222,768	7,195,262	7,158,488
>65	4,725,054	4,857,522	4,986,578	5,112,342
Total	29,509,197	29,565,885	29,607,899	29,673,665

Source: *Istituto Nazionale di Statistica (1992)*

Note: The source does not give the number of female population according to age groups, but this is calculated by subtracting the male population from the total population

TABLE 2
LIFE EXPECTANCY

Year	Females at Birth	Males at Birth	Females at 60	Males at 60
	Years	Years	Years	Years
1981	77.8	71.1	21.4	17.0
1982	78.2	71.5	21.7	17.2
1983	78.1	71.4	21.5	17.0
1984	78.1	71.6	21.5	17.1
1985	78.6	72.0	21.9	17.4
1986	78.8	72.2	22.2	17.7
1987	79.4	72.7	22.4	17.9
1988	79.7	73.2	22.7	18.2
1989	79.1	72.6	n/a	n/a
1990	n/a	n/a	n/a	n/a

Source: *OECD (1991)*

TABLE 3
GROSS DOMESTIC PRODUCT AND HEALTH CARE EXPENDITURE

Year	GDP	GDP per Head	Total Health Expenditure	Total Health Expenditure per Head	Total Health Expenditure
	Lire tn 90	Lire '000 90	Lire tn 90	Lire '000 90	as % of GDP
1981	1,000	17,705	66.4	1,174	6.6
1982	1,003	17,712	68.6	1,212	6.8
1983	1,014	17,847	70.6	1,242	7.0
1984	1,045	18,337	71.0	1,246	6.8
1985	1,072	18,772	74.7	1,309	7.0
1986	1,100	19,230	76.2	1,332	6.9
1987	1.131	19,728	83.1	1,449	7.3
1988	1,180	20,542	89.1	1,551	7.6
1989	1,217	21,157	91.9	1,598	7.6
1990	1,248	21,003	94.4	1,637	7.6

Source: *OECD (1991)*

TABLE 4
SOURCE OF FINANCE OF THE ITALIAN NATIONAL HEALTH SERVICE (Current Expenditure)
(Billions of Lira)

	1981	1982	1983	1984	1985	1986	1987	1988	1989	1990
Social Security Contributions	**7,986**	**13,830**	**16,372**	**17,863**	**19,668**	**25,540**	**26,483**	**27,120**	**33,231**	**42,462**
Employee contributions	4,898	8,788	10,021	10,568	12,885	17,074	17,282	17,717	22,546	36,612
Self-employed contributions	1,187	2,038	2,434	2,865	2,720	3,594	3,842	3,723	4,244	5,850
Other contributions	1,901	3,004	2,917	4,430	4,063	4,872	5,359	5,680	6,441	0
Taxes	**13,274**	**11,193**	**16,618**	**17,668**	**18,172**	**13,618**	**19,333**	**23,958**	**23,472**	**18,843**
Fiscal contribution	5,601	6,871	7,981	8,746	8,958	8,160	7,421	7,430	5,747	1,122
FSN integration	7,673	4,322	8,637	8,922	9,214	5,458	11,912	16,528	17,725	17,721
Other Inflows	**609**	**687**	**1,296**	**1,804**	**1,360**	**1,699**	**1,449**	**1,572**	**3,008**	**3,411**
Local financing	0	0	1,101	1,004	750	950	550	750	2,074	1,572
Regions with special status	0	0	0	0	0	0	0	0	0	972
Others	609	687	195	800	610	749	899	822	934	867
Total FSN	21,869	25,710	34,286	37,335	39,200	40,857	47,265	52,650	59,711	64,716
Total Expenditure by USL	22,911	28,172	34,286	37,170	43,393	47,320	54,540	61,678	67,448	80,262
Current Deficit	(1,042)	(2,462)	0	165	(4,193)	(6,463)	(7,275)	(9,028)	(7,737)	(15,546)

Source: NERA Calculations, based on *Camara dei Deputati* (1992)

TABLE 5

HEALTH CARE EXPENDITURE BY USLs BY SECTOR (Lira million)

Year	Expenditure on Personnel	Expenditure on Goods & Services	Expenditure on Pharma-ceuticals	Expenditure on Primaryon Health	Expenditure on Ambulatory Care	Expenditure on Contracted Hospital Care	Expenditure on Contracted Specialists	Other	TOTAL
	Lira mn	Lira mn	Lira mn	Lira mn	Lira mn	Lira mn	Lira mn	Lira mn	Lira mn
1985	17,058,698	7,397,800	7,415,513	2,804,899	462,728	4,167,115	1,353,545	1,048,383	41,708,681
1986	18,122,090	8,222,022	7,729,694	2,845,561	480,550	4,582,964	1,368,152	1,258,189	44,609,222
1987	21,521,779	9,267,873	9,494,620	3,665,328	625,519	5,397,655	2,120,389	1,529,679	53,622,842
1988	24,411,640	10,578,439	10,834,043	4,178,344	667,681	5,915,827	2,924,051	1,973,345	61,483,370
1989	26,228,266	12,135,387	11,744,366	4,175,960	735,412	6,784,110	2,641,114	2,390,856	66,835,471
1990	31,354,637	14,212,486	14,112,113	4,827,826	944,873	7,850,838	2,631,243	3,498,461	79,432,477

Source: *Camara dei Deputati (1992)*

577

TABLE 6
EXPENDITURE ON PRIMARY HEALTH

Year	Total Expend on Primary Care Lire mn	Total Expend on Primary Care as % of Total Health Expend	Public Expend on Primary Care Lira mn	Public Expend as % of Total Expenditure in Primary Health	Public Expend on Primary Care as % of Public Health Expend	Non Public Funded Expenditure on Primary Care Lira mn	Non Public as % of Total Primary Care Expend
1981	13,697,712	27.2	10,748,366	78.5	26.6	2,949,346	21.5
1982	14,528,591	27.9	11,359,833	78.2	27.5	3,168,758	21.8
1983	14,793,689	27.6	11,714,806	79.2	27.6	3,078,883	20.8
1984	15,173,203	28.2	11,888,889	78.4	28.2	3,284,314	21.6
1985	15,753,000	27.8	12,252,000	77.8	27.9	3,501,000	22.2
1986	16,100,372	27.9	12,376,394	76.9	28.1	3,723,978	23.1
1987	18,258,319	29.0	14,381,786	78.8	29.3	3,876,533	21.2
1988	20,494,633	30.4	16,194,880	79.0	30.6	4,299,753	21.0
1989	21,208,075	30.4	16,545,807	78.0	30.6	4,662,268	22.0
1990	n/a	n/a	n/a	n/a	n/a	n/a	n/a

Source: OECD (1991)

Note: The final two columns assume that what is not funded by public expenditure is privately funded, ie by private health insurance.

TABLE 7
NUMBER OF HOSPITALS, BEDS, LENGTH OF STAY

Year	No of Hospitals	No of Public Hospitals	No of Public Beds	Independent Contracted Beds	Average Length of Stay (days)	Occupancy Rate (%)
1989	1,881	1,224	368,909	72,733	10.4	70

Source: *Consiglio Sanitario Nazionale (1992)*

TABLE 8
PHARMACEUTICAL SECTOR IN THE ITALIAN HEALTH SERVICE

Year	Total Expend on Pharmaceuticals Lira mn 85	Public Expend on Pharmaceuticals Lira mn 85	Public Expend on Pharmaceuticals as % of Total	Total Expend at 1985 Pharma Prices Lira mn 85	Pharmaceutical Real Price Index 100 = 1985
1981	7,312,092	5,102,941	69.8	6,800,912	107.5
1982	8,329,149	6,011,158	72.2	7,994,645	104.2
1983	8,716,019	6,237,864	71.6	8,570,406	101.7
1984	8,703,704	6,056,645	69.6	9,058,957	96.1
1985	10,190,000	6,940,000	68.1	10,190,000	100.0
1986	10,610,595	6,678,439	62.9	11,405,594	93.0
1987	11,874,781	7,883,538	66.4	13,127,783	90.5
1988	12,298,927	8,273,328	67.3	14,144,349	87.0
1989	12,821,429	8,507,764	66.4	15,549,906	82.5
1990	14,161,220	9,397,967	66.4	n/a	n/a

Source: *OECD (1991)*

579

ANNEX 7.2 BIBLIOGRAPHY

Arcangeli, L. et al (1988), "Pensioni e sanità", *Queste istutuzioni*, no. 74.

Bariletti, A. (1991), "Riforma del Servizio Sanitario nazionale e governo della spesa sanitaria", *Rapporto di previsione*, Bologna, Prometeia, December.

Bevan, G., France, G. and Taroni, F., (1992) "Dolce Vita" in *Health Service Journal*, 27 February.

Blendon, R., Leitman, R., Morrison, I. and Donelan, K. (1990), "Satisfaction with Health Systems in Ten Nations", *Health Affairs*, (Summer), pp. 185-92.

Bollini, P. et al (1988), "Revision of the Italian Psychiatric Reform: North/South Differences and Future Strategies", *Social Science and Medicine*, 27:12.

Borgonovi, E. and Meneguzzo, M. (1990), "Opportunities for the Development of Competitive Elements in the Italian Health Care System: "Public Competition", Private Health Insurances, Non-profit Organisations - A Personal View", in Casparie, A.F. et al, *Competitive Health Care in Europe*, Dartmouth, VT.

Bos, M. (1991), *The Diffusion of Heart and Liver Transplantation Across Europe*, London, King's Fund Centre.

Brenna, A. et al (1988), *Analisi della spesa e della risore nel Servizion sanitario nazionale*, Rome, Ministero del Tesoro, Commissione Tecnica per la Spesa Pubblica.

Buglione, E. (1991), "Local Taxation in Italy", in Farrington, C. (ed.), *Local government taxation: the proceedings of the first European conference of the Institute of Revenues, Rating and Valuation*, London, Institute of Revenues, Rating and Valuation.

Buglione, E. and France, G. (1984), "Skewed Fiscal Federalism in Italy: Implications for Public Expenditure Control", in Premchand, A., Burkhead, J. (eds), *Comparative International Budgeting and Finance*, New Brunswick, Transaction Books.

Burstall, M. (1992), "¿Que sucederá con la industria farmaceutica despues de 1992?" in *Efectos del proceso de integracion europea sobre la salud y los sistemas sanitarios*, Asociación de Economia de la Salud, Madrid.

Buzzi, N. et al (1991), "Italia salute", *'ISIS new - mensile di sanità'* pubblica, anno VI:12.

Camara dei Deputati (1992), "Rapporto sanità", in Ministro del Bilancio, Ministro del Tesoro, *Relaizone generale sulla situazione economic del Paese* (1991), vol. III, Rome. (Also included: Rapporti sanità for 1986, 1988, 1989, 1990.)

Capri, S. and Cislaghi, C. (1989), *Public Competition Versus Privatisation in the Italian Health Care System*, Paper prepared for the European Conference on Health Economics, 18-21 September.

Capri, S. and Ricciardi, W. (1992), *Public/private Mix and Internal Competition: Aftermaths on the Single Market. The Case of Italy*. Paper prepared for the Second Annual Public Health Forum "Europe without Frontiers. The Implications for Health", London, 12-15 April.

Citoni, G. (1992), *Distribuzione dei costi di finanziamento dei servizi sanitari*.

Consiglio Sanitario Nazionale (1992), "Relazione sullo Stato Sanitario del Paese - 1989" Volume 1, Rome.

Desideri, C. and France, G. (1991), *Health Care Providers in Italy: the Public-private Continuum*, Paper prepared for the IISA Round Table, Copenhagen, 2-5 July.

Dirindin, N. (1992), *Armonizzazione delle aliquote, regressivita' e fiscal drag nel sistema di finanziamento del SSN*, Paper prepared for Workshop di Economia Sanitaria, Rome, 7-8 May (papers and proceedings in press).

Duriez, M. and Lequet, D. (1991a), *Alcoolisme at premiers indicateurs d'evaluation de la cirrhose dans une perspective comparative*, Versailles, Eurosante.

Duriez, M. and Lequet, D. (1991b), *Convergence des politiques de maitrise des depenses de sante e risques d'inegalites d'acces aux soins: Belgique, Italie, Luxembourg, Pays-Bas*, Versailles, Eurosante.

Fausto, D. (1990), "Italy" in *Advances in Health Economics and Health Services Research, Supplement 1: Comparative Health Systems*.

France, G. (1988a), "Emerging Policies for Controlling Medical Technology in Italy", *Journal of Technology Assessment in Health Care*, vol 4.

France, G. (1988a), *Privatisation of Welfare in Italy: Old Wine in New Bottles?*, Paper prepared for the Annual Conference of the Association for the Study of Modern Italy "The welfare State in Italy", University of London, 18-19 November.

France, G. (1989), "Il controllo delle tecnologie mediche alla luce della sentenza n. 992/1988 della Corte Costituzionale", *Nomos*, n. 3.

France, G. (1991a), "Cost Containment in a Public-private Health Care System: Italy", *Public Budgeting and Finance*, 11:4.

France, G. (1991b), *Contracting Out Hospital Care in a National Health Service: the Case of Italy*, paper prepared for Conference on International Privatisation Strategies and Practice, St. Andrews University, St. Andrews, Scotland, 12-14 September.

France, G. (1991c), *Intergovernmental Fiscal Relations in Italy, the Search for a Balance*, Paper prepared for OECD Seminar "Fiscal Federalism in European Economies in Transition", Paris, 2-3 April, (in press).

France, G. and Taroni, F. (1987), "Economic Appraisal of Health Technology in Italy", in M.F. Drummond (ed.), *Economic Appraisal of Health Technology in the European Community*, Oxford, Oxford University Press.

Garattini, L. (1992), *Italian Health Care Reform*, University of York/King's Fund College/CERGAS.

Gerdtham, U-G. and Jonsson, B. (1991), "Price and Quantity in International Comparisons of Health Care Expenditure", *Applied Economics*, 23:9.

Getzen, T. and Poullier, J-P. (1991), "An Income Weighted International Average for Comparative Analysis of Health Expenditures", *International Journal of Health Planning and Management*, 6:1.

Istituto Nazionale di Statistica (1992), "Annuario Statistico Italiano" (Eddizzione 1991), Rome.

ISIS (1991a), *Mensile di Sanità Pubblica*, Rome, July.

ISIS (1991b), *Stima regionale del disavanzo di spesa corrente delle USL per L'anno 1190 e prospettive per il 1991*, Rome, July.

King, R. L. (1987), "Regional Government: the Italian Experience", *Environment and Planning C: Government and Policy*, 5:3.

Kirchberger, S. (1991), *The Diffusion of Two Technologies for Renal Stone Treatments across Europe*, London, King's Fund Centre.

LABOS (1987), "The Situation of Psychiatric Care Since the Reform Law in Italy within the Context of Cultural and Institutional Changes and Legislative Aspects, Description of State of Implementation of Psychiatric Services, Problem Areas and Proposals Aimed at Supplementing the Current Laws", Rome, May (mimeo).

Lovestone, S. (1986), "The Trieste experience", *The Lancet*, 1 November.

Lucioni, C. (1991) "Il costo dell'assistenza farmaceutica pubblica" in *Economia Pubblica*.

Lucioni, C. (1991), "Spesa pubblica e modalità di controllo del prezzo dei farmici: Aspeti metodologici e confronto internazionale", *L'Industria*, XII no. 4, Oct-Dec.

Lucioni, C. and Rossi, F. (1991), "Economic Evaluation of Drug Prescription Monitoring Systems in the Extra-hospital Environment" in *Annuali dell'Istituto Superiore di Sanità*, vol. 27 no. 2.

Mapelli, V. (1992), *Bisogni di salute, scelte dei consumatori ed equita': una ricerca empirica*, Paper prepared for Workshop di Economia Sanitaria, Rome, 7-8 May (papers and proceedings in press).

Ministero della Sanità (1987), *Proposta per la deliberazione del Comitato interministeriales della programmazione economica: riparto del FSN 1987*, Rome, Ministero della Sanità', Servizio Centrale della Programmazione Sanitaria, January.

Ministero della Sanità (1992), *Proposta per la deliberazione del Comitato interministeriale della programmazione economica: riparto Fondo sanitario nazionale 1992*, Rome, Ministero della Sanità', Servizio Centrale della programmazione sanitaria.

OECD (1991), "OECD Health Data: Comparative Analysis of Health Systems" (software package), Paris.

Paci, P. and Wagstaff, A. (1991), "Le riform del Servizio Sanitario Nazionale", in G. Vitaletti (ed.), *La previdenza sociale ed il suo finanziamento*, Rome, Ministero del Lavoro, (in press).

Passerini, G. (1990), "Medicina di base: practica di gruppo ed assistenza sanitaria agli anziani", *Prospettive Sociali e Sanitarie*, 6.

Pringle, M. (1991), "General Practice in Italy", *British Journal of General Practice*, November.

Quaranta, A. (1985), *Il sistema di assistenza sanitaria*, Milan, Giufre.

Repetto, F. et al (n.d.), *Public and Private Mix in the Regione Lombardia, Italy. A Case Mix Analysis*, (unpublished).

Robb, J. H. (1986), "The Italian Health Services: Slow Revolution or Permanent Crisis?", *Social Science and Medicine*, 22:6.

Sanesi, O. (1990), "Millenium - prospettive dell' informatica in medicina generale", *Medicina Generale*, 3.

Scheiber, G. et al (1991) "Health Care Systems in Twenty-four Countries", *Health Affairs*, Fall.

Schenkluhn, B., *Hospital and ambulatory care in National Health Systems: England and Italy in comparative perspective*, Paper prepared for the Conference on the Division of Labour in the Health Sector in the Light of New Challenges, Max-Planck Institut für Gesellschaftsforschung, Cologne, 19-20 November.

Schenkluhn, B., Webber, D. (1988), *Steering the Health Sector in Switzerland, West Germany and Italy*, Paper prepared for Workshop in Guidance, Control and Coordination in the Public Sector, ECPR Joint Sessions, University of Bologna/Rimini, 5-10 April.

Schneider, M. et al (1991), "Italy", *Health Policy*, (special issue on health care in the EC member states), vol. 20:1-2.

Senato della Republica (1992), *Sanità*, Rome Senato della Republica, Servizio del Bilancio (internal document).

Sofio, A. D., Spandonaro (1992), *Finanziamento regionale del SSN: alcune riflessioni in termini di tollerabilita' ed equita'*, Paper prepared for Workshop di Economia Sanitaria, Rome, 7-8 May (papers and proceedings in press).

583

Stocking, B. (1991), *"Factors Affecting the Diffusion of Three Kinds of Innovative Medical Technology in European Community Countries and Sweden"*, in Bos (1991).

The Medical Letter (1992), Centro per l'Informazione Sanitaria, Milan, Anno XXI no. 2, 15 June.

Traverwa, G. (ed.) (1989), *Il ruolo della medicina di base nel SSN e le prospettive di cambiamento*, (unpublished paper).

Veronesi, E. and Torroni, G. (1992), *Una metodologia di previsione a breve termine della spesa corrente del Servicio sanitario nazionale (SSN)*, Paper prepared for Workshop di Economia Sanitaria, Rome, 7-8 May (papers and proceedings in press).

Wagstaff, A. et al (1990), "Equity in the Finance and Delivery of Health Care: Some Tentative Cross-country Comparisons", *Oxford Review of Economic Policy*, 5:1.

CHAPTER 8

THE HEALTH CARE SYSTEM IN JAPAN

Richard T Rapp

National Economic Research Associates
New York

Kyoko Shibuya

William M. Mercer Limited of Japan
Tokyo

8.1   SUMMARY

Structure

The Japanese social insurance system derives from the health insurance tradition of Bismarckian Germany.   Coverage expanded over time, and the remaining gaps in universal coverage were filled in 1961 with the establishment of a residence-based system of insurance, called "National Health Insurance", to cover those not covered under occupation-based insurance.

Prices for all health care goods and services are fixed by regulation.   These prices are uniform throughout the country.   Although highly regulated by the Ministry of Health and Welfare (the MOHW), the system is not unified, but rather reflects a history of irregular, stepwise development.

As a result of the accessibility and technical excellence of medical care, the high *per capita* income, the high rate of literacy, a favourable diet and the low rate of violence, the health status of the Japanese is arguably the best in the industrialized world.

Aggregate Level of Expenditure

Since the end of the 1970s, the MOHW has successfully kept the growth of health care expenditure within a target range, which is less than the growth rate of national income.   However, the health care system runs on fee-for-service pricing so strict budgetary limits are difficult to set.   The adoption of the growth target coincided with the end of historically unprecedented high rates of economic growth in Japan.   Whereas this growth sustained the rapid expansion of the health care system in the 1960s and 1970s, the focus during the 1980s turned to controlling growth.

The MOHW has implemented various cost-containment measures.   Most notably, the MOHW has reduced the incentives for conducting laboratory tests, sharply cut reimbursement prices for prescription drugs and structured the spread of sophisticated medical equipment.

Incentives

Providers: Most provider institutions are privately owned.   The fee-for-service reimbursement system gives health service providers an incentive to treat as many patients as possible.   There is no price competition between medical

587

service providers, who maximize their revenues by maximizing the number of patients they see and the number of tests and prescription drugs they provide. Since all doctors are treated equally under the fee-for-service system, doctors do not specialize to the extent observed elsewhere in the world.

Patients: Copayments (10-30 percent) provide some incentive for cost containment. Long waiting times substitute for higher prices as a rationing mechanism for high-quality care at popular institutions. A lack of quality differentiation leads patients to seek even the most basic primary care at large hospitals rather than local clinics.

Medicines: The prices of prescription drugs are fixed under the universal insurance reimbursement fee schedule. Recent reimbursement prices for drugs have been based on a calculation designed to squeeze the margins doctors and hospitals earn on dispensing. Japan is the only developed country where drug prices have been consistently and rapidly declining.

Issues

- Japan is the most rapidly aging society in the developed world, and the birth rate has been dropping precipitously. The increasing burden of health care for the elderly, both now and in the future, is a major concern.

- Some insurers, such as society-run Employee Health Insurance (EHI) plans, are financially strong due to the high incomes and relative youth of their insured. Other insurers, such as National Health Insurance (NHI), insure many self-employed people, the unemployed and the retired, and thus face higher costs for a population that is relatively poor. Therefore those most able to pay, pay relatively lower insurance contributions as against their income.

- Price-setting under the Reimbursement Fee Schedule is unrelated to the conditions of supply and demand. Rather, the Ministry of Health and Welfare analyses the frequency of all the types of medical services and goods consumed in order to plan future budgetary needs. The most fundamental objectives of the parties to the price-setting process is the preservation of providers' shares and incomes.

- Patients are detached from any ability to influence the price or availability of medical goods and services, except by roundabout political means.

- Evidence of shortages and the effect of mispricing is widespread:

  - a confusion of specialty and general care facilities. Hospitals have an incentive to treat primary care patients as this is equally or more profitable;
  - use of hospitals for elderly care;
  - over-medication and too much testing;
  - queues and waiting times for hospitals; and,
  - excessive hospital stays.

Current Reforms

The MOHW is trying to promote a division of labour among medical institutions, to strengthen the provision of advanced care and of long-term care for the elderly, by establishing specialised hospitals for these purposes.

Over the recent years, the MOHW has increased reimbursement fees for primary care and fees for doctors to visit patients at home, reforms which affect only the incentives for providers. Patients, in contrast, are almost completely unaware of the fees before they receive care and pay only a minor portion of fees as copayments. Given that physicians control treatment, with little patient participation, it is unlikely that increasing copayment would control costs without restricting 'needed' care. A more promising tack might be to shift certain reimbursement rates to cost-per-case pricing.

The MOHW is sensitive to the need for reform. In 1992 it charged the Medical Insurance Council (*Iryou Hoken Shingikai*) with devising a reform program including:

- funding;
- the definition of the guaranteed health care package (GHCP), including the place of hi-tech medicine; and
- the use of novel, cost-per-case payment methods.

NERA's Reform Proposals

What elements of reform would make sense in this setting, considering that, despite the above distortions, the system works well from the standpoint of both cost control and health outcomes?

Ultimately, any reform must allow the health care system to meet demand, while at the same time allowing the government to maintain tight control over the state share of health care expenditure. Reform should shift to the private sector those aspects of medical care that are discretionary and for which limits on access would not violate the conditions of social solidarity.

Our main recommendation for near-term reform in Japan involves converting selected parts of the Reimbursement Fee Schedule from a uniform schedule to 'balance billing'. The uniform fee system, under which no one may charge more than the uniform fee, obliterates quality differentiation in the system. Patients who would willingly pay extra for higher quality service go unsatisfied. Balance billing would not require the abandonment of the Reimbursement Fee Schedule. Rather, a lifting of the fee ceiling would allow health care providers to offer additional higher levels of service for a premium.

We also recommend that long-term care be separated from the medical sector and fully 'privatized'. Currently, distortions push the elderly into hospitals. Instead, the private sector should be free to establish purpose-built nursing care institutions to be priced by the market. This change would ultimately reduce the fiscal burden of elderly care, once modifications in the insurance system allowed individuals to set aside a portion of their wages to pay for care during old age.

Our other major recommendation is to remove inequities among the existing insurance plans by equalizing the premiums, basic benefits and copayments among society-managed and government-managed plans.

With regard to the pharmaceutical sector, we recommend a continuation of efforts to separate the dispensing function from the prescribing function. This process will almost certainly lead to a decline in the volume of medicines sold.

In our view, fundamental reform in Japan implies an 'opening' to the preferences of patients of what is now an administratively closed system. This will require an increase in funding from sources outside the government. Movement in the direction of the NERA Prototype system implies this as well.

8.2 STRUCTURE OF THE HEALTH CARE SYSTEM

8.2.1 The Health Care System in Context

The Japanese social insurance system has its roots in Bismarck's Germany. The basic principle was to provide protection for certain occupations, such as seamen and factory workers in large manufacturing enterprises. Originally, mutual benefit societies provided health services privately to these groups. During the first half of the twentieth century, coverage was broadened in an irregular, stepwise fashion to include ever larger numbers of employees with premiums shared between workers and their employers. In 1961, the Japanese government achieved its goal of universal coverage by adding to the residence-based NHI individuals not previously covered under health insurance plans (see the chronology of the development of the Japanese social insurance system in Annex 8.2).

The Japanese health care system is remarkable in that it achieves universal coverage at comparatively low cost while preserving some degree of choice for patients. Patients have their choice of doctor and hospital and, within narrow limits, may exercise control over the quality of care they receive. Mandatory health care insurance affords the population universal coverage with a high degree of equity (limited quality differentiation and broad basic coverage). The system does not depend upon the State employment of medical personnel and is free from the bureaucracy and other common problems of nationalized health care systems.

The MOHW exercises responsibility for the overall planning and administration of the universal health insurance system. The MOHW relies on councils (*Shingikai*) for planning and proposing amendments to health care laws. The Medical Service Council (*Iryou Shingikai*), formerly called the Social Insurance Council (*Shakai Hoken Shingikai*), has been the most important council in terms of the formation of the universal health insurance system. While the so-called 'council politics' (*Shingikai Seiji*) provide a forum for debate regarding proposed changes in the health care system, the MOHW effectively controls the councils' deliberations and ultimately retains full decision-making power.

Under the Medical Service Law (*Iryou Hou*), doctors certified by the Minister of Health and Welfare can open clinics or hospitals anywhere in Japan. An insured individual can receive primary care at any such clinic or hospital merely by showing their health care insurance certificate (*Hoken Sho*). Insured individuals can also receive any medical services available under the National Uniform Reimbursement Fee Schedule (the Reimbursement Fee Schedule) by paying a copayment that amounts to 10-30 percent of the total cost of service depending upon the insurance plan and on whether the patient is the subscriber or a dependant.

Medical institutions send claims for the remainder of their fees to the Social Insurance Medical Reimbursement Fund (the Fund).[1] The Fund checks the claims and, on behalf of insurers, reimburses clinics and hospitals on a fee-for-service basis. The actual fees are calculated by the Fund based upon the Reimbursement Fee Schedule.[2]

This administrative mechanism is considered one of the most efficient characteristics of the Japanese health care system. The fact that almost all claims are processed by the Fund creates economies of scale and limits the filing of false claims by hospitals and clinics.

The Reimbursement Fee Schedule is uniform throughout Japan; all providers of medical services are paid exactly the same fees for each individual type of service. Moreover, along with the patient copayments, the reimbursements from insurers provide the overwhelming majority of the income for hospitals and clinics.[3] As a result, the Reimbursement Fee Schedule is the most important determinant of incentives for providers to the Japanese health care system. The uniform nature of the schedule also enables centralized administration of the reimbursement process.

The Reimbursement Fee Schedule is maintained and revised by the Central Social Insurance Medical Council (*Chuikyo*),[4] an advisory council to the

---

[1] The Fund (*Shakai Hoken Shinryou Houshuu Shiharai Kikin*) was established by the MOHW in 1948 as a special non-profit corporation (*Tokushu Houjin*). While nominally independent, the Fund performs quasi-governmental functions and its operating costs are paid for out of the national budget. Employees of the Fund are not national government employees, but rather are recruited by the Fund from outside of government; the top management positions, however, are filled by former officers of the MOHW. The data collected by the Fund for administration purposes are a major source of statistical information on the health care system.

[2] See Section 8.2.2.3 for more details of the payment mechanism.

[3] The Japanese government has only a minor role in providing direct subsidies to financially troubled medical institutions.

[4] *Chuou Shakai Iryou Kyougikai* = *Chuikyo* (abbreviated term).

Minister of Health and Welfare. *Chuikyo* is a 20-member advisory body consisting of eight representatives of the payers, eight representatives of medical service providers, and four representatives of the public interest. Those representing the payers are typically the representatives of labour unions and business owners. Those representing the public interest are drawn from academia and from among renowned medical experts. Those representing medical care providers are typically individual physicians, dentists, and pharmacists.

The JMA remains the most influential political interest group in the Japanese health care system, although its power has waned since the 1970s. One of the ways the JMA exercises influence is by officially endorsing political candidates running for election to the National *Diet*. The JMA thus maintains influence with the ruling LDP, especially with LDP members belonging to the *Diet*'s Social Committee which deals with medical issues in Japan. MOHW takes notice of the positions expressed by the JMA and by LDP *Diet* members, and those MOHW officers who are medical doctors often strongly support the positions taken by the JMA. MOHW officials from non-medical backgrounds are less supportive of JMA positions.

Judging by traditional measures of health status, the Japanese health care system ranks among the best in the world. The system achieves excellent health outcomes at comparatively low cost — total national health care expenditures represent just 6.8 percent of national income in 1990.[5] Against the successes, however, one must array a list of serious problems arising largely from the high degree of administrative control over global health care budgets and the prices of medical goods and services. Among these problems:

- excess demand at current prices;

- mispricing by the political price-setting mechanism, resulting in an over-supply of medicines, tests and procedural services and the under-provision of consultative services and care;

- inadequate consumer/patient participation both in the political process that determines resource allocation and in relations with physicians and other providers.

---

[5] Ikegami (1992). If private expenditures on health care were included, overall health care expenditures may be as high as 7.5 to 8.0 percent of GDP; however, that figure is still low by international standards. See "Health Care Survey," *The Economist*, July 6, 1991, p. 15.

While the MOHW has recognized these problems and is initiating reforms in tandem with other agencies, there are limits to the ability of an administrative agency to solve these problems. The challenge facing Japan is to preserve the low level of inflation in health care costs while improving delivery to those who need it most, especially the growing elderly population.

8.2.2 General Features of the Finance System

The vast proportion of medical care expenditures in Japan are covered under the universal health insurance system. The system itself consists largely of a patchwork of government and private employment-based plans, and residence-based plans.

Private insurance plans can cover the cost of certain peripheral medical services that are not covered by universal health insurance.[6]

8.2.2.1 Overall Sources of Funding

There are five major sources of funding for medical care in Japan:

1. participants' premiums to the various insurers;
2. employers' matching contributions to EHI on behalf of their employees;
3. patient copayments to hospitals, clinics and pharmacies;
4. national government subsidies; and
5. local government subsidies.

In 1990, total medical expenditures under the universal insurance system were ¥20.6 trillion ($103 bn 1990).[7] Of this total, premiums accounted for 56.3 percent, patient copayments for 12.1 percent, expenditures from the national

---

[6] As discussed elsewhere, the MOHW does expect an increasing role for private insurance, especially in providing coverage for the elderly and controlling public expenditures on health care.

[7] This figure, calculated by the MOHW, includes reimbursement amounts to the medical institutions, co-payment portions of the payments, and government expenditures on the welfare program. The costs of administering the various health insurance programs are excluded. Also excluded are (1) healthy delivery of children; (2) health check-ups, including day-long health check-ups; (3) preventive inoculations; (4) payments for access to health promotion facilities for the elderly, such as rehabilitation facilities; and (5) additional room charges for hospitalization. However, costs for embalming are included in the figure. All data from the MOHW are based on a fiscal year that runs from April to March.

budget for 24.6 percent, and local government expenditures for 6.8 percent (see Chart 8.1).[8]

Chart 8.1
National Medical Expenditure in Japan, Fiscal 1990

By Source
Total Spending: Yen 20.6 trillion

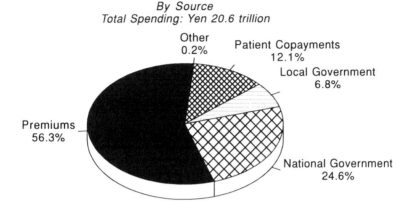

Other 0.2%
Patient Copayments 12.1%
Local Government 6.8%
Premiums 56.3%
National Government 24.6%

Source: Ministry of Health and Welfare (1992a)

8.2.2.2 Organization of Funding

The basic categories of health insurance in Japan are as follows:

• Employee Health Insurance (EHI);
• National Health Insurance (NHI);
• Health Service for the Elderly; and
• a group of minor government insurance plans for individuals in special occupations, such as national government employees, local government employees, seamen and private teachers.

Chart 8.2 shows the proportion of the total population covered by each type of insurance.

Private insurance companies are only allowed to provide very limited policies, to cover expenses which are not covered under the universal coverage system.

---

[8] These shares are calculated based on total premiums of ¥11.6 trillion ($55 bn 1990), patient copayments of ¥2.5 trillion ($12 bn 1990), national government expenditures of ¥5.1 trillion ($24 bn 1990), and local government expenditures of ¥1.4 trillion ($7 bn 1990). Data published by the MOHW, June 29, 1992.

Chart 8.2: Share of the Population Covered Under Each Type of Insurance (1991)

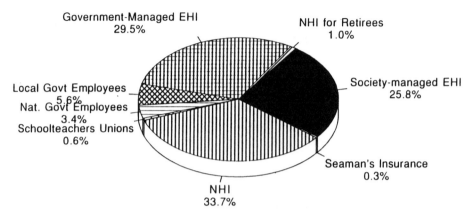

Government-Managed EHI
29.5%

NHI for Retirees
1.0%

Local Govt Employees
5.6%
Nat. Govt Employees
3.4%
Schoolteachers Unions
0.6%

Society-managed EHI
25.8%

Seaman's Insurance
0.3%

NHI
33.7%

Source: *Health Insurance Bureau, Ministry of Health and Welfare*
Notes: *EHI for Day Labourers (<0.1%; Not shown)*

8.2.2.2.1   EHI

EHI is based on the Health Insurance Law (*Kenkou Hoken Hou*) of 1922. The basic premise of the law was to provide blue-collar workers with coverage in the event of work-related illness and injuries.

EHI covers employees of large firms (over 300 employees) or of companies who are members of a trade association-related society or a society that covers a group of affiliated employers. Between employees and their dependents, EHI covers approximately 55.3 percent of the total population. EHI plans are, generally speaking, financially strong.

There are two major subtypes of EHI: government-managed EHI and society-managed EHI.[9] Government-managed EHI covers employees of small-to-medium sized companies (29.5 percent of the population).[10] Employees contribute 4.2 percent of their basic monthly salary[11] as premiums, which are then matched by employers on behalf of their employees. Together, employee

---

[9]   The third and very minor type of EHI is EHI for Day Labourers.

[10]   The average number of employees per company was 15 in 1989.

[11]   The average monthly basic salary for the insured under government-managed EHI was ¥263,687 in 1990 ($1,320 1990); under society-managed EHI, the average salary was ¥327,023 ($1,635 1990).

premiums and employer contributions constitute the bulk of the funding for government-managed EHI (see Chart 8.3).

Chart 8.3
Government-Managed Employee Health Insurance (EHI)

Total Income: Yen 6,311 billion (1989)

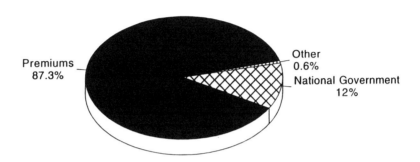

Premiums
87.3%

Other
0.6%

National Government
12%

Source: Social Insurance Agency

EHI premiums are collected by local Social Insurance Offices (*Shakai Hoken Jimusho*), which are located in metropolitan wards, cities, and towns. These small local offices are administered by local prefectural governments. These prefectural governments are, in turn, overseen by the Social Insurance Agency (*Shakai Hoken Chou*), an external agency of the MOHW.

Large companies, or affiliated company groups, can establish health insurance societies; as of 1991, there were 1,822 such societies covering 25.8 percent of the population.[12] Societies collect premiums and pay out benefits, managing the process by using outside trust banks. Under society-managed EHI, employees bear less of a financial burden than under government-managed EHI, contributing on average 3.6 percent of their basic salary as premiums. Employers, meanwhile, provide slightly more than matching contributions, amounting on average to 4.6 percent of employees' basic monthly salaries. Society-managed EHI also offers more extensive benefits. Some plans even provide supplemental income indemnity benefits. As with government-managed EHI, employee premiums and employer contributions are the predominant source of funding for society-managed EHI (see Chart 8.4).

---

[12]   *Kenkou Hoken Kumiai Rengoukai* (1991).

Chart 8.4
Society-Managed Employee Health Insurance (EHI)

Total Income: Yen 4,874 billion (1990)

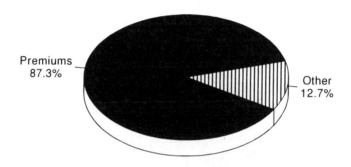

Premiums 87.3%

Other 12.7%

Source: National Federation of Health Insurance Societies

8.2.2.2.2   NHI

NHI was introduced in 1939 to cover farmers in rural areas and the unemployed. Neither group had previously been covered by health insurance, and both groups faced a high incidence of tuberculosis. Eventually, NHI developed into a safety net to protect those not covered by other types of health insurance. Today, NHI mainly covers the self-employed, the unemployed, retirees, and their dependents. NHI plans are managed by local government authorities for the residents of the region. The premiums are determined by local governments on the basis of individuals' income and wealth. NHI premiums are considerably higher than EHI premiums[13] because of NHI's disproportionately large share of elderly insurers (see Chart 8.5), who generate high claims.

Because the average NHI participant's ability to pay premiums and copayments is limited, the NHI plans are financially weak and must be subsidized to make up revenue shortfalls (see Chart 8.6). Roughly half of the subsidies to NHI plans come from the national government, a quarter come from prefectural governments, and the remaining quarter come from town and city governments.

---

[13]   Whereas those covered by government-managed EHI pay an average of ¥118,000 ($560 1990) per insured year and those covered by society-managed EHI pay an average of ¥121,000 ($575 1990), those insured under NHI pay an average of ¥142,000 ($675 1990).

Chart 8.5
Number of Elderly per 1,000 Insured

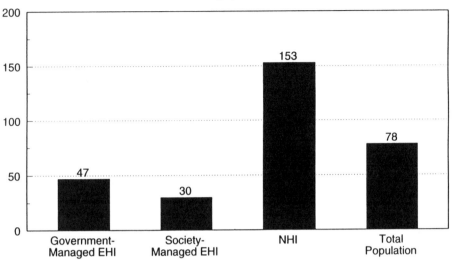

Source: Health Institute Bureau, Ministry of Health and Welfare

Chart 8.6
National Health Insurance (NHI)

Total Income: Yen 6,491 billion (1989)

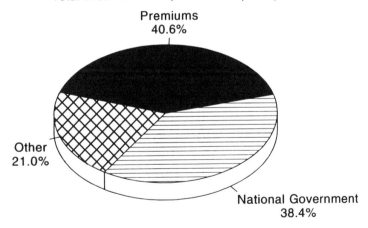

Source: Health Insurance Bureau, Ministry of Health and Welfare

8.2.2.2.3   Health Services for the Elderly

Retirees are advised to participate in NHI for Retirees.[14] This is a local-government managed NHI plan, but benefits are higher for retirees than for the typical insuree under NHI. In addition, copayments are only 20 percent under NHI for Retirees versus 30 percent under regular NHI. The 20 percent copayment is defined so that the increase from the 10 percent copayment under EHI will not be too drastic for financially weaker retirees to bear. The cost of these upgraded benefits for retirees are prorated and covered by contributions from the original EHI insurer. The NHI assumes a large portion of the burden of funding health expenditures for the elderly, with prefectural governments providing additional subsidies. Since 1990, each type of insurance bears a prorated burden based upon their share of the total insured population, rather than their shares of the elderly insured population.[15] That is, the percent of the total burden for the elderly borne by each insurer is based on the percent of the total population insured by that insurer, rather than the percent of the elderly insured by each insurer. Elderly individuals pay only a small copayment at the time of delivery of medical services (currently ¥900 for out-patients, $4.26 1990), and receive otherwise free medical care at the clinic or hospital of their choice.

Every Japanese citizen over the age of 70 (or over 65 and bedridden) is covered separately[16] under Health Service for the Elderly, which was established in 1987 with the passage of the Health Service Law for the Elderly (*Rojin Hoken Hou*).

8.2.2.2.4   Other Employment-Based Insurance Plans

The other four employment-based insurance plans cover particular occupational classes. One, Seamen's Health Insurance, has a very long history

---

[14]   At age 60, retirees automatically are switched from EHI to regional (residence-based) NHI for retirees. Age 60 is the mandatory retirement age for national government employees; Japanese companies basically follow this practice.

[15]   This provision can have an adverse effect on a plan's expenditures. For example, a plan which insures 10 percent of the population, but has no elderly participants, will nevertheless pay 10 percent of the total burden for health care expenditures for the elderly.

[16]   Some elderly over age 70 are also listed as dependents under other types of insurance.

of operation based on the same principles as EHI.[17] The other three cover national government employees, local government employees, and private school teachers.[18]

Premiums differ only slightly among the four plans. In 1990, employees' premiums fell within a range of 3.975 percent to 4.4 percent of basic monthly salaries, and employers contributed at least matching amounts on their behalf.

8.2.2.3 General Description of the Payment Mechanism

Clinics and hospitals are reimbursed on a fee-for-service basis. Insurers do not pay medical fees directly. Rather, the insurers entrust special organizations with responsibility for examining doctors' reimbursement claims and paying them. The Fund mainly handles fees and payments related to the categories of health insurance that cover the employed.[19]

Each month, individual medical care institutions claim fees from the Fund for the services they have provided in the previous month. The Fund examines these claims, calculates the fees according to the Reimbursement Fee Schedule, and then bills the adjusted fees to the insurers, while making payments on behalf of the insurers to individual medical care institutions. Charts 8.7 and

---

[17]   Seamen's Health Insurance, which originated with the Seamen's Health Insurance Law of 1939, was enacted to protect seamen from work-related illnesses and injuries. Premiums under this plan are collected either by local Health Insurance Offices (*Shakai Hoken Jimusho*), local offices of the Public Employment Agency (*Kokyo Shokugyou Anteijo*), or local offices of the Seamen's Employment Agency (*Senin Shokugyou Anteijo*).

[18]   The Mutual Unions for National Government Employees were established based upon the Law for the Mutual Unions for National Government Employees enacted in 1983. Premiums for government employees are collected at their respective ministries. With some exceptions, the Ministry of Finance supervises all administration and planning in regards to this program.

The Mutual Unions for Local Government Employees were established based on the Law for the Mutual Unions for Local Government Employees enacted in 1962. Premiums are directly collected by the Police Agency (*Keisatsuchou*), the Ministry of Education, and the Ministry of Home Affairs for their respective employees.

The Mutual Unions for Private School Teachers were established based on the Law for the Mutual Unions for Private School Teachers enacted in 1953. The Ministry of Education is responsible for all funding, planning, and administration.

[19]   The Fund also handles the collection of premiums and the disbursement of allowances for Health Service for the Elderly. The Central Federation of National Health Insurers (the Federation) reviews the claims and pays the fees for NHI. From *The Social Insurance Agency of Japan* (1991), pp. 123-127.

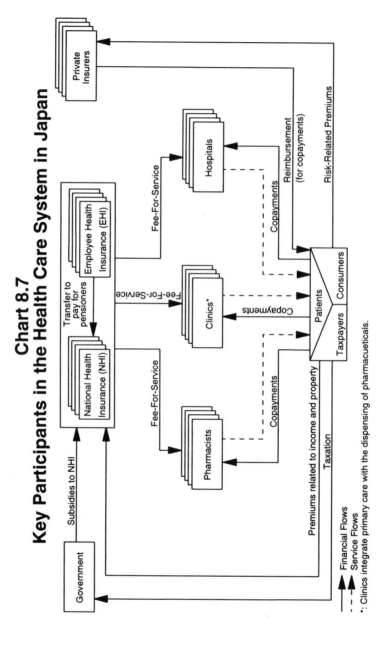

Chart 8.7
Key Participants in the Health Care System in Japan

8.8 show the flow of national medical expenditure among the various parties and detail the payment mechanism.

Chart 8.8
The Payment Mechanism

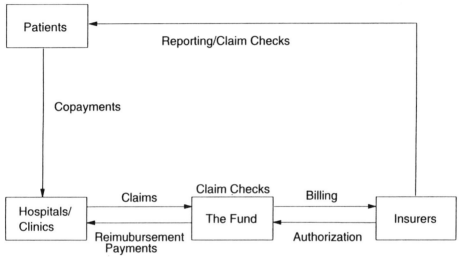

Using a new information service system, the insurers inform insured persons by mail about the individual medical services they have received over the year and the actual amounts paid to the doctors for these services. This confirmation of medical services provided to each patient is designed primarily to counteract false claims by clinics and hospitals. This program is also intended to promote cost-consciousness on the part of the insured and their dependents.

8.2.2.4 Benefits

The different schemes which comprise universal health insurance generally cover the same medical services, including medical and dental care in both in-patient and out-patient settings and expenses related to hospitalization, nursing, and the dispensing of drugs. All plans exclude from coverage inoculations, health examinations, non-prescribed medicine, premium hospitalization room charges (for upgraded or private rooms), and payments for access to health promotion facilities for the elderly.[20]

---

[20]   Payments for eyeglasses are also excluded from coverage.

603

A typical benefit package for EHI and other health insurance systems for the employed is as follows:

- **In Kind Medical Benefits:** For the insured, 90 percent of payments for medical services for out-patient care and hospitalization costs are covered. For dependents of the insured, 70 percent of payments for medical services are covered. Total copayments are capped at ¥60,000 per month ($284 1990), i.e., copayments in excess of this ceiling will be reimbursed.

- **Income Indemnity Benefits:** Allowances are provided, e.g., injury allowances, child delivery allowances, child-nursing allowances, and funeral condolence allowances. The injury allowances are based upon the standard remuneration amount of the insured.

In contrast, NHI covers 70-80 percent of medical costs depending upon the financial condition of the locality. NHI generally does not provide allowances for injury, sickness, normal child delivery, or child-nursing.

8.2.3   General Features of the Delivery System.

As of the end of 1990, there were 211,797 national government-certified doctors—one doctor for every 580 Japanese citizens and roughly double the number that existed in 1960. Of this total, 41.5 percent worked for hospitals as employees, 28.9 percent were owners of hospitals and clinics, 7.9 percent were employees of clinics, and 17.9 percent worked for medical teaching institutions.[21] As a result of the growth in the number of doctors, which out-paced even the growth in the GDP, medicine's status as a profession and with it medical school applications—has declined. This has aided the government's current effort to limit the number of doctors by reducing the number of candidates admitted to medical school.

Under the Medical Service Law, government-certified medical doctors are traditionally guaranteed the right to establish a clinic or hospital when and where they choose. 'Clinics', which are defined as medical facilities with fewer than twenty beds, are typically owned and operated by general practitioners (GPs). Because of the strong trend towards young doctors serving as employees rather than trying to open their own clinics — in 1990, 67 percent of all doctors were employees — the average age of clinic-owning doctors is

---

[21]   Rather than classification by specialty, doctors are typically grouped by employment status: whether they work at hospitals or clinics and whether they are the owner or an employee.

rising rapidly. Due to the low degree of specialization, the distinction between GPs and specialists is ill-defined and clinic doctors may claim to be specialists. Japan lacks board certification such as that found in the United States and other means for distinguishing specialties.

Japan also does not have an 'open delivery system' such as that found in the United States, in which doctors can both maintain private offices and enjoy access to hospital facilities. Clinic doctors do not have admitting privileges to hospitals. Hospital doctors and clinic doctors do not generally cooperate with one another in serving patients.

Recently, patients have come to prefer university hospitals and other large hospitals to smaller hospitals, and smaller hospitals to clinics. This tendency is attributable to the recognition that physicians working at major teaching hospitals are more legitimately 'specialists' — that is, more highly trained and expert than those in smaller facilities and clinics. Hospitals send out other quality signals as well. They are, as a rule, better equipped than clinics and they are typically more flexible in providing a range of services, as almost all have large in-patient and out-patient departments. Given that the prices of medical services are no greater in hospitals, it is no surprise that patients have gravitated to them in preference to sole practitioners' clinics. Patient preference has led to the overcrowding and misuse of secondary and tertiary care facilities like teaching hospitals, and has made the management of smaller private hospitals especially difficult.

In 1990, medical expenditures at hospitals accounted for 59.8 percent of the total national medical expenditures, while medical expenditures at clinics accounted for 27.4 percent of the total. In 1990, there were 10,096 hospitals and 80,972 clinics.

8.2.4   Inputs and Outputs of the System

8.2.4.1   Expenditure

In 1990, total national medical expenditure was approximately ¥20.6 trillion ($103 bn 1990).[22] This represents an increase of 20 percent since 1955. One of the more important reasons for the rapid growth in medical expenditures during this period was the increase in spending on pharmaceuticals. Pharmaceutical's share of total expenditures peaked at 46 percent in 1973, and then began to fall in response to the government's efforts to contain costs starting in the early 1980s through the revision of the drug price schedule.[23] By 1989, this ratio had decreased to 31.3 percent.[24]

During the 1960-1987 period, Japan had one of the highest real *per capita* rates of economic growth — adjusted for health care inflation and population growth — among the major OECD countries. The increase in real *per capita* growth was estimated to be 8.18 times or 8.1 percent annually.[25] (By contrast, the rate of increase was 2.78 times or 3.9 percent annually for the US.)[26]

Of the ¥20.6 trillion ($103 bn 1990) in national medical expenditure in 1990, 87.2 percent was spent on regular medical treatment, including drugs dispensed by doctors and hospitals, 9.9 percent on dental treatment, 2.6 percent on additional pharmaceuticals purchased in independent pharmacies, and 0.3 percent on health treatment for the elderly at medical facilities.

As indicated previously, 56.3 percent of total outlays in 1990 were financed by insurance premiums, 24.6 percent by the national government, 6.8 percent by local governments and 12.1 percent by patient expenditure (see Chart 8.1 above).

---

[22]   National medical expenditure represents the sum of all payments from National Medical Insurance to providers of medical services and medical payments by patients. It excludes expenditures for normal deliveries of babies, health check-ups, preventative medical treatments, as well as spending on facilities stipulated in the Health Act for the Aged.

[23]   Drug price reductions were: 1981 - 18.6%; 1983 - 4.9%; 1984 - 16.6%; 1985 - 6.0%; 1986 - 5.1%; 1988 - 10.2%; 1990 - 9.2%; 1992 - 8.1% (Ministry of Health and Welfare, 1992b).

[24]   Source: Statistic Information Department, Ministry of Health and Welfare, *Shakai Iryou Chonsa Houkoku* (Research on Society and Health Care).

[25]   Ikegami (1991), p. 94.

[26]   Scheiber (1990).

Excluding dental and pharmaceutical expenditures, 6.4 percent of health care outlays was spent on those fourteen or younger, 20.3 percent on those 15 to 44 years, 31.7 percent on those 45 to 64, and 41.5 percent on those over 65. Medical expenditures for the elderly exceeded ¥7.45 trillion ($37 bn 1990).

Regular medical care outlays (roughly ¥18 trillion, $90 bn 1990) can also be broken down by sector. Approximately ¥8.1 trillion (45 percent, 40.5 bn 1990) went to pay for hospital in-patient care, ¥4.3 trillion (23.9 percent, $21.5 bn 1990) for hospital out-patient care, ¥0.5 trillion (2.8 percent, $2.5 bn 1990) for clinic in-patient care and ¥5.1 trillion (28.3 percent, 25.5 bn 1990) for clinic out-patient care.

8.2.4.2   Health Status

Thanks to Japan's high *per capita* income, the accessibility and technical excellence of its medical care, its diet, literacy and its low rate of violence, the health status of the Japanese is arguably the best in the industrialized world. This is evident in the data on life expectancy, incidence of disease and infant mortality. In 1990, the life expectancy of females at birth in Japan was 81.8 years; the life expectancy of males was 75.9 years. In comparison, females in the US had a life expectancy of 78.5 and males, 71.5 years. Britain's health data showed similarly lower life expectancies: 78.1 years for females, 72.4 years for males. In 1989, Japan's infant mortality was 4.6 per 1,000 live births compared to 7.5 for Germany, 9.7 for the US and 8.4 for Britain.[27] In 1986, the heart disease death rate in Japan was 117.9 per 100,000 people, considerably less than the rate of 323.5 per 100,000 people in the US (1985). Meanwhile, the cancer death rate in Japan was 158.5 per 100,000 people, as compared to 191.8 for the US.[28]

---

[27]   OECD (1991).

[28]   Koinuma (1988), p.20.

8.3   ANALYSIS OF INDIVIDUAL SECTORS

8.3.1   Key Participants in the Health Care System

From the standpoint of the delivery of medical services, the flow of funding and the influence on the health care reform process, the important actors are:

- the MOHW;
- external advisory councils, including the Health Insurance Council, the *Chuikyo* and others;
- claim examination and payment organizations, i.e., the Fund;
- other ministries, including the MOF and the Ministry of Home Affairs;
- physicians, including clinic owners, clinic-employee doctors, hospital owners, and hospital-employee doctors;
- the JMA;
- other professional interest groups;
- the LDP;
- patients/employees; and
- employers.

The **MOHW** is by far the most important actor in the health care system. The MOHW is followed in importance by its external advisory councils and by the other organizations that are supervised by the MOHW and its advisory councils. Historically, the MOHW has wielded the greatest power due to its influence in budget decisions and control over revisions to the Reimbursement Fee Schedule. The MOHW controls the planning and administration of the health care system.

The **Health Insurance Council** (*Iryo Hoken Shingikai*)[29] was established in 1985 as a consultative body to the Minister of Health and Welfare and to the head of the Social Insurance Agency. The Prime Minister's office has a similar consultative body called the Social Security System Council.

The *Chuikyo* is another advisory council to the Minister of Health and Welfare; the council consists of representatives of the three major constituencies: the payers, the public interest, and medical care specialists. The *Chuikyo* actually determines the level of fees for the Reimbursement Fee Schedule under close MOHW supervision and control. Local Social Insurance Medical Councils,

---

[29]   As noted previously, the Health Insurance Council was formerly known as the Social Insurance Council.

subordinate councils of the *Chuikyo*, exist in each prefecture. These local councils certify medical institutions as eligible for reimbursement under the universal health insurance system.

Other important councils include the **Council for Health Service for the Elderly (*Rojin Hoken Shingikai*)**, the **Central Social Welfare Council (*Chuo Shakai Fukushi Shingikai*)**, the **Medical Service Council (*Iryo Shingikai*)**, the **Social Security System Council (*Shakai Hosho Seido Shingikai*)**, and the **Central Pharmaceutical Council (*Chuou Yakuji Shingikai*)**.

The Social Insurance Reimbursement Fund is a special corporation whose operations are supervised by the Minister of Health and Welfare. The Fund has exclusive responsibility for checking claims from medical institutions and for authorizing reimbursements for these claims. The Fund administers all claims for insurers other than local-government managed NHI,[30] including claims under Health Service for the Elderly. The centralization of this processing function provides an effective means of catching and rejecting false claims from medical institutions, and ultimately serves to enhance administrative efficiency and contain costs.

The **Ministry of Finance** is a key decision-maker in terms of the size of the total national budget and thus has influence over the budgetary amounts received by the MOHW. The **Ministry of Home Affairs** oversees local government, and thereby has strong influence over NHI, which rely upon these local governments for financing and administration.

The interests of **physicians** are articulated by organizations such as the JMA, the Japan Hospital Organization and the All-Japan Hospital Association. All JMA doctors are primary care physicians; however, their interests differ depending on whether they are clinic owners, clinic-employee doctors, hospital owners, or hospital-employee doctors. The other two articulate the interests of doctors employed by hospitals.

Other professional organizations, such as the Japan Pharmacists Association, the Japan Dentists Association, and the Japan Nursing Association, have limited but increasing influence within the medical care system.

---

[30] Claims under NHI are processed by the Central Federation of National Health Insurers (the Federation).

In the legislative branch, the **LDP** dominates the Lower Houses of the *Diet*. The LDP also dominates the Labour Committee, which comprises those congressmen with expertise regarding the health insurance system. This committee serves as the study group for the *Diet* in considering and discussing amendments to health care laws.

Although in some sense, **patients/employees** vote with their feet by choosing which types of medical institutions at which to seek care, the only established channel through which their interests are conveyed seems to be labour unions. **Employer** interests are represented by the Federation of Society-Managed Health Insurance Plans (*Kenko Hoken Kumiai Rengokai*).

8.3.2 Patients

8.3.2.1 Attitudes Toward Health Care and Expectations About the Health Care System

The MOHW regularly reviews overall health conditions in the Basic Survey of National Life (*Kokumin Seikatsu Kisou Chousa*) and the Survey of Patients (*Kanja Chousa*). In 1991, 61.3 percent of those surveyed responded that they were healthy. However, 20.6 percent responded that they felt something was wrong with their health, and 10.4 percent of these reported that they were receiving some type of medical care. Of those who sought medical care, 38.3 percent went to hospitals, 46.7 percent went to clinics and the remaining 15 percent went to dentists. Of those patients visiting hospitals, 29.9 percent were aged over 65.[31]

According to the MOHW's Survey of Patients, 6,600 out of a sample population of 100,000 went to see a doctor on one particular survey day. Thus, one of every 15.2 citizens went to a doctor. Those aged over 65 were 7.2 times more likely than those aged between 15 and 19 to visit the doctor.

Overall, the Japanese seem to be moderately satisfied with their health care system.[32] Universal health insurance offers patients easy access to health care and embodies the values of equality of provision and burden-sharing. The system is generally equitable in that patients throughout the country have access to a broad basic package of medical services at a relatively uniform

---

[31]   Health and Welfare Statistics Association (1991), pp. 80-84.

[32]   The Social Insurance Agency of Japan (1991), p. 11.

level of quality without regard to personal wealth or place of residence. The government has taken steps to ensure that those residing in undeveloped rural areas have access to roughly the same quality of medical care institutions as those living in urban areas where high-quality medical institutions are more plentiful.[33]

Under the universal health insurance system, all Japanese citizens must enrol in one of the various government medical insurance programs. Once enrolled, they may choose any primary care physician, receive treatment at any hospital or clinic in the country, and visit other medical care providers for second opinions. The access to care is made easy by the low copayments at the time of delivery.

Because of the limited cost sharing and mispricing within the Reimbursement Fee Schedule, patients have a tendency to consume more of certain medical services and make more use of certain medical facilities than they would under a market-based system.[34] For example, patients tend to opt for large, well-known hospitals because of the perception that these institutions will provide higher-quality care.[35] Moreover, the system lacks the specialization that might help to balance the delivery system and to relieve the pressure on particular medical institutions. Independent clinics and big hospitals compete in the provision of both primary care and specialty care. Neither group has an incentive to refer patients to the other.

During visits to doctors, the exchange of information is generally limited. Doctors and patients do not speak at great length, and patients are extremely

---

[33] The Medical Service Council (*Iryou Shingikai*) and the Regional Health and Medical Service Council (*Chiiki Hoken Iryou Kyougikai*) have been major promoters of health care in remote areas. See Health and Welfare Statistics Association (1991), pp. 20-22. Under a regulation called the Countermeasures Plan for Remote Areas, which originated in 1956, if there are more than fifty residents living in an area of four kilometres in diameter, and medical facilities are not available, then special health care measures are applied in order that services may be received by these people. See *Hoken, Iryou, Fukushi no Sougou Nenkan* (1991), p. 472.

[34] For example, one popular Japanese saying, "*Byouin Junrei*" or visiting hospitals as one's job, is used sarcastically to describe the tendency of the elderly to make a habit of visiting hospitals.

[35] This preference is perhaps best demonstrated by the fact that while 38.3 percent of those who sought care went to hospitals, only 7 percent of all medical institutions were hospitals.

reticent about asking questions of doctors.[36] There are cultural and historical reasons for the uncommunicative relationship between the physician and the patient. Yet this tendency is exaggerated by the reimbursement fee structure, under which the price of a simple consultation is too little to pay for anything but the most cursory examination. As a result, a typical visit to a primary care physician lasts less than five minutes, which leaves little time for dialogue and explanation and gives doctors little incentive to spend time answering patient questions.

8.3.2.2 The Role and Objectives of the Patient

Participation in one of the insurance programs is compulsory. Insured individuals can receive medical care from any doctor, dentist or pharmacist at any medical institution registered with the local prefectural governor as an Insurance Medical Care Organ (hereafter referred to as a registered medical institution). This high degree of patient choice in choosing a service provider contrasts with their near complete lack of power with regards to the selection of their insurance program, the determination of the level of premiums or the determination of the level of benefits.

Citizens have no direct means by which to affect the size of health insurance premiums or coinsurance they pay, either by shopping among insurance plans or by the exercise of political influence. In the case of government-managed EHI, the MOHW may change the contribution rate upon the recommendation of the Social Insurance Council. Officially, the representatives of the public interest on the council are supposed to represent the views of patients; however, these members are selected by the MOHW, rather than by the general public. In addition, there are no explicit communication channels through which citizens can express their views or have any input into this process.[37] In fact, the proceedings of the Social Insurance Council meetings are available to the public only at the MOHW library.

---

[36]   The lack of information and the unwillingness to question doctors is particularly severe with regard to pharmaceuticals. For example, one recent best-seller has been a "pill book," which connects pictures of medicines to their indications and effects. Doctors commonly dispense pills without identifying the name of the pill or the diagnosis. Consequently, the notion is to allow patients to obtain information about medicines and infer diagnosis from a book rather than dialogue with the doctor.

[37]   *Kenkou Hoken Kumiai Rengoukai (1990)*, p. 60. Also *Hoken, Iryou, Fukushi no Sougou Nenkan (1991)*, p. 598.

Similarly, there are no direct communication channels through which citizens can influence the determination of NHI premiums.[38] These premiums are levied on households by local governments, with the rates determined largely based upon households' income level and property. The rates also vary according to the regional financial conditions of NHI, and local prefectural treasuries provide subsidies to poorly financed local insurers in order to allow provision of equal benefits for all citizens.

The traditional attitude of the providers (and of the government) has been "*sira simu bekarazu yora simu beshi*", or "don't let them know anything so that they'll depend on you". Patients have been passive and content to have their doctors tell them what to do without explaining why it is necessary.

Despite this conservative environment, there are now some signs of change. Recently, the public health care debate has shifted its focus to finding ways of providing better medical care and increasing the amount of information available to patients. According to a 1991 MOHW White Paper, citizens are increasingly aware of the importance of their supporting initiatives to improve health care services.[39]

Meanwhile, the government is in the process of reducing the constraints on advertising by clinics and hospitals that were part of the Medical Service Law.[40] There is also a new trend, initiated by the Japan Medical Association and the MOHW Joint Study Group on the neutral rating function for hospitals and clinics, towards the development of neutral independent bodies to rate medical institutions.[41] In addition to providing an incentive for hospitals and clinics to improve their practices, such bodies may provide patients with a neutral source of information when choosing a provider.

Furthermore, by order of the MOHW, the pharmacies in designated 'model' National Medical Hospitals have been separated from the rest of the hospital. This change is intended to promote specialization within local medical service institutions by giving pharmacists an independent role. The formation of independent pharmacies, in turn, is intended to promote increased

---

[38] *Kenkou Hoken Kumiai Rengoukai (1990)*, p. 60.

[39] Ministry of Health and Welfare (1992a), p. 17.

[40] *Hoken, Iryou, Fukushi no Sougou Nenkan (1991)*, p. 13.

[41] *Hoken, Iryou, Fukushi no Sougou Nenkan (1991)*, p. 13.

consciousness among patients about medical care issues. The notion is that patients are more likely to ask questions of a relatively independent pharmacist, particularly about the medicines prescribed for them by a doctor, than they are to appear to challenge the authority of the doctor by asking questions.[42]

Despite these changes, patient-directed and patient-oriented reforms will be difficult to pursue in the absence of political and social channels through which private citizens can influence the existing system.

8.3.2.3 Benefits Under the Universal Health Insurance System

Medical benefits are provided as benefits in kind at clinics and hospitals which are registered medical institutions. The benefits include (1) medical consultation; (2) the supply of medicines or therapeutical materials; (3) medical treatment, operations and other therapeutical care; (4) accommodation in hospital or clinic; and (5) nursing.

The types of care are strictly defined by the Reimbursement Fee Schedule. The Reimbursement Fee Schedule is designed to provide one fixed fee for each category of care, and does not take into account factors such as whether the institution providing the care is located in a rural or a metropolitan area. Such differences are important from the standpoint of the provider's cost because of differing land prices. The uniform fee schedule also fails to account for differences in the quality of service. A singularly qualified specialist performing a given procedure is paid no more than a semi-qualified non-specialist doctor. Patients who require or wish to receive extended consultations with physicians can accomplish this only by repeated brief visits to the doctor. As a result, the average number of physicians visits is 12.9 (1988), compared to 5.3 (1989) in the US and 11.5 (1986) in Germany (see Section 8.3.2.1 on the frequency and duration of doctors visits).

Besides medical benefits in kind, insured individuals also receive various income replacement allowances.[43] These benefits, such as sickness and injury

---

[42]   Yutaka (1989).

[43]   For example, under EHI, an insured person who is unable to work while undergoing medical care will be paid 60% of their daily standard remuneration (reduced to 40% if the insured is hospitalized and has no dependents) for the period during which he/she is unable to work for up to 18 months (after an initial three days of incapacity for which no allowance is received). If an employee receives full or partial wages from an employer during the period of incapacitation, this payment will be stopped or reduced partially. The Social Insurance

allowances and maternity allowances, are designed to compensate for loss of income due to temporary incapacitation. The insurance plans also supply lump-sum payments for certain items, including expenses for child-birth, child-nursing allowance, and funeral expenses. Furthermore, Health Insurance Societies and Mutual Aid Associations may provide additional benefits to cover medical fees that extend beyond the prescribed amounts.

At age 60, which is also the typical compulsory retirement age for Japanese companies, the employee will have the opportunity to enrol in NHI for Retirees. This type of insurance is designed to provide better medical benefits for the insured including copayments of only 20 percent versus usual copayments under NHI of 30 percent.

Japan also has a Workmen's Accident Compensation System, which covers work-related injuries and illnesses.

8.3.2.4 Degree of Choice for the Taxpayer/Insured

Typically, an individual who works at a small-to-medium sized company is automatically enrolled in government-managed EHI; spouses and other dependents are also covered by the same EHI plan. At age 60, which is also the typical compulsory retirement age for Japanese companies, the employee will have the opportunity to enrol in NHI for Retirees.

Participation in government-managed EHI is mandatory for all employers regularly employing five or more employees; no exemptions are allowed. All employees employed by these places of work are obliged to participate in EHI regardless of their income and employment positions.[44]

Large companies with more than 300 employees are free to establish society-managed EHI plans. Employees at such companies are automatically enrolled in these plans at the time of hiring. The plans themselves usually provide employees with supplemental benefits in addition to the benefits provided under government-managed EHI. Due to the supplemental benefits, the society-managed EHI plans constitute valuable recruiting and retention tools for large companies. Furthermore, these society-managed EHI plans maintain

---

Agency of Japan (1991), p. 38-39.

[44]   The Social Insurance Agency of Japan (1991), p. 35.

their financial strength due to risk selection conducted by means of the recruiting process.

All citizens not covered under EHI or other employment-related plans must be covered under NHI. Since compulsory participation is determined largely by circumstances of employment or by the occupation of the head of the household, there is little scope for choice of scheme.

Until recently, there has been little scope for private insurers to provide health insurance of any consequence, apart from policies covering patient copayments during hospitalization and the cost of premium services such as for superior hospital rooms. A 1991 MOHW White Paper, however, encourages the introduction of private supplemental health care insurance plans with a particular focus on the provision of hospital care for the aged. Private supplemental insurance enables individuals to transfer assets from the income-producing phase of their lifetime to provide an improved standard of living in old age. As a result, the elderly can afford higher-quality meals, rooms and care in the hospital than public funds can provide. The greater reliance on private supplemental hospitalization insurance would also reduce the number of cases of elderly persons relying on available government subsidies to fund lengthy hospital stays despite the fact that they have significant pension benefits.

Although private insurance may improve the ability of the elderly to pay for their care, this situation reveals a serious flaw in the Japanese system—the misuse of hospitals as facilities for elderly care. Not only has the administrative apparatus failed to respond adequately to the needs of the elderly for chronic non-acute care, but there is a shortage of institutions suitable for the needs of healthy or only partially-disabled aged persons. Because the fee structure under-compensates consultative care, elderly patients who require advice rather than active treatments are given short shrift. There is no mechanism by which their needs are conveyed to decision-makers.

8.3.3   Payers

8.3.3.1   Funding of the Payers

There are five major sources of funding for health care expenditures under the system of universal health care coverage:

1.   participants' premiums to the various insurers;
2.   employers' matching contributions to EHI on behalf of their employees;

616

3.   patient copayments to hospitals, clinics and pharmacies;
4.   national government subsidies; and
5.   local government subsidies.

Overall, Japan's national medical care expenditures in fiscal 1990 were ¥20.6 trillion ($103 bn 1990); ¥166,700 *per capita* ($834 1990). Of this total, 50 percent goes to the doctors, nurses, and other employees of hospitals and clinics. Of the remainder, 26.5 percent goes to pay for medicine and other medical materials, and 24.5 percent goes to pay for the operational overhead of health care facilities.

Under EHI, the employer is responsible for paying the contributions of both the employer and the employee, and is authorized to deduct the amount owed by the employee from wages paid. The contribution rate for government-managed EHI is a total 8.2 percent of monthly standard remuneration, of which equal shares are paid by employers and employees (4.1 percent each). Under society-managed EHI, the contributions may vary, but on average are 3.56 percent of monthly standard remuneration for employees and 4.65 percent for employers. Under government-managed EHI, there is also a contribution rate of 0.8 percent on semi-annual bonus payments; under society-managed EHI, the contribution on bonus payments may be imposed at any rate up to that level.[45]

The amount of the contribution by a householder to NHI varies according to the local ordinances or rules of the insurer concerned. The premium is set taking consideration of (1) income; (2) property; (3) the principle of equal sharing per insurer; and (4) the principle of equal sharing per household in accordance with the solvency of insured persons. There is a limit on total contributions per year per household.

The bulk of the financial resources for EHI are derived from the insurance premiums contributed by the employers and employees. The national government, meanwhile, bears responsibility for all administrative expenses and, on average, an additional 16.4 percent of the total costs of government-managed EHI. Further, a fixed subsidy is provided from the national budget to individual Health Insurance Societies whose financial status is weak. In the fiscal 1990 budget, ¥4.85 billion was appropriated for this purpose.

---

[45]   Health and Welfare Statistics Association (1991).

The financial resources for NHI are primarily comprised of the insurance contributions paid by the insured and national, prefectural, and town/city/village subsidies. The subsidy for the NHI for Retirees is prorated based upon the number of retirees entering from EHI plans, and is collected from appropriate EHI plans through the Fund and distributed to the local NHI plan joined by the retiree.

Society-managed EHI plans tend to be in comparatively sound condition financially due to (1) the risk selection that takes place through the hiring process; and (2) the relatively high salaries received by insured persons in large enterprises. The financial foundations of NHI are not as stable due to the large proportion of the aged, retirees, and low-income people among the NHI's insured population; for these reasons, 247 out of 3,428 NHI insurers ran deficits in 1989.[46]

Premiums paid under NHI differ by region. The highest annual premiums of ¥205,900 per year ($1,030 1990) are paid by insured individuals residing in a city in Hokkaido, the northern island of Japan, while the lowest premiums of ¥55,200 per year ($276 1990) are paid by the insured residents of a village in the Tokyo metropolitan area. The huge difference between regions in the burden of premiums for residence-based NHI is a significant problem.

Currently, private insurance benefits covering patient copayments account for 18 percent of total copayments. There is also a trend towards private insurance playing a wider supplemental role within the government-dominated health insurance market. While the role played by supplemental private insurance remains small, various new types of private insurance intended as complements to existing public insurance have been introduced in recent years. Benefits usually focus on upgraded meals, rooms and simple care not requiring sophisticated medical equipment.

Another typical type of private insurance coverage provides supplemental benefits for the elderly. The emergence of such insurance packages has been endorsed by the Japanese government. In 1987, the Insurance Council of the MOHW cited the need for new private insurance to help cope with the aging population. Subsequently, a 1991 MOHW White Paper encouraged the introduction of private supplemental health insurance plans, focusing especially on hospital care for the elderly.

---

[46]   The Social Insurance Agency of Japan (1991), p. 16.

8.3.3.2   Regulation of the Payers

There are a variety of government actors involved in regulating and administering health care insurance.[47] The MOHW and its various divisions supervise and coordinate these activities. There is a high level of cooperation between the MOHW, local prefectural governments, and town and city governments which means that decisions at the top quickly cause action throughout the administrative network.

The Social Insurance Agency (*Shakai Hoken Chou*) sets premiums for EHI and NHI within a range set by the Medical Service Law based on employees' standard monthly salaries. The Social Insurance Agency reviews financial conditions of EHI plans and makes small adjustments to premium rates within the stipulated ranges.

The Health Insurance Bureau of the MOHW is responsible for:

- planning and drafting of changes to EHI and NHI;
- overall coordination of health care insurance schemes;
- research regarding the development of health care insurance schemes;
- guidance and supervision of Health Insurance Societies and NHI insurers;
- guidance and supervision of medical care provided under health care insurance;
- administration of Social Insurance Medical Fees; and
- actuarial affairs related to EHI and NHI.

The Ministry of Finance plays a key role in determining the health care subsidies provided from the national government budget. The Ministry of Finance's current policy is to maintain the MOHW budget's growth at a rate less than that of each previous year. Even if applied flexibly, the budget ceiling cannot take full account of factors such as the aging of the Japanese population, the increasing cost of advanced high-technology medical equipment, the shift in the disease profile in the Japanese population from contagious to degenerative diseases, and the preferences of patients.

The Insurance Division in each prefectural government is responsible, among other things, for the execution of government-managed EHI and for the

---

[47]   The Social Insurance Agency of Japan (1991), pp. 21-25.

supervision of Health Insurance Societies and registered medical facilities within the prefecture.

Local Social Insurance Offices in wards, towns, and villages enforce social insurance schemes, including government-managed EHI. These offices receive various forms for qualifications and disqualifications of insured persons, collect contributions, and decide upon and make payment of short term benefits. The insured can apply for consultation and receipt of benefits at the nearest of the 298 such offices established throughout the country.

A Local Social Insurance Medical Council is established in each prefectural government to review and advise the prefectural governor regarding the registration of medical facilities and doctors. Each local council is composed of 20 local members in the same proportions as the Central Social Insurance Medical Council.

National Health Insurance Operation Councils in each city, town and village serve as a forum for conferring about important matters regarding the operation of NHI. Each council is composed of equal number of representatives of insured persons; of doctors, dentists and pharmacists; and of the public interest.

The Social Insurance Appeals Committee within the MOHW consists of members appointed by the Prime Minister with the approval of the *Diet*. The Committee is an administrative organization authorized to investigate and decide on questions concerning the qualification of insured persons, their standard remuneration, and their insurance benefits or contributions under EHI, Seaman's Health Insurance, Employees' Pension Insurance, National Pension Insurance and other employment-related insurance plans. The Committee conducts reviews in response to appeals by an insured person or an employer against the decisions of administrative agencies. These appeals, which must be filed within 60 days of the original decision, are initially examined by Social Insurance Referees in each prefecture. When the decision of the Appeals Committee still does not satisfy the appellant, he/she may file a suit with a judicial court.

National Health Insurance Appeals Committees are established in each prefecture to handle complaints from persons insured under NHI regarding benefits, the assessment or impositions of contributions, and other issues. These committees are composed of nine members, with an equal number representing insured persons, insurers and the public interest.

620

8.3.3.3 Economic Incentives of the Payers

The insurance plan to which a Japanese citizen belongs is determined by his or her occupation or that of the head of the household. Unemployed and self-employed heads of households and their dependents are enrolled in their local area residence-based NHI plans. Thus, there is no individual choice between plans, and the lack of individual choice largely prevents the range of difference in copayments, premiums and income indemnity allowances under the various plans from serving to promote competition. Moreover, competition is limited because the core medical benefits provided under all plans are equal. However, through the establishment of Society-managed EHI plans, large companies are able to some extent to control copayments, premiums and income indemnity allowances for their employees. This exception to the lack of choice exacerbates the problem of unequal burden sharing, as those most able to pay, the employees of large companies, are effectively taken out of the national health care system.

8.3.4   Primary Health Care Sector

8.3.4.1 Roles and Objectives of Key Participants in the Primary Health Care Sector

Once certified by the Minister of Health and Welfare, medical doctors are allowed to open clinics and hospitals when and where they choose.[48] To start a clinic, a doctor or group of doctors need only notify the local prefectural governor, whereas to start a hospital, approval from the local prefectural governor is mandatory.[49] The 'free medical practitioner system' has led to an abundant supply of medical care. This is evident in both the sharp increase in the number of medical doctors (211,797 in 1990 compared with 103,131 in 1960), the rapid establishment of new medical schools and an excessive total number of beds.

Although the total number of doctors in Japan more than doubled between 1960 and 1990, the proportion of clinic doctors—who traditionally provide the majority of primary care—decreased from 44.8 percent to 30.5 percent.[50] Of

---

[48]   This constitutes one of the basic principles of the Japanese medical system: *Jiyuu Kaigyou I Sei*.

[49]   Upon application, clinics and hospitals may become medical corporations (*Iryou Houjin*), and receive favourable tax treatment in return for accepting some restrictions on funding.

[50]   *Iryou Shisetsu Chousa* (Statistics Bureau of the Ministry of Health and Welfare of Japan, 1988).

the 211,797 doctors in 1990, almost two-thirds were salaried doctors (*Kinmu I*). This change in the composition of physicians reflects the growing dominance of hospital-based salaried doctors.[51] Because an increasing number of young physicians have chosen to work in large general hospitals rather than in clinics, the average age of clinic doctors compared to salaried hospital doctors has steadily risen. Currently, the average age of clinic doctors is 60 (see Chart 8.9).

Chart 8.9
Number of Physicians by Age and Type, 1990

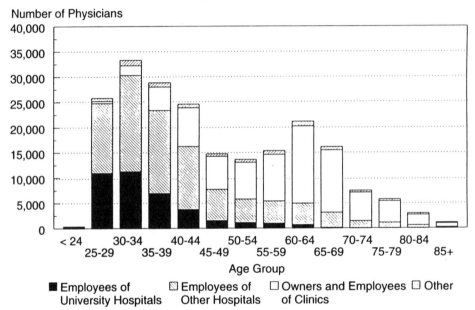

■ Employees of   ▨ Employees of   □ Owners and Employees □ Other
University Hospitals   Other Hospitals   of Clinics

Under the Reimbursement Fee Schedule, all doctors are treated alike; specialists receive the same reimbursement as non-specialists, in contrast to the situation in other countries with advanced health care systems. As a result, there is no room for price or quality competition for patients requiring primary care and only limited functional differentiation in the types of medical services provided by different types of doctors. Doctors who go into clinical practice usually undergo specialized medical training in hospitals affiliated with

---

[51]   Ministry of Health and Welfare (1990).

prestigious universities.[52]   Specialists also play the role of general practitioners or family doctors, providing both cognitive (evaluation) services and basic medical treatment.[53]

Clinic doctors are increasingly reluctant to refer their patients to hospital specialists because patients often choose to remain with the hospital physicians on an out-patient basis instead of returning to their clinic doctors.[54] Clinic doctors also resist referring patients to hospital-based doctors unless necessary because they generally have the hospital training, as well as the professional background, to provide secondary care.[55]

Clinics and clinic doctors must deal with increasingly difficult financial circumstances. Currently, the high price of land in large cities makes it difficult for new doctors even to contemplate setting up their own clinics there.[56] In addition, the requirements for establishing primary care settings have become more stringent.[57]

---

[52]   Until recently, there were few, if any, formal programs of specialization; under an unsystematic arrangement, medical students merely specialized in the fields that captured their interest. Academic associations in most fields of medicine have begun to establish such specialization programs, although these programs have yet to gain widespread approval.

[53]   Under the Medical Service Law, however, specialists are prohibited from advertising their area of expertise.

[54]   Doctors who own and manage clinics with beds have the highest income of all doctors in Japan, followed by doctors operating clinics without beds and salaried hospital doctors. The annual income of the average *Kaigyou I* is roughly three times the earnings of a salaried doctor in a general hospital. The average net monthly income for *Kaigyou I* was $22,917 while for a doctor employed by a general hospital it was $6,268. See *Chuou Shakai Hoken Iryou Kyougikai* (1990); and Yoshikawa, Shirouzu and Holt (1992), p. 14.

[55]   Physicians customarily work in hospitals for several years as salaried doctors before establishing their own private clinics.

[56]   This effect is somewhat mitigated by the fact that doctors have traditionally opened clinics in their own homes and handed down their legacies to their sons. Although such bequests are now less common, roughly one-third of all medical students in Japan are the children of medical doctors.

[57]   Most notably, the 1985 regional planning amendment that gave the prefectures control over hospital expansion had some fall-out with regard to the operation of clinics.

8.3.4.2   Patient's Choice and Access Within the Primary Health Care Sector

Patients are free to choose any primary care physician who operates under the statutory social insurance system. Although one of the strengths of Japan's health care system, this guarantee of free choice of primary care has a number of drawbacks.

First, clinics and hospitals — including national, public, and university hospitals — compete for the same primary care patients. Large hospitals, especially university hospitals, have become so popular that they are inundated with patients. One common saying, in fact, is that "one waits three hours to see the doctor for three minutes." The 1992 revision of the Reimbursement Fee Schedule allocated a higher proportion of points to primary services at clinics. This was intended to ease the over-crowded situation at large hospitals. However, since this change in incentives affects only hospitals and clinics, and not the patients who exercise individual choice between the two, this measure has not been effective in accomplishing its stated purpose. As a result of the failure of the fee schedule to distinguish among doctors by quality, "a small but significant black market has developed for patients willing to gain access to eminent specialists. This takes the form of a monetary gift to the attending physician in the range of ¥100,000 to ¥300,000 ($500 to $1500 1990) but is usually limited to patients hospitalized in the private rooms of universities and other prestigious hospitals." [58]

Second, clinics and hospitals are concentrated in large metropolitan areas, and remote areas continue to suffer from a lack of primary care institutions. Patient choice is especially limited in some areas, whereas large metropolitan areas are saturated with medical care institutions.

8.3.4.3   Funding and Regulation of the Primary Health Care Sector

Physicians are reimbursed from the Reimbursement Fee Schedule on a fee-for-service basis. Each medical service — including the dispensing of pharmaceuticals — is assigned a certain number of points; each point is worth ¥10 ($0.05 1990) for the primary care physician. For example, a first-time visit

---

[58]   Ikegami (1992), p. 616.

to a physician was worth 205-208 points (2050-2080 yen or about $15) in 1990.[59]

Each item on the Reimbursement Fee Schedule includes various service elements under a single heading. For example, the fee for each first-time visit (*Shin Ryou*) includes a physician consultation fee, a nurse fee, an administration fee, and other fees under the general heading of 'first-time visit' without any itemization of the individual fees.

Under the Reimbursement Fee Schedule, every physician receives exactly the same payment for providing each listed service. These fees remain the same regardless of the identity of the patient (including those on public assistance), the specialized experience physicians have in providing certain services, or the institution or region in which the services are delivered.

Salaried hospital doctors and other staff are generally paid uniform, experienced-based wages, regardless of their specialty. Physician owners of clinics, in contrast, can retain their profit margin after their medical claims have been reimbursed and they have covered both capital and operating costs.

Similarly, hospitals must use fee payments to finance capital expenditure, in addition to paying for the operating cost of service.[60] While hospitals generally lose money on in-patient services, they offset these losses with gains on out-patient services. Public loans are available to finance the initial capital costs for private hospitals, but these funds are not as generous as the government grants given to public hospitals.

8.3.4.4 Economic Incentives of Key Participants of the Primary Health Care Sector

The Reimbursement Fee Schedule has been skewed in the favour of services such as the dispensing of drugs and laboratory tests. As a result, physicians have an incentive to over-prescribe drugs and conduct numerous, sometimes

---

[59] Precisely speaking, there are two reimbursement system books: one called "*ko*" and the other "*otsu*". Historically, clinics have used "*ko*" while hospitals have used "*otsu*". Today, however, the differences have become minimal to the point of being virtually non-existent. For practical purposes, and unless the policy of setting fees the same for hospitals and clinics changes in the future, both books will be the same.

[60] OECD (1987).

unnecessary tests. Attempts to fix these problems by fee adjustments are under way.

Physicians also have an incentive under the Reimbursement Fee Schedule to treat as many patients as possible. Since the government decides the prices of services listed on the Reimbursement Fee Schedule, physicians are compelled to 'compete' on the basis of patient volume: the more patients they see, the more money they make. As a result, physicians normally see a huge number of patients each day. On average, out-patient physicians see 49 patients per day.[61]

Usually, the fee-for-service payment method, such as that in Japan, provides strong incentives for physicians to offer high-quality care. Japan's uniform fee schedule, however, discourages both quality maintenance and quality differentiation. Moreover, Japan lacks either the quality regulation or the specialty care industry that might help combat these tendencies.

The Reimbursement Fee Schedule also encourages widespread dispersion of sophisticated medical technology. Small hospitals and even some clinics are equipped with expensive, modern equipment. For example, 26.3 percent of all clinics have ultrasonic image testing devices, and 12 percent of clinics have gastrointestinal fibrescopes. Furthermore, approximately 70 percent of all clinics have electro-cardiographs and 60 percent have X-ray equipment.[62]

Once an investment has been made in the purchase of medical equipment, the incentives are to provide as many tests as possible to patients. There is no third-party checking mechanism in regards to the quality of medical services. The lack of cooperative use of sophisticated equipment is a major concern to the MOHW.

8.3.5   Hospital Sector

8.3.5.1   *Hospital Formation and Management*

A hospital is defined as a medical care institution with 20 or more beds, while a general clinic is defined as a medical care institution with 19 or less beds. As stipulated in the Medical Service Law, the approval of the local prefectural

---

[61]   Ministry of Health and Welfare (1985).

[62]   Yoshikawa, Shirouzu and Holt (1992), p. 21.

governor is required to open a hospital. Hospitals voluntarily apply to the prefectural governor to become registered medical institutions in order to be eligible to treat those insured under EHI and NHI.

Hospitals may be established by:

- the government;
- public organizations, including municipalities and organizations approved by the MOHW;
- medical legal entities either corporate or foundational; and
- individuals.

Official approval from the prefectural governor is required to establish a medical legal entity (*Iryou Houjin*). Article 7 of the Medical Service Law states that if a hospital is established or operated for the purpose of creating profits, a prefectural governor may withdraw its medical legal entity certification. Meanwhile, Article 54 of the Medical Service Law stipulates that the private allocation of any surplus funds of medical legal entities is forbidden.[63]

Given the rather recent development of hospitals as institutions, physicians have retained their central role in all aspects of the health care system. At general clinics and some small hospitals, doctors often double as managers and supervisors. Physicians are also in managerial command throughout the hospital system. The Medical Service Law provides that heads of hospitals (*Byouincho*) must be physicians which means that hospital administrators generally will have academic backgrounds in medicine rather than management. Even at the large hospitals, administrators are strongly influenced by the hospitals' doctors, who always head the institutional hierarchy. In this type of setting, administrators trained in business and management techniques have limited scope for independent action and advancement. Consequently, hospitals do not attract seasoned managers, and many hospitals are unable to cope with the rapid and complex changes affecting modern medical care management. MOHW has expressed a desire to make professional hospital management a recognised occupation in Japan.

---

[63] A 'special medical legal entity' (*Tokutei Iryou Houjin*) is afforded a unique tax status under Article 67 of the Special Tax Treatment Law (*Souzei Tokubetsu Toushiho*).

8.3.5.2   The Roles and Objectives of the Key Participants in the Hospital Sector

In the West, hospitals originated as charitable institutions where doctors were invited to provide treatment to poor and sick people in isolation from the community.   In contrast, Japanese doctors traditionally accommodated sick people at home-based 'clinics'.   Therefore, although the Medical Service Law (*Iryou Hou*) stipulated the right of patients to visit both clinics and hospitals for primary care, hospitals originally provided advanced medical care.[64]   The primary care function only later expanded into hospitals.[65]   Patients have come to prefer visiting hospitals, especially university hospitals, for primary care due to their strong reputation as providers of both advanced and comprehensive services.

National and other public hospitals receive subsidies from the national government.   Private hospitals and clinics have to compete with these subsidized institutions without the benefit of such subsidies, and cannot differentiate themselves on the basis of price due to the universal Reimbursement Fee Schedule system.

The problems with hospital management have been worsening for some time. The incidence of hospital bankruptcies peaked in 1984, when 68 hospitals went into receivership.   The continuing failures of hospital management are attributable to inadequate accounting and financial supervision and rigidity in the face of rapid change.   Although some hospitals have started to utilize outside management consultants who specialize in hospital administration, the practice remains rare.[66]

8.3.5.3   Patient's Choice Within the Hospital Sector

Insured persons are entitled to medical services at any registered medical institution.   Despite the freedom of choice, patients often opt for the large hospitals because they believe these facilities provide better medical treatment. As a result, patients face long waiting periods at large hospitals — particularly hospitals that are famous or have reputations for providing good medical treatment.   There are four stages of waiting: (1) when reporting to the

---

[64]   In principle, general clinics cannot hospitalize patients except in special and urgent cases, when they are allowed to hospitalize for up to 48 hours.

[65]   *Hoken, Iryou, Fukushi no Sougou Nenkan* (1991), p. 105.

[66]   *Hoken, Iryou, Fukushi no Sougou Nenkan* (1991), p. 108.

reception; (2) for medical diagnosis and treatment; (3) to make payment; and (4) to receive medicines from the pharmacist. Often there are not enough seats in the waiting rooms at these various stages.

The trend towards the greater use of large hospitals for primary care is partly due to patients' lack of information about medical institutions and their distinctive roles. More fundamentally, this trend reflects the rational choice patients make between services from an institution which signals high quality (the hospital) and one which does not (the clinic), when both services cost the same.

8.3.5.4 Funding of the Hospital Sector

The primary source of income for both hospitals and clinics are the fees received under the Reimbursement Fee Schedule. Because they are paid on a fee-for-service basis, hospitals and clinics tend to maximize the number of patient visits in order to maximize their income. Some additional income is earned from medical tests and health examinations not covered by the Reimbursement Fee Schedule.

Other sources of funding include:

- Local public hospitals receive funding from the special bonds of local governments, as stipulated in the Local Public-operated Business Law (*Chiho Kouei Kigyou Hou*).

- Private hospitals can receive funding from a public corporation under the MOHW providing social welfare and medical services (*Shakai Fukushi Iryou Jigyoudan*).

- Japan Red Cross-related hospitals and Municipal Aid-related hospitals can receive funding from pension welfare public corporations under the MOHW (*Nenkin Fukushi Jigyoudan*).[67]

In the past, efficient financial management has not been a major concern for hospitals or clinics. However, due to increasing competition, increases in personnel costs, and the large facility investments necessary to provide high-technology medical care, hospitals are now being forced to consider new and innovative ways to control costs and manage resources.

---

[67]   Health and Welfare Statistics Association (1991), pp. 214-216.

8.3.5.5 Regulation of the Hospital Sector

The Medical Services Law (*Iryou Hou*) of 1948 is the basis of the current medical care system in Japan. The Medical Services Law regulates the construction, equipping, and staffing of hospitals. If hospitals fail to comply with these regulations, the governor of the prefecture in which the hospital is located can restrict the usage of hospital facilities and/or equipment for a certain period.

Those hospitals and medical clinics that provide treatment under the universal health insurance system are obliged to receive guidance provided by the Prefectural Governors, including lectures and private administrative instruction. The Prefectural Governors also audit suspicious practices regarding billing and other administrative practices, and can then issue warnings, notices, and revocations of approval as a medical legal entity. In 1988, 6,767 medical care institutions and pharmacists received private administrative guidance, and 597 underwent audits. Out of those audited, 38 lost their approvals as medical legal entities.

Prefectural Local Insurance Division Offices employ doctors to serve as medical administrative guidance officers, i.e., national public servants assigned by the national government to investigate local registered medical institutions. In the national government, the Insurance Bureau Medical Care Section of the MOHW has established an audit function, to which 16 auditors have been assigned. These are the major official checking facilities for hospital management.[68]

The Medical Services Law has been amended several times, most notably in 1985 and 1992. The 1985 amendments provided that:

- Each prefectural government should establish a Medical Care Plan and revise this plan at least once every five years.[69] Each government should divide its prefecture into separate medical areas and determine the number of beds for each area. Each Medical Care Plan should also

---

[68]   *Hoken, Iryou, Fukushi no Sougou Nenkan* (1991), p. 74.

[69]   Under Article 30-3 of the Medical Care Law (*Iryo Ho*), as part of its Medical Care Plan, each prefectural government is to establish a system for close cooperation between hospitals, clinics, pharmacies and other medical facilities. Each facility is to provide care in accordance with its original function. This is intended to allow transfer of patients from one facility to another according to their recovery process, so that the patient receives the most appropriate treatment.

ensure the provision of medical care for remote areas, provide for emergency care, and handle any other issues pertaining to the supply of medical care.

- The national or municipal government should establish and carry out necessary measures to supplement the Medical Care Plans.

- Hospitals should provide access to outside doctors for treatments and for training.

- Prefectural Governors may make recommendations to hospitals regarding increases or decreases in the number of beds or changes in bed types necessary to accomplish the Medical Care Plan.

The 1985 amendments also limited the number of new beds in hospitals.

The 1992 amendments to the Medical Services Law established the category of 'special functioning hospital' to develop, evaluate and provide high-technology medical care and equipment, and to train practitioners of high-technology medical care. The 1992 amendments to the Medical Services Law also made clear that:

- Medical treatment should preserve the dignity of human lives and show regard for the self-esteem of individuals.

- Medical treatment should be provided on a basis of trust between medical providers (doctors, dentists and others involved in medical care supply) and patients.

- Medical treatment should be provided to patients according to the conditions of their mind and body. And medical treatments including those to prevent sickness and promote rehabilitation should be appropriate and of high quality.

- Hospitals with beds for long-term care should have rooms for training of the spirit (*Ki no Kunren Sitsu*) so that long-term patients will have opportunities for comfortable recreation.

- Patients should be supplied with appropriate medical information.

An amendment to the Medical Service Law established standards to prevent the quality of medical care from suffering when 'out-sourcing' is used. This amendment was introduced because clinics and hospitals increasingly employ outsiders for functions such as laundering and catering.

8.3.5.6   Economic Incentives of Key Participants of the Hospital Sector

The current taxation scheme for medical institutions affords preferential treatment to doctors who operate their own clinics.   Tax provisions also strongly favour non-profit management of hospitals.

Pharmaceutical price differentials, also referred to as doctors' margins (*Yakka Saeki*), are one of the most controversial economic incentives provided to hospitals.   Hospitals are allowed to keep the difference between what they charge (based on the Reimbursement Fee Schedule) for the medicines dispensed to patients and the wholesale price. These margins are a significant source of income for hospitals.   In 1989, the total annual differential (including sales by both hospitals and doctors), amounted to ¥1.3 trillion ($6.7 bn 1990), or ¥10,000 per Japanese citizen ($51 1990).

Since the early 1980s, the MOHW has reduced the reimbursement prices for pharmaceuticals in the interest of containing the cost of national medical expenditures.   This trend, which continues through the 1990s under a new price-setting regime, threatens the income of hospitals.   This effect combined with the competition for patients — which often involves the need to spend money on reputation-enhancing high-technology medicine — produces severe funding and mismanagement problems. Hospitals, particularly the larger private hospitals, have a strong incentive to influence the price mechanism through *Chuikyo* in order to do whatever is necessary to hold their incomes constant.

8.3.6   Pharmaceutical Sector

8.3.6.1   The Pharmaceutical Industry and the Health Care System

The principal distinguishing characteristic of the pharmaceutical sector in Japan is the sharing of the dispensing function by doctors and pharmacies. Doctors prescribe prescription drugs and dispense these drugs at clinics and hospitals.   The MOHW has been trying to implement a separation of the functions of pharmacists and doctors, but as of 1992 independent pharmacists were still distributing only 12 percent of the total value of prescription drugs.[70]

---

[70]   The MOHW predicts that when hospitals' pharmaceutical margins are reduced to 17 percent, the economic incentive to maintain in-house pharmacists will fade away. Meanwhile, Japan continues to lack a sufficient number of qualified pharmacists which slows down the process of separating the prescribing and dispensing functions.

Doctors and hospitals derive 25 to 30 percent of their incomes from dispensing medicines. This has important consequences both for the way disease management is conducted in Japan and for health care financing. Because of the universal health insurance system, consumption of over-the-counter drugs is low. People tend to visit doctors in order to receive prescription drugs and doctors prefer treatment with pharmaceuticals to other alternatives because of the profitability of dispensing. Patients pay only 10-30 percent of the cost of medicines as copayment. These factors have led to a higher levels of pharmaceutical consumption in Japan than anywhere else in the world. Due to the high levels of revenue earned through their dispensing of drugs, doctors were criticized for "soaking the patients with drugs" (*kusurizuke*).

Following World War II, the Japanese pharmaceutical industry expanded by cooperating with foreign manufacturers in importing new drugs and new technology. Since the establishment of NHI in 1961, the demand for medical services has risen rapidly, giving rise to an expansion in drug production. During the 1970s, as the degree of coverage provided by the universal health insurance system increased so did the consumption of prescription drugs. In 1970, total pharmaceutical production was valued at ¥1 trillion ($13.6 bn 1990). With the increase in the benefit rate associated with the change in the 1973 NHI law, and increases in benefits to the elderly, Japanese pharmaceutical production mushroomed.[71] At the same time, improvements in the regulatory environment in the mid-1970s encouraged domestic pharmaceutical production.

In 1975, with the liberalization of foreign capital restrictions, foreign businesses were allowed to open 100 percent-owned subsidiaries in Japan and participate freely in its market. Although pharmaceutical firms were somewhat hampered by the need to rely on domestic wholesalers and sales forces, they participated in this trend. In 1976, the Japanese patent law was amended to afford protection for new substances. As a result of these changes, domestic production of pharmaceuticals increased to ¥3 trillion ($19 bn 1990) in 1979 and to ¥4 trillion ($21.7 bn 1990) in 1983.[72]

---

[71]   In 1973, revisions to the NHI law raised the dependent benefit rate from 50 percent to 70 percent. Also, medical service for the elderly—those 70 years and older and the bedridden aged 65 and over—was made available free of charge.

[72]   On the specifics of government encouragement of domestic pharmaceutical production through "health policy as industrial policy" see Reich (1990), pp. 124-149.

During the early 1980s, medical costs began to rise to uncomfortable levels, even as the Japanese economy was growing less rapidly than in previous years. In response, the government undertook a cost containment program that focused on reducing the reimbursement prices for pharmaceuticals. Beginning in 1981, the annual price reduction averaged 7.3 percent for the next decade.

As of 1989, according to MOHW's 'Pharmaceutical Industry Survey', Japan had a total of 1,532 pharmaceutical manufacturers. These were:

- 419 prescription drug manufacturers,
- 517 over-the-counter (OTC) drug manufacturers,
- 467 prescription and OTC drug manufacturers, and
- 75 others.

Of these, 457 manufacturers offered drugs listed on the NHI drug price list.

8.3.6.2   Patients' Choice within the Pharmaceutical Sector

Traditionally, doctors in Japan carried a medicine box when visiting patients for consultations. Despite the influence of the German model, which included the principle that physicians should not dispense medicine, Japan did not separate the functions of pharmacists and doctors from the time of its nineteenth-century origins. As a result, Japanese doctors have continued to dispense medicine up until the present.

Doctors in Japan are highly respected as professionals. Traditionally, patients have regarded a doctor's choice of medicine as something that they must accept without comment or question. Patients are asked to take, and regularly do take, substances of which they have no knowledge. The only explanation that patients receive from doctors and pharmacists is when to take medicines and what dosage to take. Generally, patients are not even informed of the names of their medicines.

In general, the fact that hospitals and doctors wish to maintain their incomes has been the major barrier to substantial revisions in Japanese prescription and dispensing patterns. As a result, without some alternative compensation mechanism, there is no obvious method for gradually reducing the incentives to over-prescribe that are built into the system. Indeed, there is evidence that as reimbursement prices have been reduced, particularly for the more high-powered and expensive drugs, prescription patterns have changed in ways that suggest substitution for the sake of maintaining doctors' incomes.[73] Traditional Japanese respect for the role of the physician and the Japanese inclination not to question doctors' recommendations have remained a constant in the face of these changes.

Patients currently can purchase over-the-counter (OTC) drugs from pharmacists. The average prices for OTC drugs are relatively high however, and patients are not reimbursed by health insurance for purchases of OTC drugs. Thus, patients have an incentive to visit doctors, even though they pay 10-30 percent as their copayment for prescription drugs dispensed by the doctor.

8.3.6.3   Pricing in the Pharmaceutical Sector

In Japan, the Reimbursement Fee Schedule, regulated by the MOHW and negotiated within *Chuikyo*, sets a ceiling on what doctors, clinics and hospitals will pay for wholesale drugs.[74] Medical institutions then obtain widely-varying price concessions from wholesalers depending on their relative market power and bargaining strength. Finally, pharmaceutical manufacturers and wholesalers negotiate over wholesale prices. The wholesale prices of drugs vary widely, as do doctors' margins, i.e. the margins between the Reimbursement Fee Schedule prices received by doctors and the wholesale prices paid by doctors. Chart 8.10 details the roles of the key actors in the pharmaceutical sector and shows the flow of funding between the relevant parties.

In the past, pharmaceutical manufacturers protected wholesalers by compensating them for shortfalls below their normal (percentage) profit margins. Manufacturers competed mainly on the basis of the services offered by marketing representatives, which include data collection to help doctors with academic articles, research, etc.

---

[73]   Reich and Hayashi (1992).

[74]   Reimbursement prices are identical for all hospitals and clinics.

Chart 8.10
The Pharmaceutical Sector in Japan

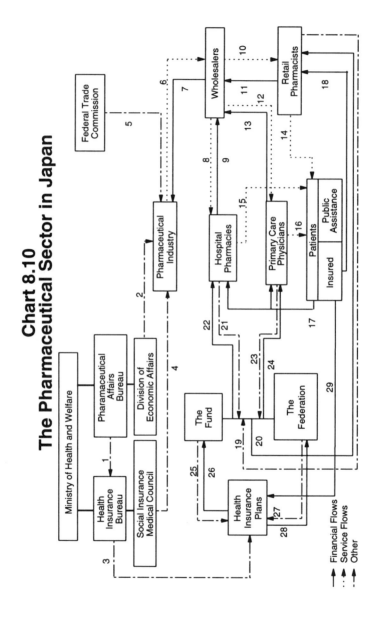

KEY TO CHART 8.10

(1) Divisions within the Pharmaceutical Affairs Bureau (PAB) make recommendations (e.g. to improve the pricing and distribution systems) to the appropriate regulatory bodies within the Health Insurance Bureau (HIB).

(2) The Economic Affairs division of the PAB is responsible for making contacts with the pharmaceutical industry on production issues. (A separate PAB division is involved in the drug approval process. This is not specifically shown in the chart.)

(3) The Health Insurance Bureau formulates the policies which regulate the health insurance plans.

(4) Within the HIB, the Central Social Insurance Medical Council sets and negotiates the drug tariffs and determines the method of drug reimbursement calculation.

(5) The Federal Trade Commission, which has tried to promote fair and free trade within all Japanese industries, has recently determined guidelines for the pharmaceutical industry's distribution system.

(6) Pharmaceutical manufacturers sell drugs to wholesalers and pay them rebates so that they will maintain a minimum final price.

(7) In return, wholesalers pay manufacturers the negotiated price (and receive rebates).

Wholesalers sell the drugs to hospital pharmacists (8), retail pharmacists (10) and clinic doctors (12). The final sale prices—indicated as (9), (11) and (13)—often include a discount. The size of the discount depends, among other factors, on who the buyer is; clinic doctors generally receive the largest discounts.

Retail pharmacists (14), hospital pharmacists (15) and clinics doctors (16) dispense drugs to patients, who make copayments (17) (18).

Retail pharmacists (19), hospital pharmacies (21) and clinic doctors (23) send their claims to prefectural review intermediaries (the Fund and the Federation) and are then reimbursed by these organizations (20) (22) (24).

The Fund and the Association then send claims to the appropriate health insurance plans—EHI (25) or NHI (27)—and receive payments in return (26) (28).

Patients also pay premiums to the various health insurance plans (29).

8.3.6.4   Regulation of the Pharmaceutical Sector

Under the universal health insurance system, the pharmaceutical sector is regulated by the government in the following ways:

* through the setting of drug Reimbursement Fee Schedule prices;

* through the approval process for new drugs and post-marketing surveillance; and,

* through regulation of the system of drug marketing.

8.3.6.4.1   The Reimbursement Fee Schedule

The Reimbursement Fee Schedule is the key regulatory mechanism in the pharmaceutical sector. The list consists of all drugs reimbursed under the insurance system and the official prices at which they are dispensed, and is uniform for all hospitals and clinics. As of March 10, 1992, the reimbursement drug price list contained 13,573 items.

In 1950 when reimbursement prices for drugs were first set there was a shortage of drugs. To increase supply (and also to discourage use of the black market), the government introduced **the bulk-line method**. This method set NHI prices on the basis of the 90th percentile or the 81st percentile in the total sales volume of a given drug whose market prices, as investigated by the MOHW, were arranged on an ascending scale.

Subsequently, the supply of drugs increased greatly; however, the variation in the wholesale prices paid by different medical service providers resulted in wide discrepancies between the average wholesale and Reimbursement Fee Schedule prices. To remedy this problem, *Chuikyo* recommended on May 31, 1991 that the MOHW abolish the bulk-line formula and adopt a **'weighted average price range method'**. On April 1, 1992, the government implemented the recommendations and introduced new calculation formulas for Reimbursement Fee Schedule prices.   The details of the new pricing methodology and their implications for price levels in the 1990s are discussed in Annex 8.1. It is known as the "Zone of Reasonableness" method — R-Zone pricing, for short.

The revision of the reimbursement price formula, in combination with the Fair Trade Commission's new guidelines regarding distribution practices, has led some to forecast an amelioration in the rate of drug price declines. This outcome, however, is by no means certain. The prices that a manufacturer will receive under R-Zone pricing depend upon the margins on drug sales of hospitals (and other medical institutions) and on their ability to sustain those margins in the face of declining reimbursement prices. Unless the permissible disparity under R-Zone pricing fortuitously equals the amount of funds from drug sales needed by medical institutions to cover their costs, or unless the government supplies funds to medical institutions in the 1990s by other means to compensate for lost margins on drugs, a continuing downward spiral of manufacturers price will ensue. The willingness of the government to set the price of new drugs relatively high and to add a price premium to drugs judged to be innovative is a countervailing, upward force on pricing. This is a strong encouragement to bring new drugs to market.

8.3.6.4.2   New Drug Approval

The manufacturing of new drugs in Japan requires approval from the MOHW. Manufacturers submit their applications to local prefectural governments, who then pass the applications on to the MOHW. The Minister of Health and Welfare and the Central Pharmaceutical Affairs Council (*Chuou Yakuji Shingikai*)[75] are responsible for actually reviewing the applications. On average, the examination period takes 18 months for ethical drugs and 10 months for OTC drugs.

The MOHW then observes the efficacy and safety of new drugs for a specified number of years after their approval (this is called the re-examination period). The re-examination period is six years for drugs containing new molecular entities, for new combination drugs, and for drugs with new means of administration. The period is four years for drugs with new indications and for drugs with new dosages and administrations. Starting April 1, 1993, the post-marketing surveillance (PMS) of new drugs required for re-examination is to be conducted in compliance with the standards of Good Post-Marketing Surveillance Practice (GPMSP).[76]

---

[75]   Established as a third party examination body based on Article 3 of the Pharmaceutical Law (*Yakuji Ho*), this council consists of 56 members (or less) drawn from academia and is under the direct supervision of the Pharmaceutical Bureau of MOHW.

[76]   Japan is/was the first country in the world to establish such standards.

8.3.6.4.3   Regulation of Drug Marketing

The overhaul of the pharmaceutical distribution system in Japan began in early 1991 when the Secretariat of the Japanese Fair Trade Commission announced the 'Draft Anti-Monopoly Act Guidelines Concerning Distribution Systems and Business Practices,' which were derived from the US-Japan Structural Impediments Initiative and were scheduled for implementation in April 1991.

The three principal aspects of the guidelines are:

1.   A prohibition against resale price maintenance except for the OTC market. Historically, manufacturers had approved purchase prices for each individual medical institution, thereby preventing wholesalers from freely setting prices.

2.   A prohibition against manufacturers' representatives negotiating directly with medical institutions. In the past, such activity effectively enabled manufacturers to decide wholesalers' prices to medical institutions.

3.   A standardization of pharmaceutical distribution practices. In the past, manufacturers' rebates constituted more than half of wholesalers' (15 percent of sales) gross margin. Moreover, the actual sales — the remaining 7 percent of the gross margin — did not even cover the wholesaler's administrative expenses (10 percent of sales).[77] In most cases, there were no documented standards for rebate payments; some rebates were arbitrary or strongly tied to quotas. As a result of the new guidelines, pharmaceutical companies have introduced 'Tate Ne Sei', under which they (1) sell at a single nationwide price to all wholesalers and (2) no longer offer compensatory rebates correcting any shortfall in the prices received by wholesalers.

8.3.6.5   Economic Incentives

The Japanese pharmaceutical industry has a large, chronic trade deficit; the dollar value of imports typically exceed the dollar value of exports by a 2:1 ratio.[78] Before 1980, the Japanese companies depended on foreign technology. Since 1980, pharmaceutical companies' R&D expenditures increased and the number of new products introduced grew. However, the dramatic slowdown

---

[77]   The numerical values are approximations, not accurate averages.

[78]   Japan Pharmaceutical Manufacturers Association (1992).

in the growth of the domestic market and continuous reduction in the Reimbursement Fee Schedule have put increasing pressure on research budgets.

Globalization has become an important concept for Japanese pharmaceutical companies as they try to spread the costs of R&D by marketing their products abroad. At the same time, the Japanese market has become a major focus for foreign pharmaceutical companies.

Pharmaceutical companies in Japan face great challenges arising from at least three sources:

- the downward pressure on prices predictable for the remainder of the decade from the R-Zone pricing formula;

- the relative financial weakness of other providers to the system, which represents a source of pressure, in the administered pricing system, to allocate resources away from pharmaceuticals; and,

- progress toward separation of prescribing and dispensing and the consequent, predictable reductions in volume.

8.3.7 Other Related Industries

Besides the pharmaceutical industry, there are three other fast growing industries related to the Japanese health care system. These are the:

- high technology medical equipment industry;
- laboratory test out-sourcing industry; and,
- disposable medical items manufacturing industry.

There has been an especially rapid increase in sales of high technology medical equipment. For example, the production of medical imaging equipment has nearly doubled since 1980. In order to maximize their income, doctors have an incentive to make the maximum possible use of their medical equipment.

Use of laboratory test out-sourcing companies has also increased drastically. This business will probably continue to grow rapidly in the future given the shortage of skilled personnel at hospitals and clinics. A potential problem relative to this industry is the lack of any institutional framework for ensuring quality control.

The manufacturers of disposable medical items constitute the third group of new players in the Japanese medical system which have arisen outside the framework of players which have traditionally been subject to strict government regulation.

8.4 INTERSECTORAL ANALYSIS

8.4.1 Major Decision Makers

8.4.1.1 The MOHW and External Advisory Bodies

The primary decision-maker in the Japanese medical care system is the MOHW, which exercises immense political influence as well as maintaining administrative control over the system. Despite what might seem to Western observers a potential for abuse in this concentration of power, the MOHW is generally considered by Japanese observers to have transcended the narrow interests articulated by various special interest groups and to have acted predominantly in the best interests of Japanese society.

The limitations of the MOHW as pilot of the system are bureaucratic. The MOHW moves slowly and listens more to well-organized interest groups than to patients. For example, the basic outlines of proposed health care legislation are often prepared by officers of the MOHW and submitted for discussion to the advisory councils. These external advisory bodies then conduct the official preliminary discussions regarding proposed amendments.[79] Council members are legally required to be representatives of the interests of 'stakeholders' such as the insurers, the insured, health and medical care specialists. While the Minister of Health and Welfare officially chooses council members, the MOHW's respective bureaus or sections are responsible for recommending prospective candidates to serve as council members.

When the *Diet* takes up consideration of any amendment to the current health care system, the Labor Committee of the Lower House serves as the major forum for discussions regarding amendments. The *Diet* determines the general framework for amendments and makes them law but the specific details are discussed and determined at the external advisory councils. Throughout the political process, the MOHW officers exercise influence over consensus-building activities and control of the administrative details, including the exact wording of legislation.

---

[79]   The important councils under MOHW are the Social Insurance Council (*Shakai Hoken Shingikai*) and the Council for Promotion of Health for the Elderly (*Rojin Hoken Shingikai*). The administration office for each council is virtually the respective section of MOHW. For example, the administrative functions for the Social Insurance Council are handled by the Planning Section of the Insurance Bureau of the MOHW.

The *Chuikyo* is in charge of discussing and proposing recommendations regarding the Reimbursement Fee Schedule. The MOHW has been successful in maintaining the *Chuikyo* as a political forum for professional discussion of the Reimbursement Fee Schedule.

8.4.1.2   The Japan Medical Association

Doctors are highly respected in Japanese society, and are considered to occupy the highest rung of the health care system hierarchy. The Japan Medical Association (JMA), in principle, is the medical doctors' trade association, although it has represented the interests of clinic doctors. The JMA maintains strong influence over the MOHW and its advisory councils, including *Chuikyo*. The JMA is also a political power, especially within the Liberal Democratic Party (LDP).[80] The increasing divergence among the interests of various groups of doctors—especially between clinic doctors and hospital employee doctors—has contributed to a decline in the influence of the JMA. While academic associations have already started to adapt to the increased specialization of doctors, the JMA has retained its traditional stance of representing the more general interests of primary care doctors.

8.4.1.3   Other Prominent Actors

The Ministry of Finance and Ministry of Home Affairs respectively are the two key decision-makers in the determination of national and local budgets. The Ministry of Finance has a strong influence over the allocation of the national budget to the MOHW. The Ministry of Home Affairs is responsible for local governments, whose financial condition affects the regionally-based NHI system.

The interests of businesses are represented by the Japan Employers Federation (*Nikkeiren*) and the Federation of Economic Organizations (*Keidanren*). These groups exercise indirect but nonetheless significant power over the Liberal Democratic Party and over the MOHW. The Federation of Society-managed

---

[80]   Often in the past, in return for accepting amendments to the health care system, JMA has traditionally demanded raises in Reimbursement Schedule fees. Illustrating the power of the JMA, in 1961 the LDP submitted a budget without any prior consultation with the JMA. The JMA chairman reacted by issuing a declaration which caused JMA members to (1) close hospitals and clinics all over Japan, (2) refuse to cooperate with public programs for promotion of health, and (3) strongly protest the attitude of MOHW. In the past decade, serious reductions in drug prescription prices have been counter-balanced by raises in Reimbursement Schedule fees to preserve physician incomes.

Health Insurance Societies (*Kenkou Hoken Kumiai Rengoukai*)[81] represents the interests of society-managed EHI insurers. These insurers are relatively strong financially due to risk selection by large Japanese employers and the adoption of advanced administrative techniques such as computerization.[82]

Ultimately, NHI and government-managed EHI are centrally administered by the MOHW, which effectively represents their the collective interests.[83] The Central Federation of National Health Insurers (*Kokumin Kenkou Hoken Kumiai Chuou Rengoukai*) represents the interests of the financially weak prefectural government-based NHI insurers.

New interest groups such as the Japan Hospital Association, which represents the interests of large national public and private hospitals, and the All Japan Hospital Association, which represents the interests of small-to-medium sized hospitals, has become increasingly vocal in recent years. These groups, however, have not yet been officially acknowledged by the government or provided with an official role in the health care decision-making apparatus.

Other interest groups include the Japan Pharmacists Association, the Japan Private Hospitals Association, and the Japan Pharmaceutical Manufacturers Association, and the Federation of Japan Pharmaceutical Manufacturers.[84] The MOHW officers welcome informal contact from these domestic interest groups. Interest groups from abroad, on the other hand, do not have strong ties into the important networks of personal relationships in Japan, and there is thus less opportunity for these groups to exercise influence through informal contacts. In a culture such as Japan's which relies heavily on verbal

---

[81] Not related to the payment organization called the Central Federation of National Health Insurers (the Federation) mentioned next in this paragraph and referred to in earlier footnotes.

[82] The Federation of Society-managed Health Insurers, aggressively opposes the MOHW's efforts to equalize the financial conditions among various types of health insurance. This interest group also articulates the views of business groups such as the Japan Employers Federation.

[83] An average, 16.4% of the expenditures of government-managed health insurers are covered by national budget subsidies. However, the financially weakest health insurance plans (NHI) depend on national and local government subsidies for 75% of their financing. While the Ministry of Finance is trying to minimize the national subsidies to NHI, the Ministry of Home Affairs opposes additional increases that would burden local governments.

[84] These groups individually meet informally with politicians and participate, for example, in the LDP Policy Affairs Research Council (*Seichoukai*) in order to pursue tax benefits for R&D investments.

communication, the language barrier is not simply a matter of difference in language, but also of difference in cultural assumptions. This gap in understanding inhibits effective communication between interest groups from different cultures.

The mass media are relatively powerless in Japan, and exercise little influence on health care issues.

8.4.2   Consistency of Objectives and Incentives

Decisions regarding reimbursement and pricing—particularly with regard to the Reimbursement Fee Schedule—are made without explicit consideration of economic incentives or economic efficiency. In addition, due to the influence of the JMA and cultural resistance to drastic changes, there is a tacit agreement that the proportion of the pie allocated to each interest group should remain constant. This inertia interferes with the rationalization of reimbursement and pricing.

The main participants in the Japanese health care system interact in administrative settings. The pilot, the MOHW, controls the promotion, development and funding of universal health insurance, regulates the providers of medical care, and administers the overall system. Currently, the primary goal of the MOHW is to contain the costs of total medical expenditures. The other major objectives deal with the insurers, medical institutions, the Reimbursement Fee Schedule and the demand for medical care.

The MOHW's goals with regard to the insurers include:

* the equalization of burden sharing on the part of the insured;
* the stabilization of financially weak insurers with the help of financially stronger insurers; and
* the equalization of benefits among different insurers.

The principle of *Jiyuu Shinryousei* states that there should be free choice of primary care institution for patients. All medical institutions, clinics and hospitals, function as primary care organizations. To promote efficiency among medical care providers, the MOHW wants to introduce the principle of functional specialization to the Japanese medical care system.

The Reimbursement Fee Schedule has been the subject of debate since Japan first achieved the goal of establishing universal health insurance coverage. The

Reimbursement Fee Schedule determines the income shares of the health care pie for all medical institutions. The MOHW, which has controlled the size of this pie, has been successful in allocating consistent proportions of the pie to major participants in the system, most notably the JMA.   However, the fundamental framework of this system, which was established more than 30 years ago, has become incapable of meeting the demand of patients.   The specific fees for service set forth under the Reimbursement Fee Schedule have brought about distortions such as the over-provision of various tests, examinations and drugs, deterioration of hospital facilities, and lack of emphasis on the provision of long-term care. Market-based Reform of the reimbursement and pricing system is necessary so that the services medical institutions provide will more nearly match the needs of the Japanese population as its demographics and disease profile continues to change. Attention to the distribution of income among providers has obstructed reform.

The primary objective of patients is to secure the provision of needed medical care at low cost. The MOHW addressed this by implementing universal health insurance coverage in 1961.   With this basic objective satisfied, patients' demands have become more diverse: humane long-term care, more attentive primary care, and more sophisticated medical treatment. Without a patients' voice in the system as "stakeholders", these demands risk going unaddressed.

8.4.3   Economic Implications for Efficiency and Equity

Under the universal health insurance system, the Japanese government has achieved a high level of equity in the provision of medical care. Even taking into account the sizeable copayment, every citizen has access to any needed medical care at any medical institution, whether large hospital or small clinic. Due to the effectively complete control exercised by the MOHW in terms of the administration, funding and supervision of the health insurance system, the administrative efficiency of health care provision is extremely high. Shortages and distortions, arising mainly from administered pricing, afflict the system, reducing its allocative efficiency and capacity to satisfy the population's changing needs.

The Japanese place a high value on equity. In 1984, MOHW attempted to separate those who were financially unable to pay NHI premiums into a separate welfare program. This was strongly opposed by almost every interest group involved. The attempt was criticized harshly for attempting to create "second-rate" citizens.

8.5 ANALYSIS OF HEALTH CARE POLICY

8.5.1 Current Health Care Policies and Proposals

At the present time, there is no active debate regarding potential health care reforms. All discussions are being conducted privately within the MOHW and other government and consultative bodies.

8.5.2 Assessment of Current Health Care Policies and Proposals

Currently, there are six major issues influencing the Japanese health care reform agenda:

- the dominance of fiscal cost control;
- distortions introduced by mispricing in the fee reimbursement system;
- the lack of quality differentiation in the Reimbursement Fee Schedule;
- the aging of the population and the under-provision of care for the elderly;
- specialization among medical care facilities;
- *bungyo*, the separation of prescribing and dispensing of pharmaceuticals.

Government expenditures on health care are governed by the principle that growth in spending should not exceed national income growth. This standard has become difficult to meet given the aging population and poor economic conditions. The most promising alternative is a greater reliance on the private sector, in the form of an expanded role for private insurance, for example. A shift in that direction would also mitigate the problems associated with inadequate consumer/patient participation in the political process that determines the allocation of resources to health care. Consumers would, instead, exercise individual control over such decisions.

The mispricing built into the national uniform fee schedule has resulted in long waiting times, an over-supply of medicines, tests and procedural services, an under-provision of consultative services and care and the physical deterioration of medical facilities. The provision of services is dictated by the reimbursement system, which favours particular types of care, and fails to account for differences between regions and between institutions in terms of the cost and quality of care. The fact that consultative services are reimbursed at such a low rate, particularly when compared to medicines, tests and procedural services, results in an under-provision of services to the elderly. Repricing may ameliorate some of these problems but as long as the

Reimbursement Fee Schedule is adjusted by political negotiations, distortions will inevitably persist.

Meanwhile, with the aging of the Japanese population, an increasing need is emerging for purpose-built institutions, particularly for providing low-intensity, long-term care for the elderly. This is part of a general demand for specialization in the provision of medical care. Another potential change could include creating separate classes of hospitals to provide primary care and high-technology medical services. In addition, there has been pressure in the direction of separating the prescribing and dispensing functions, thereby creating a more explicit division between doctors and pharmacists.

8.5.3   Reform Options Currently Under Discussion

The reforms currently under discussion focus on three areas: (1) the Reimbursement Fee Schedule; (2) medical service providers; and (3) the demand for medical services.

8.5.3.1   The Reimbursement Fee Schedule

Four aspects of the universal Reimbursement Fee Schedule are being examined in detail.

1.   *Fee for Service Pricing*: The present categorization of items on the Reimbursement Fee Schedule fails to provide economic incentives for doctors to control the cost of providing medical care.

2.   *Capital Cost Accounting*: The current Reimbursement Fee Schedule reimburses the providers' operating cost of medical services without taking capital cost into account. Thus, clinics and hospitals which need to invest have no opportunity to make provision for it in their prices.

3.   *Copayments*: Fee-for-service reimbursement encourages over-provision of medical services. Since copayments are relatively low, patients have little incentive to economize on care. Doctors, meanwhile, have an incentive to maximize the number of patient visits. Since medical insurance covers the basic costs, doctors do not hesitate to ask patients to make follow-up visits. Since patients do not have much decision-making power, it is hard to see copayment rate increases as an effective cost control technique. Because increasing copayments would reduce the burden on the state budget, if not the total demand for services, it is nevertheless under consideration.

4. *Supplemental Coverage*: Services that are not listed in the Reimbursement Fee Schedule are nearly impossible for patients to obtain. This poses a problem given that there is demand for services not listed in the Schedule, including certain sophisticated medical services that might be essential to individual patients as well as enhancing the quality of service. Supplemental private coverage is an obvious solution.

8.5.3.2 Medical Service Providers

1. *The Aging of Doctors*: The aging of Japanese society as has produced striking results among clinic doctors. In the Tokyo metropolitan area, the average age of clinic doctors is already 62. The nationwide average for such doctors is age 60. Currently, clinics and various types of hospitals such as large national and university hospitals, public hospitals and private hospitals are competing in the same market to provide primary care. This trend has been exacerbated in that young doctors tend to concentrate in large hospitals. Typically, they choose to become salaried doctors at hospitals so as to have access to advanced medical technology. The beginning of specialization in provision of medical services and the high respect accorded to specialized doctors also help encourage young doctors to stay at hospitals.

2. *Competition for Physicians*: A recent amendment of the Medical Care Law established the basic framework under which medical institutions were categorized to avoid competition for primary care physicians between large hospitals and small clinics.

3. *Intra-regional Specialization*: The MOHW is planning to institute intra-regional specialization of medical providers in order to avoid duplication and over-investment in high-technology medical equipment, emergency care facilities, and other big-ticket items. Specifically, the MOHW plans to establish centres for providing such specialty services within each region.

4. *Separation of the Functions of Physician and Pharmacist*: In 1989, the MOHW began initiatives to separate pharmacies from national hospitals. Since then, the MOHW has strengthened its influence in regard to the issue of separation. The major benefits the MOHW seeks to capture are:

    •   to enhance the role of pharmacies in region-based networks of medical services, for example, by having them maintain and check prescription records for individuals; and

- to promote cost containment by reducing doctor's margins.

An impediment to this reform is the necessity to educate qualified pharmacists to be able to deal effectively with the increasing number of prescription drugs.

8.5.3.3 Demand for Medical Services

1. *The Aging Population*: Given the rapid aging of the Japanese population, the number of those who can pay for medical services is falling. As the corresponding premium payments decrease, the expenditure on medical services must be reduced, thus reducing the quality and/or the volume of medical services. Whether it is fair for those who are now becoming dependent to receive relatively less care because their portion of the population is increasing is a matter of debate. The same issue has arisen in regards to pensions in Japan.

2. *The Unification of the Insurance Systems*: The Japanese government has achieved universal coverage, but only through a patchwork of various types of insurance schemes. Society-managed EHI is financially very strong; NHI, while the ultimate safety net in terms of health care coverage, is the weakest system financially. Even the society-managed EHI will decline in financial strength with the aging of the Japanese population. Under these circumstances, the unification of the various schemes is becoming progressively more difficult, especially in terms of the payment of medical expenditures for the elderly.

3. *Total Expenditures*: That Japanese medical expenditures are relatively low is often cited as evidence that the Japanese medical system is very efficient. However, total medical expenditure is calculated solely on the basis of the Reimbursement Fee Schedule. When it comes to international comparisons, what is and is not included in medical expenditures is a source of confusion and uncertainty about the validity of the comparisons.

8.6   CONSTRAINTS ON REFORM

The principal brakes on reform of the Japanese health care system are:

- good performance;
- a preference for incremental change;
- politics;
- Japanese concepts of social solidarity; and
- the weakness of the consumer voice.

8.6.1   Good Performance

The fact that the Japanese health care system works well in many important respects is a disincentive for fundamental change. As we have discussed elsewhere, by international standards Japan enjoys excellent health outcomes, and the health care system's cost as a percentage of National Income — less than 7 percent — is low by international standards.   There is no overt rationing of services. Administrative costs are low because of the system-wide uniformity of claims and claims processing. Access to care is universal and the level of equity is high.   Thus, changes to the system must be certain to improve performance still further in order to be held worthy of adoption.

Nevertheless, for all its virtues, the Japanese health care system best serves those who turn to the system for primary care. Those who have common diseases that can be treated at fairly low cost are well taken care of, but those who have conditions that are expensive or difficult to treat are less well served. These patients whose needs are less satisfied by the system, however, are in the minority and in no position to create pressure for change.

8.6.2   Preference for Incremental Change

Although Japanese society and the Japanese government are at times capable of drastic changes, the dominant preference of the social order, the government, and most of the principal actors in the health care system is for modest, reactive change. The *Meiji*-era revision in the health care system from traditional medicine to a Bismarckian system and the establishment of universal health care in 1961 exemplify the capacity of the Japanese government for large-scale reforms in health care. These episodes, however, are the exceptions, not the rule. They are unlikely to be repeated in the current era. The reasons are as follows:

- Since health care policy affects the daily life of Japan's subjects, administrators are disinclined to tamper massively, especially at a time when the aging of the population is beginning to increase the cost pressures on the system.

- The health care system, and particularly the Reimbursement Fee Schedule, largely fixes the income distribution among providers to the system. Reform inevitably involves changing those shares. Given the political difficulty of reforms, which would likely sharply reduce the incomes of doctors or hospitals, only incremental adjustments appear feasible.

8.6.3   Politics

Administrative entities in Japan exercise more power more freely than in other advanced countries, with the legislative and judicial branches holding correspondingly less direct influence over the regulatory process. Health care legislation in Japan determines the overall framework of the system, but the details of implementation and administration are left to the discretion of major councils and the MOHW. All changes in the health care system involve political negotiation between the MOHW and other stakeholders, and usually these negotiations are handled in the context of the MOHW-sponsored quasi-governmental advisory councils. Change proceeds through compromise among the stakeholders; the trade-offs are such that no actor loses or gains radically to the benefit or at the cost of other stakeholders in the system. This system is stable and resistant to sudden substantial change.

Since Japanese legislation does not specify administrative details, the translation of legislative policy changes into procedure always involves intricate negotiations and behind-the-scenes political manoeuvring among the stakeholders of the system. These interactions are based upon an often criticized long-term balance of accounts frequently encountered in Japanese politics and business negotiations. The object of the process is to balance the political accounts of the stakeholders. The problem with the process is that this emphasis on the protection of existing suppliers to the health care system leaves patients voiceless and intensifies the resistance to change.

Within the government, there are differing points of view about the necessity and utility of change. The Ministry of Finance is reportedly in favour of introducing the private sector into the Japanese health care system as a means of containing the size of the government contribution. The MOHW, on the other hand, is concerned about the quality of health care services and about retaining control in this sector, and so is less enthusiastic. The need to resolve these differences inhibits reform.

8.6.4   Japanese Concepts of Social Solidarity

There is a strong disinclination to alter what is at best a single-tier system and at worst a two-tier system with only small differences between the tiers. Currently, the Japanese system is universal, mandatory and presents very limited opportunities to buy more than the guaranteed health care package (GHCP). Differences may exist among plans in terms of benefits, premiums and copayment rates, but the quality of care is largely uniform. The high level of equity in the system is a source of pride. A system that creates 'second-class citizens' would be unacceptable.[85] In 1984, for example, the MOHW proposed that individuals unable to pay health insurance premiums be placed in a separate insurance pool. The proposal was strongly criticized from all quarters and defeated in the *Diet*. The disparity in benefits between society-supported plans and less-well-funded government-supported plans has not eroded the egalitarianism upon which the system is founded. Favorite physicians do receive gift payments that are not reported for personal taxation and yield preferred access for well-off patients. Queue-jumping by buying care outside the country is less common, but not altogether trivial. For the most part, however, the system has remained uncorrupted. Rich and poor receive essentially the same care. To change this arrangement requires that some fundamental equity rules be altered.

---

[85]   There are exceptions. A Ministry of Labor Official estimated that as of 1992 there were 300,000 illegal immigrants working in Japan. Although reliable statistical data on trends in this undocumented population are not available, given the economic prosperity of Japan and the continued rise in the strength of the yen the numbers of citizens of other nations working illegally in Japan is likely to continue to increase. The Tokyo Metropolitan Government and other local governments have in the past subsidized the cost of providing emergency medical care to these undocumented workers. However, a recent guideline issued by the MOHW states that local governments will no longer be reimbursed for the medical costs incurred by illegal immigrants. Currently, these costs are largely absorbed by the hospitals and clinics that provide services to these immigrants. These events imply that the strong social solidarity of the Japanese people will not be extended to the increasing numbers of illegal non-Japanese in their midst.

8.6.5   Weakness of Consumer Voice

Health care is an environment in which it is difficult for patients to make informed choices. Providers of services typically possess more information than patients, who rely on physicians as their agents. In Japan, patients operate with very little information. The idea of informed consent has been imported into Japan but has not yet been widely observed in practice. Thanks to the prevalence of the traditional view of doctors as wise, unselfish counsellors, typical Japanese patients are not accustomed to questioning their judgment. Keeping diagnostic information away from individuals is not peculiar to health care and the doctor-patient relationship. We observe, for example, that in the Japanese educational system individual academic records are not disclosed to individuals and employees in Japanese companies do not have access to performance evaluations. Under such circumstances, pressure for change will not come from below. Patients are not accustomed to behaving like consumers and do not have either economic or political means for making known their preferences and desires for change.

8.7   SHORT-TERM REFORM

In many important respects, the Japanese health care system already resembles the NERA prototype. There is mandatory universal coverage for a GHCP. Individual's insurance premiums are income related and copayments on a significant but not overly burdensome scale ensure a degree of patient responsibility. There is easy access to primary care.

Equally fundamental, however, is the fact that the Japanese health care system is removed from the influence of market forces by the Reimbursement Fee Schedule and the unique social compact that leaves the government with nearly complete control of the system.

As noted in the next section, the NERA Prototype, in its pure form with competing insurers, is incompatible with the Japanese system as it has historically developed and is now managed. We do not propose that the existing system, based on government supervision, be overthrown to make way for one based upon competition. Instead, our presumption is that the current system will be subject to continual stresses and that the NERA Prototype will serve as a guidepost toward which evolutionary change should be directed.

The most likely stress on the system in the future will be a shortage of funding and the corresponding unmet need for health care goods and services, a problem that arises when an aging population's needs conflict with treasury goals. We expect that the government's interest in increasing the flow of outside funds into the health care system will prompt an examination of new means for increasing private sector contributions. Two of our proposals will help in this respect. An initial proposal is intended to redress certain imbalances among insurance funds.

8.7.1   Equalize Insurance Funds

Tables 8.1 and 8.2 describe the current similarities and differences among the various EHI and NHI funds. As related more fully in Section 8.2.2, the funds differ in terms of their financing, the basis upon which premiums are calculated, the copayments and the benefits. One object of our reform proposals is to reduce these differences, as has already been discussed in Japan.

Table 8.1
Differences Among Japanese Insurance Plans

Plan		GHCP	Premiums*	Premium Collection / Fund Operation	Character-istics	Other Benefits	Profitability
EHI	Govt.-managed	Identical	% of salary	Centralized Social Insur-ance Agency	Employment based	Allow-ances	Money-earning
	Society-managed		% of salary (each society determines own rate)	Society-based coll-ection/fund operation		Allow-ances & Facilities	subsidy
NHI			% of income and wealth (formulas vary with locality)	Locally operated	Residence based	Limited	Money-losing
	Retirees						
	Elderly		no premiums -- just copayments				

*   See Table 8.2 for copay rates

Table 8.2
Differences in Copayment Rates
Among Japanese Insurance Plans

Type of Care	Employee Health Insurance (EHI)		National Health Insurance (NHI)	
	Society-managed	Government-managed	Retiree	Elderly
In-patient	Employee: 20% Dependent(s): 20%	Employee: 20% Dependent(s): 20%	30% · · · 20%	¥500
Out-patient	Employee: 10% Dependent(s): 30%	Employee: 10% Dependent(s): 30%	30% · Employee: 20% Dependent(s): 30%	¥900

657

Health insurance funds in Japan are at least in part publicly funded with one major exception — society-managed health insurance funds. The differences between NHI and EHI premiums are not substantial. In 1990, the average NHI premium per household was ¥142,000, whereas the government-managed EHI premium per household was ¥118,000 and the society-managed EHI premium per household was ¥121,000. Government welfare programs protect low-income subjects from an inability to pay for health care. Similarly, the differences in copayments between EHI and NHI are not considerable (see Table 8.2).

The largest difference among plans lies in so-called supplemental income-indemnity allowances provided by EHI funds (including both government-managed EHI and the society-managed EHI). Another major difference arises with respect to resort/sports facilities, which are provided almost exclusively by society-managed EHI funds.

We propose five steps to eliminate the inequities among EHI and NHI plans:

1. The first reform step would be to eliminate the differences in premiums and copayment rates between society-managed and government-managed EHI plans.

2. EHI plans provide income-indemnity allowances that are not provided by NHI plans. The provision of this type of benefit, used by employers to attract and retain employees, is an insurance function separable from health care.

3. Prorated subsidies from EHI to NHI plans, such as those currently paid into Insurance for Retirees (so that they only have to pay a 20 percent copayment rather than a 30 percent copayment), would help equalize the financial status of the plans.

4. Consolidation of the various regional NHI plans, which currently differ in terms of premium per household, would further reduce inequality. In this process, subsidies from EHI plans support financially weak NHI plans.

5. The final and most drastic step would be to eliminate the link between insurance and employment. The employer-matching premium contribution could be replaced by the comparable corporate tax to temporarily subsidize weak funds. Once consumers can shop for health insurance among different plans, the transition to a prototype system would be nearly complete.

This five-step reform program may meet opposition from large employers because the proposed reform will deprive large companies of some of their advantages in attracting and retaining employees (e.g., resorts, sports facilities and income-indemnity allowances). A prospective supporter for the reform would be the MOHW, whose interest lies in promoting equity in the financing of health care.

The short-run purpose of this reform is greater fairness in an already fair system. An additional effect is to open the door for eventually allowing subjects to choose insurers should the current system prove untenable in the long run. Since there is no necessary connection between an individual's situation of employment and his or her health insurance status, there is wisdom in anticipating the day when employment status will no longer adequately serve as a basis for assignment to a health plan. Equalizing the plans serves this purpose.

8.7.2 Distinguish Long-Term Residential Care From the Practice of Medicine

Long-term care should be split off from the medical sector entirely and its supply 'privatized'. The establishment of purpose-built institutions for nursing care should be opened to the private sector on a wider scale and priced by the free market. Currently, distortions created by the Reimbursement Fee Schedule push the elderly into hospitals, which are ill-suited to their needs and inimical to their health and well-being. Professional medical personnel at high wages are used to perform functions that relate more closely to inn-keeping than to acute medical care. A main purpose of hospitals is to confine contagion. For healthy elderly people who require assistance in living, residence in a hospital is positively dangerous as well as unduly expensive.

The idea of nursing homes unconnected to hospitals (*Rojin Hoken Shisetsu*) is relatively new in Japan. They have been around for only the last 15 years and they remain few in number. The unpopularity of nursing homes in Japan is tied to the country's traditional values which emphasize children taking care of their parents. Combine this with the lower cost to the patient and his or her family of a hospital stay and it is clear why the practice of installing the elderly in hospitals for long-term care (social hospitalization) has become so prevalent. The Specially Certified Hospitals for the Elderly (*Tokurei-Ninka-Roujin-Byouin*) have a poor reputation and some of the regular hospitals which accommodate a large number of elderly patients are said to be of low quality. MOHW is planning to introduce care-intensive hospitals to accommodate elderly patients by introducing *Ryouyou-gata-Byousyou-Gun, Kaigo-Kyoka-Byouin* and others, however within the range of medical-care services. MOHW is also supervising development of nursing homes (*Rojin-Hoken-Shisetsu*). This is proceeding very slowly however and private capital has not yet been introduced on a significant scale. Our recommendation is to develop nursing homes and open up residential care to private capital.

At present, the facilities in Japan are inadequate to cope with the rising number of elderly. Although under the Health Services for the Elderly Act in 1986 and the MOHW "Golden Plan" of 1990, the government has established new community-based, non-hospital residential care facilities, there were only 393 such facilities at the end of 1990, with a total capacity of 31,490 beds. By 1990, about 700,000 elderly people were being cared for outside the home, 80 percent of them in hospitals. Reducing this proportion by encouraging the construction and management of long-term care facilities is an important element of near-term reform.

The cost savings from subtracting residential care from the health care system would not be immediate, as might be supposed. Funds presently earmarked for paying for long-term care inside the health system would need to be diverted to subsidize patients' payments to private nursing care facilities or to subsidize residential care. With time and government encouragement, the private insurance market should take over this function so that saving for old age, such as through pension programs, includes adequate provision for residential nursing care. It goes without saying that when medical care for the elderly is required, it should be provided under the health care system as before.

A related reform involves reducing the barriers to private capital investment in hospitals and long-term care facilities and providing incentives to encourage more professional management of these institutions.

8.7.3   Institute Balance Billing

The main recommendation for near-term reform in Japan involves converting the Reimbursement Fee Schedule from a uniform schedule to 'balance billing'. Balance billing means that patients can be charged more than the reimbursement rate, with the residual amount to be paid out of pocket or by supplemental insurance. Presently, all doctors and medical institutions in Japan may charge only the uniform fee for all medical goods and services listed on the schedule. The effect is to obliterate quality differentiation in the system. Because there are patients who would willingly pay extra for perceived better service, but are prevented form doing so by the fee ceiling, patients' wants go unsatisfied and revenues are lost to the system.

This proposal does not involve the abandonment of the Reimbursement Fee Schedule, only a lifting of the ceiling. Each doctor and medical institution would remain obligated to provide its range of goods and services at the basic reimbursement fee level. They may, however, offer additional levels of service for a premium that would be paid exclusively either by separate private insurance or out of patients' own pockets. The preservation of the full range of services at existing reimbursement fees guarantees that no patient will be worse off as a result of the lifting of the cap.

Medical institutions have a high proportion of costs that are fixed and sunk. Many clinics and hospitals are now short of funds because the administratively-set prices contained in the Reimbursement Fee Schedule bear no relation to their costs. The economics of public utilities teaches that differentiating service qualities and prices is an efficient way to improve the finances of such institutions. Allowing hospitals, for example, to charge different rates for operations performed by surgeons of differing certification and reputation will bring funds into the system. Table 8.3 provides an example. Under present circumstances, a hospital receives ¥63,000 (6,300 points) for an appendectomy, of which (say) 20 percent is copayment and 80 percent is reimbursement, as shown. The doctor's fee in this circumstance is hypothetically set at ¥21,000. With balance billing, a resident surgeon would be available at the Reimbursement Fee Schedule rate. A patient, however, who wished to be operated upon by the Chairman of the Surgery Department, would be charged an ¥80,000 fee, reflecting a premium of ¥17,000 that the patient would pay either directly or through private insurance. Similarly, a large teaching hospital might charge a premium for extra services a local hospital might not offer.

Table 8.3: Balance Billing Based Upon The Reimbursement Fee Schedule

Appendectomy			
A. For any Surgeon			
Hospital Revenue		**Hospital Cost**	
Operation Fee Reimbursed Copayment @ 20%	¥63,000 50,400 12,600	Surgeon's Fee	¥21,000
With Balance Billing: **B. Chairman of Surgery**			
Operation Fee Reimbursed	¥80,000 50,400	Surgeon's Fee	¥30,000
Patient pays: - Copayment - Premium	12,600 17,000 29,600		
C. Resident Surgeon As under A above			

The surgeon's fee, naturally, would also be higher. The hypothesized ¥17,000 fee in Table 8.3 implies a division of the premium, with ¥9,000 going to the surgeon and ¥8,000 to the hospital. This proportion is purely hypothetical.

If the increases in 'quality' of the sort implied by this change threatened to produce differences in the success rates of treatment between patients who selected premium services and those who did not, a significant inequity would be introduced into the system, relative to what exists today. The emergence of such inequities, however, seems unlikely. Many health care-related goods are 'positional goods', that is goods where satisfaction is more mental than physical, more a matter of attitude than actual impact. The system could be monitored to ensure that, while inequalities in the consumption of 'status health care' might arise, real differences in rates of mortality, morbidity, and recovery do not interfere with social solidarity.

In the absence of freedom to quality-differentiate, substantial distortions in the system have arisen. The gravitation of patients away from small clinics to large public hospitals and, of late, to university teaching hospitals for even primary and out-patient care is a manifestation of the failure of the system to recognize quality differences. Larger hospitals send out quality 'signals', and patients, behaving rationally, prefer the higher quality institutions as long as there is no price difference. The introduction of functional and quality differentiation in both fees and certifications is necessary to the rationalization of the system. The most straightforward and socially beneficial means of accomplishing this goal is to move to balance billing. The proposed reform does not involve major administrative changes. There is no need, for example, for the government to engage in elaborate quality-related categorization and certification programs.

The use of honoraria or side payments in cash to secure the services of the physician of one's choosing is a widespread practice in Japan today. Naoki Ikegami, writing recently in *Science* magazine, has stated that payments of ¥100,000 to ¥300,000 are common. This practice shows that the conversion to a balance billing system is not nearly as radical as one might suppose. Although gift-giving is part of a long Japanese tradition, and it is difficult for foreigners to reckon the difference in this setting between a gift, a bribe and a market-determined premium, the fact remains that the price of these services is something more than the reimbursement. This does not mean that the adoption of balance billing would not cause significant change. Gifts to physicians are 'side payments' that pass neither through the hospital accounting system nor, in most instances, through the tax system. Balance billing channels sorely needed funds to medical institutions and tax revenues to the treasury.

Balance billing — the separation of pricing from reimbursement — may be seen as an important first step in freeing prices from *Koseisho/Chuikyo* control. At present, the worst aspect of the Japanese system is the manipulation of prices to set the incomes of providers (stakeholders) rather than to bring output in line with demand. By detaching reimbursement from pricing, balance billing creates the opportunity for less regulated pricing of medical services.

Finally, balance billing provides a market-determined method for establishing gradations of quality within the Japanese system. No administrative substitute will adequately allow for the differentiation of services by quality or serve as a means to ration the consumption of high-quality services. Moreover, balance billing is in no way inconsistent with the preservation of a GHCP that is generous and available to all at reasonable cost. Balance billing does imply, however, an expansion of the health care sector's provision of services above the basic level. The MOHW has been willing to experiment with premium service in a small way. These days, premium services are limited to better meals and rooms in hospitals and reserved appointments to avoid marathon waiting room ordeals. These modest precedents notwithstanding, there is no denying that the change to balance billing reduces the equity of the system. Whether Japan will pay this price in order to improve efficiency remains to be seen. We advocate the change.

8.7.4   Effect on Total Expenditure

Our proposals for reforming the health care system in Japan would leave in place the system's mandatory nature, in addition to its qualities of universal coverage and access for all subjects. Privatizing the long-term care function would ultimately reduce the fiscal burden, once a system of insurance arose to allow individuals to set aside money during their working life to pay for care during old age. For current generations, however, the savings from this step would come mainly from efficiencies arising from substituting purpose-built facilities and a lower-wage labor force for the medical institutions now being misused for elderly care. Permitting quality differentiation in provision and fee setting will inevitably increase aggregate expenditures on medical care. The government's expenditures, however, would not change and the increase in private payments would be incurred by those most willing to foot the bill. The existence of funding difficulties under the current regime indicates that such a revision is sorely needed even if it means that Japan loses its claim to being the lowest-cost health care nation in terms of the share of National Income devoted to this purpose.

8.8   LONG-TERM REFORM

In this section, we describe the relationship between the Japanese system of financing health care and the NERA Prototype.

A basic conclusion of our comparative research is that the NERA Prototype represents an appropriate direction towards which long-term reform should be focused in every country. The NERA Prototype, thus used, points countries in the direction of:

- universal care under a GHCP;
- mandatory insurance coverage;
- consumer choice among competing insurance funds;
- contractual relations (or vertical integration) between insurers and providers;
- government funding of the health care system limited to funding care of the indigent and supervision of the system; and
- elimination of the motive on the part of the government for administered pricing or spending caps.

As noted above, many of the most important elements of the NERA Prototype are already to be found in the Japanese system.

The vital difference between the Japanese system and the NERA Prototype is the large role of the Japanese government as:

- a source of funds;
- an insurance plan manager; and
- a price setter.

The government's large role is not an accident of history. The generally paternal role of the government in Japanese society and the cooperative nature of government-industry relations makes it harder to envision a prototype-style health care system in Japan than in other countries. Even long-term reform will leave a sizable role for the government. If, however, the system becomes increasingly subject to stress as a result of funds shortages and mispricing — as we predict — then the government's role as a source of funds and as a price setter may diminish. Its role will never entirely evaporate.

8.8.1   The Funding Side of the Health Care System

8.8.1.1   The GHCP

The Japanese GHCP currently consists of most medical goods and services, apart from prevention, normal childbirth, inoculations, physical exams and expensive, highly advanced or rarely used treatments. Costly new treatments are covered only when the price comes down and the treatments begin to be used more frequently. We do not propose that the GHCP should be changed.

8.8.1.2   The Role of Insurance Funds

The NERA prototype recommends that health care should be financed by competing insurance funds that would purchase care on behalf of their members. This recommendation would require revolutionizing the Japanese system. Currently, the funds do not compete, nor do they purchase services on behalf of their members. Instead, they simply collect premiums and pay claims. The need for contracting services is eliminated by the universal Reimbursement Fee Schedule.

8.8.1.3   The Structure of Insurance Premiums

Presently, premiums for EHI plans are calculated on the basis of standard salary as legally defined, while premiums for NHI plans are calculated on the basis of income, wealth, the number of dependents, etc. The shift to a NERA Prototype-style system, with payments in the form of both income-related fees and risk-related premiums, is feasible but not likely to occur in the near-term stages of reform. Japanese society pursues the ideal of one-tier citizenship. Any differentiation of subjects according to health status (such as that implied by the risk-related premium) will be opposed.

8.8.1.4   Services Outside the GHCP

The near-term proposal for a shift to balance billing implies an open-ended extension of the limited categories of services available beyond the GHCP. An implicit premise of this approach is that premium services offered by hospitals largely represent convenience or positional goods and do not adversely effect health outcomes. If it turned out that wealthy purchases of supplemental services enjoyed superior health care, the Japanese system would require a redress in the balance.

8.8.2   The Provider Side of the Health Care System

With the uniform fee system, the number and size of insurers and providers has no effect on the price or supply of medical services. With free pricing, insurance societies will need guarantees against over-charging and the over-provision of premium services. As a result, the sort of contracting between insurance companies and medical institutions envisioned in the NERA Prototype may arise.

8.8.2.1   Price Determination

Long-term reform necessarily implies the relaxation of the current procedures for administrative price setting in Japan. The practice of setting prices through a political negotiation among stakeholders, the objective of which is to maintain income shares, is inconsistent with the objective of meeting patients' demands at the lowest possible cost. For example, the preservation of doctors' incomes at a high level has been an important feature of the pharmaceutical price-setting regime, given the physician's role as a dispenser of drugs. Although recent ministry decisions make it clear that both pharmaceutical prices and doctors' and hospitals' margins from selling medicines will decline, the relative changes will be set by administrative fiat, largely without reference to the underlying real economic value of the goods and services being produced. Instead, the distribution of income between doctors, hospitals and other 'stakeholders' will be the main concern. In order for patients' needs to be met at the lowest cost, this system will eventually have to give way to market-determined pricing. Balance billing is a first step in that direction. The subsequent step will be reforms that reduce the level of government funding, and with it the need to control prices. Ultimately, the system of price negotiation among provider/stakeholders will give way to more market-oriented alternatives that focus on the value of treatments to patients and on costs.

8.8.3   The Responsibilities of Government

Even under a system evolving toward the NERA Prototype, the government will have an important role to play. In Japan, this role would be larger than in most other countries because of the tradition of the government as a protector of the population and because of the harmonious relations that generally exist between government and industry.

The government must continue to ensure universal access to the GHCP by:

- Obliging every individual to take out health insurance.

- Obliging insurance funds to accept enrolment on reasonable terms. This applies to NHI systems so long as the distinction exists between EHI systems and NHI systems.

- Assuming responsibility for explicitly defining the GHCP.

- Auditing and quality control. This includes ensuring that all insurance plans meet credentialling requirements and inspecting providers to insure that acceptable quality services are being provided.

- Assuming responsibility for public health issues, in particular, the prevention of communicable diseases.

- Licensing both insurers and providers, a function that will necessitate a medical approval agency.

- Acting as the payer of last resort. The government must supply funds so that those individuals who cannot pay are covered by health insurance. The government also must act as the agent of the mentally disabled and others who are unable to participate in the health care system. Such an agency would purchase health on behalf of its members and represent their interests in those matters that require a decision by the government.

Even after long-term reform in Japan these and other functions would remain with government. As long as the Reimbursement Fee Schedule is preserved, the most important government function is to try to reduce distortions. This goal can never be fully achieved under an administered-price system, but some of the more obviously perverse incentives can be corrected. The government has already taken steps to reduce the reliance of physicians and clinics on pharmaceutical dispensing and medical tests by reducing their point values and increasing the point values of consultative procedures. Further action along these lines is warranted. Of equal importance is the adjustment of hospital fees to take capital costs adequately into account.

The government should continue its policy of encouraging an independent pharmaceutical sector and the separation of the prescribing and dispensing functions of physicians. The drugs bill will go down and the need to manage the 'doctor's margin' through administered pricing will disappear. Relaxation of government controls go hand in hand with *bungyo* (the separation of dispensing and prescribing), balanced billing (the separation of pricing from reimbursement), and the privatization of long-term care.

Auditing the cost and quality and maintaining minimum standards would remain an important role for the MOHW. Under the cost-depressing discipline of competition, preventing reductions in the quality of GHCP care is important. Providing useful information to consumers is a socially useful by-product of auditing for quality.

8.8.4   The Responsibility of Patients

Japan is an example of an equitable system that relies on across the board, mandatory coinsurance to encourage individual responsibility. According to our short-term reform recommendations (Section 8.7), copayments for services included in the GHCP would be rendered uniform for all subjects, irrespective of the plan they join. The retention and refinement of copayment ceilings and relief for the needy are necessary adjuncts to reform.

To increase patient choice, insurance funds and private insurers should all be permitted to offer supplemental coverage. Today, that coverage exists only for minor amenities such as single rooms and better meals in hospitals and clinics.

The Japanese medical care system is notably lacking in consumer voice. To the extent that this stems partly from the traditional relationship between patients and doctors, there is little that can be done on an administrative level. Reform, however, should certainly include the representation by consumers in the councils that deliberate changes in the health care system, including *Chuiyko*, the council in charge of revising reimbursement prices.

There is no doubt that the changes we propose for the Japanese system over the long run — to bring it more into line with the NERA Prototype — are radical. We would note, however, that competition in health care markets needs not be of the ruthless sort that one finds in commodity markets, for example. In fact, competition already exists within the Japanese system to a significant degree. Even though prices are fixed, those physicians and medical institutions that can attract a large practice make more money. To the extent that there are scale economies or that overheads are in some degree fixed, the profitability of busier practices will be greater, assuming that patients are not added to an irrational degree. Patients also benefit from the competition between clinics and hospitals. As such, the prospect for improving patient welfare with more competition, even of a gentle sort, represents a real possibility for improvement in Japan. Although total expenditures (public plus private) under this system might be higher as a result, any change in that direction would be the result of individual preferences. Moreover, under a prototype system, the fiscal contribution of government, along with the constraints is imposes on the system, would be much diminished.

ANNEX 8.1 THE ECONOMICS OF R-ZONE PRICING FOR PHARMACEUTICALS

8.1.1 Introduction

The "Zone of Reasonableness" method of setting the reimbursement price adopted in April 1992 by the MOHW sets in motion the pricing formula that will determine pharmaceutical manufacturer's prices and margins throughout this decade. This Annex describes the methodology and predicts the outcome, within a broad range, for prices in the 1990s.

R-Zone pricing is deregulation in the sense that the reimbursement price in a given period is linked to a free market negotiation between wholesalers and hospitals in the previous period. This relationship is spelled out in Annex 8.1.2. Despite the link to market prices, the schedule of R-Zone reductions over the next six or eight years implies reductions in the prices that manufacturers will be able to charge for medicines. This is because the R-Zone formula places strong downward pressure on the reimbursement price over time. Annex 8.1.3 details the economic implications of the R-Zone pricing mechanism.

8.1.2 The R-Zone Method in a Nutshell

For any listed[86] pharmaceutical product, the general price revision formula under the R-Zone method equals:

$$NHI_T = \hat{WH}_{T-1} + (R * NHI_{T-1})$$

where:

NHI_T = the NHI reimbursement price for a listed product in a price revision year: 1992, 1994, 1996, etc.

$\hat{WH}_{T-1}$ = the wholesale price (charged by a wholesaler to a hospital, for example) for the product in the previous period. The "hat" indicates the weighted average price of all transactions during this period.

R = government-set R-Zone percent margin over wholesale price: 15% in 1992; 13% in 1994; 11% in 1996; 10% in 1998.

---

[86]   The pricing formula for new products is different and not discussed in this annex.

The formula specifies that the current period reimbursement price shall equal the weighted average of past period wholesale prices (meaning the price charged to the hospital or clinic by the wholesaler) plus a margin equal to the current R-Zone percentage multiplied by the old reimbursement price. Thus, referring to Table 8.4, for a product whose NHI reimbursement price in 1992 was ¥1000 and for which the weighted average wholesale price was ¥800, the formula specifies that the NHI price for 1994 will equal:

$$\text{NHI}_{(1994)} = 800 + (13\% * 1000) = 930$$

The reimbursement prices for succeeding years are calculated in an identical manner.

Using the reimbursement price determination formula and the assumption of a constant wholesaler margin, we can clarify the reimbursement price-setting process by use of two extreme cases, as shown on Table 8.4. Case I describes the circumstance where the hospital margin (drug price discrepancy or DPD) falls each year to a level very close to the stipulated R-Zone percentage. This variant however, is a happy story; wholesaler and manufacturer prices hold up nicely and the decline in the NHI reimbursement price is comparatively gentle and finite in duration.

Case II is an unhappy story. The new assumption is that hospitals manage to retain a constant percentage margin in negotiation with wholesalers. Note that as the NHI reimbursement price declines, this assumption entails a falling absolute margin; hospitals earn less money from each dose of the drug year after year, although the amount that they earn remains a fixed percentage of the reimbursement price. In this setting, all three prices decline throughout the decade.[87] As long as the percentage hospital margin remains substantially greater than the R-Zone percentage, the downward spiral continues, even though the R-Zone percentage stabilizes in the latter years.

Although the two cases presented are obviously extremes, the important question is: between these two extremes, where will reality fit?

---

[87] As Table 8.5 shows in Case II the average compound rate of decline is 5 percent per annum in real terms. Adding an inflation rate of 4 percent yields a nominal decline of 1 percent.

8.1.3 Economic Implications of the R-Zone Mechanism

Although the industry has endorsed the R-Zone pricing mechanism, regarding it as a source of relief from the oppressive price reductions by fiat that occurred during the 80s, R-Zone pricing has a potential for creating a harsh pricing regime for pharmaceutical manufacturers in Japan.[88]

The difficulty with the R-Zone approach to price regulation is that both the reimbursement price and the manufacturer's price depend crucially upon the negotiation between the wholesalers and the hospitals The more successful the hospitals are in preserving their margins—either by force of bargaining strength or sheer necessity—the lower will be the reimbursement price the wholesale price and the price obtainable by the manufacturer.

For the sake of the discussion that follows these assumptions are used:

- Wholesalers' margins can be squeezed, but not by much. Wholesalers will be squeezed quickly to the point where their margin will cover only operating costs plus a normal rate of return.[89] For illustrative purposes in Table 8.4, we use a margin of 7 percent, approximating the current margin; in fact, the true competitive wholesale margin may be about half that. Either way, a relatively small proportion of the total price is involved.

- Hospitals are not highly profitable under the drug price regimes of the present and the immediate past, notwithstanding the fact that hospital margins on medicines—approximately equal to the drug price discrepancy—exceeded 20 percent. The implication is that while there may be some scope for reducing the current hospital margin in the short run, further reductions will involve the bankruptcy and closing of hospitals. The only other alternative is supplying funds to hospitals by readjustment of other reimbursement rates.[90]

---

[88] Reich (1991), writing a year before the implementation of R-Zone pricing, mentions that the JPMA, the U.S. PMA and the European Business Council endorsed the method. Reich, in his own description of R-Zone pricing, however, anticipated differential impacts, noting that the method could be even harsher than the bulk-line approach for deeply discounted medicines.

[89] It is rumoured that the government is willing to encourage a degree of collusion among wholesalers in order to make the process adjustment more gradual. The implications of this odd policy, if true, are not of significance to the present analysis.

[90] Table 8.6 shows the estimated impact on hospital margins of a regime in which the hospital margin were depressed to the R-Zone level in each period. The effect is not small.

Because wholesalers operate on thin margins and have no market power,[91] it seems certain that after a few years of R-Zone pricing wholesaler margins will be pushed to a minimum by competition, leaving room only for the recovery of costs plus a 'normal' rate of return sufficient to recover the cost of capital. Whether or not wholesalers resist the compression of their margin, the numbers are too small to matter much—the difference between seven and three percent of the wholesale price or about ¥4 per ¥100 of wholesale price. Wholesaling is likely to be a competitive segment of the industry and as a result wholesalers become transparent in the bargaining process. That is, they will be price-takers on the buying side from the manufacturers and price-takers on the selling side to the medical institutions, unable in either case to have any real effect on the transaction prices.

Hospitals (and possibly other medical institutions) are in a different situation from the wholesalers, but not drastically so. Larger hospitals may be able to exercise some degree of buyer-side market power by forcing several wholesalers to bid for their business and granting the supply contract only to the lowest price bidder. Even if this were not the case, there is a limit under existing reimbursement arrangements to the ability of hospitals to sustain a reduction in their pharmaceutical sales margins. Under existing reimbursement arrangements hospitals are simply not well-funded institutions, and the margins on drugs are an important source of income. Unless it becomes a fact that lost hospital drug margins are immediately compensated by increased funding from other reimbursement sources, hospitals will simply be unable to tolerate compression of margins.

A glance at Cases I and II shown in Table 8.4 reveals that either end of the spectrum of outcomes of R-Zone pricing imply declining absolute margins for hospitals. Even if hospitals are able to sustain percentage margins, the money they reap on each prescription goes down as the reimbursement price drops. The closer the hospital margins falls to the R-Zone percentage, the more drastic is the decline in absolute margins for the hospitals. Unless the government is willing to let hospitals go bankrupt on a large scale, increases in outside funding to hospitals is inevitable. In either case, the downward pressure through wholesalers on manufacturers' prices in likely to be high. Thus, R-Zone pricing translates into a tug of war between the pharmaceutical manufacturers and other stakeholders (including the government), with

---

[91] Market power is the ability to exercise some control over price in a transaction. Firms without market power are, in other words, pure price-takers. The more competitive a market, the smaller the ability of any firm within it to exercise market power.

wholesalers and hospitals serving as the rope. Every price decline by a manufacturer represents money that the government or others need not supply to hospitals by other means.

Predictably, there are mitigating factors. Foremost among these is the well known principle of preserving the relative shares and incomes of the stakeholders in the health care system. It is already the case, in fact, that changes in reimbursement rates for hospital services have been effected in order to compensate for lost revenues from pharmaceutical sales. Second, it has traditionally been the case that the reimbursement prices for new drugs have been set at reasonable levels which mitigates to some degree the effect of reimbursement price declines later in the product's life. In addition, the new pricing format provides premiums for innovative pharmaceutical products that improve on the price advantage for new drugs. Thus, one outcome of the R-Zone system when combined with these other elements of the pharmaceutical price setting mechanism is that older drugs with close substitutes will be hurt, as they would in competition, while newer more innovative drugs will hold up better. This creates an incentive for pharmaceutical manufacturers to introduce as many new drugs as quickly as possible so as to stay level or even rise on a downward-moving escalator. As to the net effect for the industry as whole, it is too early to tell. Much depends upon the capacity of the MOHW and *Chuikyo* to adjust reimbursement mechanisms to keep hospitals afloat and at the same time to prevent the downward pressure of the R-Zone formula on drug prices from crushing the industry.

Japan

Table 8.4
JAPAN R-ZONE PRICING MODEL (MARGINS SET PRICES)

CASE I: VARIABLE PERCENTAGE HOSPITAL MARGIN & FIXED DOLLAR WHOLESALER MARGIN

	1992-3	1994	1996	1998	2000	2002	2004	2006
YEAR								
"R-ZONE"	15%	13%	11%	10%	10%	10%	10%	10%
PRICES								
Reimbursement List Price	1000	930.00	902.30	890.23	889.02	888.90	888.89	888.89
Wholesaler > Hospital	800	800.00	800.00	800.00	800.00	800.00	800.00	800.00
Manufacturer > Wholesaler	744	744.00	744.00	744.00	744.00	744.00	744.00	744.00
MARGINS								
Hospital Margin[1]								
Absolute	200	130.00	102.30	90.23	89.02	88.90	88.89	88.89
Percentage	20%	13.98%	11.34%	10.14%	10.01%	10.00%	10.00%	10.00%
Wholesaler Margin[2]								
Absolute	56	56.00	56.00	56.00	56.00	56.00	56.00	56.00
Percentage	7%	7.00%	7.00%	7.00%	7.00%	7.00%	7.00%	7.00%

CASE II: FIXED PERCENTAGE HOSPITAL MARGIN & FIXED PERCENTAGE WHOLESALER MARGIN

	1992-3	1994	1996	1998	2000	2002	2004	2006
YEAR								
"R-ZONE"	15%	13%	11%	10%	10%	10%	10%	10%
PRICES								
Reimbursement List Price	1000	930.00	846.30	761.67	889.02	888.90	888.89	888.89
Wholesaler => Hospital	800	744.00	677.04	609.34	548.40	493.56	444.21	399.79
Manufacturer => Wholesaler	744	691.92	629.65	566.68	510.01	459.01	413.11	371.80
MARGINS								
Hospital Margin[1]								
Absolute	200	186.00	169.26	152.33	137.10	123.39	111.05	99.95
Percentage	20%	20.0%	20.0%	20.0%	20.0%	20.0%	20.0%	20.0%
Wholesaler Margin[2]								
Absolute	56	52.08	47.39	42.65	38.39	34.55	31.09	27.98
Percentage	7%	7.00%	7.00%	7.00%	7.00%	7.00%	7.00%	7.00%

[1] The hospital margin is set by negotiations between the wholesaler and the hospital.
[2] The wholesaler margin is set by negotiations between the manufacturer and the wholesaler.

676

Table 8.5

COMPARISON OF HISTORICAL NHI DRUG PRICE REDUCTIONS TO PROJECTED REDUCTIONS UNDER CASE II OF R-ZONE PRICING

Year	NHI Drug Price Reduction[1]	Implicit Drug Price Index	Compound Annual Growth Rate from 1980	Case II RLP[2]	Compound Annual Growth Rate from 1992
1980		100.0			
1981	18.6%	81.4	-18.6%		
1982		81.4	-9.8%		
1983	4.9%	77.4	-8.2%		
1984	16.6%	64.6	-10.4%		
1985	6.0%	60.7	-9.5%		
1986	5.1%	57.6	-8.8%		
1987		57.6	-7.6%		
1988	10.2%	51.7	-7.9%		
1989		51.7	-7.1%		
1990	9.2%	47.0	-7.3%		
1991		47.0	-6.6%		
1992	8.1%	43.2	-6.8%	1,000.00	
1993				1,000.00	
1994				930.00	-3.6%
1995				930.00	-2.4%
1996				846.30	-4.1%
1997				846.30	-3.3%
1998				761.67	-4.4%
1999				761.67	-3.8%
2000				685.50	-4.6%
2001				685.50	-4.1%
2002				616.95	-4.7%
2003				616.95	-4.3%
2004				555.26	-4.8%
2005				555.26	-4.4%
2006				499.73	-4.8%

[1] Japanese Pharmaceutical Manufacturers Association, _Pharmaceutical Industry in Japan 1992_, citing the Japanese Ministry of Health and Welfare.

[2] Reimbursement list price (RLP) from Case II of the Table 8.4. RLPs remain in effect for two years.

Table 8.6
ESTIMATED CHANGE IN HOSPITALS' MARGIN DUE TO R-ZONE PRICING

Scenario[1]	Total National Medical Expenses[2] (Yen billion)	Share of Expenses on Pharmaceuticals[3]	Estimated Expenses on Pharmaceuticals[4] (Yen billion)	Drug Price Discrepancy (DPD) Ratio[5]	Estimated Hospital Margin on Pharmaceuticals[6] (Yen billion)	Estimated Change in Hospitals' Margin[7] (Yen billion)	Estimated Change in Hospitals' Margin[7] ($ billion)[8]
	(1)	(2)	(1)*(2)=(3)	(4)	(3)*(4)=(5)	(6)	(7)
Base Case	20,690.0	31.3%	6,476.0	21.7%	1,405.3		
15% R-Zone (1992)				15.0%	971.4	-433.9	-3.6
13% R-Zone (1994)				13.0%	841.9	-129.5	-1.1
11% R-Zone (1996)				11.0%	712.4	-129.5	-1.1
10% R-Zone (1998)				10.0%	647.6	-64.8	-0.5

[1] Years indicate when different R-Zones are due to come into effect.
[2] This figure is an estimate for 1990.
[3] Pharmaceuticals' share of total health expense in 1989.
[4] Estimated pharmaceutical expenses in 1990.
[5] Percentage difference between the NHI price and the wholesale price to hospitals. The base case uses the DPD as of March 1989. In the other scenarios, the DPD equals the R-Zone.
[6] Estimated hospitals' margin on pharmaceuticals in 1990; all calculations use the estimated pharmaceutical expense in 1990.
[7] Annual change in hospitals' margin from previous scenario.
[8] Yen are converted to US Dollars at a rate of 120 Yen per US Dollar.

ANNEX 8.2 CHRONOLOGY OF THE DEVELOPMENT OF THE JAPANESE HEALTH CARE SYSTEM

1905   First mutual benefit society formed, imitating Germany's system. Mutual benefit societies initially provided health services to the employees of textile firms. Historically, Japanese textile workers suffered from tuberculosis, the second leading cause of death at that time. This early form of health coverage was "small-scale and localized".[92]

1922   First compulsory health insurance plan established, covering those employees who had previously been covered under the Factory Law of 1905 and the Mining Law of 1911, and was financed by insurance payments divided equally between employer and employee.

1927   National Health Insurance Law enacted, featuring: (1) coverage of workers of firms with more than ten employees (dependents were not provided coverage); (2) coverage of injuries or illnesses suffered both on and off the job; and (3) coverage for a total of 180 days.

1934   National Health Insurance Law amended to extend coverage to employees of firms with more than five employees. This change fostered industrialization by stabilizing the labour force.

1938   Ministry of Health and Welfare (MOHW) established. The MOHW was responsible for implementing laws governing health and medical issues.

1938   National Health Insurance Law enacted establishing the first community-based (residence-based) health insurance plan. The plan covered those individuals who were not already covered by Employee Health Insurance; however, communities were not required to establish associations, nor were residents required to participate in the associations, once established.

1939   Health Insurance Law amended to provide optional coverage to the dependents of the insured.

1942   Salaried Employees Health Insurance Law integrated into the Health Insurance Law, unifying what had previously been two

---

[92]   Fujii and Reich (1988), p. 10.

separate schemes: one for manual workers and the other for salaried employees.

1943   National Health Insurance Law amended, making coverage mandatory for the dependents of the insured; the extent of health coverage was 50 percent of medical costs.

1944   Amendment to the National Health Insurance Law extended the duration of health coverage to two years.

1947   Workmen's Accident Compensation Insurance (*Rodosha Saigai Hosho Hokenho*) established to cover injuries and illnesses suffered on the job. Subsequently, Health Insurance Law amended to cover only private injuries and illnesses.

1948   Medical Services Law enacted to regulate the distribution, construction, equipment and manpower of medical care facilities in Japan.[93]

1948   National Health Insurance Law amended, making municipalities the insurers of residence-based health insurance. Although the law allowed each municipality to decide whether or not to establish a plan, once a plan was established, residents were obliged to join.

1953   National Health Insurance Law amended to extend the period of coverage to three years.

1956   Social Security System Council report demanding a more equitable health insurance system.[94] "Considering that illness is one major cause of poverty, and also respecting the value of human life, policy should stress as a top priority the equal opportunity for medical care as well as for education." The perceived inequities at that time, characterized by the lack of health insurance coverage for 30 percent of the population, were the result of delegating the provision of health insurance to the municipal administrations.[95]

1958   National Health Insurance Law amended to form a legal basis for universal coverage. All municipalities were required to

---

[93]   Iryo Roppo (1986); Fujii and Reich (1988), p. 19.

[94]   Social Security Council (1956).

[95]   Fujii and Reich (1988), p. 11.

	establish a health insurance plan and to provide coverage for those not already insured, extending coverage to the remaining 30 percent of the population.
1963	National Health Insurance Law amended to provide coverage for 70 percent of medical costs due to householders' injuries or illnesses and to abolish the limitation on the duration of coverage.
1968	National Health Insurance Law amended to provide coverage for 70 percent of medical costs for all insured people.
1973	The Welfare Law for the Aged amended to give free medical care for individuals aged 70 and over and disabled individuals 65 years and over. The amendment stipulated that the government would pay the copayment that had previously been paid by the elderly. The copayment rates were 20 percent for in-patient care and 30 percent for out-patient care for the dependents of individuals covered under Employee Health Insurance; the copayment rate was 30 percent for National Health Insurance subscribers.[96]
	National Health Insurance Law amended to provide coverage for 70 percent of medical costs for the dependents of the insured. High Cost Medical Care Benefits Law (*Kogaku Ryoyohi Shikyu Seido*) also enacted in the same year.
1977, 1982	Patient copayment rate and insurance contributions by both the employer and the employee increased to strengthen the financial state of Employee Health Insurance.
1982	Health Service Law for the Aged replaces Welfare Law for the Aged. The goal of the new statute was to ensure comprehensive medical services for the elderly, with any additional costs to be financed by the various health insurance plans. The new statute covered the same group as did the old law, but provided both curative medical care and preventive health services. Furthermore, the Health Service Law for the Aged endeavoured to reduce the incentive of the aged to over-utilize health services by introducing a small copayment for the elderly: out-patient care was 400 yen/month ($1.80/month) for each medical facility, and in-patient care was

---

[96]   Fujii and Reich (1988), p. 13.

300 yen/day ($1.35/day) for the first 50 days for the insured and the first 60 days for dependents.

1984   Amendments by the *Diet* to the National Health Insurance Law: (1) introduction of 10 percent cost sharing of medical care for the insured, with the maximum copayment set at 54,000 yen;[97] (2) implementation of a medical care benefits system for the retired elderly, separating the retired elderly from those covered under other insurance schemes, to be partially financed by Employee Health Insurance plans; and (3) controls on the expenditures on medical care, including a review of the certification system of health insurance medical care facilities, as well as examinations of high-cost medical bills.[98] This system of medical claim examinations has led to the practice of providers listing several diagnoses on patients' medical bills, since the review of itemized services is checked manually against patients' age, sex, and number of diagnoses. However, because the review panel is aware of the patterns in the delivery of medical care by providers, the examination of services tends to be strict.

1985   Medical Services Law of 1948 amended to control the number of new hospital beds. The goal of the amendment was to control rising medical costs by improving Japan's planning system for the supply of medical services. This was to be accomplished by the development of regional medical care plans designed by each prefecture, possibly setting a precedent for more localization in the provision of medical services.

---

[97]   Fujii and Reich, p. 16. The High Cost Medical Care Benefits Law, enacted in 1973 and amended in 1984, protects all insured people from monthly out-of-pocket copayments above 54,000 yen ($438 1990), or 30,000 yen ($230 1990) for those in the low-income group. "To qualify for the benefits provided under the current law on High Cost Medical Care Benefits, each member of a household must spend at least 30,000 yen. Therefore, if three members of a household spent 28,000 yen each in a month, that household would not qualify for any benefits, even though the household as a whole has spent 84,000 yen." See Ministry of Health and Welfare, *Annual Report on Health and Welfare for 1989* and Yoshikawa, Shirouzu and Holt (1992), pp. 7, 25.

[98]   The retrospective review of medical claims was sent to third-party payers every month, providing a complete list of claims for services provided by health care providers. If the review of claims by a designated panel of physicians found that providers had indulged in an over-provision of services or over-treatment, payment could be denied. See Ikegami (1991), p. 97.

The amendment, strongly opposed by the JMA, restricted the freedom of doctors to set up private hospitals. At first, however, the amendment gave physicians the incentive to quickly build new private hospitals before each prefecture could design its own plan.[99] Currently, it is practically impossible to build new hospitals in urban areas.

Despite its objective, the amendment does not make a provision for the reduction of the number of existing hospital beds and may even create incentives to add new hospital beds in sites where the number of beds are less than the pre-determined level. The Medical Services Law also requires all hospital managers to be physicians, prohibits the disbursement of surplus revenue in the form of dividends by health care businesses, and outlaws the use of advertisements which list physicians' medical backgrounds and specialties.[100]

1986	Amendment to the Health Service Law for the Aged. The amendment was a further attempt to control medical care expenditures—which continued the trend in increasing by 3.8 percent during the first year after the passage of the 1984 health insurance amendment and 10.3 percent during the first six months of the following fiscal year—by increasing the rate of patient cost sharing. The copayment for out-patients was increased to 800 yen/month and the copayment for in-patients was increased to 400 yen/day.[101] The impact of this new amendment on cost containment has yet to be fully determined.
1990	Administrative reforms of health insurance to stabilize costs and to introduce uniform copayment rates of 20 percent; these reforms have not yet been put fully into practice. "Gold Plan" for the elderly proposed with the objective of increasing the number of nursing home beds and day care centres.
1992	Fee revision plan raising fees of nursing services and other categories of services. Increased provision for surcharges to cover discretionary services (private rooms, special meals,

---

[99]   Yoshikawa, Shirouzu and Holt (1992), p. 11.

[100]   Koinuma (1988), p. 22.

[101]   Fujii and Reich (1988), p. 20.

treatment by appointment). Cost-per-case flat daily fee for care of elderly in hospitals.

Replacement of "bulk line" system for drug reimbursement price-setting with "weighted average price" method and R-Zone adjustment (see Annex 8.1).

ANNEX 8.3 DATA TABLES

List of Tables

TABLE 1
POPULATION ACCORDING TO AGE GROUPS
(Percent)

	1950	1960	1970	1980	1985	1990
MALE						
0-6	16.3	12.6	12.3	11.1	9.2	8.0
7-14	18.3	18.7	12.6	13.4	13.2	11.1
15-17	5.8	6.0	5.1	4.5	4.9	5.1
18-20	6.0	6.1	6.0	4.2	4.4	5.0
21-44	33.2	35.2	40.7	38.0	36.5	35.3
45-64	15.7	16.4	17.0	20.9	23.2	25.6
65 and above	4.6	5.1	6.3	7.8	8.6	9.9
Total	100.0	100.0	100.0	100.0	100.0	100.0
FEMALE						
0-6	15.0	11.6	11.3	10.2	8.5	7.3
7-14	17.1	17.3	11.7	12.3	12.2	10.1
15-17	5.5	5.7	4.8	4.2	4.5	4.7
18-20	5.8	5.9	5.7	3.9	4.1	4.6
21-44	35.0	36.2	39.4	36.6	34.9	33.5
45-64	15.5	16.9	19.3	22.4	24.0	25.6
65 and above	6.0	6.4	7.8	10.3	12.0	14.2
Total	100.0	100.0	100.0	100.0	100.0	100.0
ALL						
0-6	15.6	12.0	11.8	10.7	8.8	7.6
7-14	17.7	18.0	12.1	12.8	12.7	10.6
15-17	5.7	5.8	5.0	4.4	4.7	4.9
18-20	5.9	6.0	5.8	4.0	4.2	4.8
21-44	34.1	35.7	40.0	37.3	35.7	34.4
45-64	15.6	16.7	18.2	21.7	23.6	25.6
65 and above	5.3	5.7	7.1	9.1	10.3	12.1
Total	100.0	100.0	100.0	100.0	100.0	100.0

Source: *Statistics Bureau, Management and Coordination Agency, "The Population Census of Japan".*

TABLE 2
LIFE EXPECTANCY AT AGE X (FEMALES)

Completed Age X	1889-1903	1909-1913	1921-1925	1935-1936	1947	1955	1965	1975	1985	1990
0	44.85	44.73	43.20	49.63	53.96	67.75	72.92	76.89	80.48	81.81
1	51.17	51.24	49.42	54.07	57.40	69.34	73.13	76.56	79.89	81.15
5	51.97	52.16	50.71	54.40	57.45	66.41	69.47	72.78	76.03	77.27
10	48.34	48.51	47.00	50.47	53.31	61.78	64.62	67.87	71.08	72.32
20	41.06	41.67	40.38	43.22	44.87	52.25	54.85	58.04	61.20	62.44
30	34.84	35.72	34.69	36.88	37.95	43.25	45.31	48.35	51.41	52.63
40	28.19	29.03	28.09	29.65	30.39	34.34	35.91	38.76	41.72	42.92
50	21.11	21.84	20.95	22.15	22.64	25.70	26.85	29.46	32.28	33.41
60	14.32	14.99	14.12	15.07	15.39	17.72	18.42	20.68	23.24	24.29
70	8.77	9.28	8.44	9.04	9.41	10.95	11.09	12.78	14.89	15.76
80	4.85	5.26	4.41	4.67	5.09	6.12	5.80	6.76	8.07	8.60
90	2.36	2.61	2.04	2.09	2.45	3.12	2.96	3.39	3.82	3.85

LIFE EXPECTANCY AT AGE X (MALES)

Completed Age X	1889-1903	1909-1913	1921-1925	1935-1936	1947	1955	1965	1975	1985	1990
0	43.79	44.25	42.06	46.92	50.06	63.60	67.74	71.73	74.78	75.86
1	51.11	51.61	49.14	51.95	53.74	65.37	68.16	71.53	74.22	75.24
5	51.90	52.57	50.35	52.22	53.61	62.45	64.57	67.80	70.39	71.40
10	48.23	48.82	46.53	48.25	49.49	57.89	59.80	62.94	65.47	66.47
20	40.35	41.06	39.10	40.41	40.89	48.47	50.18	53.27	55.74	56.71
30	33.44	34.31	32.59	33.89	34.23	39.70	40.90	43.78	46.16	47.10
40	26.03	26.82	25.13	26.22	26.88	30.85	31.73	34.41	36.63	37.52
50	18.97	19.61	18.02	18.85	19.44	22.41	23.00	25.56	27.56	28.33
60	12.76	13.28	11.87	12.55	12.83	14.97	15.20	17.38	19.34	19.95
70	7.89	8.26	7.11	7.62	7.93	9.13	8.99	10.53	12.00	12.60
80	4.44	4.70	3.87	4.20	4.62	5.25	4.81	5.70	6.51	6.82
90	2.22	2.38	1.95	2.14	2.56	2.87	2.56	3.05	3.28	3.34

Source: *Ministry of Health and Welfare, "The Life Tables".*

TABLE 3
GROSS DOMESTIC PRODUCT AND NATIONAL
MEDICAL CARE COST

Fiscal Year	GDP (Y Billion)	GDP Per Head (Y 000s)	National Medical Care Cost (Y Billion)	National Medical Care Cost per Head (Y 000s)	National Medical Care Cost
1981	260,801	2,212	12,870.9	109.2	4.94%
1982	273,322	2,303	13,865.9	116.8	5.07%
1983	285,593	2,390	14,543.8	121.7	5.09%
1984	305,144	2,538	15,093.2	125.5	4.95%
1985	324,159	2,678	16,015.9	132.3	4.94%
1986	338,353	2,781	17,069.0	140.3	5.04%
1987	353,989	2,895	18,075.9	147.8	5.11%
1988	376,889	3,070	18,755.4	152.8	4.98%
1989	402,520	3,266	18,729.0	160.1	4.90%
1990	434,154	3,512	20,607.4	166.7	4.75%

Source: *Economic Planning Agency, "National Accounts".*
Ministry of Health and Welfare, "National Medical Care Costs".

TABLE 4
THE PRIMARY HEALTH CARE SECTOR

Year	Total Expenditure on Primary Care (1985 Y Mill)	Total Expenditure on Primary Care as a % of Total Health Expenditure	Public Expenditure on Primary Care (1985 Y Mill)
1981	6,249,420	34.6%	5,405,163
1982	6,503,930	34.1%	5,644,261
1983	6,744,661	33.8%	5,839,220
1984	6,773,022	33.3%	5,798,479
1985	6,945,400	33.0%	5,906,400
1986	7,305,599	33.5%	6,200,393
1987	7,887,192	33.8%	6,679,113
1988	8,246,719	33.8%	6,987,267

Source: *OECD (1991)*

TABLE 5
NUMBER OF INSURED PERSONS BY MEDICAL CARE INSURANCE SCHEME
AS OF MARCH 31, 1991

Health Insurance Scheme	Insurer (Number)	Number of Beneficiaries (000s)	Share of Beneficiaries %	Insured Dependents (000s)	Share of Dependents %	Total Insured (000s)	Share of Insured %	Elderly Share %
Government-managed Health Insurance	Government	17,983	22.2%	18,683	43.2%	36,666	29.5%	4.8%
Day Laborers Special Care Insured	Government	103	0.1%	52	0.1%	155	0.1%	
Society-managed Health Insurance	Health Insurance Societies (1,822)	14,668	18.1%	17,341	40.1%	32,009	25.8%	2.9%
Seamen's Insurance	Government	137	0.2%	272	0.6%	409	0.3%	6.2%
National Public Service Mutual Aid Associations	Mutual Aid Associations (27)	1,672	2.1%	2,609	6.0%	4,281	3.4%	
Local Public Service Mutual Aid Associations	Mutual Aid Associations (54)	2,963	3.7%	3,939	9.1%	6,901	5.6%	3.9%
Private School Teachers and Employees Mutual Aid Association	Mutual Aid Association (1)	401	0.5%	369	0.9%	770	0.6%	
National Health Insurance	Local Governments (3,258)	38,880	48.0%			38,880	31.3%	15.9%
	National Health Insurance Associations (166)	4,189	5.2%			4,189	3.4%	
Total		80,996	100.0%	43,265	100.0%	124,260	100.0%	

Source: *Health Insurance Bureau, Ministry of Health and Welfare.*

TABLE 6A
INCOME AND EXPENDITURE OF INSURANCE FUNDS (Yen Million)
Government-Managed Health Insurance

	1980	1981	1982	1983	1984	1985	1986	1987	1988	1989
TOTAL INCOME	3,520,439	3,809,669	4,027,920	4,135,847	5,129,167	5,251,769	5,355,675	5,702,343	5,905,582	6,311,418
Contribution	2,322,687	2,642,566	2,850,064	2,986,473	3,129,348	3,321,276	3,382,839	3,511,686	3,756,552	4,085,619
National Subsidy	499,980	528,305	569,665	593,305	637,229	538,074	556,846	619,440	699,057	759,749
Loan	676,515	625,509	582,640	523,190	1,334,780	1,366,346	1,378,423	1,389,482	1,407,994	1,426,251
Transfer from Reserved Fund	8,852	-	11,422	17,764	-	-	-	135,000	-	-
Miscellaneous	12,405	13,290	14,130	15,116	27,810	26,073	37,567	46,736	41,978	39,800
TOTAL EXPENDITURE	3,504,256	3,810,093	4,008,217	4,122,059	4,913,621	4,954,332	5,303,867	5,693,539	5,852,618	6,095,572
Insurance Benefit	2,810,435	3,033,255	3,234,413	2,891,623	2,857,327	2,765,011	2,876,300	2,997,044	3,147,725	3,333,483
Contribution for the Aged	-	-	41,957	540,015	539,581	567,835	719,653	963,009	916,473	945,082
Management Expense	34,579	37,955	39,933	39,683	43,949	48,081	50,024	51,998	54,173	57,243
Redemption for Loans	649,195	727,174	670,391	623,885	1,357,401	1,416,029	1,443,023	1,447,308	1,457,836	1,475,341
Health Facilities	3,530	3,938	5,898	9,807	13,199	20,432	25,678	32,696	37,726	40,505
Welfare Facilities	6,157	7,336	15,099	16,469	17,417	22,855	23,020	26,701	28,245	27,489
Contribution for the Retired	-	-	-	-	84,032	113,236	164,940	173,642	209,104	214,946
Miscellaneous	359	436	525	577	715	853	1,229	1,141	1,336	1,482
BALANCE	16,183	(424)	19,704	13,788	215,546	297,437	51,809	8,804	52,964	215,847
Transfer to Following Year	2,364	1,973	1,939	1,641	2,272	2,211	3,128	5,023	2,150	855
Transfer to Reserve Fund	13,819	265	17,764	12,147	213,274	295,227	48,680	4,698	50,814	214,992
Complement from Reserve Fund	-	2,662	-	-	-	-	-	917	-	-
RESERVE FUND AFTER SETTLEMENT	13,819	11,422	17,764	12,147	225,743	520,969	569,649	438,430	489,244	704,236

Source: *Social Insurance Agency.*

TABLE 6B
INCOME AND EXPENDITURE OF INSURANCE FUNDS (Yen Million)
Society-Managed Health Insurance

	1985	1986	1987	1988	1989	1990
TOTAL INCOME	3,312,568	3,489,526	3,626,621	3,835,616	4,132,935	4,873,993
Contribution	3,116,285	3,287,972	3,431,219	3,635,534	3,917,029	4,243,728
Special Contribution	6,035	5,692	5,676	6,475	7,831	8,758
National Subsidy	4,131	4,259	4,390	4,487	4,760	4,893
Transfer from Retirement Reserve Fund	2,600	2,529	2,936	3,090	3,355	3,103
Income of Hospitals/Clinics	29,484	32,193	34,423	35,888	38,547	41,050
Miscellaneous	154,033	156,881	147,977	150,142	161,413	572,462
TOTAL EXPENSE	3,014,324	3,247,382	3,626,801	3,836,434	4,025,470	4,452,209
Management Expense	84,956	90,829	95,330	99,439	104,645	111,700
Statutory Benefits	1,933,154	2,058,080	2,162,657	2,261,607	2,348,857	2,462,597
Additional Benefits	95,419	99,444	105,839	110,138	112,194	116,160
Contribution for the Aged	456,136	531,017	750,373	809,214	881,248	1,024,693
Contribution for the Retired	163,027	162,491	196,436	228,208	232,661	234,103
Health Facilities	213,979	234,989	244,305	254,634	271,500	303,815
Miscellaneous	67,653	70,531	71,860	73,194	74,366	199,140
BALANCE	298,243	242,144	(180)	(818)	107,465	421,784

Source: *National Federation of Health Insurance Societies.*

TABLE 6C
INCOME AND EXPENDITURE OF INSURANCE FUNDS (Yen Million)
National Health Insurance

	1985	1986	1987	1988	1989
TOTAL INCOME	5,275,788	5,680,483	5,900,402	6,145,711	6,490,617
Premium	1,976,669	2,223,921	2,419,306	2,541,731	2,637,463
National Budget	2,371,428	2,474,115	2,460,265	2,350,703	2,489,912
Transfer from Retirement Reserve Fund	351,238	406,790	491,614	497,554	549,005
Local Government Budget	45,031	44,725	41,224	43,366	44,518
Town, City, Village Budget	176,103	225,337	233,907	256,898	277,519
Transfer from Reserve Fund	63,307	53,950	20,963	22,181	28,825
Surplus in the Previous Year	204,995	165,985	144,622	233,007	242,484
Miscellaneous	87,016	85,660	88,500	200,270	220,891
TOTAL EXPENSE	5,164,751	5,639,499	5,749,290	5,960,991	6,294,770
Administration	164,002	172,022	179,799	189,250	198,466
Benefits	3,369,944	3,678,890	3,947,238	4,069,345	4,233,628
Contribution for the Aged	1,455,224	1,597,620	1,366,663	1,441,628	1,610,981
Health Facilities	15,224	17,668	19,568	22,989	26,246
Miscellaneous	160,358	173,300	236,022	237,779	225,449
BALANCE	105,037	40,984	151,111	184,719	195,847

Source: *Health Insurance Bureau, Ministry of Health and Welfare.*

ANNEX 8.4 BIBLIOGRAPHY

Ainoya, Y. (1991), *Kuni ga Iryou wo Suterutoki* (When the National Health Care System is Abolished), Tokyo, Akebi Shobo.

Blendon, R., Leitman, R., Morrison, I., and Donelan, K. (1990), "Satisfaction with Health Systems in Ten Nations", *Health Affairs*, (Summer), pp. 185-92.

Chuou Shakai Hoken Iryou Kyougikai (Central Social Insurance and Medical Conference) (1990), *Iryou Keizai Jittai Chousa* (Survey on Medical and Economic Status).

Eisenstodt, G. (1992), "The doctor's margin", *Forbes*, November 23, 1992, pp. 44-45.

Fujii, M. and Reich, M.R. (1988), "Rising medical costs and the reform of Japan's health insurance system", *Health Policy*, Vol. 9, pp. 9-24.

Fujii, Ryoji, and Ishimoto, Tadayoshi, eds., (1984), *Iryou Hosho no Kiki* (Crisis of Health Care System), Tokyo, Keiso Shobo.

Fujino, S. (1987), "Health economics in Japan: Prospects for the future", in Teeling Smith, G., (ed), *Health Economics: Prospects for the Future*, London, Crook Helm.

Health and Welfare Statistics Association (1991), comp. *Kokumin Eisei no Doukou* (Trends in National Health) vol. 38, no. 9, Tokyo, Kousei Toukei Kyoukai.

Hino, H. (1987), *Nihon Iryou no Tembo* (Perspective of Japanese Health Care System), Tokyo, Akebi Shobo.

Hoken, Iryou, Fukushi no Sougou Nenkan (1991), *WIBA '91* (The General Yearbook of Health, Medical Care, and Insurance), Tokyo, Nihon Iryou Kikaku.

Hosaka, Masayasu., (1989), *Nihon no Iryou* (Japanese Health Care System), Tokyo, Asahi Sonorama.

Iglehart, J.K. (1988a), "Health Policy Report, Japan's Medical Care System", *The New England Journal of Medicine*, Vol. 319, No. 12, pp. 807-812.

Iglehart, J.K. (1988b), "Health Policy Report, Japan's Medical Care System—Part Two", *The New England Journal of Medicine*, Vol. 319, No. 17, pp. 1166-1172.

Ikegami, N. (1991), "Japanese Health Care: Low Cost Through Regulated Fees", *Health Affairs*, Fall 1991, pp. 87-109.

Ikegami, N. (1992), "The Economics of Health Care in Japan", *Science*, Vol. 258 (23 October 1992), pp. 614-618.

Iryo Roppo (Compendium of Medical Laws) (1986), Tokyo, Chuo Hoki.

Iryou Seido Kenkyuukai (Study Group of Medical System) (1990), *Iryou no Kouzou Henkaku to Iyakuhin* (Changes in Health Care System and Pharmaceuticals), Tokyo, Life Science Medica Co.

Japan Pharmaceutical Manufacturers Association (1992), *Pharmaceutical Industry in Japan*.

Kasia Yutaka, ed. (1989), "Yakuhin no Shouraizo" (The Future Outlook for Pharmaceuticals), from Vol. I of *Kouza: 21 Seiki e Mukete no Igaku to*

Iryou (Lectures: Medicine and Health Care Towards the 21st Century), Tokyo, Nihon Hyouronsha.

Kawakami, Takeshi, and Kosaka, Fumiko (1991), *Iryou Kaikaku to Kigyouka* (Health Care System Innovation and Medical Business), Tokyo, Keiso Shobo.

Kawakami, Takeshi, and Kosaka, Fumiko (1992). *Sengo Iryoushi Josetsu* (Introduction to the History of Health Care System after W.W. II), Tokyo, Keiso Shobo.

Kawakita, H., "Healthcare Services in Japan", *The International Hospital Federation*, Vol. 24, No. 2, pp. 11-27.

Kenkou Hoken Kumiai Rengoukai (the Federation of Society-managed Health Insurance Unions), ed. (1990), *Shakai Hoken Nenkan, 1990* (Social Insurance Yearbook, 1990), Tokyo, Touyou Keizai.

Kenkou Hoken Kumiai Rengoukai (the Federation of Society-managed Health Insurance Unions) (1991), *Kenkou Hoken Kumiai no Gensei* (Current Trends in Health Insurance Unions).

Kobayashi, Y. and Reich, M.R. (1993), "Health Care Financing for the Elderly in Japan", forthcoming in *Social Science & Medicine*.

Koichi Emi, ed. (1984), *Iryou to Keizai* (Medical care and Economics), Tokyo, Chuou Houki.

Koinuma, N. (1988), "Caring More About Quality: Japan - US Health Care Comparison", *International Hospital Federation*, 24(3), December 1988.

Kokumin no Iryou to Kokuritsu Byouin, Ryoyojo wo Mamoru Chuou Renraku Kaigi (Central Committee on National Hospitals) (1991), *Kokumin no Iryou wo Mamoru* (Securing Health Care System), Tokyo, Gakushu no Tomosha.

Kurumada, Shozaburo (1986), *Gendai Iryou e no Teigen* (Suggestions to Current Health Care Practices), Tokyo, Chuou Hoki Shuppan.

Medical Friend Co. (1986), *Nihon no Iryou no Yukute wo Yomu* (Future of Japanese Health Care System), Tokyo, Medical Friend Co.

Ministry of Health and Welfare (1985), 1983 Patient Survey, Tokyo: *Kousei Toukei Kyokai*.

Ministry of Health and Welfare (1990), *Ishi, Sika-Ishi, Yakuzai-shi Chousa* (Survey on Doctors, Dentists and Pharmacists).

Ministry of Health and Welfare (1991), *Health and Welfare Statistics in Japan 1991*, Tokyo, Kousei Toukei Kyoukai.

Ministry of Health and Welfare (1991a), *Annual Report on Health and Welfare*, Tokyo, Kousei Toukei Kyoukai.

Ministry of Health and Welfare (1991b), *Kousei Toukei Youran* (Summary of Statistics on Health and Welfare), Tokyo, Kousei Toukei Kyoukai.

Ministry of Health and Welfare, ed. (1991c), *Zusetsu Nihon no Iryou* (Pictorial explanation of Japanese Health Care System), Tokyo, Gyousei.

Ministry of Health and Welfare, ed. (1992a), *Kousei Hakusho, 1991* (Welfare White Paper 1991), Tokyo, Kousei Mondai Kenkyuukai.

Ministry of Health and Welfare, ed. (1992b), Insurance Bureau, Medical Care Section (*Hokenkyoku Iryoka*), *Yakka Kijun Seido* (Drug Pricing System).

Minkan Byouin Mondai Kenkyuusho (Study Group of Private Hospitals), ed, (1990), *Shin Nihongata Iryou Taisei e no Ristorakucharingu* (Restructuring for new Japanese Health Care System), Tokyo, Minkan Byouin Jouhou Center.

Niki, Ryu, (1990), *Gendai Nihon Iryou no Jissho Bunseki* (An analysis of Current Japanese Health Care System), Tokyo, Igakushoin.

Nishimura, S., (1987), *Iryou no Keizai Bunseki* (Economic Analysis of Health Care), Tokyo, Touyou Keizai Shinposha.

Nomura, T., (1987), *Nihon no Iryou to Iryou Undou* (Japanese Health Care System and Health Care Movement), Tokyo, Rodoujunposha.

Okamoto, Etsuji (1989), *Kokumin Kenkou Hoken* (National Health Insurance), Tokyo, Sanichi Shobo.

Okamoto, Etsuji (1991), *Iryouhi no Himitsu* (Health Care Cost Scheme), Tokyo, Sanichi Shobo.

Organisation for Economic Co-Operation and Development (1987),"Financing and Delivering Health Care, A Comparative Analysis of OECD Countries", *OECD Social Policy Studies No. 4*, 1987, p. 28.

Organisation for Economic Co-Operation and Development (1991), *OECD Health Data: Comparative Analysis of Health Systems* (software package), Paris.

Powell, M. and Anesaki, M., (1990), *Health Care in Japan*, London, Routledge.

Reich, M.R, (1990) "Why the Japanese Don't Export More Pharmaceuticals: Health Policy as Industrial Policy", *California Management Review*, Vol. 32, No. 2, pp. 124-149.

Reich, M.R. (1991), "Policy Challenges Facing the Pharmaceutical Industry in Japan," April 1991 (typescript)

Reich, M.R. and Hayashi, K., (1992) *Pharmaceutical Consumption and Price Policy in Japan*, Takemi Program in International Health, Harvard School of Public Health.

Scheiber, G.J. (1990), "Health Expenditure in Major Industrialized Countries, 1960-87", *Health Care Financing Review*, Summer 1990, pp. 159-167.

Social Insurance Agency of Japan, Japanese Government, comp., (1991), *Outline of Social Insurance in Japan*, Tokyo, Yoshida Finance and Social Security Law Institute.

Social Security Council (1956), *Iryo Hosho Seido ni Kansuru Hokoku* (Recommendations on the Medical Security System), Tokyo.

Tsujimura, Akira, ed., (1987), *Iryou to Shakai* (Health Care System and a Society), Vol. 5 of *Kouza Nijyuu Isseiki e Mukete no Igaku to Iryou* (Series on Medical Science and Health Care toward Twenty-first Century), Tokyo, Nihon Hyouronsha.

Uzawa, Hirofumi, ed. (1987), *Iryou no Keizaigakuteki Bunseki* (Economic Analysis of Health Care System), Vol. 4 of *Kouza Nijyuu Isseiki e Mukete no Igaku to Iryou* (Series on Medical Science and Health Care toward Twenty-first Century), Tokyo, Nihon Hyouronsha.

Yoshikawa, A., Shirouzu, N. and Holt, M. (1992), *How Does Japan Do It?*, A Special Report Comparative Health Care Research Series, Asia/Pacific Research Center, Stanford University, Spring.

Yoshitoshi, Kazu, ed. (1988), *Iryou no Shouraizo* (Future of Health Care System). Vol. 3 of *Kouza Nijyuu Isseiki e Mukete no Igaku to Iryou* (Series on Medical Science and Health Care toward Twenty-first Century), Tokyo, Nihon Hyouronsha.

Yutaka, K. (1989) (ed), *Yakuhin no Shouraizo* (The Future Outlook for Pharmaceuticals), from Vol. I of *Kouza: 21 Seiki e Mukete no Igaku to Iryou* (Lectures: Medicine and Health Care Towards the 21st Century), Tokyo: *Nihon Hyouronsha*, pp. 145-147.

CHAPTER 9

THE HEALTH CARE SYSTEM IN THE NETHERLANDS

Graham Shuttleworth

National Economic Research Associates
London

9.1 SUMMARY

Structure

The health care system in the Netherlands is a system in transition. The current financing scheme is one of public funding through sickness funds (covering about two-thirds of the population) plus private insurance coverage for those with higher incomes (about one-third). Under the so-called Dekker reforms, approved by the government in 1988, this system will eventually be replaced by a centralised financing scheme. Private insurers and the sickness funds will attract enrollees by offering competitive premiums. Insurers will contract with providers to serve their enrollees. Providers will continue to be independent but will have greater incentives for efficiency under the new plan.

Aggregate Expenditure

Historically, total spending on health care was determined by the demands of patients and the incentives on providers in treating patients. This led to unacceptably high expenditure which, in turn, resulted in increasing regulatory constraints. These included negotiated fees and capitations for physicians, attempts to limit physicians' incomes, constraints on capital spending by hospitals, prospective global budgeting for hospitals and reference pricing for pharmaceuticals. Given this heavy regulation, aggregate expenditure has become increasingly determined by political negotiations which try to balance public budgets against patient and provider satisfaction.

Incentives

Primary Care Physicians: General Practitioners (GPs) are paid a capitation, or a fixed amount per year, for each public patient who registers with them. This encourages the GPs to pass patients to the hospital as soon as they begin to draw significantly on the GP's time and office resources, even when the least-cost site of care would be the GP's office.

Hospitals: The vast majority of specialists, or hospital-based physicians, are paid a fee-for-service which is negotiated for publicly insured patients. The incentive has been for them to provide low-benefit, high-cost services in the most expensive setting, the acute care hospital.

Since 1983, hospitals have been given a prospective, global budget in place of cost-based reimbursement, which had created strong incentives to increase costs. The newer scheme is meant to penalize hospitals which exceed their budget, essentially by forcing the hospital to make up the difference. This has not worked well. Hospitals do not control the utilization decisions of the hospital specialists or the GPs who send the patients to hospitals. Also, the hospitals have been able to increase their global budgets by obtaining approval to add equipment and capital which have, in turn, been used to justify higher revenues.

Funders: The publicly funded sickness funds lack important efficiency incentives, largely because they are the a monopoly insurer for a large share of the local population. The reforms being implemented will force the sickness funds to compete with each other and with the private insurers. Private insurers have been successful in serving those who were not eligible for the public funds. The private sector has been able to select the lower risks in the population; so much so that the private sector makes a contribution to the public fund as payment for the adverse selection experienced by the sickness funds.

Medicines: As of January 1992, pharmaceuticals are being paid for under the Exceptional Medical Expense Fund (AWBZ) instead of the Health Insurance Act Fund. This reflects the ongoing implementation of the Dekker reforms which seek to roll all health care services into one central insurance fund. Other recent reforms have introduced the GVS programme, a 'reference pricing' scheme to pay for medicines. Under this scheme, patients must pay for anything in excess of a maximum reimbursement price. Pharmacists also receive one third of any costs saved by dispensing identical products with lower prices. These features of the system encourage the use of generics (although the growth of supplemental insurance to help patients cover their copayments will reduce such incentives).

Issues

The Dutch health care system has been characterized by significant inefficiencies, especially the lack of incentives to use least-cost alternatives in health care. This has created a large and expensive hospital sector and encouraged long lengths of stay and very little day surgery by comparison with other developed countries. Government attempts to control costs during the 1980s have stabilized spending as a share of GDP but have also reduced patient and provider satisfaction with the system. All of these factors underlie the recent passage of a major reform package to restructure the Dutch health care system.

700

Current Reforms

The Dekker reforms are now being implemented in the Netherlands. The program has three main features: (1) one basic benefits package for all citizens under one financing scheme, with consumers choosing their insurer and the details of the insurance policy they most desire; (2) greater incentives for efficiency in the delivery of care; and, (3) a shift from government regulation to greater reliance on managed competition. Sickness funds and private insurers will compete for enrollees and receive a risk-adjusted premium for each enrollee from the single Central Fund. Each enrollee will pay a flat-rate (i.e., not risk-adjusted) premium that depends on the insurer and coverage plan of their choice. Funding for the basic benefits package will come largely from income-related taxes paid into the Central Fund (85 percent), with the remainder coming from the individual flat-rate premiums (15 percent) paid directly to the insurer chosen.

Political Environment

The reforms are proceeding slowly despite widespread bi-partisan support at the time of passage. In addition to the technical complexities involved in finalizing the new schemes, there is growing political opposition to the proposed changes. Higher income groups generally object to paying more under a system funded by income-related taxes than they paid for private insurance premiums. Private insurers are less satisfied with the new system because a large share of their revenues will derive from a bureaucratic formula rather than being under their direct control. Consequently, many believe that full implementation will require as much as another decade.

NERA's Reform Proposals

The current reforms are similar to our proposed reform path. Health care is already funded by a mixture of income-related premiums charged by a central fund, and additional premiums charged by the individual sick funds. Separation of providers from purchasers is long established.

However, the system reflects the main political and religious divisions in Dutch society, which have always required a careful balancing of sectional interests. These divisions have severely limited the operation of competition between sick funds and between providers, whilst the attention to sectional interests has undermined attempts at central financial control. The current reform proposal is an attempt to rectify these rigidities, but it is widely recognised that such social reforms cannot proceed rapidly.

The main thrust of the reforms is, first, to centralise the control of funds and their allocation and, second, to impose financial discipline on the major players by disaggregating budgets to ever lower levels. These reforms will allow management of the health care sector to be decentralised, by allocating clear-cut responsibilities to lower levels.

Once this decentralised system has been put in place, competition can be introduced to encourage greater efficiency in the long term. During the interim, the government may use the introduction of competition, or the threat of competition, as a way to encourage health sector professionals to adopt a more commercial, or financially responsible, approach to their institutions. However, competition can only be successfully introduced if the sector operates with clearly defined financial and management responsibilities. Until such a time, the government may need to retain certain direct controls over the sector.

At the same time, the system of patient copayments should be modified, to remove the current bias against pharmaceuticals. Patients should pay an equal percentage of all health care costs, although exemption from copayments could be granted to individual patients, on grounds of income or health status. This would replace the current system, which applies copayments to many pharmaceuticals, but exempts some forms of health care. A more uniform structure of copayments would give patients better information on health care costs and encourage them to make more efficient choices.

9.2   STRUCTURE OF THE HEALTH CARE SYSTEM[1]

9.2.1   The Health Care System in Context

The Netherlands is a constitutional monarchy. Legislative power rests with the Crown and the States-General (*Staten Generaal*) which has a 75 member upper house and a 150 member lower house. The upper house is indirectly elected by the twelve Dutch Provincial Councils for six years, with half its members being re-elected every three years. The lower chamber is elected by direct universal adult suffrage on the basis of proportional representation every four years.

There are 12 main political parties of which the most important are the Christian Democrats, Labour and the Liberals. All post World War II governments have been centrist coalitions, either Centre-Right or Centre-Left, and have always included the Christian Democrats. The most recent election for the lower house was in September 1989. The present government is a coalition of the largest party - the Christian Democrats - and the Labour Party.

The government has overall responsibility for most aspects of health policy in the Netherlands. However, the actual system is characterised by a public/private mix of finance, together with service provision from private, not-for-profit hospitals. Most doctors - both GPs and specialists - work as private practitioners. Many Dutchmen pride themselves on having developed a pragmatic 'mixed' health care system, combining the social responsibility of the British and Scandinavian public systems with the entrepreneurial efficiency of the United States.[2]

Expenditure on health care is high by international standards, and the standard of care is considered to be good. In general, patients have ready access to a comprehensive range of services and a wide choice between providers. Health status is also high. Life expectancy is long and infant mortality rates are among the lowest in the world.

Nonetheless, there are problems. The government has been particularly concerned with the rising costs of health care. Since the early 1970s, it has

---

[1]   I am grateful to Ray Robinson, of the King's Fund Institute in London, for his assistance in compiling the descriptive material in this chapter.

[2]   Saltman and de Roo (1989).

sought to control the growth in aggregate expenditure through price controls and by regulating the numbers of hospitals, hospital beds and new technologies. Overall, the results of these policies have been disappointing.[3] Total expenditure continued to increase at what was thought to be an excessive rate during the 1970s. These increases also led to increases in the share of income being spent on health care. As aggregate cost containment policies became more effective during the 1980s, other pressures emerged. Waiting lists for elective surgical procedures lengthened and there was a strike by physicians protesting about restrictions on their incomes. It became increasingly obvious that the system contained few incentives for using resources efficiently at the micro level. Moreover, some aspects of the mix of public and private funding were felt to be inequitable and to threaten social solidarity.

Faced with these shortcomings, the government appointed a committee to review the structure and financing of health care, chaired by Wisse Dekker, a former president of the electronics group, Philips International. The Dekker committee produced its report, "Willingness to Change", in March 1987. The Dekker plan had two main components: the introduction of a unified, basic health insurance package for the entire population; and the introduction of regulated competition between insurers and between providers. The proposals represent a movement towards a more market-based approach and are consistent with developments in a number of other countries and social policy areas.

After a lengthy and difficult decision making process, the cabinet presented its final response to the Dekker Report in a policy paper, "Changes Assured", in March 1988. In this paper, the cabinet accepted the main lines of the Dekker approach. Following parliamentary debates, the first steps towards a new health care system were taken on 1 January 1989. It was expected that full implementation would take place over four years and would be completed by 1992. In fact, progress has been far slower than was originally envisaged. The proposals have encountered considerable political opposition, and doubts are now being expressed about whether they will ever be implemented in full.[4]

In summary, the Dutch health care system is in the throes of a major programme of reform. This represents an ambitious attempt to introduce

---

[3]   van de Ven (1990).

[4]   Elsinga (1989).

incentives for greater efficiency while maintaining equity in terms of access to health care. At present, however, there are doubts about the extent and pace of change which can be achieved.

9.2.2 General Features of the Finance System

According to official Dutch estimates for 1992, 9.4 percent of GNP was spent on health care in the Netherlands.[5] This figure is higher than the OECD estimate of 8.1 percent (1990) mainly because it includes some long term nursing care expenditure not included by the OECD as health expenditure.

Finance is raised from three main sources. First, the entire population is covered by compulsory social insurance for the costs of serious illness or long-term disability under the Exceptional Medical Expenses (Compensation) Act, better known by its initials (in Dutch), AWBZ. Services covered include hospital stays in excess of 365 days, nursing home care, and services for people with physical disabilities, mental handicaps and mental illness. Revenue to meet the costs of AWBZ is derived from two sources: income-related payments made by employees to the tax collecting authority; and (now only to a small extent) central government grants. In 1992, AWBZ is expected to account for about 45 percent of total health care expenditure.

The second source of health care funds is social insurance payments made under the Health Insurance Act. Everyone earning below a certain wage and salary level (set at 54,400 guilders in 1992 or $23,550 1990) and recipients of social security benefits are required to contribute to this fund. These contributions include contributions related to earned income from insured people and their employers, and nominal flat-rate premiums. The over-65s remain covered after retirement if they were compulsorily insured before retirement. Funds contributed under the Health Insurance Act cover the costs of GP services, short-term hospital care, dental care and, until this year, medicines. Approximately 62 percent of the population is insured under the Health Insurance Act. In 1992, it is expected to contribute approximately 24 percent of total health care expenditure.

The third source of health care funds is payments made directly by individuals (i.e., out-of-pockets payments) and payments made by private insurers on behalf of their enrollees (the insured). These companies offer cover to the self-employed and to those individuals with earned incomes above the ceiling

---

[5]   Ministry of Welfare, Health and Cultural Affairs (1992).

specified by the terms of the Health Insurance Act. Currently, there is a wide variety of private insurance packages varying in the extent of their coverage and use of copayments and deductibles. Employees often receive a contribution from their employers towards the costs of private health insurance but, unlike in the United States, most private insurance is taken out by individuals rather than by their employers. About 32 percent of the population is covered by private insurance arrangements.

Social insurance contributions are paid into a central fund administered by the Sickness Fund Council (*Ziekenfondsraad*). This board is an independent administrative body responsible for distributing funds to about 30 private, not-for-profit sickness funds, which operate on a regional basis, and to the private insurers (AWBZ funds only). The individual sickness funds are responsible for meeting the bills submitted by hospitals and other providers, including doctors' fees, for services received by insurees.

In addition to these three main forms of health insurance, there is a separate scheme for civil servants, covering about 6 percent of the population. Also, social care - particularly long-term residential care of the elderly - is funded separately through a combination of government grants and user charges.

9.2.3   General Features of the Delivery System

In 1990, there were 120 general hospitals offering a range of short-term care. Most of these hospitals are run privately on a not-for-profit basis and each is managed by its own independent board. Many of these hospitals were developed by religious institutions. In addition, there were 36 specialised hospitals offering particular services, such as children's or ophthalmic services, and 9 teaching hospitals attached to universities, in which the training of doctors and medical research took place.

Despite the private status and autonomy of Dutch hospitals, they have all been subject to strong regulation under national planning legislation. They have not been permitted to expand or alter their activities without government approval. In general, approvals have only been granted if proposed changes conform with a hospital plan that has been drawn up by the local government and ratified by the national government.[6]

---

[6]   VNZ (1990).

Long-term care is provided in 83 psychiatric hospitals, 121 homes for people with mental handicaps and 325 nursing homes.

Family doctors (GPs) and most specialists are self-employed, private practitioners. The specialists are licensed to practise in the hospitals in which they work. As with hospitals, doctors' activities are subject to regulation by government. Until this year, local authorities had the power to restrict the establishment of new GP practices in areas in which their numbers exceeded a specified norm. This restriction has been recently abolished. There are still, however, norms regulating the number of medical specialists.[7]

In 1990, there were 1,453 pharmacists and, in addition, just over 700 doctors who had pharmaceutical facilities (from a total of 6,573 GPs).

9.2.4   Inputs and Outputs of the System

During the period of 1987 to 1992 Dutch health care expenditure as reported in the Financial Overview of the Care Sector (FOZ) by the Ministry of Health increased from 42.9 bn guilders to 52.6 bn guilders (from $19.6 to $21.3 bn 1990). This corresponds to 10.0 percent of gross national product (GNP) in 1987 and 9.4 percent in 1992.[8]   These expenditure figures, both in absolute terms and expressed as a percentage of GNP, are somewhat higher than those reported by the OECD for the Netherlands. The major reason for this discrepancy is that OECD figures do not include long-term residential care of the elderly. Both sets of data indicate that expenditure as a proportion of GNP has fallen over the period.

Chart 9.1 indicates the sources of health care finance and the distribution of health care costs between the main sectors for 1990. Hospital care and the services of medical specialists (usually provided within hospital settings) account for nearly one-third of total expenditure. This is almost double the share of expenditure devoted to ambulatory care. In fact, the predominance of hospital services is a notable feature of the Dutch health care system. Bed days per person and average lengths of stay are both high by international standards.[9]

---

[7]   VNZ (1990).

[8]   Figures for 1992 are estimates.

[9]   OECD (1991).

Chart 9.1
Expenditure on Health Care in the Netherlands, 1990

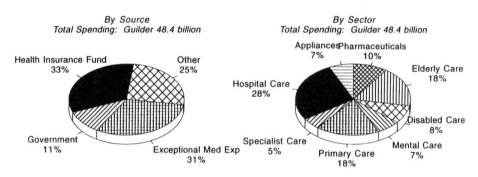

By Source
Total Spending: Guilder 48.4 billion

Health Insurance Fund
33%

Other
25%

Government
11%

Exceptional Med Exp
31%

By Sector
Total Spending: Guilder 48.4 billion

Appliances 7% Pharmaceuticals 10%

Hospital Care
28%

Elderly Care
18%

Disabled Care
8%

Specialist Care
5%

Primary Care
18%

Mental Care
7%

Source: Ministry of Welfare, Health and Cultural Affairs (1992); VNZ (1992)

The number of general hospital beds fell steadily over the period 1986-90 as did the number of beds per 1,000 population, mostly in response to cost containment regulation. Over the same period, the number of GPs grew by 4.6 percent, while the number of medical specialists increased by 16 percent.

Selected health status indicators indicate that life expectancy for both sexes and at all ages are among the highest reported by OECD countries. Favourable health status is also indicated by very low infant mortality and crude mortality rates, although the Netherlands is in the bottom one-third of OECD countries in terms of its perinatal mortality rate.

9.3   ANALYSIS OF INDIVIDUAL SECTORS

9.3.1   Key Participants in the Health Care System

The main participants within the health care system in the Netherlands that are discussed in this section are:

*   patients;
*   financing organisations;
*   providers of primary and community health care services;
*   providers of hospital services; and
*   pharmaceutical sector.

The relationships between these participants, and the flows of finance and services between them, are described in Chart 9.2.

9.3.2   Patients

Health care services in the Netherlands originated largely from private initiatives, often on a charitable basis. Although the role of philanthropy has been gradually replaced by public finance and government regulation over the years, the system is still based upon a high degree of individualism. It is not a 'socialised' system in the same sense as the British National Health Service. One manifestation of this approach is that 'rights' are rarely discussed in the health care context in the Netherlands. Rather, discussion usually focuses on 'obligations' and the ways in which different participants in the health sector are bound together by mutual, interlocking obligations.[10] Nonetheless, the concept of 'social solidarity' does figure prominently among the objectives set for social policy in the Netherlands, as in many other European countries. This is generally taken to mean that contributions to the total costs of health care should be on the basis of ability to pay and that access to essential services should be based upon some definition of need.

Since the introduction of insurance benefits under the Exceptional Medical Expenses Act and the Health Insurance Act in the 1960s, the Dutch have become accustomed to wide access to a high standard of service. There is considerable choice between GPs and hospital specialists, and care provided under social insurance is generally free at the point of service. There is a high level of public satisfaction with the health care system, as reported in a recent

---

[10]   Kirkman-Liff (1991).

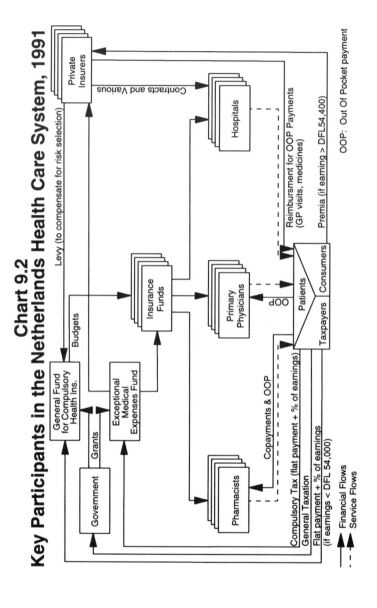

Chart 9.2
Key Participants in the Netherlands Health Care System, 1991

Private Insurers

Levy (to compensate for risk selection)

Contracts and Various

Hospitals

Reimbursment for OOP Payments
(GP visits, medicines)

Premia (if earning > DFL54,400)

OOP: Out Of Pocket payment

General Fund
for Compulsory
Health Ins.

Budgets

Insurance
Funds

Primary
Physicians

OOP

Patients

Consumers

Exceptional
Medical
Expenses Fund

Taxpayers

Government

Grants

Copayments & OOP

Pharmacists

Compulsory Tax (flat payment + % of earnings)
General Taxation
Flat payment + % of earnings
(if earnings < DFL 54,000)

Financial Flows
Service Flows

710

ten-nation survey.[11]   On the basis of a sample of 1,000 Dutch residents surveyed in 1990, the Netherlands emerged as second only to Canada in terms of the proportion of the sample (47 percent) who felt that "the health care system works pretty well and only minor changes are necessary to make it work better." The same survey showed that nearly the same proportion of the sample (46 percent) thought that "there are some good things in our health system, but fundamental changes are needed to make it better." Only 7 percent believed that the system should be entirely rebuilt.

Certainly there is evidence of dissatisfaction with some aspects of the system. In particular, attempts to control the growth of aggregate expenditure have resulted in waiting lists for some services; these include care of the chronically sick, organ transplants, and orthopaedic and ophthalmic services. The real costs of waiting lists are significant. Silver Cross (a private insurer) estimates that 20 percent of absenteeism from companies in the Netherlands is caused by waiting times in health care services.   As a result, Silver Cross has developed insurance packages which include 'accelerated treatment programmes.' These programmes allow privately insured patients to be treated in local hospitals without joining the waiting list.   In urgent cases Silver Cross guarantees treatment, even if the patient must be sent outside the country.[12]

Cost containment through reductions in hospital capacity and restricting physician services have been politically unpopular. There has even been a strike by physicians protesting at attempts to control their income. At the same time, there is a widespread view that the health care system harbours X-inefficiency; that is, costs are higher than they would be if providers and sickness funds were being subjected to competitive pressure. A majority of the public (50 percent) believe that a 10 percent cost saving could be achieved with no decline in quality, and 20 percent believe that a 20 percent cost saving could be achieved with no decline in quality.[13]

---

[11]   Blendon *et al.* (1990).

[12]   Overmars (1992).

[13]   Kirkman-Liff and van de Ven (1989).

9.3.3   Payers

9.3.3.1   The Exceptional Medical Expenses Act (AWBZ)

The Exceptional Medical Expenses Act came into force in December 1967 and phased implementation began in January 1968.   The scope of the Act is considerable.   Initially it served mainly as a means of funding long-term or high-cost care, but over the years its provisions have been extended to cover more elements of health care, many of which are neither prolonged nor expensive in nature.   In the future, coverage under the Act will be extended so that eventually it represents a basic insurance scheme covering the great majority of health and social services for the entire population.   In 1992, AWBZ is expected to cover about 45 percent of all health care expenditure, up from 31 percent in 1991.   This reflects the reform plan's shift of coverage for some health services (notably, pharmaceuticals) from the Health Insurance Act into the AWBZ fund.

Coverage under the Exceptional Medical Expenses Act includes:

*   treatment and care in hospitals after the first 365 days;
*   treatment and care in psychiatric hospitals and psychiatric wards;
*   nursing home care;
*   care in an institution for the mentally handicapped;
*   care in an institution for the deaf and those with partial hearing;
*   services for the blind and poorly sighted;
*   vaccinations;
*   services for the disabled including day centre and hostel care;
*   day care in a nursing home;
*   home-care services;
*   psychosocial care;
*   psychiatric out-patient and non-residential care;
*   medicines; and,
*   aids and protheses.

Insurance under the Exceptional Medical Expenses Act is statutory; practically the entire population is covered and must make both income-related and flat-rate contributions.   In 1992, the income-related contribution rate is 7.3 percent of income (to a maximum income level) and the flat-rate contribution is 133.2 guilders ($53.81 1990) per adult and 44.4 guilders ($17.94 1990) per child up to the age of 18 years (for a maximum of two children).

In addition to the funds provided by individual contributions, part of the costs of AWBZ are met by a central government grant. However, as a result of government funding constraints, the size of this grant has fallen considerably over recent years and is now very small.

The contributions collected by the tax authorities, together with the government grant, are paid into the Exceptional Medical Expenses Fund. This is administered by the Central Sickness Fund Council (*Ziekenfondsraad*) which makes payments to individual sickness funds and private insurers. It is these funds and insurers that are responsible for paying the bills for health care services provided under AWBZ. They are also responsible for organising payments for services covered by the Health Insurance Act.

9.3.3.2 *The Health Insurance Act*

The Health Insurance Act came into force on 1 January 1966. This provides a financing scheme for basic medical and hospital care for about 62 percent of the population. Under the provisions of the Act, everyone meeting the criteria set by the legislation is automatically insured and must pay the statutory contributions. The most important criteria is that the individual's wage or salary is below a specified ceiling, set at 54,400 guilders in 1992 ($23,550 1990). In addition to the employed, this includes the unemployed, disabled and pensioners.

Coverage under the Health Insurance Act includes:

- medical and surgical treatment by GPs and specialists;
- obstetric care;
- dental care;
- hospital care;
- transport;
- maternity care;
- audiological services;
- haemodialysis;
- services for patients with chronic respiratory problems;
- non residential rehabilitation services;
- services of a thrombosis unit; and,
- genetic testing and counselling.

There is some regional variation in the percentage of the population covered under this scheme, ranging from 56 percent of the population who are covered in the province of Utrecht to 68 percent of the population in Limburg.

Contributions for those up to the age of 65 are related to their income, whether this is earned income or income from social security. Until the end of 1988, employers and employees (or the relevant social security organisation) were each required to make payments of about 5 percent of the insured's income. However, from the beginning of 1989, contributions ceased to be entirely income-related; a part of the insured's contribution is now a flat-rate charge and so the income-related part of their contribution has been reduced. Under the Dekker reforms, the transfer of coverage for some benefits to AWBZ has also served to reduce the income-related payment. In 1992, the combined employee/employer contribution amounted to 6.35 percent of the insured's income, with a flat-rate payment of 198 guilders ($80 1990) per adult and 99 guilders ($40 1990) per child up to the age of 18 (for a maximum of two children).

The over-65s and people who have taken early retirement are subject to special arrangements. Reduced rate income-related contributions (0.75 percent in 1992) are payable from that part of their incomes which is related to the Old Age Pensions Act. Additional retirement income is charged at the full rate payable by employed people. The retired are also required to pay the flat-rate charge.

Contributions from employers and employees cover about 85 percent of the cost of benefits provided under the Health Insurance Act. The remainder is covered by government grants (about 10 percent) which were originally used to cover some of the costs of services for the elderly before they were incorporated into the Health Insurance Scheme in 1986, copayments (4 percent) and payments from private insurers (1 percent). The payments from private insurers are required to meet some of the public sector costs arising from adverse selection. This occurs because old people are over-represented within the Health Fund Scheme compared with the private insurance sector. In order to meet the extra costs arising from this imbalance, legislation was introduced requiring the private sector to make a contribution towards the costs of compulsory health insurance, as long as old people remain over-represented within the compulsory scheme.

All of these funds are paid into the General Fund for Compulsory Health Insurance. This fund is managed by the Sickness Fund Council, which makes payments to individual sickness funds. Thus, the individual sickness funds are responsible for organising payments under both the Exceptions Medical Expenses Act and the Health Insurance Act.

The sickness funds are regionally based. Table 9.1 lists the funds that were operating in January 1988, their location and the size of population covered by them. Since 1988, there has been a reduction in the number of funds through rationalisation and amalgamation. It is expected that eventually there will probably be only 10 to 15 funds.

Because the individual sickness funds are responsible for making payments to health care providers, they are in a key position - as third party purchasers of care - to influence the efficiency with which the care is provided. In fact, there is a certain amount of evidence to suggest that they have not been particularly vigilant in this respect. One reason may be that sickness funds operate as local monopolies and so there is little competition between them for subscribers. A study of the financial reports of 40 sickness funds reveals a variation in *per capita* expenses between the lowest-cost and highest-cost fund of 69 percent. Standardising for the age-sex composition of their insurees accounts for only about one-third of this variation, suggesting that there are large unexplained differences in management efficiency.[14]

The current reform programme (discussed in Section 9.5) aims to address this problem by introducing competition between insurers. It would be incorrect, however, to suggest that none of the individual funds has been active in encouraging efficiency to date. Kirkman-Liff and van de Ven (*op cit*) describe a number of initiatives which have sought to encourage greater efficiency among providers. Many of them concentrate on the role of GPs as 'gatekeepers'. Traditionally, the capitation payment system has offered little incentive for GPs to develop services for their patients. There has been an incentive for GPs to refer their patients to hospital specialists at an early stage. This decision is costless to them and avoids the costs of managing patients themselves. Thus, patients are shifted from a low-cost site of care to a high-cost site. Various sickness fund demonstration projects have sought to counteract these perverse financial incentives.

---

[14]   Kirkman-Liff and van de Ven (1989).

Table 9.1: Sickness Funds, 1988

Name	Place	Population
Noord Holland Noord	Alkmaar	313,120
Amersfoort	Amersfoort	180,335
Amstelveen CZH	Amstelveen	407,650
Amsterdam ZAO	Amsterdam	472,255
Apeldoorn en Omstreken	Apeldoorn	71,020
MZB	Bergen op Zoom	100,175
AZWZ	Breda	317,680
Zuid-Hollandse Eilanden	Brielle	111,440
DSW	Schiedam	207,385
Salland	Deventer	75,200
Drechtstreek	Dordrecht	122,635
Eindhoven en Omstreken	Eindhoven	177,815
Ziekenfonds OGZO	Goor	110,770
Gorinchem en Omstreken	Gorinchem	66,735
Gouda-Woerden	Gouda	132,600
Haaglanden	Den Haag	314,435
Azivo	Den Haag	93,185
Spaarneland	Heemstede	198,575
RZG	Groningen	357,655
Mijnstreek	Heerlen	207,165
Twente	Hengelo	354,990
Het Gooi en Omstreken	Huizen	164,885
Leeuwarden-Sneek	Leeuwarden	69,295
Leeuwarden-APFZ	Leeuwarden	228,470
Leiden-Alphen	Leiden	176,495
Zuid-Limburg ZZL	Maastricht	101,740
Drenthe Noord-Overijssel	Meppel	395,660
Midden en Noord Zeeland	Middelburg	128,910
Nijmegen BAZ	Nijmegen	136,585
Purmerend	Purmerend	171,525
Rotterdam SZR	Rotterdam	445,305
Sittard	Sittard	254,345
Tilburg Centraal CZT	Tilburg	512,130
Midden-Brabant ZMB	Tilburg	392,620
Midden-Nederland RZMN	Utrecht	400,095
Rijn-IJsselland RZR	Doorwerth	483,815
Noord-Limburg ZNL	Venlo	158,170
Zwolle RZZ	Zwolle	173,110
Apeldoorn ANOZ	Apeldoorn	⎫
Friesland ANOZ	Leeuwarden	⎪
Lingestreek ANOZ	Leerdam	⎬ 275,736
Ijsselstreek ANOZ	Zutphen	⎪
Nijkerk ANOZ	Nijkerk	⎭

Several sickness funds have invested substantial effort in improving their medical care monitoring systems. These systems typically provide individual physician data on referral rates, prescriptions for medicines and the use of diagnostic services. They enable medical advisors from the sickness funds to meet with individual GPs to discuss their performance. Moreover, various combinations of performance payments and elements of fee-for-service have been introduced in order to reduce unnecessary referrals to hospitals, to stimulate GPs to undertake more minor surgical procedures themselves and to encourage them to take on greater responsibility for long term care, such as diabetes control.

There has also been a collaborative effort between Silver Cross (the largest private non-profit insurer in the Netherlands), a regional sickness fund in Utrecht and a community health centre to develop a limited provider plan. This incorporates elements of a US-type health maintenance organisation with some of the hospital and specialist referral aspects of a preferred provider organisation.

Elsewhere, sickness funds have successfully developed programmes for Area Clinical Pharmacologists, in collaboration with medical schools. Under these arrangements, physician-pharmacologists work for the sickness funds and meet with general practitioners to discuss pharmaceutical issues. This often involves the development of prescription protocols for more cost-effective use of high-cost medicines.

Despite these initiatives, however, Kirkman-Liff and van de Ven believe that there is still major scope for sickness funds to strengthen the roles of their medical advisers and other staff involved in utilisation management and quality assurance. They cite use of prior authorisation for major diagnostic and therapeutic procedures in the United States, as well as concurrent review and discharge planning during inpatient stays, and claim that these activities could similarly encourage greater use of clinically-appropriate and cost-effective care in the Netherlands. They also claim that an alternative to introducing fee-for-service elements into general practice would be to reduce GP patient list sizes and offer higher capitation payments in return for active GP participation in quality assurance and utilisation review procedures.

717

9.3.3.3 *Private Insurers*

People earning over the income limit of 54,400 guilders in 1992 are not eligible for coverage for basic medical and hospital care under the Health Insurance Act. Most of these people take out private insurance plans with one of the more than 40 private insurers. Just over 5 million people, or 32 percent of the population, are insured in this way. About 60 percent of private insurance is taken out in the form of individual contracts, and 40 percent are group contracts. There is considerable variation among the contracts in terms of their coverage, the choice offered between providers and the use made of copayments and deductibles.

Many of the companies offering health insurance are multi-sectoral firms offering insurance in other areas in addition to health care. In recent years, there have been a number of joint ventures between private insurers. In 1989, for example, two alliances were formed by eleven of the largest private health insurers, accounting for half of the private health insurance market. Because the regional market share of private health insurers is generally low, joint ventures and mergers are seen as a way for them to develop countervailing bargaining power in relation to providers.[15]

Although the private insurers serve individuals not covered by the Health Insurance Act, their activities are not always entirely separate from those of the sickness funds. There is some joint ownership. Although formal mergers between private insurers and sickness funds are not possible at the moment, one private insurer already offers supplemental insurance business for six sickness funds. (Under the reform proposals, direct mergers will be possible - see Section 9.5).[16]

Moreover, the largest private health insurer in the Netherlands - Silver Cross, which has 650,000 subscribers - was actually founded in 1948 as the result of an initiative taken by the sickness funds. The funds were concerned about the fate of their members whose incomes reached the ceiling level and could therefore no longer be insured with them. Silver Cross was developed to offer good quality services to these groups at a reasonable price. Subsequently, Silver Cross has taken the view that insurers need to be more active in the organisation and management of care and has developed the 'Silver Care'

---

[15]   Schut *et al.* (1991).

[16]   *Ibid*

concept as an example of managed care based upon the US health maintenance organisation model.[17]

9.3.4 Primary Health Care Sector

Primary health care in the Netherlands is based upon a system of general practice doctors (GPs) who are usually the first point of contact for people with health problems. Dutch GPs are independent contractors with the sickness funds, in much the same way that British GPs are independent contractors with the National Health Service.

In 1989 there were approximately 6,200 GPs with an average of 2,350 patients each. More than half of all GPs (54 percent) are in individual practices; 38 percent work in partnerships, usually comprising two GPs; and a small minority (7 percent) work in integrated health centres alongside community nurses and social workers. Until 1992, doctors who wanted to establish a separate general practice were required to obtain a permit from the relevant municipal authority. Permits were issued based upon the GP *per capita* ratio and the spatial distribution of practices. In 1992 this system is being abolished and GPs will be able freely to choose the location of their practices.

The overall number of contacts with GPs is estimated at 4.2 per patient per year; of these, 3.2 are with the GP and the remainder with the practice secretary. Of the contacts with GPs, 17 percent take the form of home visits.[18]

GP's patients may be divided into two categories on the basis of their insurance status. First, there are those whose services are publicly insured under the Health Insurance Act. These patients can choose to be registered with the GP of their choice. The GP currently receives a flat capitation fee (not related to age or other patient characteristics) for each patient. The capitation covers only primary care services and the GP is not at financial risk for referral to hospitals or specialists. (In the future GPs will negotiate reimbursements with insurers.) Second, there are patients covered by private insurance. Some of these will have policies which include the costs of primary care. Privately insured patients generally pay their GPs per consultation and claim partial payment from their insurance companies if covered for this service.

---

[17]   Kamermans *et al.* (1991).

[18]   Groenewegen (1991).

Publicly insured patients can only obtain access to specialist and hospital care on the basis of a referral from a GP. Most private insurers also require a GP referral. GPs are, therefore, in a strong position as 'gatekeepers' to secondary care. To date, their financial incentives have been to shift patients into secondary care too quickly. Under the proposed reforms, these incentives are expected to change.

Primary or community health services are also provided by about 7,000 community nurses. The work of community nursing is concentrated in two main areas: namely, well-baby care and nursing care, mainly for elderly people. Most of this work takes place in the patient's own home. The service is organised on a national basis through 70 regional organisations and their constituent local teams, usually comprising a head nurse, seven registered nurses and two unregistered nurses. These local teams usually work within a restricted geographical area, unlike GPs who often serve scattered populations. A small number of community nurses work in integrated health centres alongside GPs and social workers.

In contrast to many other countries, patients in the Netherlands have direct access to the services of community nurses. About half of patient contacts are made in this way. The remainder come from GP recommendations (about one-fifth) and from nursing home and hospital referrals (about one-third).[19] Since 1980, the services of community nursing have been insured under AWBZ, although a membership fee is often required. The membership fee reflects the origins of the service which began through voluntary organisations.

Two other groups which contribute to the provision of primary and community care are family assistants and general social workers. Family assistants are organised within a large number of local or regional organisations. There are approximately 35,000 family assistants providing housekeeping, personal care and social support, primarily for elderly people living alone. The service is funded, as with community nursing, through AWBZ, although people have to pay part of the costs themselves, based upon their personal financial circumstances. The service is important because it enables people to live on their own, delaying admission to nursing homes or homes for the elderly, or bridging waiting times for admission to these institutions.

---

[19]   *Ibid.*

Social workers are in the salaried service of social work organisations, although they often work closely with family assistance organisations. In 1989, there were 2,000 general social workers usually providing assistance for those with psycho-social problems. They provide a major source of help for low income groups in need of mental health services. General social work is directly accessible to patients without any copayments. The costs of the service are met through municipal subsidies. The service is notable for being the only area of primary care where finance has been successfully decentralised.

Co-ordination between the various providers of primary and community care is achieved through bilateral cooperation, through loosely structured primary care teams ('home teams') and through integrated health centres. Home teams involve co-operation between a GP, a community nurse and a general social worker with regular consultations about patients and their needs. In 1989, there were 460 home teams, comprising one-quarter of all GPs, one-fifth of community nurses and two-fifths of general social workers. Health centres involve at least one GP, a community nurse and a general social worker working together in shared premises. In 1990, there were 160 health centres. They are mainly located in new towns or in new parts of towns where health care services have been built up from scratch. Relatively few have been formed by joining together existing services.

9.3.5   Hospital Sector

The hospital system in the Netherlands reflects the complicated political and religious history of the country. Many social institutions were organised either confessionally (Catholic and Protestant denominations) or politically (socialist and liberal parties). These have been referred to as the 'four pillars' of society, each seeking to maintain its own cultural identity.[20]

Although the decline of the 'pillar system' over time has led to mergers and joint ventures between different institutions, the basic landscape remains largely defined by confessional and/or political affiliations. Thus, the majority of the country's 250 hospitals are religious in character. Although about 40 hospitals were established and are operated by municipal governments, most hospitals are owned and operated by private, locally-controlled, independent boards on a not-for-profit basis. In fact, private for-profit hospitals are prohibited by law in the Netherlands.

---

[20]   Saltman and de Roo (1989).

Government policy aimed at reductions in hospital excess capacity has led to the active encouragement of mergers between hospitals, and to a steady reduction in the total number of hospitals over time. Between 1986 and 1990, for example, the number of general hospitals fell from 143 to 120 separate institutions. Some researchers question the wisdom of this policy and claim that it is likely to stifle competition.[21] However, the government seems to believe that larger hospitals offer economies of scale and that mergers are politically the most effective way of eliminating excess bed capacity.

Most hospital specialists work for themselves as independent practitioners. There are a small number of specialists working on a salaried basis in teaching and municipal hospitals. Despite their independent status, however, the majority of hospital specialists are now organised in group practices known as partnerships, usually comprising three to six members. When a new specialist enters a group, a 'goodwill' fee, usually amounting to between one and one-and-a-half times the specialist's annual gross income, is payable to the group.

Specialists are paid on a fee-for-service basis. For sickness fund patients, a detailed fee schedule is negotiated between the Association of Sickness Funds (VNZ) and the National Association of Specialists. This schedule is based upon a norm, or target income, for doctors within each specialty, which is also negotiated nationally. Payment involves a sliding scale of fees - known as 'regressive fees' - on the basis of which payments per item of service fall as the number of services provided exceeds specified limits. However, attempts to restrict specialists' incomes to target levels have been largely unsuccessful, because there is no co-ordinating system for aggregating income earned from sickness funds and private insurance companies. The available evidence indicates that doctors compensate for reductions in fees by increasing their workloads to achieve target incomes they set for themselves rather than those specified in national negotiations.

Hospitals are required to break even after taking account of all of their costs and revenues. There have, however, been some major changes in the financial arrangements governing hospital behaviour in recent years. Prior to 1983, hospitals received full retrospective reimbursement for all of the services they provided. It was an open-ended arrangement. Taken together with the fee-for-service system under which doctors were paid, there were powerful incentives to maximise the number of inpatient days. This was achieved both

---

[21]   Schut *et al.* (1991).

by high admission rates and long lengths of stay. There were few incentives to contain aggregate expenditure or to strive for efficiency at the micro level. Government attempts at cost containment were pursued through regulation of capacity and through attempts to control tariffs. Neither mechanism was considered to be particularly successful.

A major effort to address these shortcomings was launched in 1983 when retrospective reimbursement was replaced by a regime of prospective global budgeting. Under this system, each hospital received a prospective budget limit for the following year. It was intended that any over-expenditure would be met by the hospital itself and that the prospect of this penalty would encourage greater cost consciousness.

Considerable effort has been devoted to the task of devising a formula for setting hospital budgets. In the early years, individual hospital budgets were simply set on the basis of historic expenditure levels. Clearly, this did not distinguish between efficient and inefficient providers. The first attempt to address this problem was taken in 1985, when a formula was introduced which sought to identify acceptable cost levels with more precision. It did this by distinguishing between fixed and variable costs. Budgets for fixed costs are based on fixed inputs such as the number of beds and the number of specialist units within a hospital, whereas variable costs are based on variable inputs such as admissions and patient days.

The second major revision to the budgetary formula was the introduction of functional budgeting in 1988. Functional budgeting is based on the principle that hospitals should receive the same budget for performing the same function. Three main factors were taken into account in order to determine the functional budget:

- the size of the population served by the hospital;

- approved hospital capacity measured in terms of bed numbers and specialist units; and,

- 'production agreements' between local insurers (sickness funds and private insurers) and local hospital boards.

This process was expected to lead to a large re-allocation of budgets between hospitals, but was also expected, in the longer term, to increase efficiency incentives in the hospital sector.[22]

It is not clear that prospective budgeting has achieved the results expected, either in terms of aggregate cost containment or greater efficiency. A case study of two 500-bed hospitals carried out in 1987 sheds some light on the limitations of these budgetary controls as a cost containment device.[23] The study showed that for the two hospitals concerned, their budgets grew by 15-17 percent over the period 1983-1987 rather than falling by the 7 percent that official policy required. This occurred because, faced by budget limitations, the hospital managers responded by aggressively pursuing new capital investments - for which revenues were automatically approved - and by developing 'off-budget' activities beyond the regulator's grasp.

Another reason why prospective budgeting appears to have had limited impact upon the efficiency with which resources are used in hospitals is because effective internal management arrangements with hospital specialists have rarely been developed. External cost constraints may act as a stimulus for more effective hospital management but, if it is to be implemented successfully, it requires clinicians to be actively involved in the management of resources. Despite some experiments with clinical budgeting at university hospitals in Maastricht and Utrecht, for example, most medical staff have not been fully integrated into the management of services. Indeed, some researchers emphasise the independence of hospital specialists and the unwillingness and/or inability of managers to challenge their autonomy.[24]

One specific source of rising costs in the hospital sector that the Dutch government has been concerned with is the introduction of new technologies. In fact, with the exception of open heart surgery, the Netherlands does not have particularly high treatment rates in procedures using expensive new medical technologies. Similarly, expenditure on drugs and medical equipment is not excessive. Nonetheless, as in most other countries, there is concern about the impact of new diagnostic and therapeutic procedures on health expenditure.

---

[22]   Maarse (1989).

[23]   Saltman and de Roo (1989).

[24]   Saltman and de Roo (1989); van de Ven (1991).

With individual sickness funds facing few incentives for purchasing cost-effective care, most of the onus for controlling the diffusion of new technology has traditionally been assumed by the government. The Hospital Provisions Act provides two regulatory measures for pursuing this aim. Article 3 gives the government the power to control the distribution of medical specialists in the hospital sector. This can be relevant when new technologies are related to specialist functions. More directly, Article 18 gives the Minister of Health the authority to control, by licensing, the provision of certain services involving new technologies. Ten technologies have been licensed under this authority; namely, kidney dialysis, kidney transplantation, radiotherapy, neurosurgery, cardiac surgery, heart catheterisation, nuclear medicine, computed tomography, pre-natal chromosome examination and neo-natal intensive care.

More recently, the realisation that the causes of increased health care expenditure seem to lie in the more widespread use of 'common' technologies (rather than simply the introduction of new technologies) has led to an increased interest in providing incentives for cost-effective care, rather than placing reliance upon administrative regulation. Recent changes in hospital budgeting falls into this category, as does the decision of the Sickness Fund Council, in 1987, to designate certain technologies as 'emerging' and to approve them for reimbursement only following evaluations. Various transplant procedures, lithotripsy and in-vitro fertilisation were all designated as emerging technologies. Rutten and Banta (1988) argue that overall there is a growing belief that incentives are more powerful than regulation in achieving a cost-effective use of new technologies.

The development of an appropriate incentive system does rely upon the existence of accurate information on the costs and benefits of existing and new technologies. Despite an active academic community that is engaged in this work in the Netherlands - and a community which, moreover, has strong links with health policy officials - there is still an extremely limited institutional base for technology assessment. Given that the country imports about 90 percent of its technology, Rutten and Banta suggest that there is need for a clearing house that will be able to access international information.

9.3.6   Pharmaceutical Sector

The Ministry of Welfare, Public Health and Culture has broad responsibility for pharmaceutical affairs. The Pharmaceutical Inspectorate, which is part of the State Health Inspectorate, is responsible for ensuring that regulations are complied with, and for advising the Ministry.

All registered pharmaceuticals are divided into two categories; namely, prescription only (*Uitsluitend Recept, UR*) and pharmacy only (*Uitsluitend Apotheek, UA*) products. A limited number of pharmacy only products are sold on a non-prescription basis and smaller pack sizes (list V products) are available from non-pharmacist druggists.

The main outlet for prescription medicines is through retail pharmacies. These pharmacies must be owned by a pharmacist or a co-operative of pharmacists. Most retail pharmacists are members of the Royal Netherlands Pharmacy Society (KNMP). KNMP members may run only one pharmacy. However, some non-KNMP pharmacy chains have been set up. There are no regulations covering the location of retail pharmacies, although the KNMP produces voluntary guidelines. There were 1,423 retail pharmacies in 1990 according to the Central Bureau of Statistics. The State Health Inspectorate inspects these pharmacies.

In addition to these retail pharmacies, there were 758 dispensing doctors in 1990. Doctors are permitted to dispense in areas with no pharmacy but lose this right when a pharmacy is authorised in their district. In recent years, the number of dispensing doctors has fallen as the number of retail pharmacies has grown. The Ministry of Welfare, Public Health and Culture seeks to encourage a rational distribution of retail pharmacies and dispensing doctors.

Druggists sell List V products, as well as non-pharmaceutical items such as cosmetics.   There are over twice as many druggists as there are retail pharmacists and these tend to be preferred by many customers.

Other outlets for medicines are hospital pharmacies and a limited number of grocery stores which are registered to sell a restricted list of medicines. A hospital must have more than 300 beds in order to have its own pharmacy, otherwise it must rely upon local retail pharmacies.

The pharmacists' association publishes an official price list for pharmaceuticals which is used by the sickness funds and private insurers as a basis for reimbursement. Apart from supporting some voluntary price freezes, the government no longer seeks to control prices directly and, no doubt partly as a result of this, prices in the Netherlands have been high by international standards. Figures reported by Burstall (1991) show that they were nearly 30 percent above the EC average. Patients have been expected to meet about 20 percent of the cost of pharmaceuticals in the form of copayments.

High price levels in the Netherlands in comparison with other European countries makes the practice of parallel importing profitable. In fact, the government actually looks favourably upon the practice, viewing it as a useful way of keeping total expenditure in check. To this end, it allows retail pharmacists to retain one-third of the savings made through the use of parallel imports and other cheaper, but chemically identical, substitutes. Burstall (1991) notes that it is not clear whether this is legal under the terms of the Treaty of Rome.

Government attempts to reduce overall expenditure on medicines have a long tradition in the Netherlands. In 1982, the government introduced three limited lists. The Sickness Fund Council also seeks to influence prescribing through a pharmacotherapeutic guide which lists the names of all pharmaceuticals available on the market with a description and assessment by the Central Medical Pharmaceutical Committee in terms of their efficacy, indications, contra-indications, side-effects and price. The guide indicates products not recommended for prescription (because of their therapeutic value or price), new products not yet assessed for reimbursement, and also lists recently withdrawn products. It also contains products included in the Dutch National Formulary.

The volume of consumption of medicines *per capita* in the Netherlands is very low by international standards (about half the EC average). Thus, although pharmaceutical prices are relatively high, overall expenditure on medicines is relatively low. Only about 5.3 percent of total health care expenditure was devoted to medicines in 1987 compared with an EC average of 10.1 percent. There has, however, been an increase in per capita sales of medicines of on average 9 percent per year over the period 1987-1990.

In July 1991, a considerably more powerful policy for controlling expenditure on medicines was introduced. This took the form of a new pharmaceutical reference pricing system for people insured under the sickness funds. Under the new Drugs Remuneration System (GVS), medicines with the same therapeutic effect are grouped together and a maximum reimbursement price is calculated for all pharmaceuticals in the same group, based on the average of the pharmacist purchase prices in terms of the daily cost of therapy. For medicines costing more than the maximum reimbursement price, patients must pay the difference. This encourages the use of generic substitutes for patented medicines, when they are available, although the price of many patented medicines has fallen to meet the competition from generics.

Some forecasters suggest that GVS may reduce expenditure on medicines by up to 30 percent, and that sales of generic products can be expected to increase rapidly. Others, however, point out that the availability of supplementary insurance for prescription charges may act to maintain expenditure levels and that some products currently below the GVS level may actually increase in price.[25]

The new system has been criticised by the pharmaceutical industry which fears that it could have serious adverse effects on innovative, research and development companies. In response to such criticism, the Ministry of Welfare, Public Health and Culture postponed the introduction of GVS, which had been scheduled for January 1991, and set up a committee to investigate the therapeutic grouping procedure. The pharmaceutical industry association, Nefarma, sought to block the introduction of the new system through an injunction against the government in June. However, this move failed and the scheme was introduced in July 1991.

The latest major policy change to affect the financing arrangements governing expenditure on medicines took place in 1992. As part of the Dekker reforms (see Section 9.5), responsibility for reimbursement for pharmaceuticals has been transferred from the sickness funds and the private insurers to the Exceptional Medical Expenses System (AWBZ). This is part of the phased transfer of services to this fund so that eventually it will constitute the unified, basic insurance system. The changeover was not without political problems. In particular, the government had claimed that the transfer of responsibility for pharmaceuticals would result in reductions in payroll contributions and private insurance premiums for basic health insurance to offset higher patient contributions to the AWBZ fund. In fact these reductions did not materialise. After a good deal of publicity, the sickness funds and some insurance companies modified their premiums, but not by as much as the government had expected.

---

[25]   Van de Ven (1991).

9.4   INTERSECTORAL ANALYSIS

In the government's response to the Dekker Report, four serious deficiencies in the Dutch health care system were identified:

*   an uncoordinated finance structure;
*   few incentives for efficient behaviour;
*   unworkable government regulation governing volume and price of care; and,
*   insurance market failures.

In the following section, we discuss these deficiencies arre discussed in more detail. Much of this discussion relies on van de Ven (1990).

9.4.1   Uncoordinated Finance

Interrelated forms of care in the Netherlands are often financed from different sources. Thus, hospital care and care by GPs are paid for by sickness funds or private health insurers; financing of home care is based on the AWBZ; family assistance programmes are paid for by private payments as well as out of the national budget; social work is paid for by private payments and municipal budgets; financing of nursing care is based on the AWBZ; and homes for the aged are heavily subsidised from national budgets.

Separate budgetary responsibilities act as a barrier to coordinated monitoring and coordinated cost containment efforts. For instance, it is hard for the AWBZ to control nursing home spending if the fund has no direct authority or financial leverage over the physicians who make the decisions to place people in nursing homes. Thus, uncoordinated finance makes it difficult to achieve efficient substitution between different forms of care, both within the health sector and between the health care and other related social services facilities (for example, homes for the elderly and nursing homes).[26] This problem is exacerbated by the lack of incentives to providers to encourage treatment of patients in the least-cost setting.

---

[26]   Groenewegen (1991).

9.4.2   Lack of Incentives for Efficiency

The Dutch health care system contains very few financial incentives encouraging efficiency among producers of care, consumers and insurers. On the contrary, the financing system is such that efficient behaviour is often financially punished, while inefficient behaviour is financially rewarded. For example:

- the hospital finance system makes inpatient admissions much more attractive than cheaper day surgery;

- a system of fee-for-service payments to hospital doctors sometimes encourages unnecessary and inappropriate, costly treatments;

- the capitation system under which GPs receive payment stimulates them to refer patients to hospitals rather than treating them themselves;

- the majority of consumers are close to fully insured for all of the health costs they incur regardless of their choice of provider and, therefore, have little reason to be interested in the efficiency with which resources are used when treating them;

- all sickness funds receive full reimbursement for their expenditure from the central fund of the Sickness Fund Council and, therefore, face few incentives for improving efficiency;

- private insurers have stronger incentives to be cost conscious but, under the present system, the incentives tend to encourage them to insure low risk individuals rather than encouraging more efficient provision of health care.

9.4.3   Unworkable Government Regulations

Cost containment has been one of the major aims of Dutch government policy. Government regulation has been used extensively in pursuit of this goal. Examples include reductions in the number of beds, limits on hospital budgets (since 1983) and on investment in new health care facilities and even regulation of doctors' incomes. This extensive programme came under pressure in the 1980s in two respects. First, much of the legislation proved to be unworkable. Regulations often failed to recognise the complexity of health care planning and the number of parties involved, each with conflicting interests. Moreover, the regulations themselves were often vague.

Second, policies based upon tight state regulation are encountering political opposition. State intervention is increasingly being viewed as discouraging efficiency, rather than promoting it. Regulation is either ineffective, and participants in the system are able to contract around it, or it introduces unintended distortions (for example, the creation of waiting lists). A strategy more firmly based on cost consciousness and financial responsibility by those who use, provide and insure health services is considered preferable.

9.4.4 Insurance Market Failures

The partition of health insurance into a social sector, on the one hand, and a private insurance scheme on the other has given rise to a number of complexities and inefficiencies. Sickness funds generally provide insurance for people with a higher risk than those insured privately. This feature, together with the general goal of equity between different economic groups in society, has led to the need for a complex system of compensation for adverse risk selection from the private to the social sector.

Other problems in the insurance market include the lack of competitive incentives among the sickness funds (as they are essentially regional monopolies), the basic lack of choice among insurers, and transitional problems for individuals transferring from social insurance to private insurance on reaching the specified income ceiling.

9.5   ANALYSIS OF HEALTH CARE POLICY

9.5.1   Reform Proposals

The reform programme begun in the Netherlands in 1989, based upon the Dekker proposals, is far from complete, and significant political and technical obstacles remain to its full implementation. However, the general principles outlined in the Dekker Report in 1987 are still accepted as the basis for reform. The reform programme contains three main features:

- there should be one basic health package for all. This will mean that existing financing sources will be channelled into one system. Sickness funds and private insurance companies will compete for enrollees;

- incentives for greater efficiency are to be offered to consumers, insurers and providers of care; and,

- there should be a shift from government regulation to managed competition as a means of encouraging the provision of cost-efficient services. Government responsibilities, however, will still be exercised to ensure an acceptable quality of care, adequate financial and geographical accessibility for all patients, a local supply of services in relation to the needs of the population, and solidarity between social groups.

The system will work as follows:

- individuals pay an income related premium into a central fund (an expanded AWBZ);
- individuals enrol with an insurer of their choice for basic cover. The insurer must accept all comers;
- individuals pay a fixed premium, unrelated to risk, to their chosen insurer. The premium may vary from insurer to insurer, in part due to their efficiency;
- the insurer receives a risk-adjusted capitation payment from the central fund for each enrollee;
- insurers contract with providers for delivery of health care;
- individuals can take out supplementary insurance for services not in the basic package.

The relationship between the main participants in the health care system can be described as a triangular structure which highlights three sets of bilateral relationships, namely:

- the relationship between consumers and insurers;
- the relationship between insurers and providers; and,
- the relationship between providers and consumers.

9.5.1.1 Consumers and Insurers

The compulsory basic package will cover GP services, hospital treatment and specialist fees, as well as nursing homes, family care and certain forms of home health care. The basic insurance scheme will be financed approximately 85 percent from an income-related premium and 15 percent a fixed premium. The income related premium will be collected by the tax authority and paid into a central fund. Insurers will receive risk-adjusted capitation payments from the fund for the consumers who insure with them, adjusted for the main determinants of risk, such as age (Chart 9.3 shows these financial flows).

A key function of the central fund is to combine the goals of equity and efficiency. Income-related payments from contributors permit any desired degree of cross-subsidisation between high and low income groups, between healthy and unhealthy people and between young and old people. At the same time, risk-adjusted capitation payments to insurers are an attempt to neutralise the insurer's incentives for preferred risk selection (see Section 9.5.2). Competition for insurees can then focus on providing health insurance and health care to consumers as efficiently as possible.

The fixed premiums paid directly by consumers to insurers may vary from insurer to insurer, but will not depend on the risk characteristics of individuals. Variations in fixed premium levels between insurers, based upon different levels of management efficiency, are expected to be one of the main areas of competition between insurers. Consumers can save by choosing an efficient insurer who keeps premiums down or by choosing an insurance package that covers the basic services but may or may not include copayments or restrictions on choice of provider (as found in the US HMO system).

In addition, consumers will be free to take out supplementary insurance to cover health care and social service costs not covered by basic insurance. According to the 1988 government proposals, this will include such services as some of the costs of medicines, physiotherapy and dental treatment for insured people above the age of 18. There has, however, been a continuing discussion about what exactly should be excluded from the basic benefits package and this may well change. Supplementary insurance will be financed entirely by fixed premiums set by insurers.

Chart 9.3
Key Participants in the Proposed Netherlands Health Care System

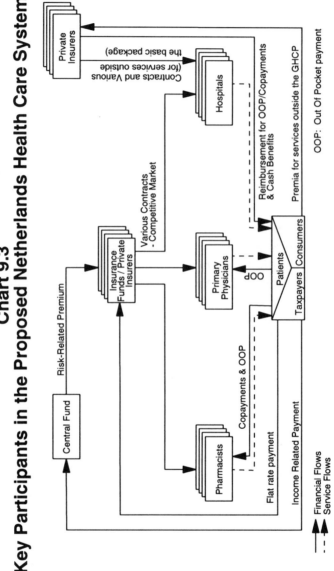

Since premiums paid to insurers out of the Central Fund will be risk-adjusted, insurers will be required to offer open enrolment; consumers cannot be refused insurance on the grounds of high risk. Insurers will not be able to price discriminate between consumers in terms of the fixed premiums they charge for either basic or supplementary insurance, although premiums are expected to vary between insurers.

Eventually, it is expected that the distinction between sickness funds and private health insurers will disappear as they both compete for customers on common terms.

9.5.1.2 *Insurers and Providers*

Under the new system, insurers will negotiate contracts with providers. Negotiations between them are expected to cover the volume, quality and price of care. Moreover, in contrast to the existing system, insurers will be able to contract selectively; that is, they may choose between providers on grounds of efficiency rather than having to accept bills from any provider who offers services. Consumers must explicitly accept such restrictions when they sign up with a specific insurer and a specific plan offered by that insurer. Insurers will presumably be free to offer plans without restrictions if consumers favour that type of insurance.

Competition between insurers for consumers is expected to act as a stimulus to keep nominal premiums as low as possible, and this is expected to improve cost-consciousness in their contracts with providers. Any threats that this might offer to the quality of care are intended to be allayed by clear specification of the services that consumers will be expected to receive. Consumers will also discipline quality through their choice of insurer. In some cases, it will be necessary for the government to lay down minimum standards. For instance, it is proposed to amend the Hospitals' Facilities Act to provide for the monitoring of large residential institutions.

Under the previous planned health care system, various regulations were used to create a cohesive and efficient network of facilities in each region, in keeping with the needs of their local populations. Henceforth, however, the government sees regional development as being primarily the responsibility of providers and insurers. Providers will be put at risk for their revenues. If they are successful in running efficient facilities, they can buy the necessary plant and equipment out of the revenues they receive.

Similarly, agreements on prices and budgets will be an essential part of the contracting process between insurers and providers. Negotiations will take place at the local level. It will no longer be appropriate for tariffs or hospital budgets to be set centrally. In some cases, however, cartels may form on either the insurer or provider side. In these circumstances, the government has made it clear that intervention through antitrust enforcement may be necessary either to stimulate or regulate the market. However, this will be very much a policy of last resort.

9.5.1.3 Providers and Consumers

Consumers will have choice between insurers and different types of policies. While choice is based in part on the level of the flat premium and the type of plan being offered, the quality of care offered by providers with whom individual insurers have contracts can be expected to be an important consideration for consumers. Dissatisfied consumers are expected to vote with their feet if quality standards with a particular insurer and/or provider are not met. The ability of consumers to express preferences provides the appropriate signals for the allocation of resources in the health care market, and provides an important check on quality. Beyond this, however, it may be necessary for the government to support quality assurance through the promotion of accreditation initiatives or other forms of quality certification.

9.5.2 Consequences of the Reforms

Van de Ven (1990) points out that the reform package will have far reaching consequences for insurers, providers and consumers.

The role of insurers - both sickness funds and private health insurers - will change dramatically. Instead of acting as administrative payers or pure indemnity insurance companies, they will need to become cost-conscious purchasers of care. Sickness funds will receive a fixed but risk-adjusted budget allocation with which to purchase care. Moreover, they will lose their regional monopoly and will have to compete with other insurers. They will be able to contract selectively with providers. Private insurers will be confronted with pro-competitive regulation such as open enrolment. Preferred risk selection should become less of a problem as a result of risk adjusted capitation payments from the central fund.

Supply side competition can be expected to develop as providers compete for service contracts on the basis of price and quality. This should increase productive efficiency in the use of resources by providers. One manifestation of this incentive for greater efficiency is likely to be further pressure to reduce excess capacity in the supply of hospital beds, presently estimated to be about 25 percent. Doctors too will feel the pressures of competition. Fixed fees will no longer be guaranteed and they will no longer be able to expect new contracts with insurers to be issued automatically.

Consumers will be permitted to choose the insurer, the insurance scheme, and, implicitly, the provider which most closely satisfies their needs and preferences. The fact that insurers and providers will be competing for enrollees means that the appropriate signals for the allocation of health care resources will be forthcoming. Open enrolment will protect consumers from the effects of risk selection to the extent that the risk adjustment is imperfect.

Van de Ven (1991) notes several problems that are likely to be involved in the transition from a centrally planned health care system to one based more upon market principles.

- There is a problem of consumers' lack of information. In particular, there is a serious shortage of information on quality. Without good information on the quality of care offered, consumers will not be able to make sound decisions between competing insurers and providers. A high priority should be attached to the task of disseminating understandable information to consumers. Ways of doing this include the establishment of independent institutes of certification for providers, encouraging providers and insurers to disseminate information and/or establishing independent organisations which would publish relevant data. As competition among insurers evolves, it is expected that the competitive process will produce substantial information as a method of convincing consumers to register with one insurer rather than another.

- Prices within the Dutch health care system are presently determined through negotiations between provider and insurer organisations and by government regulation. As such, prices are only poorly related to costs and as yet cannot be relied upon to provide the right signals for encouraging efficient resource allocation. Far better cost information needs to be generated in order to set prices in relation to actual resource costs. Competition is expected to stimulate the production of this information since providers must know their costs of managing patients if they are to bid for contracts to provide medical services.

- There are presently a number of price cartels (between, for example, physicians, dentists and pharmacists) and regional cartels (between, for example, sickness funds and GPs) that could inhibit the workings of the price system. As such, an effective antitrust policy is central to the creation and maintenance of a competitive health care system.[27]

- Management skills are seriously underdeveloped in the Netherlands. Under the old style administrative system, managers acted more like bureaucrats and were given little discretion. To be able to take advantage of the opportunities offered by a market system, they will be required to take responsibility for revenue raising, managing within budgets and managing their staff in ways that they have not been called upon to do before. Managing clinicians, who have traditionally enjoyed a high degree of professional autonomy, will be a major part of this task. Since the clinicians rely on the hospital, co-operation in bidding for insurance contracts and sharing risk with the hospital is expected.

Another aspect of the Dutch reforms that has attracted the attention of health economists is the potential for preferred risk selection, or 'cream skimming', that could arise as the result of an imperfectly risk-adjusted capitation system.[28] Cream skimming refers to the selection of good risks by insurers (those for whom the capitation payment is above the expected costs of their care) and the rejection of poor risks. It arises because of information asymmetry between insurers and those determining the capitation payments. While it is efficient for insurers to consider the risks they take on, preferred risk selection has a number of adverse consequences. Most notably, it leads to restrictions on access to care for those whose health is poor, relative to the health of others with th same basic charactristics.

Methods which insurers might potentially use to carry this out include designing benefits packages to deter poor risks, using selective advertising and mailing, using agents that are familiar with family health records and even offering 'golden handshakes' to poor risks if they disenrol.

Research evidence suggests that the potential profits from preferred risk selection are large if capitation payments are based on standard risk-

---

[27]   See Schut *et al.* (1991) for a discussion of this issue.

[28]   van Vliet and van de Ven (1992).

adjustment factors such as age, gender and location. It appears that the maximum amount of the total variance in acute health expenditure per individual which is explainable is between 15-20 percent, while the standard adjustors are only likely to explain about two percent. Prior utilisation of health care services by individuals seems to be the best predictor of future expenditure, explaining up to two-thirds of the explainable variance. Thus, with the prospect of large profits and access to predictive information that is not included in the capitation formula, insurers have both a strong incentive and the ability to engage in preferred risk selection.

Van Vliet and van de Ven (1992) suggest that the Dutch government has two policy instruments with which it could reduce the threat of preferred risk selection; namely, by refining the capitation formula to include more of the risk adjustment factors known by insurance companies and by encouraging pro-competition policies.

Their research - based upon a panel of 35,000 people - shows that global parameters, such as age, gender and location, can explain about one-fifth of the explainable variance in annual health care expenditure. If the individual's prior year's costs are added as an explanatory variable, about three-fifths of the explainable variance in costs can be explained. Further analysis, using the Dutch Health Interview Survey (with a sample size of approximately 20,000), indicates that the addition of three health status indicators and several background characteristics increases the proportion of variance explained to three-quarters of its maximum level. Taken together, this evidence suggests that, in the short term, information on prior expenditure should be included in the capitation formula. In the longer term, as information becomes available, indicators on chronic health status based upon previous hospitalisations should also be added, especially since this information would be available to insurers.[29]

Alternatively, they argue that pro-competition policies could be used to overcome preferred risk selection. The incentive to select the lowest risk enrollees would be greatly reduced, for example, if insurers were able to vary the size of the flat rate premium between individuals on the basis of perceived risk. They claim that this would probably only produce a small variation in total premium payments but that this might be sufficient to deter preferred risk selection. Socially unacceptable premium differences could be avoided by

---

[29]   van Vliet and van de Ven (1992).

setting upper and lower bounds on the flat rate premium. Van Vliet and van de Ven point out that risk sharing between the central fund and the insurers would also reduce the incentive to risk select.

Overall, van Vliet and van de Ven believe that preferred risk selection is potentially a serious problem, but there are several strategies that might be used to reduce its negative effects. At the moment they have reservations about whether the government can implement the necessary measures, because of their lack of patient-specific information on prior utilisation.

9.5.3   Preliminary View of the Reform Programme

The Dutch reform proposals represent a coherent and consistent attempt to meet the multiple objectives of their health care system. The unified basic insurance package is designed to ensure equitable access to health care for all the population. It embodies the important concept of social solidarity in which cross-subsidies flow from higher income groups, the young and the healthy to lower income groups, the elderly and the sick.

Within this environment, efficiency gains are being sought through competition between insurers and between providers. It is intended, however, that competition will be managed, or regulated, to ensure that quality, access and other dimensions of care, which may be threatened in a totally free market, are maintained. Still, consumers will have choices and will be able to register their preferences for the style and level of care they most prefer. This encourages an efficient allocation of resources in the health care system.

There are many technical aspects of the reforms which need to be addressed if they are to work as hoped. It appears that management skills are seriously underdeveloped within provider organisations. In particular, clinicians have rarely been involved in the management process. Effective integration of clinicians into management decision making is likely to be a prerequisite of greater efficiency within hospitals and other providers. Further, the development of a satisfactory risk-adjusted formula for capitation payments will be necessary to avoid preferred risk selection.

More generally, however, the political context within which these changes take place is likely to be crucial and can be expected to govern their extent and the pace at which they proceed. At the outset, the Dekker proposals gained bi-partisan support, in contrast with many past reform proposals, because they combined features that were attractive to both of the main political constituencies. The Right was attracted by greater competition, while universal basic insurance appealed to the Left. Subsequently, however, new divisions have appeared. It has become clear that income-related premiums involve a redistribution of income away from higher income groups because, under private insurance arrangements, their payments were not income-related. Some private insurers have expressed concerns about the bureaucracy with which they will have to deal in order to receive capitation payments. Continuing debate on these and other political issues has slowed the implementation of the reforms. Many informed observers now doubt whether they will be implemented to any significant extent for at least another 10 years.

9.6   CONSTRAINTS ON REFORM

The Dutch government is already trying to implement a set of reforms very close to what we recommend. Moreover, the system proposed by the Dekker Commission is not markedly different from the current one, at least in terms of the institutional structure. The Dutch population already receives most health care from independent providers; their charges are met largely by sick funds or insurance companies; and these funding agencies receive their incomes from a combination of income-related contributions channelled through a central agency and additional payments direct from the patient.

However, despite the limited need for institutional changes, the Dutch government is facing difficulties which mean the reform process could take a decade or longer. Health care reform is not just a question of forming new institutions, but also of transferring key responsibilities and creating new power structures. This process will be rather drawn out, given the pluralistic nature of society in the Netherlands.

Both the Dekker proposals and NERA's Prototype call for competition between insurance funds, and between providers. Competition can only function if the competing bodies have separate financial responsibilities.   In the past, however, the health sector has operated through a corporate planning procedure which allows associations of professionals to divide up the gross allocation between themselves. This approach is entirely inconsistent with competition, and will have to be replaced.

However, this will not be simple, as the Dutch health care system reflects a national preoccupation with politics and religion, which impose additional constraints on the division of funds. The Netherlands have been described as a 'pre-centralised' society[30] in which sectional interests negotiate over their share of resources.   Before a 'decentralised' system can be established, responsibilities must first be 'centralised'. In other words, it will only be possible to allocate funds rationally once the following rights have been established:

- the central funding agency's right to dispose of all its funds without political interference;
- the sick funds' right to allocate funds to hospitals and doctors;

---

[30]   Saltman and de Roo (1989).

- the hospital managers' right to allocate funds to hospital departments and personnel.

The government is proceeding apace with this centralisation and subsequent decentralisation, but cannot override the existing interests. Furthermore, even when the rules have been established, it will be some time before each of the players is familiar enough with the system for competition to work. Information on costs is rarely available for the construction of relevant prices, and little is known about patient preferences with regard to the definition of the Guaranteed Health Care Package. Furthermore, the institutions themselves have a tendency to prefer collusion to competition. Writing in 1991, van de Ven[31] suggests that the constraints to reform are:

- poor consumer information on the quality of services provided;
- inappropriate price signals (administered, rather than cost based);
- a tendency for institutions to merge and collude, in order to maintain regional monopolies;
- a weak management structure, in both terms of responsibilities and personnel.

He concludes that these problems must be sorted out before competition can be introduced, for example by establishing better information and by using a reinforced competition policy to limit mergers and other restrictive practices within the health sector.

However, some of these problems are not likely to be solved until the relevant institutions are under pressure from competition, particularly the problems of pricing and management, because it is competition which makes it necessary for prices and management practice to reflect market conditions. The government is therefore likely to continue pushing the health care sector towards a decentralised, competitive structure as fast as responsibilities can be reallocated.

---

[31]   van de Ven (1991).

9.7   SHORT-TERM REFORM

Interim reform of the Dutch health care sector means continued implementation of the Dekker proposals. For the most part, this requires a continued effort to strengthen controls over health care professionals, and to bring health care insurance within the scope of central funding. However, work has also begun to decentralise management of the health sector, within certain guidelines.

The thrust of the interim reforms can be divided into three headings: setting up a legal framework for the health care sector; defining the range of services to be offered under different arrangements; and rationalising funding systems. These major strands are considered more fully below.

9.7.1   Legal Framework for Health Care

The basis of health care provision in the Netherlands will be mandatory, universal provision. In order to enforce such a system, the government needs to lay down certain legal requirements, which are listed in NERA's Recommendation 11 (see Section 3.5.5). These are:

A.   Every individual must be obliged to take out health insurance from an accredited insurance company, to cover the Guaranteed Health Care Package (GHCP).

B.   Every accredited insurance company must be obliged to accept all requests for enrolment on reasonable terms.

C.   Every individual must be obliged to pay over to the central fund a premium related to his or her income, and to nominate an insurance company as recipient of a risk-adjusted pay-out; *or* every insurance company must be required to collect an income-related premium from every individual enrolled, on behalf of the central fund and in return for a risk-adjusted premium.

D.   A Guaranteed Health Care Package will be defined which will include mandatory copayments.

The Dutch system already incorporates these elements, to some degree. However, the next steps must make it clear that health insurance is mandatory for all, by removing the maximum income level for membership, which stood at Dfl 54,400 ($23,550 1990) in 1992.

744

Health insurance firms must also be required to offer non-discriminatory terms to all applicants. The GHCP must therefore be defined, in order to distinguish it from other services, so that insurers cannot use the offer of additional services as a means of preferred risk-selection.

The payments mechanism via the central fund is being gradually built up out of two funds created by the Health Insurance Act and the *Algemene Wet Bijzondere Ziektekosten* (AWBZ). In the longer term, these funds will need to be amalgamated and to start paying risk-adjusted capitation fees. In the interim, however, the funding process is likely to be less standardised.

Work is proceeding in the Netherlands on each of these items, but these issues will probably take a secondary priority, after the creation of new lines of responsibility and control over providers. However, attention must be given to the legal framework, before attempting to decentralise responsibilities within the new budgeting arrangements.

In addition, a safety net must be available to ensure that health care is provided to those individuals who would be unable to arrange individual health insurance. The safety net would apply to those with particularly low incomes (including the unemployed), or poor health, or a mental disability which prevents them from exercising the amount of choice over their health care permitted under the new arrangements. The original purpose of the AWBZ was to provide health care services in these cases. Its expanded role at the moment arises out of its use by government as an instrument of centralisation. This should not be allowed to obscure its original function.

9.7.2   Range of Services

Implementation of the proposed legal framework will require detailed attention to the range of health care services to be provided within the GHCP. This would define the services that society intends that everyone should be entitled to, regardless of their ability to pay.

This task requires urgent consideration by government. The nature of health care provided by the sector is, of course, under constant review, but the insurance funds and companies will be tempted to use risk-selection by offering different applicants different levels of service, unless there is a mandatory basic package available universally.

The GHCP should be defined in terms of 'function', i.e. the medical services to which each insured member of the public is entitled. This will require a slightly different approach from the present one, where some insurance packages are defined in terms of the providers which patients may use. This limits unduly the choice of provider, and also provides a less well defined measure of the level of service to which a patient is entitled.

Insurance firms should, of course, remain free to offer to their members services that are not covered by the GHCP, or more choice and higher quality versions of services that are covered by the GHCP. However, the government must urgently define the GHCP offered to everyone without discrimination, so that each citizen can demand the basic health care insurance package on an equal footing. Additional services will then be clearly identifiable.

9.7.3 Payments Mechanisms

The legal framework must impose a requirement for every citizen to take out health insurance, and for every insurance firm to enrol all applicants, without discrimination. Insurance firms should then charge their members a premium to cover their health care expenses for services within the GHCP. That premium should come from two sources: a fee paid to a central fund, that is related only to the income of the member; and a further contribution, paid direct from the member to the insurance fund, based on individual risk.

This approach to funding is very similar to the Dekker proposal, with the exception of the individual risk aspect of the further contribution. In principle, it has been decided that 85 percent of funding should come from income-related premiums. A central fund, or re-insurance scheme, will be set up to provide the insurance firms with a risk-adjustment service. The central fund will receive all income-related premiums paid by individuals. It will then provide insurance companies with a risk-adjusted capitation fee for each individual enrolled. However, under the present proposal the further contribution of individuals will be at a flat rate.

As part of the process of 'centralisation-and-decentralisation' described in Section 9.6, the government has attempted to combine contributions in a limited number of central funds, and to allocate these funds as firm budgets to sick funds and to private health insurance companies. The role of the central fund is currently divided between the provisions of the Health Insurance Act and the AWBZ (*Algemene Wet Bijzondere Ziektekosten*, or

Exceptional Medical Expenses Act). The current method of allocation uses a combination of historical precedent and more objective criteria.

9.7.4 Provider Budgets and Contracts

The sick funds and insurance companies are now negotiating new arrangements with providers, in an attempt to provide a means of financial control at the lower level. In the past, providers have been reimbursed in ways which offer little incentive for efficiency, such as fee-for-service contracts, or even just ex-post recognition of costs incurred (especially capital investment costs). The insurance firms must now negotiate contracts with better incentives for efficiency, with hospitals and with doctors.

One of the key areas for attention is the funding of new facilities in the hospital sector. Hospital management must be helped and encouraged to take a firmer control of resource allocation. Currently, specialists attached to hospitals are able to control the entry of professionals into any hospital; this is not conducive to efficiency in operation. Furthermore, specialists have apparently been able to side-step the hospital budgeting process, by arranging new capital investments which subsequently become part of the hospital's revenue earning base.

In the future, hospital global budgets will need to be amalgamated and then converted into contracts with purchasers. (This process is proceeding already.) Hospital managers will then need to take over control of resources (capital and staffing) within the hospital, to ensure that contracts are fulfilled and that contract revenues are used in accordance with the overall priorities of the hospital, not the priorities of individual groups of specialists. This transfer of effective control is bound to take some time, not least because hospital managers have neither the skills nor the information necessary for commercial management decisions.

Sick funds and insurance companies may want to extend the decentralisation of financial responsibility to doctors, to encourage them to prescribe efficiently. Patients will also want doctors to pay more attention to the costs of health care, if they are liable for copayments on most services (see Section 9.7.5 below). The setting of financial targets for doctors is a sensitive issue, as it suggests that doctors should gain from economising on the treatment of their patients. However, sick funds and insurance companies will need to improve their systems of financial and management control over doctors, using a variety of methods, as dictated by the nature of their relationship with the doctor, including peer review, selective lists of providers and treatments, and group targets.

Once these reforms have been completed, the government may be willing to relinquish existing controls over the supply of physicians and hospital capacity. It has been suggested that the government wishes to retain the controls for fear of 'supply-led demand growth'.[32] This no doubt reflects the lax budgeting procedures which applied up till now. Government would be wise to ensure that the hospital sector is subject to effective incentives, before relinquishing alternative planning tools.

9.7.5   Patient Copayments

Patient copayments in the Netherlands are currently limited to the purchase price of non-reimbursable over-the-counter drugs, and the *excess* cost of reimbursable pharmaceuticals, above a reference price defined for broad therapeutic categories. No similar payments apply to hospital and other services.

This approach tends to bias patient choice. The pharmacologically optimal treatment may be a drug for which the patient must make copayments. However, the patient may opt for hospital care instead, even if it is more expensive, because it is completely reimbursable. Alternatively, the patient may request a substitute from the same therapeutic category which is cheaper in the short run, but which gives rise to side effects or relapses which entail further cost later.

The economics of choosing between medicinal and hospital care will be improved when sick funds are given global budgets to fund their patients' health care, since they will have an incentive to recommend the patient to accept the option which is cheapest in the long run. However, the patient may still resist a doctor's advice, if it is possible to avoid copayments by using hospitals more intensively. Such biases can only be avoided by applying similar policies on copayments to all forms of health care.

The application of simple proportional copayments to pharmaceuticals implies the abolition of reference prices, since no expense would then be eligible for 100 percent reimbursement. This may be resisted by patients, who are used to most of the cost of any drug being reimbursed in full. To compensate, the

---

[32]   Schut, Greenberg and van de Ven (1991).

percentage copayment might have to be reduced to 5 percent or 10 percent of the total cost, instead of 100 percent of the excess cost. However, since very few drugs currently incur copayments under the GVS[33], the percentage copayment would have to be a very small proportion of the drugs price, if the total level of copayments is not to increase dramatically. This would seem to undermine both the incentive and revenue raising aspects of copayments.

One possibility is to apply a fixed sum exemption to copayments, so that patients would not be liable for copayments until their health care expenditure exceeded a certain amount. Drugs would then continue to be reimbursed in full, provided that the patient did not incur excessive health care costs. If the reference pricing system were abolished, the exemption limit would represent a budget available to the patient for spending on drugs (or other services). This budget could even be risk-adjusted, so that less healthy patients received a higher exemption. This would eliminate the tendency for copayments to be viewed as a tax on the unhealthy. Only *unexpectedly* high usage of drugs or other services would incur copayments.[34]

An upper limit would also need to be established, to insure patients against catastrophically high expenditure. The inability to pay large bills would not then be life-threatening.

The redesign of the copayments should begin with the introduction of a low percentage copayment on all health care expenses, so that all forms of health care are viewed equally by patients. Limits on total copayments (annual exemption and maximum contribution) should be introduced at the same time, although initially on a uniform basis for all patients. The limits could be adjusted for income and risk characteristics at a later stage, at which point the percentage contribution could be increased as well. Once the proportion of patient contribution provided a real incentive for selecting low price treatments, the need for an additional purchasing incentive for pharmacists might fall away. Alternatively, they could be retained to bolster the incentives

---

[33]   Nefarma estimates that about 100 drugs were priced above the reference price of their respective category in 1992.

[34]   The system would work equally well, even if the reference pricing system remained in force. If a patient followed a doctor's advice and selected one of the more expensive drugs within any category, the price premium need not incur copayments, if the patient's total copayments fell below the lower limit. The lower limit would be equivalent to a budget which the patient could spend upon drugs with prices higher than the reference price - in other words a 'Budget for Premium Drug Quality'.

for pharmacists to provide patients with information on the costs of alternative treatments.

9.7.6   Summary of Short-Term Reforms

In implementing the Dekker proposals, the Dutch Government is already trying to set up a legal and financial framework for the provision of health care on an equitable and universal basis. The first reform wave allowed the Government to centralise the control of finances in the funding agencies set up by the Health Insurance Act and the AWBZ. The next stage is to decentralise financial responsibilities to sick funds (insurance companies), providers and patients.

The allocation of global budgets to sick funds has already begun and the sick funds must now find ways to impose financial discipline on health care providers.   A key requirement is the reform of patient copayments, to eliminate the bias against certain forms of pharmaceutical treatment. Initially, copayments might simply be levied as a low percentage of all health care expenditure, with a uniform exemption and upper limit. Later, if possible, the exemption and upper limit should be adjusted for income and risk, at which point it would be possible to raise the percentage rate of copayment.

These reforms would give the Dutch health care sector a sound basis for financial control. It would also establish the basis for introducing competition between insurance companies and health care providers. However, this would be a longer term reform, as explained in the next section.

9.8   LONG-TERM REFORM

In this section we consider what changes would be required to move the existing Netherlands system towards that the structure of the NERA Prototype over the long term. The main reforms would be to open up the provision of health care and health care insurance to the forces of competition, in order to encourage greater efficiency.

9.8.1   The Funding Side of the Health Care System

For the health care insurance industry to provide universal health care on a competitive basis, the central fund must provide a comprehensive risk-adjustment service. Health care funding is currently provided by funds set up under two different Acts (HIA and AWBZ). These funds must be combined, and the allocation of funds must relate more closely to the risk characteristics of each insurance company's members.

The current budgeting process is a step in the right direction, since it would give each insurance company a known income to work with. However, the use of historic information does not provide long-term incentives to become more efficient and to compete for members. The central fund must develop a risk-adjustment formula which allows the central fund to pay insurance firms an appropriate amount of additional revenue every time they recruit another customer.

Once the risk-adjustment formula has been implemented by the central fund, the market for health insurance can be opened to competition between existing health care insurers, and new insurance companies must be allowed to enter the market. Entry into this market does not appear to be limited at present, but there is a strict legal distinction between two types of funding agency, the sick funds and the private health insurance companies, which has proved troublesome when private health insurance companies wish to bid for the customers of the sick funds. This legal distinction must be eliminated, to permit effective competition in all parts of the market.

9.8.2   The Provider Side of the Health Care System

The budgeting and contracting process described in the previous section will require sick funds to be more cost conscious, and should give hospital managers a greater degree of control over allocation of resources within any hospital.

However, there is some concern that providers will collude out of habit, and will establish regional monopolies which effectively prevent purchasers from exercising choice amongst competing suppliers. In part, the tendency to merge and collude is a remnant of an old government policy on health planning, which favoured regional integration. This policy has been discarded, but the government appears to have few legal measures to prevent regional concentration of suppliers.

The government will therefore have to enact more appropriate anti-monopoly legislation, and may have to enforce it in the health care sector, to ensure that competition can survive. The government's responsibilities in this area are discussed below.

9.8.3   The Responsibilities of Patients

The patient's relationship with a GP will be complicated by their liability for a share of the cost of treatment, if copayments become a signification proportion of expenditure on health care.

Patients will want to minimise the copayments required to maintain their health status, whilst doctors will try to minimise the call on their time or on a limited global budget. If doctors have no liability for the costs of treatment they prescribe, they may prescribe tests and treatments which save their time, but which are more expensive for the patient. On the other hand, if budgetary controls are applied to individual doctors, patients will be concerned in case doctors deliberately minimise the amount of treatment offered.

Patients may therefore feel that they need independent advice on any decisions presented by the GP, in order to minimise potential conflicts of interest. Consumers Associations could provide both general guidance on health care practice and opportunities, and specific advice on individual choices.

Consumers will also need to be involved in the definition of the GHCP, and in any revisions. Since the package is mandatory, there is little scope for consumers to indicate what range and level of services they would prefer; such issues must therefore be discussed explicitly, in some joint forum of government representatives, health care professionals and consumers. This forum might be an expanded version of the FTO discussions; apart from ensuring that development of the GHCP is consistent with advice on prescribing, it might provide a useful entry point for industry views on related issues.

9.8.4   The Responsibilities of Government

The interim reforms centralise financial control and decentralise budgets for the health care sector as a whole. The longer term reforms introduce competition, to provide a further incentive for efficiency. However, the Government will still have a role in the health care sector, to make sure that competition can work effectively. Government supervision of the market will require the following agencies:

- a licensing agency, to grant licenses to participants in the health care system (insurance firms and providers) and to approve new medicines;

- an anti-monopoly agency to oversee, and if necessary regulate, competition amongst insurance firms and amongst providers;

- an audit agency, to check that all insurance plans offered by the insurance firms meet certain credentialling requirements, and that health care providers maintain acceptable quality standards in the services they provide;

- a welfare agency to purchase health care on behalf of the mentally disabled, and others who are unable to participate fully in the health care system.

An Office of Health Care Regulation will have to be established, to carry out the licensing function. Its functions should include drawing up the risk-adjustment formula of the central fund. To allow it to operate independently of the health care industry, its licensing function should provide extensive powers to demand information from sick funds and insurance companies.

No agency is currently responsible for enforcing competition in the health sector and there is only a very limited basis in law for doing so. The health care sector is rife with agreements and practices which limit competition and a determined effort will be required to prevent regional monopolies.[35] Regional monopolies may be difficult to maintain in a country as small as the Netherlands, once entry barriers are removed. The Office for Health Care Regulation should therefore be made responsible for promoting competition in the sector.

An audit agency should be appointed, so that sick funds and insurance companies can be entrusted with the task of administering the money paid to them by the central fund as risk-adjusted capitation fees. The audit agency should also monitor provision of the GHCP, once it has been defined.

Funding the safety net for the disabled and others was one of the original roles of the AWBZ and should not be forgotten as the AWBZ is transformed into the central risk-adjustment fund. The Department of Health will also retain its existing responsibility for public health issues, in particular the prevention of communicable diseases, and for teaching and research, to the extent that they are not financed from private funds.

9.8.5   Summary of Long-Term Reforms

In the long-term, the health care sector should be opened up to competition, as a means of encouraging efficiency and containing costs. The interim reforms will provide a framework of legal and financial controls, but additional institutions will be required to ensure that efficient competition prevails, given the tendency of providers to collude. The roles of government will include: licensing and auditing of health care insurers and providers; prevention of collusion and monopoly abuses; and protection of certain disadvantaged members of society.

Competition will be enhanced and patients will be better served, if Consumer Associations also provide information on the effectiveness of health care treatments and the comparative performance of health insurance companies.

---

[35]   Schut, Greenberg and van de Ven (1991).

ANNEX 9.1 DATA TABLES

List of Tables

TABLE 1
AGE STRUCTURE OF POPULATION ACCORDING TO THE
LOW-, MEDIUM- AND HIGH-GROWTH SCENARIOS

Year	0-14	15-64	64-	Total	0-14	15-64	64-
		000's				percent	
Observed							
1960	3,443	7,003	1,034	11,480	30%	61%	9%
1970	3,557	8,152	1,324	13,033	27%	63%	10%
1980	3,158	9,359	1,628	14,145	22%	66%	12%
1990	2,725	10,322	1,904	14,951	18%	69%	13%
Low Projection							
2000	2,698	10,692	2,153	15,543	17%	69%	14%
2010	2,281	10,955	2,483	15,719	15%	70%	16%
Mid Projection							
2000	2,911	10,766	2,153	15,830	18%	68%	14%
2010	2,739	11,158	2,483	16,380	17%	68%	15%
High Projection							
2000	3,050	10,849	2,152	16,051	19%	68%	13%
2010	3,049	11,342	2,483	16,874	18%	67%	15%

Source: *United Nations (1990).*

TABLE 2
ECONOMIC ENVIRONMENT

YEAR	GDP mn guilders	GDP guilders per head	Health care expenditure mn guilders	Health care expenditure guilders per head	Health care expenditure % of GDP
1981	352,850	24,767	28,999	2,035	8.2
1982	368,860	25,771	30,981	2,165	8.4
1983	381,020	26,520	32,069	2,232	8.4
1984	400,250	27,749	32,472	2,251	8.1
1985	418,180	28,858	33,489	2,311	8.0
1986	428,610	29,413	34,879	2,394	8.1
1987	430,170	29,333	35,741	2,437	8.3
1988	449,420	30,449	36,829	2,495	8.2
1989	474,380	31,947	38,371	2,584	8.1
1990	504,300	33,746	40,803	2,730	8.1

Source: *OECD (1991)*

TABLE 3
HEALTH CARE COSTS IN THE NETHERLANDS 1987-1992

	1987	1988	1989	1990	1991 est.	1992 est.
Total health care costs (bn guilders)	42.9	44.1	45.6	48.4	51.4	52.6
Index	100	103	106	113	120	123
Increase in %	2.4	2.8	3.4	6.1	6.2	2.3
% of GNP	10.0	9.9	9.6	9.5	9.6	9.4
Sources of Financing (as % of total):						
Health Insurance Fund Act	35.3	35.3	32.6	32.8	32.9	23.9
Exceptional Medical Expenses Act	23.8	23.8	30.7	31.3	31.4	45.6
Government	14.1	13.8	10.6	10.6	10.6	10.7
Other Sources	26.8	27.1	26.2	25.3	25.0	19.9

Source: *Ministry of Health, Welfare and Cultural Affairs (1992)*

TABLE 4
EXPENDITURES BY THE HEALTH INSURANCE FUNDS, 1986-1990

Guilders mn	1986	1987	1988	1989	1990
MEDICINES AND APPLIANCES	2,140	2,365	2,536	2,315	2,743
medicines and dressings	1,924	2,121	2,223	2,315	2,743
appliances	215	244	313		
AMBULATORY HEALTH CARE	2,510	2,746	2,771	2,865	2,960
general practitioner	921	1,007	1,045	1,040	1,061
maternity	164	176	185	188	205
dental care	718	738	725	714	763
paramedical care	649	748	744	847	850
midwifery	58	77	72	76	81
SPECIALIST HELP	2,163	2,345	2,259	2,211	2,502
INSTITUTIONAL HEALTH CARE	6,427	6,851	7,049	6,296	6,361
hospital care	6,304	6,709	6,882	6,216	6,267
halfway care	123	142	167	80	94
REMAINING COSTS	999	1,006	1,070	1,186	1,065
transportation services	267	274	282	297	319
adjustment previous years	-1	-3	0	11	51
operating cost of health insurance fund	647	656	682	762	746
cost of collection of premium	25	31	33	35	51
operating cost of Health Insurance Council	20	22	20	19	n/a
Special costs	23	-3	0	0	n/a
international treaties	13	25	48	53	n/a
miscellaneous subsidies	5	4	5	9	n/a
TOTAL EXPENDITURE	14,239	15,313	15,685	14,873	15,631

Source: *ZFR and VNZ*
Reproduced in: *VNZ (1992), p.22.*

TABLE 5
CONTRIBUTIONS: HEALTH FUND INSURANCE ACT (ZFW)

	Employees	Over-65		Flat rate	
	and others	On benefits from Old Age Pension Act	On other income	Adult	Child
	(% of income)	(% of income)	(% of income)	(guilders)	(guilders)
1987	9.80%	2.95	9.80		
1988	10.20%	3.10	10.2		
1989	8.10%	1.90	8.10		
1990	7.90%	1.85	7.90	186.00	93.00
1991	7.80%	1.90	7.25	225.60	112.80
1992	6.35%	0.75	6.35	198.00	99.00[1]

1   *Up to a maximum of two children*

CONTRIBUTIONS: EXCEPTIONAL MEDICAL EXPENSES ACT (AWBZ)

	Employees & Persons on social security benefits (as % of income)	Flat rate Adult (guilders)	Child (guilders)
1991	5.8	-	-
1992	7.3	133.20	44.40[1]

1   *For all children under the age of 18 years*

Reproduced in: *VNZ (1992), p.21.*

TABLE 6

PROVIDERS OF HEALTH CARE: HEALTH CARE WORKERS AND INSTITUTIONS

Number of providers 1986-1990	1986	1987	1988	1989	1990 Number	1990 Per 100,000 inhabitants	1990 Per 100,000 compulsory insured
Pharmacies	1,320	1,352	1,391	1,425	1,453	9.7	15.8
G.P.s with pharmaceutical facilities	826	781	770	758	718	4.8	7.8
General practitioners	6,285	6,353	6,432	6,520	6,573	43.8	71.3
Maternity care	5,624	5,750	5,588	5,585	5,860	39.0	63.6
Home care services	10,638	10,992	11,398	11,433	11,800	78.6	128.0
Dentists	5,057	5,041	5,109	5,146	5,206	34.7	56.5
Physiotherapists	9,686	9,519	9,542	9,703	9,972	66.4	108.2
Speech therapists	2,340	2,338	2,410	2,488	2,619	17.4	28.4
Medical specialists	7,117	7,163	7,293	7,500	8,250	55.0	89.5
Ambulatory mental health care	6,394	6,587	6,551	6,759	7,022	46.8	76.2
Dental specialists							
- oral, mandible & maxillary surgery	123	125	126	131	135	0.9	1.5
- orthodontists	207	211	219	232	238	1.6	2.6

Sources: Ministry of Welfare, Health and Cultural Affairs (1992)
Reproduced in: VNZ (1992), p.7.

TABLE 7
NUMBER OF HEALTH CARE INSTITUTIONS, NUMBER OF BEDS
AND NUMBER OF BEDS PER 1,000 INHABITANTS, 1986-1990

	1986			1988			1990		
	No. of instit- utions	No. of beds	Beds per 1,000	No. of instit- utions	No. of beds	Beds per 1,000	No. of instit- utions	No. of beds	Beds per 1,000
General hospitals	143	55,360	3.79	130	54,133	3.86	120	52,164	3.50
Specialised hospitals	45	5,408	0.37	44	5,213	0.35	36	4,660	0.31
Universityh ospitals	8	7,715	0.53	8	7,456	0.50	9	7,292	0.49
Psychiatric hospitals	82	24,498	1.68	80	24,167	1.63	83	24,731	1.66
Institutions for the mentally deficient	119	30,461	2.08	119	30,871	2.09	121	31,561	2.12
Nursing homes: somatic	134	15,099	1.03	112	12.831	0.87	105	11,919	0.80
psycho- geriatric	81	11,692	0.80	77	11,614	0.78	72	11,212	0.75
combined	110	22,877	1.57	135	26,531	1.79	148	28,723	1.93
Total		173,110	11.84		172,816	11.67		172,262	11.57

Source: *VNZ (1992), p.11.*

761

TABLE 8
AVERAGE LENGTH OF STAY IN HOSPITALS, 1970, 1979 and 1988

Diagnostic Categories	1970	1979	1988
Infectious and parasitic diseases	24.2	17.9	13.9
Neoplasms	23.9	18.5	14.4
Endocrine, nutritional, and metabolic diseases and immunity disorders	24.8	19.7	15.4
Diseases of the blood and blood-forming organs	23.1	17.4	12.2
Mental disorders	39.6	36.0	36.6
Diseases of the nervous system and sense organs	17.1	11.4	9.3
Diseases of the circulatory system	25.1	18.3	13.7
Diseases of the respiratory system	8.4	8.5	9.8
Diseases of the digestive system	13.1	15.6	11.6
Diseases of the genitourinary system	14.0	10.5	8.9
Complications of pregnancy, childbirth, and puerperium	10.4	9.0	6.3
Diseases of skin and subcutaneous tissue	23.1	18.4	15.2
Diseases of the musculoskeletal system and connective tissue	22.7	15.8	10.8
Congenital anomalies	18.9	11.9	8.9
Certain conditions originating in the perinatal period	28.4	16.9	10.1
Symptoms, signs, and ill-defined conditions	17.3	12.6	9.8
External causes of injury and poisoning	23.9	17.5	14.2
All diagnoses	17.5	13.7	11.5[36]

Source: *OECD (1991)*

---

[36]   1987

762

ANNEX 9.2 BIBLIOGRAPHY

Beck, E.J. (1988), "An Anglo-Dutch comparison of health care delivery", *Community Medicine*, 10.1, pp. 33-39.

Blendon, R., Leitman, R., Morrison, I. and Donelan, K. (1990), "Satisfaction with Health Systems in Ten Nations", *Health Affairs*, Summer, pp. 185-92.

Burstall, M. L. (1990), "1992 and the Regulation of the Pharmaceutical Industry", *IEA Health Series*, No. 9, London.

Burstall, M. L. (1991), "Europe after 1992: Implications for Pharmaceuticals", *Health Affairs*, Fall, pp. 157-171.

Central bureau voor de statistiek, ministrie van welzijn, volksgezondheid en cultuur (1992), *Vademecum Gezondheidsstatistiek Nederland 1992*, Voorburg/Heerlen, the Netherlands, Tables 11.8, 11.9 & 11.10.

Coupe, M. (1988), "Reflections on the Dutch Experience", *Health Services Management*, June.

Elsinga, E. (1989), "Political Decision Making in Health Care: The Dutch Case", *Health Policy*, 11, pp. 243-55.

Groenewegen, P. P. (1991), *Primary Health Care in the Netherlands: From Imperfect Planning to an Imperfect Market?*, Paper for conference on "Changing Roles of Government and the Market in Health Care Systems", Jerusalem, Israel.

Ham, C., Robinson, R. and Benzeval, M. (1990), *Health Check: Health Care Reforms in an International Context*, King's Fund, London.

Kamermans, D., Kirkman-Liff, B. and Stompedissel, I. (1991), "Silver Care: Managed Care in the Netherlands" (mimeo).

Kelly, S. (1992), "A Practical Approach to Reclassification of Medicines", *Regulatory Affairs Journal*, Vol 3 No 11.

Kirkman-Liff, B. L. (1991), "Health Insurance Values and Implementation in the Netherlands and the Federal Republic of Germany", *Journal of the American Medical Association*, 265, pp. 2496-2502.

Kirkman-Liff, B. L., and van de Ven, W.P.M.M. (1989), "Improving efficiency in the Dutch Health Care System: Current Innovations and Future Options", *Health Policy*, 13, pp. 35-53.

Lapre, R.M. (1988),"A Change of Direction in the Dutch Health Care System?", *Health Policy*, 10, pp. 21-32.

Maarse, J.A.M. (1989), "Hospital Budgeting in Holland: Aspects, Trends and Effects", *Health Policy*, 11, pp. 257-276.

Ministry of Welfare, Health and Cultural Affairs (1992), *Financial Overview of the Care Sector (FOZ)*, Rijswijk.

Ministry of Welfare, Health and Cultural Affairs (1989), *Health Insurance in the Netherlands*, Rijswijk.

Ministry of Welfare, Health and Cultural Affairs (1988), *Changing Health Care in the Netherlands*, Rijswijk.

Ministry of Welfare, Health and Cultural Affairs (1991), *The Quality of Care in the Netherlands*, Rijswijk.

Nuijens, W.J.F.I. (1992), "The Collectivisation of Health Insurance", *Social Science and Medicine*, 34.9, pp. 1049-1055.

Organisation for Economic Co-Operation and Development (1990), *"Health Care Systems in Transition"*, Paris.

Organisation for Economic Co-Operation and Development (1991), *OECD Health Data. Comparative Analysis of Health Systems* (Software Package), Paris.

Overmars, P.F.M. (1992), "Must Scarcity Preclude Quality?", (mimeo).

Rutten, F. and Banta, H.D. (1988), "Health Care Technologies in the Netherlands", *Journal of Technology Assessment in Health Care*, 4, pp. 229-238.

Saltman, R.B. and de Roo, A.A. (1989), "Hospital Policy in the Netherlands: The Parameters of Structural Stalemate", *Journal of Health Politics, Policy and Law*, 14.4, pp. 773-795.

Schut, F.T., Greenberg, W. and van de Ven, W.P.M.M. (1991), "Anti Trust Policy in the Dutch Health Care System and the Relevance of EEC Competition Policy and US Antitrust Practice", *Health Policy*, 17, pp. 257-284.

Tiddens, H., Heeslers, J. and van de Zande, J. (1989), "Health Services in the Netherlands", in Raffel, M. (ed.), *Comparative Health Care Systems*, Pennyslvania State University Press, London.

United Nations (1990), "World Population Prospects", New York.

van de Ven, W.P.M.M. and van Vliet, R.C.J.A. (1992), "How Can We Prevent Cream Skimming in a Competitive Health Insurance Market", in Zweifel, P., and Frech, F.E. (eds) *Health Economics Worldwide*, Kluwer Academic Publishers, the Netherlands.

van de Ven, W.P.M.M. (1990), "From Regulated Cartel to Regulated Competition", *European Economic Review*, 34, pp. 632-645.

van de Ven, W.P.M.M. (1991), "Perestrojka in the Dutch Health Care System", *European Economic Review*, 35, pp. 430-440.

van de Ven, W.P.M.M. (1987), "The Key Role of Health Insurance in a Cost-effective Health Care System", *Health Policy*, 7, pp. 253-272.

van Vliet, R.P.J.A. and van de Ven W.P.M.M. (1992), "Towards a Capitation Formula for Competing Health Insurers. An Empirical Analysis", *Social Science and Medicine*, 34.9, pp. 1035-1048.

VNZ (1990), "The Health Care System in the Netherlands", Association of Social Health Insurance Funds in the Netherlands, (mimeo).

VNZ (1992), "Health Care in Figures from a Health Service Perspective", Association of Social Health Insurance Funds in the Netherlands.

World Health Organisation (1992), "World Health Statistics Annual 1991", WHO, Geneva.